ATLANTA and ENVIRONS

ATLANTA and ENVIRONS

A Chronicle of Its People
and Events

Years of Change and Challenge,
1940–1976

VOLUME III

HAROLD H. MARTIN

The Atlanta Historical Society
Atlanta

The University of Georgia Press
Athens and London

© 1987 by the University of Georgia Press

Athens, Georgia 30602

www.ugapress.org

Published in conjunction with The Atlanta History Center

Atlanta, Georgia 30305

www.atlantahistorycenter.com

All rights reserved

Set in Baskerville with Caslon Display

Printed digitally in the United States of America

The Library of Congress has cataloged the hardcover edition

of this book as follows:

Library of Congress Cataloging-in-Publication Data

Martin, Harold H. (1910–1994)

Atlanta and environs; a chronicle of its people and events.

Continuation of: Atlanta and Environs / Franklin Miller Garrett. 1954.

ISBN 0-8203-0913-3 (alk. paper)

Includes index.

1. Atlanta (Ga.)—History. 2. Atlanta (Ga.)—Biography. 3. Atlanta Region (Ga.)—

History. 4. Atlanta Region (Ga.)—Biography. I. Garrett, Franklin M.

(Franklin Miller), 1906– II. Title.

975.8231 19   54-14260

F294.A8 G3

Hardcover reissue 2011 ISBN-13: 978-0-8203-3906-1

ISBN-10: 0-8203-3906-7

Paperback 2011 ISBN-13: 978-0-8203-3907-8

ISBN-10: 0-8203-3907-5

British Library Cataloging-in-Publication Data available

The photographs in this volume are from

the collections of the Atlanta History Center

CONTENTS

PREFACE

SINCE their publication in 1954, Franklin M. Garrett's first two volumes of *Atlanta and Environs* have become the standard source for information about Atlanta's history up to World War II. A generation of journalists and historians has mined Garrett's pages to find facts and figures for dozens of articles and books. This long-awaited third volume, written by Harold Martin, covers the three crucial decades during which Atlanta went from being a city of regional importance to a metropolis of national rank. The two dominant themes of this period were Atlanta's physical, economic, and population growth and the city's and the South's accommodation to a changing racial order.

Newspaperman Harold Martin covered Atlanta's wartime life and postwar developments as a reporter and columnist, and now he has collected selected accounts of those times in a year-by-year chronicle of Atlanta from 1940 to 1969. Martin's descriptions provide fascinating glimpses into the major events and prominent personalities that caught the attention of Atlantans. The book was not designed to be a comprehensive narrative history. Rather, Martin's goal was to evoke a feeling for the concerns and interests of active citizens in the city's most active decades. He has indeed met that goal. One can open the book at almost any page and find an engrossing story or an amusing anecdote or a little-known tidbit of Atlanta's recent history.

On the eve of World War II, Atlanta's metropolitan population of 440,000 placed it in a similar class with Memphis, Nashville, Richmond, and New Orleans, but by 1959 the Gate City had a million people in its environs. In 1940, for example, Birmingham's metropolitan population trailed Atlanta's by only 35,000. Twenty years later the gap was an overwhelming 400,000.

In the 1940s the South and Atlanta were distinctly minor league. The city's national reputation, to the extent that it had one, was shaped by the phenomenal success of Margaret Mitchell's *Gone with the Wind*—both the novel and the movie—and by the enormous popularity of Coca-Cola, millions of bottles of which were consumed by American service men and women around the globe in World War II. By 1970 a transformation had taken place. Atlanta, with the Braves and Falcons, had become major league in business as well as in sports. A soaring skyline and sprawling suburbs characterized the booming city that had become the Southeast's transportation and distributing hub. The 1960s saw the most spectacular growth. During the decade Atlanta ranked eighth nationally in downtown construction, and all but one of the city's tallest buildings in 1970 had been erected in the 1960s.

Railroads had given birth to Atlanta, and they continued to be important, but it was Atlanta's rise as the major air traffic hub of the South that characterized the era after World War II. The municipal airport, on the southern edge of the city limits, became one of the nation's busiest. Delta Air

Lines, based in Atlanta, built steadily, becoming an air carrier of the first rank.

Two figures dominated the politics of Atlanta in this period of expansion—William B. Hartsfield, mayor from 1937 through 1961 (with a brief interruption), and Ivan Allen, Jr., mayor from 1962 to 1969. Both of these men were well connected with the civic-business-social elite that substantially shaped the politics and economy of the city. They were model civic boosters for their beloved city. As important and visible as Allen and Hartsfield were, behind the scenes no one was more important as a political advisor and philanthropist than Robert Woodruff of Coca-Cola.

Yet, as the city grew there were challenges to the dominance of this core of downtown-oriented, business-minded, white leadership. Part of the challenge came from the fact that the city of Atlanta no longer dominated the region. In 1940 more than two out of three metropolitan Atlantans lived within the city limits, yet by 1970 that ratio was almost reversed, with about 500,000 in the city and 900,000 in the environs but outside the corporate limits. Although a major annexation in 1952 had captured some of the suburban growth within Fulton County, the sprawling counties of DeKalb, Cobb, and Clayton effectively resisted annexation into Atlanta. By 1980 more than three out of four metropolitan Atlantans lived outside the mother municipality.

The other challenge to the old political order came from within the city in the form of the long-excluded black community. Atlanta in 1940 was as rigidly Jim Crow as any big city in the South, and integration did not come easily to the city. The desegregation of schools and businesses was fought long and hard, yet the Atlanta leadership, both black and white, managed to guide and restrain the struggle so that the city seemed to stay one step ahead of the rest of the deep South and one step away from violence. The well-established black colleges of the city provided the core of minority leadership. In the 1960s the growing international reputation of Nobel Peace Prize winner Dr. Martin Luther King, Jr., co-pastor with his father at Ebenezer Baptist Church near downtown, rubbed off on Atlanta.

The city's cautious and moderate approach to racial issues won Atlanta a national reputation as "a city too busy to hate." The term was coined by Hartsfield, and it contained at least as much hype as substance, but in comparison with Birmingham, Memphis, New Orleans, and several other cities, Atlanta did, in fact, seem calm and reasonable in the eyes of the northern-dominated press. Boosters were convinced that this image was good for business expansion.

Glimpses of all of these developments and more can be seen in Harold Martin's portraits of each year. Drawing mainly on the daily newspapers of the period, Martin highlights specific episodes and spotlights particular people to suggest the broader sweep of events. Each year is accompanied by a selected list of obituaries recalling some of the leading Atlantans who passed away in that year. These obituaries were prepared by Lil Salter, who also assisted Martin and typed the original manuscript. Volume III of *Atlanta and Environs* will be an essential source for those who seek to understand modern Atlanta, still the Gate City of the South.

        Bradley R. Rice, Editor
        Atlanta History, the journal of the Atlanta Historical Society

SECTION I

The Nineteen-Forties

INTRODUCTION

ATLANTA in the 1940s did not look greatly different from the city that had stood fifty years before. Horse cars had long vanished from the streets, and visions of a new and greater city were dancing in the heads of many of its leading citizens; but streetcars still clanged and rattled from the residential areas into the downtown section, and in the heart of town steam trains still smoked and whistled in the railroad gulch, parts of which were not yet covered over by viaducts.

Neither had white attitudes toward a large segment of the city's population vastly changed. The relationship of white Atlantans with black Atlantans, who in 1940 made up roughly one-third of its 300,000 population, was much the same as it had been in Scarlett O'Hara's day. Blacks had been freed from slavery by the Emancipation Proclamation and could no longer be bought and sold like mules or bales of cotton. But where they lived and what jobs were open to them and what opportunities there were for them to express themselves politically were still as circumscribed in Atlanta and in the deep South as a whole, as they had been in the days of *Gone with the Wind*. There were friendships between whites and blacks and even affection in their personal relationships. But any attempt to describe them as living side by side in "separate but equal" facilities would be a sardonic and bitter jest.

However, in the mid-forties as World War II came to an end, and on into the fifties, there had begun, quietly at first but with a growing fervor that turned into open violence in the sixties, an uneasy protest, an outspoken refusal on the part of black Atlantans to accept any longer what had been their status for nearly three-quarters of a century. And out of these years of traumatic change came the Atlanta we know today; still not a city of brotherly love, but one in which black power, both political and economic, is accepted, albeit reluctantly by some whites, and in which citizens of both races live and work, play and socialize in a relationship that would have been unthinkable only a generation ago.

A good way to introduce the decade of the 1940s is to examine an article written by Mayor William B. Hartsfield early in 1940.[1] Entitled "My Hat's Off to Atlanta," it takes the city into the forties with a proud flourish of trumpets, which naturally included a blowing of the mayor's own political horn.

He was still glowing from his and Atlanta's triumph the previous December in presenting the world premiere of *Gone with the Wind,* which focused international attention on the city, and in playing host earlier in the year to ten thousand Baptists who had gathered from many countries for a meeting of the Baptist World Alliance. But his theme now was that this was only the beginning of Atlanta's journey toward greatness.

Addressing "Mr. and Mrs. Atlanta," he wrote: "The Atlanta of today is moving forward as never before. She is growing both inside and outside of her limits, but she is growing in something more than mere brick and stone—in civic spirit, unbounded faith and optimism in her own future, still retaining that charm and courtesy which marks the precious heritage of the Old South." He cited accomplishments that had attracted no national attention but that would have a profound effect upon the city's future. These were extensive programs of street repair, a reorganization and cleanup of the police department, traffic controls that had cut the city's death rate from 87 in 1936 to half that in 1939, and a new method of financial operation that put the city on a cash basis, limiting future budgets to the past year's actual tax returns.

In the immediate future, he pointed out, Atlanta would see improvements in all fields—cultural, industrial, and civic. The Metropolitan Opera, absent from Atlanta since the Depression year of 1930, was due to come back in 1940. A small but beautiful park with a sparkling fountain had been under construction for more than a year and would be dedicated before the year was out. Streets would be widened, the airport improved. But all of these things, and all the favorable publicity the city had received, Hartsfield declared, would avail nothing if its people did not continue to welcome visitors with courtesy and friendliness, make them warmly welcome, and give them worthwhile things to see and do while in Atlanta.

To this end, Hartsfield wrote, the Cyclorama must be refurbished and improved, historic spots must be marked, their legends made available, and their locations brought under supervision of the national parks. If these things were done properly, he added, the visitors would come from everywhere pouring huge sums of money into the coffers of Atlanta merchants and businessmen.

In April of 1940, only three months after Hartsfield's prediction, a flood of free-spending visitors did arrive. The National Convention of the Fountain Sales Division of the Coca-Cola Company was held in Atlanta, and each visitor was given a handsome map of "Historic and Romantic Points of Interest" in and near the city. Overlaid on a map of downtown were sixteen sites of battle headquarters of both Union and Confederate generals, the area where the fiercest fighting took place during Sherman's invasion. Shown also were such noteworthy and historic places as the Wren's Nest, Woodrow Wilson's law office, Techwood Homes (the nation's first housing project), and East Lake Country Club, where both Bobby Jones and Charles Yates had learned to play golf. Along with these sites and the factual history connected with them were the supposed locations of the great scenes in *Gone with the Wind*—Aunt Pitty-pat Hamilton's Peachtree house where Scarlett lived in wartime, Melanie's home on Ivy Street, the old house where Rhett Butler was imprisoned, and the McDonough Road over which Rhett, Scarlett, and Melanie fled to Tara from burning Atlanta. The map and historical data were by the famous Atlanta artist Wilbur Kurtz, whose talent as both artist and historian had guided Selznick International Pictures in recreating the look and mood of wartime Atlanta.

Hartsfield did not suggest that Atlanta should seek to live on the legends of its historic past, nor on the reputations of its famous athletes. "In planning the future growth of Atlanta," he concluded, "we must not make the mistake of pushing one activity out of all proportion to the whole. It's no use to have new streets, and no equipment to clean them. New parks are just vacant lots unless properly developed. Fine schools are in vain if decreased public health service puts sickly children in them. Beautiful residential sections can be no better than the sewerage and water facilities that serve them and like the human body, we must grow in proportion. . . . And above all, Mr. and Mrs. Atlanta, let's keep our financial house in order—stay within our budget and never again run the risk of financial disaster."

The mayor's introduction to the 1940s contained an accurate prophecy for the Atlanta of today. "And what of the future?" Hartsfield asked. "Surely it was never so bright for the great metropolis of the New South. We live in a section where the nation's greatest future growth and improvement are bound to take place, and Atlanta is the logical center of that section."

NOTES

1. William B. Hartsfield, "My Hat's Off to Atlanta," *Atlanta Journal Magazine*, Jan. 7, 1940.

1940

THROUGHOUT his administration Hartsfield pushed firmly for all the matters he had discussed in his article in the *Atlanta Journal Magazine*. However, his support of airport development was particularly heartfelt, for he, in truth, as a young councilman had been one of the founders of the aviation facility that in the years ahead would bear his name and become one of the biggest and busiest international airports in the world.

Atlanta, born of the railroads, was increasingly aware as it moved into the forties that its future as a transportation center lay high in the air. In early January of 1940 figures prepared by Jack Gray, manager of Atlanta Municipal Airport, gave the picture. In 1925 Atlanta had no airport. Occasionally a flimsy single-engine plane landed at the old Candler racetrack. But now, in 1940, that track had been leveled and asphalt runways crossed it. Forty-one scheduled airplanes landed and took off every day. Atlanta had, according to Gray, more air routes than any other city in America. Military and general aviation, combined with the regular service, made Atlanta the fourth-busiest airport in the nation. More than five hundred people worked at the airport for a payroll of a half a million dollars a year.

Not only did Atlanta lead the region in air transport, it was still the main surface transportation and communication center of the Southeast. Despite the increasing competition of plane and bus, fifteen main lines of eight railroad companies were daily moving 104 passenger trains in and out, serving 14 million customers residing within an overnight haul from the heart of the city. Every day 224 passenger buses came and went, and truck lines operated seventy-five highway routes.

Atlanta in 1940 was the eighth American city in volume of air mail, and it was the third largest telephone center in the South. More impressive still, the city was also the third-largest telegraph center in the world, connecting directly with 499 towns and cities in the Southeast. (Franklin Garrett's first job in Atlanta was delivering telegrams for Western Union, and it was this that developed his geographic knowledge of Atlanta and its environs, and his profound interest in their history.)

Although transportation and communication were the keys to Atlanta's economy, manufacturing, retailing, and finance were important too. At the beginning of 1940 more than 900 factories were turning out 1,500 different commodities, valued at $165,729,836. Retail sales had reached a total volume of $172,279,000, exceeded in the South only by Dallas with $174,904,000 and Houston with $193,965,000. In bank clearings the order was reversed. Atlanta was the highest in the South at $3,430,900,000, and Dallas and Houston trailed at less than $3 billion. Atlanta's bonded debt, on the other hand, was by far the lowest, at $11,141,605—a tribute to the pay-as-you-go policy of Mayor Hartsfield.

A recitation of these figures, waxed and polished by the Chamber of Commerce, should not give the impression that all of the city's thoughts were solemn and money-centered. During the war years there were amusement facilities at every turn, designed to serve the thousands of soldiers, sailors, and airmen coming to the city on leave from the military training camps in the Atlanta area. Forty theaters seated nearly 40,000 people; eighteen golf courses were open for play all year round; and parks, squares, and open places covered more than 1,500 acres.[1]

In the forties the city was already a music center, presenting opera, both light and grand, and symphonies and concerts of high caliber sponsored by the Atlanta Music Club. The city, according to Edith Hills (Coogler) of the *Atlanta Journal,* was running Miami a close second as the amusement center of the Southeast. Nationally known orchestras, led by Tommy Dorsey, Kay Kyser, Buddy Rogers, Ozzie Nelson, Hal Kemp, Eddie Duchin, Morton Downey, Artie Shaw, Phil Spitalny, and Gene Austin, in 1940 were playing at the theaters along Peachtree, at the Grand, the Paramount, the Fox, the Capitol, and the Roxy, and in all the major hotel ballrooms. The Ansley Hotel's Rainbow Roof was an especially popular spot. Here, an innovation in dance flooring brought a flood of business. It was convertible to a rink on which famed ice skaters from all over the world performed. The Spanish Room at the Henry Grady, where the Conga was a favorite dance, was another place highly favored. The Samoan Room, newly opened at the Georgian Terrace, quickly began drawing crowds with dancers moving to the music of the "jukebox," a new name for the nickelodeon, instead of an orchestra. The town during the war years was also rich in vaudeville, notably at the Roxy, where big-name band leaders shared billing with top Hollywood stars.

Said Hills, in her *Atlanta Journal Magazine* article of March 3, 1940: "Two years ago, nobody dreamed that a sleepy-head town like Atlanta would support such entertainment. Folks in this part of the country ate a light supper, kissed the family good night, and went to bed by 9 o'clock." Saturday night, she noted, "was the only night out for Atlantans then, and most of the time it was whiled away at one of the clubs. If a fellow didn't belong to a club he had his choice of going to a movie or a juke joint—or staying at home with a good book."

Despite the changing moods and mores of the city—the soaring bank clearings, the booming night life, the streets thronged with uniformed men and women on leave from the military training camps that had sprung up nearby—there were certain elements reminiscent of Depression times, not all of them unpleasant.

In 1940, for example, cab fares from the Biltmore Hotel, a highly favored convention center, to the downtown area still held at the Depression price of 35¢, whether for one or five passengers. Trolley bus fares were 10¢ cash from Buckhead to downtown, or two tokens could be bought for 15¢. Transfers were free, and shopping tickets were downtown-and-back for a dime. On sightseeing buses the Atlanta Historical Society provided tour guides at no charge.

Other reminders of the recent Depression were the low prices that persisted, briefly, into the forties. Men's fine wool suits, from the best shops in town, were priced from $18.00 to $35.00, and famous-name brand shoes could be bought in the gentlemen's department at Thompson, Boland, Lee for $4.00. Ladies paid the better shops anywhere from $8.00 to $17.00 for a dressy dress, $8.00 for shoes, and then completed the look with a hat that was far more costly than the basics, starting at $17.50. Anyone shopping for a baby paid $1.00 per dozen for Birdseye Diapers, and little cotton, lace-trimmed gowns were two for $1.00.

Food prices were still low. At Kampers, a fancy and relatively expensive grocery store, one could buy pinkmeat grapefruit for 90¢ per dozen; twelve cans of tomato soup cost 50¢; and a homemade loaf of bread—white, whole-wheat, or raisin—was 20¢.

Haverty Furniture Company, celebrating its fiftieth anniversary, offered a three-piece metal porch glider set, consisting of a glider and two chairs, for 50¢ down and payments of $1.50 a month until the price of $19.50 was paid. A nickel would deliver a Simmons Beautyrest mattress to any home for the same financial arrangement. The total price was $19.00.[2]

In this year of 1940 men were beginning to break away at last from the old blue serge suit, white linen shirt, and soft gray felt or flat-brimmed straw hat that for generations had made up the Atlantan's business uniform. Now men wore coats and pants of other colors, and the colors were fantastic: all shades of the lighter blues and greens plus plaids, checks, and stripes. The pants were pleated and shorter in the leg, the coats three-buttoned and single-breasted with the middle button always buttoned. Ties were of garish design and were fifty inches long so that a double knot, created by the Duke of Windsor, could be tied to fill up the wide space between the new shirt collars.

It might be noted that, though men's clothing was still reasonably priced while changed fantastically in color and design, this meant little to the cotton farmers in the area who traded in Atlanta stores. Despite the looming threat of war suggesting the need for cotton fabric for millions of uniforms, the farmer in 1940 was still getting only 11¢ a pound for his cotton. Cotton had sold for 5¢ a pound during the Depression, and the low price had caused the Georgia landowner to start changing the pattern of his life in a way that had strong repercussions in the city. He was beginning to turn from cropping cotton in rows that were carved out by tenants' plowing mules to wide-field planting of feed crops—oats and wheat and rye and hay—that could be planted, tilled, and harvested by machine. This threw many tenants (and mules) out of work, and many moved their families north, seeking work in industry. This deprived the commissary and the small-town merchant of some of their trade. And this, in turn, deprived the Atlanta wholesaler of some of his small-town business. The mule was replaced by the motorized plow, planter, and harvester; Atlanta was no longer able to boast that it was the greatest mule market in the world.

Many Atlantans remembered the weather of 1940 long after the year had gone. On January 23 ten inches of snow, the deepest snowfall in the city's modern history, left 302,288 citizens within the city's boundaries, and 359,000 more in the environs, virtually immobilized. All activity came to a halt for days. In July ten days of almost steady downpour dropped four times the normal monthly rainfall and did greater damage to the city's streets and sewers than had the snow and ice storms of the winter. The year 1940 also saw three noteworthy fires, as explained in *Prompt to Action,* the official history of the Atlanta Fire Department's first one hundred years. In March the long freight depot occupied by the Seaboard Air Line Railway, the N.C.&St.L. Railway, and the Standard Milling Company, manufacturers and distributors of high-class animal feeds, burned. Fourteen engines, eight ladder trucks, and 125 firemen battled the fire with twenty-two hose streams for more than an hour, their combined efforts preventing the fire from spreading to adjoining structures—the Ten Forsyth Street Building, the old *Georgian* newspaper building, and the office of the Seaboard Air Line Railway. The damage was estimated at $125,000, and the cause of the fire was never determined.

On Saturday, June 21, 1940, a five-story brick structure at 1100 Murphy Avenue burned. The fire started on the two top floors where the Henry Chanin Corporation had stored more than 3,000 bales of cotton. The three bottom floors were a warehouse of the Piggly Wiggly Grocery Company, a subsidiary of the Kroger Baking Company. Eight alarms brought sixteen engines and seven ladder trucks, operating twenty-eight hose streams. This halted the fire's downward spread, but tons of falling water ruined the entire stock of groceries on the floor below. The loss was $200,000. The department's old water tower, designed to raise a nozzle sixty feet, played its last role at the fire. It was first put in service in 1909, but was removed from action after this fire.[3]

The most spectacular and potentially the most dangerous of the 1940 fires happened on November 11. The building superintendent of the old Auditorium Armory discovered fire in the fourth floor section used by the 179th Field Artillery as a headquarters and warned three hundred members and guests of the Disabled American Veterans holding a dance in the main auditorium. They evacuated just before explosions rent the air as small arms ammunition began to explode in the great heat. Fortunately, no big shells were stored in the building. Fourteen engine and ladder companies worked twenty-four hose streams to no avail.

Since 1909 the red brick structure had stood on a granite foundation. "For thirty-odd years it had welcomed every kind of industry and political rallies, graduation exercises, boxing and wrestling matches, basketball tournaments, roller skating derbies, dog shows. Each Spring, except in the depression years, the Metropolitan Opera had brought its great stars to the wide stage of the main auditorium which had been saved from destruction by a thick firewall separating it from the National Guard Armory. And now a carelessly flung cigarette, the firemen say, had destroyed Taft Hall and had caused damage to the extent of $200,000." Much of that loss was in uniforms and weapons of the 179th Field Artillery Regiment, the National Guard unit known as "Atlanta's Own." With the threat of war growing nearer day by day, Adj. Gen. Marvin Williamson and Col. T. L. Alexander were resolved to get the regiment re-equipped and back in training just as soon as possible.[4]

The searing heat from the Armory fire scorched newly planted trees across Courtland Street in nearly completed Hurt Park—Mayor Hartsfield's latest contribution to the city's beauty. The new park was to be a memorial to the career of Joel Hurt, pioneer financier and philanthropist. A reporter declared, "The two-acre tract has been converted from an area of rambling, obsolete run-down structures into a rolling stretch of green lawns, valuable shrubs, towering trees." The park's central attraction was a spectacular lighted fountain. All efforts by Hartsfield and the aldermanic board to provide a pleasing background for the November 23 park dedication ceremony by dressing up the fire-stained and crumpled old auditorium across the street had proved futile, though $5,000 had been spent on stucco and paint. Floodlights, which were to have been focused on the auditorium front, were turned instead to focus on the park.

The *Constitution* gave this report:

Hundreds of Atlantans last night stood in rain to dedicate Atlanta's only downtown park, the most beautiful and artistic of all the city's recreation and beauty spots, to the memory of a pioneer Atlanta builder, financier and philanthropist—Joel Hurt.

In ceremonies directed by Mayor Hartsfield, descendants of the Hurt family gathered along with city officials and with hundreds of citizens from all walks of life to open formally the local Hurt Memorial Park and to witness the first operation of the huge electrical fountain, given the city by the Emily and Ernest Woodruff Foundation.

Before Hurt's youngest granddaughter threw the switch lighting the fountain, Hartsfield thanked the WPA, officials of the General Electric Company, which installed the fountain, and others who aided in making the park possible. Atlanta acquired the site by exchanging the old city hall site at Forsyth and Marietta streets for the tract, with the city getting $50,000 in cash in addition to the park site. "About $50,000 has been expended from all sources in developing the tract," Mayor Hartsfield said. "Of this amount, the Woodruff Foundation paid $15,000 for the electrical fountain, which, of course, is the major nightly attraction, although the shrubs, trees and lawn expanses alone are exceedingly pleasing."

For Mayor Hartsfield the dedication of the little park was a heart-warming final moment in a year that to his surprise had brought him the ultimate disaster that can befall a politician—defeat at the polls. His achievements had been impressive in his first term in office. The *Gone with the Wind* premiere had brought national renown to the city and to its mayor. His skill as a financial manager had enabled him to sign checks for $800,000, which paid all of Atlanta's bills for 1939 and still left a half-million dollars in the bank. He had cleaned the crooks out of the police department, led an attack on the sale of obscene publications, and sorely harassed the lottery, or "bug," operators. He had pushed through council a new 25-mile-per-hour speed law, had improved street traffic and the waterworks, and had created a better monkey house at the zoo. He had set in motion, through City Council, a plan to create within the city a huge new sports stadium, seating fifty thousand, but such a facility would not come for twenty-five years, under Hartsfield's successor, Ivan Allen, Jr.

None of these things was easily accomplished, and in bringing them about Hartsfield inevitably made a number of enemies. Even the creation of Hurt Park, the first new park in the downtown area since the Civil War, had its opponents, notably Atlanta's downtown real estate developers, led by Ben Massell, one of the most outstanding of them.

By September 4, 1940, his political luck had run out. A hard-driving, self-confident former Chamber of Commerce president named Roy LeCraw beat him in the race for mayor. Two things, it seems, had beaten Hartsfield. First, confident that Atlanta would not reject the mayor who had brought it the *Gone with the Wind* premiere with its constellation of Hollywood stars and who had turned the city's $13-million debt into a surplus, he did not campaign with the fervor that had led him to victory in the past. More damaging, though, was LeCraw's simple, direct statement that if he was elected he would stop the "hiding police" who on Hartsfield's orders lay in ambush for speeders driving faster than twenty-five miles an hour. By such tactics, LeCraw charged, the city had collected a half-million dollars in fines. He also claimed that under Hartsfield there were 36,000 registered taxpayers in Atlanta and 20,000 tax dodgers, which meant that Hartsfield had to increase the toll on honest taxpayers by $2 million. He had also raised the water rate by 30 percent. LeCraw claimed these abuses would stop as soon as he took office.[5]

When the votes were counted on the evening of November 4, Hartsfield learned that he had lost by 111 votes—11,409 for LeCraw, 11,298 for Hartsfield. Hartsfield, naturally, was outraged, charging that the count was in error and that there had been chicanery at the polls. A final tally did show a slight discrepancy; LeCraw had won by 83 votes instead of 111—11,410 votes for him, 11,327 for Hartsfield.

Hartsfield's absence from City Hall was brief. LeCraw, a major in the Georgia National Guard, had been assured, he said, that he could go on furlough to serve as mayor so long as the United States did not become involved in war. When war did come, less than a year after his inauguration, he stepped down as mayor, put on his gold oak leaf, and in the spring of 1942 headed for Europe. In May, 1942, Hartsfield in a special election won over eight other candidates, and for twenty years thereafter the mayor's office was his.[6]

To stories of fires, floods, snow storms, and bitter political battles carried out under the growing threat of war must be added crime in a new and violent form that came to Atlanta as the forties began. The Ku Klux Klan, silent for years, was now back in the news again, and for many days in 1940 the story of Atlanta's problems with its hooded law-breakers was national news, drawing bigger headlines than the war in Europe. Tops among the year's stories, as listed by reporter John T. Carlton in the *Atlanta Journal* of December 18, was a series of floggings attributed to the Klan.

In March, reported Carlton, the body of an East Point barber named Ike Gaston was found in an open field in south Fulton County. He had died of shock and exposure following a brutal flogging, police reported, and in their effort to trace the whip, which was found nearby, police investigators discovered that the East Point chapter of the Klan maintained a "wrecking crew" that since 1936 had regularly turned out to punish drunks, wife beaters, and others accused or suspected of straying from the straight and narrow, including workers thought to be members of the CIO. Seventeen men were indicted, ten of them before the end of March, for other floggings that had resulted in no deaths. Of the first seven men tried by mid-December, six were convicted and sentenced, but as the year drew to an end the killers of Ike Gaston were still unknown.

Much history of a none too savory nature was being made in this first year of the forties. Early in the year, for example, Atlanta police and county prosecuting attorneys were complaining that lottery operators, known as "bug men," were pardoned by Governor Eurith D. (Ed) Rivers as quickly as they were arrested, tried, and sentenced. To prove the point, Fulton County Solicitor John A. Boykin named twenty-eight of these pardoned bug men as criminals of a more vicious sort. Assistant Solicitor Ed Stephens claimed that three-fourths of the bug men indicted by Fulton County grand juries were repeaters that the governor had freed.

Recoiling from the pardons controversy and a highway department scandal, Rivers turned to attack others. Early in 1940 he called in his attorney general, Ellis Arnall, and told him that he had been informed that Georgia, and notably Atlanta, was full of fifth columnists. He ordered Arnall immediately to start an "aggressive, effective campaign" to purge the state of "every possible fifth columnist under whatever color he may be sailing." Atlanta was to receive particular attention, the governor said, for he was receiving a flood of anonymous mail that told him that rumor was going about that anyone could attend a communist meeting in Atlanta any night in the week.

This concern on the part of the governor and others, that communists were peddling their schemes in Atlanta, came to a climax late in the year. In mid-September, Rivers presided at a hearing before the state Board of Education, at which charges were leveled at a distinguished Columbia professor, Dr. Harold Rugg. It was said that textbooks by Rugg that were used in Georgia and Atlanta schools contained subversive material, in that they presented Soviet goals in a favorable light. Chief accusers of Dr. Rugg were Capt. Jack Kelly, onetime state patrolman and former adjutant of the State Defense Corps, and A. L. Henson, prominent member of the American Legion. Henson read from a book called *The Red Network,* which named alleged communist sympathizers in America. Rugg pointed out that Eleanor Roosevelt was also named in this book, as were many other distinguished and patriotic Americans. Rugg's most outspoken defender was Dr. Glenn Rainey, Georgia Tech professor and chairman of the Georgia Service Commission on Human Welfare. The most effective defense, however, came from Rugg himself, who discussed his boyhood working in a cotton mill. The changes in people's relationship with their governments he had seen on his trip around the world was the basis of his decision to teach children how to recognize and meet the economic and social changes that the future inevitably would bring.

Whatever his own beliefs, Governor Rivers, presiding in the absence of Judge A. H. Freeman, chairman of the state school board, maintained a strict neutrality. When arguments grew hot and tempers short, he would interrupt saying, "Gentlemen, let's don't get personal." The decision was to hold up further distribution of the books until the board's professional textbook committee, which had approved the Rugg books once before, could go over them again.

In February of 1940 a campaign began to enlarge and improve Grady Hospital, where 384,324 people had been treated in 1939. Many Atlanta institutions were generous in their support of Grady. Members of the Fulton County Medical Society, who made up the visiting staff, gave more than $1.5 million in free services to "indigent citizens" in the course of a year. Thanks to Emory University, the city, and the WPA, $70,000 worth of improvements were made, including pediatric and gynecological/obstetrical clinics on the white side, a tunnel connecting the white and Negro units, and an eye, ear, nose, and throat clinic for the Negro unit. White and black patients at this time were still kept and treated in completely separate areas, a costly detail. In one instance of the author's experience, a white male who sought to give his cook's son a person-to-person infusion of a rare blood type was told this could not be done. The white man could not be brought to the black side and the black patient could not be treated in the white section. The white man insisted and a compromise was reached. The men were laid side by side on stretchers in a neutral corridor, and the transfusion was made. The sick man fully recovered.

The improvements listed above did much to make a decent hospital out of the ancient rookery that was Grady, but the biggest improvement was in the personal services rendered by the WPA at a cost of $85,000. Smaller but important contributions came from Gate City Lodge 144, B'nai B'rith, the

Service Guild, the Joseph B. Whitehead Foundation, and the Exchange Club. One of the outstanding gifts was $14,000 from an anonymous donor who supplied 200 modern hospital beds.

These activities, inspired by Dr. J. Moss Beeler, superintendent, continued on into 1940, when expenditures of the sum of $150,000 in WPA money provided salaries for 150 desperately needed new people. For years the student nurses had had to do all the dirty work of the hospital, so much of it that they had little time to study. The WPA provided trained housekeepers, extra orderlies, stenographers, and social workers. They also provided dieticians to help teach the people suffering from such diseases as pellagra and diabetes what they should eat and how it should be prepared. Another important accomplishment was the thorough reorganization of Grady's badly confused medical records. One woman, for example, had an x-ray of her stomach made three times in two and a half months—once at the emergency clinic, once by the medical staff, and once again by somebody else. All three showed about the same thing. But the city had spent a total of $66.00, when one picture and $22.00 would have sufficed.

Despite the dramatic improvements, Grady was far from being the great medical hospital it was to become. Six out of every ten babies born in Atlanta were born at Grady in a little room where mothers in labor lay side by side, so close there was no room for a screen between them. Sometimes, when many mothers were being delivered at the same time, babies were born in hallways, their mothers lying on stretchers. Frequently, children with slowly debilitating diseases like infected tonsils were brought to Grady suffering pain and fever but could not be admitted because there was no bed for them. They had to wait, sometimes for months, before they could return for the operation, the good food and the bed rest that they needed.

In mid-1940 the city decided to ask for a $4 million bond issue to provide money for Grady, Battle Hill Sanitarium, the Fire Department, and schools, some of which were fire traps. The voting took place on September 4, the same day that Mayor William B. Hartsfield lost to Roy LeCraw by 83 votes. The bond issues were also defeated by slim margins, not by votes against them, but by the failure of a sufficient number of eligible Atlantans to cast votes at all. Bond passage required a majority of registered voters and two-thirds of the actual ballots cast. In the vote on the $2 million for Grady Hospital, for example, the count was 19,230 for to 1,807 against, a huge majority in fact, but 127 votes short of the necessary total. School bonds totaling $1.5 million lost by 806 votes, and some $450,000 for the Fire Department failed by 396.

Many voters believed their ballots had been thrown out on technicalities, and J. P. Allen, chairman of a citizens' bond campaign committee, immediately urged a recount. However, certain members of City Council had begun to fear that the passage of the bond issue would lead to higher taxes, an increase in the water rates, and lower instead of higher salaries for city employees, despite assurances from experts that this would not happen. No recount was held. But the friends of Grady did not despair. By the end of the year plans again were under way to revive the $4 million bond issue that would, in time, create at Grady one of the great hospitals of the nation.

On May 5, before the Atlanta bond defeat, Fulton County voters overwhelmingly approved $750,000 in school bonds. Through cooperation with the WPA, this meant that $3 million would be available for new school buildings in Fulton County. Trust Company banker Robert Strickland, who helped push for the bonds, pointed out that a great move to the suburbs had begun and that the county schools were overcrowded. County superintendent Jere Wells agreed. Success of the bond issue, he said, meant that Fulton's children would no longer have double sessions, nor attend classes in Boy Scout huts, school auditoriums, and basements.

This election launched the long political career of Charles M. Brown, thirty-eight, president and treasurer of Fickett-Brown Manufacturing Company. A man well known in business, fraternal, and civic circles, he narrowly defeated incumbent J. A. Ragsdale as commissioner of roads and revenues. I. Gloer Hailey beat Clarence Dalton in the other commissioner's race, Thomas H. Jeffries won over Carlton Binns in the race for ordinary, and J. C. Aldredge beat Harry Barfield for sheriff.

In this political year another young man with a well-known name in Atlanta business and civic circles made his debut in a peripheral political role. Ivan Allen, Jr., was named by the national organization of Young Democrats as executive chairman of the Young Democrats from Georgia. His job was to organize the Young Democrats over the state and bring them to Atlanta in November in a convention to elect permanent officers. Young Allen, who was twenty-nine, was following in his father's footsteps. Ivan Allen, Sr., was chairman of the Democratic campaign for Georgia and on October 4 had been named by Fulton County Democrats as president of a newly created Roosevelt-Wallace Club.

Hughes Spalding, who called the new club's meeting to order, noted that Fulton County had gone Republican only three times in history—once for McKinley, once for Taft, and once for Hoover. This, he indicated, must not happen again. The danger lay in the fact that most Democrats did not usually vote in general elections. Thanks to the so-called white primary, there were usually no contests for state offices. "The purpose of this club is to get out the Democratic vote," said Spalding. "We don't want the Republican or any hybrid party to carry this country." Ivan Allen, Sr., called Atlanta's twelve-man Democratic Executive Committee together at City Hall and laid out his plans. "I think the county is going [for] Roosevelt by a large majority," he said, "and if it doesn't I'll be ashamed of Atlanta and I've never been ashamed of it yet. I want each of you to turn heaven and earth to get out the vote, the best vote in the history of the county." There was a real danger that FDR might be beaten in Fulton County. Willkie had a good following. Bobby Jones was one of his supporters, and there were signs that many influential Atlantans were leaning toward the Republicans. The well-planned get-out-the-vote effort worked, and in Fulton County the vote was overwhelmingly for FDR despite the opposition of many to a third term.

Working as a vote-getter for Roosevelt was not the only extracurricular activity Allen took on during this autumn of 1940. On September 4, Commissioner I. Gloer Hailey nominated him for the Fulton County Board of Public Welfare to fill the unexpired term of chairman W. E. Mitchell, who had resigned. The Board of Commissioners unanimously agreed.

Significant gifts came to Atlanta's worthy causes in this year through bequests from foundations and from wealthy Atlantans who had died. The will of Edgar Poe McBurney gave $1 million for the McBurney Decorative Arts Gallery at the High Museum, featuring art objects other than paintings and sculpture, including furniture, ceramics, laces, carvings of wood and ivory, and a magnificent collection of porcelains from the eighteenth century. Close behind this came a $500,000 gift from the Rosenwald Fund to provide training for Georgia teachers, especially those in Atlanta schools. The will of Atlanta capitalist J. Bulow Campbell created a $1 million trust fund for the promotion of "religious education and health projects" in the state. Judge Price Gilbert gave $100,000 to the University of Georgia for the construction of a hospital, and the trustees of the Joseph B. Whitehead Foundation, established in memory of one of the founders of the Coca-Cola Bottling Company, voted that approximately $282,000 in foundation funds be distributed to Atlanta charitable and educational institutions before Christmas.

The trustees of the Whitehead Foundation directed that the 1940 gifts be in memory of Conkey P. Whitehead, who died November 2, 1940, in New York. Conkey P. Whitehead was chairman of the board of the foundation and was deeply interested in its charities. A millionaire in his own right, he provided in his will $200,000 for the establishment of a Chair of Chemistry at Yale, which he had attended. He also made long-range provisions for a foundation to establish a home for indigent southern women and to furnish education for girls.

The sixteenth annual Community Fund drive, chaired by H. Carl Wolf, president of Atlanta Gas Light Company, set its goal at $572,222, some 20 percent more than the total of $482,982 that Community Fund volunteers had raised in the 1939 campaign. Over 750 of Atlanta's leading citizens made up the directorships of the thirty-four health and welfare agencies that shared in the Community Fund. The Rev. Dr. Herman L. Turner, budget committee chairman, announced that the figure was the absolute minimum that these agencies would need in 1941.

A small group of wealthy volunteers called upon the big givers, and other volunteers were organized into a phalanx of specialized divisions, including a Negro division headed by Alonzo Moton.

The first list of names of those giving over $25 was published October 18. At the top of the list was the name of Margaret Mitchell Marsh, with a gift of

$1,500—followed by fifty-three other names, all of them well known in Atlanta, whose gifts ranged from $700 down. Author Mitchell, in a letter to a fund official, made it plain that she had been reluctant to permit her name and the amount of her gift to be publicized. "However," she said, "if people think that the use of my name and the amount of my donation will be of any service to the Community Fund, I will be very happy to give you my permission."

The next day there was a Peachtree Street parade to promote the drive. Ten bands played "God Bless America," twenty airplanes dropped pamphlets over the city bearing the words of the song, and thirty-four agencies of the Community Fund marched. Alternating with "God Bless America," the bands played a patriotic paean entitled "Because We Are America," composed by Emily Robinson Head of Atlanta. By November 14 the money collected and pledged was still $133,046 under the target figure, but the Whitehead Foundation gave $50,000 to help close the gap.

On Thanksgiving Day 25,000 cheering fans watched the Georgia Tech–University of Georgia freshman football game at Grant Field, an annual event for the benefit of the crippled children of Scottish Rite Hospital. Georgia won the 1940 game 36–0. But, said sportswriter Al Sharp, writing in the *Atlanta Constitution* of November 22: "The score does not make much difference. It doesn't matter much, because all the time that strong young men are running up and down the field, there is limned in the background a smiling face. It is the face of a kid. His body is twisted. But there is that smile. It is a smile that brings tears to your eyes so that the figures running up and down the field are blurred. It's a blur that makes the scoreboard hard to see. And no one cares. As long as you can see that smiling face, it makes no difference." On November 30 the Tech varsity lost to Georgia (21–19). Thus ended the year that had begun triumphantly for Tech with a 21–7 victory over Missouri in the Orange Bowl on January 1.

World War II in Europe was beginning to help pull Georgia and the nation out of the Depression, but significant human misery remained. Grady Hospital reported treating 700 undernourished children in 1939. In February, 1940, the Fulton County Grand Jury heard from the Georgia Conference on Social Work the urgent plea that Fulton County "take the necessary steps to make available funds for the relief of the needy. . . . Fulton County, because of its size and importance, sets a standard for the rest of the state, and conditions permitted in Fulton County are consequently reflected throughout the state." Lyle Chubb of the Governmental Research Bureau of the Atlanta Chamber of Commerce and Edward M. Kahn of the Federation of Jewish Social Services pointed out that Fulton County for all its pride and wealth spent far less per month, per case, for the relief of its needy than was the national average. Around the nation the average was $23.27; for Georgia it was $5.02; for Fulton County, $4.92. Shortly thereafter, the county commissioners in regular meeting heard WPA administrator Robert L. MacDougall describe the relief work in Georgia as well as Fulton County as a "mess." "There are a lot of people here, heads of families who are desperate. We are in a jam and we might as well admit it." Some officials went to Washington, D.C., to seek more funds, and a food stamp plan modeled after that of Savannah, Macon, Columbus, and 125 cities around the nation was tried. But the welfare "mess" remained unsolved.

In 1940 a drive got under way that would have an enduring effect upon Atlanta and its character as a southern center for higher learning. The idea of making Atlanta a great university center had been stirring in the minds of Atlanta educators for nearly a decade, though its first protagonist was not an Atlantan nor a Georgian, but a northerner. In February of 1932 Dr. Edwin R. Embree, president of the Julius Rosenwald Fund, visited Emory University, made a detailed inspection, and told the faculty that in his view Emory more nearly approached Dr. Abraham Flexner's "ideal university" than any other institution. If he were putting 20 million dollars into a Southern university, he said later, he would "put it all into Emory . . . because I consider it rich in promise."

Dr. Thomas H. English, Emory historian, tells the story of the university center idea as it developed over more than a dozen years:

On all occasions, Dr. Embree pointed out that the South was dissipating its educational energies among a multitude of small, mediocre institutions; that the larger, better-established foundations wastefully duplicate offerings; that it presented few opportunities to advanced students for first-class specialization; and that as a result, promising graduate students and teachers were lured away to Northern and Western universities. He urged that Southern education consolidate its resources, and indicated the possibility of developing at least five university centers, of which Atlanta was one, where graduate work of the highest quality might be pursued. Such a movement he envisaged as a Southern educational renaissance.

In pursuance of this suggestion, President Cox, President J. R. McCain of Agnes Scott, and President M. L. Brittain '86 of Georgia Tech entered into discussions as to the possibility of establishing a university center in Atlanta. . . . A committee of educators of national distinction . . . visited Atlanta in January 1934 and . . . [recommended] seven major steps toward "the ultimate goal of making Atlanta a regional educational center for graduate and professional work on a high level." Specific recommendations were made for cooperation, consolidation, and development involving the three institutions so far concerned in the plan. Besides noting the need for new buildings, and the enlargement of library and laboratory facilities, however, it was clearly stated that only "an endowment running into millions . . . will make it possible for the proposed university center to attract and hold outstanding scholars in the several fields that are desirable to develop."

In the following years every recommendation of the report and every aspect of cooperation were given the most intensive study by committees of Emory, Agnes Scott, and Georgia Tech, with whom were joined representatives of the University of Georgia, Columbia Theological Seminary, and the High Museum of Art. As will be seen, much was accomplished by the institutions working in concert, although some specific recommendations were found impracticable. But the impetus gained from the movement toward a university center was to carry all the educational institutions of the area to higher levels than they had previously occupied.[7]

For several years nothing much happened. Progress was confined to what English described as "interminable committee meetings and the drafting of reports." Agnes Scott and Emory agreed to share their libraries, some exchange of professors was arranged, and Agnes Scott changed from a semester to a quarter system, to synchronize its calendar with Emory's. Then came the big break. Early in January of 1939 the General Education Board of New York, which shared Embree's view on the need for a vast improvement in southern education, made grants to Emory and Agnes Scott on a matching basis—$2 million to Emory if Emory would raise $4 million on its own; $500,000 to $1 million to Agnes Scott if Agnes Scott would raise $1 million. The total, $7.5 million, would be used as a general endowment for strengthening the library, natural sciences, and departments essential for the proposed graduate program. From the Emory grant $200,000 was to be used for general university center purposes, and Dr. S. V. Sanford announced that Georgia Tech and the University of Georgia would cooperate fully in the use of these funds. Columbia Theological Seminary and the High Museum's School of Art would also cooperate. Before the general drive began, the matching funds drive was already well along. Samuel C. Dobbs a year earlier had announced an unconditional gift of $1 million for Emory's College of Arts and Sciences, and in December another $250,000 was given to the School of Medicine to endow the Joseph B. Whitehead, Jr., Chair of Surgery.

Another who considered Emory rich in promise for the future was Dr. L. C. Fisher, president and treasurer of the Crawford Long Hospital and a trustee of its board. On Sunday, January 21, 1940, it was announced that the million-dollar facility was being transferred to Emory as part of its plans to develop a great medical center. Plans were also announced for the completion of a $300,000 nurse facility and maternity center on adjoining property recently purchased.

Present at the January 29, 1940, kickoff dinner meeting for the general drive were some two dozen educational and business leaders. Among these were: M. M. Benton, John A. Brice, Robert A. Clark, President Harvey W. Cox of Emory, Charles J. Currie, Dr. Dobbs, George A. Giesde, Wilbur F. Glenn, W. Eugene Harrington, Hal F. Hentz, Frank Inman, Sinclair Jacobs, Mitchell C. King, President J. R. McCain of Agnes Scott, H. Y. McCord, Jr., C. A. Rauschenberg, Jr., W. D. Thomson, the Reverend Herman L. Turner,

Roy Ulrich, George Winship, T. Guy Woolford, H. Lane Young, A. L. Zachry, and George J. Yundt. There were among these many who were not only strong supporters of Emory and Agnes Scott, but of Tech and Georgia and the other institutions. Speaking at the dinner, E. S. Papy, president of the Chamber of Commerce, termed this effort "the greatest single enterprise in the field of higher education now in process or development anywhere in the U.S."

Preston S. Arkwright was named general chairman of the drive, and he lost no time in putting his campaign teams together. By early March offices of the University Center Drive had been set up in the William-Oliver Building, and Thomas K. Glenn, Charles Howard Candler, and Robert W. Woodruff had set about making personal appeals to a selected group whom they knew would give generously to certain specific causes at Emory or Agnes Scott—the endowment of religious or surgical chairs, for example, or for building a dormitory. Special projects campaigns preceded more general solicitation. By May 15 an article in the *Atlanta Constitution* said: "The Drive to raise $1,300,000 to establish a $7,500,000 University Center in Atlanta was oversubscribed yesterday by $22,000, Preston Arkwright, campaign chairman, announced. Pledges and contributions totaling $1,322,624 had come in, said Arkwright, who described the undertaking as 'the most ambitious in Atlanta history.'" Still under way, Arkwright said, was a campaign to raise $600,000 more from out-of-town alumni of the cooperating schools.

The first building to be constructed under the University Center plan, Presser Hall at Agnes Scott, opened in November to provide a cultural center for community activities and for cooperative musical and dramatic enterprises for all six institutions sharing in the center development. According to Dr. James R. McCain, president of Agnes Scott, "The building will be used for varied functions in connection with the development of the entire university fine arts program." At the formal dedication of the $285,000 building, the Atlanta Philharmonic Orchestra played, and the featured speaker was Dr. James Francis Cooke, president of the Presser Foundation of Philadelphia and editor of *Etude*, a national music publication. Cooke's own composition, "Grand Processional at Avignon," was played by the local orchestra, and the Agnes Scott College chorus sang a medley. Presser Hall, it was noted, constituted one of the finest examples of collegiate gothic architecture in the country, and was one of the best equipped to provide instruments and space for a concert orchestra. Gaines Chapel, seating 900, contained a four-manual pipe organ and two concert grand pianos. A smaller hall for intimate recitals, the Joseph McLean Auditorium, seated 300.

Thus began the Atlanta University Center concept, which was to expand in many fields of study, not only in Atlanta and Athens but throughout the state. However, Dr. Raymond D. B. Fosdick, president of the General Education Board when the first grants were made, in his 1962 booklet *Adventure in*

Giving, pointed out that the center never developed as some of its backers had hoped:

In retrospect the affiliation of the Atlanta institutions failed to develop in any substantial way into the type of relationship originally envisioned by the General Education Board. Perhaps the concept of regional cooperation was too much of an alien idea, unsuited to the time or the occasion. Perhaps the trend toward sharing libraries, laboratories, and faculties, and away from duplicating specialities, was impeded by too many local difficulties. Whatever the reason, this particular experiment, while not a complete failure, must be written off as one of the less successful ventures of the General Education Board.[8]

Dr. English was more optimistic in his general evaluation expressed in 1966:

The benefit to higher education in the area has hardly been less than the hopes originally entertained. The University Center organization has continued, now financially supported by the participating institutions, with a quarterly conference of a Council of Presidents for the discussion of current educational problems. An Advisory Faculty Council allocates grants for research and arranges for visits of distinguished scholars and for interdepartmental meetings. In 1964–65 there were fourteen visiting scholars and twenty-four interdepartmental meetings. Finally, duplication of offerings has probably been brought to an irreducible minimum. The institutions of the Atlanta-Athens area, while not linked in an absolute cooperative relation, are actively allied for the furtherance of scholarship and academic progress.[9]

Oglethorpe University was not one of the cooperating institutions in the drive to create an Atlanta University Center. But from 1936 on into 1940, President Thornwell Jacobs and Dr. Thomas K. Peters, archivist and archeologist at the little school far out Peachtree, had been creating a unique historical project that attracted national attention. It covered thousands of years and the achievements of millions of people of all races everywhere. Against this background, the focus was on the present, the first decades of the twentieth century, its discoveries in all fields, and the people who brought them about. This came to be known as the Oglethorpe Crypt of Civilization, and "Cultural Atlanta at a Glance," published by the Junior League of Atlanta, nearly a decade after its sealing, gives a fascinating picture of its concept and its contents:

The meager information available regarding intimate details of life of the past inspired Dr. Jacobs in 1940 to preserve a complete cross-sectional picture of the entire life of our world for the people of the future. Under a cathedral-like limestone building which houses Oglethorpe's executive offices, a crypt as large as a swimming pool was created from the granite bedrock of the Appalachian mountains. It was lined with slate, roofed and capped with stone and sealed with a tablet of stainless steel, and deeded to the government of the United States, its heirs and assigns. The crypt is to be held in trust to be unopened until the year 8113 A.D.

The contents include phonograph records and sound films to preserve voices of such contemporary figures as Roosevelt, Mussolini, Hitler, Stalin and others; newsreels to immortalize ship launchings, baby contests, football games, Spain's civil war and other events; special time-proof editions of newspapers, books and magazines; an automatic micro-book machine for reading books; a mutoscope machine with metal leaves which will serve as a Rosetta stone to the English language; a moving picture machine and sound projector; a complete set of modern scientific instruments; models of people in costume; dioramas of important historical events; samples of textiles; food products and other material.[10]

Some of the items to be sealed away might seem a little puzzling to those who Dr. Jacobs hoped would open the crypt 6,000 years hence. The things typical of life in 1940, some $50,000 worth, included a pint of beer; a bottle of Coca-Cola, personally transported to Oglethorpe by Franklin M. Garrett as one of his first assignments with the Coca-Cola Company; a man's hat; all types of razors; ladies' cosmetics, including false eyelashes and fingernails; a toupee; and a set of false teeth. Also placed within the crypt were twenty-five-word greetings from seventeen distinguished Atlantans, Georgians, and Americans.

It was recognized by Dr. Jacobs and Dr. Peters that 6,000 years from 1940 there might be no "Atlanta" left on earth. So a history of the crypt and an exact description of its location were printed on special rag papers, for distribution to libraries and museums in all parts of the world. The fact there might not be an English language was considered. So history was translated into seven Oriental languages, including Japanese, Chinese, and Sanskrit, and into the languages of all European and South American countries. The creation of the crypt and its highly publicized sealing brought the little institution a certain national renown which was enhanced further scholastically in 1944. In that year another distinguished educator, Dr. Philip Weltner, took over as president and created a new and exciting approach to undergraduate education called the "Oglethorpe idea." It featured a curriculum stressing that education should deal with the twin aims of "making a life and making a living." The curriculum adopted has provided the framework of an Oglethorpe education from that day to the present, under a series of presidents who followed Weltner. They were James Whitney Bunting, Donald Wilson, Donald Charles Agnew, George Seward (acting), Paul Rensselaer Beall, Paul Kenneth Vonk and Manning Mason Patillo, Jr. In the 1940s the neo-Gothic buildings of the university were surrounded by woodlands and open fields. The great explosion of the suburbs had not yet brought stores, apartments, filling stations, and branch banks far out Peachtree Road.[11]

Another notable event in this busy year was the visit of General Evangeline Booth. On November 28 she arrived in Atlanta to celebrate the fiftieth anniversary of the date when the first little blue-clad Salvation Army band began to thump and tootle on the downtown streets, and a lassie named "Pleading Minnie" was harassed by Atlanta police because certain citizens thought a woman had no right to preach—particularly in the streets. With a display of pictures and with an awesome eloquence usually reserved for the more glamorous movie stars, the *Constitution* described General Booth:

General Evangeline Booth is like a rock that the sea beats against and breaks upon, or like a tree that will not bow or bend no matter how the wind blows against it.

She seems as ageless as earth, and as strong. She is probably 75 years old, but she looks not much more than 50, and there is no difficulty at all in understanding how she was for years, and for that matter still is, the fire in the hearts and the iron in the spine of that incredibly courageous organization, The Salvation Army. . . .

She's still battling against evil wherever she finds it, standing behind the men and women of her army wherever they are. In England where bombs have destroyed more than 100 of their shelters, in the conquered countries as best she can.

Age has not weakened her. She stands with the carriage of a soldier, her high head crowned by a mass of golden-brown hair, in which there is a touch of gray.

Her voice is sonorous and musical. Her most casual conversation possesses the dignity of an oration. Her every sentence is a sermon. If Salvation had not called her, she might have been one of the great actresses of the world.

That night at a "Golden Jubilee Dinner" at the Ansley Hotel, former governor John M. Slaton presented General Booth to an audience made up of the leading men and women of the town—judges, bankers, lawyers, ministers. Booth told them what had happened to the army in Atlanta in the half-century since its first small band had gathered at the corner of Spring and Marietta streets. She also pointed out that the Salvation Army in Atlanta was no longer a shabby little band, but the headquarters of a great organization spread throughout fifteen southern states and the District of Columbia, under the direction of Lt. Cmdr. William C. Arnold. Meanwhile, Salvation Army officers from throughout the South gathered in Atlanta to hear Booth and hold meetings.

Another noted visitor during this year was Eve Curie, author and daughter of the discoverer of radium. Sponsored by the Wesleyan alumnae group in Atlanta, she spoke in Glenn Memorial Auditorium at Emory University. Her subject was "Science and the Woman," the story of her famous mother.

Other notables were welcomed to the city with greater or lesser enthusiasm. General Louis A. Johnson, assistant secretary of war, came to Atlanta to speak at the Jackson Day Dinner at the Ansley Hotel. Clark Howell sounded the keynote for the record throng of 788 assembled Democrats that Georgia should remain firm in her allegiance to FDR. General Johnson assured his audience that the United States would be able to fight anybody in the world—in three years.

War, past and future, was the subject of a series of notables in the literary field who came to Emory on the invitation of the Student Lecture Association. Andre Maurois, a French biographer and essayist, who was an official observer attached to British headquarters during the battle of Flanders and France, addressed the question "Can England and France be Friends Again?" Adm. H. E. Yarnell, former commander in chief of the U.S. Asiatic fleet, covered "The Far East," and Philip Gardella, British historian and biographer, talked on "The World Today," telling of England under the Nazi assaults. Thomas Mann, Nobel prize winner and refugee from Nazi Germany, spoke on "The Problems of Freedom."

Aviation was in the news in the early months of 1940. In January the Atlanta airport was being considered by federal authorities as one of ten flying fields where equipment for blind landings in any weather would be installed. And in February the first school in the Southeast for training air stewardesses was opened in Atlanta. All clients had to be unmarried registered nurses, twenty-one to twenty-six years old, standing at least 5'3" in height, and weighing between 100 and 120 pounds. The plan for installing equipment for blind landings was of paramount interest to Atlantans. On January 3 an Indiana pilot caught by darkness while trying to find Candler Field was forced down on course at the East Lake Country Club.

Whoever the celebrity, and whatever the event, nothing so captured the imagination of many Atlantans, nor aroused their deeper enthusiasm, than the return to Atlanta of the Metropolitan Opera Company after an absence of ten years. From 1910 to 1930 the Atlanta Music Festival Association had provided the annual guarantees that the Met required. By 1930 the money was not available, nor did it become available again until 1940, when a kindred group of music lovers, the Atlanta Music Club, brought the Metropolitan Company back for three seasons, until the pressure of war caused it to be discontinued. Sally Forth (Winifred Rothermel), society commentator for the *Constitution*, explained in her March 3, 1940, column:

Those of you who remember pre-depression days when a whole trainload of Metropolitan Opera stars came down to Atlanta for a week's engagement every April will thrill again to the elaborate plans now under way for the return of "The Met" next month for three glorious days. Those were the days when the beloved Caruso raised his golden tones in "O Sole Mio" in gracious response to society's demand at the popular after-opera supper dances at the Capital City Club. Those were the days when Geraldine Farrar and the jovial Martinelli raised their voices in a tuneful aria at the annual barbecue at the Druid Hills Club. And those were the happy days when melodious notes issued from many a window of the Biltmore and the Georgian Terrace and you knew that Bori and Ponselle and Chaliapan and Gadski and innumerable others were "tuning up" for the evening performance.

Now history prepares to repeat itself, for the city's clubs and hotels are planning a gala social program to fill the intervening hours between the operas. . . . Again the famous stars of the Metropolitan will mingle in intimate camaraderie with Atlanta audiences and music lovers. And no doubt you will be privileged to hear the superb voice of Lawrence Tibbett and Richard Crooks combined in a familiar melody or perhaps lovely Helen Jepson will oblige you with your favorite song.

At last came April, and the stars arrived. In the *Constitution* of April 21, Mozelle Horton Young began her report on a jubilant note:

Showers of stars will be the order of this April day. . . . The company comes from New Orleans, where they have been playing a three-day season. The first of the week they were in Dallas.

It has been ten years since the Metropolitan Opera Company appeared in Atlanta—ten long years, and many had even despaired that we would ever have the Met again. For twenty consecutive years the Met was an annual festivity for which every music lover in this part of the country lived in anticipation all year long.

And now, at long last, the "good old days" are with us again! The Met will be here today—today for a three-day season beginning tomorrow! . . .

It is a civic dream come true—the return of the Met is a civic achievement of which all Atlanta should be justly proud. An indication of Atlanta's hunger for opera is the fact that the house for each of the three nights was completely sold out weeks in advance, and even last week 300 extra seats were put in the auditorium so that a few of those who were clamoring for tickets might be accommodated.

Amid the lavish serious reviews of opening night was the following observation by a former sports writer:

ATLANTA SWEEPS TO THE OPERA IN TOPPERS, TAILS AND JEWELS

On the wings of spring and the golden music of Giuseppe Verdi, opera came back to Atlanta last night after an absence of ten years. And Atlanta, in toppers and tails, and the glitter of jewels, came back to opera, 5,000 strong.

Not since "Gone With the Wind" has the town turned out in such array of gorgeous plumage, and not since the halcyon days of the fabulous twenties has it so bedecked itself en masse. The glittering hosts began to arrive an hour and a half before curtain time, and though a cat could have walked on the top of limousines and taxis down Gilmer Street and Edgewood Avenue, the combined efforts of eighteen policemen under Lieutenant J. C. Atha kept the traffic river of machines flowing swiftly and smoothly.

By sheer whistle power they kept things moving, and many a top hat was jammed down over the reddened ears of its owner as, urged on by officers, the chauffeur stepped on the gas, then stopped with a jerk. . . .

Inside, Emory students who usher with the privilege of seeing the opera their only pay, divided the river of humanity into divergent streams that led to orchestras, boxes, loge and balcony.

Those who sat in the orchestra made their entrance with sweeping, high-headed grace, but the steep ramps to the boxes were the bane of stately dowagers. They started out with the ponderous grace of galleons under full sail and reached the top white, shaky and puffing from the climb. . . .

Backstage as the crowd gathered and the orchestra tootled through its practice notes, the land of make-believe lay bare. Hurrying property men placed on tables that hold the stage in the opening scene, bowls of plaster of paris fruit and empty champagne glasses. Photographers focused spotlights onto corners where arias were to be sung, tiny dancers of the ballet pirouetted, singers in costumes breathed deeply, went "mi-mi-mi-mi" and cleared their throats. There was the chatter of voices in French, Italian, and Spanish and broken English could be heard from every side. . . .

Gennaro Papi stood upon the podium, in silhouette against the midnight blue of the great curtain. A dropped pin would have made a thunderous clatter as the baton moved in a swift downward stroke, and faintly through the breathless hush came the golden melody of a violin.

"La Traviata," that old familiar friend whose melodies fall upon the ears like a caress, told its sweet, sad story again. Something of splendor and beauty that Atlanta has missed for ten long years was back in all its glory.

Happy as some thousands of Atlantans were to bedeck themselves in jewels and silks and corsages for the opera, there were many more thousands who found equal pleasure in thronging to Grant Field on the night of May 4 for a people's music program presented by the *Atlanta Constitution*. About 30,000 of them gathered for the Greater Atlanta Music Festival. There, to the music of seventeen local high school bands, they bellowed their heads off to "Let Me Call You Sweetheart" and cheered themselves hoarse as team after team of drum majors and majorettes stomped and strutted and twirled their batons.

The program began with Graham Jackson, Atlanta's famous black pianist and accordion player, rendering a prologue on the Novachord, a newly developed electronically operated instrument capable of representing with marvelous fidelity, according to Frank Drake of the *Constitution*, the sounds of every instrument in an orchestra from a piccolo to a piano, organ or a big bass horn.

Following Graham Jackson came the Grand Parade of seventeen bands. After the bands came the folk dances performed by the children of the elementary schools, and finally a great chorus of 3,000 voices sang. All of this was down on the field, and then came the community sing with all blending in a chorus of 30,000 voices.

It had now grown dark and was time for what for many was the highlight of the evening. The audience had been told to bring matches, and at a given signal, each person lit his match—30,000 twinkling stars in a dead black night, their glow making a bowl of soft fire out of the great cup of the stadium.

A huge human American flag formed by 542 Japanese lanterns carried by elementary school children preceded the finale—the biggest fireworks show Atlanta had ever seen. The festivities reminded many who were there of how different life still was in Atlanta from that of people living in blacked-out London, Paris, or Oslo.

The appearance of Marian Anderson was another highlight of the spring. A review in the *Atlanta Constitution* of May 6, 1940, explained:

To Marian Anderson, the Negro contralto with the phenomenal voice, went the honor of closing the current concert season for Atlanta. Almost any single artist in concert would have been an anti-climax, coming immediately after a brilliant season of the Metropolitan Opera Company and a great symphonic concert by the Philadelphia Symphony Orchestra—but not Marian Anderson! Her concert last night at the city auditorium would have been a thrilling climax for any season.

Dignified, yet gracious to her large audience, with a simplicity of manner that is highly admirable, this fine-looking colored girl takes a step toward the footlights, closes her eyes, and the golden tones begin to roll. To hear her is really an experience. The timbre of her voice has an appeal distinctly individual, and the amazing range as well as flexibility of it places it in a class to itself. Not only does Anderson possess a great God-given voice, but she has the soul of an artist. Her extreme devoutness to her art is evident in every interpretation. Every phrase is polished in finest detail, and she is the master of every mood.

Julian Harris, nationally famous Atlanta sculptor, Tech graduate and native of Carrollton, was named state chairman of a National Art Week celebration to be held in Georgia November 24–30. He was appointed by Francis Henry Taylor, director of the Metropolitan Museum of Art and chairman of the National Council for Art Week. Harris was also named to the National Council. He appointed Mrs. Murdock Equen as his Atlanta chairman, and plans immediately got under way for exhibitions of paintings, sculptures, arts and crafts, to end with a colorful Beaux Arts Ball. Howard Candler, a friend of the arts, made available an empty store on Peachtree near Five Points. There more than one hundred painters, sculptors, and artists came to display their wares. It turned out to be one of the most successful art shows ever held in Atlanta; more than 5,000 Atlantans thronged to the show. A professional jury, choosing items for IBM to put in its permanent collection in New York, picked a painting by Robert Rogers, teacher at the High Museum School of Art, as best painting, and a bronze head of a black man by Julian Harris as the best piece of sculpture.

In February, Morehouse College held a four-day celebration of the seventy-three years since a handful of youngsters born in slavery gathered in one classroom in Augusta, Georgia, in 1867. They formed the beginning of what became one of the largest undergraduate Negro colleges in the South, occupying six buildings and twelve acres of land on Chestnut Street in Atlanta.

Founded as a branch of the National Baptist Theological Institute, the school was moved to Atlanta in 1879 as the Atlanta Baptist Seminary at Elliott and Hunter streets, was renamed Atlanta Baptist College in 1898, and in 1913 was named Morehouse College for Dr. Henry Lyman Morehouse, secretary of the American Baptist Home Mission Society. The focus of the anniversary celebration was the prayer to raise $400,000 to be matched by the General Education Board of New York as part of the University Center project under way in Atlanta.

On Confederate Memorial Day of 1940, as World War II raged overseas, five living veterans of the Civil War that had ended seventy-five years before appeared in Atlanta's parade. The author, then a reporter, wrote:

Down long streets lined with the Stars and Stripes, Atlanta marched yesterday in tribute to the men who died under another flag—the red-barred banner of the Lost Cause.

In honor of five crumpled old men in gray, who waved with feeble, blue-veined hands at the thousands who cheered their passing, and in loving memory of the comrades who rest on a hundred battlefields, the children of a New South paused for a little while to remember the gallantry and graciousness of an old South that is gone. . . .

It may be that *Gone with the Wind* has freshened in men's minds the memory of the days when another army—the loose-striding, bantering hosts of Old Joe Johnston, marched down Peachtree. It may be that the rumble of guns in Europe has touched with a new significance the guns that rolled past in the parade. Whatever the cause, for some reason there seemed to be a new and stronger interest in the Memorial parade this year.

Surely not in recent years has a greater crowd watched the march than that which lined the curbstone four deep from Baker Street to Oakland Cemetery, nor one which seemed to feel so strongly the implication of the squat, green-snouted howitzers that trundled at the tail of the artillery trucks and the quick-stepping hosts of riflemen that followed them.

In the minds of all who saw the trappings and the panoply one thought was uppermost. Here were men who were ready to fight—not as their grandfathers fought, brother against brother, under two flags—but side by side, for one land, never again divisible by the hatreds of civil war.

Meanwhile, in Marietta Ralph McGill found Mattie Lyon, "A young woman of 89, almost 90," and Lucinda Hardage (92), who still lived in the same house she occupied in 1864, the house where generals Leonidas Polk and Joe Johnston laid their plans for the defense of the Confederate line that sprawled across Big and Little Kennesaw and Pine Mountain. Said McGill:

The stories they tell are even more interesting than the stories told by veterans. Miss Mattie recalls the life in Marietta, the first troops to leave, the first Georgia casualty lists after First Manassas, the coming of Andrews' Raiders, the work of the women. . . .

Miss Lucinda remembers how General Joe Johnston's voice sounded. She recalls General Polk, and saw them poring over maps day after day. She recalls the services General Polk held for his men in the grove about the house. She remembers when his body was brought back after he was killed by a shell on Pine Mountain, not far from the house.

She saw some of the fighting. She heard most of it. She saw the backwash of the war. The thing she most vividly recalls is the long line of Confederate ambulances, going back the Burnt Hickory road, with the men screaming in some of them and the blood dripping from some of the ambulances until the mud was red along the road.

They are two of Georgia's most remarkable women. To be with them is a very real inspiration.

In Jonesboro, Wilbur Kurtz, an authority on the Old South, delivered the principal address at Memorial Day services held in the school auditorium under the auspices of the United Daughters of the Confederacy. City Council had declared a holiday, and many business houses closed during the program.

The celebration of national independence in 1940 was dampened by rain throughout the state. "It fell on picnics, camp meetings and politicians, automobile races, golf matches, fishing trips and outings for the family." But, the *Constitution* noted on the editorial page, there was a truly happy side to this. Georgia set a new Fourth of July record for safety. The rains, coupled with a special drive by the state highway patrol to keep down speeders and reckless drivers, saved many from injury or death.

Three celebrations ushered in the fall. On September 10 the *Atlanta Journal* made newspaper history in the South by bringing "on line" a mighty battery of new presses, almost a city block long. Then on September 17, the First National Bank marked its seventy-fifth anniversary as an Atlanta financial institution. That same week Rich's department store put on a celebration to welcome Atlanta to its new and expanded facilities downtown. Rich's had expected 5,000 but nearly 10,000 people showed up, men and women whose parents and grandparents had bought goods from Rich's. They came to wander about the new, bigger, easier-to-get-around-in, easier-to-find-what-you-want store.[12]

In its anniversary celebration First National Bank not only remembered the individuals who had shaped its career, but the Atlanta companies that had been its contemporaries in the beginning. In an ad in the *Constitution* of September 22, 1940, was a "salute to our contemporaries of 1867 and today." It listed ten firms—the Atlanta Gas Light Company, the Atlanta and West Point Railroad Company, the *Christian Index*, Georgia Railroad, Macon and Western Railroad (now, in 1940, the Central of Georgia Railway), Rich Brothers (now Rich's, Inc.), the Tommy and Stewart Hardware Company (which became Beck and Gregg), the Western and Atlantic Railroad, and the John C. Whitner Insurance Agency. (Forty years later, in 1980, all but the Whitner Agency were still in business in Atlanta.)

As some old landmark buildings were being torn down to make way for progress, another downtown building was welcoming a new, hard-driving tenant. H. K. McCann, president of McCann-Erickson, one of the largest advertising agencies in the country, announced on February 14 that his company was opening an Atlanta office. He noted that there were three things essential to the operation of a successful advertising agency—"One, to locate in a section that is growing, to staff the agency with people who know the likes, dislikes and habits of the local people, and to stress newspapers as the media through which the advertising gets the quickest response and the best results. In Atlanta, I think we have found the ideal situation." In years to come many other advertisers shared this view, and Atlanta became the advertising center of the Southeast.

Despite problems, the 1940 economy showed signs that the Depression was ending. On May 1 the *Constitution* carried the headline, "Retail Business Zooms Sharply. Building Gains. Daily Average Department Store Sales Highest on Record." The monthly business review issued by the Federal Reserve Bank showed the dollar volume of retail sales in Atlanta to be up 17.4 percent over February, and 11.3 percent above March, 1939. Sales for the first quarter rose 10.3 percent and bank clearings showed gains over both February past and March of 1939, throughout the six states of the Federal Reserve District. Construction contracts gained because of a large increase in residential building, a reflection of the influx of many new families, drawn to the vicinity of the military training camps built in the Southern states to meet the challenge of probable war.

The mule market, a special Atlanta industry, which had been faced with a slow decline as Georgia farmers mechanized their cultivation and harvesting methods, also hoped to receive a shot in the arm due to the war. The French were beginning to look to the mule to replace the horse as the burden bearer and had bought 1,000 mules from markets to the north. The Atlanta mule market on Brady Avenue, which still was handling 60,000 head of mules a year, hoped to break into this overseas market.

Word trickling down from Washington that the federal government would sponsor airplane manufacturing plants in strategic areas caused a stirring in Atlanta's outlying communities. Despite efforts by East Point and Stone Mountain, a point near Marietta was chosen. On March 30, 1942, ground was broken for the gigantic Bell Aircraft Company bomber plant, and by March 15, 1943, 1,000 employees were working there, building the huge B-29.[13]

Georgia Power Company on May 31 announced the construction of a $3.6 million addition to Plant Atkinson, its steam-electrical generating plant on the Chattahoochee near Bolton, ten miles from Atlanta. Said Preston Arkwright, president of Georgia Power: "In deciding to build the addition to Plant Atkinson, we were influenced by several factors. Most important was the relation of this plant to the national defense program. In any large-scale rearmament program, Atlanta will almost certainly be a major southeastern center of war industries. To operate these industries, an adequate supply of electric power is absolutely necessary. We decided to build a steam-electric plant in Atlanta, rather than a hydro-electric plant on one of the undeveloped water power sites in Georgia, because it is essential that the power source be close at hand, not subject to being cut off by the destruction of long-distance connecting lines."

Arkwright's prediction that a growing economy based on preparation for war would require a vast increase in power production was soon borne out. The Industrial Bureau of the Atlanta Chamber of Commerce reported that a $6 million expansion of industries and government building was going on in Atlanta, bringing employment to hundreds of laborers and increasing business payrolls by another million dollars a year. Forty-seven Atlanta factories and other businesses expanded during the first six months of the year, spending $3 million on construction. Fifty-eight new manufacturers, distributors, and service-related businesses were established in the city during the first half of 1940, and 325 others, according to Ivan Allen, Sr., chairman of the Industrial Bureau of the Chamber, were negotiating for sites in the Atlanta area.

"The military," said the *Constitution*, "is heavily involved in this expansion. The Army is expending $700,000 in expansion at Fort McPherson, the WPA is expected to approve an application of $400,000 for the development of a new airport at Camp Gordon." And thus there came into being the new Naval Air Force Station to be constructed at the airfield at Camp Gordon, of World War I vintage.

While military aviation was expanding, so was commercial air transport. Delta in March had put in operation a luxurious fourteen-passenger Douglas airliner, said to represent the last word in comfort, speed, and beauty, on all flights between Atlanta and Fort Worth and points in between. "Delta Air Line's history-making step will mean further laurels for Atlanta as an air center," the *Constitution* prophesied. "Already it is becoming known as the southeastern hub of aviation, and this new service will be another stride in its march to the head of the nation's airports."

This was only a beginning for Delta. In January of 1941 the huge $130,000 hangar at Candler Field was completed, and Delta officials announced on January 27 plans to make Atlanta the base for its fleet of 21-passenger airliners. Some of these would be used in commuter flights between Atlanta and Birmingham, plus a Charleston run, making Atlanta the Delta base for this territory. These planes were larger, faster, and more expensive than the Delta 14-passenger planes. They offered an innovation not before seen by the city's air travelers: a snack bar for the serving of delicacies and drinks. Delta announced that its passenger revenue in 1940 was 62 percent over 1939 and that in the five years before 1940 it had increased 79 percent. Its staff in Atlanta during the same period had increased from five to seventy-five men, and its payroll and land purchases were pressing $1 million. The Opry Plumbing and Heating firm was given the contract for installing $794,000 worth of plumbing at Cristobal, in the Canal Zone. About the same time Shell Oil Company announced the opening of a new division office in Atlanta, combining the areas formerly covered by the Jacksonville and New Orleans offices. The Atlanta territory served Georgia, Florida, Alabama, South Carolina, Mississippi, Louisiana, and Texas. An Atlantan, Sid Golden, former star athlete at Georgia Tech, took over as retail sales manager in the new office, where sixty-five employees, most of them Atlantans, occupied the fourth floor of the William-Oliver Building.

The Williams Printing Company became the first firm in the South to install a lithograph press, which was said to be five times faster than the speediest commercial press then in use in Atlanta.

One of Atlanta's foundation industries was also making changes designed to keep it alive and moving in a world grown more dependent on the airplane and the truck. The Southern Railway system announced that it would soon replace with new diesel-electric locomotives the old steam engines still running in and out of Atlanta on two Southern Railway lines. The diesels would be used to pull the Crescent, operating between Washington and Atlanta, and the Ponce de Leon, plying between Cincinnati, Chattanooga, Atlanta, and Jacksonville. Each of the locomotives weighed 300 tons, with a starting tractive effort of 100,000 pounds, and could maintain speeds of 100 miles per hour. The new engines, equipped with all modern safety devices, would eliminate smoke entirely, would keep up schedules, and would keep abreast of modern transportation, according to the Southern's dispatches from Washington.

Malcolm Bryan, vice-president of the Federal Reserve Bank of Atlanta, foresaw a general business boom, based on a vast public and private construction program, fathered in part by defense measures and in part by a demand for housing after ten years of depression. Bryan told Rotarians that he did not believe that the city, or the South, would gain much industry, for it would be cheaper to expand an existing factory in the industrial East and Midwest than to build a new one in the South. Southern trade, transportation, housing and hotel business, he predicted, would be sharply stimulated by the concentration of hundreds of thousands of troops in the area. And so it proved.

As 1940 moved on to its close, work was begun clearing a sixteen-acre tract of land on which a $500,000 State Farmers' Market could be built at Murphy Avenue and Sylvan Road. A market to which farmers could bring their produce by wagon, truck, or train had played an important role in Atlanta's development since the 1860s. There had been many of them springing up, both at the curb and under a roof, all over town, and each had offered fresh vegetables, eggs, and fruits to be sold at reasonable prices to Atlanta's housewives and merchants. But each had also brought noise, smells, traffic congestion, and an influx of raffish characters. So there had been a constant shifting within the city and outward, as the city grew. The Murphy Avenue installation was vigorously protested in council and court by its neighbors in the Fourth Ward. But the need for a new market was great, and the place was there. And with both state and city officials pledging that the new market would be an up-to-date, modern, well-managed, and well-policed area, the market was built and was a tremendous success from the start.

Retired Police Chief Herbert Jenkins, senior research associate at Emory University Center for Research in Social Change, tells the story in his book *Food, Fairs and Farmers Markets in Atlanta*. Built with state funds, the array of open concrete sheds cost $150,000, and during its first year of operation sales totaled more than $6 million. Then the war came along, and sales increased by as much as $5 million in a single year. Produce from forty-two states and eight countries arrived monthly, an average of 285 carlot loads and 2,000 truck loads. Its builders thought the market would serve Atlanta for twenty years. But the war, bringing the huge increase in military population at Fort McPherson and elsewhere in the Atlanta area, soon made that expectation obsolete. Jenkins wrote:

The Atlanta Market became a bedlam of trucks, people and produce. There wasn't enough space under the sheds to accommodate all the farmers, truckers and buyers. The street that ran between the market buildings was so crowded with trucks and sales stands that vehicles at times were unable to pass. During July and August farmers had to wait for hours to get on the market grounds. . . . With most covered stall space taken, traders and farmers unable to find a space had to bear the brunt of bad weather whether it was sun, hail, sleet or snow. There was no place to go except back home, but many could not go home until they sold what they had brought to the market.[14]

Obviously, a larger market in a less congested area was needed. Under the tenure of Agriculture Commissioner Phil Campbell, a new Atlanta State Farmers' Market was opened in 1959 off the South Expressway in Clayton

County, south of the Atlanta airport. The new market covered 146 acres and cost $10 million to build.

More evidence of returning prosperity came on November 21, when the paper announced the biggest after-Thanksgiving sale in the history of the city:

Atlanta tomorrow will be the city of a million bargains.

Big store and little shop, all over town, are joining hands to play host to all of Georgia at the third and biggest After-Thanksgiving Sale ever held here, launching the Christmas shopping season with a bang while shelves are crowded with new goods fresh from the factories.

Prices will be slashed—for the period of this sale only—as the best way Atlanta merchants know of saying "Thank you" and "Merry Christmas" to the friends who have brought them patronage throughout a greatly successful year.

One of the nation's most distinguished soldiers, Brig. Gen. Robert O. Van Horn, commander of Fort McPherson since 1933, retired from active duty on August 31, ending an illustrious career that began with his enlistment in 1897 and ended with his post preparing for World War II. He saw service in the Spanish-American War, in the Philippines, and in World War I—rising from the ranks from second lieutenant in 1897 to brigadier in 1933. During the war he won two Silver Stars for gallantry under fire and a Distinguished Service Medal.

Big headlines in the *Constitution* on July 21 announced that Charles F. Palmer, Atlanta real estate developer, had been called to Washington to become U.S. Coordinator of Defense Housing. Palmer resigned as head of the Atlanta Housing Authority and was succeeded by Marion Smith, who was appointed interim chairman by Mayor Hartsfield. Palmer was one of the pioneers in the field of slum clearance, having organized Techwood Homes, the first public housing development in the United States. Constructed in 1936, the project cleared away a fetid slum adjoining the Georgia Tech campus. By 1944 Techwood and a black project called University Homes had been followed by six other developments, housing 20,000 people in 4,000 apartment units at an investment of $21 million. Said Franklin Garrett, "Indeed, by 1940 federal funds have built considerably more housing in Atlanta than Federal Representative William T. Sherman destroyed here in 1864" (II, 962).

Palmer's account of his motives and his methods is given in his book *Adventures of a Slum Fighter*, quoting an address he delivered before a gathering of his fellow Methodists at the Interdenominational Theological Center in Atlanta on April 16, 1963:

My first interest in slums was to earn money through their clearance. That was in 1933. With banks closed and 15,000,000 unemployed, President

Roosevelt passed legislation providing federal funds to make jobs by tearing down and rebuilding slums.

As head of a corporation owning office buildings in central downtown Atlanta where slums were nearby as they are in most cities, I figured their removal would increase the value of our properties. Also that if I, as a broker, assembled the land there were real estate commissions to be earned.

That night I told my wife of my plan. Her immediate reaction was "But what do you know about slums?" My counter was, "I drive through them each day on the way to the office."

"Yes, you go right through them," she replied. "You look straight ahead and drive a little faster."

My wife was right. I had seen some ragged kids along the street but knew nothing of the hovels where they lived.

The next morning I stopped enroute to town. Facing away from the pleasant view of the Georgia Tech campus and ignoring the majesty of the office buildings which bordered the other end of the intervening slums, I wandered through the wretched area.

Here were sagging shacks built generations ago. Designed to wring the last cent from their use, for fifty years they had taken all and given nothing. In the rear were stagnant pools of water near an open privy serving several families. People were everywhere. It was the same block after block. Soon I'd had enough.

That afternoon I visited the police station to talk with the officer who walked that beat. He said he never made his tour alone. It was too dangerous. They always patrolled in pairs. What sort of people lived in that Techwood slum? Some good citizens who would move but they can't "because too damned poor." The others? Mostly drunks, bootleggers and whores. What about the influence on the children? "Terrible! How can you expect kids to be decent when that's where they live."

The officer had made his case, and I had seen the evidence. "There's one thing sure," I summed up. "If we clear and rebuild that mess there shouldn't be any opposition."

"I don't know about that," the policeman replied. "Look, Mr. Palmer," he said patiently as if explaining a problem to a child, "all those slum folks pay rent. Somebody gets the money!"

The prophecy by the patrolman that we would have opposition came true. The fight was one where the slum owners, under cover, used every means to stop us. But with citizens aroused we finally prevailed.[15]

Ralph McGill pointed out, in a July article in the *Constitution*, that it was fitting that the first of the new projects be named for Clark Howell. He, according to McGill, was actually the father of the local housing program. He shared Chuck Palmer's view of slum clearance and low-cost housing for the poor, and it was Howell who took Chuck Palmer to Washington to present his ideas to Roosevelt, who gave his approval. After that Howell and Palmer did not dally. Within a few weeks they were back in Washington, with the plans drawn up by architects Burge and Stevens for buildings that would replace the miserable Techwood slums with comfortable, low-cost housing.

On May 11, 450 Atlanta and area school patrolmen were en route home from Washington after marching in the ninth annual school patrol parade of the American Automobile Association. Two Atlanta youngsters and one from Cartersville had been particularly honored at the meeting when they received three of four national awards given for bravery. Lonnie Asher and William Lanier, Jr., both twelve years old and patrolmen at Peeples Street School in Atlanta, were honored for stopping a runaway automobile that was threatening the lives of several children. Charles Shaw, age eleven, of Cartersville, received his medal for snatching a younger child out of the path of an oncoming automobile.

Felix Weihs, famous Viennese sculptor, came to Atlanta early in the year, commissioned by Sir Eric Underwood of London and cousin of federal judge Marvin Underwood of Atlanta, to do a bust of James Edward Oglethorpe, founder of the state of Georgia. The bust was presented to the state in formal ceremonies in early June and was set up on the Capitol grounds.

Atlanta Law School, an independent school that produced many local attorneys, celebrated its fiftieth anniversary. The school chose to bestow honorary LL.D. degrees on a founder, Blewett Lee, and seven of its more distinguished graduates at exercises on the evening of June 7. The alumni honored were Chief Justice Charles S. Reid, of the Georgia Supreme Court; Col. Allen M. Burdett, judge advocate of the U.S. Army 4th Corps area; retired Maj. Gen. Walter A. Bethel, for many years on the faculty of the U.S. Military Academy at West Point; Judge Anton L. Etheridge of Fulton County Superior Court; Congressman Robert Ramspeck from the Fifth District of Georgia; Lawrence S. Camp, U.S. attorney; Judge Ralph McClelland, judge of the Civil Court of Fulton County; and Hamilton Douglas, dean of the school. Chief Justice Reid delivered the graduating address.

Special honors came to two Atlanta physicians in 1940. Dr. Phinizy Calhoun was elected president of the American Ophthalmological Society, only the second Southerner to be so honored.

Another distinguished Atlanta surgeon, Dr. Daniel C. Elkin, chief surgeon at Emory University Hospital, won one of the highest awards the medical profession can bestow. He was awarded the Matas medal for distinguished work in vascular surgery, the treatment of aneurism and wounds of the heart by wondrously delicate operations, which he had performed largely on charity patients at Grady Hospital. Dr. Elkin at forty-seven was only the third man in medical history to win the Matas, which was named for the famed New Orleans surgeon Dr. Rudolph Matas. It was presented only when outstanding research warranted it. Kentucky-born, Dr. Elkin was also widely known as a breeder of fine horses.

Women also received acclaim in 1940. Late in the year plans were made to create a memorial and museum to the memory of Alice McClellan Birney of Marietta, founder of the national PTA. St. James Episcopal Church announced it would sell its rectory—the old Birney home—as a site for the Birney memorial and museum. Several of her personal possessions—her mahogany desk, two chairs from her home, and the dress she wore to the first meeting of the Mothers Congress, forerunner of the PTA—were available for the museum collection.

Atlanta in October was to see its second world film premiere in ten months when Medora Field Perkerson's mystery "Who Killed Aunt Maggie?" was shown at the Rialto Theater in October. The gala celebration focused in large degree on the author herself, star of the *Atlanta Journal* staff and wife of its magazine editor, Angus Perkerson. She was also president of the Atlanta Womens Press Club, who took over the responsibility for a series of social events to honor not only Mrs. Perkerson and her movie, but the assemblage of Hollywood stars invited to attend.

An Atlanta woman broke new ground in becoming an associate editor of the *Atlanta Constitution*. Said *Newsweek* magazine on August 16:

Few women have ever held top-drawer editorial jobs on important Southern newspapers. For one thing the tradition of forthright personal editorials lives on strongly in Dixie; for another, the newspaper atmosphere is one in which the also traditional Southern lady does not readily fit. So it was news last week when Editor Ralph McGill made a by-line page 1 announcement that Doris Lockerman has been named associate editor of the *Atlanta Constitution,* in charge of women's activities and interests.

On the *Constitution* for the past three years, Mrs. Lockerman had won considerable following with her column, "Let's See Now."

Radio was holding out attractive offers, and Atlanta journalists gossiped that the *Constitution*, notorious for pinching pennies, had to do something extraordinary to keep the popular Doris on the payroll.

Atlanta, going into the forties, might have appeared to the casual observer to be concerned mainly with matters it had long considered of primary importance: the buying and selling of goods and real estate, city and county politics, Tech and Georgia football and Cracker baseball, and the amiable activities of its social set. The fact is, however, that over everything there hung the dark shadow of war. Aid to friends in Europe facing Hitler's murderous assaults by land and air could not forever be met merely by sending food and warm clothing to bombarded civilians rather than guns and ammunition to the beleaguered armies. Soon the time would come when to guns and butter must be added a final contribution: American armies ready to fight on the ground, on the sea and in the air. And as the months passed, Atlanta and the nation became aware that war was nearly inevitable.

On August 16 the lead editorial in the *Atlanta Constitution* described Atlanta's role in the days ahead:

Atlanta, in the months and years to come, will be one of the great military centers of the world. Selection of this city to be the supply center for the Army in the South will make it one of the most vital areas in the country and will impose upon the people of Atlanta and the surrounding counties a responsibility they have in times past met.

It is no accident that Atlanta is being made the supply center for the southern armies. In its early history, the capture of the city spelled the doom of a valiant army. In 1864, as today, it was the hub of communication within the South and the channel for the flow of supplies both north and south. The network of railroads, highways and sky lanes from the city today makes it the most important city, strategically, in the South. It is accessible from all sections of the nation by any number of alternate routes, and from it all areas in the South can be reached quickly and efficiently.

It will not be in the number of troops stationed here that the city will rank as a great military center. Wisely, these troops will be dispersed to localities in which they can most efficiently be trained, Fort Benning, Camp Jackson, Fort McClellan, Camp Beauregard; Fort Knox, Fort Bragg, Fort Oglethorpe and other posts away from the big cities will house the troops. Near Atlanta, however, undoubtedly will be a number of defense air fields— not fields such as Candler and the new Camp Gordon post, but the military fields that will be necessary as the defense program proceeds apace.

This selection of Atlanta does place a heavy responsibility. Vital services must be strengthened and maintained under all conditions—and these are plans which should be made now—to insure against the placing of an additional burden on the regular armed establishment in a time of emergency.

Women of Atlanta, under the leadership of Mrs. Albert Thornton and Mrs. Daniel MacDougald, formed an Atlanta chapter of the British War Relief Society, to raise money to buy ambulances, x-ray units, surgical instruments, medical supplies, and feeding units.

Though not yet taking the form of outright war, the threat from Japan inspired in some Atlanta women the urge to hurt a prospective enemy. As Tokyo joined the Rome-Berlin Axis, many American women, including Atlanta women, resolved to boycott the Japanese silk garments—the hose, underwear, night gowns, and dresses—they had been wearing for two decades. Carolyn McKenzie, writing in the *Constitution* of October 5, said:

No more silk dresses. No more silk stockings. No more silk. Let's *cottonize* America.

A theme running something like that has attacked Atlanta violently and the women, the purchasers of 85 percent of the merchandise sold, are boycotting silk.

Many of the older women say they wouldn't mind turning back to lisle hose, because they wore them in their youth with all their georgettes, silks and satins—and, they laughingly comment, they caught their "man." The younger women, especially members of the Atlanta Debutante Club, say they really prefer the processed hosiery to the silk variety but they shy away when asked if they'd wear cotton stockings. They said:

"We're for any substitute to help defeat the totalitarian idea. . . . Cotton hose are practical and can be made beautiful. . . . Anything which will give America an advantage. . . . I'd wear any kind of hose or go without them (wear socks) to boycott Japan. . . . Yes, if they're cotton 'cause I'm a Georgian." Over at the state capitol the girls all voted for the processed or rayon hose. They said: "Boycott the worm and take up the boll weevil. . . . I'd be willing to go barelegged. . . . For cryin' out loud, I've been doin' that. . . . Yes, I'm ready and anxious."

All efforts to meet war's challenges by works of charity or boycott of enemy goods were secondary to the sacrifice that Atlantans and Georgians had already made in sending 3,000 of their sons belonging to the 30th Division National Guard units off to Camp Jackson, South Carolina, for a year's training. Now came the climax—on September 17, 1940, President Roosevelt signed the draft act which would require 16.5 million young men between the ages of twenty-one and thirty-five to register for compulsory military training. Registration day was set for October 16, and by that time, draft boards were set up in 184 school houses, fire stations and other public buildings around the state. The response was fantastic.

Atlantans soon were to discover that though more than 40,000 young men had registered, there would be no sudden rush into the service. The first selective service quotas assigned to Fulton and DeKalb counties were for only twenty-six men, and the draft boards easily made up this number out of their lists of volunteers. Thus, Atlanta Draft Board Number 9 and one volunteer provided the first Atlantan to be accepted under the selective service plan. His name was Durwood Gerson of 811 Boulevard NE, a twenty-one-year-old typist and stenographer, and he admitted that the $30 a month private's pay recently raised from $21 seemed attractive to him. He passed his physical, conducted by Dr. Bolling Gay, and the first week in December he, along with his fellow volunteers, was sent to Fort McPherson for induction, classification, and then a year's military training.

Constitution reporter Jack Spalding gave the humorous side of the draft registration story:

Heroes of yesterday's registration were not those who signed up to do or die, but the school teachers. They rose before dawn and in some cases found queues of men lined up at the school doors long before seven, when registration began. And their neat schoolrooms, cozily decorated for Halloween, soon were defiled by cigarette butts, and a faint odor of stale sweat and tobacco.

There were some registrants who weren't sure what it was all about. An eager Negro signed on at North Fulton High School and asked:

"Boss man, where's my uniform?"

He explained he was ready to go, right away.

Congestion at white schools sent prospective registrants scurrying toward town, looking for a backroad, comparatively uncrowded school. . . .

Citizens turned up in overalls, sweatshirts, and every other kind of garb, up to but not including formal wear. They walked to the nearest schools, they rode in street cars or their own automobiles. At E. Rivers School, where the winding roads of the finger-bowl district converge on busy Peachtree, station wagons and expensive sedans rubbed fenders with jalopies from the old red hills out Peachtree and Roswell roads.

While the young men were registering for the draft, a number of older Atlantans were looking closely at what the draft, and the possibility of war, could do for the city and its environs in a business way. On the day before the draft registration a promotional group representing the city, county, and the Chamber of Commerce was created to press on, in Washington, with Atlanta's already active efforts to obtain a large military airbase, a $15 million army warehouse, and other defense projects—one of them the famous Bell Bomber Plant at Marietta. E. S. Papy, president of the Chamber of Commerce, organized the first meeting at which Frank Shaw, head of the Chamber's Industrial Committee, told of what had been done already, and future plans. The tone of the meeting indicated how strongly Atlanta business leaders felt that the city should miss no opportunity to grow and build for the future, even while preparing for immediate defense against an air- or seaborne enemy.

For many Atlanta businesses, the "trickle-down" from government contracts had already begun. Six Atlanta firms, for example, printed the draft registration cards and other items. The Scripto Company, a manufacturer of pencils and pens, received a contract to manufacture $1,094,000 worth of ammunition components. Before this, Scripto's role had been to polish 75mm brass cannon shells turned out in Birmingham. The new contract, according to P. S. Hauton, vice-president and general manager of Scripto, would require the company to build a new plant, in which 250 to 300 additional workers would be employed. On November 4 the War Department announced the award of thousands of dollars in clothing contracts to plants in Georgia, including Nunnally & McCrea Company, Inc., Atlanta, that would make 50,000 denim working trousers for $41,000. Holeproof Hosiery Company in nearby Marietta was to produce 204,000 pairs of cotton socks for about 13¢ a pair.

At the same time it was reported that two Atlanta firms—Hentz, Adler & Shutze, architects, and Newcombe and Boyd, engineers—had been awarded contracts for the construction of a $5 million replacement camp at Macon to house 16,500 men. The replacement center at Macon was to include headquarters buildings, post exchanges, a fire station, hospital, theater, service club and guest house, post office, radio and telegraph building, a laundry, bakery and refrigeration plant, motor repair shops, and gas and oil storage buildings. The War Department also passed the word that the Smith-Pew Construction Company of Atlanta had been awarded a $287,000 contract for the construction of the 1,000-man recruit reception center at Fort McPherson. The center would be used for outfitting and classifying men drafted under the Selective Service Act.

The increase in war business and war jobs brought into the open a quiet change in the relations between the races in Atlanta. In years gone by blacks had made little protest when they got the leavings, so to speak, in industrial employment. That pattern was beginning to change. "Negro Problems" was the subject of a series of forums held at Morehouse College in cooperation with the National Youth Administration–sponsored Statewide Public Forum Project for Negroes in Georgia. Among the scheduled topics was "The Negro and the National Defense Program."

A study made by the National Urban League and excerpted in the *Constitution* declared:

In many centers, private employers are beginning to take workers back in increasing numbers, but nowhere are we receiving any indication of impartiality by these employers. Negroes are not returning to private industry in the same proportion as the whites are being re-employed. This is due not only to the attitude of employers, but to that of many labor unions and of employment agencies, public and private, which have refused often to register Negroes in certain categories and to recommend them to employment if registered, although frequently employers have not expressed a preference as to race.

Finally, vigorous protest is made here against the discrimination which our government practices in the matter of giving employment to its citizens. We feel that the civil service should do away completely with the photograph system and depend entirely upon fingerprinting for identification of applicants. The merit system fairly administered in civil employment is a concomitant of democracy. Negroes should be given the opportunity to serve in every avenue of public service whether they are in the civil departments of the government or in the armed forces.

This short statement, of course, cannot include a discussion of all phases of the manifestations of injustices on account of race that prevail in our nation. But the above will suffice to bring to the attention of those responsible for directing our national defense activities the points where action is necessary to safeguard our democratic ideals.

During the first World War, the National Urban League cooperated closely with the War Industries Board, the United States Employment Service, and industry in preparing our nation for the part it played. We stand ready, through our national office at 1133 Broadway, New York City, and through our 45 locals, established with offices and trained personnel in many strategic industrial centers, to cooperate fully in this emergency.

The comments from the Urban League were calm and mildly phrased. Less so were the public statements of the National Association for the Advancement of Colored People. On September 28 this increasingly powerful group announced that it would take court action "to compel the Army or Navy" to accept enlistment of men refused the privilege on account of race or color. Such actions, should they become necessary, would be taken against the secretary of war or the secretary of the navy, the association said. The resolution was passed, the association said, following an exchange of correspondence between the organization, Secretary of War Stimson, and the Navy Department. Stimson was quoted in his reply as stating that "additional Negro units had been authorized, while the Navy said it had adopted the policy of enlisting 'men of the colored race' only as mess men."

So began the confrontation between white and black that the threat of war brought on, and the outbreak of war in the next year would accentuate. That this confrontation would be less fierce in Atlanta than in other cities of the South was due in large measure to the leadership, both white and black, that Atlanta boasted. The city's white and black business leaders had worked quietly around the conference tables for many years.

On August 31, an editorial in the *Constitution* expressed the racist but restrained feelings of moderate whites:

In Atlanta, as all through the South, there are two races of people, living in the same communities, friendly and useful to each other, yet totally distinct. The relationship between the superior white race and the Negro in the South is probably more nearly ideal than that between separate races in similar circumstances in any part of the world.

The Negro in the South has advanced marvellously in the past few generations. Part of that advancement is due to the understanding and sympathetic help extended to him by the better class of white southerners. And a large part of the Negro's progress as a race is a splendid tribute to his own best qualities.

Nevertheless, as must always be the case where two races live together as do the white and the Negro here, one race is the dominant, the other the socially inferior.

It is a condition, however, that imposes added obligations by the dominant race, in this case the white. By the very fact of its superiority, its better advantages and its control of the machineries of government, of justice and of the entire social order, the white race owes a special obligation to the Negro. For all those benefits and guarantees of justice that a democratic society confers upon its people, the Negro is dependent upon the white man. It, therefore, becomes all the more a sacred obligation of the white man to see that the comparatively helpless Negro is not deprived of any of the fundamental rights or opportunities he may properly expect from society.

The schools of Atlanta are in dire need of replacement, of repair and of enlarged capacity. Anyone at all familiar with the physical condition of Atlanta's public school plant knows this. . . .

It would be well, however, if the responsible, better type of citizens took thought, at this time, to the conditions prevalent in the city schools for Negro children. A little investigation will disclose deplorable conditions there.

Of the proposed $1,800,000 bond issue, only $100,000 is to be set aside to "improve and enlarge over-crowded Negro schools." Undoubtedly, that is all that can be spared at this time. But the need remains and must be cared for.

Out of eleven Negro schools in the city, 88 percent, or 149 of the 167 classes, have to operate by double sessions. Booker T. Washington High School has to hold double sessions for all the seventh and eighth grades and there are no proper facilities there for vocational training. Practically all the Negro schools are without cafeterias, library space or library facilities. Walker Street is the only one with auditorium or gymnasium.

Let us not forget that we owe a responsibility, too, to our Negro population. A responsibility all the greater because of their dependence upon us.

Noblesse oblige.

There was no hint in any of the above of any trend toward social equality, nor of other than separate schools. But there was the strong suggestion that these separate schools must be made truly equal—in itself a long stride forward toward a better relationship between white and black. The great struggle over the ultimate step of school desegregation still lay ahead. But in Atlanta, it would be less bitter and less damaging than elsewhere.

Christmas business was good for the city's two leading retailers. Davison's gave a party for 1,800 employees on December 19 and distributed more than $25,000 in bonuses. Davison's, said President Raymond A. Klein, had done the largest twelve-months' business in its history. Each month, said the general manager, was bigger than the one before, and the store's prosperity was a reflection of the general prosperity of Atlanta and vicinity. Three days later Rich's gave a party for its 2,700 workers and distributed $48,000 in bonuses, plus announcing a change in policy that provided a five-day week for most of the employees. President Walter Rich received a diamond-studded pin marking his fortieth year with the store his father had founded. He announced that Rich's gross business that year would top $12 million, making it the largest department store south of the Mason-Dixon line.

As for the City of Atlanta itself, there was cash on hand to pay the Christmas bills with a substantial sum left over for the bills upcoming in 1941. The Atlanta city government completed its year of operations with a cash surplus of $147,196.47, and the school department carried forward $11,861.31. B. Graham West, city comptroller, announced that with all bills paid and charter funds intact, there would be $700,000 set aside to meet 1941 debt requirements. William B. Hartsfield, with only a week left to serve, announced that his outgoing administration would turn over to Mayor-elect Roy LeCraw a city in the best financial condition of any in the past quarter-century.

OBITUARIES

Mrs. William H. Adkins was a member of the First Baptist Church and was a member of the DAR, the UDC, the Daughters of the Founders and Patriots, of the American Colonists, and of 1812. Her husband, who died in 1932, was for forty years an executive of the Southern Bell Telephone and Telegraph Company. Born in Talladega, Alabama, she was the former Lundie Watson, daughter of a Confederate general. W. H. Arnold, 88, former deputy tax receiver of Fulton County, died at his residence. E. C. Atkins, president and owner of the Atlanta Wholesale Floral Company, died at 44 after a long illness. A Navy veteran of World War I, he was a graduate of the University of Alabama. In Atlanta he was a Mason, an Elk, and a member of the Atlanta Athletic Club and the American Legion. Green Hill Brandon was retired president of Brandon-Bond-Condon. pioneer funeral director who brought the first private ambulance to Atlanta, and the first motor-driven hearse. Basil E. Brooks, who began his career in construction with a team of mules and became president of one of the biggest levee construction companies in the country, died of a heart attack at 56. A. C. Belcher, city health inspector for thirty-three years and a leader in the work of the Baptist Tabernacle, died at 73. Barney Bernard, auctioneer with a booming voice whose interest in city politics was such that he had himself carried to the polls by ambulance, died after an illness of six years. Truman Neal Bradshaw, socially prominent Atlanta insurance salesman, died when he leaped or fell from the seventh floor of the Candler Building; health problems and financial worries were blamed. Polish-born Max L. Bremmer, iron and steel magnate and a leader in Jewish circles, died at 61. Laura Brown, who for forty years served Mrs. John E. Murphy as a maid and was known to three generations of Atlanta society and to opera stars Caruso, Farrar, Martinelli, and Bori, died at 61.

George M. Brown, Jr., grandson of Georgia's Civil War governor Joseph E. Brown and prominent Atlanta real estate man, died at 45. For fifteen years he had served as head of Georgia Savings Bank and Trust Company's real estate and insurance department. He was a former president of the Atlanta Real Estate Board. William R. Bean, the oldest printing executive in Atlanta, founder of the firm of W. R. Bean and Son, died at 71. R. P. Burnett, a veteran police officer and the first policeman appointed head of the city traffic squad, died after three years of suffering from injuries received in an automobile accident. Morris Brandon, Sr., widely known lawyer and a member of one of Atlanta's most prominent families, died of a heart attack. Born in Delaware and educated at Yale, he had as his partners many distinguished attorneys, including Preston Arkwright and former governor John M. Slaton. At the time of his death at 77 he was a member of the firm of Brandon, Hynds and Tindall, specializing in corporation law.

Emory Brooks, food dealer, ordained minister in the Brown Memorial Baptist Church, former member of the Atlanta Board of Education and former deputy Fulton County tax receiver, died at 59. R. N. Barclay, Sr., engineer for the Southern Railway, had been with the Southern for fifty-three years when he died at 68. The Rev. L. J. Ballard, 92, former business manager and associate editor of the *Wesleyan Christian Advocate* and a retired member of the South Georgia Conference of the Methodist Church, died at his home. Dr. W. S. Bomar, 53, lifelong resident of West End where he had practiced medicine for thirty years, died at his home. A graduate of Emory School of Medicine, he was a director of the Atlanta Kennel Club. Richard Winn Courts, Sr., retired senior member of the investment banking and brokerage firm of Courts and Company, died at 69. Born and educated in Tennessee, he came to Atlanta in 1909 as commercial agent for the Illinois Central Railroad. In 1925 he formed Courts and Company with his son Richard W. Courts, Jr. Mrs. A. S. Clay, mother of Atlanta capitalist Ryburn G. Clay, died of a heart attack at her home in Marietta. She was 80, and for twenty-one years, until her retirement in 1935, she had served as postmistress at Marietta.

J. Bulow Campbell, 69, a Coca-Cola Company director and outstanding contributor to worthy causes in his native city and region, died in Baltimore where he had gone on a business trip. Born in Atlanta and educated in Atlanta public schools and at Georgia Military Academy at Milledgeville, he first became associated with his brother, Richard Orme Campbell, in Campbell Coal Company. He became chairman of the board of Rabun Gap Nacoochee School, treasurer and member of the financial committee of Agnes Scott College, chairman of the executive committee of Columbia Theological Seminary, and advisor to Emory University. Elwin Chappell, 72, who lived on Peachtree Way, was one of the pioneers in the development of the cotton mill industry in the South. He was the dean of machinery firm representatives and drew the plans for a number of large mills in the Atlanta area. A New Englander by birth, as an Atlantan he became an enthusiastic flower gardener and clubman, belonging to the Atlanta Athletic Club, the Capital City Club, and Rotary. The Rev. Samuel A. Cowan, pastor of Euclid Avenue Baptist Church, was permanent secretary of the Atlanta Baptist Ministers Conference. He was also an evangelist, bringing religion to the working man by conducting services on week nights at the shops of the Atlanta Gas Light Company, the Lee Baking Company, and the Georgia Railroad. Robert C.

Clonts, Sr., active in Atlanta business circles for many years, was onetime chairman of the Atlanta Freight Bureau and a former member of the Presidents Club, an organization of Atlanta business executives.

Rachel Canary was a maid in the home of Mayor James L. Key for twenty-five years and after Key's death a nurse in the home of his daughter, Mrs. Monroe Butler. Known to scores of Atlanta political leaders, whom she served at dinners given by the mayor, she was born at Macon, the daughter of a slave, and was believed to be between 80 and 90 years old. Mrs. Minnie Hale Daniel led the fight to admit women to practice law in Georgia and herself became the first woman ever admitted to the state bar after becoming the first to graduate from the Atlanta Law School. She was one of the founders of the Atlanta League of Women Voters. James Dobbs, the *Atlanta Journal* church editor and former program director of WSB, died after several years of failing health. He was 59. W. Guy Dobbs, former alderman and one-time mayor pro tem, for many years was active in the civic offices of West End. He was once sales manager of the NuGrape Bottling Company and was later in life a salesman for Blalock Machinery Company. J. E. Dickerson, Sr., native of Norfolk, Virginia, and owner of the Dickerson Printing Company, had been a resident of Atlanta for thirty-eight years, coming as secretary to the late Chief Justice Richard B. Russell of the Georgia Supreme Court.

Paul Donehoo, 55, was the coroner of Fulton County for over thirty-two years, despite his blindness. Coroner, musician, lawyer, master chess player, and sports fan, he died unexpectedly at his home on Huntington Road. Left totally blind by a case of spinal meningitis suffered at the age of 5½, he was sent at age 6 to the Georgia Academy for the Blind at Macon, Georgia. After eight years there he went to Mercer University, where he earned a degree in three years. His first job at 17 was as a music teacher at Waleska, Georgia, where he gave instructions in piano and violin. He left there after a year and came to Atlanta, where he got a job in a theater playing the accompaniment for the old silent films. At the age of 21 he was elected coroner, in which job he remained until his death. He attended the Klindworth Conservatory of Music, now the Atlanta Conservatory of Music, and the Atlanta Law School. He never practiced law actively, but he was admitted to the bar in Georgia and also was admitted to practice before the Supreme Court of the United States.

John L. (Uncle John) Edmondson, 79, was public relations counsel of the Coca-Cola Company. A native of Spring Place in Murray County, he came to Atlanta as a railroad law attache with the Seaboard and moved from railroading into soft drink and public relations work, traveling the South for Coca-Cola. Frank Foster, 80, ex-city councilman, charter member of the Atlanta Rotary Club, and former head of the Atlanta Convention Bureau, was regional manager of the S. S. White Central Manufacturing Company. Dr. James R. Fuller, 57, died instantly when he fell four floors down the stairwell of the C&S Bank Building. R. L. Foreman, Sr., 73, Atlanta insurance man, was past president of the Rotary Club of Atlanta of which he was also a

charter member, of the High Museum, of the Atlanta Association of Life In-
surors, and of the Chamber of Commerce. He was active as president of
Robert L. Foreman & Son and was Georgia agent for the Mutual Benefit Life
Insurance Company at the time of his death from pneumonia.

Henry O. Flipper, the first Negro to be graduated from West Point as an
Army lieutenant, died at the home of his brother, Bishop J. S. Flipper. He was
84. William H. Glenn was one of the South's leading businessmen and civic
leaders for nearly fifty years. He was chairman of the board of the Southeastern Warehouse and Compress Company and a son of Dr. Wilbur Glenn,
Methodist minister after whom Glenn Memorial Methodist Church at Emory
University was named. He was a member of the second graduating class at
Georgia Tech in 1891. He joined the Consolidated Street Railway Company,
headed by the late Joel Hurt. Rising rapidly from rod-man to master
mechanic in the street railway shop, he headed the conductor division of the
Georgia Railway and Electric Company, founded in 1902, and under his di-
rection 87 miles of new rails were laid and 63 miles of old track were rebuilt.
Judge John E. Guerry, 58, of the Georgia Court of Appeals, died at a hospital
in Fredericksburg, Virginia, of injuries suffered in a car accident.

Mrs. James R. Gray, Sr., widow of the president and editor of the *Atlanta
Journal,* died of a heart attack after climbing the stairs at her home on Peachtree
Road. She was 77. Born on Washington Street in 1862, daughter of Walker
Patterson Inman and Mrs. Cordelia Dick Inman, leaders of ante- and
postbellum Atlanta, she fled to Augusta with older members of her family
shortly before Sherman's forces took the city in the fall of 1864. She was
educated in the schools of Atlanta and at Mary Baldwin Seminary in Virginia.
In 1881 she was married to James R. Gray. In 1900 he and Morris Brandon and
the late H. M. Atkinson bought control of the *Journal,* and he became president
in 1905 after obtaining control. She and her sons were active in the paper's top
management and remained so after her husband's death, until the paper was
sold in 1939 to former congressman James M. Cox of Ohio. Wilbur Haygood,
deputy sheriff of DeKalb County, died at 76. Son of the late Bishop Atticus
Haygood, he was graduated from Emory in 1883 and was thirty-five years in
government service with the Department of the Interior, serving as head of
various Indian reservations. William Hoffman, former president of the Atlanta
Chamber of Commerce, one-time councilman and member of the Board of
Education and a former chairman of the National Recovery Administrative
Board in Georgia, died at his home. Henderson Hallman, descendant of pioneers, was an indefatigable civic worker, lawyer, historian, and engineer; he
was closely associated with such diversified activities as the supplanting of
Georgia's cotton and corn agriculture with cattle and diversified crops and the
establishment of Candler Field.

John J. Higdon, a contractor who helped construct the Cotton States
Exposition buildings in Piedmont Park and who erected the first car barn of
the old Rapid Transit Company, died at the age of 70. William B. Harrison,

comptroller general of Georgia for eleven years and one of the state's most colorful political figures, died of a heart attack as he was returning from a fishing trip to Eatonton. He was 68. Mrs. Ida Higgins, 71, who brought joy to children by repairing their damaged dolls, died at her own "Doll Hospital," which she had operated for twenty-eight years. She was the daughter of C. L. Powell, a British lock and gunsmith who moved to Atlanta when it was still known as Marthasville. J. E. Hughie, real estate and insurance dealer, was 68 and president of the East Point Chamber of Commerce. Patrick Higgins, who rose from flying a cotton-dusting plane in southern and Mexican cotton fields to become a vice-president and director of Delta Air Lines, died at 46. He was the first man to fly a Delta plane into Atlanta. Joseph Travis Holleman graduated in law from Mercer University in 1879 and came to Atlanta. Lean times followed, until he got a job as bookkeeper in a new farm loan firm, the Nelson, Barker Company. From there he went on to become one of the foremost farm mortgage authorities in America. The first man ever to negotiate a farm loan financed by an insurance company, he more than any other man was responsible for bringing eastern life insurance capital to Atlanta to develop a region left impoverished by the Civil War. He served as a director of the old Maddox and Rucker Bank, later the Atlanta National, and of the Atlanta & Lowry National Bank, now part of the First National Bank.

Steve Johnston, retired superintendent of Grady Hospital, died at 84 in the hospital he helped to build into one of the great healing institutions. Before his connection with Grady he was a real estate auctioneer, a volunteer fireman, a member of the Board of Education, a city councilman, and mayor pro tem. Harry S. (Cap) Joyner, 52, had suffered a partial stroke and died of a heart attack at his home on Rogers Avenue. Another heart attack victim was Francis Augustus (Gus) Johnson, longtime deputy Fulton County tax collector, who died as he spoke the last words of a prayer while teaching a Bible class of the Park Street Methodist Church. At the last word of the extemporaneous prayer—"Men, can you stand the test?"—he fell to the floor dead. He was 73 and a leader in Masonic circles. Dr. Allen D. Johnson, retired physician and member of one of Georgia's pioneer families, died at 86. Born on an antebellum plantation near Sandy Springs, he was educated at North Georgia A&M at Dahlonega, and at the old Georgia Eclectic Medical College in Atlanta. For twelve years he was Atlanta's official city physician. Jerome Jones, a forceful figure in Atlanta's labor movement for more than forty years, died at 86. He had been editor of the *Journal of Labor*. Jones was one of the early advocates of free textbooks and of compulsory education.

Fitzhugh Knox, Atlanta builder and one of the state's most active classical scholars, died at 74. The firm of Fitzhugh Knox and Son built some of the finest apartments in north Atlanta including the Fitzhugh on Andrews Drive, the Knox Apartment on Peachtree Street, the Knox at Peachtree and Spring, and the Knox on Piedmont Avenue. He also owned the Briary on Peachtree Road. In his late sixties he became interested in classical literature and spent many hours in the library at Emory, reading in Greek and Latin literature. He was a member of the Atlanta Historical Society and compiled a history of the Knox family. Sister M. Loyola, of the Sisters of Mercy, Superior of St. Joseph's Infirmary here for many years, died in Savannah. For sixty-three years she wore the habit of a nun, in Savannah, Atlanta, and Augusta. Thomas H. Morgan, retired senior member of the architectural firm of Morgan, Dillon and Lewis, was dean of Georgia architects. Arriving in Atlanta in 1878, he did more than any one man to mold Atlanta's skyline of the 1940s. His buildings include the old Fourth National Bank Building, the 22 Marietta Street Building, the Ten Forsyth Street Building, the Retail Credit Company Building, the Healey Building, the Fulton County Courthouse, the Atlanta National Bank Building, the Chamberlin-Johnson store building, and the J. P. Allen Building. Besides office buildings, he had designed many other structures in Atlanta, including Oglethorpe University, the North Avenue Presbyterian Church, All Saints Episcopal Church, the Fulton County Almshouse, and the Henrietta Egleston Hospital and Nurses' Home.

A. W. McClain, 56, was deputy city clerk for nearly thirty years. He kept full and complete records of all city council actions during that time. J. Sam McWilliams had been postmaster of East Point for forty-five years. For forty years he and Mrs. McWilliams, who died earlier in 1940, operated a family grocery store adjacent to the post office. James McGee, retired Fulton County schoolteacher and former superintendent of schools of East Point, was a graduate of Emory at Oxford who retired in 1937 after fifty years of teaching. John M. McCullough, retired president of McCullough Brothers, one of the largest wholesale produce firms in the Southeast, died at 68. He was a founder of the old Ponce de Leon Baptist Church, serving as deacon for many years. One of the founders of the Atlanta Athletic Club, he was a member of the Capital City Club and the Piedmont Driving Club and was a former president of Rotary in Atlanta. Edgar P. McBurney was a pioneer developer of Atlanta and a leading figure in finance and business circles for nearly half a century. He had served as officer or director of the Trust Company of Georgia, Trust Company of Georgia Associates, First National Bank, Georgia Power Company, Atlanta Art Association, and Hillside Cottage.

John N. Malone died at age 72 a month after the death of his wife. His father, of Irish birth, was one of the town's first tax assessors, and John Malone followed in his father's path, serving the city in the tax department for thirty-six years—sixteen as tax assessor. In later years he turned to real estate and was one of those who constructed the new Greyhound Bus Terminal. Dr. Pleasant Leonidas Moon, 71, known as "the praying doctor," first made his calls on foot; later he became one of the first doctors in Atlanta to use a car. A specialist in the fight against typhoid, he was the first anesthesiologist at the Tabernacle Infirmary, which became Georgia Baptist Hospital. Arthur Montgomery, one of the founders and long president of the Atlanta Coca-Cola Bottling Company, died at his home on Muscogee Avenue after an illness of a year and a half. He was 86 years old, and until illness prevented, he went to his office every day. He began the expansion of the bottling firm by establishing fifteen franchised plants in Georgia, each serving an area covered by the distance a mule could travel in a day. As trucks with their wider range became available, these plants were reduced to six. Mrs. John K. Ottley was the wife of the chairman of the board of the First National Bank. She had devoted her life to social services and education, particularly to bettering conditions among rural people. Her chief interest was Tallulah Falls School, owned and operated by the Georgia Federation of Women's Clubs, for mountain boys and girls. She was influential in obtaining passage of child labor legislation in Georgia, sponsored a Book for the Bookless Company, developed libraries in remote rural areas, and was one of the founders of the "History Class," Atlanta's oldest study club. Mrs. H. M. Patty was a grandniece of George Washington through descent from Fielding Lewis, Revolutionary War munitions manufacturer, and Betty Washington. Charter member of the Atlanta DAR, she was 87.

The Rev. H. Jack Penn was vice-president of the Atlanta Board of Education and pastor of the Northside Methodist Church. He was one of the best known Atlantans in political, civic, and religious circles. Thomas Bridgham Paine, 78, was a leading figure in the social and business life of the city for many years. Born in Charleston, South Carolina, and educated in England, he was "flawless in speech, dress, and manner," said the *Atlanta Constitution*. No Atlanta debutante felt she had been properly presented to Atlanta Society unless Paine led the Grand March at the Piedmont Driving Club, and he also entertained each debutante group at his home on Peachtree Battle Avenue. He gave parties during opera week, which all the great stars attended. He was equally well known in golfing circles, traveling around the world with Bobby Jones and "Bobby's Boswell," O. B. Keller. His business was brokerage and banking, in which he was highly successful. "Miss Nettie" Rice was Girls High principal for almost twenty years.

William M. (Uncle Bill) Rapp, employee of the city waterworks for fifty-five years, died at 69. He joined the city water department in 1885 when it had twenty-one miles of water mains and helped it grow to 700 miles of mains serving 60,000 users in 1940. At the time of his death he was superintendent of distribution. J. B. Robinson, 76, lifelong resident of Atlanta, was with High's for twenty years and with Metropolitan Life for seventeen years. He was believed to be the youngest man in the country still bearing a Civil War scar. Shortly before the Battle of Atlanta, as a small boy, he got in the way of a party of Sherman's soldiers and was accidentally struck by a Yankee saber. William Henry Schroder, district manager of the U.S. Department of Commerce Bureau of Foreign and Domestic Commerce, died at 65. His wife was the former Suzanne Spalding. Another death attracted notice as Atlantans began moving out of the city for the Fourth of July celebration. Roohanah Solomon, oldest resident of Atlanta and possibly one of the nation's oldest men, died at his Campbellton Road home at the age of 107. He was a merchant until he retired in his late eighties and was well known in Atlanta's Syrian circle. William Speer, 75, former president of the old John Silvey Company and an Atlanta social leader for half a century, died at his home. The Silvey Company, founded by his father-in-law, was one of the largest wholesale drygoods firms in the Southeast. Emil C. Seiz, Sr., architect for the Massell Realty Company, designed more than 1,000 mercantile, hotel, and office buildings in Atlanta. Among them were the Robert Fulton Hotel, the Red Rock Building, and the Chrysler Motor Company Building.

W. J. Stoddard, who developed the noninflammable fluid used in dry cleaning, died of a heart attack at his office here. He was 62 and a national figure in the dry-cleaning business. William M. Slaton, former superintendent of the Atlanta public school system and for fifteen years principal of Boys High, died at 86. He was a brother of former governor John M. Slaton. Robert Sledd, purchasing agent for the DeKalb County school system, was a graduate of Emory, where he was Phi Beta Kappa. Son of the late Dr. Andrew Sledd, noted educator and scholar, he was a grandson of Bishop Warren A. Candler. Jon Dean Steward, attache of federal courts in Atlanta for nearly half a century and clerk of the U.S. Court for the Northern District of Georgia, died of pneumonia contracted in Washington, D.C., where he had attended a convention of U.S. Court Clerks. He was 70. Claude Tolbert, known affectionately as "Gabe" to the thousands of young men he had coached in major sports at Tech High, died of a heart ailment that had plagued him since his days at the University of Georgia, where he was a baseball star but could not play football. His teams at Tech High won forty championships in three major sports in the twenty years he coached there.

Courtland Winn, 77, was mayor of Atlanta from 1911 to 1913 and for many years thereafter was assistant city attorney. He had been a leading lawyer in Atlanta for more than half a century. Mrs. Ephie Erwin Williams died at 76. She was the first southern woman to own and edit a newspaper, a social journal called *Society*, published in the early 1890s with author Lollie Belle Wylie. In addition, she taught in the Fulton County school system for thirty-five years. O. H. Wright, Sr., was private secretary to Gen. Leonard Wood, governor general of Cuba after the Spanish-American War. He was 64, and during his stay in Cuba took notes on the fever epidemic which were published by the American Medical Society and led physicians to discover the cause of yellow fever. For thirty-eight years he was a merchandising broker in Atlanta.

NOTES

1. Atlanta Chamber of Commerce, "Facts and Figures about Atlanta, Headquarters of the Southeast, 1940" (Atlanta, 1940).

2. Edith Hills [Coogler], *Atlanta Journal Magazine*, Mar. 3, 1940.

3. Atlanta Fire Department, *Prompt to Action: Atlanta Fire Department, 1860–1960* (Atlanta, n.d.).

4. *American City,* Apr., 1943.

5. Harold H. Martin, *William B. Hartsfield, Mayor* (Athens: University of Georgia Press, 1978).

6. Ibid.

7. Thomas H. English, *Emory University, 1915–1965: A Semicentennial History* (Atlanta: Emory University, 1966).

8. Raymond D. B. Fosdick, "Adventure in Giving" (1962).

9. English, *Emory University, 1915–1965.*

10. Junior League of Atlanta, Inc., "Cultural Atlanta at a Glance" (Atlanta, 1950).

11. Manning Patillo, *Oglethorpe University Bulletin,* 1982–83.

12. Celestine Sibley, *Dear Store* (Garden City, N.Y.: Doubleday, 1967).

13. Marguerite Steedman, *Atlanta Journal Magazine,* Jan. 21, 1940.

14. Herbert T. Jenkins, *Foods, Fairs and Farmers' Markets in Atlanta* (Atlanta: Center for Research in Social Change, Emory University, 1977).

15. Charles F. Palmer, *Adventures of a Slum Fighter* (Atlanta: Tupper and Love, 1955) and brochure published by Church and Community Press, Atlanta, in Palmer personality file, Atlanta Historical Society.

NOT since the prosperous years of the mid-twenties had Atlanta greeted the new year with such exuberance as it showed in bringing in 1941. It was almost as if the people knew that before this year was out they would be at war and they were determined to have one last fling. Not only in the private clubs, but all over town the revelers gathered. Traffic jammed the downtown streets and in the mild winter night the parties were crowded long past midnight.

The passing of longtime county coroner Paul Donehoo not long before Christmas, 1940, had its curious aftermath. Fifty-four persons, the largest number ever to offer for a single office in Fulton County, entered the race, among them lawyers, doctors, preachers, and one newspaperman. By election day, January 15, the list was down to 48—but one name had been added— that of Mrs. Paul Donehoo. She was an easy winner in a light election.

Not elections, but inaugurations, the swearing in of those already elected, were the big news in the early months of the year. On New Year's Day the Fulton County Commission gathered in the Commissioners Room in the courthouse to hold their organizational meeting for 1941. Charlie Brown, newcomer to the board, and I. Gloer Hailey were sworn in on a four-year term by Judge Thomas H. Jeffries, county ordinary, and Troy Chastain was named chairman, succeeding retiring chairman Ed L. Almand.

The commission soon found itself busy with matters dealing with the threat of war. On January 4 the Fulton County grand jury warned Atlanta that the waterworks must be guarded against sabotage.

On the evening of January 6 the year's top local political event took place. Roy LeCraw, with his wife and five sons looking on, was inaugurated as the forty-fourth mayor of the City of Atlanta. In his farewell message William B. Hartsfield extended "every good wish to LeCraw." In his inaugural address the incoming mayor pledged a lean and hungry financial policy. He reiterated his promise to reduce water rates to $1 for the first 800 cubic feet for city users, and to $2.50 for the same amount for out-of-the-city residents. This, he said, would save water users a quarter of a million dollars a year. He also said he would eliminate "hiding police," and would no longer require each policeman to make a certain number of arrests. He promised that he would make war on tax dodgers and that he would push hard to raise funds for a new and better Grady Hospital. Doctors' fees and private hospital rates, he said, had increased to the point that Atlantans making less than $200 a month could not pay them. At least one-third of Atlanta's population, he said, should be cared for at Grady.

Sworn in along with LeCraw were the members of Atlanta's bicameral municipal legislature. Aldermen included G. Dan Bridges, Ed A. Gilliam, L. O. Moseley, Lester R. Brewer, Frank H. Reynolds, and Raleigh Drennon.

Councilmen were Roy Bell, James E. Jackson, Jr., Cecil Hester, William T. Knight, George B. Lyle, J. Allen Couch, Joe Allen, John T. Marler, Paul Butler, John A. White, Howard Haire, and Frank Wilson. Alderman Bridges and Councilman Lyle, whom Hartsfield had tried to purge, were given high committee positions by LeCraw, and Councilman John A. White was named mayor pro tem.

Eugene Talmadge took the oath as governor on January 14 and immediately wielded the ax on twenty of Governor Rivers's employees, whom he replaced with loyal supporters. Like LeCraw at City Hall, Talmadge in the capitol nearby was wrapped up in money matters. He was determined, he said, to pay off the state's debt of $32 million and to do this without raising taxes. To begin with, he said, he planned to cut state salaries by $3 million. Talmadge also aimed at the state colleges. He was determined to remove from office and responsibility all educators, no matter how distinguished they might be, whose idea of the teacher's role differed from his own. By mid-July his actions had driven the war headlines off the front pages. Charging that Dr. Walter R. Cocking, dean of the School of Education of the University of Georgia, and Dr. Marvin S. Pittman, president of Georgia Teachers College at Statesboro, were advocating interracial education, he ordered the regents to dismiss them. The regents voted 8-4 to do this, but in the brief recess that followed President Harmon W. Caldwell quietly announced that if the two were not reinstated, he would resign as president of the university system. A hearing was set, and on June 16 Dr. Cocking was reelected by a vote of 8 to 7. Talmadge, angered, demanded the resignation of the offending regents.

Some resigned and Talmadge dismissed those who would not do his will. He appointed replacements who would do as he wished. Thus on July 14, 1941, not only Dean Cocking and President Pittman were dismissed from the university system, so were three others. This action brought nationwide attention to Georgia, all of it unfavorable.

In December, 1941, ten colleges in the university system were suspended by the Southern Association of Colleges and Secondary Schools, and the University of Georgia and Georgia Tech were removed from the approved list of the Association of American Universities. The Southern University Conference also dropped the University of Georgia from membership. This meant that the scholastic credits from the Georgia schools would not be recognized by other institutions throughout the nation. To many a Georgian it meant the unthinkable—that Georgia could not compete officially in intercollegiate athletics.

In the sometimes bitter question periods directed by Talmadge's regents to Dr. Cocking and President Pittman, books were mentioned that the governor considered subversive in that they seemed to advocate racial equality or socialism. This led Talmadge to threaten a purge of all college libraries in the state. There was one university system, however, whose library facility he could not touch. Across town at Atlanta University, a new School of Library

Science opened in September, made possible by a grant of $150,000 from the Carnegie Corporation of New York. The new school would employ the best trained black librarians available. The main library of Atlanta University would be the main training area, but black high school libraries, and, it was hoped, a white high school library in the city of Atlanta as well, would be utilized, with the Library School of Emory University being used in certain phases of study. And thus it would come to pass, in the years ahead, that white and black librarians would teach and learn together in the libraries of the city.

As Talmadge neared the end of his third term as governor, the regents made a final effort to save the accredited standing of the University System of Georgia by promising to do whatever was demanded by the Southern Association of Colleges and Secondary Schools. Their argument did not prevail, and ten colleges of the university system were suspended from the accredited list because of "unprecedented and unjustified political influence by Governor Talmadge." The edict, which would affect 11,500 students, did not take effect until the following September, and no credits earned by students prior to that time would be denied. But the Southern Association would hear no more arguments until its next annual meeting in December of 1942. By this time Ellis Arnall was governor, and the suspension was lifted.

In 1941 football Frankie Sinkwich, Georgia's flashy tailback, caused great excitement at Athens and Atlanta when he failed to report for the second day of spring practice, saying he was tired of football and just wanted to be a student. This was the third time that Sinkwich had made this decision. And again, as the season opened in the fall, he repented and played the schedule with such zest that he was named one of the outstanding backfield men of the year, finishing the regular season as the nation's leading ball carrier with a total of 1,102 yards. In the final game of the year, before 31,000 at Grant Field, Atlanta, he did not score running, but threw the three passes that beat Tech 21-0, and earned Georgia an invitation to play in the Orange Bowl at Miami against Texas Christian on New Year's Day, 1942. Again Sinkwich— "as good a football player as the South has ever seen," wrote Ralph McGill on the morning after New Year's—was the star. The score was 40-36, with Sinkwich both passing and running in a little drama, described by McGill as "the pigskin you love to touch."

In contrast to political battles and war's alarums, one change in Atlanta living took place relatively without event. After having its area divided for many years into two time zones—Eastern and Central—the entire state of Georgia was put on Eastern Standard Time.

Checking over figures prepared by the Industrial Bureau of the Atlanta Chamber of Commerce, Frank C. Gilreath, Jr., *Journal* business editor, discovered that from January 1 to June 30 fifty new factories, distributors, and sales and service organizations had taken up residence in Atlanta, and the total payroll of the newcomers totaled just under five million dollars annually.

Another aspect of Atlanta's growth was the vast increase in white-collar jobs, mainly of governmental employees. The 17,000 government employees ranged from the fine salaries of generals and commissioners to those of the clerks and secretaries and typists earning $35 to $45 and the Army private's abysmal take-home pay of $21 a month. With the more than fifty agencies of the federal government doing business in Atlanta, the town truly deserved its reputation of being the Little Washington of the South.

Physicians made news in the closing months of the year when a goal they had been striving for for eighteen years was attained. On December 16 the Fulton County Medical Society dedicated its impressive new home at 873 West Peachtree Street. More than 300 doctors attended the dedication proper in which Dr. Fred A. Rankin, president elect of the American Medical Association, read the history of the Atlanta organization from 1855 to the present.

Some interesting visitors passed through the city this year. George Peter (81), one of the six artists who painted the world-famous Cyclorama of the Battle of Atlanta, came to Atlanta June 18 to see the painting he had not seen in fifty-five years. After all the years he could recognize not only the horses and the figures of men he had painted, but the areas painted by his fellow artists whose styles he knew. His observations contributed to the history of the painting. A self-exiled German thinker, Dr. Thomas Mann, Nobel prize-winning philosopher, came to Atlanta to speak at Emory on "The Problem of Freedom." "The war," he said, "will continue. There is no thought of defeat on either side. They will fight until one side is destroyed. But out of the conflict will come a greater concept of democracy."

As war clouds gathered Atlanta was designated to serve as the supply center for all the troops stationed in the eight southeastern states. This process was begun at the old World War I depot on Stewart Avenue at Murphy Avenue SE, but this location soon became inadequate, and the War Department in October of 1940 had authorized the establishment of a quartermaster depot at Fort McPherson. Soon this, too, was outgrown. A new and, it was hoped, truly ample collection of warehouses went under construction on a tract between the Southern Central of Georgia railroads near tiny Conley in Clayton County. This facility is now known as Fort Gillem—a subpost of Fort McPherson.

Congestion around Fort "Mac," Camp Gordon, and other training areas made for fantastic traffic problems in the downtown area, and the town's best brains were put to work trying to solve them. Peachtree at Ellis was considered the worst traffic nightmare. There, between 11:00 A.M. and 7:00 P.M., 41,592 persons crossed the streets in a day, and in a full day from 7:00 A.M. to 11:00 P.M., 23,043 private automobiles moved past at a crawling speed of 6.5 miles per hour. This did not include buses and street cars. And, even at 6 miles per hour, it was discovered, four accidents had occurred and three persons had been hurt. At Five Points traffic moved smoothly and well, for there were two policemen to keep cars moving rapidly. But at Five Points II—the

Peachtree, Carnegie Way, Forsyth, Pryor Street intersection—lack of traffic controls resulted in twenty-seven violations, mostly on turns, in one thirty-minute span of the afternoon rush hour.

Frank H. Neely, chairman of the Fulton County Planning Commission, told the Atlanta Group of the American Society of Civil Engineers that twenty years from 1941 one million people would be going to and from work in newly developed industrial centers, riding buses to new shops and stores and offices, and that thousands more would be driving from home to half a hundred flying fields. Unless some master plan could be devised, the city would be choked to death by its own traffic.

From Neely's idea grew a proposal of what Atlanta would be in the near future—a city of 95 square miles with a tax digest of $450 million and a population of more than 400,000. In the Greater Atlanta that Neely advocated, a vision the City Council approved, a 5.5-mile circle radiating from West Peachtree and North Avenue was proposed for the New Greater Atlanta. It would extend from Buckhead south to Lakewood Park—east from Center Hill to beyond Kirkwood. The Neely Plan got the strong support of the *Atlanta Constitution*. Towns and municipalities that already had their own government would not be brought under city control; thickly settled areas that had no local government of their own and that were logically part of Atlanta economic and social life would be brought in. It took a decade of struggle however before Atlanta reached out to take in its adjoining territory in 1952.

To improve traffic conditions in the busy downtown area, the city made some downtown streets one way. Another solution sought by Mayor LeCraw and finally accepted reluctantly by the Georgia Power Company was the replacement of the old streetcar with the new railless, trackless trolley, mainly on the lines leading to Fort McPherson.

Though the power company might have watched the old streetcars go to the boneyard with some regret, it proudly greeted another event—the establishment of its gigantic new Atkinson power plant on the Chattahoochee River ten miles from Atlanta. Powered by steam, Atkinson operated without regard for weather and thus was protected against power shortages during droughts.

Neither Atlanta's number-one problem, tangled traffic, nor the coal smoke estimated to cost the city $4 million a year in property damage, impeded the flow of people and new business into the city proper. Some of them were part of the military and others served indirectly, contributing to the area's growing importance as a military center. Of a total of 1,317,100 men in uniform, 488,300 were in the 4th Corps Area headquartered in Atlanta. The soldiers were in camps in Tennessee, Alabama, Louisiana, Kentucky, North Carolina, Florida, South Carolina, and Mississippi as well as Georgia. By mid-June the city was a quartermaster center handling nearly half of all the food, bedding, clothing, and transport used by the army in the U.S.

Not all the business news emanating from Atlanta in 1941, however, was of the type to please the Chamber of Commerce. "Bug" racket lottery operators were temporarily derailed when "King" Walter J. Cutcliffe's company and twenty-five smaller competitors were rounded up by county police, prosecuted, convicted, and given suspended sentences for five years. Long before the five-year term was out Governor Rivers, on leaving office, pardoned them, and they were soon back in business.

The "King" of lottery was not the only criminal or senior criminal racketeer at work in Atlanta during the last months preceding the war's outbreak. Two years earlier members of the Atlanta Lawyers Club had investigated and exposed a number of companies operating loan businesses at usurious interest rates, which in some cases ranged from 240 percent to 260 percent. So grossly usurious had this small loan racket become that the grand jury, in an effort to eliminate all illegal loan businesses from the community, found little difficulty in bringing indictments against twenty-one loan firms. High on the list in this loan-shark racket was Cutcliffe, the lottery king, who with Harold J. Smoot, traded as Walter's Finance Company at 3½ Edgewood Avenue. Walter Cutcliffe, Jr., was in the same racket, doing business as Pacific Finance Company in the 202 Mortgage Guarantee Building.

The Ku Klux Klan, unmasked by its Imperial Wizard James A. Colescott in 1940, gathered in convention in Atlanta on June 7, 1941, and announced that a move to hide their faces behind hoods again had been defeated by a vote of 587 to 22. At the same time, the Klan unanimously pledged that it would strive to raise a million dollars in 1942, to promote Americanism. Thus resolved, the Klan adjourned on Saturday night to Stone Mountain, there to burn a fiery cross while the Imperial Wizard made his final speech. Delegates from thirty-eight states were present, wearing robes but not masks.

Even while moving steadily into the future, Atlantans with a sense of history were paying tribute to a colorful vignette of their past. On Christmas Day in 1855 happy Atlantans set ablaze a gas lamp newly erected at the corner of Whitehall and Peachtree streets. (Fifty others were also set aglow in a burst of civic pride.) It was burning there still in 1865 when a Yankee shell hit at the base, leaving a hole in the shaft. During the *Gone with the Wind* festivities the lamp was relighted with an "eternal flame" and was burning there on March 10, 1941, when a bronze tablet, giving the story of the historic lamp-post, was placed there by the Old Guard.

On the evening of December 5, just hours away from the falling of bombs on Pearl Harbor, the Atlanta Junior League put on its annual Follies, that year commemorating the silver anniversary of the league in Atlanta. Its title was "Nice Going," and, indeed, the performances were far beyond that expected of any group of amateurs. In the cast of 150 were 19 vocalists and specialty dancers, 21 comedians and comediennes, a male chorus of 24 cadets from the Naval Reserve Air Base, 76 chorus girls, and 16 male singers. The Follies said goodbye to Christmas joy for the duration of the war years.

In 1941–42 even the Debutante Club canceled many of the parties that in the past had been a classic part of the presentation ceremony. Instead of spending their time at luncheons, teas, and dinners, the debs set up classes in which they mastered first aid, ambulance driving, and bandage rolling.

Ringling Brothers Circus was in town the first week in November, and a bizarre story developed. In a matter of hours a veteran clown, an advance man, and three of the show's forty-seven elephants were dead of a mysterious ailment. It was believed that some chemical poison had been ingested from the grasses on which the animals grazed on their stopover in South Carolina. The men, it was later discovered, died of heart attacks. But the elephants kept on dropping, until ten of them had died. It was a pitiful sight—the big beasts standing, swaying, supported by their mates until they finally toppled. And, as Big Baby and Big Jenny dragged the bodies of the dead out of the tents to the trucks that would haul them away, the others lifted their trunks high and uttered a strange braying sound like a bugle, blowing goodbye. All along the line the surviving elephants entwined their trunks as if encouraging each other. The dead were buried together in a deep grave near Howell Station, outside of town.

December 7 came, and the attack on Pearl Harbor pushed all lesser matters to the back of the public mind. The anticipation of war had changed the city in 1940 and 1941, and, of course, the war itself would have an even more profound impact on Atlanta. War was here at last. The *Constitution* editorialized: "We are in it now. The years of doubt and wrangling are over. We have become a nation one in purpose."

The *Atlanta Constitution* of the morning of Monday, December 8, told the story of Atlantans' reactions. Mayor Roy LeCraw, a lieutenant colonel in the Georgia National Guard, immediately asked for active duty—which meant that he would give up his job as mayor, which he had pledged to do when elected, if the country should go to war. Said he, "I have every intention of entering the service of my country." "I don't care whether I am a major, a lieutenant, or what not. Every red-blooded American will rally to the cause." At the same time Mayor LeCraw joined with Colonel Lindley Camp, commander of the state's Defense Corps, and Police Chief Hornsby in ordering all Japanese in Georgia and Atlanta to stay in their homes. At the Atlanta waterworks the guard against saboteurs was doubled. Only fourteen Japanese of alien birth were found living in Atlanta, most of them cooks and waiters. One of them, Sadajiro Yoshinuma, was well known to thousands of Atlantans who patronized the restaurant and nightclub Wisteria Gardens on Peachtree Street.

It was Thomas F. Byrd (20), grandson of Mr. and Mrs. S. A. Williams of Merrits Avenue, who had the unhappy distinction of being the first Atlantan killed in the Pearl Harbor attack. The second local victim was aviation mechanic William H. Manley (23), son of Mr. and Mrs. Emory S. Manley of the Mirror Lakes section near Hapeville.

The outbreak of the war turned Governor Talmadge's thoughts in a new direction—how Atlantans and Georgians could best serve the war effort. Within an hour after President Roosevelt's signing the joint congressional resolution declaring the United States at war with Japan, Governor Talmadge named a committee of prominent Georgians as a Citizens' Defense Committee to coordinate all the war effort within the state. Hughes Spalding was named temporary chairman and other noted Atlantans called to serve were Dewey Johnson, Lucy Randolph Mason, Arthur Acklin, Lindley Camp, Robert Strickland, Erle Cocke, J. D. Robinson, and H. Lane Young.

Atlanta had already formed a Greater Atlanta Defense Council, under Charles Currie and Frank Carter; its purpose was to train volunteers in civilian defense, and with the declaration of war, this group was besieged by thousands of volunteers.

Atlantans, at first, were reluctant to begin blackout drills; the first one planned was postponed, and they did not start until mid-December. However, with no barrage balloons, few anti-aircraft guns, and few interceptor planes in the area, Atlanta had no other effective way of defending itself, other than by these passive methods.

Attired in her Red Cross uniform, Margaret Mitchell on December 23 left for the New York Navy Yard to attend celebrations commissioning the new cruiser *Atlanta,* which the famous author had christened in September, 1940. Commander DeSales Harrison, serving in the U.S. Navy, assisted his fellow Atlantan on this occasion as her naval aide.

It was in early 1941 that the military, realizing that there was to be a high concentration of troops in and near Atlanta, called upon local officials and urgently requested that suitable provision be made for the recreation and welfare of the increasingly large number of men coming into and passing through the city. Mayor Roy LeCraw requested that E. S. Papy, president of the Chamber of Commerce, assemble a committee of citizens broadly representing religious, welfare, and business groups, to be known as the Atlanta Defense Recreation Committee. Under Dr. Herman L. Turner's stimulating and inspiring leadership the committee raised the necessary funds to open the city's first Service Men's Center. It was a small second-story room on Walton Street, but it furnished information and facilities for reading, writing, and table games.

Boys in uniform had, until this time, roamed up and down the streets with no place to go, not knowing how to fill their off-duty hours, not knowing to whom to turn for needed advice and friendliness. Soon the center became the clearinghouse for many outside activities such as group weiner roasts, parties given by church, civic, and fraternal groups, sight-seeing trips, and other such entertainment. All work was done on a volunteer basis with the exception of certain personnel furnished by the Recreation Division of the Work Projects Administration. Soon the center had a full-time director and secretary.

In October, 1941, the center moved to more spacious quarters in the old ballroom and banquet hall of the Kimball House, with its marble floors, vast shadowy ceilings, and glittering chandeliers.

Electrified into intense action by Pearl Harbor, the city became the scene of feverish activity. Atlanta, like other cities, was ill prepared to meet this sudden influx of military personnel. Each day it grew increasingly necessary to expand both space and facilities for mass recreation and for overnight housing. Because it would require entire buildings to meet these demands, plans were made and sites were selected for a white service center on property adjoining the Municipal Auditorium and for a Negro center on the grounds of Washington High School on Hunter Street. The floor plans were identical, with the exception of dormitory facilities at the white center. No sleeping quarters were needed at the Negro center, since a tent city with a 550-bed capacity had already been erected by the Army. Funds for construction were jointly furnished by local and national governments.

Atlanta, now a critical area, requested assistance from the United Service Organizations (USO), the organization endorsed by the president as the proper agency to set up new programs for the welfare and recreation of the armed forces and to assist programs already in operation. Under the direction of the USO regional office in Atlanta, the USO Council was created with much the same membership as the Atlanta War Recreation Committee. The USO Council was faced with the problem of vast numbers of troops jamming the railroad and bus terminals. Two lounges, one for white troops and an adjoining one for Negro troops, were erected at the rear of the concourse at the Terminal Station.

In the meantime, the buildings to house the white and Negro service centers were completed, and on May 22, 1942, the doors opened through which over 2.5 million men and women in uniform were to pass. Mayor LeCraw was called into the army.

Almost at once, the council found that it was imperative that even more facilities be provided. Under the direction of the USO Council, the Jewish Welfare Board, the National Catholic Community Service, the Young Women's Christian Association, both the white and Negro operations of the Young Men's Christian Association, and the Salvation Army—all member agencies of USO—set up subsidiary programs.

USO offered throughout the city and its environs a well-rounded recreation program, overnight dormitory facilities, light refreshments, a wholesome camaraderie, and that most valuable of all contributions to the morale of servicemen—a feeling of belonging. The USO Service Men's Center never closed its doors at 16 Courtland Street. A jukebox played free of charge from early morning until late at night. Tri-weekly dances with local or service orchestras proved the most popular of all diversions, with an average attendance of 1,300. The girls participating in this part of the recreational program were selected through a registration system; references were required and closely checked before cards were issued. Over 8,000 girls registered for junior hostess during the six years of operation.

One of the first organizations to offer assistance was the English Speaking Union, which acted as official hosts for all members of the British Armed Forces visiting Atlanta. The British Royal Air Force trained numbers of men in Georgia, Florida, and Alabama at navy, army, and private flying schools. Each week, members of the English Speaking Union entertained numbers of these British boys in their homes, including the men of the Royal Navy who came to Atlanta from the U.S. Navy yards at Charleston, S.C., where their ships were tied up for repair. The ESU takes a poignant pride in this work, for so very few of the RAF boys who were in Atlanta survived the early mass bombing attacks on Germany. Fourteen of sixteen boys entertained by one Atlanta family were shot down.

The USO Center, at some time during the war, utilized almost every volunteer organization in Atlanta. For example, the day the Service Men's Center was dedicated, the Garden Center called on various garden clubs throughout the city to furnish and arrange flowers in the various rooms of the building. From that time fresh flowers or blooming shrubs kept the center beautifully decorated, and Christmas, Easter, and Thanksgiving were appropriately celebrated with beautiful seasonal decorations.

The volunteer staff, assigned through the Civilian Defense Volunteer office and the Red Cross, served in three shifts from 9:00 A.M. to 10:30 P.M. except on dance nights, when they stayed on duty until 11:30. In addition to staff assistants, the Atlanta chapter of Red Cross assigned a number of motorists from the motor corps to a desk at the center. They maintained a shuttle service between railroad and bus stations and were on call for transporting servicemen and their families to any point within the city limits in emergency.

OBITUARIES

Willette A. Allen was the founder of Atlanta's Kindergarten and Normal School and operator of the city's first kindergarten. J. Frank Beck was president of Troy Laundry and a city councilman for seventeen years. Dr. George T. Brown was a practicing physician since 1882 who introduced the legislative bill creating the State Tuberculosis Hospital at Alto. Gutzom Borglum was the world famous sculptor who began the Confederate memorial carving on Stone Mountain in 1920. Amy A. Chadwick, a native of England, was head of the Leonard Street Home for Orphan Negro Girls for fifty-three years. D. G. Cheatwood, 52, a construction engineer and vice-president of A. K. Adams Company. He was engineer on the Camp Gordon project in World War I and had just finished the army anti-aircraft center at Hinesville. He also built the train station on the Emory campus. Dr. D. D. Crawford, 76, was an honored leader of Negro Baptists of Georgia and president of the Morehouse College Alumni Association.

Two members of one of Georgia's most beloved families died within three months of each other, Bishop Warren A. Candler and Judge John S. Candler, brothers of Asa G. Candler. Bishop Candler was a leading figure in Southern Methodism for more than fifty years. From 1888 to 1898 he was president of Emory University. Candler had received his diploma from Emory College at Oxford in 1875 in the church where his last services were held. "As an educator he will always occupy high place in the history of Georgia. He and his brother, Asa G. Candler, planned and built Emory University. It is fitting that his funeral be held in the old church at Oxford," stated the *Atlanta Constitution*. Judge John Slaughter Candler, 80, former member of the Georgia Supreme Court, died December 9, just three months after the death of his brother, Warren A. The last of the distinguished family of eight brothers and three sisters, he had come to Atlanta as a young man and was appointed by Gov. John B. Gordon to be solicitor-general of the Stone Mountain circuit. A few years later he was elected to the Supreme Court of Georgia and served until his retirement in 1906. One of the first to erect a residence in Asa Candler's real estate venture, Druid Hills, he resided in his handsome home at the corner of Ponce de Leon and Briarcliff Road for many years. Deeply interested in religious and educational affairs, Judge Candler was a trustee of Wesleyan, Emory, Young Harris, Reinhardt, and LaGrange Colleges.

David Eichberg, 75, was a fifty-year member of the Atlanta Bar Association and a charter member of the Atlanta Athletic Club. Dr. Alfred Enloe was an instructor at Atlanta-Southern Dental College for more than twenty years. Professor Thomas Witt Fitzgerald, 55, was head of the Electrical Engineering Department at Georgia Tech. Gilbert Thomas Ray Fraser, 78, was for fifty years an agent for the old Queen Insurance Company and a charter member of the Atlanta Athletic Club. Henry Garrett, 82, one of the city's oldest employees, was deputy to Riley Elder, municipal revenue collector. Antoine Graves, pioneer Negro real estate broker, was in business for fifty-five years. Gen. M. Y. Griggs, 94, was a Confederate veteran who participated in the Atlanta battles and was a charter member of the Ku Klux Klan. Thomas Ham was the chairman of the board of Baptist Tabernacle and a well-known evangelist. Mrs. Thomas Hancock, the former Irene Johnson, was the superintendent of nurses at the Atlanta Hospital School of Nursing. Robert H. Hogg, Sr., was a retired liquor and beer wholesaler and a sportsman whose hunting dogs were national champions. Charles H. Hopson, 75, a native of England, was a church architect for over fifty years. He designed the Rock Spring Presbyterian Church and Ponce de Leon Methodist Church. George F. Hunnicutt, 80, was editor of *The Southern Cultivator*. C. Ernest Hutcheson, 64, was superintendent of the East Point Light and Water Department.

W. H. Jacks, 58, was manager of Grant Park and at one time had been the purchasing agent for the city. Frederick Reese Jones, 67, was secretary-treasurer of Country Bankers Association. He was a veteran of the Spanish-American War and for years was captain of the Macon Hussars. He was the father of Boisfeuillet Jones, state administrator of the National Youth Administration at the time of the elder Jones's death. T. K. Jones was widely regarded in southern newspaper circles as the best police reporter who ever worked for the *Constitution*. He was an honorary member of the police department. Fred Jordan, 46, was president of the Georgia Field Trial Association, a bird-dog man supreme and a conservationist. A Phi Beta Kappa graduate of the University of Georgia and Harvard Business School, he was also a member of the first officers' training camp in World War I and spent eighteen months in France. At the time of his death he was agent for the Federated Mutual Insurance Company.

N. A. Kaplan, 79, was a native of Russia who founded the Avath Achim congregation in 1890. Courtenay Kay, 40, was for twenty-five years employed by Southern Bell; he was a member of the Masonic Order and one of the old "Bell House Boys." Edward D. Kennedy, 69, established the Atlanta Show Case Company and was a partner in the Capital Electric Company. He was a member of the Capital City Club. Friends and business associates mourned the death of Clyde Lanier King, 66, member of a prominent southern family and board chairman of the King Plow Company, which he purchased in 1901, when it was the Atlanta Plow Co. For many years it was a leading manufacturer of farm implements, with a heavy export business with South America. King was a Presbyterian, a Rotarian, a member of Capital City Club, and a founder of Druid Hills Golf Club.

Walter D. Lamar, 78, was president of the S.S.S. Company, Atlanta medicine manufacturers, and vice-president of Lamar-Rankin, a wholesale drug firm, both founded by his father, Henry J. Lamar. Rev. Father Francis Larney, 67, was a member of the Society of Mary and treasurer of Marist College and Sacred Heart Church. A native of Ireland, he was a priest for over forty-five years. Joseph Lazear, 56, prominent in the drug business, was a founder and first president of the Progressive Club. Thomas J. Lyon, 62, was a widely known printing executive who formed his own company in 1920. He was a member of the Piedmont Driving Club and a life member of the Capital City Club. Fred M. McGonigal, 67, was for thirty-three years a member of St. Luke's Church and active in Nine O'Clocks, the Piedmont Driving Club, and the Capital City Club. Mattie McCrary, 81, was one of the first telephone operators in the South and one of the two operators who handled Atlanta's first switchboard, with 108 phones. Mrs. Benjamin Massell, 50, the former Fanny Wolfson, was active in all affairs of The Temple Sisterhood and was wife of one of the city's most prominent realtors. Judge Newt A. Morris, 72, was a prominent leader in Georgia politics and a member of the state legislature from Cobb County.

Louis H. Moss, Sr., 67, was president of the Atlanta Leather Company and vice-president of Atlanta Paper Company. He was a member of the Rotary Club of Atlanta and The Temple. D. R. Nesbitt, 73, was chief auditor of the Atlanta and West Point Railroad and oldest member of College Park Presbyterian Church. Robert Parker, 56, was president of the Atlanta Federal Reserve Bank and a notable figure in financial and legal circles. Clem Powers, 50, prominent attorney and a member of Jones, Powers and Williams legal firm, had served in the 82nd Division in World War I and was on the board of deacons at the Second Ponce de Leon Baptist Church. Henry Alton Purtell, 79, was a bookkeeper at the old Lowry Bank and later at the First National Bank. He was a member of the "Pioneer School Boys" and with his father, its organizer, served with Atlanta's first military company, The Fulton Blues.

Dr. Stewart Ralph Roberts, 62, professor of clinical medicine in the Emory University School of Medicine, was for more than twenty-five years one of the South's leading physicians. Widely recognized as a diagnostician and specialist in internal medicine and heart diseases, Dr. Roberts had received some of the highest honors of the medical profession, including the presidency of the American Heart Association. In World War I he was chief of medical service for the Emory unit. Dr. Roberts was born October 2, 1878, at Oxford, Georgia. His great-grandfather was a contributor to Emory College, and both his grandfather and father were Emory graduates. Charles E. Sciple, 83, was a leader in the city's social, cultural, and fraternal life and head of the building supply firm founded by his father in 1872. A founder of the Old Gate City Guard and Druid Hills Golf Club, he was also a member of the Piedmont Driving Club, the Capital City Club, and the East Lake Country Club. Col. J. A. Skelton, 95, was the last survivor of the Andrews Raid. He enlisted in the Confederate Army at sixteen and served as a guard at Andersonville. Skelton died at the Confederate Soldiers' Home. William Wilbur Carroll Smith, 69, founder and board chairman of W. R. C. Smith Publishing Company, had been president of the Rotary Club and the Atlanta Chamber of Commerce. He was a member of St. Luke's Church. J. W. Starr, 73, president of J. W. Starr Lumber Company for more than forty years, was life chairman of the Board of Stewards at Druid Hills Methodist Church.

George Stone, 52, descendant of a long line of educators, was born at Oxford, Georgia. Both his father and grandfather were professors at Emory, from which he was graduated in 1911. He was traveling auditor for the General Motors Acceptance Corporation. Patrolman J. D. Stribling, 58, a veteran of twenty years on the police force, was noted for playing Santa Claus. For many Christmas seasons he sold candy and used the proceeds to purchase food, clothing, and toys for the needy. Mrs. Bertha L. Sweat, 107, came to Atlanta when it was Terminus and was already a grown woman when Sherman burned the city. She was a charter member of the Bellwood Baptist Church. Alison Quitman Turner, 87, organized the Fulton County Police Department and served as its first chief for seven years. Brig. Gen. Robert O. Van Horn was former commandant at Fort McPherson. Enlisting as a private in 1895, General Van Horn worked his way up from the ranks serving in Cuba, the Philippines, and France.

Mrs. Willis E. Venable, 91, widow of the man who sold the first glass of Coca-Cola in Atlanta, was the mother of Edward Venable, the restaurant owner, who survived her by only two weeks. Operator of Venable's Restaurant on Forsyth Street, Edward Venable died at 71 at his home on Gordon Street in West End. His restaurant was noted for its "country cooking," roast beef and barbecue. Morris Weinberg, 58, was one of the city's leading grocers and one-time president of the Georgia State Food Dealers' Association. Mrs. George White, 67, was a former Latin teacher at Girls High School who financially helped many girls obtain college educations. She was the sister of John Smith, Atlanta automobile dealer. R. C. White, 84, started to work for the Southern Railway when he was ten years old and retired after an unprecedented sixty-nine years of service. H. T. Williams, 70, conductor for the Seaboard Railroad for nearly fifty years, was a member of the Park Street Methodist Church, a Shriner, a Mason, and a member of Knights Templar. Albert J. Woodruff, 62, was southern manager of the Frick Company and a Georgia Public Service Commissioner.

1942

THE usual revelry accompanied New Year's Eve, but of course the new year would not be a usual one because of the war. Many Atlantans—Catholic, Protestant, Jewish—responded to President Roosevelt's call to make this January 1 a day of prayer throughout the nation. Two noted Atlanta ministers set the theme at a meeting of fifty Protestant congregations held at the Druid Hills Presbyterian Church. Said Methodist Bishop Arthur J. Moore: "For this hour we need a finer spiritual temper. No Christian patriot can tolerate for a moment the belief that ultimate victory can be achieved without the help of Almighty God." Prayed Dr. Louie D. Newton of the Druid Hills Baptist Church: "Oh, Lord, look upon our nation today. . . . We come to a place where we cannot go on without Thee. . . . The burden is too heavy, the road too long, the hill too steep, the night too dark. . . . Wilt Thou come nearer and minister to Thy Children." Similar themes were heard in Catholic and Jewish houses of worship as thousands of the faithful gathered for prayer on this rainy New Year's Day.

A highlight of the first week of the new year was a triumph of showmanship. It was Rich's Diamond Jubilee Celebration, a stirring pageant of history told in words and pictures of how both the town and the store had grown together since Rich's founding in 1867. At ceremonies Margaret Mitchell unveiled five large murals that told the story. Two huge murals, painted by John M. Silton of Forsyth, Georgia, portrayed the Legend of Atlanta and the Legend of Georgia. A vast mural by Wilbur Kurtz showing how Atlantans, mainly female, dressed through the ages was also unveiled. Even more startling in its design and color was the painting by Walter Gordon showing the riotous colors of Georgia's red clay, golden autumn leaves, crimson peach blossoms, and white dogwood.[1]

While 15,000 Atlantans were pouring into Rich's to celebrate their seventy-five years of prosperity together, not only the city but the whole state of Georgia was becoming aware that they were going into the first year of the war riding the crest of one of the greatest business booms in the city's history. Figures put together by the Chamber of Commerce showed that in virtually every line of business activity the figures were rising. During the previous year 116 new factories, distributors, and sales and service organizations had been established in Atlanta; 63 new sales agencies had come in, representing out-of-town firms and bringing in 4,397 people and payrolls of $6,595,000.[2]

Spindles were humming in 175 cotton mills in Georgia, according to Theo M. Forbes of Atlanta, secretary of the Georgia Cotton Manufacturing Associates. This production of cloth, mostly for the army, was reflected in cotton consumption. Construction had climbed steadily throughout the year, the railroads and other transport had been increasing each year since 1929, retail sales were up by 20 percent, postal records were up 6 percent in Atlanta, even before the Christmas business was added and thousands of water meters, gas meters, and telephones had been installed. Bank clearings had reached an all-time high, at $4,531,500,000. (The previous high of $3.6 million had been set in 1925.) Payrolls were up by 47 percent, according to Labor Commissioner Ben T. Huiet.

To many Atlantans, though, the big and exciting news had nothing to do with business figures but with Frankie Sinkwich and his Georgia Bulldogs, who had beaten Texas Christian University 40 to 26 in the Orange Bowl.

Governor Talmadge started the year with a pair of fractured ribs. His explanation: "I was just a country man walking on those slick city floors when a rug slipped out from under me and the floor flew up and hit me in the face." He was probably less bothered by criticism of his action in purging the state school department of "books dealing with the betterment of race relations." The Metropolitan Library Council of New York charged that such potential book-burning "weakens national unity in the face of Hitler's aggression." The association concluded with the plea that Governor Talmadge do all possible to insure the improvement of race relations between the Negro and the white people of Georgia toward the furtherance of national unity and American democracy.

Dr. Marvin S. Pittman who, like the library books, had been purged by Talmadge, issued a pleasant New Year's greeting and a thinly veiled attack on Talmadge: "The schools must be kept running efficiently during war as well as peace if our democracy is to be preserved. It would be a mistake to fight on the high seas and on foreign lands for the preservation of democratic ideals and at the same time to neglect to defend them at home."

Though he made no specific reference to the teachers he had purged from the university, Governor Talmadge soon was front-page news again for the two-month probe he had been quietly carrying out of the actions of his predecessor, E. D. Rivers, and certain of his friends. For months Solicitor General John A. Boykin, his first assistant E. H. Stephens, and a special staff had been collecting evidence seeking to establish that funds had been mal-administered by Governor Rivers and some of his associates

On January 3 the Fulton County Grand Jury under Solicitor General John A. Boykin indicted former governor Rivers, his son, and eighteen others for milking the state of a sum slightly in excess of $200,000. Governor Rivers did not long remain silent in the face of the grand jury charges. On a fishing trip in Florida when the indictments were returned on Saturday, January 3, he told the press that this was all a political maneuver, worked up by Talmadge and his henchmen. Rivers said, "I have full faith in the fairness and the judgment [of the people] and they will not be swept away by such persecution and clamor." Soon, in fact, the charges all were forgotten.

Ed S. Cook was reelected president of the Atlanta board of Education for the seventh consecutive time on January 2. Also reelected were D. F.

McClatchey, vice-president, H. Lane Young, treasurer, and Fannie Mae Weston, secretary.

Mayor Roy LeCraw, pleading for a lean, hungry war-time economy, urged that city expenses be trimmed to the bone, so that no taxes or extra assessments of any kind need be added to the people.

Atlanta in early January paid special tribute to Rabbi David Marx. Nearly seventy years old, Marx had spent forty-six as rabbi of The Temple, which observed its seventy-fifth anniversary on January 9. "He was," said columnist Dudley Glass, "a human encyclopedia, a phrase maker switching from theology to Jewish history and the influence of environment upon Jewish thought." Marx arrived in Atlanta shortly after the Civil War, when there were few Jews here, and his friends in the beginning were the men of other faiths who built Atlanta. One of them was Dr. C. B. Wilmer of St. Luke's Episcopal Church, who became his life-long friend. His public activities were varied; so were his friends. Rabbi Marx was a Rotarian, as well as the representative of nearly all Jewish civic movements for many years. He was a devotee of Scottish Rite Masonry, and at a fee of $1.00 per year he served as chaplain of the U.S. Penitentiary in Atlanta. He had preached in many denominations and spoke for his people in such civic enterprises as the Community Chest and the Red Cross Campaign.

Atlantans of all ages wanted to contribute to the war effort. On January 6, Mrs. S. C. Hornbuckle of St. Charles Avenue became the first officially designated senior air raid warden. Her training, largely self-administered, centered around a huge map of Atlanta, actually a window shade on which she had drawn her particular sector, extending from Virginia Avenue to Ponce de Leon Avenue, then from Ponce de Leon Place to North Highland. On this she put red stars to show where the Red Cross nurses lived, large red dots to identify emergency status, and blue-and-white dots to identify air raid shelters. She soon was busy charting houses and recording the material of which they were made, whether quickly inflammable or not.

While Mrs. Hornbuckle was doing her work more or less on her own volition, Chairman Robert B. Troutman of the State Defense Committee announced the appointment of seven chiefs of training divisions. They were: Fire Fighting—Fire Chief D. W. Brosman of Albany; Supplementary Police—U.S. Marshal Charles Cox; Air Raid Wardens—Clint Davis of the U.S. Department of Forestry; Emergency Medical Services—Dr. T. F. Abercrombie, state health director; Rescue and Demolition—Hughes Roberts, Georgia chairman, American Association for Contractors; Public Utilities—Walter R. McDonald, chairman of the Public Service Commission, and Representative Robert L. Foreman. This group would hold schools of instruction in each of the state's ten districts.

Many manifestations of war were evident. Attracting attention in the Atlanta papers was a picture of the wrestler-clown Man Mountain Dean having his massive 280-pound carcass measured as he was being sworn in at Fort McPherson. He asked that he be assigned to the Tank Corps, provided the army had one into which he would fit. More seriously, the 3rd Air Force Headquarters in Tampa announced it was setting up an air warning nerve center in Atlanta at which some 250 highly trained women would "man" observation equipment that would register the force, direction, height, and type of aircraft moving in the north Georgia area. Those who operated the center were told not to reveal, to either their friends or their families, the location or nature of their work. Tire rationing was also ready to go into effect on January 7, according to B. C. Forbes. Some 375,000 civilian defense workers were being enrolled in a state-wide organization. Boy Scouts distributed in the downtown area printed rules on behavior in Atlanta during blackouts. And all over the Atlanta area children were being given instructions in air raid drills and instructions for safety at home.

The Red Cross received help from two widely disparate sources early in January. More than one hundred wives of army officers at Fort McPherson organized the Fourth Corps Area Auxiliary to the Atlanta Chapter. Mrs. Clifford C. Early, wife of the commanding officer at Fort Mac, and Mrs. J. P. Smith, wife of General Smith, commander of Corps Area Headquarters, led the group. Meanwhile, the men at federal prison were making what they called "merely the down payment on the obligation to our homeland that we as devout Americans feel." They gave the Red Cross a total of $1,225.50— money they had earned in prison industries, the little pocket change they got from home, the money that in peacetime they would have spent for cigarettes, candy, and soft drinks. There was only one string attached: they wanted Margaret Mitchell to accept the donation. So "Peggy" went out, dressed in the gray-blue uniform of a Red Cross volunteer, and stood up before the 2,401 prisoners and made them a little speech straight out of the times of *Gone with the Wind*. She told them of the Roberts Guards, the felons of that day, who came out of their prison cells at Milledgeville to join up with Fighting Joe Wheeler when Sherman, after capturing Atlanta, swept with his forces toward Savannah and the sea. The Roberts Guards had no uniforms, and the guns they had were sorry guns. But they did not care, she said. Fighting at first as guerillas, they killed Yankees and seized their guns all along the line, until one last fight at Griswoldville almost wiped them out. They were fighters who were more than soldiers, for freedom and liberty were sweeter to them than to men who had never lost theirs.

As Peggy Mitchell told this story you could hear a pin drop, for deep down some of these men were hoping they would be turned free to fight for their freedom. They said as much on a scroll they gave to Mitchell in thanks for her presence. Warden Joseph W. Sanford told her that nobody in America was working harder to further the war effort than the men in his prison. They had stepped up the production in the prison by more than 250 percent, willingly jumped from a forty-hour week to forty-eight to sixty hours, six-day weeks. They even worked two eight-hour shifts on New Year's Day and gave this long day's pay to the Red Cross. Evidently inspired by their example and patriotism, the prison guards and clerks added $1,500 in cash to the Red Cross fund. The Red Cross drive reflected the devotion of all concerned. By the night of January 7, half the emergency War Chest quota of $320,000 had been filled.

With the men going to the service by thousands, jobs became open to women, and that brought with it some changes. In some jobs it became necessary, from safety and other standpoints, to wear not dresses but slacks, and women who found themselves wearing the slacks on the street often became the victims of crude and irritating wisecracking. One young lady, May McCauley, a Red Cross trainee who had lived in many places, felt that Atlanta, for all its assumed sophistication, was actually callow and boorish. "There are smiles, smirks, whistles and doubtful remarks whenever I get on the bus. One night I was standing in the aisle when one of two men said: 'Ain't you going to get up and give that lady your seat?' 'I don't see no lady,' said the other one." The whole situation, she added, is "silly and maddening."

Leon Henderson of the Federal Office of Price Administration announced that Oscar R. Strauss, Jr., executive vice-president of Rich's, Inc., had been appointed director of the regional office. Strauss, associated with Rich's for twelve years, was a nephew of Walter Rich, head of the firm. Born in Atlanta, educated at Marist and at the School of Business Administration of New York University, he was a director of the C&S Bank and past president of the Atlanta Advertising Club.

On January 8 the National Youth Administration dedicated its new resident work center in Marietta. After three months of work experience and training, young men would be qualified for special jobs building ships, producing aircraft, and manufacturing armaments and precision instruments. NYA state administrator Boisfeuillet Jones, who directed the construction of the work center, told his audience of more than one hundred young workers, including eighteen women, that they should "regard their coveralls as armor, their tools as ammunition" and to ready themselves for America's growing battles for production. A message from President Roosevelt told the group, "Your country asks you to work here now, seriously and without hesitation so that when you join the production line for war, you can give your maximum in labor and ability."

Many Atlanta business houses were contemplating air raid shelter plans. The Retail Credit Company on Fairlie Street in the heart of town used 2,000 sand bags to become the first to change its basement office area from business quarters to an air raid shelter. Teams were trained in fire fighting and first aid, and with the special permission of the city, an opening was made from the basement through the sidewalk, as an escape route to the outside. The shelter would hold 300 people and would contain chairs, lanterns, stirrup pumps, hose, goggles, asbestos gloves, and buckets of sand. In a penthouse at the top of the nine-story building there was material to put out any incendiary bombs that might drop on the roof.

The shortage of rubber for automobile tires was a matter for grave concern, but Ralph McGill tried to make light of the situation. Like the tank tread and the truck tire, McGill pointed out, the girdles the women wore were made of rubber. And the areas of the Far East where the rubber trees grew were now being invaded by the Japanese. Thus the phantoms of delight which American men had become accustomed to seeing all around them, from grocery stores to cocktail parties, had suddenly become lumpy, bumpy, and wobbly in areas that should have been round and firm. There was, though, one possible advantage, McGill pointed out. "We will fight hard in the jungles as we have power to free captive peoples from Japanese domination. We will fight even harder, to reclaim the rubber that has kept our women lithe and slim and beautiful."

Banks prospered as the threat of war turned finally into reality. First National showed earnings of $1.3 million. There were increases of $25 million in deposits and $16 million in loans. The Trust Company of Georgia loaned $11,211,006 during 1941 to borrowers engaged directly in defense work, President Robert Strickland told his shareholders at their fifty-first annual meeting. The year, said Strickland, was the most successful in the bank's history, as each department reached higher levels. Loans for all purposes, including defense work, totaled $41,643,132.23 for the six banks in the Trust Company Group. Citizens and Southern also reported a good year. At Fulton National, deposits set an all-time high.

The war came one small step closer to Atlanta when a native Atlantan took command of the big guns during the Japanese attack on the island of Luzon. Maj. Gen. E. P. (Ned) King, commander of all artillery under MacArthur in the Far East, was the son of the late E. P. King, for many years secretary of the Scottish Rite Masons in Atlanta. General King's wife lived in Atlanta with King's brother. General King was a graduate of Boys High and the University of Georgia Law School. Interested in the military, he joined the Atlanta Grays and married the daughter of General Lafayette McLaws of Savannah, a distinguished veteran of the Civil War. King fought in France as a major of artillery in 1918. Just before Pearl Harbor he was chief instructor at the Army War College in Washington. He soon joined General MacArthur as commander of all artillery in the Philippines. It was a natural progression, for his uncle had been an artillery commander in the War Between the States.

Recurring rumors that Mayor LeCraw was soon to be called back into the service and would resign his post as mayor sent a surge of excitement through the local politicians. Among the prospective candidates who began laying plans for the race to replace LeCraw were Councilman John A. White, Alderman G. Dan Bridges, Mayor Pro Tem George B. Lyle, Alderman Ed A. Gilliam, Frank H. Reynolds, and, naturally, former mayor William B. Hartsfield.

In a push to provide more high school and college graduates for the armed forces as soon as possible, it was announced that DeKalb County schools would operate on Saturdays. Thus the school year would end May 7, two weeks ahead of the usual May 29. Dr. Willis A. Sutton, city school superintendent, announced that Atlanta's 60,000 school children would not go on a six-day week. To accomplish this same purpose of speeding the learning process, the University of Georgia eliminated every holiday for 1942 and proposed a new speeded-up schedule that would permit graduation in two and one-half years. Despite the shortened term, however, President Harmon W. Caldwell announced that the fundamentals of math and physics would be intensified for all students, and that daily vesper service, with religious speeches and music, would be introduced.

"The Sidewalk Snoopers," a radio program familiar to thousands of Atlantans for seven years, was taken off the air in mid-January at the request of Byron Price, censorship director. His theory was that such man-in-the-street quiz programs made it too easy for an enemy agent to send coded messages to his people back home. For the same reason, local stations could not accept telephoned requests to play specific pieces of music on the air.

It was late in January before Atlanta had its first bomb scare. Frantic Marietta Street residents thought they had been bombed, though by a dud, when a bright shining cylinder was found by Sam L. Hulsey in a vacant lot at 842 Marietta Street. It was about a foot long and an inch in diameter with a parachute at one end and powder at the other, which Hulsey removed. It was not a dud bomb, as it turned out, but a flare, dropped by a flight of nine planes that had passed over during the afternoon.

One specialized item of defense was being produced in Atlanta in greater numbers, perhaps, than anywhere else. At his training school for dogs Benno Stein was training German Shepherds to act as guard dogs in areas where human beings could not function nearly so well. A well-trained guard dog, Stein estimated, would be worth at least two soldier guards in areas such as munitions plants, factories, and homes, where an armed guard would be dangerous to innocent persons.

The shortage of rubber for tires, and the ban on the purchase of new automobiles, made many Atlantans somewhat unwillingly turn to bicycles as a more patriotic means of transport. A parade of bike riders, led by Mayor LeCraw, Governor Talmadge, Councilman Howard Haire, and *Constitution* city editor "Pop" Hines, took place February 2. The route was from the State Capitol to Piedmont Park. Editor Hines reported that the last time he rode a bicycle was when he was delivering newspapers announcing the sinking of the battleship *Maine,* and both LeCraw and the governor claimed they had not ridden a bike since the Spanish-American War.

Robert Troutman, state director of Civilian Defense, warned that in Atlanta only one-third enough persons had volunteered to give their time and effort to home defense. Speaking on the night of January 22 to the Atlanta

Convention and Visitors Bureau, he urged the leaders to offer their services and to lay before their employees and associates the dire need for home defense. He told them to "stop being amateur experts on military strategy in battle 8,000 miles away. Be an expert in your own job of helping defend your own town or city." Meanwhile, it was announced that in the previous year the Visitors Bureau had brought 76,000 to Atlanta in 445 conventions and that the visitors had spent more than $2.5 million.

Cash donations to all worthy causes were heavy as the war picked up pace. Red Cross contributions reached $235,000 by January 21, $85,000 short of its goal of $320,000. The largest single contribution yet to the Red Cross came from employees and officials of the Georgia Power Company, a total of $15,596.13, of which $13,396.13 came from individual workers on a basis of a day's pay per employee. Included were contributions specifically for the Pearl Harbor Memorial Fund, to commemorate Atlanta men killed in action at Pearl Harbor whose names would be inscribed on a plaque.

As January drew to a close, much of the impact of the war on Atlanta had been more irritating than important. Debate arose over the moving of the clocks up an hour as ordered by Washington to extend the workday, for it would also have kids walking to school in the dark and employees reporting for work at sunup. Sugar fell into short supply as careful housewives overbought and grocers installed an unofficial form of rationing. The organization of the city into eight military defense districts was moving too slowly to be effective, and there was much discussion as to whether the dairies should deliver their milk daily, as always, or every other day. These were small things, though, compared with the news that made the front page on January 22, 1942.

Enemy submarines, skulking off the Atlantic seaboard, sank the coastal steamer *City of Atlanta* (not to be confused with the light cruiser that Margaret Mitchell had recently christened the USS *Atlanta*). A former passenger liner converted into a freighter plying between Savannah, New York, and other coastal points, the *City of Atlanta* was struck off Cape Hatteras by a torpedo and went down in a matter of minutes, leaving one sailor known to be dead and forty-three others missing. It was the fifth vessel sunk by Axis submarines operating in East Coast waters, and it had a particular meaning to Atlantans. Since its launching in 1904, the *City of Atlanta* had carried many Atlantans on its regular run between Savannah and New York. An editorial in the *Constitution* on January 23 declared that the men who died as the *Atlanta* went down died in the service of their country and were as truly heroes of the war as were those who died at Pearl Harbor, Wake Island, Burma, and the Philippines.

On January 22, the day after it was announced that the Metropolitan Opera would return in April, the All-Star Concert Series presented Eugene Ormandy and the 110 members of the Philadelphia Orchestra in concert before 5,000 at the auditorium. It was the biggest crowd ever to attend a symphony in Atlanta.

Though heavy tires were hard to come by, Bishop Arthur J. Moore,

Atlanta resident bishop at Glenn Memorial Methodist Church, went ahead with an idea he had treasured for years—a plan for carrying the Gospel to those who needed it wherever they might be. On January 21, 1942, 150 Methodist pastors stood by at Glenn Memorial while Bishop Moore dedicated "The Circuit Rider"—a Methodist church on wheels. The trailer-church was the culmination of an idea born in the mind of Bishop Moore, who began his early ministry as an evangelist traveling through Georgia. When the bishop shared his dream with a few sympathetic Methodist friends, they made the money available for the purchase of the outfit. It was fifty feet long and was fully equipped with a platform, a modern public address system, and records to carry sermon transcriptions and hymns of the church. The Reverend Nat Thompson would have active charge of the trailer as it carried the Christian message from the Georgia mountains deep into Florida.

With a sense of excitement Atlanta learned that work on the mammoth Bell Bomber plant, to cost $15 million and employ 40,000, would start in Cobb County early in February, and the plant would begin turning out gigantic four-engine bombers within eight months. When going full blast, the plant would have a payroll amounting to more than $1.5 million a week. William J. O'Conner, counsel for the Bell Aircraft Company of Buffalo, joined L. M. Blair, mayor of Marietta, and George McMillan, Cobb County commissioner, in making the announcement.

Atlanta's first large-scale blackout test was held on the night of January 27 and was completed in seconds. Reported the *Constitution:* "A test blackout at the First National Bank Building last night proved that one man could turn out the lights from 3,500 lamps before you could say 'James D. Robinson, Sr.' At one second before 9:00 the 16 stories of the First National Building were ablaze from a thousand windows. At 9:00 on the tick Chief Engineer W. J. Dickens down in the basement started yanking switches and the lights started winking out in huge squares. At less than a half minute past nine, there wasn't a glimmer to be seen from ground floor to penthouse."

Despite the war and all the financial demands that it made upon the public, Atlantans continued generously to support worthwhile projects that were not directly war or defense connected. Cason Callaway, for example, traveled 3,700 miles by car, talking to friends in every corner of Georgia; he persuaded sixty of them to give $1,000 each to the State Infantile Paralysis Fund, a tangible way of congratulating polio victim Franklin D. Roosevelt on his sixtieth birthday on January 30.

The war affected but did not stop efforts to develop the Atlanta University Center concept. Declaring Emory's goal as "the development of creative minds for productive service—in war and in peace," Emory president Dr. Harvey W. Cox called for productive service to meet and overcome the "most powerful, most ruthless enemies the world has ever known. While it may not be possible for Emory at present to go forward with all her plans for buildings and for strengthening graduate work, we believe it will be possible, because of the success of our financial campaign, to do our full share in the emergency and then go forward with our plans when the war is over. We must have creative minds fired with a zeal for productive service to reconstruct a new world after this great catastrophe has passed."

To this Dr. Goodrich C. White, vice-president of Emory, added his views on the need of developing in the South such universities as were projected under the University Center program, adding that "it is no narrow sectionalism nor false pride that makes me long for the day when the South can take its place on terms of equality with other regions, educationally, culturally, intellectually. We of the South have something to give that the nation and the world need," he added, "but we cannot give in full measure so long as the educational status, like our economic and political status, is one of colonial dependency."

Before 1942 was over there were at least fourteen civilian defense organizations functioning, and it seemed that nearly every Atlantan not subject to military draft was taking part in some specialized form of civil defense. One of the more important was the Civil Air Patrol. A call for pilots got an immediate response from all over the state, including six Atlanta "lady-birds," who were veteran civilian pilots.

For those not in uniform, life at home was rapidly becoming more complicated. In Atlanta, gas pumpers at filling stations were being laid off regularly because of tire and gas rationing, but progress in the construction of the great Bell Bomber plant at Marietta held out the hope that before their jobs were lost and hunger struck, they would be trained to build bombers at a higher rate of pay than they had known before. Taxi drivers were losing their cars, and even those who kept wheels rolling were not doing well at a fee of 25¢ to 35¢ for the first two miles. But the women who left their cars in the garage had to travel downtown to market somehow, and they increased the transit business of the Georgia Power Company by 25 percent over the previous year. Every piece of rolling stock the company owned was in service, including old one-man streetcars long retired. The fleet in active daily use consisted of 272 trolley cars, 70 trackless trolleys and 116 motor buses. Forty-six more trackless trolleys and motor buses were on order to be delivered within the year.[3]

After considerable discussion, Atlanta schools, businesses, and industrial plants agreed to stagger their opening and closing hours to accomplish two purposes: to give maximum cooperation to the federal government in conservation of power during the national emergency and to prevent overloading of transportation facilities during rush periods. Under the system of staggered hours, schools would open at 9:30 instead of 8:45; the city hall would open at 9:00 instead of 8:00, and business houses in general would set their opening an hour later than their practice in the past. Thus some of the larger stores would open at ten o'clock instead of nine. The change to a later opening was a reflection of the newly installed daylight saving time, ordered by Roosevelt, which advanced the clock by an hour. To keep this system without moving up an hour, many school children in Atlanta and workers, too, would be going out in the dark.

Atlanta in 1942 was responsible for many things in which it could take pride, but there was one thing that caused concerned citizens deep embarrassment. Atlanta was the syphilis capital of the South. When the U.S. Public Health Service examined the medical records of the first million draftees, it found that over the nation as a whole, 45 men out of every 1,000 were suffering from syphilis and were, therefore, unfit for military service. In Georgia, the number was 132 per 1,000, fourth after Florida, South Carolina, and Mississippi. But when they checked the figures on the cities, they found that Atlanta was number one: 162 out of every 1,000 had syphilis, meaning that Atlanta led all its sister cities of similar size from Baltimore to Houston.

The question was "Why?" A committee of a dozen Atlantans headed by a young dermatologist soon found the answer. They found that the laws of Fulton and DeKalb County for the control of syphilis were adequate but were not being enforced. They found that the hospital founded for the treatment of syphilis in Atlanta was completely inadequate, haphazard and limited in size, equipment, and personnel. This was not the fault of Atlanta doctors and nurses but of the lack of support the city gave to a treatment program. The city of Chicago in 1941 spent more than $828,000 treating 9,613 cases, using a staff of 623 persons. Atlanta, with twice that many needing treatment, treated half as many people at a fraction of that cost, using a staff of 20 specialists. A minimum average cost per person was $50. Atlanta spent $10. The report made clear that Atlanta was spending thousands of dollars for every lame, blind, and insane person on the relief rolls because of syphilis, and the charity wards of the hospitals were full of patients whom syphilis had made prey to other illnesses.

The investigators, of course, did not view with alarm and drop the matter there. Both the Senior and Junior Chambers of Commerce jumped headlong into the battle against VD. Strong recommendations went out to the mayor and council, the Fulton County commissioners, and the health services of both city and county. Throughout 1942 and 1943 several things had to be done. First was a drive to recognize and treat the hundreds of prostitutes who walked the streets of Atlanta. Next was to build a $100,000 treatment building next door to the present inadequate clinic, fully equipped and staffed with specialists in the field of venereal disease. Third was to set up a staff of field nurses and employ a social worker who could follow up bedridden patients and check on those who failed to show up on schedule for treatment. Also, clinics for treatment of all diseases, including syphilis, were to be set up in at least two black and one white housing project. As a result of nearly two years of effort, the Chamber of Commerce in a report entitled "What we have done in 1943" was able to announce proudly that VD was on the run. The army reported that VD in Atlanta was no longer the serious problem it had been.[4]

Atlanta was becoming more and more a regional headquarters center for all the military services. The joke started going around that "Dixie" would soon become the official Marine hymn instead of "From the Halls of Montezuma." The Southern U.S. Marine Division was transferred to Atlanta from New Orleans, where it had functioned since 1916. Recruiting headquarters staff set up in the Atlanta National Building. Maj. Meigs O. Frost, the public relations officer, was a former reporter on the New Orleans *Times Picayune* and a winner of the Sigma Delta Chi Distinguished Service Award for general reporting. The Atlanta commander—Lt. Col. Adolph Bradlee Miller—was a distinguished fighting Marine in France during World War I. On February 2 the Corps moved along Peachtree Street as they put on Atlanta's first big military parade of World War II. The crack Marine regimental band came in from Parris Island, South Carolina, to lead the grand march and to give a free concert at the Municipal Auditorium to which the public was invited. Called the "Remember Wake Island Parade," this military show moved through town from Peachtree and Baker to Whitehall and Alabama.

Some other "touchdowns" scored in Atlanta during this war year, as reported by the Chamber, were the establishment of 110 new industries and manufacturing plants, 51 resident representatives and out-of-town agencies, and 37 new federal departments and agencies. These 198 new developments employed 4,824 people, with an annual payroll of $8 million. Eleven companies, the report noted, had applied to the Civil Aeronautics Administration for thirty new air routes, and at the Chamber's urging the National Housing Administration instigated construction of 1,900 new dwelling units and the establishment of an Atlanta-Fulton-DeKalb War Housing Center for essential civilian workers, funding of which was shared by the city and the two counties. The *Journal of Labor* reported that by September of 1943 the Southern Bell Telephone Company had 117,471 telephones in operation, a third more than the 88,587 phones in service in 1940. In 1940, 139 operators handled long-distance calls. By 1943 the number was up to 229 long-distance operators, and according to the manager of Southern Bell, the total number of operators had risen from 200 in 1940 to 861 in 1943. "Years of long-planned engineering," he said, "was accomplished almost overnight."

Two members of the President's cabinet arrived in Atlanta on January 28, 1942, on the same train but on different missions. Attorney General Francis Biddle came in to inspect the Atlanta Federal Penitentiary and to thank the 2,000 prisoners there for the fabulous production of cotton canvas, used by the military. Claude Wickard, secretary of agriculture, came in to speak to Georgia farmers about how to increase their production of food crops by at least 15 percent under wartime circumstances.

For gallantry and intrepid action beyond the call of duty, a twenty-three-year-old native of Atlanta, 2nd Lt. Alexander B. Neninger, became the first soldier in World War II to win the nation's highest military honor. The Congressional Medal of Honor was bestowed posthumously on him on recommendation of General MacArthur. In hand-to-hand combat while under heavy rifle fire and grenade explosions, he fought his way alone deep into enemy lines. Only 1,723 men had won this high honor in all the wars prior to World War I, and only 95 of the more than 4 million men involved in that conflict had received it. Born in Atlanta in 1918, Neninger grew up in Florida. His paternal grandparents were well known in Atlanta, where they had lived for many years.

Atlantans celebrated President Roosevelt's sixtieth birthday on the night of January 30 by dancing the whole night through at a series of balls to raise the $320,000 goal set for the Infantile Paralysis Fund. The revelry took place at the auditorium, where Perry Bechtel's Orchestra played, at the Ansley where Curley Hicks's Band furnished the music, at the Henry Grady with Nu Nu Chastain, the Capital City Club where Jimmy Vincent's Band played, at the Biltmore where Harry Hearn furnished the music, at the Piedmont Driving Club with Bill Manley's Orchestra, and at the Standard Club with Bill Mayfield's Orchestra. Atlanta's pro rata portion of the total was $97,000.

The revels in Atlanta were only a few of the estimated 12,000 parties held throughout the United States; the president delivered his birthday message by radio. His message carried with it the strong prediction of imminent victory in the war. Equally meaningful as a quality of the American character, he said, was the fact that many thousands of dollars, despite the demands of war, had been raised for the relief of children crippled by polio. "That means very definitely that we have an abiding faith in the future. . . . Even in time of war this nation which still holds to the old ideals of Christianity and Democracy is carrying on services to humanity which have little or no relation to torpedoes or guns or bombs. We're going to win through to a peace," he said, "which will bring with it continuing progress in our efforts for the security and not for the destruction of humanity."

On February 18, 1942, fire in the upper floors of the sixteen-story Winecoff Hotel at 176 Peachtree Street in the heart of town trapped dozens of persons in their rooms above the eleventh floor. It was 6:00 P.M., and thousands of home-going Atlantans crowded Peachtree and Ellis streets, so firemen struggled through the choking smoke, and bellboys kept the elevators moving as they moved from room to room. Many women fainted and had to be carried into the lobby and there revived. Particularly helpful was Dr. C. Raymond Arp, who at the sound of firebells rushed from his office in the Candler Building to go into the smoke-filled rooms, bringing out and treating those who had fainted. Guests hung halfway out their windows, gasping, and one guest, Capt. John Ord of Fort Monmouth, Virginia, clutching his briefcase, stood for nearly thirty minutes on a narrow ledge outside his window on the fourteenth floor. By passing a ladder across the narrow alley between the back of the hotel and the Mortgage Guarantee Building, firemen were able to crawl across to rescue two New Yorkers who were trapped in their rooms. In the hotel along with the firemen, manager L. O. Mosely and bellhops Murphy Lyle, Burton Watts, and Omer Dyer felt their way along smoke-filled corridors inspecting every one of the hotel's two hundred rooms. The lobby filled with choking, strangling, fainting guests. But none died. This fire, spectacular as it was, was only a precursor of the Winecoff Hotel fire of 1946 in which 119 people died.

Eleanor Roosevelt came to Atlanta to speak at a civilian defense rally, and many Atlantans were somewhat concerned to note that the rally was to be open to Negroes as well as whites—though the blacks were to sit in a special section.

An item of great interest to Atlantans came on February 20, when Secretary of War Stimson announced that the famed old 82nd Army Division of World War I would be ordered back to service on March 25. First made up of southern men, many of them Atlantans, the 82nd was organized at Camp Gordon on August 25, 1917, under command of Maj. Gen. Eben Swift. Southern officers remained in command, and as the 82nd's southern fighting men went on to fight and to suffer great casualties in the St. Mihiel and Meuse-Argonne offense, they were replaced by draftees from New England. Since the end of World War I the division had existed only on paper—but the memories of its survivors were vivid, particularly of their twenty-six days under continuous fire in the Argonne advance, which was the war's record for unrelieved combat action.

Another action of the War Department had a greater effect on the future of Atlanta and its environs than the rebirth of the famous fighting 82nd. As had been expected, with eagerness by many, with anxiety by some, on March 3, 1942, Mayor Roy LeCraw was ordered to report for duty with the Army Chemical Forces. On March 13 he offered his resignation to City Council. In his farewell message to the council, LeCraw called on the city to continue his policies—to preserve the city's finances, refuse to raise water rates or tax rates, keep the traffic reforms his administration had put in, continue to improve the police department with police training schools and the selection of officers on the basis of merit, continue the smoke abatement programs, preserve the civilian defense set-up, deemphasize all nonessential government functions, and plan a postwar improvement program for the city.

As he finished, Councilman Roy Bell leaped to his feet to urge that LeCraw's resignation not be accepted. He should, instead, be granted "leave of absence" for the remainder of the year. Bell was supported in this by Councilman Paul Butler, Councilman Howard Haire, and Alderman L. O. Mosely. Councilman J. Allen Couch then paid warm tribute to LeCraw's splendid character and honesty but added that "the Mayor needs saving from his friends," urging that his sacrifice for his country not be marred by a "leave of absence," which was illegal under city law. In this LeCraw himself joined, urging he be allowed to resign. When it came to a vote, the "leave" motion was dead, and LeCraw's resignation was accepted. That afternoon he went back to his City Hall office, changed from his mayor's suit into his major's uniform, and went over to the Bona Allen Building to report for duty to Col. Alfred L. Rockwood of the Chemical Warfare Division of the 4th Corps area. For LeCraw it was a personal triumph. As a youth he had volunteered for service on the American border and helped General Pershing chase Pancho Villa; after LeCraw was kicked by a mule, he was dismissed from service in 1916. In World War I he had applied for officer training and was accepted, but that war had ended almost immediately thereafter. He had joined the Georgia National Guard and he served there from 1922 until 1941, when he became mayor. And now, here was a third opportunity to fight staring him in the face, and he was determined not to let this opportunity slip by.

LeCraw's departure from City Hall set off a flurry of excitement among Atlantans ambitious to take his place. His chair at City Hall was still warm when Councilman John A. White and Dewey L. Johnson, city electrician, announced their candidacy for the $8,000-a-year job. They were followed by aldermen G. Dan Bridges, Ed A. Gilliam, and Frank Reynolds, councilmen Howard Haire and J. Allen Couch, and retired businessman and former councilman Jim Backman. Also in the race was Mayor Pro Tem George B. Lyle. And, confidently, ex-mayor William B. Hartsfield, still smarting over his narrow defeat by Roy LeCraw fourteen months earlier, put his name in the pot.

Hartsfield's confidence was justified. The vote was held on May 27, 1942, and it was a walk-away, with Hartsfield winning over the other candidates in the largest field of mayoral candidates in the city's history. Out of the 41,157 voters registered, 23,289 cast their ballots—12,630 of them going for Hartsfield. G. Dan Bridges was far back with 4,867, and Dewey L. Johnson came in third with 2,328. Councilman White was next with 1,158. Hartsfield polled more votes than his combined opponents by a majority of 1,971. Mayor Pro Tem Lyle, serving in City Hall since LeCraw's departure of March 14, polled 752. Others were Haire, 666; Backman, 595; Reynolds, 273; and Jimmy Vickers received 48 votes.

Roy LeCraw's career after 1942 was one of military practice mixed with politics and, finally, religion. In the Army Air Force he rose to a colonelcy, serving not only in World War II in Europe but in Korea as well, winning a Bronze Star. With no wars to fight, he returned to his basic profession, the law, and his basic interest, politics. At the end of the war he lost a bid to unseat Hartsfield and return to city hall. In 1948 at age fifty he represented Fulton County as state senator. In 1954 he ran for Congress and lost. Thereafter, he confined his interest mainly to his law practice in DeKalb County and to real estate. Then in the 1960s his deeply religious nature came to the fore and for years thereafter, as he moved on into his eighties, he concentrated on building churches in countries he had come to know as a soldier. An elder of the North

Avenue Presbyterian Church in Atlanta, he raised money from churches in this country with which he helped to build more than 130 churches in Korea, Taiwan, and Japan.[5]

For Bill Hartsfield, the departure of LeCraw was a political triumph he never forgot, but he soon learned that as wartime mayor he would have troubles that he had never dreamed of in the years he served before the conflict. During his first term of office, the roof of the old City Auditorium had fallen in during a heavy rain. He quickly had it repaired. Then just before he was to go out of office, the front section of the building burned. The WPA had made a good start on replacing the old structure with a fireproof shell of steel and cement, but as the war came along, building materials for nonessential purposes were impossible to obtain. He was faced with the prospect of boarding up the windows or finishing it off with wood. His decision was to make the best of whatever materials were available. It was this philosophy that guided him and Atlanta through the war. "Steering a city through troublesome times is like piloting a ship through stormy waters," he told a *Journal Magazine* writer. "You don't know what you are going to run into, but you are going to be ready for anything. You may have to go through obstacles, or around them. Or you may try to zig-zag."

One thing in Hartsfield's philosophy had not changed—his determination that Atlanta be kept free of professional crooks, members of the organized underworld, which would be attracted to Atlanta by the big payrolls of new industries and the thousands of troops that were coming in. Atlanta, he told his police, had to rid itself of all such loafers and idlers and criminal parasites. The result was that Atlanta got the reputation of being a good leave town where a soldier with a few dollars in his pocket, looking for a few beers, could be sure he would not be mugged, rolled, or served a Mickey Finn in a local bar.

Troops also found the people of Atlanta extremely friendly—and many lifelong friendships were established between them and the local population. And this, it proved, was one of the things that caused so many of the military people who had served in the area to come back to Atlanta after the war.

On a Saturday night in July of 1942 the Atlanta Historical Society paid tribute to sixty-six living Atlantans, descendants of the 120 settlers who were living here one hundred years earlier when the town changed its name from Marthasville to Atlanta. Ruth Blair rang the city's oldest school bell to summon the guests to dinner at the Biltmore Hotel. Franklin Garrett brandished the cane used by Marthasville's first town marshal as he introduced the speakers, including Mayor Hartsfield, Judge John D. Humphries, Dr. Glenn W. Rainey of Georgia Tech, President Goodrich C. White of Emory, and Dr. Major F. Fowler, president of the Fulton County Medical Society.

The war had a way of bringing people together, as Celestine Sibley explained: "War—the same war that has their sons fighting on far-flung battlefields of the world, the same war that is beginning to make small dents in the thick structure of the old complacent way of life, is restoring to at least one group of Atlantans an ancient, almost forgotten gift. It is the gift of neighborliness, of actively working together at a homely task, and accomplishing it with pride and satisfaction." She then cited what was going on at the home of Mrs. O. C. White on Lookout Place, "a quiet, treesy little street east of Peachtree," where an entire neighborhood joined together to create a basement first aid center, complete with homemade stretchers, sheets and pillows, cots, iron beds, blankets, all contributed from home supplies, and bandages and drugs they bought with their own money. Sixty-seven neighbors, many of whom had not known each other before, joined in this enterprise, led by Mrs. White, Mrs. John P. Coleman, and Mrs. H. L. Hackett. "And," said Miss Sibley, "even if the war never hurls a casualty into the basement first aid center, the project has been many times worth the effort they put into it," for it brought people together in love and understanding, and in the pioneer spirit of an earlier day.

Near the end of the year fighting in the Pacific brought a symbolic loss to Atlanta when the cruiser named for the city was sunk by the Japanese. Hanging in the Atlanta Historical Society near a portrait and a large-scale model of the *Atlanta* is a placard that tells the tale:

The Light Cruiser, whose model is shown here, was built by the Federal Shipbuilding and Dry Dock Company, a subsidiary of the United States Steel Corporation, at Kearny, New Jersey. The keel of the vessel was laid on April 22, 1940 and the ship was launched on September 6, 1941. The sponsor was Mrs. John R. Marsh (Margaret Mitchell, author of *Gone with the Wind*) of Atlanta. The vessel was delivered to the United States Navy at the New York Navy Yard on December 23, 1941, and commissioned the next day with Samuel P. Jenkins in command.

The U.S.S. *Atlanta* had a short but distinguished war record. It participated in the battle of Midway June 4 to June 6, 1942, in the landing of the United States forces upon Guadalcanal Island on August 7, 1942 and in the Battle of the Eastern Solomons on August 24, 1942.

In the Battle of Guadalcanal the U.S.S. *Atlanta* was one of a group of five cruisers and eight destroyers which engaged a superior Japanese force which included two battleships. United States ships opened fire at 1:48 A.M. November 13, 1942 and shots from the U.S.S. *Atlanta* sank a Japanese destroyer and helped to set afire and eventually sink a Japanese light cruiser.

Shortly thereafter, the U.S.S. *Atlanta* was struck by a Japanese torpedo and its rudder was damaged. In this helpless condition, the U.S.S. *Atlanta* circled toward the enemy, powerless and under heavy fire of a Japanese heavy cruiser. As the battle action moved away, the U.S.S. *Atlanta*, blazing from stem to stern, lay dead in the water. The enemy forces eventually fled in defeat but the U.S.S. *Atlanta* was damaged beyond salvage. It was abandoned and sunk.

The U.S.S. *Atlanta* and its gallant crew received the following Presidential Unit Citation:

"For outstanding performance during the action against enemy Japanese forces off Guadalcanal Island, November 12–13, 1942. Struck by one torpedo and no less than 49 shells, the U.S.S. *Atlanta,* after sinking an enemy destroyer and repeatedly hitting a cruiser which later went down, gallantly remained in battle under auxiliary power with one-third of her crew killed or missing, her engine room flooded and her topside a shambles. Eventually succumbing to her wounds after the enemy had fled in defeat, she left behind her a heroic example of invincible fighting spirit."

Immediately, with Hartsfield and Margaret Mitchell Marsh leading the way, the city began a war bond drive to build a new *Atlanta*. The goal was $35 million and as a measure of how the local people felt, $165 million in bonds were sold. Hartsfield immediately suggested to the secretary of the navy that Margaret Mitchell again be asked to be the sponsor. She, in turn, suggested that Hartsfield, for his diligent labor on behalf of the bond sales, be asked to be a member of the party. The launching of this, the fourth ship to bear the name "Atlanta," took place at Camden, New Jersey, on December 3, 1944. It served through the closing days of the war and joined in the bombardment of Japan. Hartsfield was a sentimental man about anything that had to do with the history of Atlanta. The silver punch bowl that the city had given the third *Atlanta* had been lost when the ship was sunk off Guadalcanal, but the ancient bowl that had been part of the silver service to the *Atlanta* built in 1886 was floating around somewhere in navy storerooms. Hartsfield found it, and at his request it was placed aboard the fourth *Atlanta*. When, after the war, the ship was retired from service, the bowl finally came home in 1959 as a gift from the navy and, like the model of the third *Atlanta,* is now at the Atlanta Historical Society. In a gesture of gratitude, a replica of the silver service that was lost when the third *Atlanta* was sunk was presented to the navy by the city and the Coca-Cola Company.

Several items from 1942 stood out. A Census Bureau report showed that the Atlanta metropolitan area had a population of 503,000 in May, 1942, an increase of 23,000 in the twenty-five months since April, 1940. W. Zode Smith, general manager of the city waterworks, reported that in the twelve months prior to December 28, 1942, the city had pumped 15 billion gallons of water to its more than 400,000 users—an average of 37,000 gallons a year per customer, and enough to cover the 34.4 square miles of Atlanta's surface to a depth of 25 inches.

An unexpected result of the population increase was the increase in divorce suits, 117 more than the year before. The Fulton County Court of Domestic Relations heard 4,600 cases, according to J. H. Bush, clerk of the court. Curiously, only half a dozen cases involved persons in the armed services. Some of the cases were memorable. The marriage of longest duration that terminated in divorce in 1942 was that of a man of seventy-nine, married to a woman of sixty-nine for more than fifty-four years in which they raised ten children. She secured her divorce on the grounds that she had discovered that he had started seeing another woman. A woman filed a claim for alimony twenty-five years after being divorced. The court ruled she had waited too long. Mrs. Floyd Woodward, divorced wife of the former "Bunco King," was luckier. She was granted $40,000 in alimony. Another woman, married for thirty-two years and a grandmother, asked for a divorce and a restoration of her maiden name. Both requests were granted.

The early war years led to emerging change in the attitudes of the black man and woman toward white society and their place in it. In the Urban League Bulletin appearing in the *Constitution* of December 27, 1942, for example, it was reported that Rachel Pruden Herndon, secretary to attorney Austin T. Walden, had passed the bar examination to become Georgia's first Negro woman lawyer. The only Negro candidate, she was one of the eighteen who passed among the sixty-eight who took the examination.

In October of 1942 Negro leaders from ten southern states met in Durham, North Carolina, to study the effect of war on Negro-white relations, and to establish a broad base for interracial cooperation. Among them were two well-known and respected Atlanta Negro educators, Dr. Benjamin E. Mays, president of Morehouse College, and Dr. Rufus Clement of Atlanta University. In a report, the committee asserted that the effect of the war had been to make the Negro the symbol of every other minority in America and in the world at large. Under the heading "Political and Civil Rights," the group in measured tones listed "obvious social and economic inequities which Whites continue to defend on the grounds that any effort to change them represents an effort by 'the predatory ambition of irresponsible Negroes to invade the privacy of family life.'" The report then went on to list the changes needed if the two races were to live in peace and harmony. The ballot is a safeguard of democracy, and to preserve it, the poll tax, the white primary and "all forms of discriminating practices, evasions of the law and intimidation of citizens seeking to exercise their right of franchise must be discontinued."

The committee also struck at exclusion of Negroes from jury service, and "the abuse of police power by White officers of the law." Lynchings had been fewer in recent years but still occurred in some areas of the South—a fascistic expression of white supremacy that must be abolished by effective law enforcement. Equality in kind and quality and in character of service for Negroes on common carriers and at terminals had to be established. In industry and labor there should be the same pay for the same work, and service workers should be organized into unions.

The report, though not stressing the integration of schools, called strongly for the improvement of Negro schools, which would require that the southern states spend much more money on their Negro schools.

Though the report applied in the main to the urban Negro, it also spoke for the black farmer. The tenant, the committee recommended, should work under written contracts, under longer lease terms, and the day laborers should receive higher wages.

In conclusion, the report noted "the present hysteria" of many house-wives who were losing poorly paid servants to better-paying war industries.

The importance of this meeting was not lost on Atlanta's editorial writers nor their reporters. Said Ralph McGill in his *Constitution* column December 18, 1942: "It will be most unfortunate if the Southerner does not discuss calmly and intelligently the basis for inter-racial cooperation as advanced by this group of Southern Negroes. . . . This is the very first vocal expression by a united front of Southern Negro leadership [and] it is important and signifi-cant." McGill then went on to point out the southern group was not demand-ing "social equality—though it did oppose in principle the practice of segre-gation—but was merely asking for "simple effort to correct social and economic injustices, with both races cooperating in the advancement of a sound policy aimed at the improvement of race relations within the Demo-cratic framework."

Early in 1943 McGill served as chairman of a meeting at which some two hundred white Atlantans in all fields of civic and political life considered the Durham Report and compiled an answer that was, in effect, an agreement. It said in part that the statement of the Durham Group was "so frank and courageous, so free of any threat or ultimatum, and at the same time shows such good will that we gladly agree to cooperate." Later McGill read the complete statement by the white southerners to a directors' meeting of the Atlanta Chamber of Commerce. So impressed were they that many signed in agreement, and the full text was included in the Chamber's minutes of May 3, 1943. The text follows, in part:

We do not attempt to make here anything like a complete reply to the questions raised nor to offer solutions for all the vexing problems. We hope, however, to point the pathway for future cooperative efforts and to give as-surance of our sincere good will and desire to cooperate in any sound program aimed at the improvement of race relations.

These Negro leaders rightly placed emphasis in their statement on dis-crimination in the administration of our laws on purely racial grounds. We are sensitive to this charge and admit that it is essentially just. From the Potomac to the Rio Grande there are some ten million Negroes. While all citizens are governed by the same laws, it is recognized that Negroes have little voice in the making and enforcement of the laws under which they must live. They are largely dependent upon the will of the majority group for the safety of life and property, education and health, and their general economic condition. This is a violation of the spirit of democracy. No Southerner can logically dispute the fact that the Negro, as an American citizen, is entitled to his civil rights and economic opportunities.

The race problem in any Southern community is complicated by our economic limitations. The factors which have kept the South a tributary section have also kept it poor and lacking in sufficient industry to develop and to provide enough jobs and enough public funds for every public need. Yet the only justification offered for those laws which have for their purpose the separation of the races is that they are intended to minister to the welfare and integrity of both races. There has been widespread and inexcusable discrimination in the administration of these laws. The white Southerner has an obligation to interest himself in the legitimate aspirations of the Negro. This means correcting the discrimination between the races in the allocation of school funds, in the number and quality of schools, and in the salaries of teachers. In public travel where the law demands a separation of the races, primary justice and a simple sense of fair play demand the facilities for safety, comfort and health should be equal. The distribution of public utilities and public benefits, such as sewers, water, housing, street and sidewalk paving, playgrounds, public health and hospital facilities should come to the Negro upon the basis of population and need.

It is recognized that there is often practical discrimination by some peace officers and in some courts in the treatment of Negro prisoners and in the abrogation of their civil rights. There is no such discrimination incorporated in the laws of any of the Southern states. False arrests, brutal beatings and other evils must be stopped.

In the economic field, unquestionably procedures should be undertaken to establish fully the right to receive equal pay for equal work. To do otherwise works a wrong to our entire economic life and to our self respect. With so large a proportion of our wage-earning population belonging to the minority race, if we cannot plan for a well-trained, well-employed and prosperous Negro population, the economic future of the South is hopeless.

Most of the Negroes in the South are on farms and in rural communities. Failure to provide for them all the facilities for improving agricultural practices through schools, county agents, supervision holds back all of the South. Fair wages, longer tenures of leases and increased opportunities for farm ownership are also necessary.

All men who believe in justice, who love peace and who believe in the meaning of this country are under the necessity of working together to draw off from the body of human society the poison of racial antagonism. This is one of the disruptive forces which unless checked will ultimately disturb and threaten the stability of the nation. Either to deny or to ignore the increased tension between the white and colored races would be a gesture of insincerity.

That there are acute and intricate problems associated with two races living side by side in the South cannot be denied. But these problems can be solved and will ultimately disappear if they are brought out into an atmosphere of justice and good will. If we approach them with contempt in one group and with resentment in the other group, then we work on hopeless terms. The solution of these problems can be found only in men of both races who are known to be men of determined good will. The ultimate solution will be found in evolutionary methods and not in ill-founded revolutionary movements which promise immediate solutions.

We agree with the Durham Conference that it is "unfortunate that the simple efforts to correct obvious social and economic injustices continue, with such considerable popular support, to be interpreted as the predatory ambition of irresponsible Negroes to invade the privacy of family life." We agree also that "it is a wicked notion that the struggle by the Negro for citizenship is a struggle against the best interests of the nation. To urge such a doctrine, as many are doing, is to preach disunity, and to deny the most elementary principles of American life and government."

And so over the next three decades, in Atlanta at least, there came peacefully into being most of the changes black and white southern leaders had recommended in this their first calm expression of their hopes, changes that, particularly in Atlanta city government, went far beyond anything either white or black could have dreamed of in 1943.

OBITUARIES

James T. Adams, believed to be Atlanta's oldest railroad man and enjoying the distinction of being the conductor on the last run made by the Texas of Andrews' Raid fame, died at 82. J. C. (Mott) Aldredge, 56, was a former railroad man, city alderman, and sheriff of Fulton County since 1938. Samuel Carter Atkinson, justice of the Georgia Supreme Court and one of the most widely known figures in Georgia public life, died at 78. Mrs. William Y. Atkinson died at 84. The former Susie Cobb Milton, she was one of Georgia's most noted women and was responsible for the founding of the Georgia State College for Women. She was the widow of former Gov. William Y. Atkinson. J. L. Beavers was a forty-three-year veteran of the Atlanta Police Department who rose from patrolman to chief and on to president of the International Association of Police Chiefs. Madison Bell, father of Georgia's first child labor law and a legislator for six terms, died at 62. Bartow M. Blount was the first mayor of East Point and a founder of the Capital City Club.

Martha Berry, born to wealth in Rome, Georgia, was the founder of the Berry schools, which are dedicated to giving opportunities to young people, especially those from the north Georgia mountains. Dr. Joe P. Bowdoin was a practicing country doctor for more than thirty years, a state health officer, and the oldest *Atlanta Constitution* correspondent, a post he was appointed to by Henry Grady. Dr. Luther O. Bricker, noted clergyman, author, and founder of the Peachtree Christian Church, died at 68. J. W. Bridwell, "Uncle Billy," was a pioneer leader in the labor movement in Atlanta and the Southeast and was the second president of the Atlanta Federation of Trades.

He died at 76. Sally Eugenia Brown was a member of civic and patriotic organizations and was the surviving child of Georgia's wartime governor Joseph E. Brown. William H. Brenner, pioneer electrical engineer and world renowned employee of Edison's laboratory, installed the electricity in the palace of the Japanese emperor and the Japanese street railroad system. Mrs. Fannie A. Cosby, 104, was married before the Civil War and left sixty-seven descendants. Dr. John B. Crenshaw, for thirty-eight years head of the modern language department at Georgia Tech and college teacher for sixty-one years, died at 81. A pioneer in southern intercollegiate athletics, he was faculty director of athletics at Georgia Tech.

Ernest M. (Dinky) Dallis, well-known over the South as advertising agent for sugar, oil, steel, and railway industries and Atlanta commercial agent of the foreign and domestic commerce division of the U.S. Department of Commerce, was 61. Emil Dittler, president of Dittler Printing Company, one of the South's largest business establishments, died at 65. Col. C. M. DuPress, a veteran of the Battle of Atlanta and a resident of the Home for Confederates, died at 95. W. W. DeLany, 74, was superintendent of Southern Bell and head of DeLany Insurance Company. He was a charter member of the Atlanta Athletic Club and the East Lake Country Club. Sam E. Finley, 70, was a former president of the Community Chest, a trustee of Egleston Hospital, and head of a road construction firm that has done thousands of miles of paving. Cameron Douglas Flanigen, vice-president and board member of the Georgia Power Company and designer and builder of hydroelectric plants, died at 87. George Jefferson Foster, who drove the first electrically powered streetcar in Atlanta and who was a thirty-four-year veteran of the Georgia Power Company, died at 76.

Henry W. Grady, Jr., son of the famous editor and orator and himself active in civic, fraternal, and business organizations, died at 69. He was president of the Southern Engraving Company. Bryan M. Grant, Sr., well-known Atlanta businessman, sports enthusiast, and father of the famous tennis player Bitsy Grant, was a grandson of Col. Lemuel P. Grant, who gave the site of Grant Park to the city. George Harris was a three-term mayor of College Park, Georgia. Louis D. Hicks, well-known Atlanta businessman and president of Ruralist Press, was dead at 67. Judge John D. Humphries, distinguished member of the Georgia Bar and judge of the Superior Court since 1919, died at 69. He was an enthusiastic amateur astronomer.

Mrs. Joel Hurt, wife of the late pioneer Atlanta developer and the former Annie Bright Woodruff, sister of Atlanta philanthropist Ernest Woodruff, died at 87. C. J. Keith, former banker with the old Atlanta National Bank and then tax assessor for the city, died at 86. Walter Wallace Kilpatrick, retired Southern Railway mechanic who invented the device to heat railroad passenger cars, died at 84. Victor Emile Lambert, the oldest florist in Atlanta and son of the first florist in the city, died at 79. Lambert and his father planted the magnolia trees around the lake in Grant Park and the famous Lombardy poplar trees on the street that became Lombardy Way. Macon T. LaHatte, dean of Atlanta printers and at one time mayor pro tem of the city, died at 86. Dr. J. Sprole Lyons was one of the best loved and most highly respected ministers in Atlanta. For many years he was pastor of the First Presbyterian Church, and he was instrumental in bringing the Presbyterian Seminary to Decatur and in obtaining the stained glass windows of his stately church, most of them made by Tiffany. Rev. Benjamin F. McCoy was a Confederate veteran who had carried his troop's flag at the Battle of Kennesaw Mountain. Later a merchant and a Baptist minister, he died at 94.

The Rt. Rev. Henry Judah Mikell, bishop of the Episcopal Diocese of Atlanta and one of the South's outstanding clergymen, was an authority on the history and liturgy of the Episcopal Church. At the time of his death he was chancellor of the University of the South. "Bishop Mikell was genuinely loved and deeply admired by all who knew him," the *Atlanta Constitution* declared. "Famous as a scholar, he was recognized as a preacher of great force and humor." Guido Negri was proprietor of Herren's Restaurant, maître d'hôtel of the Atlanta Biltmore when it opened, and manager of the Piedmont Driving Club. He was talented with more than food, for this son of Italy spoke seven languages and was a creditable musician, composer, and painter. J. B. Paris, 75, was for many years clerk of the old Milton County Superior Court, and after the merger of Milton and Fulton counties, he became a tax assessor. Jacob Wilmore Patterson, who came to Atlanta in 1908 to manage the Miller Union stockyards and who succeeded in making Atlanta the mule capital of the world, died at 78. Dr. Nathaniel Palmer Pratt, founder of N. P. Pratt Laboratory for Analytical and Technical Chemistry and onetime president of Georgia Tech, died at 84. Maj. Trammell Scott, prominent Georgia sportsman, was onetime president of the Southern Baseball Association and a judge of sporting dogs in field trials. Fred Loring Seely, 70, was the founder of the old *Atlanta Georgian*, which he sold to William Randolph Hearst. He then moved to Asheville, N.C., and built the Grove Park Inn.

Mrs. Ophelia Standard, born in Atlanta when the town was called Marthasville and a charter member of St. Paul's Methodist Church, died at 86. Margaret M. Waite was owner of a book and gift shop in the Atlanta Arcade since 1919 and was also active in civic affairs. Stephen West was president of West Lumber Company and chairman of the board of stewards of Glenn Memorial Church. L. P. Whitefield was the Atlanta manager of the Burns Detective Agency and chief investigator for the defense in the Leo Frank Case.

NOTES

1. Henry G. Baker, *Rich's of Atlanta* (Atlanta: School of Business Administration, Atlanta Division, University of Georgia, 1953).

2. Atlanta Chamber of Commerce, "Facts and Figures" (Atlanta, 1942).

3. Georgia Power Company file, Atlanta Historical Society.

4. Atlanta Chamber of Commerce report, Chamber file for 1943, Atlanta Historical Society.

5. *Atlanta Journal-Constitution Magazine,* July 2, 1978.

1943

Walled
WAR or no war, Atlanta's citizens gave the usual New Year's attention to parties and football. Georgia's two big-time football schools had both earned major bowl bids. With Frankie Sinkwich starring, Georgia beat UCLA 9–0 in the Rose Bowl in what the *Constitution* called one of the most exciting games ever played in the big saucer at Pasadena. Held scoreless for three periods, Georgia's vaunted Bulldogs seized two scoring opportunities in the last period and cashed them in for a safety and a touchdown. Atlanta's "home team" came off less well in the Sugar Bowl at New Orleans. There, the Georgia Tech Yellow Jackets went down 14–7, before the massive hardcharging line of the Texas University Longhorns.

While Atlanta warmly welcomed the soldiers, sailors, and airmen from other cities who trained here or came on leave, Atlantans in service abroad were by no means forgotten by the folks at home—notably by Mayor Hartsfield, now back in City Hall in 1943 and determined to stay there. Taking up his old habit of roaming the city by night and taking pictures, he sent copies of these to the more than nine hundred Atlanta city employees who were now in the armed forces, and who kept his incoming mailbox filled with homesick letters. He tried to answer all who wrote, giving them a private report on what he was doing to keep the city functioning smoothly under wartime shortages and restrictions.

The mayor's main interest in this war year, however, was in increasing Atlanta's status as an aviation center. Late in 1943 he wrote Ivor Sikorsky of United Aircraft, telling him that Atlanta was the pioneer city in the development of aviation and that he was determined to keep it ahead of other cities by creating landing areas for Sikorsky's invention, the helicopter, whose marvelous capabilities had been proved by the war. Sikorsky answered Hartsfield's questions about where and how helicopter landing pads could be placed; ever since, the skies over Atlanta and surrounding areas have been the route of the whirlybirds. Nor did he neglect his first love—the airport. He acquired 800 acres of adjacent land so the runways could be extended to handle bombers that might need an alternate airport in bad weather—as on a cloudy day at Marietta. And these runways could handle the bigger aircraft that would come along after the war.

Hartsfield, moving about the country, discovered that Atlanta during the war was accomplishing a great deal in the way of civic improvement that other cities still looked upon as postwar projects. Grady Hospital, for example, set up a clinic for the treatment of syphilis by fever therapy, which it was hoped would rid Atlanta of its unhappy reputation as the venereal disease capital of the universe. He pushed for parks and playground areas for both white and Negro citizens—segregated, of course. He paved fifteen miles of city streets and built a fine new detention hospital at the old City Prison

Farm. Most dramatic of all, perhaps, he had restored the fire-burned and fallen front of the old Municipal Auditorium by the use of Georgia marble, concrete, and fine walnut wood, none of which were on the wartime restricted list.

Atlantans other than Hartsfield were also working hard to keep Atlanta moving forward under wartime conditions. In 1943 the Atlanta Chamber of Commerce polled 3,515 educators, business people, ministers, civic leaders, and professionals, asking them what in their opinion were "Atlanta's greatest needs." A brochure listing their answers was published.

One of the strong suggestions was obviously influenced by the dialogue on race relations going on in this year between southern Negro and white leaders. On race relations the booklet said: "There is a golden opportunity for Atlanta to be a pioneer in developing justice for the Negro and there is a challenge to tackle the matter of race relations with vision and daring."

The other needs had to do with a faster plan for moving traffic through and around town, more parks and playgrounds, adequate school buildings (Boys High and Tech High's portable buildings were derisively referred to as "shacks"), improved health facilities—particularly a hospital where black patients could be treated by black doctors—more low-cost housing, more slum clearance to rid the town of diseased and crime-building slum districts, and the modernization of downtown buildings.

Other needs of the 1940s that were to be met in the ensuing two decades were better schools at all levels with higher pay for teachers and improvement in all transit facilities for crosstown bus lines to an expanded airport. Many urged the merging of Fulton, DeKalb, and Atlanta city governments and the annexation of outlying areas as they were built up. The goal was for neighborhoods to be served by "one health system, one law enforcement system, one water system, one sewer system, one park system, and, if possible, one school system." There were those who wanted the city to lay aside money for postwar expansion, and there was much interest in the conversion and retention of war plants, particularly those in aircraft and allied industries, so that the highly skilled newcomers—and their ample payrolls—would become a permanent part of the Atlanta community.

The poll showed that there was strong opposition to freight rate differentials. Many felt that they should be abolished or Atlanta and the Southeast would find wartime industries "drying up" after the war. Completion of the famed memorial on Stone Mountain was favored. An effective smoke-abatement program was urged, as was a general cleanup of the City of Atlanta, where houses were run down, streets dirty, and vacant lots littered with weeds and junk.

One great need the booklet listed was a "revival of interest in spiritual matters." Others were the expansion of the library, the creation of a symphony orchestra, and a "garden more beautiful than Magnolia Gardens."

Through nearly all of the suggestions ran a common thread—the need for a revival of the "Atlanta Spirit"—with all organizations and classes of Atlantans pulling together on any worthwhile project. Said one in conclusion: "My suggestion is that with the enormous growth of Atlanta, and the necessary increase and multiplication of organizations, we should not lose that old time effective capacity for sinking differences and getting together and pulling together."[1]

Chamber president Carlyle Fraser commented after grave and careful study of the suggestions, "I am sure that these expressions are indicative of the thinking of Atlanta. They are a clear cut mandate to all of those in places of responsibility to translate these expressed needs into definite achievements. The people of Atlanta have made it clear that they expect leadership of the Chamber of Commerce—of those in public office they expect honest, constructive and progressive service to make this the kind of community it should be."

"Atlantans," Fraser continued, "above all want a planned and orderly community—a comprehensive metropolitan place—as against the unplanned and disarranged community in which we now live." Second in their thinking, he added, was a strong demand for simplification of local government. An urgent appeal for improvement in race relations occupied third place.[2]

Lily Pons, the Metropolitan Opera star, arrived in town to give a concert at the Municipal Auditorium, its facade now renovated. Her purpose was to create support for the second war bond drive, and the result was highly satisfactory. Atlanta's goal was $50 million. Total subscription was over $52 million. The state as a whole, in fact, gave exceptionally strong support to the bond drive. W. S. McLarin, Jr., president of the Federal Reserve Bank of Atlanta, said that the quota for the state was nearly $61 million. The total raised was more than $83 million.[3]

In June Madame Chiang Kai-Shek paused briefly in Atlanta to have breakfast with Governor and Mrs. Ellis Arnall. Madame Chiang was en route to Macon to receive an honorary degree from Wesleyan College, which she had attended thirty years earlier.

The vicious murder of a distinguished Atlanta banker left the city shaken. In recent years burglars had preyed on the residences of the well-to-do in the better neighborhoods, but no death had resulted. But this, according to Police Chief Herbert Jenkins, successor to the veteran police chief Marion Hornsby, was the most bizarre murder case he had ever worked. The victim was Henry C. Heinz, vice-president of the C&S Bank, who with his wife Lucy, the only daughter of Asa G. Candler, the founder of the Coca-Cola Company, lived in a beautiful Mediterranean style mansion on Ponce de Leon Avenue in Druid Hills. At 9:50 on the night of September 29, 1943, an intruder shot Heinz to death in the library of his home. And thereafter ensued one of the most incredible gun battles in the history of crime in Atlanta. Upstairs Mrs. Heinz, who was retiring for bed, heard her husband call, telling her that he heard someone in the house and urging her to come quickly and bring his gun. (After being burglarized twice before, Heinz had bought guns and had begun target practice.) As she started down she heard Heinz cry out again, and there were two shots. In the library, she saw her husband struggling with a Negro man. She ran into another room to get the gun and ran back into the library to see Heinz on the sofa, obviously wounded. The intruder had disappeared. She ran to the phone, called Grady Hospital, the police, and her son-in-law, Dr. Bryant K. Vann, who lived on Lullwater Road, just back of the Heinz mansion. Vann, in pants and pajama tops, arrived almost simultaneously with the police, carrying his Army .45. In the darkness and confusion each thought the other was the intruder and opened fire. Neither policeman was hit by Dr. Vann's fire, though one officer was struck by bits of concrete ricocheting from near-misses that struck the stucco wall of the driveway. The other officer broke an ankle when he leaped off the porch trying to get out of the line of fire. Dr. Vann had been less fortunate. A bullet had broken his wrist, but he kept on firing until finally both officers converged upon him, knocked him to the ground, and beat him with their gun butts until they learned to their dismay who he was.

They backed away in stunned amazement, and shortly thereafter Herbert Jenkins arrived. Jenkins, captain in charge of the evening watch at the time and senior police officer on duty, immediately began trying to bring some order out of the tragedy. As he remembers it, "People were rushing to the estate from everywhere. A phalanx of Atlanta police and DeKalb police were on the scene. Neighbors and curiosity seekers attracted by the commotion and the gunfire began to invade the premises. A streetcar had been passing in front of the house when the shots were fired and the motorman stopped the car and began to investigate. All the passengers filed out behind him to see what had happened. Relatives began to come from their own homes in Druid Hills. It would be long after midnight before family and friends, police, and the plain curious departed from the estate. I have never seen anything quite like the confusion at the Heinz home that night." Jenkins saw that Heinz had been shot several times and evidently had died instantly. Dr. Vann, who had put up a terrific fight against a pair of fine policemen, was treated by Grady ambulancemen and was rushed off to the hospital, shot in the chest and right wrist. Mrs. Heinz still seemed hysterical and was sent home with a relative.

During the night, as news of the murder spread, panic gripped the Druid Hills neighborhood. Residents began to flood the Atlanta and DeKalb police stations with calls, reporting prowlers on their property and burglars in the house.

In the library where Heinz's body lay, Jenkins began a search for clues among the disarray of overturned floor lamps and disarranged furniture, evidence that Heinz had put up a terrific struggle. To carry out his search, he had to drive out the press and the host of intruders who were interfering with the work of his men.

There were two significant clues; the inner works of a smashed wristwatch lay on the floor, and Heinz did not wear a wristwatch; and clear fingerprints were lifted from the venetian blind in the library. A year and four months later, these clues led to the arrest and conviction of the Heinz murderer. Police arrested a black man named Horace Blalock for questioning in regard to the burglary of the home of Atlanta attorney Hughes Spalding, and Blalock's fingerprints matched a print lifted from the venetian blind in the Heinz library. A jeweler identified the watch that Blalock was wearing as one that Blalock had brought to him two weeks after the Heinz murder, asking him to replace the inner workings, which he had done.

Faced with this evidence, Blalock confessed and described in terrifying detail his fierce struggle with Heinz. It was, he admitted, the third time he had robbed this house. When asked why a man who had a $200-a-month job with the railroad felt he had to turn to burglary, he explained: He played the "Bug"—gambling about $15 a day—and he nearly always lost. And when he won, he put it all in the numbers the next day—and lost.

Before some thirty witnesses he reenacted his entry to the library, his attack on Heinz, his flight down the path in the rear of the house. He was convicted and sentenced to life imprisonment. On May 18, 1955, having served ten years, he was paroled by the Georgia Pardon and Paroles Board. In 1957 he was working as a painter for an automobile agency in Vidalia, Georgia. And that, said Chief Herbert Jenkins, "was the last we have heard of him."

Though Horace Blalock may be long forgotten, the name and the good deeds of the man he killed are still remembered in Atlanta. Though he was born in New Haven, Connecticut, his father and grandfather had been native Atlantans. As a young man he began his career in banking, with the Central Bank and Trust Company, which had been founded by his future father-in-law, Asa G. Candler. When this bank merged with the Citizens and Southern in 1922, Heinz became a director and vice-president of C&S, the position he held at the time of his death. His civic services were myriad, particularly in the aid he gave to the less fortunate of Atlanta's citizens. He was a founder of the Atlanta Boys' Club and was president of the organization at the time of his death. He was city chairman of the banking division of the third War Loan Drive, and just moments before his death he had heard over the radio that the drive had reached its goal. In fact, it was to hear this report that he had stayed up beyond his usual bedtime.[4]

Another Atlantan, a Druid Hills neighbor of Heinz, made news in a different way in the closing months of 1943. Ernest Woodruff, moving into his eighties and in failing health, on November 20 received the Atlanta Chamber of Commerce Certificate of Distinguished Achievement. The citation declared:

Farsighted, a sound planner, courageous under all circumstances, a quiet worker who did not ask or expect praise. He developed enterprises which brought prosperity to his associates and created continuing benefits for thousands of others. The Foundation established by him and the capital created through his enterprises, now provide support for much of the charitable and educational work of this community. His construction work strengthened the fabric of the city and state.

For this service to his fellow man, a type of service the fundamental importance of which is not often enough recognized, and in special recognition of the fact that he employed his talents and his resources in this community and section, we tender this testimonial of our grateful appreciation. November 29, 1943.[5]

In the closing months of 1943 nearly a score of young Atlanta doctors left for the battlefront.

The School of Medicine furnished an Emory Unit for World War II as it had for World War I (See II,743). The 43rd General Hospital was activated on September 1, 1942, and sent for training to Camp Livingston, Louisiana. The Commanding Officer was Col. LeRoy D. Soper, an army career physician. Colonel Ferguson was chief of surgery and Col. H. Hugh Wood, chief of medicine. The unit was "essentially Emory University Hospital transferred to the field," said Emory historian Dr. Thomas English. The unit served in the European theater from October, 1943, through the end of the war.

For some eighteen months following Pearl Harbor, *Constitution* editor Ralph McGill, restless and fretting, stayed in Atlanta attending sessions of the draft board to which he had been appointed. Finally came the chance to cover the war firsthand that he had been waiting for. In July of 1943, he flew secretly to London. From there his column to the *Constitution* described that dark, hungry, battered city. The days of the great blitz, the dreadful nights when the German bombers came and went away almost unchallenged were over. Now American and British were flying by night against the Reich, "and the great gray elephants of the barrage balloons, whose mahouts were all women," were defending London. The people who touched him most deeply were the bomber crews, the young Americans taking their flying fortresses across the Channel, defying the German fighters and braving an incredible eruption of anti-aircraft fire. To Americans at home, the war was still far away, even though their sons were fighting around the world. But McGill's columns in the *Constitution* brought it to their breakfast tables and made them hear it, see it, smell it, feel it, as the English had endured it for four long years.[6]

In the closing months of 1943 Atlanta paid tribute to a longtime teacher and said good-bye to one distinguished educator. In November, Ira Jarrell was elected superintendent of Atlanta schools to fill the unexpired term of Dr. Willis A. Sutton, and in December Dr. Thornwell Jacobs, founder of Oglethorpe University, resigned as president and was replaced by Dr. Philip Weltner.

While the war brought many new businesses and thousands of individuals to Atlanta, two agencies that had served the city well over a period of years were closed down because their services were no longer needed. On April 30, 1943, the WPA (Work Projects Administration) closed down its office after eight years in which it spent $179,085,920 on the state for labor and materials to be used on public improvement projects. Now, WPA labor and materials were both needed in defense work. In the eight years Fulton and DeKalb counties had received a total of $134,357,419 for use on the metropolitan sewer system, and the City of Atlanta auditorium had been remodeled at a cost of $3,193,218. Peak of WPA employment was in 1938, when 44,214 persons were on its payrolls in Georgia.

At the year's end another agency that had served the city well closed its doors. The National Youth Administration was abolished by Congress in June. The organization in its eight years in Georgia had spent $16 million training thousands of young men and women for useful work, and it had had a distinguished leadership throughout its function here. Raymond Paty, the first director, had moved on to become president of the University of Alabama.

The closing of the local offices of these two bastions of the New Deal symbolized that World War II had indeed brought an end to the Great Depression. But as 1944 approached, Atlantans knew that the end of the war was not close at hand. Indeed, over nineteen months of war remained.

OBITUARIES

Milton Ailes, onetime newspaperman working in southern cities for the Associated Press and then public relations director for the Georgia Power Company, died at 65. Edwin L. Anderson, president of the Anlo Coal Company, had been a member of the American Rifle Team in the Stockholm Olympics. Judge Marcus W. Beck, 81, was an accomplished linguist, scholar of the law, and presiding justice of the Georgia Supreme Court. Ernest Garfield Beaudry, founder and owner of the motor company that bears his name and employee of Ford Motor Company since 1915, died at 61. Russell L. Beutell, 52, widely known Atlanta architect, was fatally burned at his summer home at Helen, Georgia. Charles Birchy, an organizer and vice-president of Atlanta Terra Cotta Company, died at 71. He was noted for his architectural sculpture, which included the ornamental work in the Erlanger Theatre, The Temple, the First Christian Church, and Glenn Memorial Chapel. James G. Brandon, manager of the Piedmont Hotel, died at 67.

Mrs. C. E. Brantley, member of the pioneer DeKalb Kelly family, was an organizer and director of the first PTA in the Panthersville District, where she lived. Corrie Hoyt Brown, daughter of George M. Brown, former president of Georgia Savings Bank, was the granddaughter of Joseph E. Brown, Georgia's wartime governor. J. T. Brown, pioneer Atlanta contractor and builder of many fine residences and business structures including the Georgia Power Company's steamheating plant on Butler Street, died at 92. Dr. Charles Edward Buchanan, a graduate of Atlanta Dental College, was a prominent musician who had played the violin in Victor Herbert's Pittsburgh Symphony Orchestra. Under Buchanan's direction the Yaarab Temple Shrine Band came to be known as "the million-dollar band." Hugh H. Caldwell, one of the South's foremost educators and for more than twenty years registrar and secretary at Georgia Tech, died at 63. Patrick Calhoun, grandson of John C. Calhoun and principal in the last duel fought on Georgia soil, died at 87.

Mrs. Moses G. Campbell, the former Maude Smith and widow of a prominent Atlanta physician, had participated in religious, social, and civic affairs for more than fifty years. Mrs. John H. Candler, the former Elizabeth Brandon, was an active member of St. Luke's Episcopal Church and the Junior League. Mrs. Warren A. Candler, widow of Bishop Candler, onetime president of Emory College at Oxford, died at 83. Born Antoinette Curtright in LaGrange, she was a graduate of the LaGrange Female College. She was long interested and instrumental in the organization of old Wesley Hospital, now Emory. Jason Cannon, a retired conductor for the Southern Railway's Crescent and a fifty-year Mason, died at 84. Dr. W. Harvey Clarke, for fifty years a missionary to Japan from the First Baptist Church, was a son of a Baptist missionary to Africa. Dr. Charles D. Daniel, 61, was southeastern manager of D. C. Heath & Company, publishers; he had been a professor of English at several southern colleges.

Archibald H. Davis, retired attorney and accomplished organist and composer, died at 80. He was one of the earliest members of the Piedmont Driving Club. Mrs. Mamie L. Davis, head of the Primary School at Washington Seminary for many years, died at 78. William Cox Dickey, son of James L. Dickey, president of Dickey-Mangham Insurance Company, died at 47. He had served in the Ambulance Corps in France in World War I. Edward Emmett Dougherty, widely known southern architect who specialized in church buildings and designed the Druid Hills Baptist Church, died at 67. Edward James Duncan, native of London who served with the British army in India and Egypt and followed the profession of tailoring in this city, died at 78. Mrs. Willis M. Everett, the former Mary Catherine Gillette, was a well-known church and civic leader for over sixty years. Willis M. Everett, attorney and chairman of the executive committee of home missions of the Presbyterian Church, died at 80, two months following his wife's death. Lucy Farr, a seamstress employed by Rich's and Grady Hospital who had witnessed the burning of Atlanta, died at 88. Mrs. Robert L. Foreman, eldest daughter of Evan P. Howell, first editor of the *Atlanta Constitution*, and widow of the general agent for Mutual Benefit Life Insurance Company, died at 72. Her life was a long career of public service.

Dr. John Shaw Foster was a professor emeritus of homiletics and practical theology at Columbia Theological Seminary in Decatur. Hugh N. Fuller was professor of sociology and director of research in social science at Emory University. George K. Hanjaras, Greek-born restaurant operator who worked untiringly to send relief to Greece during Nazi occupation, died at 48. George Washington Jenkins, Sr., was a member of the first graduating class of Georgia Tech and was a retired grocer. James M. Johnson, Confederate veteran who participated in the Battle of Atlanta, died at 96. Alfred W. Jones, artist in stained glass and authority on religious symbols who designed the windows of Westminster Presbyterian Church and Gammon Theological Seminary, died at 75. James Kempton, who published the *Fulton County Daily Reporter*, died at 78.

Sam Greenberg, pioneer Atlanta funeral director and an organizer of the Kiwanis Club, died at 66. William W. Griffin, 85, was a pioneer Atlanta builder and head of Griffin Construction Company, one of the oldest construction firms in the state, whose buildings included the Cathedral of Christ the King, The Temple, Ten Pryor Street Building, and the Atlanta Coca-Cola Bottling Company. Maj. Robert J. Guinn was an agent for New England Mutual Life Insurance Company and at one time was superintendent of Fulton County schools. Sigmund Guthman, pioneer printer and founder of the Atlanta Envelope Company who was highly regarded for his charitable character, died at 71. Mrs. Joseph R. Lamar, the former Clarinda Pendleton and widow of the Supreme Court Justice, for many years was national president of the Society of Colonial Dames. Edward Spaulding Lewis was a well-known architectural engineer and a member of Morgan, Dillon and Lewis. He had also been associated with H. J. Carr, Contractors, builders of the Terminal and Brookwood stations. George Lindner, German-born concert violinist, composer, and teacher, died at 65. His activities had included directing the Atlanta Conservatory of Music and conducting the Atlanta Philharmonic Orchestra.

Dr. L. B. Longino, former superintendent of the state hospital for the insane, died at 64. Homer and Lewis Logue, 70-year old twins, inseparable in life and death, died within twenty-four hours of each other on May 1. They had been employed by the Atlanta Milling Company since 1898. A high point in their life was their participation in the parade connected with the premiere of *Gone with the Wind*. Arthur Lucas, national figure in the motion picture business and theater owner and operator, died at 65. Mrs. George McAliley, 70, the former Ida Howell and daughter of Evan P. Howell, was the widow of one of the South's outstanding pediatricians. Active in the affairs of Peachtree Christian Church, the Red Cross Service Group, and the Planters' Garden Club, she also participated in many charitable endeavors. Henry Y. McCord, religious and civic leader and founder of McCord-Stewart Company, wholesale grocers, died at 89. He was an active sportsman and the last surviving charter member of the Homosassa Fishing Club. As a Methodist layman he was particularly interested in the development of Emory University.

Joseph Alexander McCord, retired capitalist and former chairman of the Mortgage Guarantee Company of America, was an organizer of St. Mark's Methodist Church. He died at 86. Mrs. V. A. S. Moore, who received her early education at the West End Academy and Shorter College, died at 70.

Historian of her UDC chapter and regent of the DAR chapter, she was an accomplished genealogist. Dr. Eglan Thomas Morgan, the first dentist in Atlanta to use gas for dental surgery, died at 82. Ernest Neal, Georgia's second poet laureate, died at 83. Henry Alexander Newman, prominent Atlanta attorney and a member of the Nine O'Clocks and the Piedmont Driving Club, died at 55. James Robert Holliday was former secretary to Henry Grady and national advertising manager of the *Constitution*. Linton C. Hopkins, practicing attorney in the city for forty years who started practice with his father, Judge John Hopkins, died at 71. An organizer of the Sheltering Arms Nursery, he was also president of Family Welfare and chairman of the Atlanta Library's board. Sarah Huff, 86, one of the city's oldest residents and long an authority on the history of Atlanta, died in the house on Huff Road, where she had been born. She was witness to skirmishes in the Battle of Atlanta and wrote prolifically about the city's history.

Maude Andrews Ohl, widow of J. K. Ohl and society editor of the *Constitution* for many years, died at 80. William Thomas Perkerson, vice-president and trust officer of the First National Bank, died at 68. His grandfather was the first sheriff of Fulton County. Mrs. Harry G. Poole, the former Jimmie Stewart and widow of one of the city's best-known funeral directors, died at 62. She was a life member of the Atlanta Woman's Club. O. R. Randall, president of NuGrape Manufacturing Company and considered one of America's foremost authorities on the soft drink business, was 68. Otto Schwab, one of the founders and chairman of the board of Southern Bed Spring Company, was 87. Simon S. Selig, who established the Selig Company and served as president of the National Sanitary Supply Association, died at 64. Mrs. Alma A. Shaw, secretary for quarter century to the Secretary of State and an authority on land grant records, died at 68. L. P. Skeen, Atlanta attorney and member of the Georgia Public Service Commission, died at 77. Dr. Simon H. Smith, graduate of the old Atlanta Medical College and president of the Atlanta Association of Jewish Doctors and Dentists, died at 42. Alonzo C. Sowell, 71, was deputy marshal for forty-two years and onetime sheriff of Henry County. Justice Alexander W. Stephens was associate judge of the Georgia Court of Appeals and a grand-nephew of Alexander H. Stephens. George W. Stevens, court reporter for the Supreme Court, died at 82. L. L. Stevens, who operated the First National Bank Barbershop for forty-five years, died at 63. T. O. Sturdivant, retired Atlanta police chief and for many years an ace detective, died at 63.

Rev. Charlie D. Tillman, 82, widely known Georgia Methodist evangelist and songwriter, was the author of over one hundred hymns, including the famous "Life's Railroad to Heaven." Dr. Theodore Toepel, well-known physician and advocate of physical education, died at 73. For many years he donated his time to Atlanta city schools, teaching physical education until the course was adopted into the schools' curriculum. E. Walter Tripp, onetime deputy collector of revenue and secretary to Gov. Hoke Smith, died at 69.

Dailey Homer Vandergriff, general chairman of the DeKalb County ration boards and owner of the DeKalb Laundry, died at 51.

Lt. Col. William Slaton Waldo, prominent insurance man in business with his father, A. L. Waldo, died on duty in Latin America at 40. Lt. Col. Lamar (Pie) Weaver, widely known as a fine basketball player, served in World War I, and continued his career in the army until his death. Capt. Jere Wells, Jr., son of Fulton County school superintendent, was killed in a plane crash. Sara Willcoxon was for many years a teacher in Fulton County schools including Garden Hills and R. L. Hope. Mrs. R. Wayne Wilson, for sixty-five years a strong influence on musical circles in Atlanta and a respected voice and piano teacher, died at 89. Mrs. Courtland Winn, widow of Atlanta's mayor in 1911–1912, died at 80. Walter Gilbert Withers, president of Withers Foundry and son of Julia Carlisle, first child born in Atlanta, died at 76. H. B. Young, Seaboard Railway employee for forty years and chairman of the Seaboard Chapter of the Brotherhood of Locomotive Engineers, died at 66. Charles Zattau, long prominent in civic and business affairs, was formerly the president of Foote and Davies.

NOTES

1. Atlanta Chamber of Commerce, "The Greatest Needs of Atlanta and Georgia, A Summary of Opinion" (Atlanta, 1943).

2. Ibid.

3. Ibid.

4. Herbert Jenkins, "My Most Bizarre Murder Case," *Atlanta Journal-Constitution Magazine*, Aug. 22, 1971.

5. Atlanta Chamber of Commerce Annual Report, 1944.

6. Harold H. Martin, *Ralph McGill, Reporter* (Boston: Little, Brown, 1973).

WHILE Atlanta's sons in early 1944 were giving their blood in battle in the Pacific and in Europe, Atlantans at home were establishing here one of the biggest and most efficient blood donor services in the country. For her work in organizing and directing this center which was awarded the Army and Navy E for its performance, Mrs. Francis Abreu was named the city's principal Woman of the Year as well as being named Woman of the Year in the War Effort. A native of Atlanta, Abreu was by profession an interior decorator.

Mayor Hartsfield, as in years gone by, found occasion to point with pride to the management of the city's finances. There was more than $1 million in the city surplus fund, he told City Council in his annual message on January 4, and he urged the council to support a government that would conserve and increase this surplus so that it could be used for postwar development.

Hartsfield's report on the city's financial condition was supported in some detail by the little booklet, "Facts and Figures about Atlanta," issued annually by the Chamber of Commerce's Industrial Bureau. Here Atlanta was listed as having the lowest bonded debt, at $8,294,000, of any of the ten leading cities of the Southeast. (New Orleans was highest at over $66 million and neighboring Birmingham had a debt of over $20 million.) Atlanta's bank resources as 1944 began also led the South at $721,143,637, with Houston next at $680,277,000. Bank clearings in Atlanta were also strong at $6,560,573,000, with Dallas trailing at $5,377,914,845.

The city had spent $12,157,367.99 in general disbursements in 1943—with the bulk of it, $4,331,063 going to the schools, $1,880,534.46 to Public Safety (police, etc.), $1,084,586.54 to hospitals, and $1,116,363 to serve the public debt. In one area the figures in Atlanta, as in every other city, were dropping because of wartime restrictions. Building permits in 1940 had been $14,558,861, highest since the great upsurge of 1928, when the figures stood at $27,580,541. By 1943 they had fallen to $1,827,219, but permits picked up strongly in 1944 to a total of $3,958,296.[1]

For sports lovers in Atlanta 1944 began most auspiciously indeed. In the Sugar Bowl at New Orleans, Georgia Tech beat Tulsa 20–18 when a dazzling performance by Eddie Prokop, Tech halfback, proved too much for the Oklahomans.

Atlanta lovers of America's Sweetheart got their own kind of thrill when Mary Pickford came into town on January 9 to support a fund drive of the National Foundation for Infantile Paralysis. She spoke to an audience viewing the Russian Ballet at the City Auditorium, and visited the Scottish Rite Hospital. "I am thrilled to be even a small part of such a great movement," she told reporter Jane Malone before moving on to Warm Springs.

The new cruiser *Atlanta* was set to go into service on February 6, with

Margaret Mitchell doing the honors again. On February 3 Ralph McGill announced that a Liberty Ship would be named for the late Clark Howell, Sr., editor of the *Atlanta Constitution*, who had died in 1936. McGill observed that those who knew "Papa" Howell knew how fitting it was that a Liberty Ship, constructed in a Georgia shipyard, should be named for him.

Matters of local politics and forms of local government were much in the minds of Atlantans in this year of 1944. *Constitution* political reporter Herman Hancock reported that First Ward Councilman James E. Jackson, Jr., was urging the creation of a joint city and Fulton County committee of representative citizens to study a plan for the consolidation of the governments and to create the "City and County of Atlanta, Georgia." Hancock indicated that there was much agitation for the merger of specific government functions, which of course, as the years passed, did take place by the process of annexation favored by Mayor Hartsfield.

Several Atlantans, distinguished in their service to the city over a period of many years, chose to retire in 1944. Among them was John A. Boykin, solicitor general of the Atlanta Judicial Circuit for more than a quarter-century and one of the best known prosecuting officers in the South. He announced in February that he would retire at the end of the year and indicated that he would support his assistant, E. E. (Shorty) Andrews, as his successor.

At Georgia Tech, Dr. M. L. Brittain resigned early in the year. He had served as Tech's president for twenty-two years and was named President Emeritus by the University System Board. Col. Blake R. Van Leer was named to succeed him, to take over on July 1. Under Van Leer's administration three new dormitories, eight apartment houses, and a new west stand at Grant Field were built.

Dr. James Edgar Paullin, Atlanta physician and past president of the American Medical Association, was named to receive the Chamber of Commerce Certificate of Distinguished Achievement on November 21 at an awards ceremony that Rear Adm. Ross T. McIntyre, President Roosevelt's personal physician, would attend.

On November 15 Atlantans were reminded that the city had suffered directly from war itself in the past. Gen. William T. Sherman's forces had burned the city, leaving a smoking ruin as they headed toward the sea. Said reporter Sterling Slappey in the *Constitution*: "Eighty years ago today this city felt the shock of war as severely as any other city in all history has felt it."

The recurring feud between advocates of slum clearance and Atlanta realtors flared up again in the fall of 1944. The Atlanta Real Estate Board filed a report with City Council urging that the council and housing authority study the problems relating to housing and enact new ordinances to correct them. The building code, the realtors said, should be amended so that more open area between dwelling units would be required than was then permitted by the City Planning Commission. This, it concluded, would eliminate the congestion that contributed to slum conditions. The most striking part of the report was the contention by the realtors that public housing was not being used to house the poverty-stricken. Instead, they claimed, employees of the federal government, the city, and of leading business firms, some of whom were in managers' positions, were living in the public housing units.

Federal prisoners who early in the war had earned high praise for their extra labors in support of the war effort and the Red Cross drive for funds, which had brought them praise and a personal visit from Margaret Mitchell, now showed another side of their nature as 1944 moved toward its close. Late in the evening of December 4, twenty-five of them took over an area of the prison's segregation unit and seized four guards as hostages. Their complaint was that they were being quartered with Nazi spies and saboteurs who had been arrested in the Atlanta area.

Three days later, on December 7, they asked that Morgan Blake of the *Atlanta Journal* be permitted to come to the prison to act as an arbitrator for them. Blake, famed as a sports writer, was also a Sunday school teacher at the Baptist Tabernacle. A deeply religious man, he often visited the prison on welfare missions. Blake met with the prisoners, and for forty-five minutes he pleaded with them to free the hostages. They promised they would—if he would write the story of their grievances. But this conference came too late. At 2:00 P.M. on December 7, the three-day siege was over. Attorney General Francis Biddle ordered that the prisoners be seized and placed in solitary confinement, and this was done.

Three months later, on March 4, 1945, Atlanta's Federal Prison inmates were back in the news again, not in revolt but as volunteers in a medical experiment designed to find a cure for malaria. Along with the prisoners in state prisons at Joliet, Illinois, and the New Jersey Reformatory at Rockaway, they submitted to experiments by the Division of Medical Science of the National Research Council, which was testing over 800 new drugs. For this, the prisoners received no reward.

In 1944 Atlantans were not only getting reports from such local correspondents as Ralph McGill and Wright Bryan, they were hearing from their own sons and daughters, working or fighting around the world. An article by Eileen Hall, for example, reported on four Atlanta girls working out of Edmonton, Alberta, as civilian employees of the Army's Northwest Service Command, which was building the Alaska Highway.[2] Carl Newton, a former *Journal* sports staff member, wrote of his adventures as the ball-turret gunner of a B-17, dropping its bombs in fifty-two missions over Germany. A Seabee, T. R. Walker, serving with the Marines in the Pacific, sent to his wife Nell in College Park a fantastic collection of souvenirs. One was a Japanese sniper's bullet from Guam, a carved mahogany letter-opener from Bougainville, coins from New Zealand, Japanese money, bookends and ashtrays made of artillery shell casings, and a sleeping mat from Samoa.[3]

A shortage of domestic help, due to the departure of cooks and maids and yardmen, had its effect on Atlanta housewives, making it necessary for them to take over some of the labors that were performed by their pioneer grand-mothers. In an amusing article in the Sunday paper, Mrs. Toulman Hurt wrote of her experiences in cleaning, cooking, and doing other housekeeping chores at her home on North Rock Springs Road, N.E. "The pampered dar-ling," she said, "has gone forever, and women can no longer be called the weaker sex. Anybody who is trying to run a house in these hectic days de-serves a medal. . . . [But] now I have a feeling of independence. It's nice to know that you can take care of your family all by yourself, and that you are so desperately needed."[4]

Robert Whitaker, superintendent of Emory University Hospital, wanted 1944 to be a banner year for the continuing effort to make Atlanta one of the outstanding medical centers of the country. Already, he noted, its reputation in the Southeast brought more than 10,000 people a year to seek treatment in Atlanta hospitals, but there was still much that needed doing. According to Dean R. H. Oppenheimer of Emory University School of Medicine, money for budget and equipment could be fairly easily obtained from friends of Emory in Atlanta. "First, though," said Dr. Oppenheimer, "we would get something else much more important—confidence. When the people of the Southeast learn that Atlanta medics can be relied on to give them whatever service may be needed, as effectively and as cheaply as anywhere else in the country, we shall not be able to build hospitals fast enough." To bring about this public awareness of Atlanta's special place in the medical world, said Dr. Oppenheimer, "we must bring more medical students into our educational and service projects. But in order to attract such men to our schools and hospitals, we must show them that the schools and standards of Atlanta medi-cine are so high that they will add to their prestige by associating themselves with the work here."[5]

Since September, 1944, Emory had enhanced its status as a dental teaching center when the old Atlanta Southern Dental College became the Emory University School of Dentistry, though it continued to occupy its premises at Forrest Avenue and Courtland Street. In the same year the Emory University Hospital School of Nursing was elevated to college rating. Since 1941 and as late as 1943, Emory had turned back a determined effort by Oglethorpe University's newly organized and nonaccredited medical school to join with Emory in the operation of Grady Hospital. Emory considered Grady too small to accommodate two medical schools.[6]

Georgia Tech had already gained some national renown as a place where high-quality service, not in medical but in technical fields, could be obtained. It was chosen by the navy as a part of its V-12 program. Under this program, enlisted veterans who had proven their capacity for leadership under the stress of battle by remaining cool, alert, and functional were pulled out of the ranks and sent to college, there to meet the educational requirements of naval officers.

One group of specialists remembered long after the war was the Atlanta

Promenaders, a dance group who gave exhibitions at USO centers, schools, and church recreation halls. Led by Fred Collette, they dressed in costumes of many colors and danced the romping dances of many lands—including the polka, the schottische, and the Swedish mambo, taught them by a Norwegian native. When the group danced the traditional square dances of the Georgia hills to such music as "Turkey in the Straw," Atlantans of all ages often joined in happily.

One of the most important events of 1944, other than the city's contributions to the war effort, came when the City Council commissioned H. W. Lochner Company of Chicago to make a study in detail of "all phases of the city traffic patterns, and to make a detailed report based on this study which would recommend a major street layout to be built after the war was over, which would take care of Atlanta's traffic needs far into the future." Thus there came into being the pattern known as the Lochner Plan, accepted in 1946. The plan called for an interstate highway system that would begin in Atlanta as the central city, and that would provide direct links to Birmingham, Montgomery, Macon, Chattanooga, and Spartanburg, with an additional route to Augusta. Under this plan two traffic lanes would run in each direction, divided by a broad center mall, and with a space on either side for an additional lane to be built in the future, if needed. "Downtown connectors" would tie the main routes together outside the business district. This plan, it was estimated, would cost $48 million.

Intown street improvements would call for the widening of certain streets and the creation of a smoothly flowing artery system by the elimination of jogs and the separation of grades. Other Lochner recommendations would eliminate cars parked on the curbs in the central business districts and the construction of a modern bus terminal in the heart of the business district, plus the construction of a major Union passenger station. Thus the traffic patterns of future generations of Atlantans would begin to take shape in the late 1940s.

In the war the most significant event of 1944, of course, was the Normandy invasion, and an Atlantan was one of the first civilians to see and tell about part of the invasion. Wright Bryan, managing editor of the *Atlanta Journal,* in a feat of journalistic enterprise that brought him national fame, sent back to station WSB and the world the first eyewitness broadcast of the landing of U.S. troops in France on June 6, 1944. His opening words: "In the first hour of D-day, the first spearhead of Allied Forces for the liberation of Europe landed by parachute in Northern France." Bryan retained a tape of that historic broadcast, which he modestly claims came about purely as a piece of luck. While the other correspondents jockeyed for a place with the invasion forces landing from the sea, Bryan decided to go over with the paratroopers, the first wave of invasion forces. It was a gamble, for he was not going to jump, and he was not sure he could see from the air what was going on below. He was in the air over the coast of Normandy for only eleven minutes of a moonlit night, but that was long enough for him to see and understand the magnitude of what was happening.

While the other correspondents were still filing canned releases from the high command, Bryan remembered, he was back in London handing the text of his report, line by line, to a government censor. And by 3:00 A.M. Atlanta time, Bryan was on the air across the nation.

"The Battle of Europe has begun," he wrote, "and our nation has delivered the first foot soldiers to this scene of action."

He went on to witness the capture of Paris, and then this fighting reporter was captured by the Germans and held prisoner for ten months in German-occupied Poland. Released by advancing Soviet troops, he was returned to the U.S. Army's First General Hospital near Paris, where in longhand he wrote to the *Journal* about his experiences as a prisoner-of-war. While in Paris, he was looked after by Atlanta friends. Maj. Charles Reiser of the hospital staff and Col. (later Brig. Gen.) William Plummer, commander of nearby Orly Airport, brought him newspapers and visitors. Among them was Senator Walter George. In May, shortly after V-E Day, Bryan left the hospital and returned to Atlanta. On November 20, 1947, General Eisenhower pinned on Wright Bryan's lapel the Medal of Freedom.

Wright Bryan ended 1944 in the confines of a German prison camp not knowing what would happen to him, but Atlantans at home ended the year and started 1945 confident that victory was near.

OBITUARIES

Dr. Hulett H. Askew was the team physician for the Georgia Tech football squad and was a Fellow of the American College of Physicians. Mrs. Harry M. Atkinson, widow of the chairman of the board of Georgia Power Company, was the daughter of one of Atlanta's premier boosters in the nineteenth century, Richard Peters. Edward Austin was a retired employee of Southern Bell and had been secretary of the Capital City Club for thirty years. Luke Lee Brown, a longtime resident of Atlanta and a thirty-year veteran engineer with the N.C.&St.L. Railway, died in a train crash. Lt. Col. B. M. Bailey, Jr., a graduate of West Point, died in action in France. He was a son-in-law of Mr. and Mrs. Cason Callaway. Wiley Ballard, owner of Phenix Supply Company and W. P. Ballard Company, was a longtime member of Rotary and the Piedmont Driving Club. Dr. Stephen T. Barnett was an active physician and civic leader in Atlanta for fifty-three years. Dan Bridges was alderman for the First Ward and was active in state politics.

Patrick Henry Calhoun, 93, was clerk of the Fulton County ordinary's office for fifty-three years and the son of Atlanta's mayor during the Civil War. Dr. Edward Randolph Carter, who died at 86, was the son of slaves. Encouraged by Henry Grady to get an education, he successfully pastored

Friendship Baptist Church for sixty-two years and was a founder of the Baptist World Alliance in 1905. Lt. Col. Robert S. Clinkscales, sometime pilot for General Douglas MacArthur, was killed in action. Dr. Harvey W. Cox, chancellor of Emory University, served as president of that school for twenty-two years. Coming to Emory in 1920 when it was just being established in Atlanta, he increased the school's physical size and academic standing; it was accepted into the Association of American Universities during his administration. Milton Dargan, 82, was nationally known and respected in the insurance field and was a founder of All Saints Episcopal Church. He was the oldest living past president of the Piedmont Driving Club. W. E. Dendy, Sr., had been an educator and school superintendent in Atlanta and DeKalb County. Pittman Wesley Derrick, who served on the staff of the Georgia Court of Appeals for thirty-eight years, died at 73.

Dr. William S. Elkin died at 86. He was principally responsible for the Atlanta Medical College becoming the Medical Department of Emory University. Lt. Col. George F. Eubanks, a proctologist, died while on duty in England. Joseph Flipper, who was born in Atlanta in 1859, had been a bishop of the African Methodist Episcopal Church for thirty-six years. Mrs. Frank Foster, the former Julia Toombs Rankin, was head of the Atlanta Public Library until 1911, when she married and moved to England. She was a daughter of the founder of Lamar-Rankin Company. Clint W. Hager was U.S. attorney for the Northern District of Georgia. Dr. Michael Hoke was the first surgeon of Warm Springs Foundation and founder of the Scottish Rite Hospital for Crippled Children. He was an eminent physician in the field of orthopedic surgery.

Vincent John Hurley had been organist at Sacred Heart Church since 1906. Edgar H. Johnson, 71, was dean emeritus of the School of Business Administration at Emory University. Dr. Daniel Noble Johnson, son of pioneer Atlantans Daniel and Elizabeth Chandler Johnson, was born in Johnson Estates in 1851 and attended Georgia Eclectic Medical College in 1881. He was a founding member of Rock Spring Presbyterian Church, where he was a deacon seventy-two years. James B. Jones, well-known north Georgia jurist and chief attorney for the state income tax department, died at 80. J. P. Kennedy, the physician who founded the Atlanta Health Department and oldest member of the Fulton County Medical Society, died at 80. Forrest E. Kibler, former member of Atlanta city council, died at 74. W. F. McLendon, electrical contractor and founder of the Dixie Electric Company, died at 61. Six of his ten children were serving in the armed forces. Mrs. James B. McNelley was supervisor of music at Druid Hills School and daughter of the poet-laureate of Georgia. The former Emily Melton, she was a graduate of Wesleyan College and Peabody Conservatory. Dr. Wightman F. Melton, 77, poet-laureate, teacher, author, poet, and veteran head of the English Department at Emory University, died two days after his daughter. Royall Miller, a retired physician and surgeon and honor graduate at the University of Georgia Medical College in 1880 where he received his M.D. degree at 19, died at 84.

Eugene Muse Mitchell, 78, outstanding authority on Atlanta's history, distinguished legal counsel, and father of Stephens Mitchell and Margaret Mitchell Marsh, died at St. Joseph's Hospital June 17. "Great was his contribution to the progress and culture of the city. He served during his long and illustrious career as president of the Atlanta Bar Association, the Atlanta Historical Society, the Young Men's Library Association, and the City Board of Education. It may well be as an historian that he will be best remembered in the years to come. For his was a consuming interest in the history of Atlanta and Georgia and he has left not a few authentic treatises on the past life of this section which will be of great and increasing value to historians in the future," said the *Atlanta Constitution*.

Sam Moscow had been district manager of Columbia Pictures since 1931. He was active with the Variety Club and died at 59. Charles Naegele, a portrait painter of national renown whose works hang in the National Gallery, died at 86. Howard W. Pitts, one of the city's best known barbers, died at 87. A pioneer Atlanta citizen, he was born in slavery. For more than fifty years he was employed by Herndon's and was known to hundreds of Atlanta gentlemen as "Major." George Pratt, retired chemical engineer and son of Nathaniel P. Pratt, noted chemist who had charge of the gunpowder plant at Augusta during the Civil War, died at 74. William Brown Reeves, retired cotton dealer and onetime manager of the New York Coca-Cola Bottling Company, died at 67.

Capt. Lawrence Wood Robert was one of Georgia's pioneer railway engineers and builders. His first job was with the Georgia-Pacific Railway, now the Southern Railway, between Atlanta and Birmingham. He built many of the railroads that played a large part in the economic progress of Georgia and her cities. In 1918 he came out of retirement at the request of his son, "Chip" Robert, to become secretary of Robert and Company, Inc., Architects and Engineers. He saw it grow to one of the largest firms of its kind in America. Frank Elgin Shumate, retired vice-president in charge of legal matters at the Georgia Power Company, died at his home at Sea Island. He was 71. Burton Smith, a practicing attorney for thirty-four years and brother of Hoke Smith, died in Washington at 80.

Harris McCall Stanley, also known as Hal M. Stanley, was long the State Commissioner of Labor and Secretary of the Georgia Press Association, died at 77. Dr. C. R. Stauffer, for nearly twenty years pastor of the First Christian Church of Atlanta, died at 62. Dr. Paul Stegall, 69, was professor of anatomy at the Dental College of Emory University (formerly, the Atlanta Southern Dental College). Mrs. Thomas D. Stewart died at the home of her daughter, Mrs. Ewing Dean. The widow of a Georgia state senator, financier, and partner in the McCord-Stewart Company, she was 88. Dr. W. F. Shallenberger, one of the best-known abdominal surgeons in the South, died at 63. Julian Thomas, prominent attorney and a member of Spratlin, Harrington and Thomas, died at 57. Mrs. Sara Torbert was a former teacher and for twenty years a prominent Atlanta lawyer. Mrs. C. D. Tuller, Sr., was the former Mamie Metcalf and widow of the president of the Exposition Cotton Mills. William Van Houten was known as "Uncle Billy" to thousands of Georgia Tech students. Foreman of the Tech foundry since 1898, he was the oldest faculty member at Georgia Tech. Mrs. W. R. B. Whittier, the former Miriam Fletcher, was the widow of the man who brought Whittier Mills to Georgia. She was 75.

The Reverend Theodore S. Wills, rector of All Saints Episcopal Church, died at 58. Hugh M. Willet, general agent for the Penn Mutual Life Insurance Company, died at the home of his son, Lawrence Willet. Willet was very active in civic affairs, being the first president of the Atlanta Community Fund. He was a lifetime deacon at Second Ponce de Leon Baptist Church. J. B. Withers was the son of Julia Carlisle Withers, the first white child born in Atlanta. He was a lifelong employee of his father's company, Withers Foundry and Machine Works.

Ernest Woodruff, industrialist and philanthropist, died at 81. The *Atlanta Constitution* said, "Ernest Woodruff came to Atlanta as a young man. He devoted the rest of his long and active life to promoting the city's progress and growth. It would be well-nigh impossible to trace the many industrial developments in which his creative genius found expression. Atlanta's street railway system, the Trust Company of Georgia, the Atlantic Ice & Coal Company, the Continental Gin Company, and the Atlantic Steel Company are but a few thriving monuments to his foresight and ability. And it was, of course, under his capable direction that Coca-Cola has become well known 'round the world. . . . [Woodruff] took a deep and abiding interest in educational and cultural matters. And he leaves, in passing, the Emily and Ernest Woodruff Foundation, dedicated to the educational, medical and religious development of the South. The Foundation, set up in 1938 and augmented several times since, now becomes the largest such philanthropic undertaking in the South."

NOTES

1. Atlanta Chamber of Commerce, "Facts and Figures About Atlanta" (Atlanta, 1944, 1945).

2. Eileen Hall, *Atlanta Journal Magazine*, Oct. 27, 1944.

3. Carl Newton, "A Seabee Reports," in ibid., Sept. 17, 1946.

4. Mrs. Toulman Hurt, "The Southern Lady Disappears," in ibid., Sept. 8, 1944.

5. Robert Whitaker, "Atlanta Medical Center," in ibid., Oct. 22, 1944.

6. Dr. Thomas H. English, *Emory University, 1915–1965: A Semicentennial History* (Atlanta: Emory University, 1966).

1945

IN ATLANTA, in the nation, and around the world 1945 was a memorable year. On April 12 Franklin Roosevelt died at the Little White House at Warm Springs. At the very moment when Madame Elizabeth Shoumatoff, a famous portrait artist, was reading his life story in his face and putting in color on canvas what she saw there, he reached a shaking hand to his forehead and slumped in his chair, stricken by a massive cerebral hemorrhage. Complete in all but its final details, the painting still rests on the artist's easel in the room where Roosevelt was posing.

Atlantans, however, remember equally vividly another picture, not of FDR but of his friend and favorite minstrel, Graham Jackson of Atlanta. It shows Jackson, tears streaming down his face, playing "Going Home" on his accordion as Roosevelt's funeral train left Warm Springs en route to Washington by way of Atlanta. In Atlanta the eleven-car train pulled into Terminal Station at 1:30 P.M. for a forty-minute halt. Steel-helmeted soldiers stood at attention at the station, and thousands of Atlantans filled every inch of open space around the terminal as the train, pulled by two engines with their bells clanging mournfully, passed slowly by. As the train stopped, Mayor Hartsfield, Maj. Gen. Frederick E. Uhl, commanding officer of the 4th Service Command, and newspaper and radio men gathered at the last car in which lay the flag-draped casket of the late president. Stephen Early, White House Secretary, stepped from the train to greet the Atlanta group, and Mayor Hartsfield, expressing Atlanta's deep sorrow, presented Early a basket of white gladioli and red roses. The flowers were placed at the head of the casket, which was guarded by two sailors, a soldier, and a marine. There were no other flowers in the car.

In the adjoining Pullman car, which was blacked out, the Mayor and General Uhl expressed their sorrow to Mrs. Roosevelt, who was there with Grace Tully, the president's secretary, and Mrs. Early. "There are no words which can express our deep sorrow today," the Mayor said. "I understand," said Mrs. Roosevelt. Only the presence of the president's little dog Fala broke the mood of mourning. Walking up and down the platform on a leash held by a black serviceman traveling with the funeral train, Fala wagged his tail politely at all the bystanders who had greeted him.

Throughout the city flags were flown at half-mast, and all stores, except grocery and drug stores, were closed throughout the day. In school auditoriums, in schoolrooms, on playgrounds, and in churches, more than 50,000 Atlanta children bowed in silent prayer in tribute to the man who had died. And as his train pulled slowly out of Atlanta in mid-afternoon thousands of people of all ages lined the tracks to bid him a last farewell.

As Roosevelt's train moved north for funeral services in Washington and final interment services at Hyde Park, the papers carried glowing headlines telling of the great victories of the Allies over the by now obviously beaten Germans. By mid-April the American armies driving from the west were within forty miles of Berlin. On the east the Soviets were only thirty miles away, and soon the two armies joined south of the city. For two weeks the siege went on, a great aerial bombardment. And then on April 20 the Associated Press released a story, based on an interview with a "high official," that said that the Germans had made an unconditional surrender.

In Atlanta, New York, and all over the nation, thousands took to the streets. Bars, liquor stores, theaters, restaurants closed, afraid to keep open in the face of what might turn out to be a host of rampaging revelers.

But the report was premature. After two hours of nervous waiting, President Truman announced that he had talked to General Eisenhower at his headquarters in France. The report of a German surrender was "unfounded." The city took up the normal pace of life again. Bars, theaters, restaurants opened, and the three hundred policemen Chief Marion Hornsby had called in to take to the streets if needed were sent home before midnight.

For a week the tension continued. And then at 8:00 A.M. Atlanta time on Tuesday morning, May 8, President Truman in Washington and Prime Minister Churchill in London went on the air simultaneously to announce that, at last, Germany had surrendered. The papers had been signed in the "little red school" house in Reims, France, which was headquarters for General Eisenhower, commander of the Armies of the West.

In the intervening days between April's premature celebration and the final victory announcement, Atlantans had time to think of what was past and what lay ahead. Prayers of thanks seemed more appropriate than mindless shouting in the streets. Too many people could not forget sons killed or wounded in the war in Europe and Africa, and thousands of men still capable of combat were almost immediately sent on to join their brothers still fighting in the Pacific.

The war was still far from over.

President Truman in his V-E Day proclamation recognized this fact. He called upon all Americans to observe Sunday, May 14, 1945 as a day of prayer: "I call upon the people of the U.S., whatever their faith, to unite in offering joyful thanks to God for the victory we have won and to pray that He will support us to the end of our present struggle and guide us into the way of peace."

That mood of gratitude and reverence prevailed in Atlanta. Though thousands in London and New York surged in the streets again as Churchill's and Truman's voices came on the air, in Atlanta the mood was "calm, reverential," wrote Sterling Slappey, as the "real" V-E Day arrived with the leaders' announcement. The people did not wait for Sunday to express their gratitude in prayer. Said Slappey:

The sky over the state was clear and warm and the May sun was bright. No clouds marred Atlanta's weather [and] prayers of thanks, of hope, went up to those clear skies from Atlanta's people and the children of the city. As they had done in tribute to President Roosevelt on the occasion of his death, children in Atlanta's schools gathered to pray and sing and read the Scriptures. Churches all over the city were open for prayer and meditation, and the chimes of Peachtree Christian Church rang in a two-hour victory program. Workers at Bell Bomber Plant at Marietta celebrated by putting in a full day's work, in contrast to plane builders in Nashville; and at a service station and parking lot at Spring and Luckie Street, Roy Livingston provided "on the house" parking all of V-E Day. Business went on as usual all day except for the liquor stores, which were closed.

The greatest outward change in the city's appearance was in the downtown theater district. Here the marquee lights had been turned off for weeks, for fear that a desperate and vengeful Germany might attempt one last bomber strike. Now all along Peachtree they were ablaze again, a signal that peace in Europe had come at last, and fear was gone.

With Germany defeated, the army began to put into effect its plan for discharging soldiers with the longest service. This meant that the original members of Atlanta's most venerable and most noted unit, the Governor's Horse Guards, which was inducted into active service as the 101st Air Transport Anti-Aircraft Artillery Unit, would soon be on its way home. The unit was called in on February 10, 1941, and trained at Camp Stewart. It sailed for Australia and the southwest Pacific on February 15, 1942. There it earned four battle stars in New Guinea, the Dutch East Indies, and the Philippines. This service gave most of the members enough points to bring them home. Of the 750 Georgians who originally went overseas with the 101st, 250 were still members of the organization, including about 100 from Atlanta.

The war in Europe was over, but Japan was still fiercely defensive in the Pacific, and expenses would remain heavy until they were conquered. Atlanta and Fulton County volunteers, therefore, joined heartily in the drive for a Seventh War Loan, which got under way on Monday, May 14. The national goal was $14 billion. Of that sum, Atlanta and Fulton County had pledged to raise $43.2 million.

Georgia's most noted soldier, Gen. Courtney Hodges, native of Perry and commander of the famous 1st Army, arrived in Atlanta on May 24 to receive homage that royalty might have welcomed. In what was officially termed "Heroes Day," General Hodges and his party of fifty 1st Army veterans landed at Atlanta's Army Air Base at the municipal airport. They were met by Mayor Hartsfield and Governor Arnall.

Twenty Mustang fighting planes, forty-six P-46's, and a flight of forty B-29's from Marietta circled overhead as the parade passed through town en route to a banquet at the Georgian Terrace, where wounded veterans from Lawson General Hospital waited to greet General Hodges. Also waiting across the street at the Fox Theater parking lot were 105mm field guns that announced the arrival of the general with a 17-gun salute.

The passage of the general and his party through town from the airfield to the Georgian Terrace took forty-five minutes. Tumultuous crowds lined the route, flinging confetti at the car in which the general rode, and thirty bands at different intersections played martial music as he passed. Here at last Atlantans had cause and excuse to celebrate V-E Day as joyously as they could wish. Here was a man and an army to whom they could pay joyful tribute without shame. Hodges's 1st Army had, indeed, been a "first" army in the truest sense.

"His Army," wrote Dupont Wright in the *Constitution* of May 23, 1945, "was first on the bloody beaches at Normandy, first to cross the grey flowing Seine, first to reach the Ardennes. There he caught the full impact of the flower of the Prussian Army . . . yielded part of his advance under the hammer blows of Von Runstadt's last desperate thrust, but contained it, and then surged forward to be the first to find a vulnerable spot in the Siegfried Line. He was first to storm the beetling ramparts of the Rhine, first in the wild dash across Germany to join the Russians at the Elbe."

And finally, Wright concluded, Hodges's army was the first of the conquering legions to make history in Germany, and now he was ready to lead his fighting men across the Pacific to join in the war against Japan.

As he spoke to an evening crowd at the City Auditorium, General Hodges was in a reminiscent mood. He recalled another return to Atlanta after a victory over Germany twenty-five years earlier at the end of World War I, when he came home to Georgia as a major in the 5th Division. He recalled also that he was only nineteen years old when he came up from his home in Perry, Georgia, to enlist as a private at Fort McPherson, and he had never been out of uniform since. For all these years, he said, Atlanta had always been a favorite city of his. He had one brief informal message for the city and his home state of Georgia. It had to do with the Seventh War Loan Drive, just two weeks under way, in which Georgia was pledged to raise $121 million, of which Atlanta and Fulton County's share would be $43 million:

As you are aware, this is just a pause for me and the men of the First Army. We are on our way to the Pacific, and speaking for myself and other Georgians in our outfit—I can tell you this—the men of the First Army will go back to battle successfully, come-what-may, but they will go with much less reluctance if they know that the homefolks know how important it is. I can think of no more sincere and effective way of making sure that message gets across than in holding to the light the actual thermometer of civilian support—war bond purchases.

Far more than anything that could be done for us personally would I vote the pocket book sincerity, the war bond sincerity, of my neighbors and fellow Georgians. I would like to carry a message from Georgia to the men of the First Army and I would like for it to read like this: "I have been home to Georgia. They don't think the war is over in Georgia. They didn't tell me that. They showed the hard way—for civilians. They showed me in war bond deeds—and you can't argue with that!" In other words, I want to tell my men that the smart money is on our side, and there's plenty of it!

I know this—every Georgian in the Armed Services would be proud to learn that Georgia was the first state to meet her war bond quotas in this mighty Seventh War Loan Drive.

The war in Japan indeed was not over, but Japan was crumbling fast. It was now an air war. On the day that General Hodges arrived in Atlanta, in fact, headlines announced that 550 bombers had dropped 9 million pounds of fire bombs that had set the industrial heart of Tokyo aflame. This was the greatest of many raids so far.

Finally on August 15 the headlines in the *Constitution* read: "WAR WEARY WORLD AT PEACE AS BEATEN JAPS SURRENDER." The story that followed gave a dramatic picture:

Atlanta plunged thunderously into the post-war world last night. The darkness which had lain over the city for three years, eight months and one week—the war years—was lifted with dramatic suddenness when President Truman announced that Japan had surrendered. Then Atlanta went wild. Never in the city's history had it given itself over so unreservedly to such an orgy of joy and celebration. But the people had reason to "blow their top." All day long and for the past four days their nerves had been strained to the breaking point as the news seemed to change as with the wind—now good, now bad. But Atlanta's day of days had come at last. It was time for celebration, for joy that knows no bounds. . . .

The surrender news hit the city just as thousands of office, shop and war workers were filling the streets.

There was a moment of calm at first . . . like the calm before the storm. Then it broke loose. By six o'clock 100,000 people were jammed into the theatre district of Peachtree Street, overflowing into the cross-thoroughfares.

"Tear the roof off," Mayor William B. Hartsfield advised them—and they did. Shouting, cheering, waving flags, hats and bottles, making whoopee in the biggest sort of way. Atlanta welcomed the era of peace. As if by magic, horns and other noise makers began to appear. . . . Sirens blew, automobile horns hit sustained notes. Motors were raced and mufflers were burst. Some shot firecrackers. The scene was one of bedlam. They beat washtubs, blew bugles, beat pans, and streetcars clanged their bells. They were singing in the streets "OH SAY CAN YOU SEE" . . . and there were dancing conga lines slinking in and out. Sailors kissed girls, girls kissed sailors and bands played . . . jam and jive. So the dances, hundreds of people long, snaked through the crowd as tons of confetti and torn paper showered down on the crowd. . . . Soldiers and sailors commandeered automobiles and piled in and on top to ride through the throngs of walking merry makers. One motorist even knocked the top off his automobile to accommodate more sailors. As many as thirty would pile onto one automobile, breaking the springs. Streetcars were not only jammed, shouting sailors rode through town on top. One nameless man did his own thing. He walked from Cain Street to the Candler Building—backward.

The next day, Thursday, August 16, the city was back to normal—almost. Department stores decorated their windows with victory slogans but remained closed to trade, according to L. L. Austin, secretary of the Retail Merchants' Association. Furniture and chain groceries and many independent shops were open. So were the banks of the Atlanta Clearing House Association, headed by Freeman Strickland. Bell Bomber plant employees, who worked all V-E Day, were closed. Liquor stores stayed open, as did the State Capitol, but all city employees except policemen, firemen, and garbage collectors took a holiday on order of Mayor Hartsfield. Charlie Brown, chairman of the Fulton County Commission, kept the courthouse open but with only necessary services operating. All over the state, employment offices, under State Labor Commissioner Ben Huiet, were open. And with gasoline rations free at last, and seemingly plentiful, Atlantans flocked to the filling stations to utter the almost forgotten cry, "Fill 'er up."

On Sunday, September 2 the Japanese delegation, wearing top hats and formal civilian dress, climbed from a small dinghy to the deck of the battleship *Missouri* lying in Tokyo Bay. There they signed the document of surrender, which was accepted by General MacArthur and by representatives of the other Allies. The twenty-minute ceremony marked the final and formal victory over Japan—the official V-J Day, already celebrated so riotously in the United States. Looking on was Gen. Courtney Hodges, commander of the 1st Army, last seen by Atlantans as he paraded down Peachtree Street in the wake of victory in Europe. And among the 383 warships lying off Tokyo was the fourth cruiser *Atlanta*.

So ended the war. Atlantans, and the nation, turned their thoughts to other things, to politics, business, and civic progress.

One other victory, set in motion by Ellis Arnall when he was attorney general, combined in its effect on Atlanta and the South most of the elements named above. In 1942 Attorney General Arnall had filed suit against Dr. Hiram W. Evans, imperial wizard of the Ku Klux Klan, charging that the Klan and the asphalt companies that supplied road-building materials to the state had fixed prices in violation of the antitrust laws and should be liable for treble damages.

The defense argued that the antitrust law applied only to any "person" injured in his business or property by reason of anything forbidden in the antitrust laws. But a state was obviously not a person and therefore could not sue. In Atlanta the district court dismissed the case, holding that the state, indeed, was not a "person," and the Fifth Circuit Court of Appeals upheld the lower court. But Arnall stubbornly fought on—and supported by the attorneys general of thirty-five other states, he carried the case to the Supreme Court. There his argument prevailed—that every person, corporation, partnership, and city could file suit under the antitrust law, that the federal government could impose criminal sanctions against conspirators, and that thus it was "unthinkable" to believe that Congress, in using the word "person," meant to deny the states any redress against injury. The Supreme Court agreed. Georgia was a "person" under the antitrust law.

This case opened the legal doors to the case that was, indeed, closest to Arnall's heart—a suit against the nation's railroads, charging them with a conspiracy to fix transportation rates that kept the economy of Georgia and Atlanta, indeed of all the South, in a state of arrested development. In 1944 Georgia had filed an antitrust action against the Pennsylvania and twenty-two other railroads. As Arnall remembered it years after, "The railroads were deeply amused by what they considered no more than a petty annoyance."

The case was set for oral argument on January 2, 1945, and nearly three months passed before the decision came down—to the consternation of the railroad lawyers. The Supreme Court would accept jurisdiction over Georgia's case and, in a 37-page opinion written by Justice Douglas, said what Governor Arnall himself had been arguing for many years: "Discriminating [freight] rates are but one form of trade barriers. They may cause a blight no less serious than the spread of noxious gas over the land or the deposit of sewage in the streams. They may stifle, impede or cripple old industries, and prevent the establishment of new ones. They may arrest the development of a state, or put it at a decided disadvantage in competitive markets."

With this, Arnall remembers, the Interstate Commerce Commission began to stir. There had been a freight-rates case under consideration by the ICC since before World War II began—with no action taken. Then, on May 15, 1945, in a decision nearly 300 pages long, the ICC agreed with nearly everything Arnall and the advocates of equal freight rates for the South and West had been contending—that discriminatory freight rates were unfair and unjust, and that rates on southern manufactured products must in the future be no higher in the South than in the North. The equalization of rates would become effective on August 30, 1945.

The railroads fought back, of course, taking to the Congress their argument that they should be exempt from the antitrust laws. The Senate agreed on June 18, 1947, and the House on May 11, 1948. The Reed-Bullwinkle bill was passed, and President Truman vetoed it, but the Congress overrode his veto and the bill became law. But the ICC had already equalized the freight rates in Georgia's case against the railroads, and the new law was not retroactive.[1]

A northern reporter, Arnall later recalled, once asked Stephens Mitchell, brother of Margaret Mitchell, what were the most important things that had happened in the South during his lifetime, expecting, evidently, some reference to *Gone with the Wind.* "Only two important things have happened," Mitchell answered. "One, the boll weevil destroyed the South's cotton economy, and two, Ellis Arnall broke the freight rate shackles that had kept the South from becoming industrialized."

Arnall at thirty-four was not only the youngest man ever to serve as Georgia's governor, he was the first to serve a four-year term, and his accomplishments other than the equalization of freight rates attracted national attention. During his term a new state constitution banished the poll tax and lowered the voting age from twenty-one to eighteen. His achievements, in fact, set stirring in his mind and in the mind of many Georgians the idea that the constitution should again be amended, to permit him to succeed himself for another four-year term. After a bitter struggle in the state house, the "Draft Arnall" proposal was defeated, due in the most part to opposition by former governors Talmadge and Rivers, and Speaker of the House Roy Harris. The vote, on January 25, 1946, was 126 for the pro-Arnall amendment, 74 against—which was 11 votes short of the necessary two-thirds majority.[2]

For all of Georgia and the South, and for Atlanta in particular, Arnall's freight-rate victory had come at a particularly opportune time. Thousands of young men from all over the nation had trained in the Atlanta area or visited during the war. Many had come to like Atlanta, its climate, and its people, and when mustered out wanted to come back to live and work if they could find jobs. The elimination of the "class" freight rates on manufactured articles held out the promise that manufacturers in the North and East who wanted to expand into the South, but who had hesitated to open southern branches because of discriminatory freight rates, would now do so. Thus jobs would become available to hundreds, perhaps thousands, of the former military men and women.

And so it came to pass. In 1945 Atlanta's 905 factories were turning out 1,500 different commodities. By 1947 that figure had risen to 1,350 factories turning out 2,000 different commodities, and by 1950, 1,575 manufacturing plants were producing 3,000 diversified items, with no single industrial group dominating. Population had grown in proportion. In the 1940 census the population of the city of Atlanta was 302,288, and in 1950 it was 327,080—an increase of only 24,802, or 8.2 percent. But the metropolitan area, including Fulton, DeKalb, and Cobb counties, had jumped from 518,100 to 664,033, an increase of 145,933, or 28.1 percent.[3]

Payrolls reflected this growth in population and by 1946 had reached an estimated $28 million. Two of the largest employers soon to add to this figure were expanded plants installed by General Motors and Ford, at opposite ends of the metropolitan area. The General Motors plant for assembling of Buick, Oldsmobile, and Pontiac automobiles occupied a 386-acre site at Doraville.

Dedicated in June, 1948, the $7 million project had a roof area of more than seventeen acres and a production line capable of holding 550 automobiles at once. Its combined payroll and purchase of Georgia products represented an annual expenditure of some $27 million in the Atlanta area. Ford Motor Company had dedicated an equally modern plant at Hapeville in December, 1947. It occupied eighty-three acres and employed more than 2,300 workers, at an annual payroll of $5 million. Meanwhile, at the existing General Motors Chevrolet and Fisher Body plants, operating on McDonough Boulevard near the federal prison since 1928, production had been steady until the beginning of World War II, when the entire facility was devoted to war production. The first postwar truck rolled off the line late in 1945. By 1947, 1,500 employees, in 360,000 square feet of working space, were turning out thirty passenger cars or forty-five trucks in an hour. In twenty years of operating its assembly plant in Atlanta, Chevrolet had built more than 1 million cars and trucks. At Ford's first assembly plant in Atlanta on Ponce de Leon Avenue near Sears, the first Model T rolled off the line in 1915. This plant was sold in the early 1940s to be taken over by the War Assets Administration.[4]

At a dinner honoring the centennial of John C. Calhoun's prophecy of Atlanta's coming greatness, transportation and utility leaders tried their hands at predicting what the Atlanta of the future might be. Charles Hammond, assistant vice-president in charge of sales forecasting at the Georgia Power Company, predicted that Atlanta would be a cleaner city due to smoke control, and Fred Turner, vice-president and treasurer of Southern Bell Telephone and Telegraph Company, foresaw the day when nearly every house would have its own television set—with Ma Bell providing the facilities. There was general agreement that in twenty-five years—by 1970—Atlanta would be a city of a million people. (Indeed, the census of 1970 showed the Atlanta metropolitan area to be well beyond this mark—reaching 1,434,676. The city proper numbered 495,039.)

The Finance Committee of City Council announced it was considering a resolution that would make Atlanta the "dogwood capital" of the nation. The plan called for the purchase of 15,000 dogwood trees that would be planted in the parks and along the streets.

The city not only wanted its trolley riders to have something beautiful to look at as they rode, they wanted them to be comfortable as they traveled. As a result, in the heat of August, the first air-conditioned trolley began a three-day test run on the Peachtree-Oglethorpe line, moved on to the Stewart Avenue run for four days, and then to the College Park–East Point line for four days. Cost of each bus was $17,000.

One party that attracted considerable attention was the fiftieth anniversary of the founding of the Piedmont Driving Club on May 22, 1895. Five original members and their wives were the honorees at the anniversary event. They were Mr. and Mrs. Frank Inman, Sr.; Mr. and Mrs. Gordon Kiser, Sr.; Mr. and Mrs. Robert F. Maddox, Sr.; Mr. and Mrs. John K. Ottley, Sr.; and

Mr. and Mrs. Hugh Richardson, Sr. The Driving Club included in its membership Atlantans who were leaders in business, the professions, and the arts.

The year 1945 ended with some Atlanta servicemen still overseas, but most were home, and most Atlantans wanted to put the disruption of war behind them. Consumer products were again becoming widely available. Some business people feared that 1946 might bring a postwar depression, but their concerns turned out to be largely groundless.

OBITUARIES

Lawrence W. Arnold, who for years had taught at Southern Business University, died at 74. Mrs. W. Frank Bird, widow of a retired A&WP Railroad engineer, had been president of the Missionary Society of Inman Park Methodist Church. Mrs. Milton (Effie) Dargan, Sr., widow of the chairman of the Executive Committee of Cotton Insurance Association, died at her home. William Charles Dumas was head of Dumas Chemical Laboratory and husband of Floye, principal at Washington Seminary. Ben Fortson, Sr., was assistant reporter of the Georgia Supreme Court. Emory University professor Dr. Nolan A. Goodyear died at 62. Troy G. Chastain was a member of the Board of Fulton County Commissioners from 1938 until 1942. He was president of Atlanta Chemical Company.

Hon. Warren Grice, associate justice of the State Supreme Court, died at 70. Mrs. Arthur W. Harris, wife of the president of Harris Manufacturing Company, was the former Pauline Crawford. William (Billy) Hartsfield, grand-nephew of Mayor W. B. Hartsfield, was accidentally shot to death. Mrs. R. V. Haslett, the former Cora Knox, was the wife of the president of Crystal Pure Carbonic Company. William R. Hoyt, Atlanta pioneer and president of W. R. Hoyt Insurance Company, died at 84. The Rev. John Hughes, a Methodist minister for seventy years, died in Hapeville. He was 96. Mrs. Enrico (Matilda) Leide, wife of the well-known musician and symphony conductor, died at 60.

Chief Charles H. Millans had been director of the State Department of Public Safety and Fulton County police chief. Dr. J. H. Savage, was a long-time physician in the West End area. Robert W. Schwab had been president of Southern Spring Bed. Mrs. John Marshall Slaton was the former Sally Fanny Grant. Her interests included the High Museum, St. Cecelia's Circle at St. Luke's Episcopal Church, the Colonial Dames, the DAR, the UDC, the Daughters of the Colonists, the Daughters of 1812, the Daughters of Colonial Wars, the Huguenot Society, the Atlanta Historical Society, the Every Saturday History Class, and the Woman's Club. Hon. Alexander W. Stephens was presiding judge of State Court of Appeals. Mrs. E. K. Turner, the former Frances Lee, was a well-known artist and wife of an Emory professor. Judge Edgar Watkins was a member of the legal firm of Watkins and Watkins. Sidney M. Wilson was credit manager of Wofford Oil Company and an active member of Central Presbyterian Church and Georgia Association of Credit Men. Dr. W. W. Young, of Emory University, was a professor of psychiatry and neurology.

NOTES

1. Speech by Ellis Arnall to the Atlanta Historical Society, Feb. 2, 1982.

2. Howard Lawrence Preston, "The Georgia Gubernatorial Campaign and Democratic Primary Election of 1946" (M.A. thesis, Atlanta University).

3. Atlanta Chamber of Commerce, "Facts and Figures about Atlanta" (Atlanta, 1940, 1945, 1951).

4. Paul W. Miller, *Atlanta, Capital of the South,* American Guide Series (New York: Oliver Durrell Press, 1949).

THE need for capital improvements in the metropolitan infrastructure convinced the voters of Atlanta and Fulton County to pass a $40.4 million joint bond issue. Similar efforts had failed several times in years past. But now the city would receive $20.4 million—$9 million for schools, $4.1 million for traffic improvements, $3 million for airport improvements, $1.7 million for libraries, $1 million for sewers, $600,000 for auditorium improvements, $500,000 for parks, $300,000 for fire station improvements, and $200,000 for each of the city's garages.

The county figures, totaling $20 million, included: $12 million for traffic, $2.5 million for a courthouse annex, $2 million for sewers, $1 million each for auxiliary airports and parks, $500,000 for health and community centers, and $250,000 each for garbage disposal facilities and police and fire department improvements.

The victory was hailed by Mayor Hartsfield and Robert L. MacDougall, chairman of the Citizens Bond Commission, as a mandate from the voters to keep metropolitan Atlanta the business, commercial, and educational center of the Southeast.

Talk of the bond issue brought forth Dr. Thomas Dick Longino, whose 100th birthday was on September 7. He recalled that in 1899 he had introduced in Council a bond issue bill calling for $1 million for civic improvements. It did not pass, but five years later the growing city finally voted in favor of a $3 million issue for schools and Grady Hospital improvements.

Bankers, as in years past, were much in the news in Atlanta in 1946 as their young men came back from the wars and their older men laid down their burdens. At the Trust Company, for instance, President Robert Strickland (51) died of cancer in early August, and two months later chairman of the board T. K. Glenn also passed away. The bank's top lawyer, John A. Sibley of the firm of King and Spalding, was named chairman shortly before Glenn's death, and he became president following Strickland's passing. One of his first moves was to bring George Craft, organizer of the Emory University School of Business, back into the bank's hierarchy. Among others Sibley brought in was Ivy Duggan, President Truman's chairman of the board of the Federal Land Bank, which handled billions of dollars in loans to farmers. Duggan took over the bank's agricultural development program.

Sibley, in his efforts to get the bank going under new management, had the support of a board of directors representing some of the best business and financial brains in Atlanta. Among them were Ivan Allen, Sr., civic leader and businessman, who had developed his office supply business into a national concern; Charles H. Candler, former president of the Coca-Cola Company and son of Asa G. Candler; Carlyle Fraser, who founded the Genuine

Parts Company; and John N. Goddard, president of the Conklin Tin Plate and Metal Company.[1]

Under the management of Sibley and his board and the team of officers they had in training, Trust Company made the transition from a war to a civilian economy with great success. By the end of 1947 the capital, surplus, and undivided profits had risen to over $8 million, and Marshall Hall, president, and George Craft, vice-president, took over a strong and vigorous institution. By 1949 the company decided it could go ahead with its plans for opening a branch office in Atlanta at West Peachtree and Third streets, a white-columned structure that was reminiscent of the old governor's mansion at Milledgeville. Here the first "drive-in" teller window in Atlanta was opened.

Not all of the news in Atlanta during this time was joyfully onward and upward. In the *Atlanta Journal Magazine* of April 26, 1946, Mayor William B. Hartsfield described an increase in juvenile crime. He attributed it to a "wave of materialism sweeping over the whole country" and blamed "so-called progressive education" for the sudden upsurge in juvenile delinquency. Atlanta's junior hoodlums were both boys and girls, many in their teens, and some as young as twelve. Also, Hartsfield discovered, many were not poor, black, nor hungry. They were the sons and daughters of well-to-do Northsiders, and richly furnished homes on the affluent Northside were often robbed, ransacked, their fine furniture and objets d'art smashed and floors and carpets smeared with eggs and tomato ketchup.

Hartsfield called for strong measures: (1) the construction of new juvenile prison facilities, so that no offender would be released because there was no place to put him; (2) to rewrite and enforce stricter laws on juvenile delinquency, including strong punishment for adults who contribute to that delinquency; and (3) to make public examples of youthful offenders, even if they were underage, thus reversing the newspapers' ban on using the names of juvenile offenders in the belief that the young are entitled to protection.[2]

In his book *Atlanta and the Automobile*, retired police chief Herbert T. Jenkins described the activities of four young "thrill wreckers," sons of middle- and upper-income families residing in Druid Hills. They did not rob and vandalize their neighbors' houses for excitement; instead, they wrecked automobiles for the thrill of it. They would find a car parked on a hill, release the brakes, and let it roll until it crashed into a tree, a fire hydrant, a power pole, or a wall. In this manner they wrecked twenty-eight automobiles in the Buckhead–Northeast Atlanta area in one two-week period. Of the four the youngest was sixteen, the oldest nineteen. One was a student at Georgia State, another at Emory, one was an assistant scoutmaster, and the fourth was the son of a Baptist preacher. They were eventually caught and their names and pictures were printed in the papers, for they all were of legal age. They were fined, placed on probation, and their parents made restitution to the owners of the damaged cars. And the police department, which had paid little attention to youthful crime, since it heretofore had been relatively rare, now established a Juvenile Bureau, and a juvenile investigator was appointed.[3]

The year 1946 marked the entry of the World War II jeep into civilian life. When in early summer the War Assets Administration offered 2,700 jeeps for sale at the Conley Depot, veterans came from all over the South to buy them. Most of these, of course, were put to work at honest utility tasks— rough jobs of pulling and hauling heavy and dirty loads. However, Capt. Neal Ellis of the Atlanta Traffic Department pointed out that the snub-nosed machines were so adept at traffic weaving and tight parking that Atlanta police were inclined to look upon them, and their owners, with suspicion. For numerous reasons, the jeep never became as popular a civilian vehicle as many people had expected it would.

Other products of wartime development helped revolutionize hospital care, and some were seen at the newly opened Conkey P. Whitehead Surgical Pavilion at Emory University Hospital. There were shadow-proof lights over the operating tables, and new and highly effective forms of communication between the operating rooms and the chief operating nurse's office. During delicate operations doctors, interns, and nurses could send orders for personnel or equipment without having to touch a telephone, buzzer, switch, or any other nonsterile instrument. A combination loudspeaker and microphone hung above the operating table and was activated by pressure of a footpedal just above the floor. Another product of the war years was an air-conditioning "brain" that provided cool air for the east side of the hospital in the morning when the sun lifted the temperature there, and did the same thing to the west side in the afternoon.

A far less happy by-product of the war years was an upsurge in the KKK mentality, brought on perhaps by the greater visibility of the black man as he put on the uniform of his country. The black male was no longer the simple plowhand, the tenant farmer. The all-black regiments had been dissolved, and black and white soldiers by the war's end were beginning to eat and sleep and fight side by side. Long before integration had taken place in southern schools, it had taken place in the military.

As a result of this—combined with the Supreme Court's striking down of Georgia's "white primary" laws and the prejudice stirred by the campaign for governor discussed below—there was revived in the hearts of some white southerners, Georgians among them, fears and angers that soon became manifest in brutal, often seemingly meaningless, lynchings. One of the most cruel of these occurred some miles east of Atlanta in Walton County near Monroe, on the night of July 25, 1946. Weeks earlier a white farmer had been stabbed by a young Negro who worked on a farm, when he tried to break up a fight between the man and his wife. The wound was serious, but not fatal, and the youth was convicted and released on bond to another white farmer. Loy Harrington, who needed help on his farm, had posted $600 bond. Harrington was driving the young black man and his wife and another young Negro couple to his home. On the way in the darkness they were halted by an armed, unmasked group of twenty white men. The former prisoner and the other youth, who had served for five years in the military overseas, were marched off the road into the woods, lined up against trees with their wives, and at the count of one, two, three all four were brutally shot to death.

Monroe is not Atlanta, nor was Walton County considered part of the metropolitan area. But Atlanta, and all of Georgia, felt that "this brutal act had placed them in a pillory before the world." The reaction by the Atlanta and statewide press was one of incredulity and horror, and the cry rose up to the officers of the law to find and convict and severely punish the perpetrators of this act of inhumanity.[4]

A federal grand jury was convened on December 3 at Athens. It questioned approximately one hundred persons, but on December 20, 1946, the headlines told the story: "JURY FAILS TO UNCOVER WALTON MOB." The jury announced that it was "unable to establish the identity of any person guilty of violating the civil rights statute in connection with a July 25 lynching of four blacks."

The Monroe lynching had one result that gave an insight into the shape of the future. Among the hundreds of letters to the *Atlanta Constitution* in the two weeks following the murder in July, one was from a seventeen-year-old student at Morehouse College. In this letter young Martin Luther King, Jr., without referring specifically to the lynching, outlined the goals and dreams that would inspire and guide him until he too would be killed by an assassin's bullet on April 4, 1968:

We want and are entitled to the basic rights and opportunities of American citizens: the right to earn a living at work for which we are fitted by training and ability; equal opportunities in education, health, recreation, and similar public services; the right to vote; equality before the law; some of the same courtesy and good manners that we ourselves bring to all human relations.

M. L. King, Jr.
Morehouse College

The Walton County incident was symptomatic of a mood that gave rise to a resurgence in the KKK and gave birth to an organization known as the Columbians, a neo-Nazi type group whose members hated Jews and wore armbands bearing the drunken thunderbolt design used by Hitler's Elite Guard. Their openly admitted purpose was to execute the Jews and to send the Negroes back to Africa. Neither the Columbians nor the Klan caught on to any great degree in Atlanta of the postwar 1940s. This was in large measure due to the powerful editorials and columns Ralph McGill wrote in the *Con-*

stitution, denouncing them and all they believed in. Equally effective was the fact that McGill had informers planted in both organizations, who gave him detailed reports on meetings, telling him who was there and what they said.[5]

One of the brightest happenings of the year was a world premiere film at the Fox Theatre on November 12. The combined magic of two men, one living, one dead, produced the movie "Song of the South." Br'er Rabbit, Br'er Fox, and Br'er Bear took on the status of film stars.

Joel Chandler Harris, Atlanta's gentle genius of the storybook "critters," and magical Walt Disney seemed to be made for each other. In Harris, Disney recognized a writer who had the fantasy, the humor, the human understanding, and the timeless flavor that are requisites of Disney films.

It was the hard work of many Atlanta Junior League members that brought the two together. In 1944 Mrs. Frank Boston had the idea that a perfect event for a league-sponsored money-raising project would be a Walt Disney movie featuring the Uncle Remus stories. Mrs. Ivan Allen, Jr., was president that year and wrote the initial letter to Disney suggesting the idea. The indefinite reply gave impetus to Mrs. James Fraser's further request, and during her term of office plans were formulated and Hollywood agreed that Atlanta would be the ideal place for the premiere. It was Mrs. Hugh Dorsey who had the pleasure of presiding on opening night.

This movie was the realization of a dream that many people had shared over a long span of years. Joel Chandler Harris, Jr., said, "For years the members of our family have been keenly desirous of having the stories of Uncle Remus given an impetus on the screen to be immortalized further for the older generation and brought more keenly into the minds of the younger generation who seem to get so many more of their ideas from the screen than from books."

And so Atlantans awaited with keen anticipation the big event—opening night. To those who had grown to middle age and beyond, the stories of Uncle Remus were more than enchanting folklore. They were the bright dreams of childhood, stirring the embers of memories of a bygone South, waking a nostalgia for a gentle way of life lost in the rush of years. It was the hope of all the league women and of Disney's staff that "Song of the South" would inspire a great resurgence of interest in Uncle Remus, for the war-weary world needed, as never before, its homespun philosophy, its rich imagery, and its "Laughing Place." From the first strains of "Zippity-Do-Dah," it was off and running and successful all the way.

Co-sponsors of the happy event with the Junior League were the women of the Uncle Remus Memorial Association, headed by their president, Mrs. W. M. Jenkins. This organization until recently maintained the "Wren's Nest," the Harris home in West End.

One of the most bizarre episodes in the political history of Georgia unfolded in 1946. With Gov. Ellis Arnall constitutionally unable to succeed himself, the Democratic primary for governor became a crowded race. Former Governor Eugene Talmadge, campaigning on the issue that if he were elected governor no black would thereafter be permitted to vote in Georgia, played on these fears—and won. He defeated James V. Carmichael by 242 county-unit votes to 146—though Carmichael's popular vote was 313,389 to 297,245 for Talmadge. Hoke O'Kelly and E. D. Rivers both trailed far behind. Then Talmadge died of cancer on December 21, 1946, at Piedmont Hospital, before his inauguration in February could take place. This led to the incongruous three-governor squabble. The state's political system was in a ludicrous muddle from which at first it seemed there was no rational solution. Melvin E. Thompson, lieutenant governor, had assumed that he was the legal successor. But the Talmadge faction, knowing that the elder Talmadge was nearing death and wishing to keep the office in the family, wrote in the name of his son, Herman, in the general election in November. Followers of James V. Carmichael did the same for their man.

But to Georgia voters the Democratic white primary was still *the* election. They were not used to voting in the general election, and they turned out in minute numbers. In a controversial count, there were 775 write-ins for Herman Talmadge and 669 for James V. Carmichael. On the basis of this victory Herman Talmadge claimed the governorship, and the General Assembly named him to the office when his father died a month thereafter. But Ellis Arnall did not believe the legislature had this power, and even though it had been ruled that he could not succeed himself, he refused to give up the office until the State Supreme Court could rule on the issue. The court ruled that Thompson was the governor, and he was sworn in for a two-year term. Two years later, in 1948, Herman Talmadge was elected governor, serving until 1955, when he moved on eventually to his long career in the U.S. Senate which ended in 1980.

Carmichael's defeat in the state primary had been a bitter disappointment to many Atlantans. They had known and admired him as a highly competent businessman who in the last years of World War II had managed Bell Aircraft Corporation at Marietta—Georgia's busiest and biggest wartime enterprise. After the war and his unsuccessful race for governor, he returned to Scripto, Inc. to put it back in the pencil-manufacturing business. There he served as president of Scripto until his election to chairman of the board in 1964. He was appointed to the Board of Regents by Governor Carl Sanders in 1965.

Curiously, after the fire at the Winecoff Hotel described in the 1942 chapter, nothing much took place, except cleaning, to put the old hotel back in shape. When another and far more tragic blaze touched off about 3:00 A.M. on the sixth anniversary of the Pearl Harbor attack, the fire raged through a building that still had no fire escapes or sprinkler systems—though W. F. Winecoff, who built the structure, lived in the hotel on the fourteenth floor and with his wife died in the fire.

The most accurate account of the dreadful event is taken from the official files of the Atlanta Fire Department's history, *Prompt to Action:*

The hotel was situated at the southwest corner of Peachtree and Ellis Streets on the highest eminence of downtown Atlanta. It had been built in 1913 by the William A. Fuller Company of New York. The architect was W. L. Stoddart, also of New York. The cost at the time it was built was in excess of $350,000 and at the time of the fire it had an estimated value of from $750,000 to $1,000,000.

The structure occupied a plot 63 feet by 70 feet at grade, with the main entrance and marquee on Peachtree Street. It was fifteen stories (approximately 155 feet in height) with a full basement and a small sub-basement. The floors were numbered from one to sixteen but, as is the case in many hotels, there was no "13th floor". . . .

The construction classified at the time as "fireproof" included protected steel frame with the roof and floors of concrete on tile filler between protected steel beams and girders. Dividing walls between rooms were of hollow tile, plastered on both sides. Exterior walls were twelve-inch brick panel type.

The elevator shafts were enclosed in tile with openings on each floor protected by metal doors and wired glass panels. The stairway was not enclosed, a fact that may have been the primary factor in the spread of the fire. The stairway rose about the elevator shaft to the roof penthouse.

The fire was believed to have originated on the third floor from as yet an undetermined cause, and there was quite a bit of confusion over the discovery and the delay in transmitting the alarm.

The rapid extension of the fire vertically was mystifying to all the fire experts who conducted the probe and who still express wonderment over the speed with which the fire spread. It may have been the wall coverings which were freshly painted burlap becoming involved and creating combustible gases, progressing the intensity of the flames as they traveled upward; and of guests simultaneously throwing open their windows upon the arrival of the first fire companies, creating the necessary draft to speed up the combustion of the flammable gases.

In any event the heat reached a high degree of intensity which may have been in excess of 1,500 degrees as it melted light bulbs, fused electric ceiling fans, twisted metal doors, and cracked porcelain bowls.

The Fire Department responded on a telephone alarm which was sounded at 3:42 A.M. . . .

Additional alarms were snapped in rapidly and the final one was the general-alarm which brought out the entire Fire Department and all members of the off-duty platoon. The entire metropolitan area of Atlanta was mobilized at the scene.

The fire fighters were quick to bring into operation all of the aerial ladders of the department and every life net was employed to catch jumping guests.

Guests were endeavoring to escape the searing flames by improvising escapes with knotted bed sheets and other bed clothes, but many jumped to their deaths. One struck Fireman A. J. Burnham, injuring him critically. Several of the life nets were demolished after the initial impact of bodies. Ladder bridges were erected between the burning structure and the adjacent Mortgage Guarantee Building.

Of the several hundreds of guests and employees in the building, 119 were killed and over 100 injured. Mr. W. F. Winecoff, original owner, lost his life in his rooms of the hotel that bore his name.

The Fire Department used a total of thirty-three fire streams from surrounding buildings, aerial ladder pipes, and deluge sets. Penetration of many of these streams was limited due to the extreme vertical angle necessary from the narrow streets and towering heights.

Eight out-of-town engines operated at the fire and three filled in at No. 1, No. 5, and No. 8. The total number of engines at the fire was thirty-two; aerial ladder trucks, five; city service ladder trucks, six; a salvage-rescue truck, and the floodlight truck. The total number of pieces of equipment operating at the fire was forty-nine.

Departments from out of town which responded on the urgent request were Fort McPherson, East Point, College Park, Decatur, Avondale, Druid Hills, Hapeville, Marietta, and the Naval Air Base, and Conley Motor Base.

Chief officers in command were Chief of Department C. C. Styron, Sr., First Assistant Chief W. B. Fanning; Second Assistant Chief F. J. Bowen; Battalion Chiefs W. A. Fain, C. D. Reed, H. G. Pierce, and J. G. Webb.[6]

The recollections of Robert L. Snee added more detail:

Chuck Hosch, a reporter for the Associated Press, stated in the Atlanta *Journal* as regards the safety nets used to catch people "Of the fifteen or twenty that I saw jump, none walked away. They hit the nets with such force that firemen couldn't hold them in most cases, managing only to check their leap." Said Chief M. A. Hornsby, "At least twenty-five or thirty persons lost lives leaping from windows." Of the 51 boys and girls in town for a youth conference, twenty-eight perished.

By 6:04 A.M., the fire was out and a room by room, floor by floor search began for remaining survivors. Also begun was the reconstruction of the fire's origin.

In a three hour time period, one hundred and nineteen people had lost their lives; twenty-six people either fell or jumped to their death; forty-one persons died of burns and thirty-two of suffocation. Causes of death for the remaining twenty people were not available from the Bureau of Vital Statistics.

The cause of the fire remains of an undetermined origin, but most likely started from a carelessly thrown cigarette into an innerspring mattress stored near Room 326. The floors most completely involved in the fire were the 8th through 12th floors, with very little fire encountered below the 3rd floor. Fire damage gradually increased up to and including the ninth floor and lessened from that point to the 15th floor. On the top floor the damage was limited to the hallways and was small. . . .

The official fire report states that it was impossible to center the death toll in a particular section of the hotel. Bodies were recovered on all but the 1st and 2nd floor.

In a monthly routine inspection by the Atlanta Fire Department just one week prior to the fire, the Winecoff was found to be in reasonable conformance to the fire code.[7]

The blaze was believed to have been arsonist in origin, but a long investigation made by the Fulton County Grand Jury and the state fire marshal was never able to reach a conclusion as to how it began. The building was sold three days after the fire, but it stood empty, a grim monument to horrible death, for four more years. More than three million in damage suits filed by relatives of those who died were fought through the courts; final settlements were in the neighborhood of a quarter of a million dollars.

In 1950 the building was reconstructed and re-equipped with safety features, including fire escapes. The old name was abandoned. It became the Peachtree on Peachtree Hotel.

In 1967 owner Fred Beazley and his Beazley Foundation in Norfolk gave the hotel to the Georgia Baptist Convention, with the provision that the Baptists establish a home for old folk and a ministry for the aged on this site where so many had lost their lives. In 1981 Georgia Baptist Homes, Inc., sold the building for $2 million to Ackerman and Company, an Atlanta real estate firm, which owns or has owned such important downtown properties as the Candler and Carnegie buildings.

OBITUARIES

Dr. W. S. Belyeu, 77, was the first dentist in Atlanta to use nitrous oxide gas as an anesthetic when pulling teeth. He started the practice in 1892. In addition to being a dentist, Belyeu also owned a drug store and invested in real estate. Dr. G. E. Clay, 57, was one of the South's pioneer oculists. His work was widely published in medical journals, and he served as an officer in several medical associations. A former president of the Emory University alumni association, he worked hard to build up the medical school. Thomas K. Glenn, 78, retired in 1946 as chairman of the board of Trust Company of Georgia. He had been with the bank since 1902. He was also chairman of the board of Atlantic Steel Company and a member of the board of Coca-Cola. He was a strong promoter of Atlanta as a medical center and had served as chairman of the Emily and Ernest Woodruff Foundation. He was a Mason, a

Shriner, a Rotarian, and a member of the Capital City Club, the Piedmont Driving Club, the Atlanta Athletic Club, and several others. Leopold Jacob Haas, 73, was the founder of the insurance company bearing his name. A life-long Atlantan, Haas was a member of the Hebrew Benevolent Congregation.

Mrs. Samuel Martin Inman, 79, was the widow of a prominent Atlantan who died in 1915. She had received many awards for her civic and phi-lanthropic work, including an honorary doctor of laws degree from the University of Georgia. Inman was a pillar of the Georgia Federation of Women's Clubs. She served as a trustee of Agnes Scott College and Tallulah Falls School. She was in the DAR. Mrs. Wilbur G. Kurtz, wife of the noted artist and historian, died after a long illness. With her husband she acted as technical advisor for the movie version of *Gone with the Wind*. She was active in the Atlanta Historical Society, the Uncle Remus Memorial Association, and the Ladies Memorial Association. Charles B. Lawson, a veteran of the Battle of San Juan Hill in the Spanish-American War, died at 69. For many years he had worked for the city as a street construction foreman. Mrs. Charles H. Morris was president of the Presidents Club of the PTA. She worked hard as a leading lobbyist for PTA-backed legislation for child welfare. Helen M. Prescott, 85, was a genealogist and one of the founders and charter members of the Habersham Chapter of DAR.

Edward A. Stephens was one of the prosecutors in the infamous Leo Frank Case. From 1911 until his retirement, Stephens, 73, had been assistant solicitor general of Fulton County. He was a Methodist and a Mason. Nan Bagby Stephens, writer of "Roseanne," which ran on Broadway in 1924, and several other plays and books, died after a long illness. Stephens was a native of Atlanta and a graduate of Girls High. She was a member of the Cathedral of St. Philip. Eugene Talmadge was governor-elect at the time of his death in December. The death of the three-time governor on the eve of his return to the capitol set off a controversy concerning who would assume the governorship.

NOTES

1. Harold H. Martin, *Three Strong Pillars: A History of the Trust Company of Georgia Bank* (Atlanta: Trust Company of Georgia, 1974).

2. *Newsweek,* Apr. 1, 1946.

3. Herbert T. Jenkins, *Atlanta and the Automobile* (Atlanta: Center for Research in Social Change, Emory University, 1977).

4. Bulletin, Catholic Layman's Association in Georgia, Aug. 24, 1946.

5. Harold H. Martin, *Ralph McGill, Reporter* (Boston: Little, Brown, 1973).

6. Atlanta Fire Department, *Prompt to Action: Atlanta Fire Department, 1860–1960* (Atlanta, n.d.).

7. Robert L. Snee, "The Winecoff Fire" (MS, Atlanta Historical Society).

1947

IN AN optimistic report Dr. Allen D. Albert, Jr., head of the Department of Sociology at Emory University and a noted authority on city planning, detailed the status of Atlanta and its environs as of 1947. Though the city of Atlanta itself was limited by municipal boundaries, Albert declared that "Greater Atlanta" had passed the half-million mark and was rapidly on the way to making it a million. The advantages enjoyed by Atlanta as to population and income "derived from the two revolutions, one agricultural, one industrial," said Albert. However, he went on to note, "another trend is added to make the city great: the tendency in this society to develop regional capitals. The greatest of these is, of course, New York, but every region is in the process of developing its own, and Atlanta is rapidly becoming the capital of the Southeast." He cited the classic reasons for Atlanta's promise of future growth: "Its location as an air, rail and highway hub, its strong and broad-visioned local banks, functioning under a progressive Federal Reserve Bank with a breadth of vision as to the South's future, and the growing influence of branch offices from all over the nation that are coming into the city in increasing numbers."[1]

Mayor William B. Hartsfield, of course, agreed wholeheartedly with Albert's analysis of Atlanta's virtues and strove tirelessly to create a political and governmental climate in which they could thrive. He renewed in 1947, unsuccessfully, his effort to bring the suburbs into the city through large-scale annexation. He appointed a charter commission to sponsor legislation that would revise the city charter, giving him as mayor power to appoint department heads for an indefinite term—subject to confirmation by council, along with the right to appoint all boards, commissions, and committees of the various city offices. The changes sought by the mayor would have confined the elected council to a purely legislative function, giving Hartsfield, in effect, control over all city departments. After much debate, the decision was made not to carry out Hartsfield's proposed changes at that time.[2]

Hartsfield, however, was allowed to appoint his own executive secretary, private secretary, and the deputy recorder.

Fulton County in 1947 was somewhat more successful in changing its government structure. The county manager plan went into effect; A. E. Fuller was named to coordinate the many functions of county government. Under this arrangement the county manager would handle administrative details for the five county commissioners, leaving the commission to function primarily as policy makers. During the manager's first year there were improvements in the budgeting system and in purchasing responsibilities regarding uniforms, a strengthening of the civil service system, and a reorganization of the Public Works Department. The efforts of years past to combine many city and county functions continued, but two separate governments still existed side by side, one in City Hall, the other in the nearby Fulton County Courthouse. Nor did the county manager's job, in its original form, survive past 1949. (Fulton County does have a manager form of administration today.)

Perhaps more important to Atlanta as a city than these administrative changes was the subtle change taking place in the mind of the mayor. His attitude toward Atlanta's black citizens was undergoing a gradual conversion. He began his political career as a typical segregationist, and his first efforts to become "mayor to all the people" were tentative. Instead of removing the "white" and "colored" signs from restrooms at the airport, for example, he had them reduced until they could barely be seen. He required City Hall clerks, when sending letters to black citizens, to address them to Mr., Mrs., or Miss. (By southern custom a black man could be addressed as Doctor, or Professor, but not Mister.) The mayor grew suddenly bolder after the U.S. Supreme Court decision outlawing the white primary in 1946. This was not a matter of social relations. This to Hartsfield was politics, and he immediately recognized what he must do. He spoke at the black nerve center in Atlanta— the Butler Street YMCA—to those black leaders he respected—Grace Hamilton, A. T. Walden, Warren Cochran, and others—and told them that once they and their people had registered to vote, they could sit anywhere on the bus they wanted to sit—and many other avenues would be opened to them as well. Come to him with 10,000 registered voters, he told them, and he would be glad to listen to any project they proposed.[3]

Under previous voting restrictions only a few hundred Atlanta blacks had bothered to register. Now, spurred on by Hartsfield, led by Grace Hamilton, and guided by Dr. Clarence A. Bacote of Atlanta University, they put 18,000 names on the voting list in fifty-one days.

This shift in political attitudes was not lost on the black leaders of Atlanta University Center. There, Dr. Bacote was elected the first chairman of an All Citizens Voter Registration Committee. Other University Center faculty members who played important roles in the effort were Dr. William Boyd, chairman of the Political Science Department and president of the Atlanta chapter of the NAACP; R. O. Johnson of the School of Education; Dr. Joe Pierce, head of the mathematics department; and Morehouse English professor G. Lewis Chandler. A network of black workers was organized, mass meetings were held, speeches were made, and by 1949 there were 25,000 blacks registered.[4]

Meanwhile, Hartsfield had kept his promise. The greatest tension between the races rose from the relationship of the black man to the white police. Since Mayor Key's time, the black leaders had urged the creation of a black police force to patrol the black community, but fear of Klan reprisals had prevented this being done. Now the time had come. Hartsfield's first police chief was Marion Hornsby, who died on January 4, 1947, after ten years as chief. Herbert Jenkins succeeded Hornsby immediately. Both had purged the police force and kept it free of Klansmen and Columbians. Backed by Councilman Ralph Huie, Hartsfield and Jenkins made their move, and in the spring of 1948 eight black police donned uniforms and began walking their beats in Atlanta. At first they reported for duty at a separate precinct station on Butler Street under a white sergeant. They were not allowed to wear their uniforms when not on duty, nor were they permitted to arrest a white person. That was soon changed, on Hartsfield's argument that if you catch a burglar in your house you don't care if the policeman who comes to arrest him is white or black.

The appointment of black policemen was the first real breakthrough in race relations in Atlanta. It led on, in a few years, to a black police commissioner and a police force with one of the largest numbers of black patrolmen of any major city.[5]

While Atlanta's black community struggled for its political rights, Atlanta's women lawyers were carrying on a campaign on behalf of their sex, urging the legislature to pass laws permitting women to serve as jurors. The bill had been killed twice before, but the women lawyers in 1947 had the backing of a Supreme Court decision, handed down in December of 1946, in which the court ruled that the Constitution required that a jury shall be a cross-section of a community—and if women were excluded, jurors could be drawn from only half the community. Thus, the General Assembly was finally persuaded to require jury service of women as well as men.

Though jury duty for women was slow in coming, women lawyers in Atlanta had long been recognized as highly skilled practitioners of the legal profession. Atlanta's Woman of the Year in the Professions—who was also chosen as *the* Woman of the Year 1946 on the evening of January 15, 1947, at a banquet at the Biltmore—was a woman lawyer, Frances Craighead Dwyer. A graduate of Agnes Scott with an A.B. degree, of the University of Michigan with an M.A., and of Emory University with a law degree, she was largely responsible for the revision of the child labor laws, which prohibited Georgia's children from exploitation and hazardous occupations. She also for a long period was general counsel for the Legal Aid Society, a Community Chest Agency that gave advice and legal representation to some 3,000 indigent persons a year.

Women were also recognized for their business acumen and for other talents. In January, 1947, Mrs. Frank Lowenstein was named Woman of the Year in Business for 1946. She had been president of Norris Exquisite Candies, Inc., since the death of her husband in 1928, and 1946 was the best year in the company's history. Katherine Comfort was named Woman of the Year in the Arts. She had headed the Art Department of Girls High for twenty-one years and taught thousands of Atlanta girls to appreciate art in all its forms. Mrs. Robert H. Jones, Woman of the Year in Civic Affairs, was president of the Atlanta Federation of Women's Clubs. Dr. Catherine Sims was named Woman of the Year in Education, and Florence Van Sickler, who had headed the Child's Welfare Association in Atlanta for ten years, working to give homes and security to thousands of neglected and orphaned children, was named Woman of the Year in Social Welfare.

The grand award of the evening, though, was given to a woman who was not an Atlantan, though her good deeds and warm heart had made her worthy to be called one of Atlanta's most "notable women of years past or years to come." She was Lettie Pate Evans of Hot Springs, Virginia. A former Atlantan whose husband was the founder of the Coca-Cola Bottling Company, she had carried on the charitable work of her two sons, both now dead. Through the foundations she founded in memory of her sons, Joseph B. Whitehead and Conkey Pate Whitehead, she had aided in the distribution of millions of dollars to Atlanta hospitals, religious institutions, orphans' homes, and the Community Chest. More than one-fourth of these gifts had been for the benefit of children. The Conkey Pate Whitehead Surgical Pavilion at Emory, combined with the Joseph B. Whitehead Chair of Surgery, had helped to make Atlanta a medical center of national renown.

In 1946 a wave of juvenile hoodlumism, as described earlier, had swept over Atlanta and the surrounding area. The incidence of other crimes of violence was increasing, too. There were 97 murders in Atlanta that year, and 58 in Fulton County. There were 351 cases of aggravated assault, and 20 of rape.[6] This wave of terror continued on into 1947; 747 Atlanta police evidently were unable to stop it.

The case that held the attention of the Atlanta police, press, and public for the longest time of any of the 1947 tragedies was the drama of the Refoule Case. Not since the murder of banker Henry Heinz in his home in Druid Hills in 1943 had the town been so stirred to anger and fear. On Wednesday, May 14, the body of Margaret Alston Refoule was found in the shallow waters of Peachtree Creek behind her home on Howell Mill Road. She was lying face up, her arm twisted behind her back, her feet tied together with her shoelaces.[7]

Mrs. Refoule, known as Peggy to her friends, was the daughter of an old and socially prominent Atlanta family. In the mid-1930s she had gone to school at the Sorbonne in Paris, and there she met Paul Refoule, a young artist. They married on January 19, 1937, and went back to Paris to live. At the outbreak of war, Paul Refoule joined the French Army. He was taken prisoner. In December of 1944 he escaped from the Polish camp and made his way across Europe to Orleans, where he joined his wife and son.

In August of 1945 they came to Atlanta, where Paul got a job teaching art at the High Museum and at Oglethorpe University. He also had his own private studio. The Refoules bought an old woolen mill that had been standing since 1882 alongside Peachtree Creek, and they converted it into a striking, modern home. On Wednesday, May 14, 1947, when their son Jon (9) came home he found the front door of his home locked but the back door open, and he noticed muddy footprints on the small back porch. His mother was not in the house. Paul Refoule came home about an hour later to find that his wife was not there. Thinking that perhaps she was visiting friends, he did not worry for a while. By 8:10 she still had not returned, and many phone calls gave no trace of her, so the Fulton County Police Department was called. Tracking dogs led police to the body in the water. Marks on Mrs. Refoule indicated she had been strangled. Her plain gold wedding ring was missing from her finger, but she often removed it when doing housework. However, also missing were two diamond rings in unusual settings, a lady's wristwatch, and an inexpensive camera.

Police at first concluded that Mrs. Refoule had surprised a burglar in her home and had been murdered by him. Throngs of people, hearing the news on the radio, swarmed in, trampling any footprints that might have existed and wiping out any fingerprints the murderer might have left.

The investigation continued, and wild rumors and false reports sent nine Fulton County police officers off in all directions, checking leads that led nowhere. Then, finally, a nineteen-year-old art student of Refoule's at the High Museum told police that she had had sexual relations with her teacher—and that he had told her he was unhappy with his marriage.

This, it seems, was all that Chief Neil Ellis and his men of the county police needed. From then on, the burglar theory seemed forgotten, and all the attention focused on the artist himself, particularly on his sex life. Refoule under questioning by police was said to have admitted that his marriage to Peggy had lost its luster, and that he had indeed had an intimate relationship with the art student.

By now the shocking headlines in the papers had Atlantans in a frenzy of curiosity, and as they had done in the Heinz case, thousands of Atlantans stormed through the Refoule home and grounds.

The police spent their time gathering all the evidence they could against Refoule. They went to Oglethorpe University and had all the students in Refoule's art class make notarized statements. The statements were nearly all the same: Refoule was at Oglethorpe teaching on the afternoon of the murder, and though he left the classrooms, he did not leave the building. "It should have been obvious to anyone that Refoule could not have murdered his wife," wrote James S. Jenkins, son of Chief Jenkins.[8]

After questioning the Oglethorpe students, the police went to the High Museum and interviewed the faculty and students. What they learned about life among students was a shock to the straitlaced police, according to Jenkins. "Needless to say, the police were operating in a rather unusual environment for them and what they learned about artists and art schools was a terrific shock. They thought it deplorable that models posed in the nude. They listened wide-eyed to stories the students made up about wild sex parties and loose morals which they knew would startle the cops."

On Thursday, July 8, 1947, through his attorney Hal Lindsay, Refoule went into U.S. District Court in Atlanta and asked the court to prevent any further illegal detention or questioning. At the same time he entered a $50,000 damage suit against Chief Ellis and other Fulton County police officers, alleging harassment and physical brutality. The unfounded charges, he claimed, had caused him to lose his teaching and art jobs. For the first time, the artist and ex-POW issued a public statement: "I have been accused of murder by the police. This charge is not true and the police know it is not true. They know that reliable witnesses have accounted for every minute of my time on the day of the murder. Instead of accepting this proved fact, and making a real search for the murderer, they have reverted to the old Nazi trick of accusing a person of sexual perversion if they cannot prove him guilty of some other crime."

The hearing on Refoule's charges against Captain Ellis and the Fulton police lasted seven days in an un-airconditioned courtroom. Everybody came, Jenkins reported, "housewives with babies, summer school students playing hooky, young matrons wearing big straw hats, and a scattering of farmers in overalls. . . . Refoule and his lawyer entered by a side entrance and managed to evade the crowd outside, but they had to go up in the regular elevator and there they were besieged by a throng of screaming teenage girls, mad as if Refoule was a Hollywood celebrity."

The mother and father of Paul Refoule had come from Orleans, France, to be with their son, but according to Jenkins's report, the incredible behavior of the Atlanta crowd and the sweltering heat was too much for the older Refoules. After their first day in court, the dignified old couple left for New York and thence to Paris.

The trial had gone on for several days when the presiding judge ruled out testimony on Refoule's love life; he told the crowd: "I don't think the proceedings will be of much interest to you from here on out." Nor were they. Gradually the crowds diminished, the hate-Refoule mail to the newspapers began to subside, the headlines shrieked less loudly.

In October of 1947 the federal judge issued an injunction forbidding the Fulton County police from questioning Refoule further about the case unless he was placed under arrest for murder. And in November of 1947 the morals charge against Refoule was not pressed by the Fulton Superior Court. The reason, according to Solicitor General Paul Webb: The principal witness, an art student on whose testimony the charges of sodomy were based, had left the state with her soldier husband and would not agree to return. Therefore, there would be no trial.

Refoule, in a long and deeply emotional statement, demanded that he be tried. He sought "judgment of acquittal [to] which I am entitled under the law." But the authorities refused to bring the case to trial—and Refoule was by now too ill for further protest. Shortly after his last statement he went into the hospital and underwent two operations, for kidney stones and hernia. While he was there, doctors discovered that he had a cancerous lung and removed it. Two weeks later, on February 13, 1948, he died.

"To this day," wrote James S. Jenkins, "most Atlantans don't really know what to make of the murder of Peggy Refoule. It was, and remains, one of Atlanta's most baffling murder mysteries." Jenkins concluded: "Any impartial investigator must conclude that those who still insist on implicating Refoule will not or cannot separate in their minds the act of murder from what is, to them, a peculiar life style and/or profession, and probably for some the two cannot really be separate. The fact is there is no evidence linking Paul Refoule with the murder."[9]

Refoule's death was not the only tragic event of this troubled year. In April, 1947, Lindley Camp, solicitor of Fulton County Superior Court, and seven Delta Air Lines officials were killed in a plane crash at Columbus. This was a severe shock to Delta management. With headquarters in Atlanta, it was preparing to complete a million-dollar expansion project that was to contain a general office, hangar, and modern testing and maintenance shops.[10]

Army aircraft had been flying from the city airport since 1929. During the war the city leased more land, and the army expanded its operations until more than forty permanent buildings had been constructed and long concrete runways had been built to serve the thousands of army and navy flyers who used the facilities as a stopover for fueling and repairs. In 1947 the U.S. Army deeded the original twenty-seven acres of property back to the city and moved military air forces to Marietta. Meanwhile, Fort Mac became headquarters of the 3rd Army, with Lt. Gen. Alvin C. Gillem in command.

When the army turned over its airport facilities to the city, Mayor Hartsfield and airport manager Jack Gray were given their chance to expand. A huge hangar-like building, designed by Hartsfield and Gray and built almost entirely of surplus war materials, was constructed. It cost only $270,000 and was one of the most modern passenger terminals in the nation when it opened for operation on May 9, 1948. Its 250,000 feet of floor space provided all passenger comforts, including a 24-hour restaurant, observation platforms, and, at Hartsfield's insistence, plenty of toilet facilities to serve the 250,000 passengers who passed through every month. It served the city for over a dozen years before it gave way to a new building.

During 1948 construction of three new runways totaling 20,000 feet was begun as part of a $6 million expansion program. Also approved during this year was a $150,000 dual radar system, designed to permit all-weather flying in any season.[11]

On what would have been Hartsfield's eighty-first birthday, March 1, 1971, City Council passed an ordinance urging that the Atlanta Municipal Airport should henceforth be known as the William Berry Hartsfield Airport. Six months later that name was changed to acknowledge Atlanta's growing status as a global air center. It became the William Berry Hartsfield International Airport.[12]

While airport development was going on apace, new building permits in and around Atlanta slumped sharply in the first three months of 1947, as compared with the building boom that had lasted throughout 1946. However, existing downtown business property increased in value greatly.

In 1947 the *Atlanta Constitution* moved from its old location next to Rich's department store to a new building across the street. It featured a sculptured mural by Julian Harris that depicted reporters, photographers, and printers at work. WCON, the *Constitution*'s new radio station, was on the top floor of the new building.

The moving of the *Journal* and *Constitution* from their old locations was a wrenching experience to many veterans on both papers, for the venerable structures had given office space to many literary figures over the years, among them poets, playwrights, and novelists as well as journalists. Included were Margaret Mitchell, Don Marquis, Ward Greene, Ward Morehouse, Erskine Caldwell, Laurence Stallings, Vereen Bell, Hal Steed, Harry Stillwell Edwards, Evelyn Harris, Sam Tupper, Wilbur Kurtz, Margaret Steedman, and Minnie Hite Moody.

The current crop of editors, reporters, and photographers was not inclined to brood over past glories, however. On the *Constitution* they followed the lead of Ralph McGill, editor, Major Clark Howell, publisher, Hugh Trotti, vice-president, Ralph Jones, columnist and associate editor, Yolande Gwin, social reporter, and Doris Lockerman, who was made an associate editor in 1948. Young associate editor and columnist Jack Tarver was beginning his rise in the field of newspaper management.

The *Journal*'s staff in these years of change were even more widely known locally. Among them were Editor Emeritus John Paschall, W. S. Kirkpatrick, managing editor, and Ed Danforth, sports editor. The latter two were refugees from the old *Georgian*; O. B. Keeler, Morgan Blake, Ernest Rogers, the unofficial "Mayor of Peachtree Street," Medora Field Perkerson and her husband Angus, Frank Daniel, Helen Knox Spain, and Edwin "Ole Timer" Camp were other stars of the *Journal*.

Postwar traffic in Atlanta increased beyond expectations. Georgia Power Company, operator of the transit system, estimated that the number of streetcar riders after the war would revert to the 87.6 million passengers hauled in 1941. Instead, in mid-1947, the company was rushing to complete a $7.3 million modernization program to care for a volume of traffic estimated at 153.8 million passengers a year—and still moving rapidly upward. Part of this program of improvement would be the installation of trolley buses, which would require some adjustment in traffic patterns. Trolley buses used overhead wires but needed no tracks, since they rolled on rubber tires. The city, of course, was glad to cooperate with its biggest single taxpayer. In 1946 the Power Company had paid $531,615.89 into the city treasury.

When the highly competent teacher Ira Jarrell took over the Atlanta Public Schools on January 1, 1944, she immediately began a program of change designed to bring out what, to many Atlantans, were radical reforms in teaching patterns and methods.

By 1945, explained Philip Noel Racine in his doctoral dissertation, it was decided that coeducation must be introduced into all the high schools and that they should be made "community schools," if the rapid growth and development necessary to meet contemporary standards was to be attained. This was made possible when, in the huge $42 million bond issue finally passed in 1946, $9 million was allocated to city schools. Thus the change to coeducational schools came to pass, although the faculty of both Boys High/ Tech High and Girls High was strongly against it—and so were many graduates. Yet the arguments for change were too strong to be overcome, and in September of 1947 the changeover was made. Students no longer had to commute all the way across town, jamming public transportation morning and afternoon and clogging the flow of traffic of downtown Atlanta. Actually, by the time the change was made, Boys High and Girls High were not the schools they had traditionally been. Increasingly, commercial and vocational courses had been introduced into these schools to accommodate the increasing needs of boys and girls who did not find college preparatory work appropriate. This fact alone had changed the character of the schools.[13]

The name of Girls High was changed to Roosevelt, in honor of the late president, and Boys High/Tech High became Grady High for Henry W. Grady. Each, however, remained in its old building—Girls High in the big brick building on Rosalia Street where it had been since 1925, Tech High/ Boys High in the newly named Grady High School between Ninth and Tenth on Parkway Drive (later Charles Allen Drive) across from Piedmont Park.

The change in name and attitudes toward scholarship did not go unnoticed. On May 10, 1947, at the end of the last school year under their old identity, more than one hundred alumnae of Girls High held one last sentimental luncheon meeting, looking at old pictures, remembering old friends, honoring old teachers, remembering old pranks and jests. Margaret Steedman in an article in the *Journal* on May 11, 1947, the day after the luncheon, recalled some of those jests: Before 1925 Girls High had been near the state capitol, the Second Baptist Church, and a boarding house. This produced a crossroads which showed Girls High, representing Education, bound by Legislation, Salvation, and Starvation. At the new school (on Rosalia Street) there was nothing to joke about except the city stockade and federal prison, both in full view.

The Steedman article traced the history of Girls High from 1872 to the last year, recounting the changes that took place as the school moved from one old building to another. Some of the things remembered were the art lessons taught by Katherine Comfort and the lessons on "How to be a Lady" learned under the quiet guidance of Jessie Muse. One musical tradition was continued to the last: the Triumphant March from Verdi's *Aida,* as the first two girls, president of the school and of student government, entered for the traditional graduation ceremonies.

Tech High took no formal notice of its passing as a separate school, its melding in with its old scholastic neighbor and bitter athletic rival, Boys High. But for years after the merger, Tech High graduates met to salute each other and to honor the teachers who had meant most to them. On March 21, 1957, ten years after the end of Boys High, two hundred loyal alumni, including old football stars Bob Randolph, Bill Fincher, and "Coot" Watkins, met to do honor to Dr. Willis A. Sutton, Tech High's first principal, and Dr. W. Cheney, president in 1947. Also present, in his wheelchair, was Tech High's most famous athlete—Bobby Jones, the world champion golfer.

In an article in *Atlanta* magazine called "Boys High Forever," Pat Watters, distinguished Atlanta essayist, told what it was like to have been a student at Boys High in the 1940s. The old, proud shout of "Boys High Forever" did not last beyond 1947. Watters wrote: the closing of Boys High revealed "the forces of progressive education, of sameness, and blandness finally triumphing over an institution that had held out for individuality and old-fashioned academic standards and for an anachronistic brotherhood of male exclusiveness."

Watters did admit that "by the time I got to Boys High, in 1945, in the midst of World War II, the academic standards had slipped [in this he agreed with Philip Racine] and a long tradition of hell raising had perhaps gotten out of hand. But, we felt still the Boys High Spirit. It was one of pride in achievement; of solidarity; of being of the best." He turned to Douglas G. McRae, retired assistant superintendent of Fulton County Schools and a graduate of the Boys High Class of 1924, for words that, to Watters, "captured the essence of the Boys High Spirit." McRae had written: "Boys High School, with a superb teaching staff, literally tatooed on our minds the elements of English and Algebra, and Latin and Physics and American History. Many schools could have done this, but Boys High did more; her teachers in some inspired way, taught us about Truth and Honesty, and Justice and Humility."

"The point is," McRae continued, "that Boys High convinced us there was pride and honor in having to work hard. The old school was for most of us both test and forge of will. And, when Will accomplished what Wit alone could not, we felt a warmth of satisfaction surging through us. We knew we had done a job well, that we could wear the ribbon of pride, and the badge of honor."

Boys High produced no world-famous leaders, with the possible exception of Dean Rusk, the former secretary of state. It did, however, produce some men outstanding in Atlanta and the nation. The class of 1935 produced two of these. One was George Goodwin, who as a *Journal* reporter in 1948 won the Pulitzer Prize for his investigation of Telfair County voting frauds. Another was architect Cecil Alexander, who in the 1970s designed the Coca-Cola Building, the Southern Bell Building, and the MARTA Five Points Station.

One of the most remembered characters of Boys High was its longtime football coach. Says Watters: "Coach R. L. (Shorty) Doyal, who began coaching at Boys High School in 1925, was a genius at football. Doyal's record, when he left in 1946, the year before the school died, was 200 wins, only 41 losses, and 12 ties." For all of that, the last issue of the *Boys High Tattler* on

June 2, 1947, recorded that even under Doyal, Tech High had won eighteen games to sixteen for Boys High. Doyal produced a string of great players who went on to star at college, among them the great broken-field runner Clint Castleberry, who made All-American in his freshman year at Georgia Tech and later was killed in World War II.

OBITUARIES

Henry A. Allen was the city attorney of Hapeville for twenty-five years. Alfred C. Broom, former city attorney of College Park, died at 70 following a long illness. He was a graduate of Emory Law School and had lived in the Atlanta area since 1901. Mary M. Connally, 92, was an active worker in Methodist missionary circles. She served for many years as treasurer of the Atlanta Children's Home. She was a life member of the Uncle Remus Association. Clarence L. Duncan, 51, was the chairman of the Fulton County Commissioners. He had served as a commissioner since 1943. He was active in civic organizations, including the Optimist Club and the Masons. Mary Wilbanks Herndon, 90, was the daughter and wife of Civil War veterans. Her husband was wounded in the Battle of Atlanta.

Dr. M. Ashby Jones, 78, was the retired pastor of the Ponce de Leon Baptist Church. Jones was the son of a chaplain who rode with Gen. Robert E. Lee in northern Virginia. An indication of his wide scope of influence was the fact that Rabbi David Marx and Dr. William Holmes Borders, pastor of the Negro congregation at Wheat Street Baptist Church, spoke at his services. Dr. Thomas D. Longino was a 100-year-old Civil War veteran and longtime Atlanta physician who practiced into his eighties. A graduate of the Medical College of Georgia, Dr. Longino served on the City Council for seven years. Thomas A. Rainey, 80, was retired conductor of Southern Railway's Piedmont Limited. Affectionately known as "Capt. Tom," Rainey worked for the Southern for fifty-three years. He was a Mason and a Shriner. Victor L. Smith, 80, was a prominent Atlanta attorney. He graduated from the University of Georgia and was admitted to the state bar in 1889. He was involved in organizing the Atlanta Music Festival and was a member of the Piedmont Driving Club.

W. M. (Bill) Turner worked for the *Atlanta Constitution* for sixty-four years, rising to foreman of the pressroom. He was 83. Dr. Joseph C. Wardlaw was director of the Division of General Extension of the University System of Georgia and former superintendent of Atlanta schools. He was a Kiwanian, a Mason, a Shriner, and an active Methodist layman. He served as an officer in several educational associations and was a member of Phi Beta Kappa. Judge Garland Watkins of Fulton County Juvenile Court, 58, died after a three-month illness. He had served as juvenile judge since 1920. Mrs. John C. West was a prominent civic worker and daughter of the founder of North Georgia College. She was especially involved with the Florence Crittenden Home and the Cascade Baptist Church. She was a member of DAR and UDC. Edna L. Whitmore was the Director of Choral Music for the Girls High School and then Roosevelt High. She also was the organist at Westminster Presbyterian. Richard Robert Wright, born in slavery on a Georgia farm, died at 94 in Philadelphia. He was principal of the first Negro high school in Georgia and had served as president of Georgia State College in Savannah. In 1921 he moved to Philadelphia and was involved in founding one of the largest black-owned banks in the nation.

NOTES

1. Paul W. Miller, *Atlanta, Capital of the South*, American Guide Series (New York: Oliver Durrell Press, 1949).

2. Ibid.

3. Harold H. Martin, *William B. Hartsfield, Mayor* (Athens: University of Georgia Press, 1978).

4. *Atlanta Historical Journal* 25, no. 1 (Spring 1981).

5. Martin, *Hartsfield*.

6. *Newsweek*, Apr. 1, 1946.

7. James S. Jenkins, *Murder in Atlanta* (Atlanta: Cherokee Publishing, 1981).

8. Ibid.

9. Ibid.

10. Miller, *Atlanta*.

11. Ibid.

12. Martin, *Hartsfield*.

13. Philip Noel Racine, "Atlanta's Schools: A History of the Public School System, 1869–1955" (Ph.D. diss., Emory University, 1969).

I N 1948 the Georgia legislature enacted a building safety law, in direct
response to the Winecoff Hotel fire of 1946. It sought to provide methods
for enforcing national safety standards in public buildings, not only in
hotels but in office buildings as well. The Atlanta Fire Code was even more
stringent than the state law, and the city's chief of building inspectors,
O. Marvin Harper, was recognized nationally as one of the "most conscien-
tious exponents of fire safety and maintenance of construction standards in
public buildings." In the months following the Winecoff fire a systematic and
thorough inspection of all buildings affected by the local codes was tabulated,
recommendations were made, and most owners were cooperative in making
construction changes without delay. And in the winter of 1948 Atlanta engineers began preparing an entirely new building code for the city.[1]

In September the need for codes and their continued enforcement had
once again been dramatically demonstrated when E. Rivers School at Peachtree and Peachtree Battle Avenue was destroyed by fire. There were no injuries reported, and the school was soon replaced by a modern building.

The two major downtown department stores had not yet in 1948 begun
the flight to the suburbs, and each made substantial investments in its central
city physical plant. On March 19, 1948, Rich's opened its spectacular new
Store for Homes, featuring the glass-enclosed bridge five floors above street
level, over which throngs of shoppers moved from the main store across Forsyth Street. Here is where "The Great Tree" would be lighted at formal
services thereafter on Thanksgiving night to launch the Christmas season.
Davison-Paxon, not to be outdone by its old rival, constructed a five-story
addition at the rear of the main store and provided a separate entrance on
Carnegie Way.[2]

In the fall of 1948 a survey done by the Greater Atlanta Traffic Improvement Association showed that more than 415,816 people were in the downtown area between 7:00 A.M. and 7:00 P.M. on any given business day. The
maximum number of vehicles downtown on any average day at 2:00 P.M. was
14,500. To help move these cars in and out of the city, work was started on a
$40 million expressway system, the beginning of hundreds of millions of dol-
lars of freeway construction to follow. One disturbing effect on a city proud of
its history was that some of the historic old houses that were in the path of the
approaching expressway would have to be taken down or moved. One of these
was the home of Patrick Lynch, a gigantic Irishman, who owned a blue-stone
quarry and built his house on Simpson Street with the rock from his quarry. It
is not recorded exactly when he built the house, but he bought the land in
1860 (24 acres for $1,230) and died in 1870. His weight was said to be 300
pounds, which had kept him from serving in the Confederate Army. It is

thought to be this, plus the fact that he was a Catholic, that caused Sherman to spare his house.

Another and more widely known of Atlanta's old homes was the brown granite mansion built by John Silvey at the corner of Marietta and Spring streets in 1885. Mr. Silvey, a wealthy merchant, foresaw the fact that his house might one day stand in the way of the city's progress, so he bought a tract of land out Peachtree Road and provided in his will that at his death the house should be moved there. And this was done in 1900–1902. Every arch and artifact of the twenty-room house, its Tiffany stained glass windows, mahogany paneling and carvings, and Italian tile fireplaces, along with a covey of cement ducks, all were moved to the new location at 1611 Peachtree Road. And there, by the end of 1948, progress caught up with it again. Silvey's daughter, Mrs. W. A. Speer, age ninety, was moving out, making way for the demolition crews that would raze the house and clear the land for an expressway.

The growth of the Atlanta area suburbs was dramatized when the population within East Point's corporate limits was estimated at 22,000, almost double that of the 1940 census report of 12,403.

Among events of more than passing interest in 1948 was the dedication of the stadium at Morris Brown College. A bowl seating 15,000 fans, it could be enlarged to 25,000 by using temporary stands on the open sides and was equipped with lighting for night games.

The Atlanta Athletic Club, a landmark on Carnegie Way, celebrated its Golden Anniversary in 1948. The club started in 1898 when sixty-seven members petitioned the Fulton County Superior Court for permission to incorporate.

A reflector of Atlanta's growth in new residents moving in from far-off places was the fact that in December Atlanta-area doctors set up an emergency night call service. One hundred thirty-eight physicians, members of the Fulton County Medical Society, were to participate in the night call service. The purpose was to provide medical service, in emergencies only, for newcomers to Atlanta who had not yet established a doctor-patient relationship with a private physician.

Atlanta was a town that valued its trees and flowers and shrubs and those who knew how to grow them. Southern horticulturist H. G. Hastings was honored by the Atlanta Men's Garden Club. He was presented the Johnny Appleseed Award of 1948, a national award sponsored by the Men's Garden Clubs of America.

The Hastings firm still serves the city's gardeners from its headquarters on Cheshire Bridge Road near the northeast expressway.

Another Atlantan known and loved by many received a fine tribute in the newspaper. His name was Joe McElroy and he was ninety-six years old. For many years he had been the "Uncle Remus" of the Joel Chandler Harris

Memorial Association's annual festival. He died on December 21, 1948. Said the *Constitution:*

An ex-slave, "Old Joe" had been a cook supreme for several Atlanta families since he came here as a boy from his plantation home near Griffin. Mrs. Perry Blackshear remembers him when he used to cook for her mother, Mrs. Philip Breitenbucher, many years ago. Later he worked for Dr. and Mrs. E. C. Barnette while Dr. Barnette was pastor of the First Presbyterian Church.

Mrs. Carl Dodd remembers that Joe never missed a meal for 25 years while he worked for her family, the A. P. Hallmans on North Avenue. Joe was a friend of every boy who went to Georgia Tech. Known more often as Joe Hallman than by his real name, McElroy, he was continually taking food to the students in the Tech dormitories "whether they needed it or not." He supervised and made their party refreshments for 35 years. "He was crazy about Tech boys," Mrs. Dodd said.

Selected by the Uncle Remus Association as a perfect Uncle Remus, he graced the float depicting the Joel Chandler Harris character in the parade in honor of the opening of the Disney film, *Song of the South,* and attended the premiere as a personal guest. To Joe it was reminiscent of the parade in honor of Grover Cleveland's election to the Presidency in the 1880's.

Retired for the last fifteen years, Joe still remembered his old families. Said Mrs. Dodd, "To them, and to many others who knew him, and remember him, there will be something missing this Christmas."

OBITUARIES

L. M. Anderson, executive in the Arcade Merchants' Association, died at 72. He was owner of a millinery store in the Arcade and was also active in the Retail Merchants' Association. Thomas H. Bloodworth, retired conductor for the Southern Railway, died at 74. He was well-known on his favorite "run"— Atlanta to Jasper, Georgia. Mrs. Sarah Elizabeth Burnett, who claimed to be the city's oldest resident, died at 102. She was known as "Granny" Burnett. W. Evans Chambers, retired, was formerly Purchasing Agent for the City of Atlanta. He was 67. William J. Davis purchased the Atlanta Title and Trust Company in 1918 and was its president until his retirement in 1938. His memberships included the Atlanta Athletic Club, the Ten Club, and the North Avenue Presbyterian Church. He was a director of the Trust Company of Georgia.

John Robert Dillon, architect and authority on steel construction, died at 77. He designed some of the buildings at Oglethorpe University, at the University of Chicago, and the Atlanta Masonic Temple. Mrs. T. W. Estes, the former Lucille Reeves, died at 53. A school teacher for thirty-one years, she had taught at West Fulton for fifteen years. She was a graduate of Oglethorpe and Bessie Tift College. L. T. (Pat) Gillen, former speaker pro tem of the Georgia House of Representatives, died at 49. He was a graduate of Mercer University and was instrumental in a revision of the Georgia code. J. Dozier Lowndes, an associate of Courts and Company, died at 60. He was the son of Mr. and Mrs. George Lowndes of Atlanta and was a graduate of the University of Georgia. He belonged to the Nine O'Clocks, the Piedmont Driving Club, the East Lake Country Club, and the Homosassa Fishing Club.

Mrs. Richard Charles Martin, who in her first marriage was Mrs. Paul Donehoo, died suddenly in New Orleans. Assistant to her first husband, who was noted as the "blind coroner of Atlanta," she succeeded him at his death and won in an election over forty-seven males. She was the former Margaret Dolvin and had graduated from State Teachers' College and the University of Georgia. She was noted as being the nation's only woman coroner. Arthur E. Sortore, manufacturers' representative and an active member of Holy Trinity Episcopal Church, died at 62. He was active in the Rotary Club. William E. Tippen, retired motorman and veteran employee of Georgia Power Company, died at 77. He was active in the Grant Park Baptist Church.

NOTES

1. Paul W. Miller, *Atlanta, Capital of the South,* American Guide Series (New York: Oliver Durrell Press, 1949).

2. Ibid.

1949

ROUNDING out the decade of the 1940s, Atlantans could look back with considerable contentment at the progress made since World War II, and with confidence that the future would be equally prosperous. Each year the Chamber of Commerce profiled the city in a booklet, "Facts and Figures about Atlanta." In 1946, the first full year of peace after the victory over Germany and Japan, the city's population stood at 350,000—up 47,712 over 1940, a 15.8 percent gain. Going into 1950, the city population was an estimated 363,000. Surrounding counties also had made good gains during the war years. In 1947 Fulton's estimated population was 485,000, up 23.4 percent from 1940; DeKalb's was 110,000, up 26.5 percent; and Cobb's was 56,500, up 43.7 percent. By the end of the decade Fulton's population had moved up to 525,000, DeKalb's to 124,000, and Cobb's to 59,500, for a metro-wide total of 708,500.

Part of Atlanta's appeal was its mild climate. Its altitude, 1,050 feet, is the highest above sea level of any southern city, which helps account for the fact that its mean annual temperature is 62°F, lower than any southern cities except Nashville and Richmond.

Atlanta in 1946 had 104 passenger trains moving in and out every day. By 1950 the trains were down to 92 a day, but Atlanta held its own as the largest railroad city in the South. Atlanta's business lead on the Southeast was unchallenged, but the Texas metropolises of Dallas and Houston exceeded Atlanta in many measures. Atlanta's retail sales in 1946 had totaled $375,257,000, trailing Dallas, Houston, and New Orleans, which registered more than $400 million each. At the end of the decade Atlanta's retail sales were up to $715,505,000, but Dallas and Houston were still leading—Dallas at $759,244,000 and Houston at $857,581,000. In bank clearings Atlanta was tops in 1946, with $9,886,579,000. Its closest rival was Dallas at $8,688,884,300. In 1949, even though Atlanta bank clearings had reached $11,573,153,000, Dallas had slipped past, to lead at $12,259,101,700. In 1946 Atlanta's bonded debt, at $11,187,373, reflected the conservative views of both Mayor Hartsfield and Roy LeCraw. Only Jacksonville and Nashville owed less money. However, by December 31, 1949, the bonded debt had doubled—to $22,349,815, putting Atlanta well up among the big spenders, though still far back of Dallas with its $49,835,386 in bonded debt and Houston with $59,438,642.

In 1946, 95,000 trucks and automobiles were registered in Fulton County. In 1949 this figure had pushed up to 133,694. At the municipal airport 160 mail and passenger planes arrived and departed daily, making 342,700 landings and take-offs a year. On city streets Georgia Power Company operated 540 streetcars carrying 460,000 passengers 61,500 miles a day over 240 miles of route. In addition, Southern Coach Company carried 4 million passengers a year over

124 miles of route. There were 142,532 telephones in town. Atlantans and their visitors could call one of 135 Yellow Cabs, 40 Veterans Cabs, or 116 Cars for Hire.

By 1950 the Georgia Power Company had turned over its street transportation facilities to a spin-off—The Atlanta Transit Company, which now was operating 593 trackless trolleys over 244 miles of route, carrying 370,000 passengers an average of 52,833 miles a day. The growth reflected the effect of an $8 million modernization program involving the largest fleet of trackless trolleys in the world plus motor buses; it was one of the few completely modern transit systems in the nation. In addition, the Suburban Coach Company operated forty-five buses carrying 4 million passengers a year over 124 route miles. Cabs were fewer—Yellow Cab now operated 122, Veterans Cabs had 80, and there were 150 Cars for Hire.

Atlanta as a telephone center was the largest in the South and the third largest in the world, handling 540,000 outgoing calls, 487,000 through calls, and 776,000 incoming long-distance calls each month. A new form of communication came to town in September when WSB, the "Voice of the South," added television service.

In the hustling, bustling postwar years these figures told the story of a bold drive toward the top. By 1950 automobile and truck registrations had jumped past 147,000 from the 95,000 of 1946. But landings at the municipal airport had dropped from 342,700 in 1946 to 180,000 in 1949—a reflection of the decrease in military flights. Air mail in 1949, however, amounted to 2,507,560 pounds, up from the 1946 figure of 1,583,797 pounds.

At the end of 1946, Atlanta had 1,350 factories turning out more than 2,000 different commodities. Going into the 1950s, factories numbered 1,575, turning out more than 3,000 commodities. Manufacturing employed 267,000 workers, mainly in apparel, textiles, and food products.

Waterworks figures and electric meter installations reflected the growth of the city in the first four years after the war. Atlanta's water, the softest and lowest in minerals in sixty major U.S. cities, was drawn from the Chattahoochee, which flows at the average rate of 500 million gallons per day. The Atlanta Water Works, valued at $30 million in 1946, pumped 50 million gallons in an average day—with a maximum capacity of 65 million gallons. Going into 1950, the waterworks was pumping 55 million gallons daily and had increased its capacity to 75 million gallons. Water meters connected had risen from 77,474 to 87,718 in 1950. The number of electric meters had also increased. In 1946, 109,109 were in service; in 1950, 140,417. Georgia Power Company served the city from Plant Atkinson, a huge steam plant near Atlanta turning out 240,000 kw. Plant Yates, a new 200,000 kw steam plant forty miles from Atlanta, would go into service late in 1950.

Natural gas from the Atlanta Gas Light Company was making rapid inroads. In the twelve months ending September 30, 1949, 95,707 homes,

8,971 commercial establishments, and 1,221 industries used more than 33 billion cubic feet of this modern fuel. The number of meters increased from 83,000 in 1946 to 108,000 in 1950.

City General Fund Disbursements in 1946 and 1949 gave a picture of postwar growth. In 1946 the assessed valuation of property in Atlanta was $393,853,444, with an ad valorem tax rate of 16 mills. In 1949 the assessed valuation was $528,707,436 and the millage rate was up to 28.5 mills, though this included 1.5 mills countywide school tax and .5 mills for the Hospital Authority. In 1946 General Fund Disbursements for general government, public safety, conservation of health, sanitation, streets and highways, charities, corrective institutions, education including libraries, recreation, public service enterprises, pensions, and public debt service totaled $14,703,080.45. In 1950 the total was $19,429,449.86. In both years the heaviest expenditures were in education and public safety.

Atlanta was a regional leader in hotel space for convention visitors. In twenty hotels there were just under 5,000 rooms. Visitors wishing to shop could do so in 23,300 shops and stores. There were 330 white churches, representing forty creeds and denominations. Many churches had congregations numbering more than a thousand, housed in magnificent buildings, and the total membership was 175,000. There were also more than 150 Negro churches, with an aggregate membership exceeding 75,000.[1]

The Chamber of Commerce's "Facts and Figures about Atlanta" publication gave an accurate picture of Atlanta's growth since World War II—a modern-day equivalent of the upward surge of the city after the Civil War. But there were many things still to be done, and on December 8, 1949, Elbert P. Tuttle, president of the Chamber of Commerce, outlined a plan designed to "Keep Atlanta Ahead" for the next years and beyond.

Work had already begun on Plan 1, a basic study leading to the development of a master metropolitan plan for the one thousand square miles surrounding Atlanta. The idea was to relate all the elements of the community to each other and to the whole in a well-ordered pattern that would prevent further destruction of existing property values and would create new values. The second point, the development of a coordinated system of local streets, through highways, and bypasses, also was already under way, with the north-south leg of the expressway taking shape. Most important, $24.6 million in city, state, and federal funds was available to continue construction.

Already, said the report, Atlanta had adopted the most up-to-date traffic organization in the nation, combining off-the-street parking for 3,272 cars, curb parking on ten streets, and rush-hour parking bans on those streets. The result was a much faster traffic flow.

Other suggested programs, many already under way, included a continued modernization of the public transportation systems and redevelopment of worn-out fringe areas, with special attention to new Negro residential areas and new industrial areas to relieve a shortage in both fields. Enlarged water, power, gas, and communication facilities were needed, and great progress in providing additional facilities had been made in 1949. The power company had spent more than $11 million; the gas company nearly $3 million, and the telephone company nearly $6.5 million. A railroad belt line, a joint railroad freight terminal, and enlargement of the Union Railroad Passenger Station were in the offing.

The development of the Chattahoochee River basin in combination with the Flint and Appalachicola river systems would provide power, flood control, navigation, recreation, and water supply. Construction of Buford Dam, an integral part of the system, started in 1950. The Fulton County Airport for private flying went into service in 1950, and an east-west 7,500-foot runway was already in service in 1949 as part of the Atlanta Municipal Airport.

Commercial expansion was part of the plan for downtown, with a thousand additional first-class hotel rooms needed—but no progress was reported as 1949 came to an end. On the other hand, great progress was being made in the construction of 500,000 square feet of new office space; a six-story building at Peachtree and Seventh streets would contain nearly 300,000 square feet to house federal agencies. The half-million-dollar reserve Armory was dedicated in 1949, and the Municipal Auditorium Annex with three commodious exhibit halls was opened, financed by city bond funds.

In various ways, the city began to move toward its new personality as an international city. The city's World Trade Council compiled a directory of Georgia's exporters and importers; it was printed for domestic and foreign distribution. The council entertained numerous foreign visitors and promoted the Havalanta Sports Meet held in Havana in 1949—to be held in Atlanta in 1950—and sponsored World Trade Week. At Emory University a foreign trade clinic was held.

In the field of health, the plans were to make Atlanta a great medical center. Medical schools and hospitals in the area would work cooperatively and a new public hospital run by the Atlanta-Fulton County Authority would be constructed. A contract for a new Negro hospital was let in December. Numerous health centers were established, and there was an intensified promotion of health education, with a study made of nursing and convalescent homes. The study, it was held, would lead to the city's being given broader authority and control of such establishments.

Atlanta had a strong interest in the folk who lived on the farms in the surrounding area. The Chamber of Commerce's Farmers Club sponsored the Third Annual North Georgia Farm Improvement Contest in thirty-three north Georgia counties. Forty-five thousand people in 135 rural communities participated in this self-help program.[2]

There was indeed a need for tax revision. An analysis of Fulton County's tax digest and population figures subdivided into geographic areas disclosed that taxpayers of the city of Atlanta and unincorporated Buckhead paid 87.9 percent of the net taxable digest. Indeed, studies showed, they paid more in taxes than they received in services. The Buckhead area paid $2,272,000 in county taxes and received $2,141,000 in county services. Atlanta city residents paid $9,838,000 in county taxes but received only $6,082,000 in county services. Despite this analysis, a joint study of municipal tax rates completed and issued by the Bureau of Government Research and the U.S. Conference of Mayors indicated that Atlanta's overall tax rate was the lowest of any city in the nation having 100,000 or more population. (Atlanta was twenty-ninth in population nationally.)

In other areas than taxes the financial news pertaining to Atlanta was cheerful. James H. Therrell, director of the Atlanta Housing Authority, announced that a 2,000-unit Negro housing project to be developed in the Lakewood area had been given top priority in the new public housing program. (President Truman earlier had approved a $500,000 loan for the Atlanta authority to begin preliminary planning on a new $30 million housing program for Atlanta. The Lakewood project alone would absorb $16 million of this.)

Atlanta's Jewish community was much in the news in this closing year of the 1940s. On November 23 the impressive new Standard Club clubhouse at Brookhaven was dedicated. Less than a month later Jewish citizens of Atlanta celebrated Hanukkah in new surroundings. A million-dollar Atlanta Jewish Community Center was created around a remodeled mansion at 1745 Peachtree Road NW. The center was situated on a nine-acre tract that had been transformed into play areas, softball diamonds, tennis courts, baseball diamonds, basketball courts, and a place for archery. There was also a picnic and barbecue knoll. The remodeled mansion, which in time would be replaced by a bigger structure, already contained a fully equipped nursery school, a game room, arts and crafts workshop, and administration offices.

Members of the Jewish community were not the only Atlantans to find themselves in new surroundings. In 1948 the *Atlanta Journal* moved from its red-brick building at 7 Forsyth Street, where it had operated for thirty-eight years, across the street to the shiny marble walls of 10 Forsyth Street. Here huge new presses, which cost $1.25 million and were capable of turning out 245,000 papers each weekday and 300,000 on Sunday, were installed with windows looking down upon them so that passersby on the street could see them in roaring action. Here, unseen but busy at their special tasks, were nearly a thousand employees, many of them reporters known to most Atlantans. Among them were Wright Bryan, editor of the *Journal;* John Mebane, his assistant; Edwin Camp, associate editor; John Paschall, editor emeritus, with the paper for forty-seven years; and William Cole Jones, assistant editor and distinguished editorial writer. Others included W. S. Kirkpatrick, managing editor; Ed Danforth, sports editor; and Bob Collins, city editor. Telegraph editors Martin Luther and LeRoy Fuss picked up their top stories from Associated Press and United Press wires, and state news editor Ralph Newton and two assistants handled more than one hundred correspondents in counties outside the Atlanta area.

Equally well known to Atlanta readers were the members of the staff who turned out the *Atlanta Journal Magazine* for Angus Perkerson, its editor for thirty-seven years. The move into the new quarters was one month short of the anniversary of Perkerson's first magazine, produced in February, 1912, from a desk in a corner of the city room. One of his early reporters was Margaret Mitchell, who from 1922 to 1926 wrote on widely ranging subjects, from Confederate generals to debutantes.

On September 23, 1949, a statue memorializing the late Eugene Talmadge was unveiled at the state capitol. Talmadge's grandsons, Eugene and Bobby, did the unveiling, and their father, Herman Talmadge, accepted the statue "with great pride and humility as Governor of Georgia and a member of the Talmadge family."

The event of 1949 that struck most deeply into the hearts of many Atlantans was the death of Margaret Mitchell. Franklin Garrett summed up that tragic moment:

The city, the state and the nation were stunned when, shortly after noon on August 16, 1949, word went out to the world that Margaret Mitchell was dead. She had been struck down by a speeding auto, driven by an off-duty cab driver, at Peachtree and Thirteenth Streets, just after 8 o'clock on the night of August 11. The famed author and beloved Atlantan made a gallant five-day fight for life, but to no avail.

On the morning of August 18, at beautiful Spring Hill, Dean Raimundo de Ovies, in the black and white vestments of his office, read the service for the dead from the Book of Common Prayer. Then, as the cortege moved slowly through the streets to the ancient hallowed precincts of Oakland Cemetery, the sorrow and grief of a native populace became starkly evident— in the blank, stricken countenances of everyday Atlantans, white and colored, who lined the curb, and stood on porches, and in windows and doorways, to gaze silently upon the last journey of a great lady. (II,1005)

In his 1977 book police chief emeritus Herbert T. Jenkins told the story of Peggy's fatal injury in shuddering detail. He also described the effect her death had on Atlanta traffic laws, particularly as they applied to cabs and cab drivers:

The death of Margaret Mitchell created an outcry for reform of the traffic laws and enforcement of ordinances regarding cab drivers when it was learned shortly after the accident that Hugh Gravitt (the offduty cab driver) had not only been charged with drunken driving, but had been cited for a total of 24 traffic violations *prior* to the Mitchell accident. The public was outraged. . . .

The Police Department was besieged with calls denouncing Gravitt and demanding an investigation of him and all cab drivers. . . . And police, concerned with Gravitt's safety, moved him to a private area of City Jail for fear that some other prisoner or even an outsider might do him harm. . . .

Atlanta City Government immediately responded to public demands and took steps toward imposing new regulations in a sweeping investigation of 350 persons holding taxi permits, and more stringent laws governing issuance of such licenses was ordered by City Council. . . . Following lengthy investigations by the police, 64 taxicab driver had their permits revoked because of past bad driving records.

Hugh D. Gravitt was indicted on charges of involuntary manslaughter, and on November 15, 1949, the trial began. Gravitt was convicted, and he served four months in jail.[3]

Millions of words were written in tribute to Margaret Mitchell after her death. Most referred to her mainly as the author of *Gone with the Wind;* there were some, however, who spoke of her other contributions: of the Red Cross drives months before the war began, of her charity, of the first cruiser *Atlanta* in World War II that was sunk by the Japanese and her drive to raise the money to build a second *Atlanta,* and, above all, of her unsung aid to hundreds of European civilians caught in the path of war, to whom she sent food and clothing as well as encouraging words. A journalist who was a family friend wrote one of the more revealing tributes.

"She was," he wrote, "for all her friendliness, and for all the fame the book brought her, a shy and unpretentious person." The writer continued:

"I remember . . . the night of the premiere, when the whole town was crazy and the lights were blazing down and the glittering stars from Hollywood were causing the public to swoon. Peggy came in, composed as a tiny queen, pleased of course that her home folks liked the book she had written and the picture that had been made from it, but still as calm and poised as if she were merely another spectator come to see the show. Outside the theater I caught [her husband] John Marsh for a moment and asked him a question or two—hunting for something that could go in the story about the premiere I was doing for the paper. He didn't have much to say. So I told him thanks, and as he turned to go, I said:

"I guess you are pretty proud of Peggy tonight."

And he turned and stopped and laid his hand on my arm, and said:

"I was proud of Peggy before she ever wrote a book."

So I put that in the story, just as he said it, and afterward Peggy wrote me a little note, saying that of all the thousands of words that were written about the premiere, and of all the praise of the critics for her book, the line that touched her deepest and pleased her most was John's simple statement that night as he walked into the theatre before the show.

And all of us who knew her understood how he felt. For we would have loved and respected her for the wonderful person she was, if she had never written a line.

The news of her passing has been told in many nations, in many languages now. And around the world, folk whose hearts she touched through her great novel are calling upon whatever God they believe in to bless and keep her on her journey.

As Mitchell passed on, the movie made from her great book was still going strong around the world. On December 11 the *Constitution* announced that it would be taken off the market for a three-year period beginning December 31, 1949; but in this its fourth reissue, it had played in 13,500 theaters, taking in more than $4 million.

OBITUARIES

Robert Lide, district manager of the Chrysler Corporation, died at 49. Mrs. Evart A. Bancker, the former Cornelia Williams, died at 76. Her father, James Williams, was mayor of Atlanta during Reconstruction, and her husband had been president of Atlanta Lowry National Bank. Mrs. Bancker was a communicant of St. Luke's Episcopal Church. Miss Wilhelmina Schikan, daughter of pioneer citizens and a charter member of St. Anthony's Church, died at 86. Mrs. George Mosley, retired president of the Blosser Enterprises, died at 59. She was a member of All Saints. O. D. Bartlett, widely known realtor and owner of the firm bearing his name, died at 58. He developed the Colonial Homes project and was an active member of First Presbyterian, the Masonic order, and the Shrine. Robert M. Anderson, a retail grocer for many years, died at 57. He was a member of the Sardis Masonic Lodge and Bethel Church. William Manning Smith, a graduate of North Georgia College and University of Georgia Law School, was a well-known practicing attorney. He was early associated with Aldine Chambers.

Mrs. Marcus Loeb, chairman of the board of the Marcus Loeb & Company, where she succeeded her husband, was a native of Germany. She came to Atlanta in 1880 and was active in The Temple, the Temple Sisterhood, the Council of Jewish Women, Hadassah, and the Standard Club. Mrs. L. D. Teackle Quinby, 72, was a daughter of former mayor William A. Hemphill, one of the early owners of the *Atlanta Constitution*. She was past president of the UDC and a graduate of Lucy Cobb. Leroy Webb, lifelong Atlantan, was an assistant probation officer for Fulton County. He was a Shriner, a Mason, and a deacon in the West End Baptist Church. Edgar Roberts, retired executive of Provident Life and Accident Company, died at 62. He was a Mason, Shriner, member of Druid Hills Methodist Church, and the Georgia Division of Order of Railroad Conductors.

All Atlantans mourned the death of a former Atlantan. The Rev. Peter

Marshall, chaplain of the U.S. Senate and onetime minister of Westminster Presbyterian Church in Atlanta, died in Washington of a heart attack. He was serving as minister of New York Avenue Presbyterian Church at the time of his death. C. S. Drennon, vice-president of Drennon Food Products, died at 35. He was a graduate of Tech High, a veteran of World War II, and an active member of Morningside Baptist Church. He was a Mason and a Shriner. Mrs. Mary T. Kinsey died at her home on Ashby Street. She was 102 years old and the widow of a Confederate veteran. She was the oldest member of Park Street Methodist Church.

Mrs. E. Bates Block, née Julia Porter, was the daughter of Fannie Lowry and James Henry Porter, pioneer Atlantans. A graduate of Washington Seminary and the Lebre School in Baltimore, she was presented to Atlanta society on Christmas Day, 1900. In 1908 she married Dr. Bates Block. Mrs. Block was a member of many civic and cultural organizations, including the Atlanta Art Association, the English Speaking Union, the Advisory Board of the Georgia Society of Historical Research, and the High Museum of Art. She was a regent of the Atlanta Chapter of the DAR and had been president of the Atlanta chapter and state vice-president of the Colonial Dames of America. She was a member of the Every Saturday Literary Club, the Atlanta and National Societies of Pen Women, and a charter member of the Georgia Women's Radio Guild.

NOTES

1. Atlanta Chamber of Commerce, "Facts and Figures About Atlanta," (Atlanta, 1947, 1948, 1949, 1950).

2. Atlanta Chamber of Commerce, "Keep Atlanta Ahead" (Atlanta, Dec. 8, 1949, a report by chamber president Elbert P. Tuttle).

3. Herbert T. Jenkins, *Atlanta and the Automobile* (Atlanta: Center for Research in Social Change, Emory University, 1977).

SECTION II

The Nineteen-Fifties

1950

GOING into the 1950s Ralph McGill, editor of the *Constitution*, wrote that "Atlanta is a city that is always moving, yet never in a hurry." An excerpt of his summation, an excellent portrait of the town as seen by a man who had learned to love the place, follows. He pointed out that some cities smell—of acid and smoke, or stockyards, or the marshes and the sea:

But Atlanta! When you come off a plane and stand at the top of the steps and draw in the first breath of air—that's something! Clean and full of hope and welcome. It has a soft dry smell and tastes like a very dry white wine. . . . There are those who call us a Yankee town—it is, and isn't. But it is better off because of the Yankees in it and I hope more of them keep coming. They do the town good. They are part of the leaven that makes us what we are. They come to us full of plans and they walk very fast, even though they are not in a hurry to get where they are going. After a while they slow down their walk, but they keep their plans, having learned that in Atlanta they can take time to live and still get things done. Atlanta is a Georgia city, a Southern city and a Yankee city. It attracts people from the small towns, the big towns and the farms. It brings them in from the North, East and West. It brings them in from foreign countries. I like Atlanta because of the fine citizens from Greece and their kids; the Syrians who have been fine for us, too; and the smaller number of other nationalities including the Chinese and some others from Oriental lands. They fit right in. They are one reason for our tempo—a blend of the South, the Yankees and a pinch of foreign herbs—that gives us a tempo faster than the rest of the South—but not too fast.

I like it because we are not an old city. Atlanta is not a city of magnolias and mockingbirds looking at the past and mourning for it. It never was that sort of a city. It wasn't too long ago—1837—there were Indians not far from Peachtree. We are a city always looking ahead and going places. We were that when Sherman came and burned the town—we were a frontier railroad town, a little touchy and hard to handle, but going places. . . .

I like it because it is a busy manufacturing town but one which knows it must be, and wants to be, a part of the transition of the state from the poverty of a one-crop system to one of grasses and cattle and livestock which already has doubled our wealth. I like it, too, because we are going ahead to make a channel up the Chattahoochee so that someday we shall confound those friends who have said that if Atlanta could suck as hard as she could blow she'd have the Atlantic Ocean at her doorstep. We are going to do just that. Plenty of us living now will see ocean barges at our doorstep in the years ahead. [This dream, of course, never came to pass.] . . .

I like it because it is beginning to be a great medical center . . . because it reads books—because it has an art gallery and artists; because it has good cooking and fine cosmopolitan restaurants as well as good luncheon places for busy people who want good food quick.

I like my town, too, because since the war it has kept on growing and planning. It is building new streets and it is cooperating with the county to do that job and others. Atlanta isn't going to stand still. It is in no frenzy or precipitate rush.

Atlanta—DO I like it? Man, I love it. It is my home town and I don't see much wrong with it and what is wrong we know how to fix.[1]

Though McGill's description of his city was a bit excessive, it was not too grossly exaggerated. The town could look back with pride on what had been accomplished in 1949, and look forward with confidence to 1950 and the years beyond. One important item concerning the citizens was a seven point plan, brought out by the Local Government Commission. Based on a year's study by Dr. Allen Albert, the plan would triple the area within city limits, increase population and reduce taxes. The commission would eventually submit its plan to the General Assembly, and the people would vote on the final product. The commission said the net effect of its proposal would be a reduction of $241,000 in the amount of property taxes then required by both governments. Moreover, it claimed that the plan would insure the people's getting more for their tax dollars.

Keynote of the sweeping changes would be increasing the present area of Atlanta from 35 square miles to approximately 117 square miles. Two new wards would be added. Such an annexation would add about 87,000 to the total city population.

George Goodwin of the *Atlanta Journal* described the anticipated changes:

The plan would eliminate duplications of city and county services by definitely assigning specific functions to one government or the other. To the city: police, fire, garbage collection and disposal, inspections, parks and recreation, and airports. To the county: public health. The city would continue its functions of water distribution, sewage disposal, library service, the auditorium, and the office of traffic engineer.

The county would continue to operate courts, public welfare, agriculture, the sheriff, coroner, ordinary, surveyor, and the operation of the almshouse.

Schools and street and road constructions would continue as the functions of the separate governments, but with their territories of course changed by annexation.

Consideration of the plan continued into 1951. Finally the voters did approve the proposals, referred to in the campaign as the "Plan of Improvement," and the long-sought annexation of some areas peripheral to Atlanta came about in 1952.

The refusal of the surrounding area to be "taken in" by Atlanta in the past had been bitter enough, but the most bitter battle of all in the early 1950s was over the long-controversial county-unit system, which had roots in colonial days when the governor was elected by the legislature. Since 1896 the state Democratic party had allowed two delegates for each house member, and each county cast its vote as a unit. But as population increased greatly in some counties and declined or remained static in others, the ratio of county votes was not altered to correspond. Fulton County had only six units for a population exceeding a half-million, whereas a tiny county such as Echols with fewer than two thousand residents received one unit. Naturally, such cities as Atlanta railed against this diluting of the franchise, but to no avail.

Many efforts to break down the system were made, and failed. In 1950 two top-flight lawyers, Morris Abram and Hamilton Douglas, Jr., carried the case before a federal tribunal made up of Judge Samuel Sibley of Marietta, Judge T. Hoyt Davis of Vienna and Macon, and Judge M. Neil Andrews of Atlanta and Rome. Judge Davis and Judge Sibley ruled that the county-unit system was a matter of party politics in the state and therefore of no concern to the federal court. Judge Andrews dissented, holding that it was a violation of the Constitution for a DeKalb County citizen living on one side of Moreland Avenue to have the voting power of five Fulton County citizens living across the street. The case was appealed, and on April 18, 1950, the U.S. Supreme Court by a vote of 7-2 upheld the view that it was a matter for the state to decide.[2] The issue would come back into the public eye in 1952.

Statistics showed that Atlanta was doing well as the new decade began. Home construction reached a new high for Atlanta alone: 10,120 units in 1949, 8,900 of them being single-family homes.

The city could again boast it started off a new year with money in the treasury—some $1.5 million. Fulton County was in fairly good financial shape too. T. Earle Suttles, county tax collector, announced on January 1, 1950, that his office had collected $13.2 million in taxes—more than enough for the tentative 1951 budget, which called for $10,786,999.

Payrolls in Atlanta were higher by $7,884,000, the result, according to the Chamber of Commerce Industrial Bureau, of the many new plants, branch offices, and warehouses that moved into the city in 1949. In 1950, the chamber said, at least fifteen new factories and warehouses were to begin construction.

In the schools the news was both good and bad. More children were staying in school and more were being graduated, according to Ira Jarrell, superintendent of city schools. Atlanta schools at the beginning of 1949 had an enrollment of 60,916 students and a staff of 1,700 teachers. Value of school property had reached $15,296,497, or $300.34 per pupil. On August 19, 1949, many of the high school students and their parents—28,000 in all—gathered at Grant Field stadium, the biggest crowd ever assembled for a high school athletic contest in Atlanta's history. The event was the Seventh Annual North-South Georgia All-Star Football Game, cosponsored by the Georgia Athletic Coaches' Association and the *Atlanta Journal*.

The 1949–50 school year for Georgia Tech saw an enrollment of 13,856 students, an all-time high. Tech official Dr. James E. Boyd attributed the boom to the postwar rush to college by returning veterans.

Dorothy Orr, a teacher with forty-three years' experience in the city school system, was named Atlanta Woman of the Year for 1949—the same year that her school, Kingsberry, was changed from white to black. Mayor Hartsfield announced her selection at the annual banquet. When introduced as Atlanta's Woman of the Year, Miss Orr responded with the 100-year old toast: "To education, the security against oppression. If we have no other legacy for our children, let us bequeath this, for it is wealth that cannot be squandered." Orr, school principal, teacher, researcher, history book author, and true friend of hundreds of Atlanta school children, was cited for "conspicuous, meritorious and outstanding service in the field of education."[3]

The first summer Pops Concert opened July 9 at the Fox and attracted 5,000 music lovers. The program was dedicated to Margaret Mitchell, and Mayor Hartsfield paid tribute to Mitchell by saying: "This program is dedicated to the great lady of the whole world. The closing music is that of the wonderful film made from her glorious book." Albert Coleman conducted the fifty-piece orchestra.

Atlanta's aged streetcars, which had been shunted aside for the new trolley buses, found a new home in Pusan, Korea. Their clang and rattle soon fell with nostalgic impact on the ears of Atlanta soldiers serving in the Korean War.

The year 1950 was significant for Grady Hospital; early in February the hospital began offering a new service. Fulton County judges could commit prisoners with mental problems for treatment, which would be provided by Emory psychiatrists under the direction of Dr. Carl Whitaker. The results of the psychiatric exam would be considered by Fulton's Criminal and Superior Court judges before passing sentence on a convicted person. A few weeks later the Fulton-DeKalb Hospital Authority authorized chairman Hughes Spalding to appoint a joint committee of white and Negro citizens to advise the authority on operation of the new $1.5 million Negro hospital at Grady—though it was made clear that the role of the Negro members would be only advisory. Despite rapidly rising costs the hospital managed greatly to expand its resources while still staying comfortably within its budget during the year. The board of directors adopted a 1951 budget of $2,640,000, of which $649,000 was earmarked for the building fund.

There was, of course, a darker side. Public housing and Grady Hospital development brought into focus both the friendship and the tension that existed between black and white Atlantans in this year of 1950.

In early March Atlanta moved to a Metropolitan Planning Commission to look into the opportunities for civic development for both races that were offered by the National Housing Act. The commission was headed by Robert H. White, Jr., a former vice-president of the Chamber of Commerce and a member of the local government commission. On March 5, 1950, the Federal Housing and Home Finance Corporation announced that Atlanta had been granted $2,705,710 for its Slum Clearance Program. The Atlanta Housing Authority acted immediately. On March 11 it applied for $2,940,000 to support a program that provided for the purchase and clearing of slum areas. The cleared land was then to be sold to private investors for development in accord with a master plan for the city.

Not all plans for slum clearance met with complete approval. In late March of 1950, whites of the Gilliam Park and Woodlawn Avenue area strongly protested the construction of 376 new Negro housing units near them. After a conference at City Hall, the result was a compromise. Developers of the $1.5 million Gilliam Park and Woodlawn Avenue area project agreed to try to buy new land, to allow a greater separation from the white residents in the area.

In other areas whites supported developments for blacks without protest. On May 1, 1950, Fulton County officials dedicated Anderson Park on Anderson Avenue in West End as a new playground for Negroes. The park consisted of eighty acres, a summer playground, ball park, Scout campground, and picnic areas. A new swimming pool and a nine-hole golf course were to be built within the year.

Much of the growing understanding of the needs of Atlanta's black citizens can be attributed to the efforts of Mayor Hartsfield. In early June of 1950 he asked the City Planning Commission "to give Negro leaders opportunity to be heard where all questions of policy and overall planning concerning Negro areas are involved." A group of Negro citizens had called on the mayor, urging his support. They represented the Atlanta Business League, whose housing committee consisted of T. M. Alexander, chairman, J. W. Dobbs, W. H. Aiken, R. A. Thompson, J. H. Calhoun, and A. T. Walden.

By the end of the first quarter of 1950, Atlanta and Fulton County had spent half of the $50 million in bonds the city had voted in 1946. The program had included work in traffic, schools, sewers, parks, health, library and auditorium improvements.

Matters of lesser importance than street widening, parks, hospital buildings, and slum clearance occupied the minds of many Atlantans in this brisk and busy year—for example, the city's need for elephants. In April 9, 1950, Asa Candler, Jr., contributed $3,000 toward the purchase of a $5,000 elephant that was to take up residence at the Grant Park Zoo. The remaining $2,000 came from school children and other sources.

In one of the big business events of 1950, James C. Cox, former governor of Ohio and owner of newspapers in Dayton and Springfield, Ohio, and Miami, Florida, bought the *Constitution* and merged it with the *Journal* under the name of Atlanta Newspapers, Inc.

News and editorial operations of the two papers were kept entirely separate, so the news and editorial staffs could give their own interpretation to events. The *Journal* magazine section under Angus Perkerson became the *Journal and Constitution Magazine*. Though the editorial, typesetting, and photographic work was done in the Atlanta office, the magazine was printed on high-speed rotogravure presses in Louisville, Kentucky. Each paper had its separate women's department, sports department, and editorial department, but the engraving, composing, stereotyping, pressroom, mail room, circulation, photo, research and marketing, reference, and business departments served both papers.

This huge and complicated operation functioned smoothly. Six huge presses, each able to print up to 52,000 64-page newspapers an hour, turned out 202,000 *Constitution*s a day and more than 250,000 *Journal*s. More than 90,000 tons of newsprint traveled through the presses each year, printed with 250,000 gallons of black ink and thousands of gallons of colored ink.

OBITUARIES

Judson P. Bowen, an executive of Penn Electric Switch Company, died at 47. He attended Tech High and was a member of the board of stewards at Peachtree Road Methodist Church. C. J. Brownlee, dance band leader well known to New York, Miami, and Atlanta audiences, died in East Point. G. T. Butler, 77, had served as an Atlanta police officer for thirty-four years. He was a member of Gordon Street Baptist Church. Henry Otis Camp, U.S. marshal for the Northern District of Georgia, died at 69. Fred Cockrell, president of the Atlanta Cotton Exchange and owner of a brokerage firm, died while attending a meeting in Texas. D. Felton Collins, retired railroad conductor for the N.C.&St.L., died after forty-two years of service. He was 71 and a member of the Baptist Tabernacle.

John Faith, onetime Atlanta councilman and alderman and longtime employee of Remington Typewriter Company, died at 80 at the family home. He was a member of Martha Brown Methodist Church. M. C. Farrar, 66, postmaster of Avondale Estates for fifteen years, was also manager of a general store in Scottdale. Mrs. E. W. Farrior, wife of the district manager of Eli Lilly & Company, was a member of Peachtree Christian Church and the Druid Hills Country Club. Harold M. Heatley was a nationally known architect who designed several stores for Davison-Paxon, including those in Macon, Columbus, and Augusta. He had been in business for himself and was also associated with Henry Toombs. W. H. Johnson, chief engineer for Hurt Park, died at 63. He specialized in the construction of airports and was a member of the Cathedral of Christ the King. Ella Parker Leonard, English teacher at Murphy High for twenty-three years, was a graduate of Wesleyan College and had taught at Brenau.

Rev. Charles A. Linn, 59, Lutheran pastor and church official, died of a heart attack at his home. He was president of the Georgia and Alabama Synod of the Lutheran Church in America. He was a graduate of Roanoke College, Newberry College, and Hartford Theological School. Mrs. Marvin M. McCall, Sr., active in the DAR, the UDC, and the Methodist church, died at the home of her daughter, Mrs. Lloyd Chapin. She and her sister, Mrs. D. P. Holland, presented the altar to the Episcopal Church of the Epiphany as a memorial to their father, J. C. Higgins. John Newton McEachern, chairman of the board of Life Insurance Company of Georgia, died at 59. McEachern made his home in Powder Springs, where his Gladstone Farms produced show horses. He had been active in Life of Georgia all his adult life, and he had directed an expansion program that spread operations of the company into eleven southern states. He attended Atlanta public schools and Georgia Tech and was a founder of the Atlanta Historical Society. He also belonged to the Masons, the Shriners, the Piedmont Driving Club, the Capital City Club, and First Methodist Church. His mother, Lula Dobbs McEachern, died in May of 1949 and his wife died in June 1950.

Mrs. Rose W. Riley, 84, lifelong Atlantan, was the daughter of pioneer citizens Capt. James R. and Louisa O'Callaghan Wiley. Harry Sallis, a native of Greece, had been a restaurant owner and grocer in Atlanta for more than forty years. Mrs. Parker Sanford, wife of a retired vice-president of the Retail Credit Company, died at 57. Thomas R. Sawtell, retired meat packer and ice manufacturer, had sold his family business in 1910 to the Atlantic Ice and Coal Company. He was an active horseman and member of Central Presbyterian Church. Mrs. I. M. Sheffield, Sr., the former Genevieve Ward Modena and second wife of the cofounder of the Life Insurance Company of Georgia, died after a lifetime devoted to musical pursuits. She was soloist at Second Ponce de Leon Baptist Church. William A. Slate, 82, was a retired railway conductor with fifty-seven years of service to Southern Railway. His last position was conductor on the Atlanta-Chattanooga run. A Mason, he had also been a member of Yaarab Temple for forty-two years.

E. D. Smith, Sr., prominent Atlanta attorney and banker, had been appointed solicitor for the Southern Bell Telephone and Telegraph Company in 1919 and later was made general counsel, vice-president, and a member of the board of directors. After his retirement from Southern Bell in 1942, he became vice-president of the Trust Department of Fulton National Bank, on whose board he had long served. He was a Phi Beta Kappa graduate of the University of Alabama and received his law degree from Georgetown University. Mrs. Sam W. S. Smith, wife of the owner of Smith Grain Company and Snapfinger Farm, died after a year's illness. She had been active in the UDC, the DAR, and the East Lake Garden Club. Mrs. J. P. Stevens, pioneer Atlantan and widow of the founder of J. P. Stevens Engraving Company, died at 95.

She was the daughter of Confederate surgeon and early Atlantan Dr. James F. Alexander. She was a charter member of North Avenue Presbyterian Church and was the granddaughter of Richard McAllister Orme, editor for fifty years of the *Southern Recorder*.

Thomas L. Stokes, a cofounder of Davison-Paxon, Stokes, forerunner of Davison's (now Macy's), died at 79. He was an active Rotarian and a member of the Atlanta Retail Merchants Association. He was the father of Tom Stokes, Washington correspondent and author. He was a longtime member of West End Baptist Church. Henry Shelton Stringer, retired railroad engineer, had been with Southern Railway over fifty-five years. He most recently had served on the Florida Sunbeam and the Royal Palm Special. A Mason and a Shriner, he was also a member of Sylvan Hills Baptist Church and the Brotherhood of Locomotive Engineers. He was 71. Mrs. Laura Tallulah Ward, widow of Dr. A. C. Ward, pastor of Oakland City Baptist Church, died at 90. Charles G. Warren, real estate broker and dealer in roofing supplies, died at 76. William Eugene Wilburn, state Parole Board member and a leader in the state Democratic party, died at 64. He had been chairman of the Highway Board under Gov. Eugene Talmadge.

Sarah Waldo Wilson, widow of Arthur McDermott Wilson, was the daughter of pioneer Atlantans Annie Mae Slaton and A. L. Waldo. She was a guiding force for the Colonial Dames, the DAR, the UDC, the Uncle Remus Memorial Association, and the Huguenot Society, and she was an honorary member of the Old Guard of the Gate City Guard. Samuel F. Wood, chief clerk of the Railway Express Company, died at 60. He was a member of Park Street Methodist Church.

NOTES

1. Ralph McGill, "What I Like About Atlanta" (Atlanta: Chamber of Commerce, 1949).
2. Ben Fortson and Carroll Hart, *Georgia's Official and Statistical Register 1973–74* (Atlanta, 1974).
3. Woman of the Year of Atlanta Collection, Atlanta Historical Society.

AND so Atlanta moved on into 1951, its citizens confident that all
would be well in the coming year. And in most cases this was true. On
January 10 Capital Airlines inaugurated its first nonstop flight,
northbound to New York City. Mayor Hartsfield christened the four-engine
Lockheed Constellation "The Atlantan" by pouring a two-foot bottle of
Coca-Cola over its nose. Capitol Airlines president J. H. Carmichael looked
on. Forty-two passengers made the flight in the 47-passenger plane. Prior to
the flight of the nonstop southbound trip from New York, there was a similar
ceremony at LaGuardia Field, with former Postmaster-General James A.
Farley, now an officer of Coca-Cola Export Corporation, as the principal
figure.

Delta Air Lines, which in the years just after the war had had financial
and labor problems as well as two tragic accidents, by 1950 had begun to
show strong signs of the vigor that was to characterize it in years to come.
Profits were up, and 637,386 passengers were carried in 1950 as compared
with 525,839 in 1949—a gain of 21 percent. Based on this record, Delta directors in March authorized the purchase of ten Convair-liner 340 transports, for
delivery in 1952. The planes cost an estimated $6 million. The financial prog-
ress shown in 1950 continued in the first quarter of 1951. Passenger business
gained 47 percent, and the net profit for the quarter was $710,819. The rise in
business continued, and third-quarter figures were 31 percent above the same
period of 1950.

Eastern Airlines was also doing well. In November it reported net earnings for the first nine months of $3,980,993, as compared with 1950's net
earnings of $1,746,000. This was an increase of 123 percent over 1950 and was
the seventeenth year that Eastern had shown a profit.

While Atlanta's airlines were pushing onward and upward steadily, bus
traffic was also increasing, and in November Atlanta's City Council gave
approval for the construction of a new $450,000 motor bus terminal on Spring
Street.

The increase in business in nearly all fields was reflected in the tax di-
gests. In August Fulton County announced a net increase of nearly $40 mil-
lion in taxable assets over the 1950 figures, and DeKalb County's tax digest
for 1951 was $18,452,963 ahead of the previous year. Tax Commissioner
W. Fred Nash told the *Journal* on August 2 that the 1951 total was
$114,738,860 compared with $96,280,895 for 1950.

The Atlanta YWCA was also prospering under the presidency of Mrs.
Joseph C. Read, Jr. The organization celebrated its fiftieth anniversary in
Atlanta by moving into a new building on Edgewood Avenue and Ivy Street.

The Atlanta Speech School began its fall 1951 term in a new location. In
the Sunday *Journal-Constitution* on October 14, 1951, Margaret Turner told the

story of the Junior League and its years of service to the deaf children of Atlanta:

On a hot June day thirteen years ago a line of anxious parents and small children crowded the long hall of a downtown building. They were hopeful of what might lie beyond the door of the new Speech School just opened by the Atlanta Junior League. . . .

Today deaf children and those with halting speech have within their reach the most complete school and clinic for speech and hearing defects in the entire South.

A far cry from its humble origin, the Speech School began its 1951 fall term in the palatial old home of the late J. J. Haverty at 2020 Peachtree Road, recently purchased by the League. It has an aural rehabilitation clinic open to anyone in need of having his hearing tested and has been carefully planned by scientists from the leading medical centers in the United States. . . .

"We visited the finest clinics in the country before we decided definitely on our new equipment," Mrs. William G. Hamm, founder of the Speech School, said. "We now have a place where the large number with hearing loss (an estimated 60,000 in greater Atlanta) can be accurately tested and proper hearing aids recommended, if needed, and treatment provided."

Mrs. Hamm, who has worked feverishly for the development of this program, stressed that no charge is made to anyone having a hearing test at the clinic. . . .

Mrs. Edwin McCarty, lifetime board member and finance chairman, says that in addition to the $125,000 paid for the building, the League has spent an additional $80,000 for remodeling and new equipment. The annual budget of $60,000 for operating expenses of the school comes from profits of the Junior League Nearly New Shop and the League's endowment fund.

Last year the Speech School gave training to more than 800 children and adults; it is expected to train at least 1,000 this year under the new setup.[1]

The year was an exciting one for the league in other ways. The Nearly New Shop, founded by Mary Elizabeth Schroder, president of the League in 1949–50, and Anne Carr, ways and means chairman, netted $13,995.85. For the fifth consecutive year the League joined with the Music Festival Association in sponsoring the Metropolitan Opera in Atlanta, netting $10,583.69 from advertising in the programs, and at the High Museum of Art the League sponsored the Southeastern Art Exhibit. All income earned by the League was used to support not only the Speech School but other community services—Egleston Hospital, Crawford Long Hospital, the Tuberculosis Society, Hillside Cottages, the Red Cross, and the Community Fund.[2]

Another handsome old Atlanta home, the white colonial Cator Woolford mansion on Ponce de Leon Avenue, was put to a useful public purpose when it was renovated and equipped with an elevator to become the first child rehabilitation center in the South. The Cerebral Palsy School moved in in

March. (In later years the mansion was leased to the Atlanta Hospital Hospitality Home, which provided lodging and meals for families and friends of patients in Atlanta hospitals who came from outside the Atlanta area.)

Several public functions expanded in 1951. In June the Atlanta Waterworks Department dedicated its new $350,000 construction and distribution building. A new city-county Public Health Department was created and Dr. Roy W. McGee was elected commissioner. On Sunday, July 1, the new Fulton County Juvenile Court facility was dedicated. It contained not only courtrooms but a detention home where young prisoners could be kept separate from older and more experienced felons. The new building was located in the immediate rear of the Courthouse, at the intersection of Central Avenue and Mitchell Street. The Fulton County Juvenile Court was founded in 1908 as a children's division of the Superior Court.

Schools and school people were, of course, in the news. Devereaux F. McClatchey who had served as a member since 1937 was elected president of the Atlanta Board of Education on January 2, 1951. He was an attorney and a graduate of Emory Law School. In the fall, Atlanta school superintendent Ira Jarrell reported that the enrollment figures for September, 1951, showed 73,588 students enrolled in Atlanta and Fulton County schools—up by 3,755 over 1950. The increase included 2,784 white students and 991 Negro students.

Integration of Atlanta's public schools was still a decade away, but on the college level Negroes were pressing, quietly but firmly, for admission to Emory. The reaction of Emory students was divided. Students at the Candler School of Theology favored the admission of blacks. However, their dean, H. B. Trimble, announced after the student council poll that "there are no plans afloat to admit Negroes to the School of Theology." Student council members in a joint statement said: "We think we are morally obligated to make the opportunity for equal education in religion available here. We are tired of giving first class propaganda to communism by continuing our failure to practice what we preach." A month later, in March, the Lamar School of Law at Emory voted unanimously against admission of Negroes to any graduate school at Emory. State law at that time provided that any private school which accepted a student of other than the white race would lose its freedom from state taxes. This obviously applied only to integration of blacks, for Emory and many other colleges had Oriental students.

It was ten years, however, in 1962, before the bars were let down and two black women were admitted to Emory University School of Nursing. (According to Emory historian Dr. Thomas H. English, the thirty black nurses who graduated from Grady Hospital Nursing School in 1951 were not connected with Emory University and they did not endanger the university's tax status.)

The courts accepted blacks as jurors before the schools accepted them as students. In September of 1951 the DeKalb County jury commission asked DeKalb citizens and civic groups to submit the names of Negroes to the commission, in order that these names might be placed in the grand jury, or trial jury boxes. This was in obedience to an order by Judge Clarence Vaughn and Judge Frank Guess of the DeKalb Superior Court, who had ruled that blacks henceforth should sit on juries in DeKalb County.

In mid-July four Negroes, seeking to test the ban on their use of city parks, sought admission to Bobby Jones Golf Course and were denied entry by the pro, Bill Wilson. Their response was to take their case to federal court, basing their suit on the Fourteenth Amendment and federal civil rights laws. The four were Dr. D. H. Holmes, his sons Oliver W. and Alfred F. Holmes, and Charles Bell, a real estate dealer.

Progress in opening up the city to smoother flowing traffic continued steadily in 1951. On April 17 Colonel Mose Cox, engineer for the joint Atlanta-Fulton County Bond Commission, spoke to a group of traffic experts and civic leaders at the Capital City Club. He told them that 10.5 miles of the Metropolitan Expressway System had been completed, or was under contract, at a cost of $22 million—and that 87 miles could be completed by 1955 at a cost of $48 million. In late July, Colonel Cox reported that state and federal authorities had agreed to provide $400,000 to purchase the right-of-way for a 3.4-mile northeast leg of the expressway.

Sears Roebuck caused a mild stir in the business community when it announced plans to build a second complete department store in Atlanta. The new facility would cost more than $3 million and would be located at the corner of Gordon and Ashby streets in West End.[3]

The big business news of the year, however, came from the radio and TV stations. By the end of February, 1951, there were 20,000 TV sets in Atlanta, and three tall new towers were rising above the city, or were under construction, as WSB-TV, WAGA-TV, and WCON-TV strove for greater range that would give them wider coverage. WSB radio, the "Voice of the South," had been the first radio station in the South and it became the first TV station in the Atlanta area. It had presented its first audiovisual program on Wednesday evening, September 29, 1948, and now in March of 1951 it became the NBC affiliate, sending out its signal over a new tower 550 feet high.

WAGA-TV began operating shortly after WSB, its tower rising 499 feet above ground. WCON-TV's tower would eventually top them all, according to the station's owner, the *Constitution*. It would rise 1,056 feet above the ground, making it the highest tower in the world.

All TV and radio stations in Atlanta had something exciting to look at and talk about on August 27, 1951. On that date the city welcomed home Dorothy Kirby, who after thirteen years of striving had won the National Amateur Women's Golf Championship. Crowds greeted her at the Chattahoochee River bridge, and she rode from there to City Hall in an open car with Bobby Jones—"The King of Golf." She was welcomed officially by Mayor Hartsfield, who had proclaimed this "Dot Kirby Day," and by Governor Herman Talmadge.

In fields other than golf Atlanta women made their mark. In politics Mrs. S. Robert Norsworthy of Decatur defeated a three-term city commissioner to become what was believed to be the first woman to serve on a municipal governing body in greater Atlanta. She received 1,011 votes to 642 for attorney Roger Bell. In journalism, *Journal* reporter Margaret Shannon won the Georgia Associated Press newswriter's award for 1950 for a series of fifteen articles on the improvement of Georgia schools.

One school showing a new vitality in 1951 was the High Museum's School of Art, which in early January changed its name to the Atlanta Art Institute. The school originally opened in 1926 in two rooms of the High Museum, and by 1951 it had grown to more than a thousand students. According to Robert S. Rogers, director of the institute, who along with artist Ben Shute was one of the most effective teachers during the quarter-century of growth, the executive committee of the Atlanta Art Association felt that "the growth of the school merited a name of its own which would serve to identify it with the Atlanta Art Association."

On June 18, 1951, *Atlanta Journal* writer, later editor, Jack Spalding published an impressionistic account of Atlantans and their longtime mayor, describing the mayor as a "prototype of his constituents." Spalding said:

The character of the citizens largely determines the quality of their government and because Atlanta fundamentally is a white-collar heaven whose citizens pay their bills, love their homes, fear the Lord and respect the law, the city government is what it is.

The average Atlantan, according to William B. Hartsfield, the city's white-collar mayor, is several degrees above the average citizen of most large American cities.

He brings home a decent paycheck, shares ownership of his home with a mortgage company, admires a good salesman, wants his children to go through college, prefers stability to excitement and probably is proud of being an office worker.

His life is an even one. He expects no hurricanes or earthquakes from nature, his boss, his neighbors, his church or his government. His social habits are discreet, and visitors from rowdier climes find him a sound, if dull, fellow.

This devotion to the American middle-class ideal on the part of the electorate sent Bill Hartsfield into the city hall in 1937 when the city was bankrupt, and with one short exception he has been there since.

His ability to bring something resembling corporate order to a political entity is widely admired by the managers and salesmen who are the main economic force in the city, and his easy charm, his ready wit, captivate enough of the rest of the voters to keep him in power.

The mayor also is straightforward in the best business tradition. The way he puts his foot in his mouth, his occasional lack of finesse, and his fondness for a direct answer when an indirect one is indicated, makes him a lot of enemies, but saves him a lot of time.

"I've got some swell enemies," he says, "but I've also got some swell friends."

In a city of salesmen, the mayor is something of a supersalesman himself. When the president of a national concern visits his Atlanta branch, the mayor can be counted on to greet him, and impress him with the vast potential of the region served by the city. An hour with the mayor has been described as more effective than all the promotion literature the Chamber of Commerce has put out since its foundation. . . .

Mr. Hartsfield took over the mayor's office from James L. Key. Mr. Key had been a great mayor, but the combination of the national depression and the mayor's poor health had brought Atlanta to a state bordering on anarchy.

There was around $3,000,000 in floating debt, about half of it in relief bonds, the banks had refused the city further credit, and employes were being paid in scrip. There also was strong evidence of corruption, particularly among the police.

The new regime's first act was to call in the bankers and draw up a model budget law. Generally speaking, it prevents Atlanta from spending in any one year more than 99% of the preceding year's income. This law has worked beautifully.

For the last fourteen years the city has operated in the black, and its long-term obligations are regarded as very tasty things indeed by the nation's bankers and bond buyers.

Born five blocks from Five Points, and a resident here all his life, Mr. Hartsfield may be said to be in tune with the desires of his fellow townsmen, and often knows what they want before council does.

While still an alderman in 1926, and long before a lot of people thought aviation was here to stay, he sponsored the municipal development of Candler Field, and his airmindedness has meant much to the city.

For this particular project, he became the first politician to win the Chamber of Commerce's Certificate of Distinguished Achievement. He received the same award later, after the premier of *Gone With The Wind*.

Mr. Hartsfield was re-elected for another four-year term in 1949. He already has served longer than any other mayor in Atlanta's history. Whether he will go on and on forever is not certain.

His tenure would not last forever, but it did stretch for another decade. Probably the most important civic achievement of 1951 in all its variety was brought about by the Local Government Commission, which formulated and won public approval of the Plan of Improvement, and the Fulton and DeKalb County legislatures, who after years of controversy and misunderstanding finally wrote the plan into law. When the Local Government Commission began its work, opposing factions, the *Atlanta Journal* reported, faced each other in an apparently insuperable deadlock as to what might be done to eliminate duplication and overlapping to improve services and to effect economies in Atlanta and Fulton County. As beneficial as the plan might be, its potential was limited from the outset because DeKalb County legislators would not allow their county to be included in any annexation or service realignment. Consequently, a significant portion of metro Atlanta would not be affected by the plan.

For many years every effort to extend Atlanta's corporate limits to cover an area comparable in some degree with the physical growth of the metropolis had been blasted. Then in 1949, through the leadership of Representative Luther Alverson, the legislature established the Local Government Commission and selected its personnel. The citizens on the commission, serving without pay, employed capable research men to obtain all pertinent facts and worked out a plan that provided for a major extension of Atlanta's city limits—but only on condition that it be accompanied by a rational allocation of responsibilities and burdens between city and county. Under the guidance of the commission, when the plan was explained in detail, the people in the affected areas gave it their approval. They voted for the plan in an advisory referendum—and ratified conditional amendments to carry out certain of its details. The plan was approved by the public and the legislature by February of 1951. The commission that had brought about this incredible act of agreement between warring factions disbanded and its members went back to managing their own affairs. Leaders of the commission were Elfred S. Papy, who began the work and was forced by illness to relinquish his post, and Dr. Allen Albert, who succeeded him as chairman. The other members were F. M. Cannon, Kelsey D. Howlington, A. C. Lawrence, Douglas McCurdy, Arthur Pew, Jr., and Malcolm A. Thompson.

Most of the legislative agreements the commission had worked out took effect on January 1, 1952. Wrote Albert Riley of the *Constitution* on that date: "The new year 1952 brought into being at 12:01 A.M. Tuesday a new and greater Atlanta. . . . The City of Atlanta tripled its area to 118 square miles and added approximately 100,000 new citizens to make its population 428,299, based on the 1950 census. Thus in one gigantic stride, the City broke the rusty chains of corporate limits that had restricted its growth for twenty years. It was one of the truly great moments comparable almost to the city's rise from the smoldering ashes Sherman left behind him. . . ."

OBITUARIES

Clarence Bell, retired judge of the Civil Court, was the son of George L. Bell, judge of the Superior Court and the grandson of Hiram Bell, a former U.S. representative. A graduate of Boys High and the University of Georgia, he read law with the late Judge Charles L. Pettigrew. He was appointed to the bench in 1928 after having practiced with Frampton Ellis and was retired in

1948. He was a member of Peachtree Road Methodist Church and Sardis Masonic Lodge. Jesse Love McLure, 96, of Fairburn, was survived by eighty-four descendants. He was one of Campbell County's oldest citizens. William C. Haire, Sr., was retired traffic manager of Western Union and had been a resident of Atlanta for more than fifty years. Charles Thomas Wurm, 90, well-known musician who was affiliated with the First Baptist Church, had been in Atlanta since 1872. He was connected with the southern department of the Royal Queen Insurance Company. Mrs. James Alva Walton, 55, the former Laura McClellan, was a granddaughter of General George B. McClellan, commander of the Army of the Potomac in the Civil War. She was a graduate of Agnes Scott and the University of Georgia and was a member of Inman Park Presbyterian Church. Mrs. Montgomery Folsom, 90, the former Frances Edna Crost, had six brothers in the Confederate Army. She and her husband, a writer for the *Constitution*, were close friends of Henry Grady and named their second child for him.

Dr. Julian G. Riley, 51, was one of the city's outstanding surgeons and a graduate of Emory Medical School and the University of South Carolina. Chief of surgery at St. Joseph's Hospital, he held memberships in the Nine O'Clocks, the Piedmont Driving Club, the Capital City Club, and the Peachtree Golf Club. He attended the Cathedral of Christ the King. Dr. J. Gaston Gay, 53, was an authority on thyroid gland operations. He was a graduate of the University of Georgia and the Johns Hopkins University. He was a member of First Presbyterian Church and the Piedmont Driving Club. Princess Donna Eugenia Ruspoli, 81, was a sister of Martha Berry and Mrs. J. Bulow Campbell, and daughter of Confederate Army colonel Thomas Berry. Her first husband was Henry Burton, head of the American Snuff Company, and her second husband was an Italian nobleman. She owned the historic castle of Nemi in Italy. Dr. Charles William Daniel, 76, was former pastor of First Baptist Church and had been president of the Southern and Georgia Baptist Conventions. Dr. Claude A. Smith, 77, was world famous for his research on hookworm. He was pathologist at Grady Hospital and city bacteriologist for many years. Dr. Charles G. Giddings, Sr., 89, had practiced medicine in Atlanta for more than fifty years and was the father of Dr. Glenville Giddings. Mrs. Julius L. DeGive, widow of an Atlanta investment executive, was the former Gertrude Louise Westmoreland. Her grandfather, John Westmoreland, founded the Atlanta Medical College. Arthur Heyman, 84, had been a practicing attorney in Atlanta for more than half a century. He belonged to Phi Beta Kappa, the Hebrew Benevolent Congregation, and the Standard Club.

Rev. John Franklin Blackburn, 92, died at the home of his daughter in West End. As a child he lived next door to Abraham Lincoln in Springfield, Illinois, and remembered being bounced on the great man's knees. Blackburn was the representative in Atlanta for the Congregational Publishing Society, which sold religious literature. Orman L. Jernigan, son of pioneer Atlantans, was founder of the Lester Book and Stationery Company and retired after more than fifty years as a dealer in books and stationery. Mrs. Thomas Richards, the former Emma Johnson, had been an employee of the Coca-Cola Company for more than thirty years and was secretary to Harrison Jones. Annie Forsyth, 88, was the oldest living member of the First Presbyterian Church and was active in the Pioneer Women and the Ladies Memorial Association. Her parents came to Atlanta in 1851 from Glasgow, Scotland. Mrs. Ella Buchanan Gunn, 80, had been one of the South's leading hat designers for more than fifty years, having started her business in Atlanta in 1890. She was a member of Kirkwood Methodist Church. Charles Edwin Shepard, 80, was a retired executive of the Gulf Oil Corporation and had been in the petroleum business for fifty years when he retired in 1948. He was active in Boy Scout work and belonged to Rotary, the Piedmont Driving Club, the Capital City Club, and St. Philip's Cathedral.

Dr. John W. White, 88, practiced medicine in the Oakland City section for more than sixty years. He was a graduate of the Eclectic College of Medicine and was a member of the Fulton County Lunacy Commission. William E. Arnaud, 72, attorney and musician, was choirmaster and organist at All Saints Episcopal Church for twenty-four years. He was often called the "godfather of the Atlanta Symphony." Maj. Graham Johnson, 73, had been a military aide in the White House to President Taft. His memberships included Piedmont Driving Club, the Capital City Club, and the Chevy Chase in Washington, D.C. Dr. John Moore Walker, rector of St. Luke's Episcopal Church in Atlanta, was a native of Macon, Georgia. He was ordained in 1914 and began his work in the Diocese of Atlanta in 1931. In April of 1942 he was elected Bishop of Atlanta to succeed Henry Judah Mikell. He was succeeded by the Very Rev. John B. Walthour, who died in 1952 after less than a year as bishop. The Rt. Rev. Randolph R. Claiborne, Jr., then served through the duration of the 1950s.

Edward J. Hardin, 57, a vice-president of Retail Credit Company who had been with the firm since 1922, was a veteran of World War I. He was a member of the Piedmont Driving Club and the Capital City Club. Otho J. Parker, 78, fire chief from 1933 to 1938, had been with the Atlanta Fire Department since 1897. He was an elder at the Gordon Street Presbyterian Church and a Mason. Mrs. Frances Gordon-Smith, a daughter of Confederate general John B. Gordon, was active in Atlanta's civic life and was a member of many patriotic organizations. She was decorated by General Pershing for meritorious volunteer service with the Red Cross in France during World War I. Dr. James Edgar Paullin, nationally known Atlanta physician, 69, was a former president of the American Medical Association. During World War II he was a consultant to the medical department of the Navy. Dr. Paullin had been called to Warm Springs to treat Franklin Delano Roosevelt when the president suffered a fatal stroke. Rev. D. P. McGeachy, Sr., 79, had been minister at Decatur Presbyterian Church from 1918 to 1942. He was a graduate of Davidson College and Union Theological Seminary.

Mrs. Frederick Winship Cole, the former Clara Rawson Boynton, died at 91. Her father established one of the city's first department stores in 1860— Chamberlain, Cole and Boynton. She was educated at Wesleyan College and attended Trinity Methodist Church, founded by her uncle, Atticus G. Haygood. Her husband was the first president of the Georgia Association of Insurance Agencies. Joseph D. Ratteree, a veteran of World War II and a graduate of Emory University, was killed in a PBY crash while on Naval Reserve duty. He belonged to the Nine O'Clocks, the Piedmont Driving Club, the Capital City Club, and St. Luke's Church. Mrs. John J. Woodside, Sr., daughter of pioneer Atlanta citizens, was the widow of the founder of Woodside Storage Company. She was a member of First Presbyterian and a life member of the Woman's Club and the DAR. Twice she served as president of Florence Crittenden Home. Walter Simeon James, Jr., vice-president of Clement A. Evans brokerage company, died at 46. He was graduated from Georgia Tech and Yale and belonged to the Nine O'Clocks, the Piedmont Driving Club, and the Episcopal Church. Mrs. Charles T. Parker, known as "Aunt Sadie," died at 104. She was the city's oldest citizen.

James R. Gray, son of the editor and president of the company publishing the *Atlanta Journal*, died at his winter home in Florida. Albert Rhodes Perdue was president of A. G. Rhodes Enterprises, Rhodes Development Company, and Perdue-Collins Real Estate. He was a member of the board of the A. G. Rhodes Home. His memberships included the Capital City Club, the Piedmont Driving Club, SAE fraternity, and Peachtree Christian Church. Josiah Tyron Rose, 82, was an Atlanta attorney and the city's collector of internal revenue from 1921 to 1933. He was a Civitan, a Mason, and a Shriner. Also he was a member of the Burns Club and St. Mark's Methodist Church. He had been a trustee of the Atlanta Historical Society. Dr. Joseph D. (Jerry) Osborne, 65, was a native of Savannah and a graduate of Georgia Tech and the Atlanta Southern Dental College. He served in World War I as a member of the Emory Unit. He was a member of the Piedmont Driving Club. Dr. William Gilmer Perry, professor of English at Georgia Tech for forty-seven years, died at 74. A graduate of Davidson College, he came to Tech in 1902.

Mrs. Charles J. Haden, the former Annie Llewellyn Bates, noted civic, religious, and social leader, died at her home. She was a graduate of Wesleyan and had served as president of the Atlanta Woman's Club, YWCA, and the Wesleyan Alumnae Association. She was a member of First Methodist Church and many patriotic and social organizations. Frank Troutman, Sr., a member of the legal department of the Coca-Cola Company, died at 51. A graduate of the University of Georgia and the University of Michigan, he had been with Coca-Cola twenty-eight years. He was active in Boy Scout work and the affairs of St. Philip's Cathedral. He was a member of the Piedmont Driving Club. John G. (Jake) Johnson, Jr., member of a pioneer family in the Morningside-Johnson Estates area, died at 51. He operated a garage at Piedmont and Boulevard.

Walter McElreath, chairman of the board of Atlanta Federal Savings and Loan Association and one of the leaders responsible for the business growth of Atlanta over the years, died at 84. As an attorney for more than fifty years, he was an authority on the Constitution of Georgia. Perhaps his greatest achievement was the contribution he made to the growth of mutual savings institutions in the state. He was a director and chief counsel of Life Insurance Company of Georgia. A leader in civic affairs, he had been founder and first president of the Atlanta Historical Society. He was a trustee of the Atlanta Art Institute, and under his leadership the buildings of Grace Methodist Church were erected on Ponce de Leon. Eventually, his estate would go to the Atlanta Historical Society, and McElreath Hall and its beautiful surroundings would stand as a living testimony to his life and his love for Atlanta's history.

Edgar A. Neely, noted attorney, died at 73. Senior Warden at St. Luke's Episcopal Church, he was also active in the Legal Aid Society, the Shriners, the Piedmont Driving Club, and various legal societies. Mrs. George P. Howard, Sr., member of a pioneer Georgia family and long active in civic and religious affairs of Atlanta, died at 81. She was the daughter of Confederate general Alfred Holt Colquitt and was born in Edgewood, a suburb of Atlanta. She had been president of Sheltering Arms Day Nursery, First Methodist Church, and the Alfred Holt Colquitt Chapter of the UDC. Hugh Richardson, owner of real estate and builder of several downtown projects in the city, including the Rialto, died at 82. He attended Southwestern Presbyterian College and in 1894 was graduated from Princeton. He married Josephine Inman, daughter of Hugh Inman, and in 1925 built his home, Broadlands, at Northside and West Paces Ferry Road. He was a member of First Presbyterian Church and the Piedmont Driving Club. Mrs. J. O. Gilbert was the former Kate Johnson and widow of one of Atlanta's pioneer physicians, Jeremiah Gilbert. Mrs. James Osgood Wynn, prominent in civic and social affairs, was the widow of the manager of Prudential Life Insurance Company. She held memberships in many patriotic organizations and was an officer in the Colonial Dames.

NOTES

1. Margaret Turner, *Atlanta Journal-Constitution Magazine*, Oct. 14, 1951.
2. Junior League of Atlanta, *Peachtree Papers*, various 1950 issues.
3. Jouett Davenport, *Atlanta Journal-Constitution Magazine*, Mar. 4, 1951.

AS THE Plan of Improvement began to take effect in the Spring of 1952, Atlanta did indeed become, in Albert Riley's words, "A new and greater Atlanta."[1] And a year later, on Sunday, March 22, 1953, the entire *Journal-Constitution Magazine* was made up of a series of articles titled "Atlanta, An All-American City, Reports to its Citizens." In thirty-two pages of pictures and text it described in detail what happened in 1952, and who made it happen. It was described honestly, not as a journalistic report in detail but as an "advertisement," printed, said Mayor Hartsfield, as a public service to the City of Atlanta. His Honor's goals were clear: "Let us go forward together as citizens of a great city, with pride in the past, action in the present and faith in the future."

The form of Atlanta's city government was still the bicameral body, composed of eighteen councilmen and nine aldermen, representing the city's nine wards. It would not change its form until January 1, 1954, when the number of wards would be dropped to eight. Councilmen as such would disappear, and each ward would be represented by two aldermen. The city at large would elect the president of the Board of Aldermen, who as a "vice mayor" would replace the present mayor pro tem. The legislative function of the new, smaller aldermanic board would be similar to that of the old—to make the laws, appropriate the funds, set the tax rate, adopt the annual budget, issue special licenses, make contracts, and grant franchises. Aldermen would choose department heads, election managers, and members of the public library board. Most of the work was to be done through committees, appointed by the mayor, who would be an ex officio member of each committee or division. The mayor had no vote, but he could veto any action the council took of which he did not approve. His veto could be overridden only by a two-thirds majority.

The most important official action of any year is to set up the annual operating budget. Legally, it could not exceed 99 percent of the actual receipts of the year before. To be sure there would be no deficit, the council generally set a budget of roughly 95 percent of the previous year's receipts. This practice had been followed for fourteen years, and as a result the city in each year had a sufficient cash carryover at the end of the year to operate on a strict cash basis, without having to borrow operating funds from the banks.

The total operating budget of the city for the year 1953 would be $21,957,999. The schools would get the largest share of the city's funds—about 30 percent—and they also had to operate on a sound cash basis.

The three top men in this first year of the Plan of Improvement were Mayor Hartsfield, Councilman R. E. Lee Fields, mayor pro tem, and Alderman D. B. Donaldson, provisional mayor pro tem. Aldermen were E. A. Gilliam, R. C. Ailor, Milton Farris, Raleigh Drennan, L. O. Moseley, Cobb

Torrance, Colie B. Whitaker, and Lester Hardy. Councilmen were Arthur Johnson, R. M. (Bob) Clark, William T. Knight, John A. White, John T. Martin, Douglas Wood, Jimmy Vickers, T. Wayne Blanchard, Ralph Huie, Charlie Leftwich, Dean Callaway, H. I. Sargent, Jesse Draper, Ogden Doremus, James E. Jackson, Jr., Joe Allen, and Robert S. Dennis.

Also important to Atlanta citizens were the department heads who actually ran the day-to-day operation of the city, a task suddenly grown more arduous and more complicated in 1952 with the sudden increase in population and area under the Plan of Improvement. Elected by the council, department heads served four-year terms; exceptions were the police and fire chiefs, who were elected for life so long as their conduct and efficiency remained satisfactory. The superintendent of schools was chosen for a four-year term by the Board of Education, and the library director was elected for an indefinite term by the Library Board.

J. R. (Jack) Gray managed the Atlanta airport, where growth had been phenomenal since the war. More than 32,000 persons were employed there during 1952, for an annual payroll of $18 million. Approximately $6 million had been spent in the previous few years, half from Atlanta bond issue funds and half from the federal government. With this money a new runway system, one of the most modern in the world, had been developed. In 1952, 900,000 passengers boarded airplanes in Atlanta. At least 350,000 passengers a month used the temporary terminal.

J. C. Settlemeyer, head of the Library Department, had charge of the main library, seventeen branches, a bookmobile, and book department stations conveniently located to serve Atlanta and Fulton County. Approximately 1.5 million books were borrowed annually for home use, and the reference department in the downtown library answered more than 150,000 questions a year.

William Wofford, building inspector, headed a staff of fourteen experts who inspected not only buildings under construction but old buildings to be sure that they conformed to the building code so far as safety was concerned. They worked with the Fire Department to enforce fire safety laws and also controlled heating and ventilation systems, slum clearance, and air pollution controls.

J. R. Richardson, the city clerk, was one of the busiest of Atlanta's employees. He had to write minutes of council meetings, furnish copies to all departments affected by an act of council, and record, file, and preserve all original papers in which the mayor and council took official action.

J. C. Savage, city attorney, with his highly competent staff represented Atlanta and all its boards, both as prosecutor and defendant. He passed on the validity of all titles to real estate acquired by the city, prepared or approved contracts, and prepared or assisted in the preparation of all legislation to be submitted to a general assembly.

H. B. Andrews, the land agent for Atlanta, bought and sold all real estate needed by the city for its many operations, doing business of about $1 million a year. This included expansion at the airport, sites for new fire stations, and rights-of-way for the expressway.

Ernest J. Brewer was head of the Purchasing Department, which was also housekeeper for the city, buying everything from aspirin tablets to heavy machinery. In 1952 his office handled purchases totaling $6,371,436. The department also handled the mailing machine for all departments in City Hall, numbering 488,888 pieces of mail.

Karl Bevins's traffic engineers installed 1,800 parking meters in 1952 and put in traffic signal timers at the most complicated intersections such as Lee and Whitehall streets. They built traffic-channeling "islands" at Park Drive and Boulevard and other intersections where the motorist had to be guided along a certain path. The islands also provided a refuge for the pedestrian hurrying to cross at an intersection. For the first time in the city's history, every legal crosswalk in the downtown section was painted. The maintenance of crosswalks, center lines and load lines, truck loading zones, and yellow curbs was a major project of Bevins's department, for they had to be re-painted every four to six months. Atlanta, also for the first time, set up its own sign production and refinishing department. Hitherto, the signs, once they faded, were thrown away and new ones were bought—an extravagance. By law, all money collected from parking meters had to be spent for traffic im-provements such as these. The Traffic Department with its three-point pro-gram of education, engineering, and enforcement touched daily life in many ways. Education was carried out by the press, radio, and TV and by the Police Department, through school safety patrols and driver-training classes in the high schools. The Greater Atlanta Traffic and Safety Council, made up of five department heads and seven private citizens approved by the mayor and serving without pay, passed on engineering principles that could make the greatest return in freedom of movement and safety per tax dollar invested. It put official management on a business basis.

L. A. James, city comptroller, operated a modern centralized accounting system for all nonschool city departments and issued approximately 120,000 salary checks annually.

Riley F. Elder, the municipal revenue collector, in 1952 was given the duty of supervising all tax collections. In his office were the "fi-fa" (tax lien) division, the street improvement collections division, and the cashier's divi-sion. The fi-fa division collected past due taxes and delinquent business li-cense payments. The street division collected for paving, curbing, sidewalks, and construction of sewers and water mains. The cashier's division handled all money that came into the city from any source.

The Municipal Court was divided into two divisions—the General Court and the Traffic Court. Presiding in Traffic Court were Judges Paul Bynum, Wilson Brooks, and J. Frank White, who in 1952 handled 71,500 cases. Pre-siding over General Court were Judges A. W. Callaway and Luke Arnold, who handled cases involving intoxication, disorderly conduct, and code violations. They also sat as commitment judges in cases bound over to county courts or to the grand jury.

The Atlanta Police Department, under Chief Herbert T. Jenkins, was considered in 1952 to be one of the most modern in the country in its personnel training program, its radio control system, and its personnel, which in 1952 was made up of both men and women, black and white. New recruits were trained for eight weeks, full-time, in a program accredited by the FBI Police Academy. The course included instruction in firearms, gymnastics, Red Cross, first aid, traffic control, and all elements of modern police science. Curiously, this modern police headquarters was housed in a building at 175 Decatur Street SE, which was constructed in 1892. Much expanding, remodeling, and repainting had ensued over the years, and civic groups were often impressed not only with its age, but its cleanliness.

The Fire Department, under Chief C. C. Styron, put five new 500-gallon pumpers in service in 1952, and new 1,000-gallon pumpers were put on order. A rescue wagon, manned by trained men, answered the same type of emergency calls as those answered by hospital ambulances. Atlanta firemen were young men—80 percent of them were under thirty-five—and their training in firefighting, fire prevention, and arson investigation had given Atlanta one of the lowest fire rates in the country.

Atlanta also was one of the best lighted cities in the United States in 1952, under the supervision of Dewey Johnson, the city's electrical engineer. In 1952 mercury vapor street lights were installed in the Luckie, Cone, Poplar, Williams and Fairlie Street areas, and the Georgia Power Company was employed to install 1,623 modern street lights for the area brought in under the Plan of Improvement.

Atlanta was also a "well-watered city" under Paul Weir. In 1952 the Water Department engineers were installing eighty-one miles of water mains, serving 6,600 new meters. The department also installed 600 fire hydrants and built a 50-million-gallon-per-day steam centrifugal pump at Hemphill Pumping Station. The biggest pump ever installed by the city, it cost $600,000. A 30-million-gallon steam turbine pump at the Chattahoochee River station was rebuilt at a cost of $126,000. With the development of the Chattahoochee River and the great Buford Dam thirty-five miles north of Atlanta, the city was preparing to serve an Atlanta with a million population.

H. H. Gibson kept a wary eye on the city prison farm, off Highway 42 at Key Road, where city prisoners served their short twenty- to sixty-day sentences working on 350 acres of farm lands and pastures. Built to accommodate 850 prisoners, the prison had 700 workers in 1952. They contributed 92,000 workdays on city streets and parks and produced farm crops valued at $72,000, which was enough to feed half the prisoners for a year. Church services were held in the chapel on Sundays, there were two television sets, and the prisoners were free to have visitors.

Under the Plan of Improvement, the Municipal Planning Commission under Wyant B. Bean studied and made recommendations for an orderly development of the city—and the county also. The Commission recommended where streets should be built and what buildings should be permitted in residential areas.

Carl T. Sutherland was responsible for the Personnel Department, which was recognized throughout the nation for its highly effective merit system. City employees were selected on the basis of merit, and the department sought to establish an equal-pay-for-equal-work system. There were 4,500 employees working under the Personnel Department.

George L. Simons directed the Parks and Recreation Department, whose activities both for whites and Negroes were more extensive than many Atlantans realized. Many yearly citywide projects had become a part of Atlanta life, such as the Kite Contest, the Tulip Festival, the Lantern Parade, the Arts and Crafts Fair, and the Festival of Nations. There were three eighteen-hole golf courses and four nine-hole courses. The department operated ten swimming pools. Visitors from all over the world visited the Cyclorama, the zoo, and the greenhouse and conservatory in Grant Park. Joel Hurt Park at the approach to the city was a mass of color during tulip time, and Plaza Park in the downtown business section was a restful haven for the weary shopper.

Most park programs were for children, featuring box hockey and tetherball tournaments, Easter egg hunts, pet shows, Mother's Day programs, marbles tournaments, Play Day, Nature Week, and Story-Telling Week. Community centers were operated in parks, gymnasiums, and churches. Teen clubs, on the City Youth Council, conducted activities for teenagers and planned citywide social events and activities such as square dancing, folk dancing, table tennis, and arts and crafts.

The Parks Department also maintained and operated historic Oakland Cemetery, where members of noted Atlanta families have been buried since before the Civil War.

One of the less glamorous but most important of Atlanta's departments was that of Sanitation, headed by S. W. Graydon, the chief garbage collector. His other duties included street cleaning, rubbish removal, sewer flushing, and premise inspection. Of 129 city trucks, 103 collected garbage on regular routes with a driver as foreman and three laborers on each truck. Atlanta's sanitary tax rate, at $7 to $8 per year per household, was believed to be the lowest in the nation for a city of 200,000 population. There were 750 employees in the department, which had an annual budget of approximately $2 million. The nation's most modern garbage incinerator, also located in Atlanta, operated at an annual profit of $70,000 realized from the sale of steam and reclaimed cans.

The Construction Department, under Clarke Donaldson, in 1952 installed nineteen miles of curb and gutter, eleven miles of sidewalks, nine miles of resurfacing, and four miles of subdivision paving. The department also installed nine miles of sewer. A total of thirty-four miles of sewer was added to the metropolitan system—DeKalb County installing eleven miles and private contractors thirteen miles. Resurfacing of Ivy, Mitchell, Tatnall and Hunter streets was completed in 1952, and the Virginia Avenue Bridge and approaches were rebuilt by the city and the Southern Railway.

The Motor Transport Division under Homer W. Townsend employed eighty persons, who saw that the city motor equipment kept rolling. Some activities were tire repair, gasoline services, blacksmithing, chassis and engine overhaul, and operation of a complete machine shop. The department's stations at Hunter Street, Hill Street, and North Avenue dispensed more than a million gallons of gas annually. Brooms for the city's street sweepers were also made by this department.

The Municipal Auditorium, under the supervision of R. H. Neibruegge, was an all-purpose structure, used for trade and automobile shows, industrial exhibits, and all types of entertainments from opera to the city's symphony to wrestling matches. More than a million people visited the auditorium each year, and more were expected once a quarter-million dollar air-conditioning system was installed.

Ira Jarrell continued as Superintendent of Schools. Under the Plan of Improvement, thirty-nine schools with a total student body of 18,000 were added to the Atlanta system, bringing the total enrollment past 90,000. The city was participating in a state funded project totaling $7 million. Construction projects were in progress or being planned for new high and elementary schools, both white and black, to take care of an additional 13,000 children expected to come into the system by 1955, with 23,000 more expected by 1960. This meant that additional teachers and equipment would be needed; a future bond issue would provide between $12 million and $15 million. Working to meet these expectations in 1952 were Atlanta Board of Education members J. Austin Dilbeck, president, E. S. Cook, honorary president, and Dr. D. F. Miller, pastor of Druid Hills Presbyterian Church, chaplain. Other members were P. L. Barden, A. C. Latimer, J. C. Shelor, J. H. Landers, D. M. Therrell, and Devereaux McClatchey.

Progressive programs being developed by the board included coeducation in all the schools, the growth and acceptance of community high schools, equal salaries for elementary and high school teachers, and equal salaries for black and white teachers. The teachers' salaries were moved from a previous minimum of $90 a month to a maximum of $231 to the 1952 scale of a minimum of $210 a month and a maximum of $430. The Atlanta School System was going into 1953 busily working out the organization of a special teachers' corps to teach the handicapped. City teachers were in training for this at the Junior League Speech School, Aidmore, Grady Hospital, and the Cerebral Palsy School.

Each school in the Atlanta area now operated its own cafeteria where well-balanced, wholesome and nourishing meals were sold to students at 25¢ a plate.

The city's finances at the end of 1952 were in good shape. Receipts were $28,685,000, most of which (54.68 percent) came from property taxes, and expenditures were $27,850,000, nearly a third of which (32.15 percent) was spent on education. From 1937 to 1952, the first year of the Plan of Improvement, the city did not increase its ad valorem or property tax rate. One board of assessors served both the city and county; Atlanta members were Leo Sudderth, chairman, J. Sid Tiller, W. N. Blankenship, and C. A. Hinson, Jr. Fulton County was represented by Robert Remington, Sam Callaway, and Charles Boynton.

Money that had been raised for capital improvements such as expressways, schools, libraries, parks, aviation facilities, and the auditorium came to a total bonded indebtedness of $29,913,000 in 1952. The legal limit for the bonded debt was $48,249,000. Thus the debt at the time was about 62 percent of the limit set by law. This happy situation gave Atlanta one of the best credit ratings of any city in the entire nation.

In addition to hired professionals and other workers more than one hundred Atlanta citizens served on various advisory examining boards and commissions. Many of the boards represented both Atlanta and Fulton County.

Many things happened in Georgia in 1952 that directly or indirectly affected Atlanta and its people. Celestine Sibley, after a poll of her fellow journalists, listed the biggest events in the *Atlanta Constitution* of January 1, 1953. The number-one news story of 1952 was "Ike." Sibley described the Eisenhower phenomenon: "His campaign brought him to Atlanta in September, the first Republican candidate in many years to invade the Democratic stronghold of Georgia. His election in November pulled the highest Republican vote this state has ever cast—and the day after election he and his family flew straight to Augusta, Georgia for rest, relaxation and the newsmaking conferences which were an early indication of his cabinet selections."

The second most important story of the year impacted most directly on farmers but still affected Atlanta. Sibley explained: "Drought: For two long summer months rainfall over Georgia was either scarce or nonexistent, precipitating what national farm leaders called the 'worst agricultural disaster in 20 years.' Georgia shared heavily in the Southeastern crop loss estimated at $500,000,000. Temperatures soared to 104 in Atlanta and to 112 in Louisville in Jefferson County. Ten persons died in one weekend as a result of the heat and despairing farmers sold off beef and dairy cattle and hogs at a sacrifice because of parched pastures. The blow to agriculture and to Georgia economy generally brought the nation's farm leaders to Atlanta in August to declare an emergency and to plan for disaster area relief loans from the federal government."

The third story on Sibley's list was the controversy over the county-unit election system. "Gov. Herman Talmadge, who won national approval at the Democratic convention in Chicago and was named chairman of the Southern Governors Conference, met his first major defeat at home when his county unit amendment was licked at the polls in November. The measure, bitterly fought out during the summer campaign, would have written Georgia's unique county unit system into the state constitution. It was defeated by a vote of 278,882 for and 309,170 against."

Evidently encouraged by a 1950 decision that upheld the county-unit Democratic primary, the county-unit advocates, led by Talmadge, sought to amend the state constitution to extend the county-unit system to the vote in the general election. Talmadge in his arguments revealed matters that in the years after World War II had become of deep concern to Atlantans, as well as to all Georgians. In a letter sent on September 11, 1952, to the judges and ordinaries of all Georgia counties, Talmadge urged them to vote for Amendment 1, which if passed would write the county-unit system into the State Constitution—thus making it applicable to the general elections as well as the Democratic primary.

"The County Unit System," Talmadge wrote, "stops political machines at each county line. It will keep political power in the hands of the majority of people throughout the state, instead of turning it over to a highly organized group of bloc voters, led by the Negro lawyer, A. T. Walden, within the city of Atlanta."

The opposition to the county-unit system, Talmadge charged, was supported by the *Atlanta Constitution* and the *Journal*, and led by Walden, "because they want to gain political control of our state through manipulation of the bloc voting elements. Then you will see mixed schools within our state, you will see boss rule, through the manipulation of these bloc votes. . . . I urge you to protect the majority of the people of our state from turning their political power and influence over to a group of selfish individuals and organized bloc voters within the city of Atlanta." By "bloc" Talmadge, of course, meant Negro.

Urban Georgians, especially Atlantans, tended to oppose the county-unit method of election because it gave disproportionate clout to rural citizens in lightly populated counties. Leading the fight against the county-unit amendment were Atlantans Judge M. Neil Andrews, chairman of the group, Julian LaRose Harris, associate chairman, and Mrs. William C. Pauley of Decatur, secretary-treasurer. Strong support for the anti–county-unit forces came from the League of Women Voters, which under the direction of Mrs. Tom M. Byrd, Jr., president, and Mildred Hulse, director, put out a brochure called *Facts* that showed voters how to read the huge and complicated ballot for the November 4 general election. Parts of both the Plan of Improvement and the County Unit Amendment were included, as was the list of presidential electors. Another brochure, *Georgia Voters,* also published by the League of Women Voters and edited by Mrs. Philip G. Hammer, was more specific. It spoke out strongly for a vote against Amendment 1.

The Plan of Improvement won, but the county unit amendment lost. The day after the election, Charles Weltner, later congressman and judge, wrote Judge Andrews: "It looks like our candidates are free from the county unit system for at least two more years. May I offer my congratulations to you for the work and talent you have devoted so successfully to this end."

On the same day Weltner wrote to Morris Abram, later advisor to John F. Kennedy and member of the U.S. Civil Rights Commission: "Now that it is assured that Amendment #1 has been repealed, I want to extend to you personally my heartiest congratulations. There can be little doubt that your splendid efforts have been a very substantial factor in obtaining the vote. For the victory, you deserve the commendations and thanks of a great many people, including myself."[2]

It was not until 1962 that the U.S. District Court for the Northern District of Georgia ruled that the Democratic party of Georgia could not use the county-unit system in the Democratic primary, which was still tantamount to election. The 1962 primary elections were held on a popular vote basis. The case was appealed, but on March 18, 1963, the decision of the Supreme Court confirmed the decision of the lower court. Thus, after years of struggle, the county-unit system finally faded at last into the mists of history.

In a town famed for its interest in golf and its high regard for golf champions, blacks decided to make the links a minor legal battleground. Atlanta was not yet ready to integrate its golf courses. In mid-July of 1951, four prominent black leaders were refused permission to play at Bobby Jones course. They brought suit in federal courts, based on federal civil rights laws. In response to this the city tried the "separate but equal" tack. In April of 1952 a joint meeting of the Parks Committee of City Council and the Citizens Parks Advisory Committee earmarked a fund of $75,000 for the purchase of land on which an eighteen-hole golf course for Negroes could be laid out. The course would cost around $200,000 upon completion. Eventually, Hartsfield quietly desegregated the courses.

In the aviation field Delta Air Lines spread its wings in the spring of 1952 when it announced its plans to consolidate Chicago and Southern Airlines. Delta's home office in Atlanta thus would become the major base of an extensive system of air routes, operating with the top airlines of the country. C. E. Woolman, president of Delta, would be president and general manager of the new company, to be known as Delta-C&S Air Lines. Financial phases of the merger were arranged by Courts and Company, an Atlanta firm.

Bell Telephone was also reaching out in this year, extending its Radio-Relay, a "super highway of communication," to link Atlanta and Charlotte with Washington, D.C. A series of towers tied in at Washington with the transcontinental radio-relay route that carried the first collect call west in

1951. Thus Atlanta's telephone users could now speak to the West Coast or far Northeast in any weather, in a matter of seconds.

Women received recognition long denied them when Dr. Blake R. Van Leer, president of Georgia Tech, announced that women would be admitted to Tech's classes in all fields of engineering and architecture at the beginning of the fall term in 1952. The Board of Regents had voted by the narrow margin of 7-5 to allow them to enter on a limited basis.

President Van Leer's wife had studied architecture and his daughter was an engineering graduate, and he had long been in favor of admitting coeds to Tech. His wife, in fact, was one of the leaders in the drive to go coed. A petition circulated by the Women's Chamber of Commerce in Atlanta finally brought the matter before the Regents, according to Tech historian Robert B. Wallace, Jr.

There was a considerable amount of grumbling among the male students, who were determined that no Tech tradition would be changed because of the presence of women. Said Ronald Holt, president of the senior class: "If they come here to study engineers instead of studying engineering, they won't last long."

The first two women admitted were Elizabeth Herndon, a World War II widow with a nine-year-old son, and Diane Michel, from Houston, Texas, whose ambition was to become an engineer. The two entered Tech in September of 1952. Michel graduated in 1956, along with Shirley Clements, an electrical engineering transfer student.[3]

The halting steps toward coed status obviously had no effect on the engineering school's position as one of the nation's consistent football powers. Celestine Sibley explained: "Winning Season of the Georgia Tech Football Team: Georgia Tech's Yellow Jackets improved on their unbeaten record of 1951 by going untied as well during the 1952 season. They won eleven straight games to extend their victory string to 25 games and then accepted their second straight Bowl invitation—this time to meet the University of Mississippi in the Sugar Bowl." Tech won 24-7. In 1951 the Yellow Jackets beat Baylor in the Orange Bowl, 17-14. In the 1953 Sugar Bowl they defeated West Virginia 42-19.

OBITUARIES

Thomas Dent Meador, son of pioneer Atlantans, was a member of Georgia Tech's class of 1898. He was founder and president of Meador Construction Company, which had laid countless miles of city sidewalks. His memberships included the Piedmont Driving Club, Elks, Chamber of Commerce, and the First Presbyterian Church. Henry B. Kennedy, one of the organizers and executive vice-presidents of Fulton National Bank, died at 73. In addition to banking, he served as treasurer of the City of Atlanta and president of the Atlanta Clearing House Association. He was also president of the Bell House, life member of the Capital City Club and member of the Piedmont Driving Club, Masons, and Shriners. Dr. Charles A. Sheldon, Jr., organist and choir director for the First Presbyterian Church, died at 65. He was also organist for the city and The Temple. He had designed and built more than sixty-five organs in various sections of the country. He was a member of Rotary and the Masons. Harry Park Woodward, an executive of Southland Coffee Company and well known in business circles, died at 58. He was a graduate of Georgia Tech and belonged to the Piedmont Driving Club, Druid Hills Golf Club, Capital City Club, Peachtree Christian Church, and American Legion. John R. Marsh was the widower of author Margaret Mitchell. Gen. William Bush was Georgia's last Confederate governor.

Dr. Walter Wright Daniel, prominent Atlanta physician and past president of the Fulton County Medical Society, died at 55. He was a graduate of Wofford College and Emory Medical School and had been on the staff from 1923 to 1927. He was also head of staff at Crawford Long Hospital. Joseph R. Palmer, a machine pattern maker by trade, died a week after his 100th birthday. Dameron Black, vice-president, secretary, and treasurer of the Trust Company of Georgia until his retirement in 1949, died at 70. He had been an auditor for the A&B Railroad and the Georgia Railway and Electric Company before joining the Trust Company. He belonged to St. Mark's Methodist Church, the Capital City Club, and the Atlanta Athletic Club. J. Frank Fair, food broker and past president of Atlanta Food Brokers Association, was a founder of Massey and Fair. He was a member of Second Ponce de Leon Church, Kiwanis, and the Atlanta Athletic Club. Dr. Thomas Collier, Sr., Atlanta anesthetist, was the son of Mr. and Mrs. A. J. Collier of Atlanta. He attended Gordon Military Academy, Georgia Tech, and Emory Medical College. He was chief anesthetist at Wesley Memorial Hospital and then Piedmont. He was a past president of several societies dealing with his profession. Gabriel Haas Schoen, president of Schoen Brothers and POM Chemical Industries, died at 50. He was a director of Lakewood Heights Boys Club and a member of The Temple, Masons, Shriners, and Elks.

Lafayette Johnson Magill, former president and chairman of the board of the Atlanta Hosiery Mills, died at 89. He was a member of First Presbyterian Church for fifty years. Tomlinson Fort Newell, well known Atlanta insurance man and grandson of Confederate general Alfred Colquitt, died at 77. W. Chester Martin, lifelong Atlantan who had risen from clerk to vice-president of the Trust Company of Georgia, died at 44. Miss Rusha Wesley, retired principal of Lee Street School for twenty-two years and of John B. Gordon for ten years, died at 71. A graduate of Agnes Scott, she also attended Emory, Harvard, Chicago, and Columbia universities. She had been a member of Trinity Methodist Church since 1900 and served on the board of stewards. James Edwin Warren, 73, was formerly president and board chairman of Southern Bell. He advanced within the company from stenographer, and his career spanned forty-three years. William Danner Thompson, Atlanta attorney and president of Atlanta Title and Trust Company, died at 75. He was executive vice-president of Emory University's board of trustees and had been a member since 1915. A graduate of Emory at Oxford, he was a past president of the Atlanta Bar Association. Judge Ralph McClelland, who occupied the bench of Fulton County's Civil Court, died at 59. Thomas Guy Woolford was a founder, past president and chairman of the board of Retail Credit Company, which he started with his brother, Cator, in 1899.

Leonora Raines was a former war correspondent and staff member of the *New York Sun*. She was a founding member of the Atlanta Historical Society and contributed many stories on Atlanta's earlier days to the organization's bulletin. She was also a founding member of the Atlanta Art Association. She attended Sacred Heart Church. Dr. William Stockton Nelms, professor of physics at Emory for twenty-two years, died at 59. He was a Ph.D. graduate of Columbia and a longtime steward of Decatur Methodist Church. Warren T. Hunnicutt, retired North Georgia Methodist Conference leader and former pastor of five Atlanta churches including Wesley Memorial, died at 89. He was a graduate of Emory at Oxford. Dr. James Ryan Garner, retired Atlanta physician and railroad surgeon, died at 75. A graduate of Emory at Oxford and University of Virginia, he became surgeon for Atlanta and West Point Railroad, Western Railway of Alabama, Georgia Railroad, and Atlanta Joint Terminal.

Mrs. William A. Gregg, the former Lizzie Jones whose father Oliver was city marshal during the Civil War, died at 93. The oldest member of Trinity Methodist Church, she was the wife of a founder of Beck and Gregg. Benjamin Elsas, former president and chairman of the board of Fulton Bag and Cotton Mill, died at 80. He was a native Atlantan and the son of pioneer citizens Jacob and Clara Elsas. Educated at Harvard, he became president of Fulton Bag at the death of his brother, Oscar, in 1924. He was an ardent supporter of musical groups and the High Museum and was a member of the First Church of Christ Scientist. Mrs. Kurt Mueller was a native of Germany. She and her husband were co-directors of the Atlanta Conservatory of Music. Rufus Clark Darby, founder and treasurer of Darby Printing Company, died at 71. He was active in Boy Scout work, the Rotary Club, the Atlanta Chamber of Commerce, and St. Mark's Methodist Church.

Mrs. Isaac Newton Ragsdale, widow of a former Atlanta mayor, was a witness to the Battle of Atlanta. She was a member of the first graduating class of Girls High School and a charter member of the Atlanta Woman's Club. She died at 91. Mrs. Wade H. Blanchard, the former Kate Slaton, sister of Gov. John M. Slaton, died at 95. She had been a resident of Atlanta since 1875. Mrs. August C. McHan, the former Lillian Robinson, daughter of Joseph L. and Louise Fleming Robinson, pioneer Atlantans, died at 72. She attended Miss Ballard's School and was a charter member of the Lullwater Garden Club. Rt. Rev. John Buckman Walthour, bishop of the Episcopal Diocese of Atlanta, died unexpectedly at 47. He had been dean at the Cathedral of St. Philip since 1947 and was consecrated bishop, succeeding John Moore Walker, in 1951. Palmer Walthour, pioneer bicycle salesman, co-founder of Walthour and Hood and a brother of famed bicycle racer Bobby Walthour, died at 80. He was active in business and civic affairs and was an elder at Westminster Presbyterian Church. Cecil A. Alexander, Sr., long associated with Alexander Hardware Company and benefactor of the SPCA, died at 75. He was a member of The Temple and B'nai B'rith.

NOTES

1. Albert Riley, *Atlanta Journal-Constitution Magazine,* Mar. 22, 1953.

2. Charles Longstreet Weltner Papers, Atlanta Historical Society.

3. Robert Wallace, *Dress Her in White and Gold: A Biography of Georgia Tech* (Atlanta: Georgia Tech Foundation, 1969).

ABOVE: Atlanta became the state capital in 1868, and the present capitol building was dedicated in 1889. This view shows the state capitol dome about ten years before it acquired its distinctive coating of Dahlonega gold in 1958. The Church of the Immaculate Conception is in the left foreground.

LEFT: Standing just across the street west of the Capitol is the Atlanta City Hall completed in 1930.

Several military installations surrounded Atlanta during World War II, but the most economically significant one was the Bell Bomber Plant that produced B-29s like these on the plant's runway.

The Bell Plant employed over 20,000 workers, including many women as this posed photograph of fuselage work shows.

Gone with the Wind author Margaret Mitchell celebrated the centennial of Atlanta's 1847 incorporation as a city by serving Mayor William B. Hartsfield a slice of birthday cake. Former mayors Robert F. Maddox and Walter A. Sims are to Mitchell's left and right respectively.

President Franklin D. Roosevelt often passed through Atlanta on the way to and from his retreat at Warm Springs, Georgia. On April 13, 1945, a funeral train brought him through the Gate City one last time.

ABOVE: Beginning in 1943, the Woman of the Year awards honored Atlanta women in several categories of service. In 1955 Mayor William B. Hartsfield congratulated Miss Ruth Blair, the overall winner for that year.

LEFT: Coca Cola's Robert Woodruff was known as "Mr. Anonymous" because of his millions of dollars of anonymous contributions to worthy causes. In the woods of his south Georgia plantation, Woodruff joined President Dwight Eisenhower in a drink of Atlanta's most famous product.

LEFT: Whisper-quiet trackless trolleys that ran on rubber tires and drew power from overhead wires still plied the streets of downtown in the early 1950s when Plaza Park was new. As the center of activity moved northward in the 1960s and 1970s, Plaza Park became a haven for street people. By 1963 diesel buses had replaced the trackless trolleys.

BELOW: The Buckhead Sears-Roebuck store sold the appliances and expensive black-and-white televisions characteristic of a well-equipped middle-class home in 1951.

It did not rival Times Square, but Peachtree Street north of Five Points boasted its own white way in the 1950s. *Gone with the Wind* had premiered at Loew's Grand in December 1939.

From 1915 until the 1970s, the Lakewood Park Fairgrounds on the south side hosted the Southeastern Fair. Until the last few years of its operation, the fair was racially segregated; and, as in this 1950 scene, only whites walked the midway except on designated "colored days."

Lenox Square, which opened in 1959, was Atlanta's first major outlying shopping mall. By the time of this photograph in 1968, Lenox had become a magnet for surrounding development as it would continue to be into the 1980s.

From 1909 to the 1960s, the Municipal Auditorium was Atlanta's center for such events as a Shrine convention and the appearances of the Metropolitan Opera. The city dedicated triangular-shaped Hurt Park in 1940. The area in the upper right of the photograph would later be developed for Georgia State University, and the front portion of the auditorium building would become the university's Alumni Hall.

HOWEVER fast it might be progressing as an aviation center, Atlanta in 1953 was still the busiest railroad city in the South. Some 8,500 people in the metro area had jobs in railroad-related occupations at an annual payroll of almost $35 million a year. Fifteen lines radiated from the city. The Southern operated five, the Atlantic Coast Line two, Atlanta and West Point one, Central of Georgia one, and the Nashville and Chattanooga and St. Louis and the Seaboard Airline each two. Each day 83 passenger trains arrived and departed from Atlanta and 109 freight trains operated out of the terminal area—giving Atlanta a freight volume greater than any other city in the Southeast. To handle the daily traffic, 150 switch engines were needed.

Atlanta's desire to become the South's leading medical center received strong impetus in the year. Early in January Dr. Hugh Wood, dean of the Emory Medical School, announced that seventeen doctors had formed a partnership and organized a new Emory University Clinic. Dr. Wood described the new clinic as "simply a partnership arrangement by a group of physicians who want to teach medical students and carry on research in the medical services while continuing their own medical practices." Other officials at Emory described the organization of the clinic as an "important new step toward the development of a great medical center for the Southeast, with Emory's teaching and hospital facilities in medicine, dentistry and nursing at its heart."

The next year, in 1954, a grant of $1 million was made for construction of a new clinic building on Clifton Road. By 1956, when the building was partly completed, the clinic staff of teacher-doctors had swelled from 17 to 34, and by 1965 the number had increased to 104.[1]

While improvements in medical facilities were being made at Emory, great changes were also in the works for Grady Hospital. In mid-April the Fulton County Commission agreed with the Fulton-DeKalb Hospital Authority that a new, fireproof Grady Hospital should be constructed. The commission agreed to underwrite $20 million in revenue certificates to accomplish this.

A glowing editorial in the *Atlanta Journal* declared: "The County Commission Has Done Right By Grady." It went on:

The Atlanta area apparently will get a new Grady Memorial Hospital. One that is fireproof and with beds and facilities adequate to meet the demands of this heavily populated section.

The Fulton County Commission made the new 1,000-bed building possible when the commissioners signed an agreement with the Fulton-DeKalb Hospital Authority to set aside approximately $1,180,000 annually to amortize the revenue certificates that will be sold to pay the cost of construction.

Grady Hospital's present plant was built to care for a city of 100,000 people, and now must provide service for nearly 750,000. It is overcrowded, and in constant danger of fire.

Plans for a new Grady have been drawn for years. First one thing, then another, blocked its construction. Finally, only the question of financing it without raising the tax rate remained, and that question has been solved.

Like the actions of all political bodies, some of the decisions of the County Commission have come in for sharp criticism. Guaranteeing the construction of this great public hospital is one deed for which the present body will be blessed for years to come.

In this same month of April trustees of Piedmont Hospital launched a drive to raise $1.5 million to assist in paying for a new hospital that would cost $3.5 million. Piedmont in 1953 was operating a 132-bed facility on Capitol Avenue. Envisioned was a 238-bed facility, to be constructed on a ten-and-a-half-acre lot at Peachtree and Collier roads.

One Atlanta doctor had long been deeply concerned with the problems faced by the poor when they needed medical care. When the will of Dr. Luther C. Fischer, cofounder of Crawford W. Long Hospital (originally Davis-Fischer), was probated, it was discovered that he had left most of his extensive estate in a "trust for hospital care for the poor and needy in Georgia."

There was increasing need in Atlanta for hospital facilities not only for the poor but for the aged, a fact that was recognized by the Georgia Heart Association. Greater Atlanta's population had been growing steadily older since 1930, according to a report by the Metropolitan Atlanta Community Services. In 1930 there were 13,419 persons sixty-five years of age or older in Fulton and DeKalb counties, representing 3 percent of the population. In 1950 there were 37,107 such persons, representing 6 percent of the population. In the fifty years since 1900 average life expectancy had gone from forty-eight to sixty-eight years of age. With these facts in mind, the Georgia Heart Association, at its annual meeting in Savannah in September, provided funds to pay professors and finance research in cardiovascular disease both at the Emory University School of Medicine and the Medical College of Georgia at Augusta.

While these changes were taking place in the medical school, Emory was taking one other step to keep pace with modern trends in education. In April, Frances B. Atkinson enrolled in the College of Arts and Sciences to become the first "official" coed in the 119-year history of the university. When the fall session opened in September, seventy more women were enrolled, in all the schools and divisions of the university. Forty were freshmen and thirty-one were in the upper classes. Actually, women had attended Emory in various capacities for years. For example, as part of the "University Center" idea for Atlanta, Emory and Agnes Scott worked out an exchange program. According to Dr. Thomas H. English, the school had seen limited coeducation from the start. Every division at one time or another enrolled women students and granted them degrees. The formal acceptance of women officially acknowledged that which had long been Emory's policy—to recognize the need of women for more than a nursing education. (In her obituary in 1953, it was noted that Mamie Haygood Ardis, daughter of the president of old Emory College, graduated there in 1885.)

Under the new arrangement, however, women students had their own female advisor, Barbara Ames, and all university activities were open to them. For instance, Emory scholarships could now be theirs, and thirty-four of the seventy-one entering in the fall of 1952 had already been awarded scholarships. Enrollment figures in the various schools in 1952 showed 4 women to 145 men in the Law School. The Dental School had a 3 to 300 ratio, the Medical School 4 to 279, and the Theology School 1 to 387.

While Emory was moving more rapidly into the coeducational pattern, Agnes Scott, which had provided many of the unofficial Emory coeds prior to 1953, was being chosen as one of the top ten women's colleges in the nation as a producer of top-ranking scholars. The ranking was based on a study of records of college graduates who had earned Ph.D.s and large fellowship awards from 1945 through 1951. The results were published in an article entitled "Where Do the Top Students Go?" by authors Robert Knapp and David Greenbaum.[2]

Robert Cheeseboro, an eighteen-year-old Negro freshman at Morehouse College, decided he would prefer to go to Tech instead. His application for admission was not rejected by the Board of Regents in so many words; instead, he was offered financial aid which would permit him to go to a school outside of Georgia, where he would not be denied admission because of his race. He rejected this. Cheeseboro, from Columbus, was the second Negro to make application for admission to Tech. Calvin W. Jackson, who listed Atlanta as his home, applied in 1952 and also was offered out-of-state aid by the Board of Regents. The Regents heard nothing from them thereafter. Cheeseboro, Jackson, and Horace Ward were the only three Negroes to seek admission to the university system up to that time. And Ward *was* heard from after admission was denied. He filed suit in federal court in Atlanta in an effort to force the authorities to admit him to the Law School at the University of Georgia.

The university's problems with the Horace Ward case were not reflected in enrollment figures at the university's Atlanta division—precursor to Georgia State University. Freshman enrollment was at an all-time high of 1,867. Total enrollment was 4,507, and 1,017 of these were veterans of the Korean War. The School of Business Administration had the highest attendance, with 2,849 students.

In the field of business 1953 was in many ways a history-making year. The value of construction projects in Atlanta was estimated at more than $70 million. One of the more impressive of these projects was the new Trailways Bus Depot, which was dedicated in October. It represented a $500,000 investment for the three Georgia corporations using it. These were Modern Coach Lines, Inc., Crescent Stages, Inc., and Smokey Mountain Stages, all members of the National Trailways System.

As Trailways increased Atlanta's status as a national bus terminal, Delta Air Lines in May added to the city's renown as an aviation center by merging with Chicago and Southern Airlines after months of negotiations. The Civil Aeronautics Board approved the consolidation for May 1, 1953. The merger included top management and line personnel, as well as air routes, and it made Delta the fifth-largest domestic air route in the nation. Delta's big ads touting its merger with Chicago and Southern were perhaps the inspiration for Eastern to put on a show stressing its services to Atlanta in years gone by. On May 1, 1928, Captain Eugene R. Brown of Decatur, an Eastern Airlines pilot, had flown the first daily airmail flight between Atlanta and New York. Twenty-five years later, on May 28, 1953, Captain Brown, still an Eastern pilot, planned to duplicate his trip in the same kind of plane—an open cockpit Pitcairn Mail wing.

Retail business in Atlanta was expanding quickly into outer areas. Many large specialty shops and department stores were moving into the suburbs in an effort to capture business at its source. Among the stores that opened branches in areas more accessible to public demand were Franklin-Simon, Sears, Roebuck, and J. C. Penney. In the winter of 1953 Belk-Gallant Company was planning to open an outlet in Buckhead. Atlanta's banks in this year also were seeking to make life simple for their customers. On June 3, 1953, the First National Bank of Atlanta opened its first all-automatic bank, serving the drivers who did not wish to get out of their car, at the corner of Piedmont and North Avenue NE. Officials estimated that two hundred cars a day could be handled at the drive-up window. The bank also had a walk-up window.

Busy and bustling Atlanta and Fulton County residents prospered in the first year of the Plan of Improvement to the degree that they paid one-fifth of all the state taxes paid in Georgia in 1952. Georgia's tax collections totaled $227,387,964 and Fulton residents paid $124.27 per capita—or a total of $48,822,943. The heaviest impost was in state income taxes. Individuals and corporations filed 76,121 returns totaling $9,631,332—or 26 percent of the total.

Mayor Hartsfield won a substantial victory over Charlie Brown in the city's primary in May, thereby assuring his fifth term as mayor.

Music, as in the past, held many Atlantans in thrall. The Atlanta Symphony Guild's 1953–54 season was described by one journalist as the "most colorful and varied listings since its beginning." The Atlanta Opera Company season consisted of four traditional operas, one popular operetta, and a musical play. The opera season at the Fox was again a success. By May 3 Atlanta opera lovers were saying farewell to the stars at two good-bye parties. The

Chastain Park amphitheater hosted programs, and August 9 was "an evening to remember," according to *Constitution* writer Paul Jones. The Atlanta Pops Orchestra and the Southern Ballet offered a program of music and dance based on Broadway shows such as *South Pacific, Oklahoma, Song of Norway, Carousel,* and others. "Some 2,000 people had an enchanting evening," said Jones.

One black Atlantan went far afield from business and far from home geographically to win high acclaim. Mattiwilda Dobbs, age twenty-five, made her debut as a singer at Milan's LaScala Opera House in the role of Elvira in Rossini's opera *Italian Woman of Algiers*. She was the first Negro singer to appear at LaScala and her performance was termed a huge success. The British magazine *Opera* called her the "outstanding coloratura of her generation," and indeed she did go on to greater and greater fame, singing in the years ahead with the Metropolitan and most of the great opera companies of the world. She sang solo roles in many great cities, including her native Atlanta. She was born in Atlanta, the fifth of six daughters of John Wesley Dobbs, a railroad mail clerk at the time, who worked extra jobs to put his six daughters through college. She graduated from Spelman College. Her five sisters became college professors, and Mattiwilda herself became a teacher as well as a singer. Her father went on to become the national vice-president of the National Association for the Advancement of Colored People. Her aunt was the first black to apply for a card at the Atlanta Public Library. When her nephew, Maynard Jackson, became mayor of Atlanta (1973), she sang at his inauguration. A month after her LaScala debut she married a Spanish journalist, who died a year later. In 1954 she sang at Covent Garden for Queen Elizabeth II and Prince Philip, and was decorated with the Order of the North Star by King Gustav Adolf of Sweden.

In 1957 Dobbs married Bengt Janson, public relations director of the Swedish Ministry of Health and Welfare. She moved to Stockholm with him and lived there for eighteen years, meanwhile singing in concerts all over the world, including the Soviet Union, where the critics described her voice as "genuine aesthetic perfection." In 1975 she returned to the United States to live and teach. She taught in Texas and Illinois and at the University of Georgia before settling into a teaching post at Howard University in 1977. In March of 1976 she was featured in a concert with the Atlanta Symphony under the direction of Robert Shaw.[3]

Many of the racial problems of the South have been modified greatly during the generation that Mattiwilda Dobbs wandered the world as a singer. And the year of 1953, when she made her debut at LaScala, saw one landmark in the diminution of many of the old antipathies.

In another step forward the Atlanta Negro Voters League, organized in 1949, got the support of white leaders to run a black candidate for the Atlanta Board of Education. Dr. Rufus Clement, president of Atlanta University, was selected to run, and he won a decisive victory over T. H. Landers. Landers, a white, had served on the board since 1927, but Clement won with 22,259 votes to Landers's 13,936. Said Clement: "It isn't a personal victory, it's a victory for the people." He added that "the white population is ready to work constructively with the Negro population."

Clement's race had not been easy, for charges before the Democratic City Executive Committee that Clement was "un-American" first had to be investigated and dropped. Files of the U.S. House Un-American Activities Committee were studied, and after a lengthy hearing in which A. T. Walden, Negro attorney, and Hughes Spalding, distinguished white attorney, represented Clement, the charges were dropped by a vote of 5-4. Clement had been associated with the American Civil Rights Congress, the Southern Conference for Human Welfare, and the Southern Negro Youth Congress but had withdrawn his membership and support of these organizations when he learned they had been infiltrated by Communists.

Another notable event of 1953 was the construction of the F. W. Olin School of Industry for Negroes as a branch of Carver Vocational High School. The school was the result of a gift of $610,000 from the F. W. Olin Foundation. The brick building cost a half-million dollars. It contained fifteen classrooms, nine shops and laboratories, reference rooms, science rooms, and athletic locker rooms. It could accommodate 1,200 to 1,500 students and a staff of twenty-five teachers. Classes would offer young blacks training in business, landscape design, plastering, lathing, woodwork, radio and TV, furniture upholstery, carpentry, painting and decorating, drafting, and food service. The Olin Building was dedicated on September 15, 1954, and has been functioning since.

Carver, a vocational high school of which Olin was a part, was founded in 1946 on 59.8 acres of land along Capitol Avenue that was purchased from Clark College for $55,000 by the City of Atlanta and Fulton County. The seven old buildings on the land had been brutally vandalized, but they were redesigned and renovated to form the nucleus of Carver.[4]

Other projects designed to make the lot of the Negro in Atlanta a happier one came about when the Negro Advisory Committee to the Atlanta Housing Authority dedicated the $10 million Carver Community on Pryor Road SW. Over nine hundred Negro families could be housed at reasonable rents. Mayor Hartsfield and members of the Housing Authority were present at the dedication on April 26, 1953.

In August, 6,000 delegates to the Negro Elks' National convention paraded through downtown Atlanta. Crowds cheered as bands, floats, and more than one hundred military units moved up Whitehall and Peachtree streets. Robert H. Johnson of Philadelphia, the Negro Elks' exalted ruler, led the parade, whose marchers had come from all over the United States.

At the end of their five-day convention, the black Elks expressed their "hearty thanks and appreciation" for the gracious reception they had received from the people of Atlanta. One phase of this reception that was particularly pleasing to the black Elks was the medical care provided for the visitors, including more than 1,400 free chest x-rays and ten first aid stations scattered about the city.

However, the fact that a political, financial, and social gulf still existed between white and black races was not concealed. The convention formally ended with an appeal by Walter White of the National Association for the Advancement of Colored People for Negroes to continue their fight for racial equality. He asked that "one great effort be made to clear up remaining discrimination and segregation based on race or color." Resolutions urged the federal government to pursue its efforts to abolish segregation in all parts of the country; commended the armed forces for beginning to end its segregation of blacks and whites in separate units; and urged Negro Elks to exercise the right to vote as "the most potent remedy available" for achieving the political recognition of Negroes.

The next month another group of blacks, younger and smaller than the Elks, gathered in Atlanta. The nineteenth annual convention of the New Farmers of America, Negro branch of the Future Farmers of America, convened at the City Auditorium. Forty-nine delegates from sixteen states attended the convention. Mayor Hartsfield made the welcoming address at the opening meeting, well aware of the fact that the support of the black community had given him a resounding victory over Charlie Brown in the race for mayor in May.

Meanwhile, the Atlanta school board was aware of the U.S. Supreme Court's consideration of school segregation. So that the board would be ready, no matter what the decision, school board member A. C. Latimer proposed the appointment of a committee of five to "make a thorough and exhaustive study as to what the board should do if the Supreme Court handed down a decision which does away with segregation in the public schools." After considerable argument the committee was formed, then abolished, and formed again on a resolution with a slight but significant difference in wording: "Resolved that we instruct the school administration to make a detailed study of the varied school facilities and the school population of all schools in the Atlanta area and bring this information to the board in order that we may be in a position to intelligently meet any possible decision that the Supreme Court might render in connection with the school segregation cases."

National events intruded on Atlanta in 1953 in other ways, too. In April there began an exchange of prisoners of war between the United States and its allies and the Communists in Korea. Among the more than 3,300 Allied prisoners to be returned in the following months were several Georgians, including Atlantan Pfc. Ray Hendrick, son of Betty Hendrick of Pulliam Street.

One of the most amazing and in the long run most humorous events of 1953 involved an alleged UFO. Three Atlantans reported that on U.S. Highway 78 near Austell a flying saucer was seen with "space creatures" emerging from it. The men reported that they killed one of the creatures as it sought to return to the spacecraft, and they produced the body. It was twenty-one inches long and looked like a hairless monkey—which on careful examination, it turned out to be.

The main aviation story of the year was no hoax, but a tragedy. On December 6 four Atlanta National Guard pilots were killed instantly when their four F-84 Thunderjets, flying in close formation, crashed to earth.

OBITUARIES

J. Henry Porter, a grandson of Atlanta banker W. M. Lowry, died at 76. He was a director of Georgia Savings Bank and Trust Company of Georgia. He twice had been president of the Atlanta Athletic Club, of which he was a founder. Hiram C. Blair, 58, was traffic manager of Atlantic Steel Company. He was a veteran of World War I and a member of St. Mark's Methodist Church. He was a brother of historian Ruth Blair. Dr. Oscar H. Matthews was chief of staff of gynecologists and obstetricians at Georgia Baptist and a staff member of Grady, Piedmont, and Crawford Long hospitals. He was raised in Gwinnett County and graduated from Emory. He was active in the Masons and Shriners and was a member of St. Luke's Episcopal Church. Mrs. Luther Z. Rosser, the former Sarah Emily Dorsey and wife of a Civil Court judge, had lived in Atlanta all her life and was a graduate of Lucy Cobb Institute. She was a member of First Methodist Church and was one-time president of the YWCA.

Mrs. Wilmer L. Moore, long identified with civic and cultural life in Atlanta, died at 82. She was a granddaughter of two Confederate generals, T. R. R. Cobb and Henry R. Jackson. She and Mrs. Robert Maddox organized the first day nursery in Atlanta and named it Cornelia Moore Day Nursery. As president of the Atlanta Music Club, Moore helped to make it one of the most substantial and influential cultural groups in Atlanta. Walter Preston Warren, 78, was a graduate of the Boys High Class of 1890 and the University of Georgia in 1893. He served as an attorney for N.C.&St.L. Railroad and then in an administrative capacity for the University of Georgia. Waldo W. Mallory, executive vice-president of Clement A. Evans & Company, died at 56. He was a graduate of Clemson and Columbia and served as a vestryman of All Saints Episcopal Church. He held membership in the Piedmont Driving Club and the Oglethorpe Club in Savannah. Mrs. Sam Finley, the former Mary Virginia Powell, known to thousands of children as "Mother Mary," died at her home in the Biltmore Apartments. For many years she worked tirelessly for children's organizations and successfully ran her husband's business after his death in 1942. John Alvan McCrary, Atlanta engineer and banker who was the only surviving member of the original board of directors of Fulton Reserve Bank, died at 82. He was a graduate of Georgia Tech and member of Decatur Methodist.

Asa G. Candler, Jr., financier and one of the city's most prominent citizens, died at 72. He was a son of the founder of the Coca-Cola empire. Herbert J. Haas, long active in Atlanta civic and legal circles, died at 68. He was a graduate of Boys High and Columbia University and had practiced law nearly fifty years. He was a lifetime trustee of the Jewish Orphans Home and vice-president of the Hebrew Benevolent Association. Mrs. James L. Dickey, prominent in religious and civic affairs, died at her home. She did volunteer Red Cross work during both World Wars and was interested in the Home for the Incurable. Gilbert Francis Beers, prominent Atlanta building contractor and owner of Beers Construction Company, had been in business in Atlanta for more than thirty years. He was a graduate of Phillips Exeter Academy and M.I.T. Stuart Bird, former vice-president of Foote and Davies, for whom he had worked fifty years, died. A Mason and an Elk, he was a member of the Capital City Club and St. Luke's Episcopal Church. He was secretary-treasurer of Notchaway Hunting Club.

Lee Ashcraft, internationally known financier, Atlanta philanthropist, and chairman of the executive committee of Ashcraft-Wilkinson brokerage firm, died at 82. Past president of the Chamber of Commerce, he was also chairman of the English Speaking Union, a life deacon at Ponce de Leon Baptist, and belonged to Rotary, the Piedmont Driving Club, and the Capital City Club. Mrs. John S. Spalding, the former Mary Connally, granddaughter of Georgia's wartime governor Joseph E. Brown, died at 75. She was active in civic and religious affairs and had been a member of Second Baptist since 1888. She was a member of the Atlanta Historical Society, the DAR, and the UDC. Dr. Edgar DeWitt Shanks, longtime physician and editor of the *Journal of the Medical Association of Georgia*, died at 64. John T. Thompson, one of Atlanta's oldest real estate brokers, died at his office. He had resided at the Atlanta Athletic Club for the past thirty-five years and had his own firm for over thirty years. Thompson's firm had developed Winnona Heights and Emory Grove.

Isham M. Sheffield, Sr., one of the South's leading insurance executives, died at 82. He was vice-president and director of Life Insurance Company of Georgia, which he founded in 1891 with J. N. McEachern. He was a life deacon at Second Ponce de Leon Baptist and a Mason and a Shriner. Much of his time was directed to philanthropic and church affairs. Harold T. Hagan was owner of Pig 'n Whistle and Peacock Alley. The son of Atlantans Mr. and Mrs. Lee Hagan, he was a graduate of Washington and Lee and a veteran of World War I. Thomas Croom Partridge, Atlanta lawyer who was active in Georgia and Atlanta bar associations, died at 50. He was a trustee of the Atlanta Historical Society, president of the English Speaking Union, and a member of the Piedmont Driving Club, the Atlanta Athletic Club, and St. Mark's Methodist Church. Oscar R. Thompson, prominent shoe retailer and president of Thompson, Boland and Lee, died at 69. A Mason and a Shriner, he was also a member of the Capital City Club.

Beverly M. DuBose, prominent Atlanta insurance executive and widely known Atlanta historian, died at 67. A graduate of the University of the

South, he came to Atlanta to join his cousin, Thomas Egleston, in the insurance business. They were southern general agents for Hartford Insurance. With a keen interest in history, DuBose collected an outstanding and invaluable store of information and documents pertaining to the Atlanta area. He was past president of the Atlanta Historical Society and a trustee of the High Museum, Egleston Hospital, and the Atlanta Stove Works. He held memberships in the Piedmont Driving Club, the Masons, and Civitan, and was a communicant of St. Philip's Cathedral. Dr. Paul D. Selman, Atlanta druggist for more than fifty years, died at 69. He was the oldest member of the Georgia Pharmaceutical Association and a member of the Second Ponce de Leon Baptist Church. Mrs. Joseph K. Hines, widow of the Georgia Supreme Court Justice, died at 86. She was the former Cora McBride and was a member of the DAR and the First Methodist Church. W. Zode Smith, general manager of the Atlanta Water Works before his retirement in 1947, died at 78. A city employee for fifty-seven years, he spent forty of them as a waterworks manager. Mrs. William J. Hobbs, wife of the president of the Coca-Cola Company from 1946 to 1952, died at 49. Daniel MacDougald, attorney and chairman of the board of directors of Georgia Power Company, died at 70.

Dr. Luther C. Fisher was president and treasurer of Crawford Long Hospital, which he had started in 1906 as an eighteen-bed sanitorium. After graduating from Emory, he did medical study in Vienna and Berlin. He joined with Dr. E. C. Davis to found Davis-Fisher Sanitorium, and in 1931 the hospital's name was changed to Crawford Long. He was well known as a rose grower. Hyman Kessler, 80, a native of Poland, was owner of an Atlanta department store and had been an active merchant since 1914. His store was at the corner of Whitehall and Hunter streets. He was a Mason and a member of The Temple. Dr. and Mrs. T. R. Staton died in a plane crash. He was a leader in Atlanta medical circles, a graduate of Emory and a past president of Druid Hills Golf Club. They were both members of Peachtree Christian Church.

John Paschall, editor-emeritus of the *Atlanta Journal*, who had worked for the paper since the turn of the century, died at 74. He was a graduate of Vanderbilt. He played an important part in the introduction of radio to Atlanta, presiding over "The Atlanta Journal Editorial Hour" on WSB. James A. Branch, Jr., Atlanta attorney and a partner in the law firm of Spalding, Sibley, Troutman and Kelley, died at 35. He was educated at Marist, Georgetown, and the University of Georgia. He was a member of the Cathedral of Christ the King and the Society of St. Vincent de Paul. Mrs. Patrick J. Bloomfield, the former Elizabeth Lynch, daughter of pioneers Peter and Julia Lynch who came from Ireland, died at 79. She was the widow of mortician Patrick Bloomfield, partner in Greenburg, Bond and Bloomfield Funeral Home.

Mrs. Adolph Montag, the former Helen Loeb, was the widow of a founder of Montag Brothers. She was a member of The Temple, the Sisterhood, and the Council of Jewish Women. Fred A. Scheer, operator of one of Atlanta's oldest established jewelry stores, died at 58. Mrs. David Marx was the former Eleanor Rosenfield and widow of the Rabbi David Marx. She was a graduate of Girls High School and was a member of The Temple, past president of the Temple Sisterhood, and a member of the Council of Jewish Women. Hugh Nunnally, retired vice-president and treasurer of Nunnally & McCrea Company, where he was employed from 1929, died at 48. He was a member of the Piedmont Driving Club, the Capital City Club, Peachtree Golf Club, and Homosassa Fishing Club. He was a graduate of Boys High and the University of Georgia.

Oliver Perry Adair, realty broker and state and southern amateur golf champion, died at 53. He was a son of George W. Adair. He was dubbed "The Little Gamecock" because he was a superior competitor in golfing tournaments and always a crowd pleaser. Frank Winecoff, retired Atlanta real estate executive, died at 61. He was a son of William Fleming Winecoff, builder of the famous Atlanta hotel bearing his name. Dr. John Gordon Stipe, vice-president of Emory University and one of its most distinguished graduates, died at 67. Holder of many academic honors, he also held high offices in numerous educational associations. He was graduated in 1907 and had been with the university since 1911. Dr. Richard Eubanks, a graduate of Atlanta Dental College, had been in dentistry since 1911. A colonel in the Old Guard of the Gate City Guards, he was also on Governor Talmadge's staff.

Charles DeWitt Herren, son of pioneer Atlantans William and Sara Little Herren, died at 68. Noted as a restaurateur, he founded Herren's in 1934 and the Brass Rail later. Dr. Marion Luther Brittain died at 87. He became president of Georgia Tech in 1922 after many years in the field of education, including teacher at Boys High, principal at Crew Street School, superintendent of Fulton County Schools, and State Superintendent of Education. He was educated at Emory, Mercer, and the University of Chicago, and he was the author of several publications. He was a Knight Templar, Rotarian, Kappa Alpha, and a member of Phi Beta Kappa. William Winston Gaines, who had been an attorney for more than sixty years, died at 86. He had been chairman of the City Board of Education and served as registrar of Fulton County. A graduate of Georgetown University, he was also a charter member of Capitol Avenue Baptist Church.

Eugene M. (Beau) Hudson, a resident of Atlanta for nearly seventy years, died at 87. He was associated with H. Y. McCord and McCord-Stewart Company, of which he was vice-president and general manager. He was on the advisory board of C&S Bank, a director of Thomaston Cotton Mills, and a member of the Homosassa Fishing Club. Joseph Priestly Orme, great-grandson of Sir Joseph Priestly, the British scientist, died at 78. His grandfather, Joseph Thompson, was one of Atlanta's first physicians. He was a member of the Piedmont Driving Club, the Capital City Club, and the Nine O'Clocks.

Dr. Cyrus W. Strickler, Sr., distinguished physician and surgeon and a specialist in internal medicine, died at 80. For over half a century he was a student, teacher, and leading practitioner of medicine. The son of Dr. and Mrs. G. B. Strickler, he came to Atlanta as a boy, when his father was called to be minister at Central Presbyterian Church. He attended Washington and Lee and was graduated from Atlanta Medical College in 1897 with first honors. He was a member of many medical societies, Phi Beta Kappa, the Atlanta Athletic Club, and the Capital City Club. He served with the Emory Unit in World War I and was executive officer in command on its return to America. Dr. Strickler was on the committee that organized the Medical Service Bureau in 1932 to provide medical services to low-income groups.

Dr. Harry B. Johnston, Sr., noted Atlanta dentist, died at 73. He served as a member of Emory University's dental faculty, and he was widely known for finding and perfecting endodontia, a method of sealing off tooth infection. Morgan Blake, retired sports editor of the *Atlanta Journal* and widely known in southeastern religious circles, died at 64. He became a sports writer locally in 1916 after his graduation from Vanderbilt. Samuel Francis Boykin was president of Coca-Cola International and past vice-president, secretary, and treasurer of the Coca-Cola Company. In 1899 he joined Pratt Laboratories as a bookkeeper and successfully worked his way up to president. The firm merged with Coca-Cola in 1919. Boykin was a director of Wilmington Trust Company, a trustee of Emory University, as well as a member of the Piedmont Driving Club, Rotary, and the Capital City Club. He had been a steward at St. Mark's Church. Mrs. Oscar Newton, active in the work of North Avenue Presbyterian Church and a member of the Piedmont Driving Club and Capital City Club, was the widow of a president of the Federal Reserve Bank. Toulman T. Williams, retired vice-president of J. M. High Company and a lifelong resident of Atlanta, died at 74.

William Schley Howard, lawyer and DeKalb County legislator, died at 78. During his long legal career of more than half-a-century, Howard served as prosecutor, legislator, and congressman, but it was his remarkable role as defense attorney in capital cases that made him famous. It was estimated by his son, Pierre, that he had defended more than 500 murder cases. He was born in Kirkwood in 1875, the son of Thomas Coke Howard, postmaster of Atlanta during the Civil War. His mother was the former Susan Harris of Savannah. The only formal education he had was received at Neil's Academy in Kirkwood, where he attained the fourth grade. Howard read law at every opportunity, studying with Alex Daley, and was admitted to the bar in 1896. He served in the Spanish-American War, and after it was over he was elected to the legislature from DeKalb County. He was associated with James Branch from 1919 until 1935, when he formed the firm of Howard, Tiller and Howard. Howard was noted over the state as a great hunter and fisherman and owned many fine bird dogs.

Mrs. James Gillespie, formerly Mary Fitzgibbon and born in Atlanta in

1858, died at 95. She was hidden in the cellar during the bombardment of Atlanta. She was a member of Sacred Heart, the Atlanta Historical Society, Pioneer Women, and the Atlanta Woman's Club. A. C. Miller, founder of A. C. Miller & Co., Inc., one of the city's pioneer designers and builders of truck bodies, died at 95. He began his career as a blacksmith's helper and apprenticed for three years. In 1889 he opened his business as a carriage builder and switched to wagons, then trucks. Richard Louis (Dick) Hull, president of Irvindale Farms, Inc., and chairman of the Fulton County Board of Health, died unexpectedly at 51. The milk products business he operated was founded by his father-in-law, Gen. A. R. Glancy. Hull was a member of North Avenue Presbyterian Church, the Piedmont Driving Club, Rotary, the Capital City Club, and the Nine O'Clocks, and was past master of foxhounds of the Shakerag Hunt.

Dr. James Samuel Guy, former chairman of Emory's department of chemistry, died at 69. He had been head of the department for thirty-two years and had also served as chairman of the DeKalb Board of Education. He was active in the Red Cross and Boy Scouts and was vice-president of the Atlanta Community Fund. Everard D. Richardson, Jr., a veteran of World War II and practicing attorney, died at 45. He attended old Tech High and was graduated from the University of Alabama. He was a member of American Legion Post #1, Yaarab Temple, the Piedmont Driving Club, the Nine O'Clocks, and Allatoona Yacht Club. James W. (Jim) Little, veteran southern newspaperman and copy editor of the *Atlanta Journal,* died at 45. His wife, Celestine Sibley, is a writer for the *Atlanta Constitution.* Mrs. Stoney Drake, Sr., the former Lillian Gregory, was the wife of the president of a textile chemicals firm. She was a member of the Atlanta Symphony Guild, Atlanta Music Club, and Brookwood Garden Club, and was a life member of Egleston Hospital Auxiliary.

John C. (Uncle Calvin) McElroy, DeKalb County's oldest citizen, died at 100 on the old family farm in Doraville where he was born. A lifelong farmer, McElroy tended crops until the year before his death and had been an elder in Doraville's Presbyterian Church since 1875. W. Grover Lamb, retired assistant secretary of the Coca-Cola Company, died at 66. He was a member of St. Mark's Methodist Church. Ben E. Ragsdale, vice-president of Commercial Credit Corp. and a son of Judge and Mrs. W. M. Ragsdale, died at 64. He was a veteran of World War I and attended Decatur First Methodist. He had been a member of the Atlanta Athletic Club for more than forty years.

Albert E. Thornton, financial, civic and social leader, died at 67. A native Atlantan, he attended Atlanta public schools and was a graduate of the University of Georgia and Yale. He received his law degree from Columbia in 1909 and for a few years practiced law with King and Spalding. A son of Albert Thornton, Sr., and grandson of Gen. Alfred Austell, he discontinued his law practice to tend his business interests. He was on the board of directors of First National Bank from 1912 and was vice-president and director of

Elberton Oil Mills and Southern Mills. His memberships included the Piedmont Driving Club, the Capital City Club, and All Saints Episcopal Church.

Dr. Thomas Callahan Davison, one of the outstanding surgeons in the South and a national medical figure, died at 69. He had served as chief of surgical services at Grady and Georgia Baptist hospitals and was associate professor of surgery at Emory University, his alma mater. He served as a major in World War I. In 1931 he served as president of the Fulton County Medical Association. He was a member of the Piedmont Driving Club and the Second Ponce de Leon Baptist Church. Judge Edgar E. Pomeroy, judge emeritus of the Fulton County Superior Court, died at 75. At All Saints Episcopal Church he had been a member of the vestry for many years. A graduate of the University of Georgia, Judge Pomeroy began practice in Atlanta in 1899. He went to City Council in 1906, served as alderman from 1908 to 1910, and was mayor pro tem from 1907 to 1913. He served as county attorney from 1914 until 1926, when he became a superior court judge.

George Mathieson, retired chief of the Fulton County Police, died at 75. He attended Atlanta's public schools and Creighton Business College, joining the police force in 1900. He became chief in 1913. His memberships were in Knights Templar, Buckhead Century Club, Sardis Masonic Lodge, and the Second Ponce de Leon Baptist Church. Albert D. Thomson, former city councilman and executive secretary to Mayor Asa Candler, died at 76. Educated at Emory at Oxford, he was a member of Sigma Alpha Epsilon fraternity and was a Mason. William E. Pitts, retired supervisor of the Atlanta Joint Terminal, died at 83. Mrs. Morris Benjamin, the former Amelia Eichberg, daughter of pioneer Atlantans, died at 92. She was a member of The Temple and a charter member of the Council of Jewish Women. John L. Harper, Atlanta realtor and flower company associate, died at 69. A founder of Harper's Flowers, he had also owned Harper's Realty Company.

Winfield Payne Jones, Atlanta lawyer and a graduate of Georgetown and the University of Georgia Law School, had been an attorney since 1903. Norman P. Cooledge, member of a socially prominent Atlanta family and a widely known business, civic, and financial figure, died at 63. A native Atlantan, he was a graduate of Boys High and Princeton. William Roulhac Prescott, southern manager of Hartford Fire Insurance Company, died at 86. He served as director of the old Lowry National Bank and the Trust Company of Georgia and had been board chairman of Henrietta Egleston Hospital since 1928. He was member of the Capital City Club, Piedmont Driving Club, Atlanta Athletic Club, Druid Hills Golf Club, and All Saints Church. Abraham Holzman, founder of Georgia Diamond Merchants and one of the first diamond setters in Atlanta, died at 87. He was the oldest man in the Hebrew Benevolent Congregation.

Dr. Frank K. Boland, Sr., Atlanta surgeon, died at 78. A graduate of the University of Georgia and Emory Medical School, he had practiced in Atlanta since 1903. He served as professor of surgery at Emory and was a lieutenant colonel while serving as chief surgeon of the Emory Unit in World War I. He held membership in a long list of medical organizations and served as president of the Southern Medical Association in 1937. He was a member of Phi Beta Kappa, the Piedmont Driving Club, Chi Phi, and Rotary Club. Mrs. Letitia Pate Whitehead Evans, widow of Joseph B. Whitehead and mother of Joseph Brown Whitehead, Jr., and Conkey Pate Whitehead, died at 81. As president of the Whitehead Foundation, she had given over $3 million to Emory University Hospital as a memorial to her husband and sons. In recognition of her many gifts to Atlanta, the Woman of the Year Committee voted her a special citation in 1947.

Joseph Samuel Slicer, Atlanta attorney and charter member of the Shakerag Hounds Hunt Club, died at 73. He was past master of the hounds for the Keswick Hunt Club in Virginia. Mrs. I. M. Sheffield, Jr., the former Margaret Ransom and wife of the board chairman of the Life Insurance Company of Georgia, died at 51. She was a member of the Junior League, Rose Garden Club, and Shakerag Hounds and was an ardent golfer. She was a graduate of North Avenue School and Agnes Scott College. Walter A. Sims, former mayor of Atlanta and a lawyer for over fifty years, died at 73. Homer S. Prater, who operated his own food brokerage firm in Atlanta for over fifty years, died at 76.

NOTES

1. Thomas H. English, *Emory University, 1915–1965: A Semicentennial History* (Atlanta: Emory University, 1966).

2. As reported in *Atlanta Constitution*, Jan. 6, 1953.

3. *Who's Who in America* (1974–75), vol. 1.

4. Interview with Dr. Walter Bell.

1954

EARLY in this year it became clear that the election of Dr. Rufus E. Clement to the school board had been a stroke of good fortune. With the expansion of the city limits under the Plan of Improvement, three new members, A. C. Latimer, J. C. Shelor, and P. L. Bardin, were added to the board from the outlying areas. A rivalry soon formed between the newcomers and the members of the board from the old Atlanta wards. In the years ahead Dr. Clement served as a mediator, compromiser, and smoother of ruffled feathers. This talent was demonstrated soon after he joined the board in January. By April it was reported that the Board of Aldermen was setting up a bond issue of $10 million, with $5 million allotted to three schools. Latimer wanted the whole $10 million to go to the schools. Ed S. Cook felt that it would be unwise to ask for any more money at this time. Dr. Clement came forward with a compromise—"thank the Aldermen for the $5,000,000, but point out that this would barely scratch the surface, and the schools must have more money as soon as possible." On July 11, 1954, the bond election was held and by a vote of 13,136 to 1,819 the schools were awarded $5 million for a building program.[1]

On May 17, 1954, the long-anticipated Supreme Court decision outlawing segregation in the public schools came down, setting off a strident summer-long debate over the passage of a constitutional amendment that would convert Georgia's public schools into private schools and thus nullify the integration issue. In the November election the amendment did pass, though later it was rescinded. The Supreme Court's decision also gave impetus to gubernatorial candidate Marvin Griffin's summer-long barbecue-cooking, watermelon-cutting crusade to keep the schools segregated and the county-unit system intact. He won a first-ballot victory in the Democratic primary held on September 9 over former acting governor M. E. Thompson.

When the Supreme Court handed down its school desegregation decision, Dr. Clement's talent for compromise again was manifest. It was he as much as any other school board member who sponsored the "go slow, go easy" procedure Atlanta followed in bringing its public school system into line with the court's decision. In so doing, Atlanta avoided in large degree the violent confrontations between reluctant whites and impatient blacks that took place in other cities.

As Dr. Clement, president of Atlanta University, made his debut in city politics, another president of a black college quietly moved into retirement. Dr. Florence M. Read completed her twenty-sixth year as president of Spelman College in 1953 and turned the position over to Dr. Albert E. Manley, dean of the College of Arts and Sciences at North Carolina College. Under Dr. Read, Spelman had been accredited by the Southern Association of Colleges and Secondary Schools. She had been instrumental in bringing about the affiliation of Spelman with Morehouse and Atlanta University in the Atlanta University Center. Later, Clark College, Morris Brown College, and Gammon Theological Seminary also became associated.

Another distinguished Atlantan, not a teacher but a judge, became a private citizen going into 1954. Judge A. W. Callaway, called by Keeler McCartney of the *Constitution* "one of the best known and most respected men in the public life of Atlanta," resigned his post as municipal judge after thirty-one years on the bench. In that time he estimated that more than 2 million accused persons had passed before him—and he had sent at least 1 million of them to the city prison farm. Said Keeler McCartney:

On the judicial bench, the veteran judge has looked down on the great and small, the rich and poor, the humble and meek, as well as the arrogant during their worse moments. For almost a third of a century he has observed the seamy side of the people living in a great city.

Has the experience created bitterness in the man?

Not at all. The judge still has a merry twinkle in his bright blue eyes and his trim figure and sandy hair would do credit to a man of fifty, much less seventy.

"You know," he says, "I'd be willing to tackle it all over again.

"People are not really bad. They sometimes find themselves caught in the web of circumstances. But a little correction laced with sympathy and human understanding generally sets things right. There are some good points in everyone." . . .

One thing of which the judge is most proud is a campaign promise of thirty years ago. He pledged the people of Atlanta that if elected to the then position of recorder [municipal judge], the door to his office would never be closed.

Judge Callaway has always found time to keep the promise. Facing dozens by the day and thousands by the month, he must speedily and impartially administer justice.

The tall, friendly man who was born at Woolsey, in Fayette County, the son of a typical Georgia dirt farmer, came to Atlanta at the age of fifteen to clerk in a store and later operated a store of his own. He has this word of advice for young people:

"If you move around, you're going to step in mud. When you do, pull your foot out as gently and carefully as you can. Don't stir it up."

So closes the public career of a man which started when he joined the city police force as a patrolman in 1916. He was appointed to municipal court upon the death of Judge George E. Johnson in 1922 and later was elected to his first term in office.

What will he do when the gavel bangs out his final moment on the bench next Thursday afternoon?

"That's the $64 question," he smiles.

In this year, as in years past, the weather had Atlantans and Georgians panting and perspiring. In Celestine Sibley's roundup of the top events of the year, she said: "Drouth, a July to October spell of searing days and nights, took a toll which Georgia farmers won't recover from for five years or more. . . . Atlantans experienced the rigors of the drouth. Wells dried up and many Northside Atlantans found themselves carrying cooking pots, buckets, garbage cans, anything that will hold water, to a big spring located just off the 6000 block of Northside Drive."

Atlanta went into the autumn season with the blare of trumpets and the thump of drums, with 1,700 young musicians and the prancing and pirouetting of some 300 cheerleaders in shakos and short skirts. First of these big musical assemblies came on November 20, 1953, between the halves of the Grady-Sylvan contest for the city football championship. This contest was made up only of high school bands, playing a concert of football songs, but at the suggestion of Kenneth Rogers, a *Constitution* photographer, Ira Jarrell, superintendent of schools, decided to go all out. She invited the nine-to-thirteen-year-old youngsters of the four elementary school bands as well as the high school bands to jam the Georgia Tech Stadium with all the school bands in town. The results were that on December 23, what was possibly the largest group of musicians ever assembled in Atlanta marched and countermarched and played to the thunderous applause of thousands of friends and assembled music lovers.

In his article describing this rare event Willard Neal pointed out that the Atlanta Symphony Orchestra, recognized as one of the finest civic groups in the country, was made up largely of graduates of the Atlanta high school bands—and that most of these high school bands were filled with youngsters who had learned to play in elementary school.

The symphony since its founding in 1945 under Henry Sopkin may have been made up of former high school musicians, but by 1954, said the *Atlanta Journal*, it had "come of age in the quality of its work and the abilities of its members." In proof of this the orchestra was asked to go on the air for a coast-to-coast broadcast over NBC on February 6, 1955, the tenth anniversary of its first concert. In the following winter the orchestra, now grown to eighty-two musicians, would offer forty-seven concerts in surrounding states.

One event that attracted little notice at the time but that in the years ahead had great effect in the field of engineering in Atlanta, in Georgia, and in the nation as a whole took place at Georgia Tech. In 1954 Dr. Blake R. Van Leer, president of Tech, named Dr. James E. Boyd associate director of Tech's Engineering Experiment Station. The station, a subject of campus controversy since its founding in 1934, had had a troubled financial and scholastic existence under a series of directors. Boyd began in 1954 as assistant director and was made top man three years later when his predecessor, Dr. Paul Calaway, returned to teaching. Said author Robert B. Wallace, Jr., in his Tech history, *Dress Her in White and Gold:*

Calaway's administration of the station marked the rise to prominence of the man who would . . . develop the station to its highest point in history. He was Dr. James E. Boyd, creator of Tech's first major electrical research program and chief of the physical sciences division, largest of the Tech research divisions. . . . Before Boyd left he saw to it that the research income to the station had more than doubled during the greatest growth period the station had ever experienced. Boyd, a dynamic and respected researcher and teacher, developed the nuclear program, fought for new facilities . . . revised the administration of the station and within two years he brought the station's income up to $2,958,000. . . .

In January of 1961 Boyd, too, was hired away from Tech, as so many of his predecessors had been. In August he left to become president of West Georgia College, another unit of the university system. At the end of his last year as head of the Engineering Experiment Station, its income had gone over the $4 million mark.[2]

While Tech was striving to master new techniques in engineering, another Atlanta institution was trying to master one of the oldest of all engineering and construction problems—how to keep a convicted felon behind bars.

On September 16, 1954, two convicted bank robbers disappeared from the federal penitentiary on McDonough Boulevard, SE, an event that had not occurred there in thirty-one years. Warden W. H. Hardwick identified them as George Ellis (20), serving twenty years, and Charles L. Stegall (36), serving twenty-five years. The warden considered both men dangerous. The last prisoners to escape from the prison were a machine-gun killer, George (Dutch) Anderson, and Gerald Chapman, a notorious mail robber; both escaped in 1923. Charles Stegall did not remain long at large. He was captured September 19 near Buchanan, Georgia, when FBI and federal officers identified the 1950 Ford he was driving as being one that was stolen outside the penitentiary.

The biggest throng to assemble on Peachtree since the parade of the Negro Elks in 1953 gathered there on September 20. Police estimated that 250,000 people crowded the curbs to watch Fulton County celebrate its one-hundredth birthday, with all the bands and floats. Reporter Bill Diehl described the scene at Five Points as "looking like Times Square on New Year's Eve."

"Atlanta's skyscrapers snowed confetti, an occasional stream of ticker tape floated into the street, a deck of cards drifted down from one high window, paper airplanes scooted out of the sky and crashed silently among the litter."

Another anniversary was celebrated somewhat more quietly. Southern Bell Telephone and Telegraph Company, founded, said reporter Jimm Walker, "in the days when Atlantans spoke and listened through the same tube and had to water their own telephone batteries," celebrated its seventy-fifth anniversary on December 20, 1954. On December 20, 1879, the day it set up shop, it was called the Georgia Branch of the National Telephone Company. A call to Decatur was long distance and cost 15¢. The company started out with ten subscribers in a tiny exchange, in a room at the Kimball House, and grew rapidly into the thousands. The city had 1,077 phones in 1879 and 254,000 by 1954. One early ad in the *Constitution* said, "The voice is plainly recognized and the conversation will not be heard by a third party. You can order goods from the grocer or butcher, call a carriage, call your physician, . . . of course saving immense time and exertion."

A bell that had nothing to do with telephones did have a visual and an aural impact on Atlantans in the closing days of 1954 and would for years thereafter. On December 22, North Avenue Presbyterian Church installed a bell in its bell tower, which had been empty since the church had been built, fifty-six years earlier. Plans called for the bell to be rung for the first time on Christmas morning. After that it would be used before all worship services as a call to prayer at noon every day, and before weddings and other special events in the church.

Made of bronze and weighing about 775 pounds, the bell was cast in Holland by the Royal Van Bergen Bell Foundries, a company that had been making bells for 150 years. Dr. Vernon Broyles, pastor, pointed out that such bells were practically indestructible, staying in tune forever, even though they were kept out-of-doors. Purchase of the bell was made possible by a bequest from the gift of Mrs. Elma S. Norton, a member of the church, and it would be erected as a memorial to her.

A memorial of a different sort had been dedicated a few days earlier to Atlanta's famous and justly beloved author of *Gone with the Wind*. On the evening of December 15, the Margaret Mitchell Memorial Room was opened in simple ceremonies at the Atlanta Public Library. Some one hundred friends of Mitchell came to the alcove on the second floor, where glass display cases lining the walls displayed souvenirs, awards, and trophies presented to the author. They included the Pulitzer Prize, her honorary degree from Smith College, her own library of Civil War books, and copies of her book in many foreign languages.

A four-foot picture of Mitchell looked down upon the group as Alma Jamieson, reference librarian who helped the novelist research the book, conducted the dedication ceremony. "Margaret," she recalled, "wanted to know if antebellum ladies used perfume or scent, if iodine was used in hospitals then." Margaret Mitchell's brother, Stephens Mitchell, said that the memorial room "is the one thing on earth my sister would have been most proud of." And Mayor Hartsfield, accepting the room from the library board president W. F. Floyd, Jr., called Mitchell "a little lady who wore her honors modestly and becomingly."

Honors of various types came to other Atlanta women over the year. A historic moment came on April 19 in Fulton Superior Court when the first woman in the county—and only the second in Georgia—served on a jury. She was Frances Smith, a secretary. The eleven men on the jury elected Smith the forewoman, and it was she who announced the verdict in a $7,000 settlement of a damage suit.

The first woman ever to serve a Georgia jury was Mrs. Bell Tinius, a White County grandmother, who cast her ballot with eleven men jurors on April 13, 1951, finding a man not guilty of making whiskey. Mrs. Tinius's name was placed on the list by mistake, but the judge let her serve anyway.

Another judge who believed in women jurors was Fulton County's Civil Court Judge A. L. Henson. Studies made by the American Bar Association, he said, showed that women jurors were more attentive than men while the trial was in progress and were not hardheaded in the jury room when the verdict was under discussion.

"Women," said Judge Henson, "will listen to all the evidence and be just as serious about a 15¢ verdict as about $10,000."

Women also were highly skilled in other fields as well. Jewell Mitchell, in charge of the biology laboratory at Grady Hospital, was named as Georgia's first "Medical Technologist of the Year."

As the year drew to an end, another distinguished Atlanta organization looked back upon years of service and forward to the celebration of its birthday. The Fulton County Medical Society was preparing to celebrate its fiftieth anniversary. Said the *Journal*:

Honor will be paid to those consecrated members who have ministered to the ailing for fifty years or more. Medicine has come far in these eventful fifty years. Professional ability has improved along with the tools. Drugs have been developed to strike back at the deadly germs about which we had so little knowledge fifty years ago.

The doctors know the germs now. They have seen them under the microscope. They take pictures of them. They know which medicine has shown tremendous tenacity in fighting them—research, constant improvement, triumph in many fields. Surgery has kept pace. Modern day miracles have become commonplace in the operating rooms of Atlanta's hospitals. On the roster of Fulton County Society are names known everywhere as leaders in the profession.

Only a dozen or so are living of the doctors who were members of the Society fifty years ago. Men like Dr. W. L. Champion who first rode with saddlebags, then in a buggy, and on to hand-cranked automobiles. He still comes to his office every day except Friday and Sunday.

Fifty years ago, the Society had 150 members. There were only 686 physicians in the entire state. Now the County Society has a membership of 2,820.

Fifty years of service to mankind. Fifty years of effort to give the people of Fulton County freedom from pain in illness. It is achievement at the highest.

OBITUARIES

S. H. Kulbersh, a native of Poland, died at 75. He came to Georgia in 1902 and was in the shoe business for over forty years. He was a founding member of Shearith Israel congregation. C. A. Gillespie, a former director of the Alcohol Control Unit of the Georgia Bureau of Internal Revenue, died at 77. He was a member of Decatur Methodist Church. J. A. Miller, attorney, writer, and president of the Atlanta Labor Temple Association, died at 75. He was a graduate of Atlanta Law School and the University of Michigan. He was a charter member of the Old War Horse Lawyers Club and a member of Central Congregational Church. C. Carpenter, an executive with Conklin Tin Plate and Metal Company, was a graduate of Young Harris College and a member of the Atlanta Optimist Club. He attended Druid Hills Methodist Church.

Dr. Thomas W. Ayers, 95, was a physician, journalist, and the first Southern Baptist medical missionary to China. Onetime publisher of the *Anniston Hot Blast* and *Franklin County Register,* he was the founder of two Baptist hospitals in China and was decorated by two Chinese presidents. He was the second living man to be honored with a monument in China. He was field secretary for his church's Foreign Mission Board in the United States. Another of the city's journalists died this year: Lawrence D. Hale, former editor of *The Courier,* the newspaper of the Atlanta and West Point Railroad. He was a member of the Virginia Avenue Baptist Church.

Mrs. Charles Frederic Stone, wife of the board chairman of Atlantic Steel, was the former Virginia Butter. She attended Washington Seminary and graduated from Agnes Scott in 1904. She had been chairman of the Woman's Auxiliary of North Avenue Presbyterian Church. J. M. Fluker, retired president of Johnson-Fluker Candy Company, was a lifelong resident of Atlanta and Sea Island. He was active in Druid Hills Methodist Church. A. R. Lord, Sr., principal partner in A. R. Lord and Sons, manufacturers of woodworking machinery, died at 63. He was a Mason and a member of Wesley Memorial Methodist Church. Mrs. Ethel Crowe Griffen, wife of the executive secretary of the Atlanta Christian Council, died at 47. Her special interest was the baby clinic at Central Presbyterian Church. R. E. Sidwell, southeastern district manager of the film department of E. I. DuPont, died at 55. He was a graduate of Drexel Institute of Technology and a member of the Atlanta Athletic Club, Atlanta Sales Executives Club, and East Lake Country Club.

John M. Owen, attorney and former city councilman, died at 76. He was a graduate of Mercer University and Atlanta Law School, and his specialty was title law. A member of many legal professional groups, he also was a member of Capital City Club and the Shrine. Mrs. Robert P. Stahl, widow of the vice-president of Davis-Freeman Jewelers, was a member of the DAR and of the Atlanta Woman's Club. Frank Hawkins, one of the founders of Atlanta Steel Hoop Company, forerunner of Atlantic Steel Company, died at 98. He was a founder and president of the Third National Bank, which merged with C&S. He was a member of the Capital City Club, the Piedmont Driving Club, and St. Luke's Episcopal Church. Mrs. W. F. Chester, daughter of Dr. A. H. Redd, Confederate Army surgeon, and granddaughter of the first president of Alabama Polytechnic Institute, died. She was a member of the UDC, the DAR, and the Methodist church. John F. Holcomb, retired N.C.&St.L. Railway engineer for forty-four years, died at 65. He was a member of the Brotherhood of Railroad Engineers and the Baptist church.

Mrs. Robert D. Woodall, the former Amelia Reeder, daughter of Dr. Nathaniel Reeder, Confederate captain, died at 92. She was a leader in temperance and women's suffrage groups and was president of the first women's suffrage organization formed in Atlanta in 1909. Dr. J. L. Pittman, Atlanta urologist and associate professor of urology at Emory University, died at 52. He had been on the staff of Emory since 1929 and was a member of many professional groups. On the staffs of Emory, Grady, Piedmont, and Crawford Long hospitals, he was also a member of the Piedmont Driving Club and the Capital City Club. Dr. J. W. Elliott, an osteopathic physician in Atlanta since 1919, died at 88. A. T. Butler, 84, was retired chief of police of Fulton County and had served on the force for forty years. L. O. Kimberly, retired principal of Hoke Smith Junior High, who had been a teacher and school official for forty-five years, died at 84. J. C. Dunlap, a former president of the Piedmont Driving Club and a member of North Avenue Presbyterian Church and the Capital City Club, died at 52. Mrs. Price Gilbert, well-known Atlanta club woman, also died. She was chairman of the Commission of Historic Sites of the Georgia Society of Colonial Dames.

Katherine Wood, ordained a deaconess at All Saints in 1903 and leader of the Holy Innocents Mission on Sixteenth Street, died at 90. She was a lifelong Atlantan and the only Episcopal Deaconess in Georgia. Mrs. William Early Beckham, widow of a prominent Atlanta real estate man and a resident of this city for fifty years, died at 78. She was active in the DAR, the Atlanta Historical Society, the Daughters of American Colonists, and was a member of St. Mark's Methodist Church. Mrs. Frank Adair, also a widow of an Atlanta real estate man, and a native Atlantan, died at 66. She was a graduate of Washington Seminary and Lucy Cobb Institute and was a member of the Peachtree Garden Club and the First Methodist Church. She was also a member of the Piedmont Driving Club and the Capital City Club.

H. W. Dent, a former city councilman and practicing attorney in Atlanta for fifty-five years, died. He was a steward of St. Mark's Methodist Church and a trustee of the Methodist Children's Home in Decatur. He was graduated from Emory at Oxford and the University of Virginia Law School. I. M. Weinstein, president of National Linen Service Corporation, died at 66. A leader in Atlanta's Jewish community, he was formerly president of the Atlanta Jewish Welfare Fund, chairman of the Atlanta State of Israel Bond Committee, and was awarded Israel's Distinguished Service Award in 1952.

He was a member of the Progressive Club, the Standard Club, and The Temple. Paul H. Dobbins, prominent insurance executive and a partner in the General Agency of Aetna Life Insurance, died at 71. He was a member of First Presbyterian Church. Mrs. Charles King, member of the Atlanta Historical Society's board of trustees, the UDC, the DAR, and St. Luke's Church, died at 74. She was a lifelong Atlantan and the widow of the sales manager of Bethlehem Steel Corporation. Dr. Herbert L. Reynolds, prominent Atlanta physician and associate professor of medicine at Emory for twenty years, died at 69. Dr. Reynolds was a specialist in internal medicine and a graduate of the University of Georgia and the Atlanta College of Physicians and Surgeons. He was a member of the Piedmont Driving Club and All Saints' Episcopal Church.

Mrs. Edwin P. Ansley, widow of the developer of Ansley Park and a member of First Presbyterian Church, died at 91. Mrs. Wooten Townsend, a graduate of the Boston Conservatory of Music and formerly director of music at Cox College in College Park, died at 86. For a quarter-century she served as director of music of Atlanta Public High Schools. Mrs. Paul Adams, the former Adelaide Howell, daughter of Capt. Evan and Georgia Howell, died at her home in New York, where she was soloist with Paul Whiteman's Orchestra. Dr. Franklin N. Parker, dean emeritus of Emory University's Candler School of Theology, died at 86. One of the outstanding figures in Methodism, Dr. Parker joined the Emory faculty in 1915 and was named dean in 1919. He was a Phi Beta Kappa graduate of Vanderbilt. Mrs. William Tennent, the former Kathryne Kay, died at 75. She was an active member in many areas of interest in Central Presbyterian Church.

Atlanta's famed "Lady in Black," Lucy Gartrell, died. Miss Lucy, one of the city's best known citizens, died at her home. She was a retired music teacher. When her sister died, Miss Lucy became a living memorial by wearing nothing but black. She was an active member of St. Luke's Episcopal Church. W. B. Farnsworth, assistant to the president of Georgia Power, a civic leader and member of the Atlanta Athletic Club, died at 53. He was a graduate of Georgia Tech and a member of St. Philip's. Lelia Garcia, lifelong Atlantan, was former assistant principal of Ivy Street School and later principal of Boulevard Elementary School. She was a communicant of St. Philip's Cathedral. Ernest L. Dennard, employee for twenty-nine years of the Southern Railway, died at 64. He was a member of Capitol Avenue Baptist Church. Henry Lee Ayers, Atlanta resident for fifty years, had been a train dispatcher for N.C.&St.L. and Seaboard Airline for half a century.

Ward Wight, Jr., was a prominent real estate executive and president of Ward Wight Realty Company which he founded in 1922. Ella Luckie, widow of Eugene Luckie for whose family Luckie Street was named, died at 77. She graduated from Berea College and was a Christian Science practitioner. Claude E. Buchanan, lifelong Atlantan and a manufacturer's agent, died at 82. He was a graduate of Georgia Tech and a member of the Piedmont

Driving Club. Mrs. Joseph W. Shelor, the former Lena Buchanan, daughter of pioneer Atlantans and widow of the freight agent for the Atlanta Joint Terminal, died at 79. She was a member of the DAR, the UDC, and Jackson Hills Baptist Church.

Dr. J. H. Crawford, eye, ear, nose, and throat specialist, died at 75. A graduate of old Boys High School, Alabama Polytechnic Institute, and the Atlanta College of Physicians and Surgeons, he was on the staff of St. Joseph's and Georgia Baptist hospitals. Dr. Eliot Fay, associate professor of Romance languages at Emory University and an outstanding French scholar, died at 52. He was a magna cum laude graduate of Harvard and Cornell and was an author and editor. Orme Miller, proprietor of Miller's Book and Office Supply Company, was a lifelong Atlantan and a graduate of Sewanee Military College. He died at 62. George Carpenter Jones, Sr., vice-president of J. M. High Company for forty years, died at 82. He was the first president of Ansley Park Golf Club and a graduate of Eastman School of Business. W. C. Alexander, retired Southern Railway engineer, died at 74. He attended Purdue University and had been with Southern forty-two years. He was a member of North Avenue Presbyterian Church. Mrs. James A. Beasley, one of the oldest members of St. Luke's Episcopal Church, died at 94. She was a native of England and the widow of a prominent physician. Mrs. Henry Kaufman, widow of a well-known merchant, was the daughter of Sam and Sarah Cohen of Albany, Georgia. They came to Atlanta during the summer of 1864 and she witnessed the burning of the city. Mrs. Kaufman was 92 years old and a charter member of The Temple Sisterhood.

R. B. Blackburn, oldest active member of the Atlanta Bar Association and former member of the Fulton County legislature, died at 88. He was an active member of St. Luke's Episcopal Church for over seventy years. Herbert Raymond Salter, son of pioneer Atlantans and employee of Southern Railway, died at 67. He had been a member of Atlanta City Council. C. F. Collier, Atlanta native and a member of one of the city's oldest families, died at 78. He was an employee of Fulton County for over fifty years and was a member of Sardis Methodist Church. C. B. Howard, active in the textile business and a cotton broker in his own firm, Inman, Howard and Inman, died at 87. He was past president of Rotary, a member of Capital City Club, Piedmont Driving Club, Druid Hills Golf Club, and the Atlanta Athletic Club. He attended Peachtree Christian Church.

Mrs. T. M. Brumby, widow of a mayor of Marietta and president of Brumby Chair Company, died at 69. She was a member of Planter's Garden Club and held several high offices in state and regional garden clubs. She belonged to Colonial Dames and was a member of North Avenue Presbyterian Church. Dr. Charles A. Wilkins, one of the nation's leading skin specialists, died at 74. He was a graduate of Emory and the Atlanta Medical College in 1902. He was on the staff of several hospitals and was a member of Druid Hills Golf Club. Mrs. Howard McCall, lifelong Atlantan and widow of the president of Paragon Box Company, died at 83. She was active in civic and patriotic organizations and held many offices at state and national levels, including state president of the UDC and parliamentarian of the Georgia Federation of Woman's Clubs. She was a charter member of Ponce de Leon Baptist Church.

Mrs. R. Irving Gresham, president of Gresham's Flowers and a leader in the social and civic affairs of the city, died. She was the former Juanita Stovall Tyler, daughter of John E. and Clara Stovall Tyler, and was a member of All Saints' Episcopal Church. Gresham had assumed presidency of the company on the death of her husband in 1938. Mrs. J. Hixon Kinsella, the former Dorothy Jones of St. Louis, died of injuries received in an auto accident. She was the wife of the vice-president of D'Arcy Advertising Agency and was a member of the Capital City Golf Club and the Lake Laurel Pistol Club. Langdon C. Quin, president of the insurance firm of Hurt and Quin, died at 67. He was a member of St. Philip's Cathedral. Dowdell Brown, manager of Commercial Union Assurance Company, Ltd., died at 78. He was a director of C&S Bank, member of East Lake, Capital City, and the Piedmont Driving clubs and Rotary. He was a communicant of Christ the King.

Dr. W. C. Humphries, last surviving member of the class of 1888 of the old Atlanta Medical College, died at 89. He belonged to a pioneer family of Marthasville, and his uncle operated the famous Whitehall Tavern. He was a veteran of World War I, a Mason, and a former mayor of Acworth. James M. Moore, active churchman and longtime Atlanta grocery dealer, had moved to Atlanta in 1890. He was the oldest living member of Central Baptist Church. Dr. Joel Thomas Hutchins, Atlanta physician for twenty-five years, died at 53. He was a graduate of Emory Medical School and was a member of St. Paul Methodist Church and Ansley Park Golf Club. Carson Lewis, an authority on Atlanta history at the turn of the century, died at 75. He was associated with Penn Mutual for thirty years. Mrs. Mamie Barnhart, Atlanta fashion designer in the 1920s and 1930s, had sewed for many of Atlanta's most prominent ladies. She was the owner of M. W. Barnhart Modiste Shop, which employed twelve seamstresses. Frank Carter, prominent attorney for forty years, died at 61. He had been president of the Atlanta Chamber of Commerce and the Atlanta Bar Association.

William T. Rich, 67, Atlanta business and religious leader, died unexpectedly. He was the son of Daniel and Julia T. Rich, and his father was one of the three brothers who founded Atlanta's best-loved department store. A director of Rich's, he was also president of Hygena Company and vice-president of Jacobs Drug Store. Rich was a graduate of Georgia Tech and a past president of The Temple. He was a member of the Standard Club and a Mason. Charles J. Holditch, retired official of Southern Bell, died at St. Petersburg. A native of England, he began his telephone career in Atlanta in 1903, becoming vice-president and general auditor. E. A. Minor, one of the major contributors to the development of East Atlanta, died at 92. He was the oldest living former city councilman. He was a Mason and a member of Martha Brown Methodist Church. Mrs. Robert S. Griffith, the former Emily Reynolds, was a member of Ivy Garden Club, the Piedmont Driving Club and St. Philip's Cathedral. T. A. (Uncle Lon) Burdett, oldest resident of the Sandy Springs community and prominent civic leader, died at 86. He had been a deputy sheriff of Fulton County and was the oldest member of Sandy Springs Methodist Church, which he had attended for sixty-three years.

NOTES

1. Melvin Ecke, "From Ivy Street to Kennedy Center; A Centennial History of the Atlanta School System" (Atlanta: Atlanta Public School System, 1972).

2. Robert Wallace, *Dress Her in White and Gold: A Biography of Georgia Tech* (Atlanta: Georgia Tech Foundation, 1969).

1955

THE year 1955 could well go down in history as the year of the nurse, the doctor, and the medical researcher. As summer ended, the *Constitution* on August 8 issued the following report:

Hospital, health and medical facilities in the Atlanta area are being greatly expanded by building projects which will cost a total of more than $45,000,000.

Some of the construction projects are still in the planning stage—and others are nearing completion.

Five big projects to improve local health facilities are:

1. The new Grady Hospital to cost about $24,000,000—now under construction.

2. The new Piedmont Hospital to cost in excess of $4,000,000—under construction.

3. Communicable Disease Center headquarters, U.S. Public Health Service, to cost $12,000,000—still in the planning stage but scheduled to start before the first of next year.

4. Georgia Baptist Hospital Professional Building erected at a cost of about $1,750,000—near completion.

5. Emory University Clinic Building to cost an estimated $1,000,000—begun in May.

In addition, plans are in the mill to build a $1,500,000 Tri-Cities Hospital to serve Hapeville, College Park and East Point, a $250,000 hospital at Fairburn to serve South Fulton County and part of Fayette County and a $500,000 hospital to serve North DeKalb County.

Construction of the 1,000-bed, 20-story Grady Hospital building is "slightly ahead of schedule," Frank Wilson, superintendent of the hospital said.

The new Grady is scheduled to be completed in October 1956. Piedmont Hospital's new building at 1968 Peachtree Road will be completed "about a year from now," said G. R. Burt, superintendent of Piedmont.

The five-story hospital building will have 260 beds, Burt pointed out. He said construction is "proceeding according to schedule."

The professional building adjacent to Georgia Baptist Hospital is slated to be completed "within the next sixty days," said E. B. Peel, administrator of the hospital. He pointed out that more than 100 physicians will have offices in the new building.

Construction of the new home for the Communicable Disease Center, U.S. Public Health Service, will start about the first of the year (1956) and require about thirty months. The six-building center will be located on

Clifton Road near Emory University and will comprise one of the largest medical and scientific centers in the nation.

Favorable action by the Senate Public Works Committee on July 28 cleared the way for the tremendous project. The central and largest building will consist of a five-floor laboratory section surrounded by an eight-story office section. Completion of the project will permit consolidation of many of the center's widely scattered activities, now housed in eleven structures (many of them temporary).

The Emory Medical Clinic under construction across from Emory University Hospital will house the offices of 35 physicians. The clinic building is a five-story structure with 38,000 square feet of floor space. It is expected to be completed in a year.

The five-year-old South Fulton Cities Hospital Authority has been reorganized as the Tri-Cities Hospital Authority. Trustees hope to build a hospital with not less than 100 beds—and they estimate the total cost will be about $1,500,000.

A fund campaign is under way in the Fairburn area of South Fulton County to raise $250,000 for a 25-bed, non-profit hospital in Fairburn. The hospital will be known as the Campbell Memorial Hospital and serve part of Fayette County as well as extreme south Fulton County.

Private contributions supported much of Emory's expansion. In January, 1955, Emory University received two grants amounting to $5 million from an anonymous foundation; $4 million went for the School of Medicine, and $1 million went for a clinic. There were other gifts to Emory in this year; $2 million was from the Rockefeller Foundation, and $435,000 from the will of the late Mrs. Frances Winship Walters, for a memorial chair of pediatrics. Also, the Emory School of Nursing celebrated its Golden Anniversary this year. The nursing school's affiliation with Emory began in 1933, when the Wesley Memorial Hospital moved to the Emory campus. The dean was Ada Fort.

In December, with the building about half complete, Atlanta celebrated the laying of the cornerstone for the new Grady Hospital. An airtight copper box 4 × 6 × 14 was sealed in concrete behind the cornerstone. It contained copies of the *Journal* and the *Constitution*, copies of all reports of the Fulton-DeKalb Hospital Authority since its activation in 1946; a list of all current employees of Grady, and copies of the Hospital Authority contracts with the governments of two counties. Also sealed in for the benefit of future historians was a copy of the prospectus relating to the sale of $20 million in revenue certificates that financed the building of the new Grady.

There were no elaborate ceremonies or speeches—which could not have been heard anyway, according to reporter Katherine Barnwell, because of the roar of construction machinery in the background.

Another fiftieth anniversary took place in May of 1955. On May 13, 1905, the Atlanta Terminal Station was dedicated on Spring Street, and the event was remembered fifty years later in a nostalgic article in the *Atlanta Journal*. Modeled after an "ornate Mexican cathedral," according to writer Margery Smith, the structure in its active half-century had seen thousands of soldiers from two world wars and the Korean conflict pass through its doors. FDR took his last journey through the terminal, and thousands of other famous and infamous people have memories of Atlanta and its terminal. Among them were Presidents Teddy Roosevelt and Warren G. Harding and vice-president-elect Calvin Coolidge, plus scores of opera and stage stars.

Architecturally, the station looked the same until well into the 1940s, when civic officials decided it should be cleaned up and renovated. Up to 1947 little had been done to modernize the station, except to remove two ornate superstructures above the twin towers that had often been struck by lightning and were regarded as architectural monstrosities and to replace the old train sheds with "butterfly sheds." In 1947 H. A. Bondurant, president of the Atlanta Terminal Company, announced a $330,000 modernization program, "designed to turn the Terminal into an up-to-date depot." And thus the terminal was to survive its fiftieth birthday until at last, in 1971, with few passengers left to use it, it was torn down. In 1955, however, it was still a fairly busy place, though passenger traffic did not approach the 30,000 a day who had passed through there during the war years.

There were fifty-eight regularly scheduled trains going in and out of the terminal daily. Four hundred people were employed there, handling 2,000 to 3,000 bags and 40,000 to 50,000 pieces of mail daily.

As noted earlier, however, the competition of the automobile was having its effect on passenger train traffic, and the development of the expressways planned through Atlanta, linking the inner city with a national system of interstate highways, would hasten the process.

"It's definitely on the record," wrote Jouett Davenport in the *Journal-Constitution* of January 2, 1956, "that 1955 was by far the best year ever experienced by Atlantans and Georgians in virtually all segments of the economic picture. . . ." He continued:

Perhaps the most spectacular gain was in the retail sales. Total volume of such sales, in the metropolitan area were estimated by Joe Heyman, vice president of the Trust Company of Georgia, at a high of $1,075,000,000. Heyman said this represented a 12% gain over the total of $963,000,000 recorded in retail sales in the three county area in 1954.

Figures on Atlanta's industrial growth showed that there were 44 new plants established here in 1955, representing a total of approximately $41,000,000 in new capital investment for buildings and equipment.

Frank Malone, chairman of the Industrial Bureau of the Atlanta Chamber of Commerce, pointed out that these projects were in addition to the expansion, costing many millions of dollars, which was carried out by existing Atlanta industries.

At the same time, Malone reported, 106 new offices and warehouses were set up here along with 81 new resident representatives. These new institutions brought 2,509 additional jobs to the Atlanta area and increased the total annual payroll here by $10,028,000.

Scott Candler, secretary of the State Department of Commerce, reported that new facilities in Georgia as a whole represented a capital investment in excess of $150,000,000. Georgia now has some 8,000 plants in operation and the total value of manufactured products in the state last year came to more than $4,000,000,000—a new high. Total non-farm employment also was at record levels in Atlanta, and Georgia as a whole, in the year just ended. Best available estimates put the figure at 330,500 workers in Atlanta and 953,000 in the state as a whole.

Georgia Labor Commissioner Ben T. Huiet said that there are some 25% more persons working in Georgia now than at the wartime peak, and the total on the job is up by 50,000 over 1954.

Davenport also noted the rapid growth of public utilities: Georgia Power Company reported that total sales of electricity increased in Georgia from 6.6 billion kilowatt hours in 1954 to 7.1 billion in 1955, a gain of more than 7 percent. Company president Harllee Branch said that more than 22,800 electric customers were added to the lines of the company, bringing the total now served to more than 576,000. The additional customers included more than 20,000 new homes, more than 2,000 small industries and commercial establishments, and 33 large industries. The company's sales totaled 1.9 billion kilowatt hours to residential, industrial, and commercial users. There was a gain of more than 146 million kilowatt hours over the 1954 total. To take care of this expanded business, the Power Company invested some $31 million during the year in new facilities. The company's tax bite for the year was estimated at $20 million, an increase of $2 million over 1954.

The Atlanta Gas Light Company also carved out an extensive expansion program in the Atlanta area. This included the addition of 1,277,454 feet of new gas mains and 16,944 new meters—10 percent more than had been added during the previous year.

O. M. Eberhart, district manager for Southern Bell Telephone Company, said that 297,000 telephones were now serving the Atlanta district, 31,000 more than in 1954 (which had been the seventy-fifth anniversary of the company in Atlanta). Statewide, 49,000 new phones were added to the company's exchanges in 1954. Expenditures in Atlanta came to $12 million.

Atlanta's automobile assembly plants also rolled to new production records in 1955, as payrolls and local expenditures reached new high levels. GM reported that its Chevrolet plant in Atlanta produced 153,255 cars and trucks, while the Buick, Oldsmobile, and Pontiac assembly division at Doraville turned out a total of 192,511 units. Goods and services purchased by GM in Atlanta and other parts of Georgia totaled $50 million during 1955. Employment figures for GM in Atlanta totaled 7,584 persons at work, compared with 6,211 in 1954, and 1955 payrolls were $41,008,000, sharply ahead of the 1954 aggregate of $24,736,081.

Ford's assembly plant at Hapeville turned out 113,437 automobiles and trucks in 1955, compared with 96,796 during 1954, and the all-time high payroll in Atlanta totaled $9,154,000 as against $7,602,234 in the previous year. Average weekly earnings of workers rose from $90.45 in 1954 to $110.62 in 1955. Ford's local purchases added up to $20,783,483, double the $10,081,869 purchases for 1954.

Another milestone for women occurred in 1955 as Mrs. Anton Flynn of College Park became the first woman to serve on a federal court jury in Atlanta. As noted earlier, in 1954 Frances Smith was the first Atlanta woman to serve on a superior court jury. Judge Boyd Sloan expressed a special welcome to Flynn as she took her place on the jury box to hear a damage suit.

In the field of music, native Atlantan Harry Kruger was named assistant director of the Atlanta Symphony Orchestra. From 1946 to 1949 Kruger played the flute with the symphony and was also guest conductor of the Youth Symphony. In his new post he would also teach instrumental music in the city schools. There he would find the number of prospective musicians greatly increased—a reflection of the increase in the school's population. Ira Jarrell announced that approximately 107,000 students would register when Atlanta schools opened in the fall, with a total of 186,300 registering from Atlanta, Decatur, Marietta, and from Fulton, DeKalb, and Cobb counties beyond the Atlanta limits. The increase in Atlanta's enrollment would be 6,000 over 1955, and it seemed likely this increase would continue in years to come.

While new structures rose to give a new cast to the city's features, old buildings rich in history went down before the bulldozer if they stood in the path of progress. Atlanta's Washington Seminary, a school for girls, was demolished in 1955 by the Continental Wrecking Company. The school was located at 1640 Peachtree Road NW and was noted for its main building, with its twenty-six great white zinc Corinthian columns.

"The Seminary," one loyal alumna told Frank Daniel, "was no mere matter of pillared porticos graced with fluted shafts and capitols of stylized acanthus leaves. . . . The Seminary was an Atlanta institution before it was a school building. For a lot of Atlanta women it is a very special place and it will endure a long time in the hearts and the habits of its alumnae, in the memories of many young women and their mothers, and their grandmothers." Founded in 1878, in 1953 the seminary was merged with Westminster Schools under Dr. William Pressly. In 1959 the high ground on which it had stood on Peachtree was occupied by the Riviera Motel.

One Atlanta institution that continued to push steadily onward in the mid-fifties was the Atlanta Section of the National Council of Jewish Women, which celebrated its sixtieth anniversary on October 11, 1955, at the Progressive Club.

St. Philip's Cathedral sponsored a bell choir of dedicated teenagers, and they were featured on the Ed Sullivan television show on Christmas Eve of 1955. Before that, they had appeared on Christmas programs at the Cathedral Church of St. John in Wilmington, Delaware, and two Episcopal churches in New York City—St. John's and the Church of Heavenly Rest. Dressed in medieval costumes, the young Atlantans played specially made bells, designed in England many centuries before, and still manufactured there. Said the *Constitution* in an editorial: "these youngsters will give to some 14,000,000 Americans another aspect of Teenage activity than that usually found in the headlines. They will bring honor to the whole city."

The Supreme Court decision of May 17, 1954, requiring the states to lay out plans for the desegregation of the public schools, caused anger and dismay among many whites in Atlanta as well as throughout the South. However, city officials and the black businessmen who felt a mutual respect for each other were handling the situation gingerly, and for the most part calmly.

On May 31, 1955, the Supreme Court again ruled that racial segregation in public schools must be ended "with all deliberate speed" but again set no deadline. The reaction of top officials in Georgia was mixed. Senator Walter F. George thought the court was "saying to go slow, but to go; to proceed with care." Governor Marvin Griffin pledged that Georgia "will continue to run our schools as we always have," and former Governor Herman Talmadge said that desegregation "would not be feasible in Georgia for a long, long time." On the other hand, the National Association for the Advancement of Colored People (NAACP) was "gratified" by the decision and seemingly was encouraged to push for early compliance with the court's decision.[1]

On June 3, four days after the decision was made public on May 31, Atlanta school authorities were asked to "take immediate steps" to abolish school desegregation. The request, contained in a petition bearing the names of nine Negro children, was filed by the Atlanta Branch of the NAACP. It pointed out simply that the Supreme Court had ruled that "the maintenance of racially segregated public schools is a violation of the Constitution" and that "in the field of public education the doctrine of separate but equal has no place."

Meanwhile, national and state leaders of the NAACP met at the Wheat Street Baptist Church on Auburn Avenue to work out general policies as to how integration might be carried out. In Atlanta for the meeting were national Negro leaders, among them NAACP attorney Thurgood Marshall, executive secretary Roy Wilkins, and some fourteen NAACP presidents. A letter accompanied the petition and called attention to the fact that a suit had been filed in 1951 in U.S. District Court in Atlanta seeking an end to segregation. If school authorities would take action, there would be no need for pressing the court action further.

Defiant reaction by Georgia's state education board was not long in coming. On July 11 the board voted unanimously to revoke the salary and license of any teacher "who supports, encourages, condones, offers to teach, or teaches 'non-segregated' classes." But teachers who refused to obey the order of any superior who ordered them to teach a mixed class would be paid a salary for the full term of their contract.

In Atlanta the Negroes' efforts to achieve equality were also directed toward areas other than the schools. In June of 1955 attorney A. T. Walden, a black, Johnny Gousram, a white man, and three other blacks asked that Negroes be permitted to use the main library downtown. The Atlanta Library Board indicated it would take the request under advisement. The result was a bookmobile to serve the black areas.

In county government, however, blacks made some progress. On June 15 the Fulton County sheriff's office added two Negroes to the staff. Sheriff T. Ralph Grimes announced the appointment of Willie Lee Armour and Vesper McKinney to the force. The sheriff said the two would be working on the fourth and fifth floors of Fulton Tower, where only Negro prisoners were housed.

Later, on November 7, the Supreme Court opened another door through which blacks soon began to pass. The court by unanimous decision banned racial segregation in publicly financed parks, playgrounds, and golf courses. This decision upheld a lower court decision for segregation at beaches and bath-houses operated by Baltimore and the State of Maryland—and overturned two lower court decisions against Negroes using city-operated golf courses in Atlanta. Reaction in Atlanta was instantaneous. Georgia Attorney General Eugene Cook charged that the NAACP could get from the Supreme Court "any decision respecting segregation that is designed to further its program to force intermarriage." The next day, November 8, Governor Marvin Griffin announced in Atlanta that the state would get out of the parks business before allowing a breakdown of segregation and intimacy on the playground.[2]

In compliance with the Supreme Court decision of November 7, U.S. District Judge Boyd Sloan signed an order declaring the desegregation of Atlanta's city golf courses. On December 23 five black men played golf at Atlanta's North Fulton course. They were Alfred Holmes and his brother Oliver, who along with their father, Dr. H. M. Holmes, a seventy-one-year old physician, had filed suits protesting segregation in the Atlanta public courses. Three other players were T. D. Hawkins, head teller for the Citizens Trust Company, and C. T. Bell and E. J. Peterson, real estate men. The Holmes brothers reported that the white golfers on the course that day "made positive, friendly statements" to them.

Governor Griffin's reaction was that it was "regrettable" that Atlanta chose to allow Negroes to play golf rather than disposing of the courses, but the state could not do anything about it. He then went on to say that "this is but a foretaste of what the people can expect in those communities where the white people are divided at the ballot box and where the NAACP holds the balance of power on election day."

The opening of the golf courses was not the only break in the walls of segregation, which Atlanta and Georgia were to experience as 1955 went into its final days. On December 5 the Board of Regents, over Governor Griffin's vigorous protests, had voted 14-1 to permit Georgia Tech to play in the Sugar Bowl against the University of Pittsburgh, which had a Negro substitute full-back, Bobby Grier, on its squad. Pitt, on November 22, had accepted an invitation to play in the Sugar Bowl with the understanding that Grier, its only Negro player, would not be barred and that segregation of the spectators on a racial basis (customary in Louisiana) would not be carried out in Pittsburgh's section of the stands. Governor Griffin immediately demanded that Tech be forbidden to carry out its Sugar Bowl contract as the Southeastern Conference representative, warning, "Georgia cannot make the slightest concession to the enemy in this dark and lamentable hour of struggle." Tech president Blake R. Van Leer refused the governor's demand and the regents backed him up. However, they did adopt a new directive, saying that Georgia state colleges might not play home games with teams on which "the races are mixed," and had to respect the laws, customs, and traditions of the host state in games outside Georgia. Governor Griffin's attitude and utterances aroused Tech students to disorderly demonstrations against him on December 2 and 3 in Atlanta. A message of "apology" went out to Pitt from students, and Tech's alumni groups voiced their protests to the governor. His answer was that he was "satisfied with the Regents' forthright declaration of policy; but was unalterably opposed to the unsegregated conditions of the 1956 Sugar Bowl Game."[3]

Despite his protests, the game was played in New Orleans on January 2, 1956, and Tech won 7-0. And so began the entry of the black man into collegiate sports competition in the Deep South, forerunner of the day when black athletes would be looked upon not as pariahs, but as heroes.

This eventful year in race relations saw the passing of Walter F. White, native Atlantan who more than any other man was responsible for the NAACP. He died in New York of a heart attack on March 21. He was sixty-one, and had been in Atlanta a year before when he addressed the convention here of Negro Elks. By coincidence, on the day after his death, the Supreme Court on March 22 announced it would open hearings on methods of enforcing its decision against racial segregation of public schools. And three days before White's death, on March 18, the Georgia Education Association, made up of teachers and school officials, had met in Atlanta to announce a policy of "equal but separate schools"—a policy opposed by the NAACP on the grounds that separate schools could never be equal. The following is a summary of White's career:

"Blonde, blue-eyed, variously described as '1/64 Negro' and 'of 5/32 Negro descent,' he chose to live as a Negro, although he could have passed as white in appearance." Born July 1, 1893, son of a postman, White graduated from Atlanta University in 1916. Briefly an insurance salesman, he became NAACP assistant secretary in 1918. His courageous investigation at the scene of Elaine, Arkansas, race riots in 1919 helped win freedom for seventy-nine imprisoned Negro men (twelve under death sentence) whose cases were appealed to the U.S. Supreme Court by the NAACP.

White became acting secretary of the NAACP in 1929 and executive secretary in 1931. He gained national prominence in the 1930s as a campaigner for Negro rights and antilynching laws. He staged Marian Anderson's 1939 open-air concert in Washington after the Daughters of the American Revolution refused to let her use Constitution Hall. White drafted FDR's executive order on fair employment practices in industry during World War II. He served in many governmental advisory posts; he was consultant to the U.S. delegation at the U.N. organizing conference in San Francisco in 1945 and at the 1948 General Assembly session in Paris. He was an advisor to President Truman on his civil rights stand that caused the Dixicrat bolt from the Democratic party in 1948.

White was a *New York Post* war correspondent from 1943 to 1945. He wrote five books and over 100 magazine articles.

On Christmas Day the city celebrated the one-hundredth anniversary of its first gas street lamps.

"Today," the *Journal-Constitution* noted, "the city has only one gas lamp remaining. It burns at Alabama and Whitehall Streets. The Atlanta Gas Light Company keeps it there to commemorate a bygone era, a century ago, when Atlanta's 6,000 citizens found their way at night along streets lighted by hundreds of them."

OBITUARIES

Augustus Harvey Turner, 75, southern manager for eleven nationally known insurance companies, died at his home in the Biltmore Apartments. He was a member of the Capital City Club. Mrs. E. D. (Aunt Ann) Rainwater, 97-year-old grandmother of sixty-five persons and one of the oldest residents of Fulton County, died in Fairburn. Her entire life was spent within three miles of her birthplace. L. M. Nolan, former College Park councilman and chairman of the street committee and the utilities committee, died at 68. For forty-one years he was a telegraph operator for the Central of Georgia Railroad and was a member of the Brotherhood of Railroad Trainmen and the Telegraph Operators' Union. C. B. Beaullieu, 64, associate architect of the Fulton County Courthouse, Terminal Station, and the Healey Building, had served as president of the Atlanta Builders' Exchange.

Former governor John Marshall Slaton, distinguished legal and political figure, died at 88. He had served as the sixtieth governor of Georgia and had served as speaker of the House and president of the Senate in the Georgia legislature. He is probably best remembered for commuting Leo Frank's death sentence to life imprisonment, and many political observers felt the act swept him from the Georgia political scene for all time. Governor Slaton was born in Meriwether County on Christmas Day in 1866. His father, Maj. William Franklin Slaton, was an educator who served as an officer in the Confederate Army and then moved his family to Atlanta after the war. He became superintendent of Atlanta public schools, which his son, John Marshall, attended. The young man worked his way through the University of Georgia and graduated in 1886 with highest honors. After graduating in law he was admitted to the bar, and in 1898 he married Sarah Frances, daughter of Capt. William D. and Sarah Frances Reid Grant. John M. Slaton entered the field of politics early in life, being elected to the legislature in 1896 and serving through 1909, being speaker of the House for the last four years. From 1909 to 1913 he was a state senator and president of the Senate. When Hoke Smith resigned as governor in 1911 to become a United States senator, Slaton served as governor ad interim until Joseph M. Brown was elected to fill the unexpired term. Slaton was elected governor in 1912, and his administration was a notable one. He left the finances of the state at a high point. During World War I, Governor Slaton devoted himself to various patriotic causes and was a powerful figure in the various Liberty Loan campaigns. He was a member of many patriotic organizations, was a Scottish Rite Mason, a Shriner, and a devout Methodist, for many years serving as chairman of the board of stewards of Trinity Methodist Church. Noted for his hospitality, the governor was a member of the Capital City Club, the Atlanta Athletic and Piedmont Driving clubs, and of the Atlanta Chamber of Commerce.

Dr. Alex Batchelor, widely known Presbyterian minister and former secretary of the Sunday School Administration for the Presbyterian Church, died at 63. He was a graduate of Columbia Seminary, the University of South Carolina, and had a Doctor of Divinity degree from Presbyterian College. John Lewis Asbell, North Georgia District supervisor for Southern Bell and a member of the Municipal Planning Board, died at 60. He personally maintained the special telephone equipment installed for President Roosevelt on his many visits to Warm Springs.

Emily Prather, a descendant of Jean Jacques Verdery, counselor to Louis XVI of France, died at 93. Her father published *The New Era*, the first Democratic newspaper to be printed after the Civil War. Carroll Theodore Greer, executive vice-president of the Bank of Georgia, had been a banking officer for three decades and was well known in professional organizations. Mrs. Alexander King, Sr., 96, was one of the oldest native Atlantans and was long prominent in the social and civil life of the community. She was the widow of Judge King, who was appointed solicitor general of the United States by President Woodrow Wilson and later served as U.S. Judge of the Fifth District Court of Appeals. Mrs. John W. Rice, the former Ethel Mell, was the daughter of an old Atlanta family. A civic leader, she had been president of the Uncle Remus Memorial Association and the Atlanta Ladies Memorial Association. She was state president of the Confederate Southern Memorial Association and regent of the Atlanta chapter of the DAR. Mrs. Walter Sheffield, 47, was the former Callie Brown. She was secretary-treasurer of the Needlework Guild of America, vice-regent of the Cherokee chapter of the DAR, and past president of the Atlanta Tulip Club.

Dan Plaster, 62, was an Atlanta lawyer and construction analyst for the Veterans Administration. He was a fifth-generation Georgian and a member of a pioneer Fulton County family. He was instrumental in the development of the Piedmont–Rock Springs section of Atlanta. Joseph S. Shaw, Atlanta real estate appraiser, banking official, and civic leader, died at 68. He was vice-president of First Federal Savings and Loan Association and a charter member of International Society of Residential Appraisers. He had served as president and was a life member of its board of governors. Iva McWhorter, widely known nurse in obstetrics, was a graduate of Georgia Baptist Hospital Nursing School. She had made over 600 dolls for children in various hospitals. Dr. Anderson Scruggs, 57, professor of dentistry at Emory, was widely recognized as a poet and author. Dr. John F. Denton, 77, widely known obstetrician and gynecologist, had been in practice in Atlanta for 48 years. For many years he was a professor at Emory University Medical School and a member of many professional organizations.

John S. Blick, Sr., a founder and president of the Boys Club of Atlanta, died at 69. He was the owner of several bowling alleys in Atlanta and was a trustee of Hillside Cottages. He was a Mason and belonged to the Kiwanis Club. John S. Cowles, 91, was a widely known insurance salesman and noted for being the first in the South to write a $1 million policy on the life of an individual. He was southeastern district manager for Mutual Life. Mrs. Edgar Poe McBurney, Atlanta clubwoman and widow of a prominent Atlanta investor and developer, was the former Helen Sterett. She was known as Atlanta's first "Tulip Lady." Roy G. Booker, manufacturers' agent and civic leader, died. He was on the board of the Boys Club and belonged to Rotary, Elks, and Big Brothers. Mrs. Nellie Dodd Orme, daughter of Gus Dodd, died at 56. She was president of the Red Rock Company and a member of the Junior League.

Mrs. Robert F. Maddox, Sr., social and civic leader, was the wife of the former mayor. She was a charter member of the Peachtree Garden Club, a national director of the Garden Clubs of America, and held memberships in the DAR and Colonial Dames. Lynn W. Werner, Atlanta social and music leader, died at 77. He was the only honorary member of the Nine O'Clocks and was one of the first patrons of the Atlanta Music Festival Association and the Metropolitan Opera Company. Bessie M. Carter, 81, was a veteran nurse who served in the Spanish-American War and then went to work at Grady, where she nursed several generations of Atlantans. At the time of her retirement Mrs. Carter was supervisor of the Steiner Clinic at Grady. Carlos H. Mason was a pioneer Atlanta furniture store operator and president of Mason Furniture Co., located at Whitehall and Mitchell streets. He was a director of the First National Bank, a trustee of the Rabun Gap–Nacoochee School, and for fourteen years served as chairman of the old Atlanta Police Board.

Sidney E. Goldberg, 41, was owner of the National Supply Company. A graduate of Emory, he was national supreme master of Alpha Epsilon Pi social fraternity and was an officer in the Ahavath Achim Congregation. Active in Jewish civic affairs, he was also a member of the Mayfair Club. James L. Gwin, 78, had been associated with the Orkin Company for many years. He was an enthusiastic member of the Men's Garden Club and was the father of Yolande Gwin, Atlanta newspaper columnist. E. Allison Thornwell, prominent business and civic leader, died unexpectedly at 69. He was a veteran of World War I, and shortly after his service formed his own business as a manufacturers' agent for machinery and electrical equipment. A member of Rotary, he had been president of the Atlanta Athletic Club and also belonged to the Piedmont Driving Club and the Capital City Club. He was a communicant of Trinity Presbyterian Church.

Dr. Trevor Arnett, responsible for many of the physical developments at Spelman College and Atlanta University, died unexpectedly while visiting in Florida. The prominent Negro educator had been chairman of the board of Atlanta University and Spelman and was a trustee of Morehouse. James Raymo Cowan, chairman of the board of directors of Georgia Marble Company, died at his home in Marietta. Active in political affairs, Cowan was chairman of the Cobb County Republican party. He was a director of the Atlanta Transit System and was a member of the Masons, Capital City Club, and the First Presbyterian Church in Marietta. C. J. Shannon, vice-president and director of Robert and Company, died at 59. He was one of the outstanding textile engineers in the country.

Atlanta lost several religious leaders in 1955. Father Panos Constantinides, outstanding Greek religious leader in the South and pastor of the Greek Orthodox Church for more than twenty years, died at 62. He received his primary education in Smyrna, Turkey, and studied at the Theological Seminary in Constantinople. He was awarded his divinity degree from the University of Athens. He was a member of the National Council of Christians and Jews. Bishop William A. Fountain, senior bishop emeritus of the African Methodist Episcopal Church, died at 84. He had been president and chancellor of Morris Brown College. He was a graduate of Allen University, Northwestern, and the University of Indiana. He was a member of Allen Temple AME, where he once had served as pastor. Monsignor James J. Grady, 44, pastor of the Shrine of the Immaculate Conception and former chancellor of the Savannah-Atlanta Diocese, died while playing golf in Augusta. He was a graduate of St. Charles College and St. Mary's Seminary. Outstanding among his accomplishments was the restoration of Immaculate Conception, the oldest Roman Catholic church in the city.

Mrs. George I. Walker, lifelong resident of Atlanta and daughter of the late Capt. W. H. Brotherton, pioneer merchant in the city, died at 81. She was a graduate of LaGrange College and was a member of the Cathedral of St. Philip. Mrs. Charles A. Goddard, the former Harriet Eliza Guess, daughter of DeKalb pioneers E. H. and Jane Paden Guess, died at 81. Her death occurred at Emory Hospital, the site of the Paden homeplace near what is now the intersection of Clifton and North Decatur roads, where she was born. She was a member of Decatur Presbyterian Church. Mrs. C. W. Strickler, Sr., widow of a well-known physician and herself active in social and civic affairs, died at 75. She was a member of Central Presbyterian Church and was especially active in the affairs of the baby clinic there. Mrs. William Alexander Speer, a native and lifelong resident of Atlanta, was the daughter of pioneer merchant John Silvey. When the John Silvey Company closed in 1931, it was the end of a seventy-nine-year career—the oldest wholesale dry goods firm in Atlanta. Dr. Reuben C. Hood, dean emeritus of the Southern College of Pharmacy, died at 85. He was a founder of the school and taught there for more than five decades. He was the author of two pharmaceutical manuals for the laboratory.

The nine widows of Confederate veterans living at the Soldiers' Home on Confederate Avenue were reduced to eight with the death of Mrs. Joseph Henry Roberts, 98. Her paternal grandfather, Andrew Jackson Miller, was president of the Georgia Senate for twenty years. Dr. Paul Deneen McCormack, a leader in Georgia dental circles, died at 44. He was a graduate of Emory's School of Dentistry and did postgraduate work at Northwestern University. He was a Phi Delta Theta, a member of the Capital City Club and St. Martin's-in-the-Fields Church. Mrs. W. Earl Quillian, the former Laurie Mae Cassily and wife of an Atlanta physician who had been in practice fifty-six years, died. She was a member of Druid Hills Methodist Church, where she organized the Susannah Wesley Class. She was a member of the Women's Auxiliary of the Civitan Club and the Rhododendron Society.

Lewis Palmer Skidmore, former director of the High Museum of Art and the only man to take pictures of the actual rescue of *Titanic* passengers, died at 78. He was a young art student on his way to study in Italy when his ship, the *Carpathia,* rescued those in the lifeboats from *Titanic.* He made photographs and sketches of the tragic event. Skidmore was a graduate of Yale and the Pratt Institute. He served as director of the High Museum from 1929 until 1948. T. L. Johnson, well-known businessman and sportsman, died at 55. A foremost Southeastern Conference football official, he was also founder of Atlanta Blue Print Company. He was a Mason, Shriner, and member of the Atlanta Athletic Club.

H. Carl Wolf, president of the Atlanta Gas Light Company from 1938 to

1945, died at 63. He was a graduate of the University of Illinois and a veteran of World War I. He had served as director of the Community Chest Appeal, Central Atlanta Improvement, and First National Bank. He was a member of the Piedmont Driving Club and the Atlanta Athletic Club. He was a Mason, Shriner, and member of the Cathedral of St. Philip. Dr. Rufus Askew, Atlanta physician and official medical man for the Georgia Tech football team, died at 48. He attended Boys High and Emory University and was graduated from Northwestern University's medical school. He was a communicant of St. Philip's Cathedral. Dr. Ryland Knight, a leading Baptist minister for more than fifty years, died at 78. Called to Atlanta in 1932 to be pastor at Second Baptist Church at Mitchell and Washington streets, he later was named pastor of Second Ponce de Leon Baptist when Second Ponce de Leon and Buckhead Baptist churches merged in 1932. Dr. Knight was a cum laude graduate of Princeton in 1896 and received his D.D. from Richmond in 1910. He was a Mason and president of the Christian Council of Atlanta in 1941 and 1942. Dr. Edwin S. Byrd, a graduate of Emory University and practicing physician in Atlanta for more than a quarter of a century, died at 62. He had been a consultant for the U.S. government in heart and lung diseases and was on the staff of Grady and Georgia Baptist hospitals.

Byrd Blankenship, Atlanta's Woman of the Year in War Effort in 1944, died at 82 at the home of her sister, Mrs. Thomas D. Meador. For more than thirty years she served in a voluntary capacity at Red Cross headquarters, accumulating more than 40,000 hours of volunteer service. She was a member of the UDC, the DAR, the DAC, and the Sons and Daughters of the Pilgrims. She was an Episcopalian. Dr. William Hayes Bookhammer, Jr., prominent Atlanta chiropodist, died after a thirty-two-year career in this city. He was a graduate of Temple University and was in practice with his uncle, Dr. S. A. Bookhammer. Robert B. Pegram, retired vice-president of the Southern Railway System, died at 80. He had served the railroad for fifty-four years, beginning as a utility clerk. He was a director of First National, president of the Atlanta Terminal Company, and member of the Capital City Club, the Ten Club, and St. Luke's Church. Ens. William Hart Sibley, Jr., 1955 honor graduate of Georgia Tech, died at 21. A member of one of Georgia's most prominent families, Ensign Sibley was overcome by a lack of oxygen in a ship's storage area, where he was making a routine inspection. He was a graduate of Episcopal High School in Alexandria, Virginia. Dr. William H. Trimble, an internist and Atlanta physician for more than a quarter of a century, died at 52. He attended the University of Pennsylvania, Emory, and Vanderbilt. A member of the Emory Unit in World War II, Dr. Trimble was a member of several medical fraternities and St. Mark's Methodist Church.

Mrs. Oscar Strauss died at 73. She was the former Ruby Rich, daughter of Emanuel, one of the founders of Rich's. She attended Washington Seminary, was a member of The Temple, the Council of Jewish Women, and the

Standard Club. Gustave B. Sisson, president of A. K. Hawk Optical Company, died at 70. He was a son of Vardy Sisson, an editor of the *Constitution* in its infancy. He was a charter member of the Atlanta Athletic Club and belonged to Kiwanis, the Men's Garden Club, and the Cathedral of St. Philip. Paul Hardin, traffic manager of the Coca-Cola Company, died unexpectedly at 55. A veteran of World War I, he had been with Coca-Cola since 1923. He attended Riverside Military Academy, North Georgia College, University of Georgia, and New York University. Mrs. William Anderson Parker, the widow of the president of Beck and Gregg Hardware Company, died at 85. She was the former Alberta Abbott, daughter of William Lindsay Abbott and a lifelong resident of the city. A graduate of Girls High School and Lucy Cobb Institute, she was an active member of the First Baptist Church.

Gus Dodd, lifelong Atlanta resident and developer of the Red Rock soft drink organization, died at 88. In 1885 he joined John and Lee Hagan in a soft drink firm that produced ginger ale. Dodd was made vice-president, and in 1929 he became sole owner. He was a member of St. Mark's Methodist Church, the Piedmont Driving Club, and the Capital City Club. Judge William Harman Black, former attorney and retired Justice of the Supreme Court of New York, died at 87. Judge Black was a graduate of Atlanta schools, where he had come in 1870, and after graduation he was personal secretary to Senator Joseph E. Brown. He obtained a law degree from Columbia and returned to Atlanta to form a partnership with his brother, Eugene R. Black. His career in New York State began in the early 1900s, and he remained there until his retirement at 65, when he returned to this city. W. Daniel Alexander, founder of W. D. Alexander Company, distributor for General Electric, and former president of Alexander-Seewald Co., died at 60. He belonged to the Masons, the Shrine, the Atlanta Athletic Club, and the Peachtree Christian Church. Mrs. Allen D. Johnson, the former Ida Cook and widow of an Atlanta physician, died at 95. Her parents were Judge and Mrs. D. A. Cook, and her grandparents, the Merrill Colliers. She belonged to the Atlanta Historical Society, the UDC, the DAR, and the First Methodist Church.

Henry Francis (Frank) West, Atlanta pioneer and veteran real estate dealer, died at 88. He was the son of Confederate captain Andrew J. and Eugenia West. He was a veteran of the Spanish-American War and World War I. His memberships included the Atlanta Historical Society, Piedmont Driving Club, and St. Luke's Episcopal Church. He was the oldest member in point of service in the Yaarab Shrine Patrol. Robert Hamilton Martin, long prominent in Atlanta's automobile business, died at 67. He was a dealer for Nash and later for Cadillac-Oldsmobile, and also had been associated with Buick and Pontiac. Frank Garson, a native of Austria and president of Lovable Brassiere Company, died at 68. A leader in the Jewish community, Garson was an organizer of the Home for the Aged, Jewish Community Service, Jewish Social Service, and was a member of the Mayfair Club. Lt. Col. Worth

E. Yankee attended Boys High and was a 1936 graduate of the University of Georgia. In the Army since 1940 with the Military Intelligence, he was stationed in Cambodia. He died after contracting polio.

Andrew Metteaur Kennedy, president for more than twenty years of the B. M. Grant Realty Company, died unexpectedly at a Tech football game. He was 65. An expert tennis player, he was state champion at one time. A graduate of Mercer and a veteran of World War I, Mr. Kennedy was a member of Capital City Club and the Cathedral of Christ the King. T. Wayne Martin, vice-president of the investment firm of Clement A. Evans, died after a thirty-five-year career in investments. A graduate of Boys High and the University of Georgia, he belonged to Piedmont Driving Club, Capital City Club, and the North Avenue Presbyterian Church. John F. Glenn, retired executive of Bethlehem Steel Company, died at 76. A graduate of Georgia Tech, he was the son of the late Wilbur Fisk Glenn and the late Flora Harper Glenn, for whom Glenn Memorial Church was named. He had held memberships in Piedmont Driving Club and Rotary and was a communicant of St. Luke's Episcopal Church.

Mrs. John W. Grant, widow of one of Atlanta's most prosperous realtors and builder of the Grant, 22 Marietta Street, and Plaza buildings, died at 83. She and Grant were married in 1893 and were leaders in the city's civic and social life. A member of First Presbyterian Church, she was superintendent of its Sunday school for many years. During World War I she was a leader in Red Cross volunteer work. Her memberships included the UDC, the DAR, and Peachtree Garden Club. Frances Woodberry, faculty member and sister of the founder of Woodberry Hall, died at 61. She was supervisor of cultural activities for the City of Atlanta's Parks and Recreational departments. She was an accomplished soprano soloist. John Wightman Bowden, longtime Atlanta attorney and father of the president of the Georgia Bar Association, Henry L. Bowden, died at 83. He practiced for more than half a century with offices in the Healey Building. He was a charter member of the Druid Hills Methodist Church. Mrs. Felix de Golian, active in patriotic societies and a board member of Red Cross volunteers, died. She was a member of Christ the King.

William E. Plunkett, Sr., superintendent of the Atlanta Joint Terminal Railroad Yards, was killed when struck by a freight train. It is believed he suffered a heart attack and fell under the wheels. He was 66 years old and had been in railroading since 1908, when he started as a clerk in the yard office of the Atlanta Terminals. He was a member of St. Paul Methodist Church. Mrs. Frederick W. Patterson, active in the city's church and civic affairs and wife of the owner of H. M. Patterson & Son, died at 59. She was the former Lee Barclay. Mrs. Patterson belonged to Second Ponce de Leon Baptist, Primrose Garden Club, and was a board member of the Church's Homes for Girls. Mrs. B. F. Hilderbrand, widow of a prominent grocer, died at 98. She was the daughter of pioneer Atlantans Calvin and Fannie Jett Garmon. Augustus

Theodore Peacock, former teacher at old Tech High School and Georgia Tech, died at 88. He was machine shop instructor at both schools. His first job in Atlanta was with the Continental Gin Company. Peacock was an elder in the West End Presbyterian Church.

Mrs. Julian de Bruyn Kops, longtime Atlanta music teacher and widely known in state music circles, died at 72. The former May Woodberry, she had studied at Smith College and Columbia after graduating from Lucy Cobb. For twenty-five years she served as music director at Brown High School and was a soloist at St. Philip's Cathedral. She was a member of many cultural groups, including the Atlanta Historical Society, Atlanta Music Club, and the High Museum of Art. Edwin Camp, retired veteran newspaperman whose writings under the nom de plume of "Ole Timer" enriched the pages of the Atlanta *Journal,* died at 73. One of the outstanding figures of southern journalism, Camp had been writing since 1902. He attended Boys High and the University of Georgia and had done news broadcasting over WSB in the early days of radio. George Kearsley Selden, retired Southern Bell Telephone Company official and prominent in civic affairs, died at 73. He attended the University of Tennessee. He had been senior warden at St. Luke's Episcopal Church, had headed the Atlanta Community Chest, and at the time of his death was chairman of USO. He was a member of the Piedmont Driving Club. Alfred Quinton Smith, retired Atlanta contractor and formerly president of Smith and Pew Construction Company, died at 65. He was the son of early Atlantans Fred C. and Ella Smith and was a 1912 graduate of Georgia Tech. He was a communicant of St. Luke's Episcopal Church.

NOTES

1. *Facts on File* (New York: Facts on File, Inc., 1955), passim under "Education and Religion."

2. Ibid., p. 369.

3. Ibid., p. 404.

1956

GOING into the last half of the 1950s, Atlanta had accomplished much it could be proud of in the decade following the war. Men and women from all over the nation who had served in or around Atlanta in the 1940s remembered the city and its people and its promise. And they came back to share in that promise, to make their names here, and to go into business, the professions, and the arts.

In an article reprinted in the *Journal-Constitution* on January 29, 1956, *U.S. News and World Report* told the story. "ATLANTA: Hub of Prosperity . . . A growing market" was the headline; and the story summed up why this was so:

Main port of entry to the "new" South is Atlanta, now reaching for the million mark in population and spilling into the surrounding counties on every side.

Atlanta has recaptured the atmosphere of a boom town. You can sense it as soon as you set foot on the busy airport.

Here the North and South collide, but gently and politely. Clipped New England accents mix with Southern drawls.

A visitor to Atlanta calls five hotels before finding a room. Southeastern shoe retailers are in town, followed by the furniture men or the garment manufacturers. Convention badges sprinkle hotel lobbies. There is waiting for tables at some restaurants. Cabs are hard to find. In public places, men talk over plans for new factories, draw crude diagrams of plants on restaurant menus. "Two million . . . four million . . . six million," the dollar talk goes.

Fifteen main railway lines, sixty truck lines, ten major air routes pour passengers and goods in and out of Atlanta. They put the city at the crossroads of the awakening South.

The five states reached most readily from Atlanta—Georgia, Florida, Alabama, Tennessee and South Carolina—are doing 56 billion dollars' worth of business a year. A fat slice of this passes through Atlanta. Georgia itself did 14.2 billion in business in 1954 and of that, 6.3 billion was done in Atlanta.

One big industry in the Atlanta area—the Lockheed Aircraft Corporation—paid out 72.2 million dollars to 15,500 people in 1954. That was two-thirds as much money as Georgia got from its whole cotton crop. The Lockheed payroll is running even higher now. It goes to 17,000 people and is putting 1.5 million dollars a week into the Atlanta market area.

In Georgia and the other states that fit into the Atlanta trade orbit, business volume is now six times what it was in 1939. Since then, deposits of Georgia's biggest banking system, the Citizens & Southern National, have increased almost fourfold.

As in a good many prospering sections of the United States, war plants have given the South its first real shot in the arm. The shift from cotton and tobacco has helped the process.

In Georgia alone income from cattle, hogs, poultry and dairy products now is much bigger than from sales of cotton and tobacco. And the armed services continue to lavish contracts on the South; Georgia, for instance, got 120.6 million dollars in defense construction in the last four years.

With new money in long-empty pockets, Southerners are spending it fast for pent-up needs.

In wide reaches of the Deep South, poverty has been normal for ninety years. This backlog of need, with the new prosperity, makes the South perhaps the greatest potential consumer market in the country.

Of the 1.4 billion dollars of Atlanta incomes in 1954, 1.2 billion went for consumer products. The Southern appetite for new cars especially is sharp.

Once a dumping ground for the North's second-hand discards, the Deep South itself now trades in plenty of used cars for its lots. And in the first eleven months of 1955, dealers in the five states sold 22% more new cars than in all of 1954.

The new folding money, rustling in Southern jeans, is the reason why eighty percent of the new factories in the South have been built to fulfill the needs of Southerners exclusively.

Such plants make everything from pots and pans to the air-conditioning assemblies that are doing so much to change sleepy Tobacco Road or Magnolia Row into places where men work harder in year-round comfort.

Southerners with cash to spend are bringing the Yankees back again, this time to stay; in Atlanta alone, two-fifths of the newcomers between 1946 and 1953 came from outside the states of the old Confederacy. Other Southern cities report the same influx. Baton Rouge is full of Northerners. In Greenville, Mississippi, one businessman said: "Half the service station managers in town have Yankee accents."

There are three types of newcomers. Some of them are in high-income groups. They are officials and managers of Northern plants and agencies. They buy fine homes, showplaces with acres of grounds.

But more numerous are the younger Northerners who got their military training in the South during World War II or the Korean War. Many married Southern girls, and came back to live "easier."

There is still another class of newcomers: the young men whose fathers grew up in the South and went North because the opportunities were better there. A good many of these young "step-Southerners" are coming back to the Dixie soil and settling on or near it. They seem fascinated by the land.

This infusion from the North seems to be flattening the Southern accent little by little. It also appears to be changing some eating habits. You still get grits for breakfast in most of the South. But veal and baby beef are becoming popular in meat markets which used to sell more pork than anything else.

Of course, a lot of Southerners sigh for the old days. Still more like the new, or in any event are reconciled to its inevitability.

"Everything is changing," said one Atlantan. "A lot of things have been happening down here since General Sherman's soldiers got careless with matches back in 1864."

The same issue of the paper reported on the fantastic increase in traffic at the Atlanta airport during 1955. The number of travelers moving through the terminal made an almost unbelievable jump, from 1,205,736 in 1954 to 2,166,773. According to Grady Ridgeway, manager of the city-owned airport, this meant one passenger arrived, departed, or changed planes every fifteen seconds, night and day, for the entire year. To Mayor Hartsfield this was only the beginning. Soon Atlanta would be handling jet planes, and it would no longer be the eighth busiest airport in the nation, behind Chicago, Detroit, Los Angeles, Miami, New York, San Francisco, and Washington. It would be among the leaders.

While Hartsfield and other Atlanta boosters were looking forward to a future in the air, Mary Williams was looking back upon the Atlanta of horse-car days. Her husband, Marian Williams, started off as a horsecar driver and was promoted to motorman on the first electric streetcar ever to run on Luckie Street, she recalled. Mrs. Williams, mother of fourteen children, nine of whom she had survived, was pink-cheeked and white-haired and almost without wrinkles as she prepared to celebrate her 100th birthday on February 3, 1956.

Hartsfield's prediction that Atlanta soon would have to extend its runways to serve the new jet aircraft going into passenger service was given support by the fact that Georgia's Air National Guard was being equipped with fifty F-84 Thunderstreaks. Half of these new military jets would be based at Dobbins Air Force Base at Marietta, and the other twenty-five would be at Travis Field, Savannah.

Officials discovered that the population and traffic estimates on which Atlanta's expressway program was based were far too low. Traffic experts had estimated that it would be 1970 before Atlanta's north expressway would be carrying 44,000 vehicles daily. A traffic count by the state highway department showed that in late 1955 the expressway just north of Fourteenth Street carried 49,500 cars. The south leg of the expressway was expected to carry 25,000 vehicles daily by 1970. It was already carrying 22,500. Atlanta's traffic engineer Karl Bevins estimated that each lane of the expressway could carry 12,000 to 15,000 vehicles per hour, a capacity that was obviously insufficient.

Atlanta's population growth had also taken the experts by surprise. Greater Atlanta entered 1956 with an estimated four-county metro population of 862,000, an increase of 27,000 over 1955. At this rate it was obvious that the city's future needs for gas, electric power, telephones, streets, sewers, water mains, transit, schools, and health facilities would have to be carefully revised if Atlanta were to meet the challenge of tomorrow. Putting their heads together, the Chamber of Commerce's Metropolitan Population Study Committee and the Metropolitan Planning Commission were determined not to make the mistake made earlier—underestimate Atlanta's growth. The earlier estimate had been that Greater Atlanta would have a population of 1 million by 1970 and 1.5 million by 1980. (The fact: Going into 1970 the population was 1.3 million and the population in metropolitan Atlanta in 1980 was 1.6 million.)

The year moved on in infinite variety. Much happened that could give the city-proud a warm glow—but in one area, at least, housing for the poor and needy, there was reason for deep concern. An *Atlanta Constitution* editorial column, for example, expressed the view that "the spirit has died out of the Atlanta Slum Program." The writer elaborated:

Here where the sociological and economic value of slum clearance was first proved, where the idea of slum eradication was pioneered with Techwood, University Homes, the Clark Howell project and those which came after, the clearing of the slums has come to a halt. There is new building in plenty. Downtown, magnificent new office buildings arise, old and shabby buildings are being renovated and rebuilt into modern, clean, efficient structures. Around the periphery of the city new factories are going up.

All of which is fine. It proves that the city is full of life and vigor, there is no economic stagnation here, that the town and those who look into the future view the future with confidence.

But in the shadow of the new buildings downtown, the shabby slums still lie like skin cancers on a strong-limbed body. We stopped our great slum clearance program when it was hardly begun. In a little more than twenty years we built decent public houses for only 23,000 people. Grand juries for the past two years have been pointing out that in the city of Atlanta, there are 100,000 people who still live in some of the nation's foulest slums.

The grand juries have also reported that from these slum areas come nearly 100% of the city's criminals, from them come the greater part of the juvenile delinquents, from them the charity wards of Grady draw their daily grist of misery.

Yet in the face of these reports the Atlanta Housing Authority has reported that with the completion of the Joel Chandler Harris project in West End, the slum eradication program will become dormant; the Housing Authority will take on an administrative housekeeping role, putting aside whatever plans may exist for further development.

"What happened to the Great Crusade which Atlanta pioneered?" asked *U.S. News and World Report.* There are several answers. The *New York Times* in an editorial said:

"As with many a good crusade that has somehow mellowed with age, slum clearance housing is suffering from the lack of strongly dedicated leadership." But why, in Atlanta, is this true? What happened to the successors of Major John S. Cohen, Clark Howell, Sr., Dr. M. L. Brittain, Chuck Palmer— all those who led the fight for slum clearance twenty-odd years ago?

The fact that any great crusade loses its steam in two decades is only part of the story of why Atlanta abandoned its battle against the slums. There is perhaps a deeper meaning. Harry Barnes, Britain's great housing authority, probably put his finger on it when he said:

"There is no money in housing the poorest people well. There has always been money in housing them ill."

In Atlanta, as elsewhere, Chuck Palmer points out, many a great estate, held in trust for heirs, receives heavy income from slum property. The banks and trust departments which administer these estates are not sociologists and reformers. They are businessmen. It is their bounden duty to protect the estates entrusted to their care. It is not to their interest, as trustees, to convert slums into public housing, no matter what benefits might accrue to the community as a whole.

Which may be part of the explanation why, when $26,000,000 in federal bonds for public housing in Georgia became available, Atlanta asked for, and received, not a penny of it.

Nor does anyone greatly care—except the grand juries, which see the slums as breeding places for crime and disease. Except 100,000 people who live in the slums. Except Chuck Palmer. The old slum fighter has not yet given up. Right now, his moustaches bristling, he is needling Adlai Stevenson and the Democrats with facts and figures showing that in this richest of all nations there are still 20,000,000 Americans—5,000,000 families—living in slums.

Mr. Palmer hopes that Mr. Stevenson, if elected, will hear his plea, and initiate a building program which in ten years could eliminate slums altogether. And he hopes also, if the great crusade catches fire again, that Atlanta, which led it once, will wake from its doldrums and step back into the thick of the fight.

The editorial quoted above was inspired by the fact that on October 2 Atlanta's latest, and evidently its last, low-rent housing project would open its doors. It was the 510-unit Joel Chandler Harris Homes, located in West End and available to white tenants only. Said the *Constitution* article reporting this newest project:

Opening of the newest development may be the end of an era in Atlanta. The $7,566,691 Harris project is the last low-rent project now on the boards of the Atlanta Housing Authority, which recently has directed its prime effort to urban redevelopment and redevelopment may largely replace public housing in Atlanta. . . .

Completion of the Harris Homes will mean that eleven low-rent housing projects will have been constructed in Atlanta since Techwood Homes, the first federal government financed low-rent homes built in America, which were completed in 1936.

With the addition of the 37.6 acres covered by Harris Homes, 516.8 acres of slums had been swept clear of substandard structures, hundreds of them dilapidated houses unfit for human habitation. They had been replaced by "apartments as new as tomorrow" for low-income families.

Normally some 25,000 persons would be housed in the eleven projects, but records showed that 27,081 were living there. Of these, 13,944 were children under eighteen, and of the 6,984 families housed, 2,301 were families of veterans or servicemen. Broken families accounted for 2,256 of the tenants, and the average income of occupants was $2,077 a year.

The airport and airlines serving Atlanta continued to make news in this busy year. Delta Air Lines of Atlanta announced on February 2 that it had bought four Constellation Airliners from Pan American World Airways. Delta president C. E. Woolman said the Constellations would be used to augment service on Delta's new route to Washington and New York. The Delta fleet was now fifty-eight planes, with fifteen more on order.

Five days later Captain Eddie Rickenbacker, chairman of the Eastern Airlines board of directors, announced that Eastern would spend $500,000 at the Atlanta terminal to provide nineteen new independent gate positions, pending the completion of the new airport terminal. The new gate would eliminate double and triple plane parking. Eastern was also going ahead with its plans for a $3.5 million hangar, to be completed before the new terminal was finished.

Military aviation on the grand scale also was in the news in 1956. On October 4 the *Journal* reported that A. C. Kotchian, general manager of Lockheed, had announced that a new $100 million contract with the U.S. Air Force would keep Lockheed's 20,000 workers busy for many months. The payroll at Lockheed, Georgia's biggest manufacturing plant, poured about $100 million into the state's economy every year. Lockheed would deliver its last B-47 Stratajet bomber in February of 1957, and after that would concentrate on the C-130 Hercules, a 62-ton, high-flying, high-speed prop jet airplane which would carry ninety-two fully equipped troops or would airdrop 25,000 pounds of cargo. Lockheed officials expected the total C-130 order to total half a billion dollars.

Anticipated growth of the Atlanta area was reflected in a number of ways in 1956. In the *Journal* of October 9 Margaret Shannon foretold the creation of the great city-girdling four-lane, limited-access highway that in time would become known as I-285. (The news that Lockheed would be busy building aircraft in the years ahead stimulated interest in this circumferential road, for a perimeter highway would make it easier to get to and from Lockheed.) Other factors were equally compelling, as listed by Shannon, the highway being needed for two main reasons: (1) The fast growth of the Atlanta area. If the likely route was not blocked out as soon as possible, barriers might arise in the form of new industrial, business, or residential developments. (2) All that federal road money obtainable under the new multi-million-dollar program. The United States at that time paid 90 percent and the state only 10 percent on approved projects. It was a good time to build expensive roads.

As envisioned by the state highway department, the route would be approximately fifty-five miles long, cost around $40 million, and circle through Fulton, DeKalb, Clayton, and maybe Cobb counties.

The idea of a perimeter road went back several years; 1954 was a decisive date because that was the year the route was approved as eligible for federal interstate highway funds. The thought behind a ring route was simple. At the time, all the main east-west and north-south highways went through Atlanta. It would be easier on through traffic—and on Atlanta too—if it could go around the city instead.

The expressway system could be expected to help out some in moving traffic through Atlanta. But officials already were nervous about heavy loads on the freeways. The system did not need the extra burden of through traffic.

The circumferential route, as sketched out by state highway department engineers, was the shape of a ragged egg. Starting below College Park, it would shoot east and gradually curve north. It then would go east of Avondale Estates and west of Clarkston, circle around the northeast fringes of Doraville, and head west on the north side of north Atlanta. Then it would turn southwestward, crossing Roswell Road south of Sandy Springs, and roughly follow the course of the Chattahoochee River. In the vicinity of Riverside the route would plunge due south, skirting East Point on the west and finally intersecting itself.

In a city as big as Atlanta had become an individual might not know any of the needy ones personally, but by helping through the forty-two red feather services of the Community Chest, most of them could be reached. The money goal for the 1956 campaign was $2,105,401, and to raise this sum many Atlantans gave their time and effort. Heading the budget committee were Mrs. Roff Sims, Hughes Spalding, Jr., and Robert F. Woods, who had collected data on each agency and had determined its needs. They led a group of forty volunteers, also well known and respected in the city, who would spearhead the fund raising. General chairmen of the volunteers were Inman Brandon, John Bradbury, Joseph Heyman, and George Goodwin, who had been working since February to recruit an army of 12,000 house-to-house, office-to-office, fund gatherers who hoped to reach everyone in Atlanta who might be a contributor.

Some Atlanta boosters were also thinking earnestly of a World's Fair. The *Atlanta Constitution* reported in October:

For some years now a great idea has been buzzing around in the heads of two young Atlanta architects, Cecil Alexander and Bernard Rothschild. Their thoughts they have translated into drawings, the drawings into models built to scale. The result is something that should capture the imagination of all Atlantans who are proud of their city's past and have faith in its future.

Their idea in essence is simply this:

First, the city redevelopment agency, working with the financial help of the federal government, would tear down the worst of the city's central slums—the 200-odd acres of depressed housing lying east of the downtown business district from Piedmont Avenue to Boulevard, from Butler Street to Forrest Avenue.

On this cleared site another agency made up of leading citizens would erect the buildings and facilities to house a great World's Fair—the cost financed by public debentures, by the state, the city and the national firms who would display their products there. The central theme of the Fair would be the atomic age, the impact of the atom—not in its destructive capabilities, but in its peaceful uses—upon the world of the future. . . .

The fair would run for two years. The 14 million people which they estimate would visit it in that time would leave not only stimulated by the promise of the atom but dazzled by the South and its own potential, and the spirit of its capital city.

The area on which the fair would stand in years to come would itself be an illustration of how a modern city can resist the forces which cause it to decay at the heart. The main buildings at the fair would be permanent. After the exposition had ended the central structures would be converted into a handsome fine arts center and an exhibition hall. A huge stadium would remain, and a new city park surrounding a beautiful lake formed in the low lands adjacent to Butler Street. . . .

It's all a dream so far, of course, a set of plans, some models. But it could come true, its proponents say, if some men of vision got behind it.

And so it remained a dream as the decades passed, though most of the good things its architects visualized—the cleared slums, the new buildings in a rejuvenated downtown, the stadium, and the downtown parks—did come to pass in time, through the work of Atlantans of vision. (And a quarter-century later, in 1982, Cecil Alexander and his firm FABRAP—Finch, Alexander, Barnes, Rothschild and Paschal—designed the U.S. pavilion at the Knoxville World's Fair.)

Atlanta saw a change in 1956 in its post office. Some thirty-odd mail routes, formerly served by foot-postmen who delivered everything from postcards to packages to the addressee's door, were converted to "curb-service" deliveries by postmen driving small right-hand drive trucks. All mail on these routes was being placed in mailboxes beside the street. One happy result of this changeover was that the number of dog bites suffered by walking postmen was greatly reduced!

Both individuals and institutions in Atlanta passed significant anniversaries in this year. The head of the children's department of the Atlanta Public Library, Mary Frances Cox, retired on November 1, 1956, after thirty-one years of service. Coming to Atlanta from Chicago in 1925, she had the responsibility of selecting books for the children's department in fifteen branch libraries and the bookmobile. To do this, she had to read about forty books a day, week after week, totaling some 12,000 books a year. She found that there had been a great change in children's literature in the previous twenty-five years. Fairy stories once were most children's favorites. But now the children liked science fiction—which would help them later on when they must study the actual scientific subjects. Biographies had been made more digestible; the lives of the famous were being described in simple language. But the most sought-after books in the children's department were mysteries and short stories. However, *Journal* reporter Alice Richards, who interviewed Cox on her last day at the library, discovered that "no murder mysteries are permitted, nor any books that make crime in any form seem attractive. Miss Cox is an ardent foe of crime comics."

The life and amazing deeds of Robert Woodruff, recently retired, were described for the first time in full detail by Ralph McGill in the *Atlanta Journal-Constitution Magazine* of August 19, 1956. Though the story covered Woodruff's genius as the global businessman who developed Coca-Cola into a "symbol of what is best in the American competitive system" around the world, its main thrust was the miracles Woodruff had wrought in the use of his personal millions to build hospitals and medical schools and support of medical research. These gifts from Woodruff and the Woodruff Foundation amounted to more than $14 million. Woodruff's initial effort was a program to fight malaria, pellagra, and hookworm, and its success pushed him on. Wrote McGill:

Inspired by her son's enthusiasm, his mother, a sweet and gentle woman, persuaded her husband to establish the Emily and Ernest Woodruff Foundation. A few years later Mrs. Woodruff succumbed to cancer. Most of her fortune, several millions of dollars, went into the Foundation, which was created to minister chiefly to the health and educational needs of the South.

Woodruff himself personally established and endowed the Robert Winship Clinic at Emory Hospital. Named for his mother's father, Robert Winship, it was patterned after and staffed by doctors from Memorial Hospital, New York. It was, and is, devoted entirely to research and treatment in the field of cancer.

Woodruff spent more of his time digging into medical needs. One of his discoveries was that a medical student's tuition pays less than half the cost of a year's education. Emory University's medical school was operating, as were most of those in the nation, at a deficit.

For about 10 years Woodruff picked up the annual deficit tab of about $200,000. He managed to get some help here and there, but each year he shouldered most of the bill which, in the decade under discussion, was about $2,000,000. Being a businessman, he argued that the deficit should be funded.

The Woodruff Foundation made a capital gift large enough for the interest to care for the deficit. Being a good listener and also an asker of questions, he and his friends arranged for other income for the medical school through the establishment of a clinic especially fitted to the teaching and income needs of the school and hospital.

This was a successful development and the need arose for a building to house it. Woodruff, and the Foundation which bears his mother's and his father's name, presented it to the hospital at a cost of more than $2,000,000.

When Crawford Long [Hospital] became associated with Emory, its buildings were old and inadequate. Woodruff moved to meet what had been a long-standing emergency. He and the Foundation presented a large and magnificent, many-winged building and memorialized his mother by naming it the Emily Winship Woodruff Memorial Building. . . .

He and the Foundation constructed and equipped a tremendous research building on Emory campus. It will house the Robert Winship Cancer Clinic and its important research, along with general research in all designated fields. It is easily the finest research facility in the Southeast. The cost here was in excess of $2,000,000.

Woodruff's personality is forceful and his enthusiasm persuasive. Emory University Hospital badly needed expanding. While Woodruff brooded over this he was visited by Mrs. Lettie Pate Evans, an old friend. She had become infected with his medical-building bug and wanted advice. The result was the Conkey Pate Whitehead Surgical Pavilion, a large, magnificently modern wing costing in excess of $2,250,000. In addition, the entire front of the hospital was changed for architectural reasons, and the lawn landscaped.

These contributions, plus others of a lesser, though substantial nature, mean that Woodruff and the Woodruff Foundation have put about $12,000,000 into medical buildings at Emory Hospital. When to this is added the several millions given by his friends who were inspired by him, the result is indeed a major one.

Woodruff and the Foundation have given most generously to educational institutions, both secondary and college. . . . He personally has been one of the chief supporters of the annual cancer and polio campaigns. His benefactions in all fields of charity have been generous, and like his major one, unsung. His wife, Mrs. Nell Hodgson Woodruff, shares his enthusiasm for work in the medical field. She has always been interested in nursing. . . .

As far as I know this is the first summing up of the impressive multi-million-dollar contribution by Woodruff as a "builder" of the metropolitan Atlanta city and area. Because of his insistence on no publicity, the public is almost totally unaware of the magnitude and worth of his participation.

McGill concluded: "Among those who have helped—and who continue to assist—in building an even greater Atlanta, none has a higher place than Robert Winship Woodruff."[1]

Atlanta business houses, industries, and educational institutions all were part of the continuing upward surge in the mid-fifties, and many individuals were honored with new responsibilities or recognized for high achievement in the past.

In 1956 the Retail Credit Company moved from its old home office at 90 Fairlie Street NW to a handsome new five-story structure at 1600 Peachtree Street NW. Founded in 1899 by Cator and T. Guy Woolford to provide information to business houses on the credit rating of individuals, the company had expanded its operation to 210 branch offices extending around the world from Canada into Latin America, with a total of 6,500 employees. Approximately 600 of these would be housed in the new Atlanta branch office building along with the home offices of three subsidiary companies.

Emory, with the unfailing support of Robert Woodruff, as already noted, as in years past was busy building and expanding and beautifying its tree-studded campus in a program that would cost the school more than $3.3 million, with an additional $14 million to be spent on Henrietta Egleston Hospital and the CDC, to be located on nearby sites made available by Emory.

Ben Massell, Atlanta developer, gave the Jewish Social Service Federation of Atlanta a dental clinic to serve the city's poor and needy. It was equipped by the federation with the aid of the Bertha Hirshberg Memorial Fund. A large number of Atlanta dentists volunteered to serve the clinic without fee, and there were thirty-five volunteer receptionists. The clinic was operated on a nonsectarian basis, though black patients were treated by Negro dentists. The clinic opened in February.

Looking back to the year just past, the Atlanta Chapter of the Georgia Society of Professional Engineers named ten outstanding engineering achievements—all of major importance. Listed alphabetically, they were: the Atlanta and Fulton County Heating and Ventilating Code, the Atlanta Water Works mechanization program, the expressway (northeast leg to Buford Highway), the Fulton National Bank Building, the Georgia Power Company's 110,000-volt Butler Street substation, Lockheed's C-130 transport cargo carrier, Rich's Electronic Computer Center at Georgia Tech, Seaboard Airline's centralized train control system, Southern Bell's modernization program, and the new WSB and WSB-TV building.

Not mentioned in the list but a landmark nevertheless in Atlanta and Georgia was Tech's introduction of a course of graduate studies in nuclear physics. Governor Marvin Griffin allocated $300,000 so the school could keep abreast in this field. He also announced his plans to support a multimillion-dollar atomic reactor at Tech.

Tech's advance into this new area of science might have been reflected in an increased enrollment for the fall of 1956, for the school then reached the largest enrollment in its history, according to registrar William L. Carmichael. A total of 5,544 students registered for the fall quarter, the highest enrollment since 1947, when 5,402 were enrolled.

Other news from Tech marked the passing of a campus institution. The

Georgia Tech Yellow Jacket, the campus magazine often banned from distribution over the years because of the "off-color" nature of some of its humorous material, was replaced by a new "clean" picture magazine called *The Rambler.*

On Saturday night September 29, hundreds of members of the Ku Klux Klan gathered in a pasture near the base of Stone Mountain, burned three crosses about twenty feet high, and shouted that the KKK was "As Solid as Stone Mountain." They were robed and hooded but unmasked, and judging from the tags on the some 1,200 cars parked nearby, most of them seemed to have come from Alabama, Tennessee, South Carolina, and Mississippi.

The Klan gathering at Stone Mountain attracted little public notice, but it did draw down upon the heads of its leaders the wrath of the *Atlanta Journal* in an editorial entitled "Let KKK Roost Far Away." The unidentified author said:

Swaddled in gold and bonneted in red, white and blue, Imperial Wizard E. L. Edwards of the Ku Klux Klan climbed upon a truck bed near Stone Mountain and informed the foolish-looking followers of his sheeted order that the City of Atlanta had injured his feelings.

"We ought to get our capitol moved out of that buzzard roost," declared the Wizard.

It seems that the City taxed the Wizard's patience by refusing to give him a police escort for the KKK motorcade.

Good for the City of Atlanta.

Much of the fun will be drained from the Klan's didoes as long as the players are denied masks. More of the boyish bubble will be punctured as long as they are denied the sirens and red blinkers of the escorts they covet.

Leave the skirted squads to pick their way unheralded through the briar patches. Let them hold their squalid huddles as far away as they can hike from Georgia's capital.

There ain't nobody here but us buzzards, Wizard.

An Atlanta woman made history when she was sworn into the Georgia National Guard: 1st Lt. Ellen L. Jones, a nurse at Georgia Baptist Hospital, became the first woman member of the 199-year-old organization when she was inducted into the Georgia Air National Guard 116th Tactical Hospital Arm at Dobbins Air Force Base.

Georgia Republicans showed signs of gaining strength in this year, but not enough to unseat Fifth District congressman James C. Davis. In an election that sent a record 141,943 people to the polls, Representative Davis was winner over Randolph Thrower, Republican, by a margin of 26,319 votes. Thrower's strong try indicated to *Journal* political reporter Ralph Bryan that the Republicans were gaining strength in the Fifth District, despite their loss. Thrower got 40.7 percent of the vote. Two years before, when Republican Charles Moye opposed Davis, he got only 35.6 percent of the vote cast in that election.

At City Hall coming events cast their shadows before them. On November 21 the aldermanic board held a heated debate over the proposed construction of a $15 million shopping center on a seventy-acre tract at Lenox and Peachtree Road. Sponsors of the shopping center estimated the project would be valued at more than $100 million when it was in full operation. Aldermen Jesse Draper and R. M. Clark, in whose ward the project would be, urged its approval over the protests of a group of citizens.

The Lenox proposal was part of the growing move of Atlanta residents and Atlanta business to the suburban areas. A month earlier, though, the city had learned from real estate editor George Erwin that though this flight from the city was well under way, at the time 40 percent of the $2 million spent daily by Atlantans—for such items as food, clothing, furniture, and other consumer items—was still being spent in stores and shops located in the "heart" of the city, the central business district. This area, according to Erwin, was defined by the Census Bureau as bounded by North Avenue NE on the north and Memorial Drive SW on the southern boundary, with Walker, Nelson, Ellis, Cain, Williams, Moore, Butler, Courtland, and Currier streets and Piedmont and Edgewood avenues forming the exact boundaries.

Here in this "core" of the city, Atlantans brought $263,191,000 of the estimated $673,193,000 spent in the entire city. This represented 39.1 percent of the total, a drop from 55 percent spent in the central city in the year just after the war. Thus, despite a falling percentage, business in the central city was still rising. Figures made available by Merrill C. Lofton of the Atlanta office of the Department of Commerce showed that since World War II food sales in Atlanta had risen 76.7 percent; apparel and accessories, 13.3 percent, including a 77.1 percent gain in shoe stores. Furniture, home furnishings, and appliances gained 50 percent; automotive goods, 30.6 percent; lumber, building material, hardware, and farm equipment, 167.7 percent; drugs and prescription medicine, 40.7 percent; and sales in gasoline service stations, 110.4 percent. So, the inner city was still a busy place, despite the suburban flight of stores and customers to shopping areas on the perimeter.

The first units of Atlanta's first downtown motel, the Heart of Atlanta Motel, opened on September 5 at Courtland and Baker streets NE. It was declared by its sponsors to be the most luxurious motel of its kind from New York to Chicago to Miami. Its 120 units covered an entire city block and cost approximately $1,504,000 to build. All stockholders of Heart of Atlanta Motel, Inc., were Atlanta business and professional men. The Glass House Restaurant was managed by a Chicago firm, Interstate, which operated a chain of 150 restaurants all over the United States.

The new motel was only one addition built by private capital that was changing the face of the city and increasing its services to visitors and residents alike. The forty-five-year old State Employment Office Building at 79 Marietta Street went under the wrecking ball as Massell Enterprises, commercial building developers, razed it to make room for a 300-car parking garage. Leveling of the old building continued the effort to provide space for the thousands of autos pouring into the city every day. Many a former building had been pulled down to be replaced by faceless decks of concrete. Said the *Journal-Constitution* of September 15:

A parking garage for 500 cars now occupies the site of the old Atlanta Theater, torn down in 1954. The old J. M. High Building at 120 Hunter Street, SW, is now a 90-car open-air parking lot. The site of the old Masonic Temple on Peachtree, which burned in 1950, is now a store with a 200-car parking garage atop.

The same story goes on daily throughout the business district, where parking garage space has increased 72% within the past eighteen months. At the beginning of 1955, only 5,274 indoor parking spaces were available downtown. Today there are 9,082. During the same period, parking lot space inched forward only 3% to 12,461.

Karl A. Bevins, Atlanta traffic engineer, attributes this trend toward under-cover parking to a favorable real estate market. Owners of old buildings are finding it more profitable to convert to parking garages than to remodel for modern office space.

Even the railroad air rights at 15-17 Broad Street are being used to satisfy the unending demand for parking space. . . .

One unique part of the trend is that private capital has done it all. Atlanta is one of the few major cities that has not issued bonds to provide public parking facilities.

The city had promised at the time of the 1952 annexation to provide improved northside services, and on the evening of October 3, Mayor Hartsfield dedicated a new 5 million gallon water reservoir at Adamsville. He said that the giant tank, costing $85,000, was part of the $13 million spent by the city to extend water into the annexed areas. And this and other water facilities created by the bond money, he said, would save all Atlantans, in the annexed area as well as the central city, more than a million dollars a year in lowered fire insurance rates. Alderman James E. Jackson, Jr., master of ceremonies for the dedication, said that the new tank was the largest in the city and would quench the thirst of the citizens for generations to come. Another huge tank, Hartsfield said, would be built on Moore's Mill Road to supply more water to the northern area.

Also changing and growing with the city was Atlantic Steel Company, founded in 1901, and one of the city's major manufacturing enterprises ever since. The week of November 14 Atlantic Steel put into operation a new $8.5 million rolling mill with the potential of producing 2,000 tons of steel products a day. Said the *Constitution*: "The new rolling mill was made necessary by the increased demand of customers—a cheerful note that Atlanta is happy to hear. More buyers of Atlanta products is the sure road to prosperity."

The *Constitution* itself seemed on the road to prosperity. On December 20,

1956, it announced that in November its circulation had reached 198,446, the highest in its history.

Bobby Dodd, Georgia Tech football coach, was to pay tribute to "the greatest man I ever knew" when on Saturday, October 27, he took part in the dedication of Alexander Memorial Center to the late "Coach Alex"—William A. Alexander, Dodd's predecessor, friend, and mentor. The vast new structure—gymnasium, field house, and basketball court—replaced the old Tech Gym on Third Street, which had been in use for more than twenty years.

Atlanta's black community paid tribute to one of its leaders early in 1956 when John H. Calhoun was named president of the Atlanta Chapter of the National Association for the Advancement of Colored People. In accepting, Calhoun, an Atlanta real estate dealer, said his objective would be "full citizenship for every Atlanta Negro through the fearless promotion of an effective program." It would not be carried out with violence, he indicated, but "with prayerful reverence to God through which the organization will stay within the framework of law and order." Calhoun said that he accepted the responsibility of the post with "dauntlessly courageous humility."

Dr. Harmon W. Caldwell, chancellor of Georgia's sixteen state colleges and universities, testified in Federal District Court in Atlanta on December 18, 1956. He said that he would recommend admitting a qualified Negro to a white college although he knew that such a view, if announced publicly, might result in his dismissal as head of the university system. Testifying in September of this year against Horace Ward, who after six years was still striving to enter the University of Georgia Law School, Caldwell said that he did not oppose Ward entirely on racial grounds, but because he was not qualified from the educational standpoint.[2]

By the end of his first year as head of the Atlanta Chapter of the NAACP, John H. Calhoun found himself in trouble with the law. On December 14 he was jailed by Superior Court Judge Durwood Pye for contempt of court for refusing to produce the chapter's financial records, and the chapter was fined $25,000. After a few hours in jail Calhoun agreed to produce the records. The records were sought by state officials to determine whether the NAACP should continue to be listed as a tax-exempt corporation.

Martin Luther King, Jr., another black leader with an Atlanta background, was somewhat more successful in his efforts to bring blacks and whites together on a peaceful basis. In Montgomery, Alabama, on December 20, federal marshals served state, city, and bus company officials with injunctions prohibiting segregation on the buses. Thereupon, the Negroes called off a year-long boycott of the buses. On December 21 blacks and whites rode together on unsegregated buses for the first time.

King, a minister in Montgomery, was boycott leader and an earnest advocate of nonviolence. When the boycott ended, therefore, he urged his followers to keep their tempers, remain silent, or reply without rancor to the sneers or insults they might receive from a few white passengers. Thus, thanks in great degree to Martin Luther King, Jr., the Montgomery integration of the buses came off quietly, though on the night of December 23 an unidentified gunman fired a shotgun blast into the front door of King's home.[3]

Though racial matters on the city level in Atlanta were handled fairly quietly throughout 1956, the issue of school integration still hung over the city and the state. One action was dramatic. On December 10 members of the Atlanta Public School Teachers Association voted unanimously to separate from the American Federation of Teachers, an affiliate of the AFL-CIO. The national organization had demanded that the Atlanta local open its membership to black teachers by December 31, 1957, or have its charter withdrawn. Roger Derthick, president of the Atlanta group, said that this simply meant that the Atlanta association would revert to its original status as an independent association of white school teachers.

Founded in 1905, the Atlanta union joined the national AFT in 1919, which itself at that time was a union for white teachers only. The national union had since changed its by-laws to prohibit segregation in its local affiliates. The same order that was sent to the Atlanta unit went also to the Fulton County teachers organization, which voted to postpone a decision until the 1957 summer convention of the national federation. The Atlanta answer, however, was prompt and blunt. A resolution drafted by a committee headed by Elliott Herrington noted that members of the Atlanta local "are governed by the same state and local laws, mores, customs and traditions" as they were in 1919.

In an approving editorial the *Constitution* noted that the Atlanta teachers' withdrawal from the national association would do no harm whatever to the local union. "It is as strong or stronger locally than it ever was before." The national union, though, "is weakened by the secession of one of its most vigorous, solvent locals." The editorial also suggested that the demand to one of its subgroups that it "integrate, resign, or be expelled," might have a detrimental effect on the AFL-CIO itself, which had just celebrated its first birthday as a combination of unions.

While Atlanta's white teachers and most of its white citizens held out strongly against racial integration in the schools, either as students or as teachers, southwide surveys showed the walls of segregation slowly crumbling, for the most part peacefully. By February 1, 1956, more than 500 Negroes had been enrolled in former all-white state-supported colleges and universities from Texas to Virginia—with the exception of four states. In Mississippi, Alabama, Georgia, and South Carolina the first efforts to enroll blacks in white institutions of higher learning had brought on violent demonstrations. In Louisiana there were more Negroes enrolled in white colleges and universities than in any other southern state. The total was 350. Texas had more than 100 enrolled, and blacks were well represented in both Kentucky and Arkansas schools. Ten had entered at the University of North Carolina; seventeen were at Virginia colleges and two at a state college in Tennessee.

Though school matters were still at issue in Atlanta, Negroes were making short strides forward in various fields. The Atlanta Public Library would start operating its first bookmobiles for Negroes in the spring of 1957, according to library director John C. Settelmeyer. The three Negro branches of the library, he said, were not sufficient to offer services to the growing black population. A second bookmobile would also be added to the white area.

Permission had also been granted for the construction of the city's first drive-in theater for Negroes, on Simpson Road near New Jersey Avenue. The zoning committee of the city Aldermanic Board voted 3-1 in favor of the drive-in after hearing strong arguments both for and against by large delegations. Alderman Hamilton Douglas voted against the petition, which was presented by Bailey Theatres, owners of six Negro theaters in Atlanta.

The committee also granted permission to the U.S. Klans, Inc., to operate a lodge building under special permit, on Seaboard Road, near the intersection of Osburn Road.

Two Atlantans, one black, one white, both famed for the zest with which they lived far beyond their allotted three-score years and ten, died in 1956. Uncle Charlie Cade, who was "'most grown-up" when Sherman marched through Georgia, was found dead in his chair before a two-eyed coal heater in his shack. The fire had burned out. According to Detective W. D. Browning, records at Grady showed Uncle Charlie to be at least 106 years old. For longer than most Atlantans could remember, he and his mule Jericho had plowed all the gardens of the neighbors around him in the Rockdale Park area. And from his own fine garden he was always ready to give a "mess" of fresh vegetables to those who needed them. When the cold drove the old man indoors, the neighbors cared for him, bringing him hot food, building up the fire in his coal-burning heater, and looking after his mule. And then one night—the fire burned out.

Piromis Hulsey Bell, who would have been 99 years old on March 19, died on November 17 at a rest home on West College Avenue in Decatur. A retired lawyer, Bell at the time of his death was the oldest living alumnus of the University of Georgia, the oldest member in the nation of the SAE fraternity, and the oldest graduate of the old Boys High School. He was graduated from the University of Georgia in 1874. After retirement from his law practice in Atlanta in 1900, he farmed on land that he inherited from his father on Flat Shoals Road near Decatur. His father, Marcus Bell, was one of Atlanta's pioneer real estate dealers.

OBITUARIES

Thomas B. Arnold, son of the late Reuben and Virginia Lowry Arnold and grandson of the founder of Atlanta-Lowry National Bank, died at 81. He was an attorney with Reuben and Lowry, his brothers. Alvin Harlan Underwood, well-known insurance agent and communicant of Druid Hills Methodist Church, died at 75. He was a Phi Delta Theta and a member of Ansley Park Golf Club. Charles R. Hartsfield, a pioneer in the installment loan business in the Southeast, died at 72. He was a member of the Capital City Club and St. Mark's. Dr. Clarence Eugene Boyd, Sr., retired professor of Greek language and literature, died at 79. He was a graduate of Wofford College, the University of Missouri, and the University of Wisconsin. He had been a professor at Emory since 1910. Clifford Marvyn Stodghill, Sr., president of a chemical firm and a former consulting pharmacologist of the Army and Navy, died at 64. He was a member of Kiwanis and Second Ponce de Leon Baptist Church. Arthur Smith Benton, manager of the Atlanta division of Westinghouse Air Brake Company, died at 55. He was a graduate of Purdue, where he had been a swimming and diving champion; later, he founded the Georgia Amateur Athletic Union.

Mrs. T. Guy Woolford, 72, a native of Frankfort, Kentucky, was the widow of a founder of Retail Credit Company. She was a past president of the YWCA, charter member of the Atlanta Music Club, past president of the Needlework Guild, and a member of the board of Hillside Cottages and Rabun Gap School. She was active in Moral Rearmament, a world ideological movement. Mrs. W. F. Kennemore, Sr., the former Olive Farmer, was the mother of five sons who served in World War II. She died at 70. James Houston Johnson, a former consulting engineer for the Georgia Public Service Commission and author of a history, *The Western and Atlantic Railroad*, died at 89. A former member of the Civitan Club and engineering societies, he also attended All Saints' Episcopal Church.

Mrs. Henry G. Kuhrt, 92, was the former Mary Ryan, daughter of an Atlanta pioneer. She was a member of Sacred Heart, the UDC, and the DAR. Mrs. Gordon F. Mitchell, the former Isabelle Thomas, was editor of the women's pages of the *Atlanta Journal* from 1913 to 1919. Her activities included membership at St. Luke's Episcopal Church, the Atlanta Historical Society (of which her husband was board chairman), and the Saturday Morning History Class. Rev. Father George S. Rapier, president of Marist College from 1911 to 1914, died at 83. Ordained to the priesthood in 1901, he served as principal of the school until he became pastor of Sacred Heart Church in 1911. Mrs. William J. Davis, the former Lucy Dougherty, was the daughter of one of Atlanta's early dry goods merchants. Their home was a landmark at the corner of Baker and Peachtree streets. Mr. Davis was president of Atlanta Title and Trust Company.

William Madison Cunningham was the retired advertising manager of Atlanta newspapers. A veteran of World War I, he was a member of the Atlanta Athletic Club and the Elks. Dr. Edward George Mackay, a native of Scotstown, County Monaghan, Ireland, and graduate of Emory at Oxford, died at 70. Dr. Mackay had served as pastor of three Atlanta churches, Druid Hills Methodist Church, First Methodist, and Glenn Memorial Church, and later was superintendent of the Decatur-Oxford District of the Methodist

North Georgia Conference. He was the father of Rep. James Mackay, DeKalb County legislator. Aaron Jacobson, retired Atlanta haberdasher and a native of Latvia, died at 78. He was a member of The Temple and father of radio and TV star Bert Parks. Edward M. Gordon, vice-president and founder of Gordon Foods, noted locally for its potato chips, died at 71. He had been with Nunnally Candy Company for thirty years before starting his own company in 1938.

Rhoda Kaufman, long a leader in social welfare professional work, had been executive secretary of the Georgia Department of Welfare. She was Woman of the Year in Social Work in 1943. Dr. William M. Boyd, head of the political science department of Atlanta University and president of the state NAACP, died at 39. He was a graduate of Talladega College, was a Ph.D. graduate of the University of Michigan, and a Rosenwald Fellow in 1942. Dr. Boyd also served as a news analyst for radio station WERD. Dr. Robert Edward Latta, local dentist and active in civic and church affairs, was a graduate of Atlanta Southern Dental College. For many years he served as dentist for the Hebrew Orphan's Home and the Home for the Incurables. Dr. Latta was interested in flower gardening and had published several booklets. He was a collector of first editions of the works of Robert Burns. Inman Knox, a lifelong resident of Atlanta who attended Boys High School and the University of Georgia, died at 61. He was associated in the realty business with his father, Fitzhugh Knox. A veteran of World War I, he was a member of the Piedmont Driving Club and St. Luke's Episcopal Church.

Mrs. Edgar F. Fincher, Sr., the former Grace Maddox, died at 83. The widow of a prominent physician, Fincher was a member of St. Mark's Methodist Church, the Magnolia Garden Club, and the Atlanta Women's Club. William J. Morrison, former president of the old Atlanta Trust Company and one-time official of the Atlanta Car Wheel Works, died at 98. His memberships included the Piedmont Driving Club, Druid Hills Golf Club, East Lake Country Club, and Capital City Club. He was a communicant of Sacred Heart Church. Mrs. J. A. Beall, widow of a former city councilman and police commissioner, died at 74. She had served as president of the Atlanta chapter of the UDC and had attended twenty consecutive meetings of the DAR in Washington. She was also a member of the Colonial Dames and attended St. Mark's Methodist Church. Hardy Padgett, building contractor and supervisor of construction over several Georgia Tech buildings, died at 76. He was associated with C. A. Adair Company.

Mrs. Willis Menifee Timmons, the former Aline Mitchell and a life-long Atlanta resident, died at 73. She belonged to many civic and patriotic organizations including the UDC, the DAR, Pioneer Women, and she was an active member of First Methodist Church. She had attended Miss Thornbury's School for Ladies. Mrs. H. F. Cobb, the former Betty Reynolds, a retired attorney and first woman to be admitted to the bar in Georgia, died at 71. She was prominent in literary circles, had been editor of *Carroll County Free Press,* and was a board member of the League of Women Voters. Mrs. Joseph Shewmake Reynolds, the former Fannie Hansberger and widow of a prominent attorney, died on her 90th birthday. She was the mother of Glascock Reynolds, the artist.

Ralph T. Jones, retired associate editor of the *Atlanta Constitution* and a native of Liverpool, England, died at 70. He joined the staff of the newspaper in 1910 and had worked in many capacities, including city editor and drama and music critic. Samuel J. Winn, district sales manager with United States Steel Co. and son of Mayor Courtland S. Winn, died at 67. He was the grandson of Lovick P. Thomas, who commanded the 42nd Georgia Infantry during the Civil War. Winn was a graduate of Boys High and Columbia University and was a member of the Governor's Horse Guard. Spotswood Dabney Grant, automobile dealer, realtor, and purchasing agent for the Georgia Highway Department from 1933 to 1936, died in Miami at 59. He was a member of the Piedmont Driving Club.

George Winship, founder and president of Fulton Supply Company and one-time president of the old Morris Plan Bank, died at 72. Dr. John Beeson, state manager for Liberty National Life Insurance Company since 1922, died at 90. He was the oldest living alumnus of the University of Alabama, from which he graduated in 1888. He was a Mason, a Knight Templar, and a Shriner. Robert Purmedus Jones, affectionately known as "Colonel Bob," was a prominent Atlanta attorney and legal counsel for the Coca-Cola Bottling Company. He was the father of golfer Bobby Jones and was instrumental in organizing the Augusta National Golf Club. Mrs. John A. Manget, the former Agnes Hardiman, had been treasurer of the Atlanta City Mission Board.

Gordon Forrest Mitchell, one of the city's oldest and most respected lawyers, died at 83. A specialist in probate and real estate law, he practiced with his brother Eugene, the father of Margaret Mitchell. His father, Russell C. Mitchell, was a city councilman, alderman and mayor pro tem. Mitchell was an authority on Atlanta's history and contributed to the publication of the Atlanta Historical Society, of which he was board chairman. William R. Sullivan, owner and president of the Nu-Grape Company, died at 79. He was an official with the Atlantic Coast Line Railroad and a member of the Church of the Immaculate Conception. James Pleasant Allen, Sr., was president of J. P. Allen's, one of the South's leading specialty shops for ladies. Dr. Thornwell Jacobs, Sr., retired president of Oglethorpe University and founder of the "Crypt of Civilization," died at 79.

Mrs. Walker Dunston, the former Willie McCarty, died at 93. She was the oldest graduate of Girls High School and the oldest member of Second Ponce de Leon Baptist Church. She had served as chaplain for both the UDC and the DAR. Mrs. Robert Willoughby Davis, widow of the founder of Atlanta Savings and Loan Association, died at 75. She was the former Henrietta Collier, daughter of Charles and Susie Rawson Collier. Her father was president of the Cotton States Exposition. Mrs. Davis attended Washington Seminary and Miss Chamberlain's School in Boston. Thomas M. Cassels, son of Raleigh C. Cassels, pioneer Atlantan, died at 50. He was a well-known sportsman associated with Walthour and Hood and was Georgia state skeet champion. Mrs. Zachary Taylor Coppedge, the former Dora Virginia Wood of Rome, Georgia, died at 92. She was the mother of J. Beauchamp Coppedge, president and owner of Sophie Mae Candy Company, and grandmother of Mrs. Julian Carr.

John Ashley Jones, insurance executive and historian, died at 82. In 1895 he began his sixty-one-year career with the New York Life Insurance Company. He was an authority on Atlanta history and Georgia's colonial history. For a number of years he served as a trustee of the Atlanta Historical Society and was an elder of Central Presbyterian Church. Benjamin Wesley Brannon, vice-president and general manager of Beck and Gregg Hardware Company, died at 62. He had been with the firm forty-nine years. Howard King Chapman, retired architect, died at 81. He was the son of Monroe Chapman and was a graduate of Georgia Tech's Class of 1896. Chapman attended Peachtree Road Methodist Church. Lester Nelson Hyatt, chairman of the board of directors of National Paper Company, died at 79. He was a member of Glenn Memorial Church.

Hal Alexis Steed, author and former feature writer for the *Atlanta Constitution* and *Journal,* died at 79. He was a graduate of Mercer University and served as a newspaperman over a thirty-year period. Steed was the author of an informal state guide titled *Georgia: Unfinished State,* published in 1942. Mrs. Elvira T. Westmoreland, noted churchwoman and philanthropic leader, died at 97. She was the widow of George Westmoreland, prominent attorney. Mrs. Westmoreland was a member of Second Ponce de Leon Baptist Church and was vice-president of the Baptist Women's Missionary Union. She had also been president of the board of the Georgia Baptist Children's Home. Mrs. Lee Kennedy, the former Ruth Wallace, was a designer of glass and china. She belonged to River Valley Garden Club, the East Lake and Cherokee Country Clubs, the Atlanta Yacht Club, and the Shakerag Hunt.

Paul Lamar Fleming, president and chairman of the board of John B. Daniel, Inc., died at 83. Founded in 1867, the wholesale drug firm was one of the oldest in the city, and Fleming had held his position for forty-two years. He was a graduate of Boys High and the University of Georgia. He was a member of First Presbyterian Church and had been superintendent of the Sunday school for more than thirty years. He was a charter member of the Atlanta Athletic Club. Mrs. Samuel Washington McCallie, the former Elizabeth Hanleiter and widow of Georgia's state geologist, died at 82. Her father, Cornelius Hanleiter, was commander of Joe Thompson's Artillery, one of the first companies to leave Atlanta during the Civil War. She was a life member of the Atlanta Historical Society and a communicant of North Avenue Presbyterian Church.

Marion Columbus Kiser, well-known Atlanta investment broker, had been with Courts and Company for more than a quarter-century. His grandparents, Col. and Mrs. William Lawson Peel, were pioneer Atlantans. He attended All Saints' Episcopal Church and was a member of the Nine O'Clocks and the Piedmont Driving Club. Loomis Pratt Grant, construction engineer and grandson of Lemuel P. Grant who designed the fortifications for the city during the Atlanta campaign, died at 64. He was a graduate of Georgia Tech, a veteran of World War I, and a member of the Methodist church. Meredith Collier, former supervisor of water distribution in the city and an employee of the Atlanta waterworks for fifty-three years, died at 88. He was a member of Central Presbyterian, a Shriner, and a Mason. George Moore, Atlanta ice-cream executive and a native of Amalias, Greece, died at 79. Moore was active in civic affairs and was president of the congregation of the Greek Orthodox Church. He was in the Elks, the Exchange Club, and on the governor's staff.

Piromis Hulsey Bell, who was almost 100 years old, died as a result of a fall. He was an active member of the DeKalb Historical Society and a charter member of the Burns Club. Arthur O. Davis, Atlanta insurance executive and vice-president of American Surety Company, died at 74. Hugh H. Trotti, who had served many posts on the *Atlanta Constitution* and most recently had been vice-president, died at 67. He was a member of the Decatur Board of Education and was on the board of stewards at First Methodist Church of Decatur.

Dr. Charles E. Boynton, Atlanta pediatrician and a member of one of Atlanta's early families, died at 84. A son of Charles E. Boynton, pioneer Atlanta merchant and a founder of Chamberlain-Boynton Department Store, the doctor was also a graduate of Boys High and Princeton. He was a member of Trinity Methodist and served in the Spanish-American War. Mrs. Thomas C. Erwin, long prominent in Atlanta's civic and social life, died after a fall. The former Elsie Campbell, she came to this city as a bride in 1899. Her husband was vice-president and trust officer of C&S Bank. Mrs. Erwin was a charter member of Peachtree Garden Club and Colonial Dames, and she attended All Saints' Episcopal Church. Mrs. Vernon S. Broyles, Jr., a daughter of Percy and Bena Maxwell Virden, died. Her husband was pastor of the North Avenue Presbyterian Church.

NOTES

1. Ralph McGill, *Atlanta Journal-Constitution Magazine*, Aug. 19, 1956.
2. *Facts on File* (New York: Facts on File, Inc., 1956), Dec. 19–25, 1956, p. 430.
3. Ibid.

ATLANTA went into 1957 feeling a warm glow of pride in a new face—a $12 million face of white Georgia marble that made a gleaming backdrop to the tree-studded square of Capitol Hill. By September of 1956 three new structures, the Agriculture Building, the Highway Building, and the Judicial, Office, and Labor Building, made up the biggest office-building program the state had ever put on. These, though, were only part of the state and city public building program that had been going on in the area since World War II. Others were the Atlanta Traffic Court at Central and Trinity, the Fulton County Health Center in the same block with Atlanta's skyscraper City Hall, and the white marble Fulton County Administration Building erected as an annex behind the Courthouse.

On the outside all the new state buildings were faced with Georgia marble, which the architect said stays clean and fresh looking, whereas limestone does not. When the Capitol was built in the 1880s, however, limestone had been used instead of marble, for the contractors had discovered it was $12,000 cheaper to bring in limestone from Indiana than to quarry and ship the fine white marble from the nearby Georgia hills.

And, indeed, Atlanta in the winter of 1957 was attracting national attention. In the month of February, for example, at least four dozen policy-level executives from throughout the country were in the city for sales meetings, trade association forums, speaking engagements, and inspection visits. Among them were John S. Coleman of Detroit, president of Burroughs Corporation, and J. H. Carmichael of Washington, D.C., president of Capitol Airlines. They came to a "Congressional Issues Clinic," sponsored by the state and city Chambers of Commerce at the Henry Grady Hotel on February 18. Their aim was to prod businessmen in a dozen cities across the country to "make their voices heard more emphatically on legislation that affects the business climate." On February 13, Simon E. Knudsen, general manager of Pontiac Motors, became the third General Motors vice-president in seven days to address a dealer sales meeting here. He followed Ed Cole, Chevrolet general manager, and Edward Ragsdale, Buick's top man. The reason for the influx of automobile executives was obvious: Ford and General Motors were expanding their Atlanta assembly plants by roughly $30 million—with Ford planning to spend $17 million to double production at its Hapeville plant.

The president of Carling Brewery, Ian R. Dowie, came from Cleveland to speak to the Southeast Council of Advertising Agencies. Carling was in the process of completing a $17 million brewery in Atlanta.

More than a score of industrial bluebloods were scheduled to gather in Atlanta for the first board of directors meeting of the Westinghouse Electric Corporation ever to be held in the South. Gwilynn Price, chairman and president, broke ground for the company's new $20 million transformer plant in

Athens. Other topflight business policy makers winging South that February were John J. McCloy of New York, board chairman of Chase National Bank, the second largest in the nation; William A. Patterson of Chicago, president of United Air Lines; and Reece H. Taylor of Los Angeles, chairman of the Union Oil Company of California. Thomas J. Hargrove of Rochester, New York, Eastman Kodak Company chairman, and Charles R. Hook of Middleton, Ohio, chairman of Armco Steel Company, were also here.

While the big national companies were looking over Atlanta, Atlanta in turn was making plans to make them welcome if they should come here, or if they should seek to expand their operations already here. Knowing that American business was growing more airborne every year, Atlanta by early May of 1957 had Robert and Company working on plans for an expanded airport—a new terminal building costing $9 million and $12 million in other improvements. Of this sum, $9,935,000 would come from city funds, and the remainder from federal matching funds or from additional revenue certificates if necessary. The new terminal would provide comfort and convenience for passengers traveling to and from Atlanta, including the many thousands of transfers—bringing out the old irreverent observation that "if you are going to heaven or hell, you have to go by way of Atlanta."[1]

Atlanta's surging postwar growth as an industrial center for the Southeast was dramatized in mid-May of 1957 by an aerial photo in the *Constitution*. It showed East Point's Empire Industrial District, four and one-half miles from downtown Atlanta, fully served with paved streets, water, natural gas, other public utilities, and railroad sidetracks. Twenty-four industries, said Fred Hartley in the *Constitution* of May 15, had invested more than $30 million and employed about 2,500 workers since the 190-acre tract was opened for development by the Central of Georgia Railway in 1948. First to purchase property in the district was Colonial Stores, followed by the Kroger Company, International Harvester Company, Purex Corporation, Ltd., Ford Motor (a parts warehouse), Pittsburgh Glass Company, International Paper Company and Rexall Drug Company. The Borden Company's cheese division was the twenty-fourth business finally to fill up the tract.

On January 7, 1957, Mayor Hartsfield in his annual message to the Aldermanic Board summed up what Atlanta had accomplished in the first five years of the Plan of Improvement.

The mayor pointed out that the plan, which tripled in size the old city limits, had required tremendous changes in the function of local government. This involved the shifting of whole departments and hundreds of employees, the assumption of millions of dollars of county school bond indebtedness and pension funds and an estimated three million dollars per year of revenues to the annexed area.

Further streamlining took place on January 1, 1954, when the old bicameral type of government, with twenty-seven members, was changed to the unicameral, or aldermanic board type with seventeen members. Atlanta's huge reorganization, the mayor said, excited the interest of government experts throughout the nation.

For the eighteenth consecutive year, he said, the city had operated on a cash basis and had come through with all bills paid, going into 1957 with a cash carryover. Not a cent had been borrowed for operating expenses, which he said was a record unequaled by any large city in the nation. On this pay-as-you-go basis, the city had saved $28,784 in cash discounts, and by keeping its surplus cash in government securities had earned $201,440 in interest.

He estimated that the city population was 503,000 inside the city limits, and 885,000 in the metropolitan area.

The Atlanta Water Works, he pointed out, had spent more than $9 million in the preceding five years to improve its service in the enlarged area. They had put in 26,359 meters and 3,288 hydrants, and in 1956 they installed 3,983 meters and 538 fire hydrants. In 1956 they had 82 miles of pipe, bringing the five-year total to 433 miles, more of it in the new areas. Citizens in the new area, said Hartsfield, were saving $375,000 per year by elimination of double rates.

Looking ahead, the city had engaged the firm of Wiedeman and Singleton to lay out a plan for handling water, sewer, and pollution problems for the next fifteen years, not only for the city limits but for the greater part of the county. The completion of Buford Dam, the filling of its reservoir, and possibly the impounding of Buford's overflow in other reservoirs downstream toward Atlanta would increase the stream flow to the city, decrease pollution, and provide supplies of cool water for industrial and power plants.

Four new fire stations had been erected in the previous five years, and another was being built at Ben Hill. Seventy-five alarm boxes had been placed in the new areas, and the department had been equipped with two-way radio. Because of the improvement in water supply and fire protection, Hartsfield said that Atlantans were now saving over a million dollars a year in insurance premiums.

For the Department of Construction, it had been a busy five years. Seventy-seven miles of streets were paved; 159 miles of curbing and 45 miles of sidewalks were laid. In 1956 alone, the Grand View Avenue extension was completed, Ashby Street was extended to Lee Street, and Tenth Street opened from West Peachtree to Peachtree. In five years five new bridges were completed, four of them in the new areas. The expressway system, now being built by the state highway department under the new Federal Highway Act, was pushing on, with the city responsible for acquiring rights of way to complete the downtown connector.

Listing a number of short bypasses and cutoffs already completed, Hartsfield added that with the steady growth of Atlanta, there must be continuous large-scale traffic improvements, with both Fulton and DeKalb counties sharing the cost with bond issues.

The Sewer Department was also busy. In five years under the Plan of

Improvement it had laid 174 miles of new sewers, 46 miles in the year just past. The Electrical Department had lighted the south leg of the expressway and installed 4,700 new lights in the area.

Traffic control had been greatly simplified in the preceding five years, with particular emphasis on off-street parking, and Hartsfield noted that all this was done by private enterprise. The Traffic Department also established a $14,000 warehouse, sign manufacturing, and parking-meter plant, saving money by manufacturing its own signs. Traffic Court had moved into the most modern traffic court building in the nation.

The Department of Parks had constructed dozens of new tennis courts, adapted a plan for a new zoo, and built three modern swimming pools. Atlanta had moved strongly in the direction of urban renewal, and the Building Inspector's Office had made progress in slum clearance. Last year, said Hartsfield, 225 buildings that were substandard had been demolished and in the past five years 2,012 such buildings had been torn down.

The airport, as already noted, was in the middle of a vast enlargement program, with some $15 million of city and federal funds being spent to give Atlanta a modern terminal, satisfactory to the airlines and to the people using them. Atlanta, Hartsfield noted, was the fifth-busiest airport in the nation; it produced 10 percent more business than Paris, and almost twice that of Rome. It gave employment to 5,500 people and poured into the community an annual payroll of more than $25 million. The city itself collected more than a half-million dollars each year in landing fees and concession receipts.

Beginning in 1957 the Atlanta school board would no longer receive 30 percent of nontax city revenues, as in the past, but would seek a share of the ad valorem tax rate necessary for its operation. Under the newly formed city-county tax assessment board, and the removal of Atlanta's tax operation to Fulton County, the mayor and board of aldermen had nothing to do with reappraisal, assessment, or collection of ad valorem taxes. They did fix the tax rate millage.

Hartsfield closed by pushing for a joint city-county bond issue "which will enrich us, to make necessary improvements and additions to our school system, our airport, sewer, water, parks, highways and bridges and other necessities of a growing community. Such bonds are necessary for the progress of Atlanta. We offer our full support to the citizens representing Atlanta, Fulton County and the Atlanta School Departments . . . to the end that Metropolitan Atlanta in a few years may enter the million class of cities, well equipped with the base needs which will insure its continued growth."

Chattahoochee improvements came about as the mayor had predicted. The dedication of Buford Dam forming Lake Lanier was preceded by the dedication of Morgan Falls Dam, which was raised to take the overflow from Buford. Located only seventeen miles north of the city, the million-dollar Morgan Falls project would store more than a billion gallons of water and was jointly financed by the city and the Georgia Power Company. It was designed to re-regulate the flow released by Buford Dam in order to give the city water during the hours when it was most needed.

Hartsfield's comments on urban renewal dealt mainly with plans for the future, but in May, Alderman John A. White was recounting, somewhat boastfully, what Atlanta had done in the preceding ten years. Atlanta had been busy clearing its slums. In the decade just past, he said, Atlanta had spent $39 million repairing or demolishing 29.76 percent of its substandard homes. Most of this was done under Alderman White's supervision in the past year and a half. "Atlanta," said White, "through the efforts of our property owners, leads the nation in slum rehabilitation. We have eliminated slums and provided standard dwellings for 133,920 people. Plumbing improvements had placed 52,801 bathtubs, kitchen sinks and flush toilets in homes which lacked them."

The future also looked brighter for certain Atlantans displaced from homes by the Atlanta expressway. The Federal Housing Authority gave the signal to construct 1,500 new houses for these persons, some of whom were also being displaced by the progress of urban renewal. These houses would be three-bedroom units, with a maximum price of $9,000, and would be financed under 100 percent FHA mortgage insurance for a forty-year period. The first group would provide 1,000 homes for blacks and 500 for whites, all in areas approved by the Urban Renewal Department. The first 1,500 would be part of a larger program of 5,100 homes, 3,900 of them for blacks, mainly in the Rockdale Park and Thomasville areas.

John F. Thigpen, state director of the Federal Housing Authority, said the program would provide $13.5 million worth of home construction for Atlanta contractors and builders. Financing on the FHA loans would carry a 5½ percent interest rate; closing costs to home owners would be roughly $200; and monthly rental payments would be about $48.50.

Traveling through the South, Milton Bracken of the *New York Times* saw Atlanta with fresh eyes. Said Bracken, describing modern-day Atlanta against the background of its history:

Any resemblance between Atlanta and "Southern" cities such as Richmond and Savannah is simply a misconception in the minds of some Northerners.

This applies in the field of society as elsewhere. For Georgia's capital has been concerned primarily with growth and prosperity. It has continued restlessly to produce and distribute, to buy and sell, to consume and expand. Thus, relatively few of its people have time for society in a formal or mannered sense.

At the same time, Atlanta is a great club town. Clubs are the common denominator of its social structure; there is one or more for virtually everyone who wants to belong.

Most influential, although not the oldest, is the Piedmont Driving Club.

This was chartered in 1887 as the Gentlemen's Driving Club. The title was changed in 1895—because, according to legend some of the members were already questioning the right of the newcomers to call themselves gentlemen. . . . The resident membership has remained limited to 800, and admission has tended more and more to depend upon direct family descent.

Out of that fact grew the newest big club in Atlanta. Its story tells a good deal about evolving social relationships in the city.

Many younger Atlantans, aware of the difficulties of getting into the Driving Club, started in September, 1955, to form a similar club of their own. Virtually overnight 900 persons had subscribed the initiation fee of $600 (now up to $840). The Cherokee Town and Country Club was in business. Barely a year after it was formed it has a waiting list of its own.

Its founders acknowledge that it was "almost impossible" to get into the Driving Club because of the limited facilities; and the Driving Club people do not look upon the Cherokees as upstarts. The distinction between the clubs is one of age, rather than social standing.

In a city of 503,000 with a metropolitan area population of 885,000 the Jewish community of 11,500 has its own club structure. The Roman Catholic population is only 19,383; it includes leaders in the Driving Club and the Nine O'Clocks.

Numerically, Baptists and Methodists dominate Atlanta, with strong Presbyterian, Episcopalian and Catholic influences in the leading Christian clubs.

A peak of the social season here is opera week—this year May 14—when the Metropolitan Opera Company makes its annual appearance. This is a visit dating to 1911 when the artists included Enrico Caruso.

The season is invariably sold out by March 1, with patrons coming from eleven states. Each night is a blaze of formal dress. But Atlantans readily concede that their love of opera week—for which ticket and program sales are handled exclusively by the Junior League—combines an appreciation of good music with a desire to make a brief social splash. Here again is the city's sense of humor and of realistic self-evaluation.

One may hear at a dinner in the fashionable Buckhead section that the debutante system is pretty silly, "as it is everywhere." And it is likely to be acknowledged that very few Atlantans cared in the least when the historic Huff House, built in 1855, was burned and buried for a $1,000,000 toy factory in 1954.

The Georgia Educational Exchange sought to preserve it as a monument. "But when history comes up against industry in Atlanta," one native put it, "it's fighting a losing battle."

The ashes of the Huff House were plowed into the red earth of Fulton County. The toy plant opened in May, 1955.[2]

The title of Bracken's article was "Atlanta—A City of Clubs, Opera, Expansion and Commerce," and many events in 1957 indicated that Atlanta's interest in expanding its commerce had in no way abated. On September 8, 1957, the *Journal-Constitution* described fantastic changes going on in the heart of the downtown business section—the first big building and renovation projects since the Depression. Said George Erwin, business editor of the *Atlanta Journal*:

The ten million dollar operation, which enhanced the beauty of the downtown area north of the viaducts, was the addition of three new and modern office buildings. They are the Fulton National Bank, 25-story skyscraper which commands attention at Forsyth and Marietta; the Peachtree-Baker Building, which spreads its bright curtain walls along Peachtree, Baker and Ivy Streets, and the Fulton Federal Buildings, 10-story marble structure just behind Five Points.

The Fulton National was the first big office building built here since completion of the William-Oliver Building at Five Points in 1930.

This one, which has three basement floors and rises 295 feet above the street level at the site of the old City Hall—later a hole-in-the-ground—is far and away the largest structure of its kind in the area. Its 527,000 square feet of space tops its nearest competitor, the Hurt Building, by more than 20%, and vertically it reaches skyward slightly more than the Rhodes-Haverty Building, the previous record holder.

When work on a new motel near Georgia Tech began, there were thirty-five motels on the outskirts of the city, but only one in the downtown area. There were, however, more than 6,000 rooms available in seventy downtown hotels at prices ranging from $6.00 to $14.00 double, and the motel rooms on the perimeter ranged from $4.00 to $10.00.

Atlanta's expansion in all fields of business and industry not only was attracting a heavy influx of strangers, it gave promise that the many new plants coming into the area would create more positions for specially trained executives and engineers who got their education here. Thus, the alarming exodus of trained men from the Atlanta area might at least be stopped.

Wrote George Erwin: "In the past the more industrialized sections of the nation have beckoned to college graduates, primarily because they provide more and better opportunities and more pay. Many home town boys would have preferred to stay here, but were forced to go to 'greener fields.'"

The Industrial Bureau of the Chamber of Commerce combined with the Georgia Tech Alumni Association to question 500 electrical engineering graduates over the past ten years. They were asked, "If new jobs, comparable to your previous one, were forthcoming, would you be interested in returning to the Atlanta area?" According to Paul W. Miller, bureau manager of the Chamber of Commerce, some 300 replied, and 90 percent indicated that they would, indeed, be eager to come back home whenever new technology or scientific opportunity was created.

Reports covering the first half of 1957 indicated that these opportunities were increasing. In the first six months twenty-four new industrial plants, providing 1,233 new jobs and an annual payroll of $4,932,000, had come into the metropolitan area. In the same period fifty-five out-of-town companies opened offices or warehouses, adding another 517 people, with a new payroll totaling more than $2 million. With seventy-five new residual representatives added to the above, the overall new industries actively in Atlanta during the first half of 1957 showed 1,825 new jobs and an added payroll of $7,375,000.

Georgia Tech obviously was aware of the challenge the future held for an engineering school and was preparing to meet it head on. In 1956 it had spent $2,250,000 on research—which made it the nation's tenth-largest research organization among the 114 universities and colleges that made up the Engineering and Research Council. It led all southern members by a large margin. Tech's high ranking was made possible by more than $1,950,000 in research and development projects sponsored by industry and government through the Georgia Tech Engineering Experiment Station. Fields in which Tech carried out research during the year included aeronautical engineering, architecture, bioengineering and public health, ceramics, chemical engineering, chemistry, civil, electrical and industrial and mechanical engineering, mathematics, electronics and electronic computers, nuclear science and medical engineering, engineering drawing and mechanics, physics and industrial development.

Engineers and scientists might design a rocket to the moon, it was pointed out, but if there were no technicians able to put them together and operate them, it would never get off the ground. Therefore, Southern Tech, an offshoot of Georgia Tech in Atlanta, had been established in 1948 in the old barracks at the U.S. Naval Air Station at Chamblee. There 600 young men were working on a two-year study in the engineering science field. Though operated under the engineering extension division of Georgia Tech, the young scholars' purpose was not to become engineers and scientists, but persons who could assist, not replace, the professional engineers. Southern Tech was the first school of its kind in the South and was a new experiment in Georgia education. Though viewed with skepticism at first, in the eight years of its existence the school had proved its merit. With a rapidly industrialized Georgia needing 5,000 technicians a year, each graduating class found itself besieged by job offers.

When its curriculum was compared with Georgia Tech's, it was obvious that Southern Tech was a "know-how" school instead of a "know-why" school. Its courses stressed building construction technology, electrical technology, gas fuel technology, heating and air conditioning, and industrial technology. But salaries for graduates averaged $599 a month, and many were earning $1,000 a month three years after graduation. Director of the young institution as it grew from 116 students in its first year of 1948 to the 1957 enrollment of more than 600 was Lawrence V. Johnson, who had been an instructor at Georgia Tech for twenty-six years.

The public school teachers, under the administration of Ira Jarrell, had created a school system in Atlanta that was superior and progressive in comparison to that of cities of comparative size and resources, but a week before registration for the fall term was to begin, Jarrell spelled out the bad news. Before the year was over total enrollment was expected to reach 113,000, but the school system was starting off the year 787 classrooms short of the number needed—and the building program for 1957 would create only 300 new rooms. For 1957, between 20,000 and 25,000 children would be in double session, though at least two communities—Ben Hill and West Manor— would send their children to schools in nearby churches.

The school system, said Jarrell, would need approximately fifty-four new elementary schools and nine high schools by 1960 if every child were to have a desk. But under the building program only half would be completed as the 1960s began.

With more men teachers going into high schools, Emory University announced that it was adding two more women teachers to its male-dominated faculty for the upcoming year—and in fields of study where men predominated. Peggie Wiegand, who taught trigonometry, and Dr. Roselin S. Wagner, a physics professor, were two of six women added to the College of Arts and Sciences faculty in 1957, the largest number hired by Emory in a single year. There were now ten women on a faculty of two hundred. The Arts and Sciences division of Emory did not employ women teachers before 1953 because, said Dean of the College Judson C. Ward, "It just hasn't been the practice to have women faculty members in a male college." Emory's masculinity had been somewhat diluted since 1953, however, when 76 women students were enrolled and in the year just past there were 496 women students in the College of Arts and Sciences.

During the 1950s Atlantans and Georgians of college age were brought into closer understanding of rural and urban mores by Georgia State College, in the heart of downtown. Of the 1,600 freshmen enrolled in 1957, there were representatives from 130 of Georgia's 159 counties, from twenty states, and from nineteen foreign countries. In forty-three years, the college at Courtland and Gilmer streets had grown from a night school with forty-seven students to the largest college school of business in the South and the sixth largest in the nation, with classes scheduled both day and night. In 1957, to get into the evening school the prospective student had to have a daytime job requiring at least twenty-five hours of work a week.

Dr. George M. Sparks, called by Charles Sopkin of the *Journal* the "president, affectionate friend, and devoted parent of the Georgia State College of Business Adminstration," announced in February that he would retire in July. He had been associated with Georgia State and its forebears for twenty-nine years, during which time it had grown from the little evening school in three classrooms to a modern institution with 5,800 students.

Rabbi Tobias Geffen was feted at a testimonial dinner at the Atlanta

Jewish Community Center on February 17, 1957. He had been the spiritual leader of the Shearith Israel Congregation for forty-six years, and a special fund was established to build a wing on the new Shearith Israel Synagogue in his honor. Another retiree was Dr. Malcolm A. Dewey, for thirty-seven years director of the Emory University Glee Club. Formerly head of the Fine Arts Department at Emory, Dr. Dewey had directed the Glee Club since 1920. Under his leadership the male choral group became one of the outstanding groups in the country.

Clarke Donaldson, who helped build Atlanta for nearly half a century, retired on July 1 as City Construction Chief. When he started, the city had a population of 154,839. There were 90 miles of paved streets and 200 miles unpaved; on his retirement there were 508,000 people in an expanded area of 130 square miles, traveling on 1,190 miles of paving and 722 miles of annexed area roads that were still unpaved. Ninety-five percent of the existing sewer system was built under Donaldson. When he started to work for the city, there were 130 miles of sewers; in 1957 there were 1,300 miles and half a dozen disposal plants for the treatment of 60,000,000 gallons a day. Donaldson had received many national honors.

Another noted Atlanta figure whose retirement brought memories to the city, particularly among sporting circles, was Ed Danforth, sports editor of the *Journal*. On February 1, 1957, Danforth wrote his farewell column in the Sunday *Journal-Constitution:*

If a man just back from a war wanted to write sports . . . and no one ever found a happier calling . . . he could not have picked a spot in the land more favorable than Atlanta in the 1920s.

That was when the shining company of athletes strode into the scene to rim with fire the years of the Golden Age. Those were the days of Jack Dempsey, Ty Cobb, Babe Ruth, Earl Sande, Bill Tilden, Gertrude Ederle, Red Grange and Tex Rickard.

We had the most magnificent figure of the all in Atlanta, Bobby Jones . . . and we walked around in that retinue.

Scarcely less glamorous and close among us were Alexa Stirling, Perry Adair, Watts Gunn, Tom Prescott, Young Stribling, Bitsy Grant, Tiger Flowers, Jake Abel . . . the Atlanta chapter of the brave array, and we kept in step with their dashing deeds.

Georgia Tech was nationally famous in football and Georgia was on the rise. Bill Alexander, H. J. Stegeman, Don McGugin, Wallace Wade, Bernie Bierman, Clark Shaughnessy and young Harry Mehre were carrying Southern football banners into foreign fields . . . .

When only two Atlanta high schools had demanded attention, now the city had 13 new units with 22 in the metropolitan area offering fresh contacts to develop. New lakes brought boating into the picture. Swimming for the young found such favor that Georgia became the most highly developed aquatic field in the AAU.

Fortunately for Atlanta and for the men who picked sports writing as their beat, the publisher of our newspapers from the start were alert to the possibilities of developing sports pages. Besides, they were fans themselves. The old flamboyant Hearst executives set a pace in the 1920s that the other two papers promptly picked up and expanded. It was a wild battle in those days and the momentum persists. . . .

Baptists made up the largest church membership in Atlanta, and even with the influx of non-Southerners after the war the Southern Baptist Convention was determined that this situation should continue. Since 1942 more than eighty new Baptist churches had been added in Atlanta, and from these in 1956 came $800,000 for all causes and $150,000 for a new Southern Baptist City Mission program getting under way in 1957. This was part of a joint effort by the Atlanta Association of Baptist Churches and the Home Mission Board to double the number of churches and missions in the Southern Baptist Convention by 1964.

Lutherans were celebrating the fact that their denomination was growing in the Atlanta area, with new congregations forming in Sandy Springs, Doraville, and south Decatur. The first Lutheran church, St. John's, was established in Atlanta in 1889. In 1957 there were thirteen churches and several missions, with an estimated membership of 5,000. The heaviest growth had been since 1948, stimulated by the influx of people from the North and Midwest who had come to Atlanta with new industries and business houses.

While many Atlanta churches were celebrating the dedication of new buildings to accommodate a growing congregation, First Presbyterian of Atlanta was celebrating a different way of spreading the gospel. On Sunday morning, April 14, the church celebrated thirty-five years of broadcasting its morning service. The broadcast, heard every Sunday at 11 A.M. over WSB Radio, was the oldest continuous church radio broadcast in the United States, and possibly in the world. Dr. J. Sprole Lyons, pastor of First Presbyterian, had launched the series on Sunday morning, April 9, 1922.

Several events involving Atlanta as a transportation center attracted attention in the spring and summer of 1957. On May 13 the first commercial jet airliner ever to visit Atlanta touched down at Atlanta Airport—only seventy-eight minutes after it left Washington, D.C. The plane, a French Caravelle, came to Atlanta under the sponsorship of Delta Air Lines.

It would remain here two days, putting on demonstration flights for airline personnel and city officials, before moving on to complete its sixteen-city tour of the United States and Canada. The Caravelle, built by SUD Aviation of France, had a top speed of 460 and averaged about 386 miles an hour in its 547-mile journey to Atlanta. Its speed sliced almost in half the scheduled air time between Atlanta and Washington. The twin-engine jet cost $1,950,000, would seat sixty-four first-class or eighty tourist passengers, and had a range with sixty-four passengers of 2,200 miles.

While the most modern of passenger airplanes was being welcomed in Atlanta, the city soon was saying sentimental farewell to one of the most venerable locomotives. "Old 290, a steam engine that had pulled The Crescent Limited on the West Point Route to Montgomery and return for nearly thirty years, finally was 'put out to pasture,'" said the *Constitution*.

The passenger trains, of course, were being replaced by automobiles, buses, and airplanes, and Atlanta was a central city in this process of change. In early January of 1957, for example, Eastern Airlines announced that it had carried its fifty millionth passenger since its first flight in 1930, and the Atlanta district sales manager announced that 4.5 million of these had boarded in Atlanta. In 1956 alone a record 727,520 passengers boarded Eastern in Atlanta. In anticipation that this growth would continue, Eastern on January 11, 1957, opened its new 900-foot passenger concourse with an air-conditioned waiting room and a rooftop ramp control booth.

While air traffic continued to grow, Atlanta was busier than ever building automobiles and continuing to construct new expressways to carry them through and around the city.

On March 6 the Atlanta Chevrolet assembly plant, a twenty-nine-year-old landmark at Sawtell Road and McDonough Boulevard, turned out its 2 millionth vehicle. It had taken twenty years for the plant to produce its first million cars—and only slightly more than eight years to produce the second million. The first car produced in 1928 was a green and black four-door, four-cylinder sedan. The last was a 1957 model Bel Air, a four-door sports sedan in Matador Red and Indian Ivory. Harvey L. Green, general superintendent of production, presented the key to Ralph Smith, zone manager of the Atlanta Chevrolet Motor Division.

The production of the two millionth Chevrolet in Atlanta "brought into a revealing and somewhat startling focus the sharp contrasts between 1928 and 1957," said the *Constitution:*

The 1928 Landau had a 35.5 horsepower four-cylinder engine with a 4.475:1 compression ratio. It weighed 2,435 pounds and measured 152.06 inches long, 66.5 inches wide and 72 inches high. Standing on a 106.5-inch wheelbase, it had a turning circle diameter of only 20.5 feet.

What a contrast with the 1957 Bel Air V8 with engines ranging from 120 to 293 horsepower and with compression ratio of 9.5:1. And compared with the Atlanta plant's first model, number 2,000,000 is 1,016 pounds heavier, 47.94 inches longer, 7.4 inches wider, 11.5 inches lower.

Also, the $2,500 plus 1957 model's wheelbase is 8.5 inches longer, and the current turning circle diameter of 41.5 feet is more than double the size of the 1928 circle.

Today, the Atlanta Chevrolet-Fisher Body plant covers more than 835,000 square feet (more than double its 1928 area), produces an average of 700 cars and trucks a day on double shift (compared with 1928 single-shift output of 300 a day) and employs 3,590 workers (compared with close to 1,000 at the start.)

Atlanta in this year of 1957 was not only building automobiles, it was riding in them for greater distances over wider highways, and in greater numbers month by month. "Metropolitan Atlanta is riding to a million population four years hence—on wheels, a *Journal-Constitution* story declared:

Prophecies which seemed like whoppers at the time made have been proved timid guesses. It may be that the seers made their biggest mistakes because they failed to reckon rightly on the role of the most common carrier of all—the passenger car.

In the four counties officially comprising Metropolitan Atlanta—Fulton, DeKalb, Cobb and Clayton—there are today an estimated 862,000 people. There are 322,172 motor vehicles.

The forecasters even missed that one. Three years ago, they calculated that the total number of cars and trucks in the four-county area would reach about 325,000 in 1960. It's about there already.

Atlanta's expressway system, although still abuilding, already is carrying more traffic than was predicted for 13 years hence. The 1970 prophecy was a traffic load of 44,000 vehicles daily but an average of 55,256 vehicles are at present using the 10th to 14th Street stretch in a 24-hour period, according to a count made recently by the State Highway Department.

Despite the gap in the expressway where the downtown connector is one day supposed to be, there is no doubt that the existing legs and just the promise of more in the future have combined with the automobile to make Atlanta spread all over the place.

Although the city lacks the usual fast transportation of the metropolis—the subway and commuter trains—Atlanta has gone out in all directions. Northeastward, where the expressway will merge into the fourlane Buford Highway now under construction, land values have gone from $200 to $300 an acre to $750 to $1,200. Northwestward, beyond Sandy Springs, land in its raw state bought in the bulk for future development has commanded a price of $600 an acre. There are comparable developments on the south side.

The pattern of Atlanta's growth has produced a result that is most welcome along automobile row: The two-car family.

There's definitely a trend that way, says one of Atlanta's biggest dealers in the popular-price field. "Almost every day we talk to someone who says he's moved out to Cobb or DeKalb or Clayton County and he's got to have a car for his wife now.

"It's increased our business," he says. "It was one of the good features of 1956. And it's growing all the time. A lot of people have three cars.". . .

Besides its effect on the suburbs, the automobile has managed to influence downtown plannning and building profoundly. One big question has been where to park all those cars that come sailing in via the expressway and other arteries, and it is about the only major traffic problem that has been solved with any degree of satisfaction. . . .

The automobile's role in Atlanta's growth has not been confined to getting people downtown. Not long ago the U.S. Department of Commerce reported: "The increased usage and flexibility of the automobile has created a climate favorable for the successful development of neighborhood and regional shopping centers."

Though speaking in terms of the nation as a whole, the Commerce Department might have been describing Atlanta in particular. Shopping centers with adjacent parking lots are to be found in every section of the metropolis. There's one in the works that will top them all with 6,000 spaces for parking.

Someday the sociologists may take the statistics apart and write the history of Atlanta's development from the standpoint of the automobile. They will find that the more the city took to wheels, the faster it grew.

In 1930, residents of the four counties of the metropolitan area owned about 86,000 cars and trucks. By 1952, they owned 236,356. The gain of 175 percent was far greater than the national gain of 105 percent in the same period.

Motor vehicle registration in Fulton, DeKalb, Cobb and Clayton went up 73,639 in the 10 years from 1941 to 1951. In the next five years—from 1951 to 1956—it leaped by 119,650.

Declaring that the next four years would be the most crucial in the city's history and that he wanted to be part of them, William B. Hartsfield announced that he would be a candidate for a sixth term as the city's primary was coming up on May 8. He made this announcement on March 7, well in advance of the qualifying date, because he said he did not want to wait until the city became involved in an upcoming bond election.

Hartsfield had already served as mayor longer than any other one man in the city's history. He was first elected in 1936 and had held the position since that time, except for a year and a half in 1940-41 when Roy LeCraw served as mayor before resigning to go into military service.

Hartsfield won in the primary on May 8, beating Fulton County Commission Chairman Archie Lindsey 37,365 to 33,630. Hartsfield then went on to win over independent candidate Lester Maddox in the December general election. Hartsfield's total vote was 41,300, while Maddox's was 23,987. The campaign centered chiefly on racial policies, with Hartsfield favored heavily in the thirteen predominantly Negro precincts, where he led Maddox by 14,209 votes to 353. In the remaining fifty-seven precincts, which were mostly white, the count was much closer—Hartsfield winning 27,191 to 23,134. The mayor carried forty of the city's seventy precincts, his greatest strength being the northside. Maddox's strength was centered in working-class white areas in the south and west of the city.

In addition to electing the mayor, voters also elected seventeen aldermen and nine members of the Board of Education. The aldermen were Lee Evans, city at large; L. O. Moseley and James E. Jackson, Jr., first ward; Ed A. Gilliam and R. E. Lee Field, second ward; Bill Knight and Jimmy Vickers, third ward; Douglas Wood and Charlie Leftwich, fourth ward; John A. White and Hamilton Douglas, fifth ward; Ralph Huie and T. Wayne Blanchard, sixth ward; Milton Farris and Jack Summers, seventh ward; and Jesse Draper and Goodwyn (Shag) Cates, eighth ward.

Board of Education members were: A. C. (Pete) Latimer, member from the city at large; Ed S. Cook, first ward; Harold Jackson, second ward; Dr. Rufus Clement, third ward; Allen L. Chancey, fourth ward; Jim O'Callaghan, fifth ward; Oby T. Brewer, Jr., sixth ward; Glenn Frick, seventh ward; and Mrs. Clifford N. Ragsdale, eighth ward.

Hartsfield attributed his victory over Lester Maddox, who accused him of being a "pawn of the NAACP," to the fact that citizens both white and black refused to be led into violent controversy over racial matters. One of Hartsfield campaign themes was that Atlanta must continue to have peaceful race relationships or "we are gone." Hartsfield expressed this view particularly strongly at the annual meeting of the Central Atlanta Improvement Association, made up of top business and political leaders of the city—pointing out that it was of special importance that downtown business maintain decent race relations and avoid violence. Listening to and evidently heeding these remarks were the association's newly elected president, Fred J. Turner, chairman of the board of Southern Bell Telephone and Telegraph Company.

Four days before Hartsfield's talk to Atlanta's civic leaders more than sixty Negroes from nine southern states gathered in Atlanta, where under the leadership of the Reverend Martin Luther King, Jr., they reviewed the whole picture of race relations in the South. Segregation on buses, King predicted, would be ended by 1960, but there were other points at issue, and these were pointed out in separate appeals to members of their own race, to white southerners, and to President Eisenhower, Vice-President Nixon and Attorney General Brownell.

The president was asked to come South and make a speech "urging all Southerners to abide by the Supreme Court's decision as the law of the land" and pointing out that "extreme violence" continued to be directed toward Negroes in the South.

"The question before the nation is no longer whether there should be segregation or integration, but rather whether there shall be anarchy or law."

The appeals to the government leaders were based on the charge that the executive and legislative branches of the federal government had failed to follow the lead of the judicial in civil matters. In its appeal to white southerners the conference statement had religious overtones, a reflection perhaps of the presence of the Reverend Martin Luther King, Jr. It asked moral support from white Christians, white churches, and white southerners of good will. It urged that southern white Christians see to it that all persons who "seek the saving Grace of Christ" be accepted as equals in churches. It urged church-supported schools and colleges to "set an example of brotherhood." The appeal to their own race was to "assert their human dignity" and reject segregation "while avoiding violent action."

Early in the year the Atlanta Christian Council had urged that the racial issue be kept out of the upcoming city elections. In commenting on this action, the *Journal-Constitution,* in an editorial on April 17, said that "Atlanta has shown itself in the past to be an enlightened community that has kept the influence of hatemongers to a minimum. The result has been a harmonious, progressive city. Racial peace and religious tolerance, supported by efforts of such groups as the Church Council, has been a trademark. We need no peddling of hate or prejudices. . . . Let those who try, learn now that Atlanta is a mature, stable city of reasonable people."

One of the first public comments on racial tension by a white Atlanta minister came from Dr. Roy McClain of Atlanta's First Baptist Church, who from his pulpit on October 6 proclaimed that "Pulpits have been paralyzed . . . the well-informed people have been quiet." Thereupon the *Atlanta Journal-Constitution* invited ministers of many faiths to write down the guidance they would give their members on the race question. Many responded and were quoted in the papers for several weeks thereafter.

Their observations reflected the tortured indecision suffered by many white Christians. Though taught by the Bible that all men are brothers, "the Christian has the innate feeling that voluntary segregation in almost every area of Christian experience," as Dr. Harry A. Fifield of First Presbyterian expressed it, "is consistent with Christian truth. We segregate ourselves voluntarily according to sex, to age, to denomination, to creed, and to race." However, Dr. Fifield added: "It ought to be noted that the majority of the major denominations, including my own, in their highest court and assemblies, have spoken out clearly to the effect that enforced segregation on the basis of color is inconsistent with Biblical principles."

Said Dr. Fifield in conclusion: "Only in an atmosphere of tolerance, patience and discussion" can Christian people possibly follow through to the complete Christian solution of the problem of segregation. Greatest obstacle to this, he observed, is "the emotionalism created by adamant extremists on both sides. Some insist this desegregation must be enforced immediately, some insisting it must never come."

Dr. Dow Kirkpatrick of St. Mark's Methodist said much the same thing—that the problem could be solved if all concerned would remain "calm, sane, prayerful and dedicated to truth and the free expression of differing opinions."

The Rev. Charles Allen of Grace Methodist boiled his discussion down to two words—the headlines in his column in the *Constitution*—"It's Brotherhood, Not Integration." Said he:

Responsible people know that men should be brothers. We are all children of one Father; we are all on the same pilgrimage through life; at the close of life's day, we all travel through the same Valley of the Shadow; we seek to spend eternity in the same Father's House. The color of our skin may differ, but under the skin we feel the same joys and sorrow, we have the same hopes and fears, we commit the same sins and we need the same Saviour.

But brotherhood is never accomplished by the making of laws, the decisions of courts, or the fixed bayonets of soldiers. Neither can brotherhood be prevented by the burning of crosses, the throwing of dynamite or the windy speeches of politicians.

Neither is brotherhood accomplished by preaching about segregation and integration. I'm tired of both those words. Nobody really believes in either one of them. We need to get up some new and better words to use. To segregate means to isolate, to seclude. We don't want that.

The word "integrate" has come to mean the amalgamation of the races. Certainly we do not want that. We do want brotherhood based on the dignity of all men, the supreme worth of every human being, love for God and for each other. That is what the pulpit today is preaching.

These opinions were followed less than a month later, on November 3, by a six-point statement signed by eighty Atlanta ministers, including the three above. It covered all the points of main concern to the white community—as the conference statement by sixty black leaders in January had expressed the aims and goals of southern blacks.

Excerpts from the white ministers' statement follows:

The signers of this statement are all ministers of the Gospel, but we speak also as citizens of Georgia and of the United States of America. We are all Southerners, either by birth or by choice, and speak as men who love the South, who seek to understand its problems, and who are vitally concerned for its welfare.

In preparing this statement we have acted as individuals, and represent no one but ourselves. At the same time we believe that the sentiments which we express are shared by a multitude of our fellow citizens, who are deeply troubled by our present situation and who know that hatred, defiance and violence are not the answer to our problems, but who have been without a voice and have found no way to make their influence effective. . . .

We are of one mind, however, in believing that Christian people have an especial responsibility for the solution of our racial problems and that if, as Christians, we sincerely seek to understand and apply the teachings of our Lord and Master we shall assuredly find the answer.

We do not believe that the South is more to blame for the difficulties which we face than are other areas of our nation. The presence of the Negro in America is the result of the infamous slave traffic—an evil for which the North was as much responsible as the South.

We are also conscious that racial injustice and violence are not confined to our section and that racial problems have by no means been solved anywhere in our nation. Two wrongs, however, do not make a right. The failures of others are not a justification of our own shortcomings, nor can their unjust criticisms excuse us for a failure to do our duty in the sight of God. Our one concern must be to know and to do that which is right.

We believe that the difficulties before us have been greatly increased by extreme attitudes and statements on both sides. The use of the word "integration" in connection with our schools and other areas of life has been unfortunate, since to many that term has become synonymous with amalgamation. We do not believe in the amalgamation of the races, nor do we feel that it is favored by right thinking members of either race.

We do believe that all Americans, whether white or black, have a right to the full privileges of first class citizenship. To suggest that a recognition of the rights of Negroes to the full privileges of American citizenship and to such necessary contacts as might follow would inevitably result in intermarriage is to cast as serious and unjustified aspersion upon the white race as upon the Negro race.

Believing as we do in the desirability of preserving the integrity of both races through the free choice of both, we would emphasize the following principles which we hold to be of basic importance for our thought and conduct:

1. FREEDOM OF SPEECH must at all costs be preserved. . . .

2. AS AMERICANS and as CHRISTIANS we have an obligation to obey the law. . . .

3. THE PUBLIC SCHOOL SYSTEM must not be destroyed. . . .

4. HATRED AND SCORN for those of another race, or for those who hold a position different from our own, can never be justified. . . .

5. COMMUNICATION between responsible leaders of the races must be maintained. . . .

6. Our difficulties cannot be solved in our own strength or in human wisdom. It is appropriate, therefore, that we approach our task in a spirit of humility, of penitence, and of prayer. . . .

There were troubled years ahead of course, and angry confrontations between blacks and whites, but the voices from some of the city's pulpits helped white Atlanta to accept in a spirit of Christian brotherhood a new relationship between the races that would have been unthinkable a few years earlier.

Even before the clergy spoke, the city fathers had recognized that in the past Atlanta's Negro banks had been unfairly treated, in that none had been used as depositories for city funds. Thus, on February 1 Comptroller Earl Landers announced that the mayor and board of aldermen had chosen the

Citizens Trust Company of Georgia, a black-owned bank, as one of seven Atlanta banks in which city funds could be deposited. Others were the old-line Atlanta banks—the First National Bank of Atlanta, the Fulton National Bank, the Bank of Georgia, the Trust Company of Georgia, the South Side Atlanta Bank, and the Citizens and Southern National Bank.

Beginning on October 31 King Hardware Company celebrated its seventy-fifth year in business in Atlanta with a gigantic anniversary sale in all its eighteen stores. It was in 1882 that George E. King opened his first little store on the corner of Peachtree and Auburn Avenue, then known as Wheat Street. There it dealt in wholesale and retail hardware, guns, pistols and ammunition, tin and wooden ware, patent bottom tinware, and agricultural equipment. King had recently opened its nineteenth store. The new facility was at Northeast Plaza. Among the first to join the flight to the suburban shopping areas, King had opened eight new stores since 1949—in Decatur, Campbellton, Piedmont, Northeast Plaza, Forest Park, College Park, and Brookhaven.

On August 1 the City of East Point celebrated what could be considered its seventieth official birthday or its one-hundredth anniversary. On that date in 1887 it was officially incorporated, but thirty-three years earlier the legislature had granted a charter for the railroad, now the Atlanta and West Point, and East Point grew around its eastern terminus, where it joined the present-day Central of Georgia from Macon to Savannah. Under Mayor J. C. Stith, East Point was a hustling, bustling community of 32,000 people. "It is not content to bask in Atlanta's glory as merely another member of the metropolitan community. It wants the world to know it is the state's eighth largest city, and has perhaps more industrial plants than any other town its size in the country."

A bright new chapter in Atlanta's medical history opened in March when Piedmont Hospital moved from its old home at 550 Capitol Avenue SW to its new building at 1968 Peachtree Road NW. Under the direction of superintendent George Burt, the transfer went off with remarkable smoothness. Sixty-four patients were transferred by ambulance from the old building to the six-story, $5 million new structure, set in the midst of spacious parking areas.

The new Grady Hospital was nearing completion by the end of the year. Celestine Sibley waxed eloquent about the change:

The Old Grady Has Its Atmosphere, But the New Grady Has Everything,

Well, now I feel better about that splendid edifice, the new Grady hospital! For three years I've watched the gold and cream towers rising against the sky and heard fabulous tales of the marvels of comfort and efficiency that were being built into it. And I shook my head sadly.

It wasn't the old Grady I knew and felt comfortable with—the shabby, smelly, sprawling old place where I've spent so many hours in years gone by.

With all its faults the old Grady hospital had atmosphere and heart . . . and I couldn't be sure about this new 20-million dollar structure.

But, as I say, I feel better now. I've just come from a grand tour of the new hospital and all they say about it is true. It's beautiful and shining and as modern as tomorrow. It would be a privilege to take your toe-ache—or even your heartbreak—to such a place. . . .

The new hospital, which has been a-building since 1954, is expected to be ready for occupancy the week after Christmas—a time chosen by Supt. [Frank] Wilson when it is likely to have the lightest patient load. . . .

When you think how gallantly the old Grady limped along, coping with all comers with not half enough room and makeshift facilities, the new hospital is a gladsome thing. It has room for everything—a full block of operating rooms, running the length of the building "from Butler Street to the expressway," as Mr. Wilson said. It has everything hospital administrators have dreamed of to make patient care easier and hospital life happy—including facilities for 72 psychiatric patients.

The kitchens and laboratories, the tremendous cafeterias and lounge, the auditorium and chapel, the delivery rooms and nursery, are models of their kind. There will be room for 1,500 patients, instead of the present Grady's 800, in the 21-story structure. . .

With the new Piedmont and Grady hospitals and the heart clinic at Emory going on line in 1957, a place of healing that was not a hospital but a school finally came into being. After three years of hard work raising money, Coach Bobby Dodd of Georgia Tech at last clipped the ribbon to open the new Atlanta Retarded Children's School, located at 843 Springdale Road NE. The school would be operated by the Retarded Children's Association, a nonprofit organization incorporated to assist the slow and mentally retarded child.

Atlanta this year began getting better service from its meteorologists than ever before, at little or no increase in costs. At the Atlanta Airport Weather Bureau, a converted B-29 radar set began scanning the skies in a radius of 200 miles. This set, its disc turning hour after hour around the clock, could "see" more in five minutes than could 5,000 human observers all over the state, according to J. C. Ballard, meteorologist in charge. Tornadoes were harder to spot, he said, until they touched the ground; but cold fronts, which cause startling shifts in Georgia weather during the fall and winter months, would show up on the radar scope as a long, ragged line of clouds, and their courses could be followed and the disturbances moving ahead of them could be predicted with great accuracy. Twenty-five forecasters manned the radar in shifts around the clock.

Thousands attended the Municipal Theater Under the Stars at the 6,500-seat Chastain Memorial Amphitheatre. The papers declared: "Blessed by the weather and a succession of good shows the Municipal Theater Under the Stars is having one of its best seasons. In all likelihood more people will have enjoyed the productions this year than ever before. . . . Atlanta owes a special debt of gratitude to Maurice B. Seltzer, who has given time, effort and considerable funds to the promotion of the theater, and to the city for its support." Though he owned Southeastern Wholesale Furniture Company, Seltzer's heart was in the theater, and at the urging of Mayor Hartsfield he took on the development of the Theater Under the Stars at Chastain Park. In 1954 he was joined by Christopher Manos as executive producer and manager of the theater on a year-round basis. On Seltzer's death in 1964, Manos became the guiding figure of Theater Under the Stars. In 1968 Theater Under the Stars became Theater of the Stars and moved indoors to the new Civic Center—not, as people believed, to get out of the rain at Chastain Park but because of the springtime change to daylight saving time.

The urban renewal matching funds program had been in effect for nearly eight years, and many cities, some two hundred throughout the nation, by taking advantage of it had moved far ahead of Atlanta in their slum-clearance programs. Augusta, Columbus, and Douglas, Georgia, were at least a year ahead of Atlanta, each with urban renewal programs costing more than a million dollars. Savannah was in the midst of a development program costing more than six million dollars.

The delay in getting the program under way in Georgia grew out of the fact that opponents had fought it on the grounds that it was unconstitutional under state law. It was legal enough for the government to condemn land to be used for government purposes, but to condemn it for resale to private enterprise was unconstitutional. The battle continued in Superior Court for more than three years before it was settled. Atlanta's troubles, however, were not over. The strongest opponents of slum clearance were not slum dwellers who would be displaced, but slum owners. Slums were among the most profitable businesses to be found in large cities.

It was predicted that by mid-summer of 1958 Atlanta would begin to move into the operational stage of its urban renewal program. It would start buying up some 598 blighted sites that had been chosen for redevelopment. Three urban renewal areas had been selected. The Buttermilk Bottom, or Butler Street area, and the Washington-Rawson Street area would be almost completely leveled, with the exception of a few buildings that could be restored. The third area, near Atlanta University, would be primarily a rehabilitation section, with existing buildings being repaired and remodeled. Atlanta's plans made up the third-largest urban redevelopment in the South. Only Baltimore and Nashville had larger plans. The urban renewal program was also tied closely with expressway development, and the difficulty in finally pinning down expressway locations would also slow down urban renewal.

OBITUARIES

Sharon Hogg—funeral services were held on the day after Christmas for this four-year-old girl whose blindness led to creation of the Foundation for the Visually Handicapped in Georgia. The foundation was the creation of a group of parents of blind children who wanted their children to go to school with normal children. Sharon's father, R. H. Hogg, persuaded the Georgia Beer Wholesalers Association to finance the foundation. Michael Angelo (Mike) Greenblatt, 73, president of the Atlanta Paper Company and arranger in 1911 of the famous Georgia Tech "Ramblin' Wreck" song, died on May 20. Harold D. Smith, native of DeKalb County and a Decatur hardware store owner, died. Mrs. Isaac X. Cheeves, the former Nellie Gilber, died at 89. She was a communicant of the Cathedral of Christ the King. Mrs. Richard H. Rich, wife of the owner of Atlanta's leading department store, died. She was the former Virginia Gleaves Lazarus of New Orleans. Charles Lucien Elyea, the first wholesale automotive accessory business owner in Atlanta, died at 88. Mrs. Paul Pressly, mother of Dr. William L. Pressly, president of the Westminster Schools, died at the home of a daughter in Statesville, North Carolina. Mildred Cabaniss, former society editor of the *Atlanta Journal*, died at her home in the Biltmore. She was 85 years old and the daughter of early Atlantans, Henry H. and Sarah Royston Cabaniss. She was a graduate of Lucy Cobb, and her debut ball was the first social event held at the Aragon Hotel, which stood at the corner of Peachtree and Ellis. She was a loyal member of the First Baptist Church. Mrs. Francis Cochran Block, widow of the owner of an early candy company in this city, died at 89. She was the former Lillie Orme, daughter of the late Dr. and Mrs. Francis H. Orme. Active in cultural affairs and the patriotic societies, she had served as vice-president of Colonial Dames, had been president of the Every Saturday Club, and was regent for the DAR. She was a member of All Saints' Episcopal Church. Gordon P. Kiser, Sr., was chairman of the board of Chattahoochee Brick Company, where he had served as president for many years. He was 89 and a charter member of the Piedmont Driving Club and the Capital City Club. A graduate of Emory at Oxford, Kiser was the oldest alumnus of the Emory chapter of Chi Phi. Mrs. Hal McCall Stanley, the former Ethel Stubbs, died at 90. Her late husband was commissioner of labor for Georgia from 1912 to 1940. She was a member of the DAR, the Mayflower Society, and the First Methodist Church of Decatur. Dr. Hugh Montgomery Lokey, Atlanta physician for more than half a century and a specialist in diseases of the eye, ear, nose and throat, died at 80. He was a former president of the Fulton County Medical Society. Mrs. Willis F. Westmoreland, widow of a prominent Atlanta physician and surgeon, was the former Nannie Woodward, daughter of Mr. and Mrs. James Woodward. Her father was a former mayor of the city.

Mrs. Robert B. Blackburn, writer of Southern folklore and columnist for the *Atlanta Constitution*, died at 87. Her husband, an Atlanta attorney, served in the legislature for seventeen years. Mrs. Blackburn was a graduate of Girls High and was a member of the UDC, the DAR, Pioneer Women, and the Uncle Remus Memorial Association. She attended St. Luke's Episcopal

Church. Mrs. Eugene J. Sterne, the former Ernestine Hirsch, was an active supporter of the Southern Ballet. She taught dancing for over twenty-five years at Lottie Hentschel's Dance Studio. She was a member of The Temple. Miss Gussie Brenner, retired Atlanta schoolteacher and principal of Davis Street, Fair Street, and Kirkwood schools, died at her home on The Prado. A graduate of the old State Normal School, she was also a member of First Presbyterian Church.

Harry L. Spring died at 57. For many years a leader in the trucking business, he had been vice-president of the American Trucking Association for the state of Georgia for seventeen years. He was vice-president and general manager of Georgia Highway Express. His memberships included Rotary, Masons, the Piedmont Driving Club, Atlanta Athletic Club, Allatoona Yacht Club, and the Atlanta Chamber of Commerce. He belonged to the Peachtree Road Methodist Church. Lewis C. Gregg, Atlanta portrait artist and former *Atlanta Constitution* cartoonist, died after a long illness. Member of an old Atlanta family, Gregg studied art in Paris after he left the paper in the 1920s. Judge Walter C. Hendrix, judge emeritus of Fulton Superior Court, died at 73. A graduate of Emory at Oxford, he practiced law and served as a Fulton County commissioner and legislator. He had served as judge since 1939. Judge Hendrix was a Mason, Shriner, Jester, and belonged to Second Ponce de Leon Baptist Church.

Harry M. Crosswell, long-time president of W. L. Fain Grain Company, died at 78. He was a graduate of The Citadel and was an elder at North Avenue Presbyterian Church. Alfredo Barili, Jr., an Atlanta architect since 1910 and designer of many schools, churches, and public buildings, died at 69. His works included the new Post Office, Courthouse Annex, Murphy High School, and Haygood Memorial Church. He was a member of Delta Tau Delta, AIA, Atlanta Athletic Club, and the First Presbyterian Church. Mrs. Philip Weltner, Sr., longtime civic leader, died at 69. The former Sally Hull, she was a graduate of Lucy Cobb Institute. She was a founder of the new Oglethorpe Presbyterian Church and was instrumental in establishing a branch library in Buckhead. Her husband was a former president of Oglethorpe University and chancellor of the University of Georgia. Frank G. Lake, Sr., retired Atlanta lumber executive, died at 86. He received his education in Atlanta schools and in 1898 formed the company that bore his name. He was president until he retired in the late 1940s. A member of the Pioneer Boys Club, Lake was also a Mason and a Shriner. He attended Central Presbyterian Church.

Cone M. Maddox, Sr., director and senior member of Ward Wight Realty Company, died at 74. A graduate of the University of Georgia, he first entered the grocery business and then became a realtor in 1922. He belonged to the Ansley Park Golf Club, the Atlanta Athletic Club, the Capital City Club, and the First Baptist Church. Mrs. Robert M. Crumley, Sr., died at her home at the Georgian Terrace Hotel. She was the widow of the owner of Crumley-Sharp Hardware Company, widely known city merchant. She attended All Saints' Episcopal Church. Mrs. Thomas J. Wesley, Sr., lifelong Atlantan, died at 84. She was the widow of the executive vice-president of the old Merchants-Mechanics Bank and was a member of St. Luke's Episcopal Church. Manuel A. (Mack) Morris, a retired railroad yard conductor, died at 73. He was a member of the Brotherhood of Railroad Trainmen. Mrs. L. P. Skeen of Decatur was born in April of 1868 and came to Atlanta as a bride before 1900. Mrs. George Mathieson, widow of the former chief of the Fulton County police and active in the affairs of the Second Ponce de Leon Baptist Church, died at her home in Buckhead.

Andrew J. Collier, veteran Atlanta real estate dealer and member of one of the city's oldest families, died. He was born in the old Collier homeplace that stood on the southwest corner of Peachtree and Collier roads. Mrs. Lyle E. Campbell, wife of an Emory professor, was past president of the Women's Council of the Peachtree Christian Church and of the Emory Women's Club. William Embree Chester, retired veteran of the Central of Georgia Railroad, died at 94. He was a member of the Brotherhood of Local Engineers for seventy years. Dr. Lawson Thornton, well known in Southern medical circles and an orthopedic surgeon, died at 72. He was a veteran of World War I and a graduate of Auburn and Johns Hopkins. He was on the staffs of Piedmont, St. Joseph, and Grady hospitals and was a member of the Piedmont Driving Club. Dr. Thornton was remembered for his beautiful saddle horses, being one of the first in Atlanta to import thoroughbreds to this area. Mrs. Milton Candler, of Decatur, the former Nellie Scott, died at 91. Her father, George Scott, was the founder of Agnes Scott College. Eugene C. Dempsey, Sr., retired yardmaster of the N.C.&St.L., died at 65. He retired in 1951 after forty-five years with his company. He was a member of the Brotherhood of Railroad Trainmen.

Dr. Marion C. Pruitt, leading southern proctologist, died at 72. He was a founder of the American Board of Surgery, Fellow of the American College of Surgeons and the Royal College of Surgeons of Edinburgh, Scotland. He was associate professor of surgery at Emory University. Mrs. William L. Percy, 78, active in civic and cultural affairs, died at her home in Inman Park. Her husband was retired from the presidency of Dobbs and Wey. Mrs. Percy was a graduate of Washington Seminary and was a member of the board of the Church's Home for Girls, Atlanta Woman's Club, the DAR, the UDC, and honorary president of the Georgia Federation of Women's Clubs. Mrs. Daniel MacDougald, Sr., a distinguished figure in social and civic affairs, died at 62. She was the widow of the chairman of the board of Georgia Power Company and was active in the Junior League, Red Cross, and Egleston Hospital. She had at one time been chairman of the Child's Services Association. Joseph W. Awtry, pioneer citizen and president of Awtry and Lowndes Funeral Home until 1955, died at 87. He was instrumental in founding Georgia Baptist Hospital and had served on the boards of the Georgia Baptist Children's Home and the Church's Home for Girls.

Madge Bigham, author of children's books that delighted two generations of Atlantans, died at 83. The daughter of Rev. Robert William Bigham, she was a graduate of Lucy Cobb Institute. Her church was Trinity Methodist. Frank M. Berry, retired Atlanta bank cashier, died at 85. Known affectionately as "The Colonel," he was born in Atlanta and retired in 1946 after fifty-five years of service with the First National Bank. He held membership in The Old Guard, Jesters, Shrine, the Second Ponce de Leon Baptist Church, and the Capital City Club. Mrs. William Joseph Mallard, the former Sallie Meador, spent all of her 86 years in Atlanta. She was a retired schoolteacher and a member of North Avenue Presbyterian Church.

Methvin Thomson Salter, Jr., son and grandson of pioneer Atlanta physicians, died at 61. A graduate of Boys High and Georgia Tech, he was a chemist for the Coca-Cola Bottling Company. He was a veteran of World War I, a member of American Legion, Druid Hills Golf Club, and St. Luke's Episcopal Church. Eugene Charles Callaway, one of the city's early business and civic leaders, died at 92. He had owned Fulton County Home Builders and built the Imperial Hotel. He was director and a trustee of the YMCA from 1908 until 1956. Mrs. George S. Obear, leader in civic, education and religious activities, was the former Minnie Tidwell, daughter of Atlanta pioneers Mr. and Mrs. R. W. Tidwell. Her memberships included Woman's Club, the DAR, the UDC, and St. Philip's Cathedral. She had been especially active in library and school work in the Little Five Points area.

Mrs. Frank Dean, the former Maybelle Lewis, died at 79. Her parents, Mr. and Mrs. Thomas Sumner Lewis, were early citizens of this city. She was a graduate of Mrs. Hannah's School for Girls and was a member of the Service Group, Atlanta Historical Society, and All Saints' Episcopal Church. Mrs. Adelaide Howell, daughter of Capt. Evan P. Howell and sister of the late Clark Howell, Sr., publisher of the *Atlanta Constitution,* died at 78. Born in Atlanta, she attended Lucy Cobb and was a feature and short story writer. She belonged to the Atlanta Writers' Club, Atlanta Woman's Club, and Peachtree Christian Church. Joseph M. Collins, a vice-president of the Coca-Cola Company, died at 50. A graduate of the University of Georgia, he went to work for Coca-Cola in 1929, serving for twenty-eight years. He belonged to the Piedmont Driving Club and St. Mark's Methodist Church. Walter Cabot Sturdivant, Sr., prominent textile mill president and bank director, died. He was president of the Montgomery and Chattooga Knitting Mills and the Farmers and Merchants Bank, both in Summerville. He was a member of the Piedmont Driving Club, the Capital City Club, and the Episcopal church.

Charles Howard Candler, a native of Atlanta and son of Asa G. and Lucy Elizabeth Howard Candler, was born on December 2, 1878. He was educated in the city's schools and then attended Emory at Oxford, graduating in 1898. In 1906 he was made vice-president of his father's rapidly growing business, the Coca-Cola Company, and ten years later was made president. He retired in 1923. In the meantime he had become president in 1917 of Asa G. Candler, Inc., and had become a director of the Coca-Cola Company, the Trust Company of Georgia, Atlantic Steel, and the Atlantic Company. He became chairman of the board of trustees of Emory University in 1929 and in his family's tradition was a heavy contributor to that institution. Candler was especially interested in the Music Festival Association. President of Rotary in 1930–31, he belonged also to the Piedmont Driving Club, Capital City Club, and Druid Hills Golf Club. He was a Kappa Alpha and Phi Beta Kappa.

Eugene Adams Yates, chairman of the board of directors of the Southern Company and director and vice-president of Georgia Power Company, died in New York. He was 76. Mrs. Richard W. Courts, Sr., widow of an investment broker, died after a long illness. The former Mary Jenkins McPherson, she married in 1895 and moved to Atlanta in 1909. She was a member of St. Luke's Episcopal Church and was active in church and civic endeavors. Francis M. Craft, retired chief engineer of Southern Bell, died at 74. He retired in 1948 after forty-three years in the telephone industry, his career beginning in 1905 with Western Electric. A member of the advisory board of St. Joseph's Hospital, Craft was also active at First Presbyterian and belonged to the Capital City Club.

Eugene C. Wachendorff, Atlanta architect for fifty-five years, died at 76. A graduate of Columbia, Wachendorff had maintained his office in Atlanta since 1905. Among the buildings he designed were the W. F. Slaton and Booker T. Washington schools and the Standard Office Building. In 1914 he was president of the Atlanta chapter of AIA. Edward M. Chapman, Sr., president and founder of Chapman Realty Co., died after a forty-year career in Atlanta real estate. Chapman first worked with Forrest and George Adair and founded his own company in 1930. Twice he served as president of the Atlanta Real Estate Board, to which he had belonged for twenty-five years. He was active in the YMCA, Lions Club, and the Men's Garden Club.

Mrs. F. Chauncey Battey, widow of a former vice-president of the Trust Company of Georgia, died at 43. She was the former Marion Smith, and her brother Hoke was a well-known Atlanta attorney. Battey headed a number of civic activities, having been director of the Symphony Guild, vice-president of Theater Under the Stars, president of Rhodes Home, and active in Red Cross and the League of Women Voters. Battey was a member of the Junior League. Alton F. Irby, Sr., chairman of the board of the insurance company that bore his name, died at 73. A lifelong resident of Atlanta, he had been in the insurance business fifty-eight years. He was a member of the First Presbyterian Church.

Rembert Marshall, who had practiced law in Atlanta since 1922, died at 65. He was counsel for the Georgia division of Southern Railway Company. He was a graduate of Vanderbilt and had his degree from its law school. He was active in legal organizations and belonged to the Capital City Club, Piedmont Driving Club, and the Peachtree Golf Club. He was a member of St. Luke's Episcopal Church. Mrs. James Walton McMillan died at 92. She was Aurelia Roach, daughter of Dr. and Mrs. Elisha Roach, and was born in 1865 on Whitehall Street. For twenty-seven years she taught in the public schools of this city and for nineteen years was principal of Crew Street School. She was the last surviving charter member in Georgia of the DAR and was a Colonial Dame and a member of the Atlanta Historical Society. Edward S. Gay, lifelong resident of the city, died after a thirty-year career as an executive with Fulton National Bank. He was a son of Capt. Edward and Sally Ewell Gay, Atlanta pioneers. He was a veteran of World War I, and his memberships included the Piedmont Driving Club and Nine O'Clocks. He was treasurer of the Episcopal Diocese of Atlanta under Bishop John Moore Walker.

NOTES

1. Minutes of the Board of Directors, Atlanta Chamber of Commerce, May 8, 1957.
2. Milton Bracken, "Atlanta—A City of Clubs, Opera, Expansion and Commerce," *New York Times*, as quoted in the *Atlanta Constitution*, Feb. 15, 1957.

OFFICIALS had predicted that there would be problems and delays in carrying out the urban renewal plans, and indeed they were quick in coming. Early in January there came a controversy over the acquisition of park sites in two Negro urban renewal projects—Butler and University Center. The cost of more than $789,000 would take two-thirds of the $1 million authorized for parks in the 1957 bond issue. Aldermen Milton Farris and Charlie Leftwich of the Parks Committee contended that the price was too high. However, Colonel Malcolm Jones, director of urban renewal, joined Alderman Hamilton Douglas, chairman of the Urban Renewal Committee, in urging action. Unless other city divisions helped the urban renewal program, they argued, the whole project might have to be abandoned. Hartsfield supported Douglas. "We have promised these people parks for fifteen years," he said. The aldermanic committee finally agreed to offer $125,000 for the Butler project and postpone any action on the University Center site.

Next came a report from Georgia's FHA director John Thigpen that the program to house some 1,500 families displaced by urban renewal plans was "lagging badly." Contractors, said Thigpen, were having great difficulty finding locations for the new low-cost homes. At a conference at City Hall between federal officials and the Aldermanic Board's Building and Electric Lights Committee, it was brought out that there was much opposition to the program on the part of the general public. Many citizens, Thigpen said, opposed the program for fear that the inhabitants of the new houses "would not be good neighbors." Also, many displaced persons were not applying for new houses. They would continue to live in their old neighborhood. It was suggested at the conference that much of the opposition would disappear if model homes could be built to show the objectors that the FHA-financed houses were not slum houses. They would be well built and roomy, with the minimum floor space of 650 to 810 square feet, as recommended by the Zoning Committee of the Aldermanic Board.

Early in 1958 the Health Committee of the Atlanta Chamber of Commerce approved a resolution calling for the addition of fluoride compounds to Atlanta's water supply. According to the resolution, the addition of one part of fluoride per million would reduce tooth decay in children by approximately 60 percent. Backing fluoridation were the major medical, dental, and public health organizations in the area. Opposing it strongly and stubbornly was Mayor Hartsfield. It was one of the rare instances when Hartsfield opposed an issue that most experts felt would be in the interests of Atlantans, and, of course, in the long run he did not prevail. But many Atlantans agreed with him, and it was 1969 before Atlanta began to put fluoride in its water.

DeKalb County, under the leadership of Commissioner Scott Candler and C. D. Alfred, a farsighted water department superintendent, had been fluoridating its water since 1951, the first Georgia county to do so.[1]

Hartsfield, of course, had problems other than fluoridation to concern him as he entered his sixth term as mayor. Some were personal. In four more years he would be seventy-one, and in the back of his mind was the thought, still unspoken except to his closest advisors, that he might retire as his term ended in 1962. His wife, Pearl Hartsfield, her eyesight failing, was no longer at his side as he spoke in public, for her interests now were solely those of housewife, mother, and grandmother. And Tammie Lee Bettis, his secretary as well as friend and counselor, now was ill and dying after more than twenty years in his service. And more compelling than all was the fact that a young and beautiful widow named Tollie Tolan was more and more in his thoughts. But could an aging mayor divorce the wife to whom he had been married for forty-five years and be elected for a seventh time? He thought not.

None of these concerns showed in his look or voice as he spoke to his aldermanic board in its first session of the year. He traced the events of the past year briefly—the $51 million bond issue the city voters had approved, the completion of Buford Dam, a new cat house at Grant Park Zoo, street improvements, and the creation of the Department of Urban Renewal. He outlined his plans for the coming year—plans that might require a tax increase if the city were to continue to operate on a cash basis, as it had for more than eighteen years. There were new schools to be built with bond money, new water works plans, and a new air terminal to be started. One suggestion startled his listeners, coming from a man who had always considered himself as Atlanta's primary spokesman. He wanted a public relations department, to tell the city's story, and an administrative assistant, to take some of the daily burden off his shoulders. He wanted the legislature to permit the city to levy taxes on value other than real estate. And above all, he told his aldermen, the city must continue to move on as it had in the past, toward the peaceful solution of all social and racial problems.[2]

Throughout the year Hartsfield kept swinging. He made open war on Georgia's county unit system for giving the rural areas dominance over the municipalities, virtually disfranchising the city voter. He set in motion a court suit to end the system, and lost the first round on April 1, 1958, when U.S. District Judge Boyd Sloan refused to convene a three-judge court to hear the case. Hartsfield and lawyer Morris Abram, backed by Atlanta attorney James O'Hear Sanders, persisted, bypassing one legal obstacle after another, and when at last the case did reach the Supreme Court, the county-unit system was outlawed. The primary election of 1962 was held on a popular vote basis.

A report in *Time* magazine that Atlanta had the highest crime rate in the United States enraged Hartsfield, and he was mollified only when, at his urging, J. Edgar Hoover wrote a letter to *Time* saying that the story had misinterpreted FBI figures. Then, reluctantly, at the urging of the Police

Committee of his Aldermanic Board, he approved a Crime Committee of leading citizens, headed by Morris Abram, to study crime in the Atlanta area and make its recommendations.

Some such overview was needed, for crime was indeed a major problem in Atlanta. An end-of-the-year report by the Atlanta Police Department showed that thieves made off with property worth $2.66 million in 1957, up from $1.18 million in 1956. Of the 1957 thefts, city police recovered goods and money totaling $1.66 million. Rape, robbery, assault, burglary, larceny, and auto theft, every phase of crime except murder, were up in 1957 over the year before. Murders were down from 85 in 1956 to 72 in 1957.[3]

The crime that most deeply shocked and outraged the city came on October 7, 1958. In the early morning hours of Sunday, October 12, The Temple, house of worship of the Hebrew Benevolent Congregation in Atlanta, was shaken by an explosion of dynamite so powerful that it shook surrounding houses on Peachtree Street and Spring Street in the Brookwood Station area and broke windows in some of them. The blast occurred at 3:30 A.M., but cruising police could not locate where it came from. At 7:30 in the morning, though, The Temple's janitor arrived and found a gaping hole where the double side doors had been. The stone columns that had stood beside the door had crumbled, stained glass windows were broken, and the administrative office and the school area in the million-dollar edifice were damaged. Police estimated that thirty to forty sticks of dynamite had been used, and estimated the damage was as high as $100,000.[4]

Newsweek, in its National Affairs section of October 20, 1958, wrote, "whatever the actual damage it was the insensate act of violence with its social implications that appalled the citizens of Atlanta and left them sick at heart. This was the city that had prided itself on racial and religious moderation. No religious building had ever been assaulted and Negroes had been elected to City Council. As for the Jewish Community, as long as Atlanta itself has existed it has been a community of stability, prosperity, civic leadership and has commanded wide respect. Atlanta has never been darkened by the ugly shadow of anti-Semitism."

To Mayor Hartsfield, who was one of the first to arrive at the bombed Temple, this was the price of rabble-rousing. The explosion meant that Atlanta at last had been drawn into the pattern of social hatreds and bigotry that had stigmatized other southern cities.

Hartsfield's outraged reaction to The Temple bombing brought him national recognition. While at the scene, he offered a $1,000 reward to be paid by the city for information leading to the conviction of the bombers and then ordered Police Chief Herbert Jenkins to go all out in his investigation. He also called upon all decent people to rise up and denounce the bombers, blaming the dynamiting on the fact that "so called good citizens" have been guilty of demagoguery. "Whether they like it or not every political rabble-rouser is the godfather of these cross burners and dynamiters who sneak about in the dark and give a bad name to the South." Hartsfield was convinced that the bombers were not Atlanta residents. "Rabble rousers," he said, "have long been frustrated by the fact they couldn't start anything in Atlanta. Our homespun rabble rousers have had to take their hate and trouble to other places." Always quick to see the hand of communism behind any untoward event, Hartsfield suggested that these dynamitings could be masterminded by people having international motives, working through local dupes who fomented race hatred and bigotry that hurt America in the eyes of the world.

For his attitude and for the "swift and efficient efforts with which Jenkins' police set about tracking down the dynamiters," Hartsfield and his administration on October 20 received a highly complimentary letter from President Eisenhower commending their "forceful and unequivocable denunciation of this despicable act." Four days after the bombing the Atlanta Executive Committee of the National Conference of Christians and Jews adopted a resolution denouncing "the hideously immoral act" as being "as much an affront to Protestants and Catholics as it is to Jews . . . our American democracy has no place for such bigotry. We see in this violence a threat to the peace and safety of our entire Atlanta community."

Police Chief Herbert Jenkins had vivid memories of the explosion and the city's reaction. In his book *Forty Years on the Force, 1932–1972* he described the explosion as the beginning of "a momentous decade of upheaval and social change in Atlanta." Said Jenkins: "A school house in Clinton, Tennessee which had integrated had been blown up by dynamite [a week before The Temple explosion]. Numbers of Negro churches had been burned. It was an atmosphere in which everyone was appalled by the spreading violence and wondering where it would strike next. Atlanta, the city of shining Southern enlightenment and an example of progress to the nation, felt immune to being touched by this kind of wanton destruction. Now the sickness had touched this city."

Jenkins quickly got in touch with J. Edgar Hoover in Washington, asking for help from the FBI. Hoover immediately relayed the message to Eisenhower, who was reached after attending church services in New York City. The president, Jenkins recalls, was outraged, denouncing those responsible for bombing places of worship and hoodlums of the gangster type. By late afternoon the day of the bombing FBI agents had joined Atlanta police in searching through the rubble for clues to the identity of the bombers.

"That evening," wrote Jenkins in his book, "the city room of the *Atlanta Constitution* received a bomb threat, as did the Jewish rabbi, from someone who identified himself as a member of the 'Confederate Underground.'"

Here, it seems, was a clue. Said Jenkins: "Certain groups in Atlanta had been distributing anti-Semitic literature. We had knowledge of these groups and kept them under close surveillance. From information provided by an informant, we arrested three persons. They were not immediately charged with the bombing of The Temple, for at that time we did not have sufficient evidence."

Nor was enough evidence to convict ever gathered. The person who lit the fuse at the bombing of The Temple was never identified, though according to Jenkins's book, five persons who planned and implemented the destruction were identified, arrested, and prosecuted in the Superior Court of Fulton County.

The trial began on December 1, and after ten days of hearings that left lawyers and jurymen alike exhausted, a mistrial was declared by Judge Durwood Pye. The jury had deliberated for twenty-six hours and remained deadlocked at 9–3. Though no one was ever convicted of The Temple bombing, Jenkins recalls, "once these people were publicly identified, attacks and bombings against churches in the South declined. There were no further bombings of any kind against any buildings in Atlanta."

Atlanta, however, was feeling the growing pressure of racial unrest through 1958. In February the Reverend William Holmes Borders and the Reverend Martin Luther King, Jr., brought to a head the segregation of the seats on Atlanta buses, where the law required blacks to sit in the back. Borders and King would lead groups of black ministers aboard a bus; the driver, on order from the transit company, would park the bus and refuse to move, and a crowd would gather, creating an explosive situation. Atlanta's and Jenkins's solution was to arrest all the bus-riding ministers for "violating the state segregation law," then immediately release them on bond. "The case was then taken to federal court, and segregation in seating was declared unconstitutional. Atlanta buses were promptly integrated and we were thus able to carry out the mandate of the federal government without provoking unduly the wrath of the state government."[5]

Atlanta's Mayor Hartsfield, however, was strongly provoking the state government in matters having to do with integration of the schools. As the year drew to a close he and many of his supporters in Atlanta were in bitter confrontation with Governor Marvin Griffin and the rest of the state. Since the school ruling in 1954, Georgia had made every possible legal effort to avoid the mixing of white and black children in the schools. Under state law all state financial support would be withdrawn from an integrated school, the school would be closed, and any person teaching in an integrated school could be charged with a felony. Now time was running out, and there was strong likelihood that Atlanta schools would be under federal orders to integrate when the school year opened in September. As a delaying action, Hartsfield asked the state legislature to allow Atlanta to hold a referendum in which the citizens themselves would decide whether they wanted to integrate their schools or to close them.

Governor Griffin was outraged. He was sure that Atlanta would accept black children rather than close the city's schools, and he was determined this should not happen. The shouting match between the mayor and the governor went on and on—and Atlanta's schools remained segregated for the 1958–59 session. But Hartsfield and the integrationists were gaining moral support.

The manifesto on race relations brought out by eighty Atlanta ministers in 1957 had been addressed to "all those who felt that we must solve the race situation in love and on our knees." Thousands of copies had been sent out by the Church Women United in Atlanta and the Executive Committee of the Church Women United in Georgia. Their beliefs were simply these—that "all Americans have an obligation to obey the law, and whether an individual might approve the school decision or not, he must abide by it until by legal process the law is changed. Above all, the public school system must not be destroyed."[6]

Nor was this the church's final salvo. At the height of the row between Hartsfield and Governor Griffin, ministers came out with another manifesto. This time not 80 but 311 Atlanta ministers supported Hartsfield's view that the schools must be saved.

Though the future of the schools was still uncertain going into the closing months of 1958, both DeKalb and Fulton County citizens expressed their faith in the future. In DeKalb County in late October, sixteen new schools were dedicated, marking the end of one of the biggest building programs in the county's history and ending a series of double sessions that had been going on for nearly ten years. DeKalb citizens had voted an $11 million bond issue to complete this program, which could now take care of 40,000; but with enrollment still growing at the rate of 4,000 a year, more growth would soon be needed. Fulton County voters, foreseeing future growth, on October 23 approved by more than two to one a new bond issue of $3,325,000 to build additional schools.

Though increasing racial tension marked this next-to-the-last year of the decade, there were many institutions and many individuals in Atlanta whose actions met the challenge of the changing times. The Fulton County Commission approved a 1958 budget of $18,954,213, a $1,749,980 increase over the year before. The largest item in the budget was $4.1 million for Grady Hospital, and though the total budgeted was more than $1.5 million over the anticipated receipts for the coming year, the commission promised that the tax levy of 19 mills was not to be increased.

Grady could well use the $4 million budgeted for its support. Within a day after its move from the old building, reported above, the $26 million, 21-story structure was in operation, serving a rush of patients and their visitors. In a floor space covering 27 acres were seventeen operating rooms, twenty-two emergency rooms, nineteen elevators, and twelve x-ray rooms. There was room for 1,100 beds, but only 750 were in service. One visitor expressed amazement that a charity hospital could be so handsome. His reference was to the $75,000 chapel, the observation balcony on the sixteenth floor with its panoramic view of Atlanta, the ten-foot high memorial to Henry Grady, and the memorial to Margaret Mitchell, who died at the old Grady in 1949 after an automobile accident. There was also a panel representing Atlanta's first grand-scale medical emergency—caring for the wounded during the Battle of Atlanta.

Though one of the most costly and the most handsome of charity hospitals, Grady soon discovered it must modify in some degree its charity policy. Late in April most Grady patients learned that they must pay for at least part of their treatment and drugs. A system of patient rates approved by the Fulton-DeKalb Hospital Authority would by no means cover the full costs of services, but it would raise about $100,000 from people able to pay something. Welfare patients and patients with incomes of $20 a week or less would pay nothing for medical care at the hospital, but they would be charged 25¢ for visits to the emergency clinic. This was to encourage them to use the appointment clinics, where there still would be no charge. Patients with income of $25 or more a week would pay $1 for appointments and $2 for treatment in the emergency clinics. (No matter how high their income, non-Grady patients brought to the emergency clinics off the street would be charged only $3 for their treatment.) Drugs would be charged at the rate of 15¢, 25¢, and 50¢ against patients in the $25-a-week income bracket, and those making $30 or more a week would pay as much as $1 for drugs. Welfare patients and those making less than $20 a week would pay nothing for drugs.

This new fee system, according to Frank Wilson, secretary-treasurer of the hospital authority, was in line with charges made by other charity hospitals throughout the country. Operating under the old "all for free" system, Grady in 1957 treated 412,671 outpatients and filled 775,000 prescriptions.

Business in Atlanta going into 1958 gave a promise of at least holding to the pace of 1957, which had set new records, but not with the powerful upward surge of 1956. In one field Atlanta, which was born of the railroads, took a backward step. In April the Atlanta Joint Ticket Office in the Piedmont Hotel at 67 Luckie Street NW was closed. To manager G. F. Slayton, only two months short of forty years with the railroads, and to J. D. Davis, forty-one years in the service, the closing was inevitable. The airplane, the automobile, and the over-the-highway bus were taking the railroads' passengers. The Atlanta and West Point, the Atlantic Coast Line, the Georgia Railroad, and the Louisville and Nashville, into which the N.C.&St.L. had been absorbed, had desks in the joint ticket office when it closed at last, at 5:00 P.M. on April 15.

Growth in areas other than railroad travel, however, had been ample enough in 1957 to guarantee that, barring some unforeseen crisis, metropolitan Atlanta's overall business and industrial development in 1958 would continue at or near the pace it had been moving since the end of World War II. Expansion plans announced by existing Atlanta area manufacturers indicated that more than a thousand new industrial jobs would be created with more than $50 million in new factory and warehouse construction upcoming in the next twelve to twenty-four months—and an equal amount of new growth would be planned during that period.

This growth, both achieved and predicted, reflected the movement of money and management from other areas to Atlanta and its environs. It also marked Atlanta's entry into the international market with Atlanta manufactured products. Five Atlanta firms during a typical month of 1958 shipped goods to Peru, Cuba, Syria, Jordan, France, the Dominican Republic, Lebanon, Italy, Ethiopia, and Libya. The goods, according to a Commerce Department spokesman, included shirts, shorts, brassieres, cooking oil, beef and calf tongues, pens, and rag waste. Wrote Bob Williams of the *Constitution* on April 28, 1958:

> Rag waste to keep Italian machinery spotless.
> Tongue to tempt discriminating French gourmets.
> Brassieres for the beauties of Cuba, Syria, Jordan. . . .
> They are all produced, processed, packaged and exported from the Atlanta metropolitan area.

These items and other exports, said Williams, taken in connection with the area's total foreign trade, gave full-time employment to approximately 12,000 to 15,000 Atlantans, according to the Commerce Department's Atlanta field office. They also added up to a $200,000 gross business for the local economy. Atlanta organizations earnestly promoted these sales to foreign countries. Among them were the Foreign Trade Associations of Atlanta, Inc., and the World Trade Council of the Atlanta Chamber of Commerce.

Atlanta's dream of becoming a truly "international city" was coming sharply into focus late in 1958, and Davison's department store contributed to the image by staging an international exposition that caught the attention of *Newsweek:*

> In Atlanta this week, French Ambassador Herve Alphand dedicated a garden, mixing the soils of all free nations, moved urbanely through a series of black-tie parties for the international set, [and] climaxed his fast-paced program by cutting a ribbon to open a full-scale 'international exposition.' Purpose of all the one-world flurry: To put some excitement back into shopping.

> The whole affair was sponsored and housed by the Davison-Paxon Company department store, and the store's new decor had even the clerks agog. Six soaring tableaus, representing European nations, rose from ledges over the main floor counters. The fifth floor contained a life-sized model of an Italian villa. Cuban statuary, replicas of the British crown jewels, a gold and diamond model of the Bastogne monument, the smallest Swiss watch in the world and other cultural exhibits were displayed on every side. On the shelves, the regular stock was supplemented with some $1,000,000 worth of imported goods, including lace gloves and haute couture hats from France, hand-blown Venetian glass, and English antiques.

"This is a sincere effort to create an international exposition in which the dimensions of culture, art, drama, and history are used to grease the wheels of merchandise selling," Davison president Joseph Ross bubbled happily.

But even more than greasing the wheels, the idea was to reverse the gears on a nationwide shopping trend away from downtown department stores into the shopping centers sprouting by the thousands across the country.

Parking problems and the migration to the suburbs, downtown retailers think, are not the only reasons for the trend. Housewives, who once considered a downtown shopping trip a treat, are now entertained by TV and soothed by labor-saving devices. Too many now view shopping trips as a chore.

Some department stores have countered by "trading down" (in price and quality), hoping to tap vast consumer groups that traditionally shopped below the department store level. But others have attempted to meet the challenge by reviving the romance of shopping. The 1954 Italian Fair at Macy's in New York was one early, successful effort. Since then, the idea has burgeoned. . . .

Prescription by Davison's Ross for making this kind of flossy internationalism pay off in Atlanta: "Excite them with a spectacle, back it with sound stock, put greater emphasis on taste and selectivity. It's merchandising show business."[7]

Atlanta in this period was also "merchandising" itself as a convention city. More than $24 million was poured into the city's economy by 194,030 visitors who attended 543 conventions, trade shows, and meetings in the city in 1957. However, according to Charles A. Rawson, president of the Atlanta Convention Bureau, Atlanta's status as a convention city might deteriorate in the future due to changing patterns in racial relationships. Many national groups formerly considered prime prospects for Atlanta, said Rawson, were now demanding that their conventions be held in towns where facilites were openly available to all races of people. (It was also learned that some national firms wishing to open branch offices in Atlanta hesitated to do so because Atlanta's racial attitude might lead to boycott of their products in other areas of the country.)

Rawson told his hearers at a meeting of the Atlanta bureau that the bureau spent less than $40,000 in 1957 to bring in the $24 million in convention money. In an effort to offset possible loss of those opposed to the city's segregated meeting facilities, the bureau would raise these promotion funds to $50,000 in 1958.

On an afternoon in early spring, Robert McKee of the *Atlanta Journal* rode with "Professor" Frank Barbera on his Gray Lines sightseeing bus to see the city as conventioneers—or at least their spouses—did:

Often it takes an expression by outsiders to give Atlantans full realization of how big and exciting their home city is.

An afternoon in a sightseeing bus filled with visitors from the North and

West is indeed a revelation. These people see the beauty that so often escapes those who reside here.

They study the lovely homes, the hedges, the gardens, the trees and the velveteen lawns, and they sense behind those walls and trees a gentle and gracious way of life. Their questions and exclamations carry a world of meaning.

Flowers and trees were the class theme the other afternoon when I made the Gray Lines tour along with a friendly and inquisitive group from Milwaukee, Chicago, Ohio and Michigan.

They were enchanted by all they saw—the budding trees in the 1300 block of Peachtree, the greenery of 15th Street, azaleas breaking out a step ahead of the dogwood, the redleaf maple at 14th Street, the elegance of the lawns at the Retail Credit Company and Piedmont Hospital, the jonquils and redbud on Peachtree Battle Avenue, the early dogwood and tulips in Habersham, the Italian rye grass greener than ordinary green and the season's last camellias.

The bus followed a course through Rock Springs Road, to the campus of Emory University and on to Stone Mountain.

This was the sideshow, not the big one, for the trees and shrubs are but a step away from their springtime glory—the dogwoods just breaking into their mass of color, abetted by a multitude of flowers for which Atlanta gardens are celebrated.

The bus passengers stared in wonderment at the two magnolia trees in Decatur, said to be more than 150 years old—gnarled and crinkled by jousts with storm and drought. (Those trees bloom in July, with flowers far larger than most magnolias.)

Final stop of the tour was at the Cyclorama where the sightseers heard the lecture and looked at the massive painting depicting Atlanta's ordeal by sword. They emerged loaded with Confederate flags and hats and booklets.

They were full of talk about the great battle that raged 94 years ago on terrain covered by their tour. Most of them traced their lineage from people who had been in that war—on the other side.

A handsome lady from Michigan has at home a sword carried through the war by her great grandfather. There were many questions about General McPherson.

Bus driver Frank Barbera answered them all, for few in Atlanta know more about the great battle, Margaret Mitchell, places of unusual interest and the flowers and trees than does the "Professor." He lectures as he drives. His mind is a storehouse of facts.

It's well-nigh useless trying to trip him with questions. Who were the generals in the Battle of Atlanta? Where were they born and when did they die? He has the dates at tongue's tip.

He gives his tours the informality of a church social by introducing people as they come aboard. One of his passengers was a pretty girl, the daughter of a major-general stationed at Ft. Knox, Kentucky. He surprised her by talking ten minutes about Kentucky generals in the war that engulfed Atlanta.

Much was going on in Atlanta and the area in 1958 that could not be immediately observed from the windows of a bus. Thousands of conventioneers—retail dealers in furniture and other household wares—came in January to the fast-growing Merchandise Mart, which in the space of a year had expanded from 24 to 248 exhibit spaces, occupied by dealers from thirty-four states. A hundred more spaces would be available at the summer showings.

The rush to Atlanta by visitors from elsewhere was reflected in business at Atlanta's airport. According to the *City Builder* in 1958, official publication of the Chamber of Commerce, the airport handled some 3,000 emplaning passengers a day, making it necessary to move ahead on the plans for a new terminal and to improve greatly the access road leading from the city to the airport.

Foresight in another area—the preservation of Atlanta's water supply—paid off handsomely in 1958. Two solid months of drought in the early fall would have left the Chattahoochee River and its tributary streams running nearly dry if it had not been for Buford Dam. "Because of reserve supplies of water turned into the river by the Buford Dam," the *Atlanta Journal* reported, the river "has been in the full flush of health. Without the dam Atlanta water users surely would have been on a rationed basis weeks ago. They should give thanks for the big impounding system and the water it doles out every day to keep the river at proper level."

Atlanta as the heart of a great metropolitan area got another boost as 1958 drew toward its close. The U.S. Bureau of the Census officially included Gwinnett County into the metropolitan population figures. Now five counties wide, the metropolitan area counted 960,000 people within its boundaries, pushing close to that magical figure of one million its inhabitants had dreamed of for so long. "Atlanta," the *Journal* declared, "is almost neurotically growth conscious . . . which is perfectly all right. As long as the city and the metropolitan area want to grow, it probably will."

Fulton County hoped to boost industrial development with the opening of a special area in the western part of the county. Fulton County commissioners signed a three-year contract with the Adams-Cates real estate firm to manage and sell property in the new 800-acre industrial district adjacent to the West Fulton airport and lying along the Chattahoochee River. Stress would be on bringing in new commercial and industrial establishments from around the country. The county commissioners would set the price for each piece of property, and Adams-Cates would receive a 10 percent commission on each sale it handled exclusively.

With new buildings going up and old buildings being torn down all over town, there was one structure, "A Beacon of Faith," that could not and would not be moved. Central Presbyterian Church celebrated its one-hundredth anniversary. The Sunday paper carried a long account of the local institution:

There is something inspiring that bolsters one's faith to see a rugged old church that has withstood years of time and change standing firm in the swirling downtown section of a great city. . . . The neighborhood into which it was born has long since moved away. The magnificent homes that once surrounded it have given way to business institutions and public buildings. It stands across Washington Street from Georgia's Capitol and nearby is Atlanta's City Hall. . . .

It has stood through testing times. During the Civil War its pastor, Dr. Robert Q. Mallard, was captured by members of Sherman's army and imprisoned. A part of the church building was used as a slaughterhouse by the Union forces. The building, however, was spared from destruction although it did bear an honorable wound when a Yankee cannonball crashed into its facade.

As residential Atlanta began moving away from Washington Street the Central Presbyterian Church bravely held its ground. True, its members had to travel longer distances to worship and some changed their affiliation but many remained steadfast and the church began adjusting its activities to the needs of the community it served.

To survive 100 years any establishment must have two things—loyal workers and effective leadership. The Central Presbyterian has had both. . . .

It has been particularly blessed by having in its pulpit distinguished leaders in the religious life of Our Town: Dr. Dunbar Ogden, Dr. Ben Lacy and Dr. W. E. Davis, among others. Its present pastor is the beloved Dr. Stuart R. Oglesby to whom great credit must be given although he would be the last to ask it.

Dr. Oglesby has served the Central Presbyterian since February 1, 1930, and the last 28 years have been perhaps the most productive in the church's history, and this during a time that has witnessed the greatest change. This man of God has grown with the times and shed the effulgence of his consecrated life not only on the membership of his own church but over the entire religious community of Atlanta. . . .

At the century mark Atlanta's Central Presbyterian Church may look back with pride on its long and honorable history while, at the same time, facing the next 100 years with courage high and faith strong and confidence that the future holds its best and most productive years.

The year 1958 was the hundredth for Central Presbyterian and the first for Savannah Street mission, one of the city's best known institutions. Celestine Sibley explained:

Well, hooray, Sister Keel is getting her mission!
You don't know Sister Keel?

A lot of Atlantans don't. If you have a relatively warm house and shoes for your feet and groceries in the kitchen there's no particular reason for you to know Sister Keel. If your children go to Sunday School and your husband stays out of jail, it's perfectly possible your path wouldn't have crossed hers.

But one of the most warming and inspiring and humbling experiences in my life was my meeting with Sister Henrietta Keel on a grubby back lot in a cotton mill section one bitter cold afternoon many winters ago. . . .

Sister Henrietta Keel is one woman who took literally Christ's admonition to a would-be follower. When her own family had grown up and no longer needed her she sold all her goods and gave to the poor and moved from a comfortable home in a pleasant section of town to a room in the slums to be close to people who needed her. She dropped the "Mrs." and became "Sister" Keel to her new friends—not for any particular religious reason but because "Sister" was warmer and friendlier and denoted a difference from social workers and policewomen.

She started with a vacant lot and made a playground. She taught Sunday School to those who didn't have shoes to wear to the nearest church. She organized a Vacation Bible School for the summer. Living frugally herself she begged from old friends and church groups so she could feed the hungry and clothe the naked. Gradually with the passage of time help has come to Sister Keel. Young people's groups from various churches pitched in to help her run the playground after school, to teach and direct. The United Church Women heard about her and began to help, sponsoring the Daily Vacation Bible School program, sending teachers and perhaps best of all, refreshments.

All along Sister Keel has longed for a building for shelter against the weather. At first the United Church Women rented a makeshift shelter for her. And now the news is that they're going to build a mission! . . . [It] will be called the Savannah Street Mission.

A landmark anniversary came to L. F. Montgomery, as on February 8 he celebrated his fiftieth year with the Atlanta Coca-Cola Bottling Company. He had been president since 1940. Born in Madison, Wisconsin, Montgomery had come to Atlanta as a boy, graduated from Boys High School, and finished two years at Emory. He was brought into the Coca-Cola Bottling Company by his uncle Arthur, who had been with the company since its inception in 1903. His first job was as an office boy in the company's two-story brick building at 78 Auburn Avenue. There the bottles were filled by foot-powered pumps, and mules and wagons were the only transportation for the bottled drinks. He was also a director of the Trust Company of Georgia and a member of the Atlanta Rotary Club and the Piedmont Driving Club. He was a vestryman and senior warden at St. Luke's Episcopal Church.

In March the *Atlanta Journal,* the largest afternoon paper in the South with a circulation of 260,109, celebrated its seventy-fifth anniversary.[8]

Honor came to William Gordon, night city editor of the *Atlanta Daily*

World, who was cited as "Atlanta's outstanding Negro citizen." Dr. Albert E. Manley, president of Spelman College, presented a plaque on behalf of the 27 Club, an organization of business, professional, and educational leaders who presented the award each year. *Atlanta Constitution* editor Ralph McGill paid tribute to Gordon as a "fine young newspaperman who has headed Red Cross, Polio, and Community Funds campaigns in the Negro community with great success."

As the year began, A. C. (Pete) Latimer was unanimously elected president of the Atlanta Board of Education to succeed Devereaux McClatchey. Glenn Frick was elected vice-president; Louise Simpson, veteran secretary, was named to a new four-year term, and the Reverend Alfred Hardman, dean of the Cathedral of St. Philip, was elected chaplain, succeeding the Reverend Harrison McManus. Independent board members elected were Allen Chaney, Jr., of the Fourth Ward, L. J. Callaghan of the Fifth, and Oby T. Brewer, Jr., of the Sixth. Others elected were Ed S. Cook of the First Ward, Harold F. Jackson of the Second, and Mrs. Clifford Ragsdale of the Eighth. Dr. Rufus Clement was the Negro member of the board.

OBITUARIES

Dr. William W. Bryan, 49, was one of the South's leading x-ray specialists and professor at several schools. He rose to the rank of lieutenant colonel in the medical corps in World War II. Joseph H. Coskey, 52, was claims manager of Crum and Forster Insurance and past president of the Atlanta Claims Association. Mrs. Katherine R. DeGive, 82, was the widow of H. L. DeGive, local business leader and longtime Belgian consul in Atlanta. Mrs. DeGive was active in World War I relief efforts, especially for Belgium. Hamilton Douglas, longtime dean of Atlanta Law School, died at 70. He followed his father as dean. He was a member of Civitan and the Capital City Club. Douglas was the founder and first scoutmaster of the first Boy Scout troop in Atlanta. He was the brother of Helen Douglas Mankin, who served in Congress shortly after World War II. L. O. Freeman was the retired superintendent of College Park schools, having served in the same position earlier in Fort Valley and Conyers.

Hardin T. Herndon was vice-president of a large scrap metal company. He played for the Atlanta Crackers Southern League championship team in 1919, and he later managed several minor league teams, including the Columbus Cardinals. He was a Mason, a Shriner, and a Methodist. Dr. Annie Hill, 76, of East Point was said to be the oldest practicing chiropractor in Georgia. S. Calhoon Noland, 64, was a former member of the Atlanta School Board and director of the Atlanta Chamber of Commerce. Benjamin Hooper Peek, 76, was the retired stationmaster of Atlanta Terminal Station, where he had worked since 1905. He was stationmaster during both world wars and saw six presidents pass through his station. C. N. Ragsdale, one of the leading livestock dealers of the South, died at 68. He was active in political and cultural affairs. His wife served on the Atlanta School Board and his father had been mayor.

Arthur Neal Robinson, 71, was an architect and engineer who designed the building for the First Church of Christ, Scientist, of which he was a member. He helped found the Georgia Engineering Society. Dr. Cecil D. Strail was the past president of the Georgia Chiropractic Association and former executive director of the National Chiropractic Board. He was an Elk, Moose, and Methodist. Caroline Sutton, 83, was superintendent of nurses at Crawford W. Long Hospital at the time of her retirement in 1944. Edwin S. Walkey, 53, was the founder and president of Economy Auto Stores. He belonged to the Capital City Club, the Atlanta Athletic Club, among others. Dr. John C. Weaver, 79, was a neurosurgeon and medical historian. He wrote several volumes, including a medical history of Georgia.

NOTES

1. Interview with spokesman for DeKalb Water Department.

2. Harold H. Martin, *William B. Hartsfield, Mayor* (Athens: University of Georgia Press, 1978).

3. Herbert T. Jenkins, *My Forty Years on the Force, 1932–1972* (Atlanta: Center for Research in Social Change, Emory University, 1973).

4. Janice O. Rothschild, *As But A Day: The First Hundred Years, 1867–1967* (Atlanta: Hebrew Benevolent Congregation, 1967).

5. Jenkins, *Forty Years.*

6. Martin, *Hartsfield.*

7. *Newsweek,* Nov. 10, 1958.

8. Ibid., Mar. 10, 1958.

1959

IN ATLANTA the events of the last year of the decade were marked more by inner tension than open conflict, but they led on to the ever-increasing violence, the freedom rides, and the sit-ins of the 1960s.

On January 10, 1959, the State Board of Regents, on a recommendation by Governor Ernest Vandiver, tried to avoid integration by temporarily stopping the acceptance of new applicants for the state's nineteen colleges. On the same date, however, Judge Boyd Sloan in the district court of Atlanta ordered the Georgia State College of Business Administration (now Georgia State University) to stop barring Negro applicants solely on the basis of race.

On the day before, U.S. District Judge Frank A. Hooper had ruled on the bus riders' case brought by two Negro ministers, the Reverends Samuel Williams and John Porter. He declared that Atlanta bus and trolley racial seating regulations were unconstitutional.[1]

In some other areas of racial conflict, separation of the races expired without event. The Atlanta Public Library, for example, quietly integrated on May 19, 1959, after a meeting attended by Mayor Hartsfield, Chief Jenkins, and City Attorney Jack Savage. Despite Atlanta's reputation for being a leader in race relations, she was only coming in line with many of her sister cities—Louisville, Knoxville, Little Rock, New Orleans, Nashville, Chattanooga, Miami, Richmond, Charlotte, and Winston-Salem. All had integrated their libraries earlier.[2]

Despite progress in certain areas such as the public library and public transportation, civil rights leaders felt that the rate of change was much too slow. The courts were not moving fast enough to suit most southern blacks and the white northern liberals who had joined them in such organizations as CORE—Congress of Racial Equality. Out of this spirit of impatience the "freedom rides" began, with whites and blacks traveling in groups to challenge segregation of interstate transportation.

Police Chief Herbert Jenkins, knowing the danger that someone might be killed, had a strong complement of Atlanta police on hand at the bus station to make sure that neither the buses nor the riders were attacked. One bus, however, after leaving Atlanta safely, was attacked soon after it crossed the line into Alabama. The riders were beaten and the bus burned. The best way to keep the angry white segregationists from committing some violent act against the protesting blacks was to let them know that the local police would not condone any such action, according to Jenkins. "If the whites who were prone to violence got the message that the police were not in sympathy with their intentions, then they would in practically all instances back away from a confrontation," he said.[3]

One Atlantan who as much as any other, black or white, male or female, strove successfully to bring about these changes in human relationships was

Eliza King Paschall. The Charleston-born granddaughter of two Confederate generals, she was a student at Agnes Scott in the mid-1930s when she had her first contact with the Commission on Interracial Cooperation, forerunner of the Southern Regional Council, when her sociology professor, Dr. Arthur Raper, she remembered, "first gave me the feeling the system could be changed for the benefit of us all, and that it was up to me to help." She attended her first interracial meeting as an Agnes Scott representative at a "peace meeting" in the basement of a Negro church. This led the president of the International Association for the Preservation of the White Race to write her parents, warning them of the dangers to young white women in Atlanta.

She married Walter Paschall, news editor of WSB radio, and continued her battles for equal rights in every field, serving first in the ranks and then as chairman of the Southern Regional Council, Inc. Following Walter Paschall's death, she married attorney William M. Morrison.

The civil rights movement was the most powerful concern of most citizens, but much else was happening in Atlanta not directly concerned with racial matters that would change for better or for worse the working, playing, traveling, and overall living habits of people of both races.

In May, the *Journal* announced that "another inch, 'relatively speaking' of the expressway was turned over to the public for use. The newest section is an important part of the legendarily slow midtown connector which someday will join the north and south legs in one long stream of bumper-to-bumper traffic. . . . It's a sign too that, believe it or not, work has been progressing all the while on this project. Rebuilding the city, which amounts to what Atlanta is trying to do, takes just as much time as it does money."

This step toward completion, declared Robert Jordan, member of the State Highway Board, was crucial because the downtown expressway would be "the hub of the entire network of interstate highways throughout Georgia."

In other ways than highway construction, Atlanta builders were busy in 1959. Office and apartment starts were up. As of June 1, more than $55 million worth of new construction had been started, which was more than $5 million ahead of the starts as of June 1, 1958, itself a record year.

Not all residents of the Atlanta area welcomed the idea of new buildings proliferating helter-skelter. In Roswell the historic Primrose Cottage was threatened by development. The first house completed in the Roswell area, it was a two-story structure that once contained a school for local children. It was famous for its fence of hand-carved wooden spindles made by craftsmen from England in the early nineteeth century. The house was saved by the Roswell Library Association. The association had come into being in 1955, when several of Roswell's leading citizens joined forces to buy an old brick apartment, built in 1839 and supposedly the oldest apartment building in the United States. It was converted into the Roswell Public Library.

One attribute of the city of Atlanta that stimulated construction of new buildings was the capacity of its firemen to reach a blaze within four minutes after the alarm was sounded. For an outlay of some $4 million a year the city supported thirty-two fire stations, where 715 men and women were on duty twenty-four hours a day. Supporting them were 3,000 feet of aerial ladders, 475 fire alarm boxes, 40 pumper trucks, 18 aerial ladder trucks, and an ambulance. Because of the city's willingness to spend money to train its people in every aspect of getting to and extinguishing blazes and resuscitating those who might have been overcome, Atlanta enjoyed one of the best fire insurance ratings in the country. Cities were rated by fire insurance inspectors on a basis of from one to ten. Atlanta was a three—as good a rating as there was in the South (Savannah, Columbus, Macon, and Augusta were also threes).

While Atlanta firemen were achieving at least Southwide recognition for their skills, Atlanta police were setting some records of their own. In the eight years preceding 1959, there were 666 homicides reported in Atlanta: 650 of them were solved, giving Atlanta the best record of any police department in the United States. Of the 16 murders still unsolved, each was still being "actively worked," according to Lt. G. H. Christian, head of the Atlanta homicide squad. In three or four of the unsolved cases police believed they knew the killers but had been unable to obtain evidence strong enough to make an arrest.

While fine new buildings were going up all around, Atlanta's famous old Kimball House Hotel finally closed its doors. The story of its past and of its last day—and night—was told by reporter Warren Bosworth in the *Atlanta Constitution*. Bosworth, a resident of the hotel at one time during its fading years, was the last guest to register on March 25, 1959, before it closed its doors at midnight. The following is from his sentimental memoir:

Atlanta's historic Kimball House closed her doors to the passing world at the lonesome stroke of midnight Wednesday and awaited the arrival of a destructive modern-day devil named Progress.

There was no fanfare nor flowery worded speeches to mark the solemn occasion as the Grand Old Lady of Five Points, once the glittering queen of the nation's hostelries, said a bitter farewell.

"They'll find that tearing down the Kimball House won't be an easy thing," C. E. Wymens, the hotel's tall, white-haired desk clerk said. "It was built when labor was cheap and materials were good." . . .

The Kimball's passing marked an end of an era.

The big hotel at No. 33 Pryor Street was first built in 1870 by a Chicago carpetbagger, Hannibal Ingalls Kimball. It was destroyed by fire in 1883.

Kimball, who had returned to Chicago to live, came back to Atlanta in 1885 and on the same site rebuilt the Kimball House into a glamorous showplace known far and wide.

The doors which were shut to tenants Wednesday night were opened first on April 30, 1885, beckoning the cream of the nation's patronage inside. The

Kimball's musty ledgers contain the names of presidents, foreign ambassadors, dignitaries of the stage and literary worlds, and countless hundreds of others. . . .

"It has been so sad around here at times during the past few weeks that I could cry my heart out," Mrs. King said as she recalled the heart-clutching scenes at the hotel's registration desk over the past weeks.

While fond recollections were going on, the Kimball House site was being cleared and foundations laid for the erection of a $600,000 five-and-a-half-story combination parking garage and retail store building.

Atlanta early in April was the site of a conference in which some sixty southeastern men of great prestige in business and academic affairs established the Atlanta Association of the Committee for Economic Development, a regional branch of the National CED. This organization was not just another business organization, according to its national chairman, Daniel K. David. It was instead "a partnership of the businessmen and the scholars in developing business and political policies to promote the interests of all the people." The CED, said David at a luncheon, "built a bridge between the ivory tower and the market place." The Atlanta Association of the CED named a local committee to plan for a fall meeting and the subjects that it might be best for Atlanta to pursue. Included in the local committee were James V. Carmichael, Harrison Jones, and Ralph McGill (all CED trustees), the presidents of Georgia Tech, Emory, and Georgia State College, and the top officials of the major Atlanta banks.

While the newly organized CED planned for the future, Atlantans, spurred on by Mayor Hartsfield, paused at mid-year to evaluate what had already been accomplished as the city and the surrounding five counties pushed on toward the long-expected population of one million. On May 26 the Metropolitan Planning Commission estimated the total at 990,000 and reported that one-fourth of all Georgians now lived in metro Atlanta.

On June 1, in order to keep up with the needs of that booming population, the metro area was engaged in at least forty-two different projects costing more than $105 million. This, according to Hartsfield, "puts Atlanta right in the middle of the biggest capital improvement project in its history." Not all this $105 million, of course, was city money, city comptroller Earl Landers pointed out. Federal and state funds would help finance such costly projects as expressway construction and the new airport. The state and federal share in all forty-two projects planned, completed, or under way in 1959 would total just over $58 million, with the city's share standing at $47,178,400.

On a three-hour, forty-five-mile sightseeing tour, Hartsfield took *Constitution* photographer Hugh Stovall and reporter Marion Gaines into every section of the city to give them a firsthand look at some of the major capital improvement projects. Gaines reported, "As the Mayor's sleek black sedan, piloted by his aide, Charlie Cook, swept down Decatur Street, Hartsfield waved his arm dramatically: 'There's the new police station ($1,300,000). It's almost finished, but few people even know it.'" Hartsfield moments later focused attention on the $30 million expressway connector from Baker Street to Richardson Street and summed up the expressway system's progress. Bonds for construction had been approved by Atlanta voters in 1946, surveys were carried out in 1947, construction had begun in 1949, with officials predicting that the construction would be finished in 1963 and the whole expressway system finished by 1967. Thus the expressway would be completed after twenty years of work. The city's participation in the expressway system, he told Gaines, "I consider to be one of the most significant contributions of my administration."

While the group was inspecting the $2 million Moreland Avenue underpass project, Hartsfield's car got stuck in the mud. Perspiring freely in the midday heat, the mayor got out and tried to push. No success. But almost by magic a city truck, manned by a crew of city workmen, came to the rescue.

As the day progressed, Hartsfield's running commentary, Gaines described, took on a "decidedly stronger, and a seemingly hurt tone; while viewing work on the $8,000,000 east leg of the East-West Expressway—from Hill Street to Candler Road—for example, he said 'Lots of people don't even know about this East-West leg work . . . especially those Buckhead boys, who don't ever see anything except the Club and the bank.'"

As the reporters and the mayor approached Grant Park, where the 1959 schedule called for completion of $1 million in zoo improvements—including a new monkey house—Hartsfield said the city "is gonna spend five or six million more out here. This zoo'll be one of the finest in the nation." And then:

Gesturing toward an expanse of naked red clay behind the feline house, the mayor said that "will be a 600-car parking lot for Grant Park visitors."

"What'll it cost the public to park there?" the mayor was asked.

"Free. Free!" he replied.

Hartsfield said he has been accused of sinking $400,000 into a house for monkeys but that it's not true.

"It's a house for people," he said. "It's an investment in the smiles and gratitude of thousands of children in the years to come."

"The monkeys just work there," he said.

Asked which project he was most proud of, the mayor replied that the "new airport terminal will be the most impressive."

Hartsfield radiated approval in all directions at the busy beehive of workers buzzing about airport manager Jack Gray at the site of the new $14,747,000 air terminal.

Access to Gray, the terminal construction work, and the present facility's runways—which were slightly hazardous to automobiles because of the continuous movement of giant airliners—was blocked to the mayor's group by a parked truck and a sign.

Again the mayor leaped out and spoke to the truck driver. The truck moved off. The mayor hauled aside a "Do Not Enter" sign, reclaimed his seat and motored up to Gray's office on the edge of the runways.

Gray led the way to the heart of the new terminal site where the skeletal foundation of the giant facility is beginning to take shape.

"About 60 acres of concrete have already been put down for the new terminal," Gray said.

Three quarters of an hour later found the mayor's vehicle zipping through northwest Atlanta toward the new water purification plant at Bolton Road and Marietta Boulevard.

"There it is, that's the baby, it's brand new," the mayor cried.

"The Bolton facility will give Atlanta two water purification plants," Hartsfield said, "and that'll help us to get more and more big industries in here."

"Some of those outfits use an awful lot of water," he said, "and they won't settle anyplace that doesn't offer a prime water supply."

Cost of the new purification plant runs to $5,050,000; feeder mains from the plant will cost $1,650,000. "And that's all financed by water certificates," the mayor said.

"Not doing anything for Atlanta?" the mayor asked, and then answered himself:

"Hell, we're making Atlanta prosperous."

If the mayor had waited another sixteen days to make his tour, he could have pointed out the site of another million-dollar project that would add greatly to the architectural beauty of downtown—not sponsored by the city, but by some 10,000 Atlanta Masons. On a rainy Thursday in 1950 a small fire at the corner of Peachtree and Cain streets had flared into a blaze that completely destroyed the seven-story Masonic Temple that had stood there since 1909. For nearly a decade the Masons of Atlanta had planned for the erection of a new temple, and finally, on June 16, 1959, ground was broken for a multilevel limestone-covered structure at 1690 Peachtree Road at the corner of Deering Road. To be finished within a year, according to temple president Oby T. Brewer, the new structure would cost about $1 million. It would cover more than 50,000 square feet in floor space and would include two Blue Lodge Rooms, one hall for York Rite groups, and a Scottish Rite Auditorium. There would also be a full stage, banquet hall, gallery, and office space. The new temple would also include the cornerstone of the three previous Masonic buildings in Atlanta.

While moving steadily ahead in the field of transportation, on land and in the air, Atlanta on May 15 took a sentimental backward look at a big day in the city's communication history. On that day in 1879—eighty years earlier—the first telephone exchange was opened in the Kimball House, with ten phones and one male switchboard operator. From the first ten phones and one exchange in 1879, Atlanta's telephone progress was swift. In 1891 there were

2,000 telephones. In 1900 there were 3,344. And by mid-1959 thirty-two central offices were required to keep Atlanta's 363,081 telephones working.

In mid-June the *Journal* reported:

The City of Atlanta has shifted its slum fighting tactics, passing a stronger housing code and creating a new slum-fighting division of city government.

In one of the busiest urban-renewal and slum-condition sessions in the aldermanic board history, the aldermen Monday gave unanimous support to several major changes in the city's inner workings.

At the same time the aldermen approved final plans for the first five urban-renewal programs. With the detailed program adopted, actual land purchase in the Butler Street (Buttermilk Bottom) area should get under way during the first part of July.

The city's ambitious planning did not go unnoticed in Washington, D.C. On July 7 Harold Davis, the *Journal*'s Washington correspondent, reported that the federal government "had signed the death warrant" of 316 acres of Atlanta slums when it put up $21.7 million to remove them. Of this, Atlanta would get nearly $7.5 million as an outright gift—the rest, totaling just over $14.2 million, would have to be repaid to the federal government when the acreage was disposed of to private interests for redevelopment. These private interests, at their own expense, were to replace the crumbling slum houses— 1,543 of them in the core of the Butler Street area—with orderly and affordable residential, commercial, and park areas. Federal urban renewal commissioner Richard L. Steiner also announced that in addition to Butler Street's 249 acres the federal government would finance the 207-acre Thomasville project.

Federal funds also arrived in the Atlanta area for other purposes. De-Kalb County announced in June that it had secured a special grant-in-aid from the federal government to build an addition to an elementary school, according to Jim Cherry, superintendent of schools. The addition would include eight new classrooms for 240 new students expected to enroll in the Kittredge Elementary School. Federal law provided that such grants could be made when the influx of federal employees into a community brought in more students than the local school system could handle. This was taking place in the Briarcliff and Druid Hills area, according to Cherry, as a result of the new Communicable Disease Center, a federal research organization being built near Emory University.

The Atlanta school system in this year was granted approximately $220,000 in federal funds for support of adult education. To meet this requirement, the Atlanta Board of Education on May 11 voted to convert Hoke Smith High School to a vocational training school, thus clearing the Smith-Hughes School for all-adult education. At the same time Inman Park School for Boys was converted into a Negro elementary school. The boys at Inman

Park would occupy a wing of the Hoke Smith building, where they would have access to shop equipment and recreation facilities not available at Inman Park. Enrollment at Hoke Smith would have dropped by approximately 600 by the fall of 1959, and those would be absorbed by Roosevelt, Murphy and the new East Atlanta High School. The conversion of the Inman Park school would relieve the overcrowded Negro school conditions in the Butler Street area.

At the same meeting at which the City Aldermanic Board agreed on a slum-clearance program, agreement was reached to go ahead with the construction of a viaduct that would carry Techwood Drive into the northwest Atlanta area over the railroad gulch downtown. It was anticipated that contracts for this long-desired improvement, which would cost some $3.8 million in 1957 bond funds, could be let in October, 1959.

The Techwood Viaduct and the projected Hunter Street Viaduct would place two long spans across the railroad tracks, and it was anticipated that the downtown business area would spread out over the tracks, providing more room for downtown stores and buildings. The city would immediately begin buying up forty-five tracts of land, much of it belonging to the Atlanta Terminal Company, the Atlantic Coast Line, the Southern, the Central of Georgia, the Atlantic & West Point, the Louisville and Nashville, and the Seaboard railroads.

The belief by many Atlantans that viaducts were as important to their city's growth as the railroad tracks they spanned was borne out by one more venerable institution. For several years from 1904 to 1906, Atlantans had urged the construction of a public auditorium, but it was only in 1906 that a mass meeting led to definite plans. In 1909 the Washington Street Viaduct, giving easy access to east Atlanta, was opened, and work was begun on what was to become the Auditorium Armory, home of the Metropolitan Opera on its visits to Atlanta for many years. At the time of its construction in 1909, it cost $190,000 to build. Fifty years later plans for a three-month overhaul, estimated to cost $130,000, were put in operation.

The old building had not only been the home of the great orchestras, but the scene of dog shows, wrestling matches, ice skating, prize fights, and presidential speakers from William H. Taft to Woodrow Wilson and Teddy Roosevelt. The daughters of two presidents, Margaret Wilson and Margaret Truman, had sung there.

As mentioned earlier, in 1959 the city had built a $400,000 primate house at the Atlanta Zoo. One of its inhabitants was a baby gorilla, bought by the city for $4,500 and promptly called "Willie B." Mayor Hartsfield, with his fine flair for publicity, knew that Willie B.'s appeal to the general public would to a degree overcome the criticism heaped upon him by his political opponents for spending so much money housing monkeys. The zoo also acquired new gibbons, baboons, and other primates.

While monkey houses, viaducts, the repair of old buildings, and "urban renewal," meaning the clearing of slums in the downtown area, occupied the minds of many in mid-1959, the city's future in another form was rapidly taking shape at Lenox Square and Peachtree Road. Here, a huge regional shopping center, as big as a small city in itself, was getting ready to open its first ten buildings and the 60-acre parking lot, which would have space for 6,000 cars. The grand opening was to take place on August 3, when thousands of shoppers were expected to stroll the sidewalks, mall, and plaza area, gaping and buying at the multitude of shops and stores. These, according to John D. Smith, vice-president and general manager of Lenox Square, Inc., ranged from bakers to brokers, from barbers to bankers, from bags to boots.

There was about 800,000 square feet of space in the ten buildings. This vast spread, according to Lenox Square president Ed Noble, was due to the fact that Lenox, unlike similar centers elsewhere, was built around two rather than one huge department store. Another sixty-odd stores and service establishments were located around the mall and plaza.

Rich's and Davison's, the two fiercely competitive downtown department stores, were the main lures to Lenox. Rich's store was the largest structure on the mall level, the Peachtree Road side. Its three floors, each with 60,000 square feet, covered close to one-fourth of the square footage of the entire center. Davison's rose highest and stretched longest and widest of all the stores on the plaza side, nearest East Paces Ferry Road. It had two floors, each with 60,000 square feet, and in both Rich's and Davison's there were open sales areas as big as football fields.

Many other leading Atlanta business houses occupied expansive space in the new center. For example, Haverty's Furniture, Kresge, Muse's, J. P. Allen, and Parks-Chambers each occupied selling space on two floors. Other tenants occupied ample space on one floor. Colonial Stores, for example, expected to operate the South's largest supermarket in its 31,500 feet of single-floor space. Oby T. Brewer of Muse's was president of the newly organized Lenox Square Merchants' Associates.

Construction had required less than fourteen months from groundbreaking to grand opening. There was, however, much building of a different type still in the contemplated or planning stage. This included a movie theater, an ice rink, and a 350-seat auditorium for social and recreational events which would be available to civic, fraternal, business, and women's groups.

Lenox, according to George Goodwin, student of Atlanta's progress and advisor to its leaders, provided the stimulus that set off the flow of business to other suburban areas.[4] In short order after Lenox opened on the north, there came Stewart-Lakewood to the south, then Belvedere to the east, and Greenbriar to the west.

Thus began that shifting of population patterns that in the years ahead was to bring on the fierce competition between the inner city and its suburban environs. Lenox and the array of malls that were soon to spring up all around the city not only lured Atlantans to the outskirts to shop—they drew them there to live, work, and worship, and to pay taxes and practice politics in many ways withdrawn from the interests of the inner city.

While moving strongly in new directions Atlanta did not forget individuals and institutions that had been meaningful to it in the past. In March the city dedicated a new Atlanta Boys Club at 1900 Lakewood Avenue SE. With more than five hundred people in attendance, the new $400,000 structure was named as a memorial to Joseph B. Whitehead. It was built mainly with funds made available by Robert W. Woodruff, chairman of the Joseph B. Whitehead and Lettie Pate Evans foundations.

Edgar J. Forio, vice-president of the Coca-Cola Company, recalled the modest beginning of the Boys Club in 1946. Harold Steele, a high school teacher, saw a group of boys playing baseball with a sock-and-rag ball in the streets. He organized them into a club and found a meeting place for them in a nearby home. The club, which had begun with thirty-two members only thirteen years earlier, now had six hundred, and director Jack Stephens expected enrollment to reach one thousand shortly. The new building, built on the site of the old club, contained a swimming pool, a gym, a basketball court, an auditorium, an arts and crafts room, and a library. Adjoining its three arched roofs were a football field and baseball diamond.

In the Atlanta school system thirteen new white principals were named and two black, though city school enrollment projected for the 1958–59 session showed an increase of 4,636 Negro and 320 white students, a significant increase over the previous September's registration of 93,482.

Students with high scholastic averages had special opportunities in the Atlanta public school system. As a result of a $45,000 grant from the Ford Foundation, Atlanta schools under the careful eye of Ira Jarrell, superintendent, had been able to offer a program for the rapid learners titled "Education for the Gifted." In 1959, 1,722 high school and 58 elementary school pupils were studying "honors courses." These classes were conducted by gifted teachers, carefully chosen for the job. Jarrell said that Atlanta had more teachers with master's degrees than any city in the South.

In mid-year the Atlanta school board began a search for a superintendent to replace Ira Jarrell at the end of her term, which would expire in 1960. Under board rules she could not be elected for another four-year term because of age limitations.

In 1959 the integration controversy confronted several white churches. The Rev. Leon Smith of the Park Street Methodist Church in the West End interrupted the reading of the scripture to tell the congregation that a Negro girl had been seated at the service, and that she would be allowed to remain. Smith noted that an usher appeared to be asking the girl to leave and he spoke from the pulpit: "This is God's House. Everyone is welcome to worship." Two men, one of them a steward in the church, got up and left. But the girl, who seemed about eighteen, remained and later went up to the altar to take communion, kneeling between two white girls who had been seated in the same pew with her.

In slavery times black families often attended church with their white owners but were seated separately in a balcony. A similar situation seemed to be developing in some Atlanta churches. Druid Hills Presbyterian, for example, in April had set aside pews for Negro worshippers, though by early June none had yet attended. At Park Street Methodist no pews had been set aside for blacks, Dr. Smith said, and ushers were told to "help Negro visitors see that it would be disturbing for them to attend church. But if they wanted to remain, they would be seated at the most convenient place."

The ambivalent attitude toward the black worshipper displayed by the churches was reflected in a poll taken by Emory University. A secret ballot taken by the student council revealed that Emory students were "opposed to segregation in education based on race," but they were also against admitting Negroes to the undergraduate college at Emory.

Late in 1957, as recounted in an earlier chapter, eighty prominent Atlanta ministers had sent out a manifesto saying that racial problems must be solved "in love and on our knees" and that no matter what their personal beliefs might be, all Americans had an obligation to obey the law—including the decision by the Supreme Court declaring unconstitutional segregation of children in the schools by reason of color. Thousands of copies of this statement were sent out over the state by the Church Women United, and later, early in 1958, 311 other Atlanta ministers came out with a manifesto saying that, above all else, the schools must be kept open.

In March of 1959 another group of fifty-three ministers came out with a manifesto expressing a different view. They took no definite stand on the closing of the schools, but their feelings were obvious. They opposed the integration of the schools on the grounds that anything that would lead to the amalgamation of the races would be a "sin against Almighty God." "Integration," said the ministers, "is Satanic, unconstitutional, and one of the main objectives of the Communist Party." Most of the signers were members of the Evangelical Christian Council, an organization of some seventy ministers formed in January "to give Bible believing conservatives a voice and agency through which to speak and work unitedly."

The Rev. W. T. Hays, dean of Immanuel Baptist College and pastor of Maranatha Baptist Church, was president and spokesman for the group, which he said included North American Baptists, Southern Baptists, World Baptists, Independent Baptists, Free Methodists, Evangelical Methodists, Wesleyan Methodists, Pentecostal, and Assemblies of God ministers. All were from Atlanta churches. The core of their statement was: "We believe the races were created and separated by Jehovah God. To start or work toward anything that would lead to destruction of these God-created races, such as the amalgamation of the races, is a sin against Almighty God." Scriptural verses cited in support of their beliefs were Genesis 28:6; Deuteronomy 7:14, 32:8; Acts 17:26, and Romans 14:23.

The statement continued with the point that people of all races should be treated in a moral and Christian manner, that all things should be done without strife or vainglory; that each race should maintain its purity and earnestly seek to develop its members to their highest state of perfection in all things—spiritually, mentally, morally, and physically. But, the statement continued, "We believe the Scriptures do not teach the universal fatherhood of God, but that they teach to become a child of God; the new birth is absolutely essential." Verses cited in support of this theory were John 1:12, 3:3, 3:7, 8:44, Acts 12:10, and 1 John 3:8. The statement concluded: "We believe integration is Satanic, unconstitutional and one of the main objectives of the Communist Party, [and] we believe the integration of the races in our schools to any extent presents grave moral, social, religious, constitutional and political questions."

Amid the growing tension, one calm voice preaching moderation, though not submission, was that of the Rev. Martin Luther King, Jr. He spoke at graduation exercises at Morehouse College, where along with the other institutions of the Atlanta University Center, there was a growing impatience for faster, stronger legal action to break down the walls of segregation. Dr. King, who led the boycott of Alabama's segregated buses, advised his hearers to "stay awake" during the current "revolution" in race relations but to remain nonviolent, to practice good will in the face of lynch and mob rule. Dr. King was a graduate of Morehouse himself, class of 1948. He told the seniors that despite the slowness of the federal courts in removing the existing barriers, segregation was fading away. Therefore, he said, today's black students must be prepared to compete in a nonsegregated society.

"Don't set out to do just a good Negro job," he told the class. "If you do, you have already flunked your entrance examination for matriculation in the University of Integration." To hurry the process, however, he said he could not recommend the way of hatred. "We must stand up with the power of love," he said. "We've broken loose from the Egypt of slavery, we have gone through the wilderness of equality, and we stand upon the Promised Land of Integration."

Two weeks after King's commencement speech, the Atlanta school desegregation case reached a critical point. The *Atlanta Constitution* spread across the top of its first page a double headline, full eight columns wide:

JUDGE ASKS CITY INTEGRATION PLAN
AND GIVES LEGISLATURE TIME TO ACT

U.S. District Judge Frank A. Hooper had confirmed his previous temporary ruling of June 5 in which he had ordered the city to prepare a desegregation plan. This final edict gave the Atlanta school board "a reasonable time" in which to submit a plan but set no definite deadline by which this was to be accomplished.

"The court," said Judge Hooper, "fully realizes the difficult position in which the defendants are herein placed. If they integrate the schools all state money under existing laws will be cut off, and it may be that such funds are necessary for the operation." He added, "However, continued operation, with discrimination as in the past, will not be tolerated."

The orders, the judge indicated, gave the school board, the defendants, a "reasonable opportunity" to submit to the court a plan that would end racial discrimination. The next point was the important one. Such a plan, the order said, may be submitted "subject to approval by the Georgia legislature," and the legislature did not meet until the following January. Thus there was granted to Atlanta what the *Constitution* described editorially as "This Year of Grace."

OBITUARIES

Marvin A. Allison, 62, was a leading attorney, publisher, and educator. He served as principal of several schools and as president of the DeKalb Teachers Association. In the late 1920s he was secretary of the DeKalb Chamber of Commerce. He represented Gwinnett County in the General Assembly for four terms and was county attorney for twenty years. He was president of the Georgia Bar Association for the 1943–44 term. He was the first president of the Gwinnett County Chamber of Commerce. Louis S. Brooke, 67, a retired director and officer of Retail Credit Company, had spent forty-eight years with the firm. He was a member of the Capital City and Piedmont Driving clubs. Cherry L. Emerson was dean of engineering and later vice-president at Georgia Tech. His father had been Tech's first dean. After graduating from Tech in 1909, Emerson worked for several manufacturing, power, and engineering firms before returning to Georgia Tech. Active in civic affairs, he was a national executive in the Boy Scouts of America. He belonged to the Capital City Club and several other clubs. He was a Presbyterian. Laurence Everhart, 82, was the founder and owner of Everhart Surgical Supply Company. He had also served as registrar of the Atlanta Medical College (Emory University) and as superintendent of Grady Memorial Hospital. He was a Mason and a Methodist.

C. D. LeBey, 63, was a leading realtor and mortgage banker. He served as president of the Mortgage Bankers Association of Atlanta and was a director of the Central Atlanta Improvement Association. Mrs. Roiwena Dickey McCutchen, 53, was the executive secretary of the Board of Women's Work for the Presbyterian Church, U.S. She supervised the activities of 340,000 women in nineteen states. Mrs. Harry S. Moore was the author of several mystery books. Her first book, *Murder Goes Rolling Along*, was published in 1942 by Doubleday. H. W. Nicholes, 87, was one of the city's most active home builders. His firm erected a substantial portion of the houses in the Druid Hills, Garden Hills, and Collier Hills areas of Atlanta. Active in the Atlanta Home Builders Association, he attended Druid Hills Baptist Church. George Traylor Northen was a leading attorney and the grandson of Gov. W. J. Northen. He was a member of the Piedmont Driving Club and the Nine O'Clocks. He had been president of the Realty Finance Company and of the Mortgage Bankers Association of Atlanta.

Dr. Alfred M. Pierce, retired Methodist minister and historian, died at 85. For six years he edited the *Wesleyan Christian Advocate,* and he wrote a biography of Bishop Warren A. Candler and a history of Methodism in Georgia. Judge David P. Philips, 83, was three-time mayor of Lithonia and judge of the City Court of Decatur. He was a Baptist, Mason, and Elk. W. Horace Roberts, 82, was the oldest member of the Atlanta YMCA, having held a card for fifty-seven years. He worked for Davison-Paxon for forty-seven years, retiring as a general superintendent. He was a Mason, a Shriner, and a Presbyterian. Judge Augustus Morrow Roan, 61, was former judge of the DeKalb Civil Court. He had held office in the state bar association and was a former president of the Georgia Sons of the American Revolution. He was a Mason. J. W. Stephenson, 66, was president of the Bank of College Park and father of the mayor of College Park. A former city councilman, he was in several civic and business organizations. He attended the First Baptist Church of College Park. Paul A. Stevenson, 78, was a longtime newspaper reporter who served as an aide to Gov. Herman Talmadge. In 1958 he was appointed executive secretary of the Georgia Commission on Education, which searched for alternatives to racial integration.

NOTES

1. Herbert T. Jenkins, *My Forty Years on the Force, 1932–1972* (Atlanta: Center for Research in Social Change, Emory University, 1973).

2. *Facts on File* (New York: Facts on File, Inc., 1959), May 21–27, 1959.

3. Jenkins, *Forty Years.*

4. Interview with George Goodwin.

SECTION III

The Nineteen-Sixties

1960

ATLANTA moved into the sixties proud of its past, as well it might be; wary of its future, as indeed it should be; but confident that the old spirit still was mighty and would prevail, whatever the changes that lay ahead, in boundaries, population patterns, and social, racial, political and business relationships.

Five counties—Clayton, Cobb, DeKalb, Fulton, and Gwinnett—now made up Atlanta's metropolitan area. Five county governments and several municipalities shared in varying degrees with Atlanta's Aldermanic Board the responsibility for police and fire protection, health services, the operation of the school systems, transportation routes, and the collection and disbursement of taxes.

Three of the significant highlights of the previous decade included the implementing of the Plan of Improvement in 1952; the building of Buford Dam in 1957, which created Lake Lanier and gave the city a vast recreation area, prospective manufacturing sites, and a bountiful water resource; and at last, in the fall of 1959, the attainment of a million in metropolitan population. The Atlanta Chamber of Commerce observed October 10 as "M" Day—celebrating the fact that the population of Atlanta and its environs at last had passed the long-anticipated one-million mark. Thus the 1,724 square miles of the five-county area with its forty-six cities and towns became first in the Southeast in population, and twenty-second in the nation. In and around Atlanta was the second fastest growing metropolitan area in the United States, adding a new citizen every eighteen minutes. Even so, writer Bruce Galphin, in a study of Atlanta going into the sixties, notes that the city was still "a giant in antique chains of distorted legislative apportionment, congressional districting, and vote counting systems." And the growing issue of segregation was still "a massive wall of state law, chipped only here and there." Nor was this likely to change while the urban areas were under control of a rural-minded legislature elected under the county-unit system.

But these things, too, were changing and changing fast, stimulated by an influx of new citizens. Soon the metropolitan area became the focal point of a whole region, providing jobs and services for people from everywhere in every field of enterprise that makes up an urban area.

A brochure—"Metropolitan Atlanta—The First Million"—distributed by the Chamber of Commerce, told the story:

In *transportation* thirteen main rail lines, fifteen major air routes, and six interstate highways served the city. Train and truck transportation gave it the largest railway and expressway shipments per capita of any U.S. city. The municipal airport, already sixth in passenger arrivals and departures, now was operating commercial jet service and undergoing a $20 million expansion; Fulton and DeKalb County airports were expanding for increased use by executive aircraft.

In *communications* it was the third largest telephone switching center and the third largest telegraph center. It was sixteenth in postal receipts.

As a *financial* center Atlanta was first in bank clearings among southeastern cities, thirteenth in the nation. It was the headquarters of the Sixth Federal Reserve District and a major insurance center.

The area's topography and altitude (1,050 feet) accounted for an exceptionally *favorable climate*. Moderate summer heat with cool nights and not too cold winters were typical.

The facilities for *education* were one of the area's major assets. There were twenty colleges and universities—and more coming—with enrollment of 20,000.

The facilities for *culture, recreation, and entertainment* were varied and numerous. A symphony orchestra, one week each year of the Metropolitan Opera, light opera and popular concerts, legitimate theater, ballet, recitals, a lecture series, public libraries with well-located branches and bookmobiles, many public parks, golf courses playable year 'round, swimming, tennis, baseball, water sports at nearby lakes and other sports—all were available.

There was a high percentage of *home ownership*, with suburban gracious living for all income groups and with major urban renewal projects underway.

More than six hundred *churches*, representing more than thirty denominations, many of them housed in beautiful new structures, were scattered throughout the metropolitan area.

The city and its environs was the biggest *medical center* in the South, with a major medical school, fourteen general hospitals, and a total of over 4,000 beds.

One hundred *hotels and motels* offered 10,000 rooms for visitors, and over 250 conventions annually met in the city, with attendance exceeding 120,000.

All these things represented growth already achieved. With the one million population mark now history, the next goal of the city builders was to move on to the second million by 1985, possibly by 1980. (Actually, this goal was reached in 1980, when the U.S. Census showed just over 2 million in the official metropolitan area.) In confident preparation for this next milestone, there were big plans afoot in 1960 not only in Atlanta proper, but throughout the metropolitan area. In downtown Atlanta five skyscrapers were already under construction, or projected, and at least eight more were in the planning stage. A great merchandise mart costing $10 million was definitely moving ahead in downtown Atlanta, and plans were under way for other major projects, including a 70,000-seat stadium, a new or at least a renovated auditorium, a civic center with a symphony hall, and a planetarium. Since 1957, city-county bond issues in Atlanta, Fulton, DeKalb, Gwinnett, and Clayton counties had totaled $130 million, the largest in the history of the South. They provided funds for building libraries, schools, water and sewer facilities, parks, and streets, and they provided for fire and police protection as the population moved inexorably on toward 2 million souls. Under construction in the early sixties were a sixty-five-mile perimeter highway around the metropolitan area and six interstate highways through the central city.[1]

The brochure inspired by Atlanta's first million was followed by another a year later that was even more eloquent in its descriptions of Atlanta. Called simply "Greater Atlanta," it emphasized the reality that Atlanta was an economic unit despite political boundaries. "To speak of Atlanta," it said in the foreword, "as a city confined within corporate limits is to leave out a part of the story of this great, growing metropolis. For the essence of Atlanta is not the city, but a community of towns, cities and counties. It now displays both the appearance and substance of one of America's true 'national cities.' "

Much of the surrounding rolling terrain was the site of planned industrial districts, where new light industry or warehousing was going up, "Greater Atlanta" pointed out. A dozen or more of these districts, in various stages of planning, were scattered throughout the Atlanta area, with some of them set aside for heavy industry's long-range needs. The city and surrounding counties were working together on these plans. Atlanta's banks were particularly interested in the development of industry in the area.

Said the "Greater Atlanta" brochure:

More and more Southern capital is underwriting the growth of old established industries and businesses, and financing the land and erection of buildings for firms moving into the area from other regions. "Atlanta money" pioneered those concepts which are standard procedure in the South today, and the city continues to hold its dominant position both in banking and insurance. Greater Atlanta's banks show combined revenue of $1,650,000,000 and life insurance in force in the area exceeds $3,000,000,000. . . .

Atlanta is the first and only Southeastern metropolitan area to qualify as a "national city"—one defined as exerting a powerful economic force far beyond its normal regional functions. Atlanta people came from everywhere and all walks of life. The college professor; the new factory worker fresh from a Georgia farm; government career employees; engineers, accountants, salesmen; job and husband-seeking young women.

Though the five surrounding counties constituted metropolitan Atlanta with its million population, the chamber brochure looked upon "Greater Atlanta" as comprising sixty counties, in an area extending eighty miles in all directions. The chamber-sponsored booklet explained: "Whatever long-range development takes place in this area will be coordinated by . . . the Atlanta Region Metropolitan Planning Commission . . . composed of representatives from the five counties and the councilmen and aldermen of the main municipalities. But their activities range all the way from urban renewal to expressway and rapid transit planning, to proper land usage, population and economic studies, zoning and the development of new industrial districts. And interest in these obviously must extend beyond the five county boundaries."

The Atlanta area's twenty-six colleges and universities offered the Southeast's most varied and far-ranging facilities for higher education, the report pointed out. Atlanta had become the region's center for technological, medical, and economic research:

Georgia Tech, at the edge of downtown Atlanta, makes three bids to fame. Academically Tech has become one of the nation's top engineering institutes. It stays consistently high in the national rankings in intercollegiate athletics. In recent years the missile-age research programs directed by its industrial development branch for business, industry and government have attracted nationwide attention.

Emory University, with its liberal arts program, medical school, hospitals and laboratories is internationally respected for its high standards. The six colleges of the Atlanta University System, five of them on a common campus, comprise the world's largest center of higher education for Negroes. Other noteworthy schools are Georgia State College of Business Administration, Agnes Scott College, and Oglethorpe University.

In addition to its highly rated public school systems, Greater Atlanta is served by some 17 accredited private, parochial and military schools.

Brochures describing Atlanta always spoke in praise of its weather, climate, and location. This one declared: "There are no closed months in the city's year around golfing, fishing, and outdoor living schedule. Professional and intercollegiate sporting events, nearby mountain and coastal recreation, theatres, concerts, opera, art shows—all help to round out the picture befitting an area containing a million people."[2]

Though both brochures described Atlanta going into the seventh decade as a happy place, a city where every prospect pleased, author Bruce Galphin gave a vivid picture of a city where "sit-ins, lunch counter demonstrations, frequent court intervention, and angry political rhetoric paralleled a remarkable flowering of Atlanta economics."

This economic renaissance, Galphin pointed out, occurred "not in spite of the tremendous social and political change, but because of it, and the way Atlanta's leaders handled it."

It was handled, actually, as Atlanta's racial problem had been handled in the past—by leaders of both and white and black communities, who sat down together to talk about what had to be done to keep the peace. They recognized that change in social relationships was inevitable. In October of 1960, for example, students of Atlanta University staged a sit-in at a food counter in Rich's, Atlanta's largest department store. More than fifty of them and their nonviolent leader, Dr. Martin Luther King, Jr., were arrested and jailed. Chanting, "Jail, not Bail," and singing "We Shall Overcome," they made no effort to be released and remained behind bars for week after week. The issue was finally settled in the classic Atlanta way. Two elderly Atlanta lawyers, one black, one white, got together. A. T. Walden, son of a slave and one of the first black lawyers in Georgia, called on Robert B. Troutman, Rich's lawyer and member of one of Atlanta's leading law firms. Their discussion led to a meeting not with the stubborn sales executives of Rich's, but with executives from some twenty-five other Atlanta stores of various types, and the students were released on bail. For more than a month, according to Galphin, there were secret sessions between whites and blacks at the Commerce Club. There a director of Rich's—president of the Chamber of Commerce Ivan Allen, Jr., soon to be mayor—was the leading instrument in working out a settlement.

Basically, it provided that the stores would desegregate all their facilities— beginning in September of 1961—a month after the court-ordered desegregation of the city's schools would take place. Ivan Allen remembers that the students were not pleased by the delay. Mass meetings were held at black churches, and there seemed to be danger that the situation would explode. Martin Luther King, Jr., who had been released from jail at Reidsville perhaps because of the request of John and Robert Kennedy, stepped in to save the day at a meeting at Wheat Street Baptist Church. There it seemed that the impassioned, shouting, younger men were going to take to the streets again. Neither the pastor, William Holmes Borders, nor Martin Luther King, Sr., could control them.

Allen, in his book *Mayor: Notes on the Sixties,* written with Paul Hemphill, described the scene:

Then at the high point of the explosion, in walked Martin Luther King, Jr. I had read about him and heard about him from his father, but I had not been able to imagine just how much charisma he actually had. No one had to introduce him, of course, because he had already become the champion of the civil rights cause. The minute he entered the church and began walking firmly and confidently toward the pulpit the shouting stopped. All eyes were on him. He took to the pulpit and stood before the crowd for a full minute, searching every face in the audience. It became deathly quiet.

Finally, he said, "I'm surprised at you. The most able leadership you could have to represent you has made a contract with the white man, the first written contract we've ever had with him. And now I find people here who are not willing to wait another four or five months, after waiting one hundred years and having nothing to show until now." He said he would hold every Negro citizen personally responsible to him for the fulfillment of the contract. "If this contract is broken, it will be a disaster and a disgrace. If anyone breaks this contract, let it be the white man." And he left, as quickly and mysteriously as he had come. I had heard him called "Little Jesus" in the black community. Now I understood why.[3]

Though King's counsel prevailed at the time, the day of the sit-ins was not over. Two years later, sit-ins were renewed on a wider scale. The targets now were not only restaurants and department store restrooms, but hotels and theaters, and though some businessmen, Galphin noted, followed the example of Edward Negri of Herren's, a famous Atlanta restaurant, and voluntarily opened their doors to blacks, many others refused.

Ivan Allen's handling of the sit-in situation convinced black leaders that here was a man they could trust—that here, in fact, would be a worthy successor to William B. Hartsfield as mayor of Atlanta. A six-point program Allen had developed for Atlanta, which he presented to the Chamber of Commerce, convinced the white community as well that Allen would make a competent mayor. The program touched on every challenge and opportunity facing the city. It urged the Atlanta Chamber of Commerce officially to endorse keeping the public schools open and actively work for the passage of the necessary legislation in the General Assembly.

The chamber, Allen said, also must use its every facility to press for a definite step-up in the tempo of local expressway construction. Progress had not been fast enough, he said, and a substantial acceleration in the expressway progress "is absolutely essential to the health and well being of the Atlanta community."

On urban renewal, Allen urged that the chamber "vigorously support the city's urban renewal and housing program across the board, and private capital must be encouraged to take advantage of the unprecedented development opportunities in urban renewal projects." The chamber, he added, must work with all agencies concerned in locating new housing opportunities for the Negro population.

He urged that the chamber should strongly support the construction of an auditorium-coliseum and a stadium. "The public wants these facilities, and there is no time to lose," he declared.

For rapid transportation he urged the chamber to take the lead in pressing for a practical, large-scale, rapid transit rail system for Atlanta (the MARTA concept). The only alternative, he pointed out, would be "more expressways than are now projected at five times the cost per mile, and even further expansion of automobile traffic loads, with a breakdown in central traffic circulation by the end of the decade."

Not satisfied that Atlanta had done all it could in the recent push to sell itself to the nation, he asked the chamber to support a three-year "Forward Atlanta" program of education, advertising, and research to carry the Atlanta story throughout the country. The program, he said, should be supported by a minimum budget of $500,000 a year, raised from the city's business community. Allen in December of 1960 was moved up from vice-president to president of the Chamber of Commerce for 1961—and his six-point program was unanimously accepted by the chamber.

With the backing of Atlanta's power structure, the business community, he felt confident that his program would be carried out. His election as mayor in 1961 over Lester Maddox, whom Hartsfield had defeated in 1957, was evidence that the affluent whites could control city hall, but only with help from black voters.

The state's brewing school desegregation crisis was moderated somewhat by the report of the so-called Sibley Commission. The group was created in 1960 by Governor Vandiver, at the urging of his chief of staff, Griffin Bell. The governor named John A. Sibley, distinguished Atlanta lawyer, banker and civic leader, to head the General Assembly Commission on Schools. Sibley and his eighteen commissioners visited every school district in Georgia, laying the facts before the people. Their message was simply this: massive resistance to the Supreme Court's ruling against the segregation of schools could not prevail. Whether Georgians liked it or not, the Supreme Court's decision would be enforced. The commission concluded its work with the recommendation to the legislature that laws outlining segregation be repealed and that children be allowed to go to the school of their choice.

The Atlanta school system, however, did not—as had been anticipated—become the first public system in Georgia to desegregate. That distinction fell to the University of Georgia, which early in 1960 was ordered by the federal court to admit two Negro students, Charlayne Hunter and Hamilton Holmes, both of whom were Atlantans. They were admitted under court order, but student riots in Athens, spurred on by die-hard segregationists, forced the two black students out of school because the university could not guarantee their safety. The government's answer was that if the state university could not guarantee their safety, federal marshals certainly could. To officials at the state capitol, this was unthinkable. Holmes and Hunter returned to school.

OBITUARIES

Reuben R. Arnold, one of the strong figures of Georgia jurisprudence, died in 1960. He was a great defense lawyer and practiced law for seventy of his 92 years. He and his brother Lowry founded their legal firm in 1892, and with the late Luther Rosser he achieved national recognition as a defense lawyer in the Leo Frank Case. He was a life member of the Piedmont Driving Club, Atlanta Athletic Club, and Druid Hills Golf Club and a member of St. Luke's Episcopal Church. Dr. Charles Ross Adams, 65, a former Fulton County commissioner and active member of the Parks Department, was a popular doctor in the West End area. As a gesture of affection officials named Adams Park for him. William Henry (Uncle Billy) Alston, 70, had an active part in the business, civic, and fraternal life of the city. At one time he had been a reporter for the *Georgian* newspaper and later became head of the International Detective Bureau. Charles Atkinson, 89, a native of England, was the son of the surgeon-general of the British forces in the Crimean War and was trained in England as a chemist. He had been manager of the Georgia Marble Company since 1924.

Atlanta lost one of her great ladies in the death of Mrs. Robert C. Alston, who was the former Caro duBignon of Savannah. She was active in the parish life of St. Luke's Episcopal Church and had served as president of the Sheltering Arms Day Nursery and the Atlanta Fine Arts Club. During World War I she was commandant of the Red Cross Canteen. Alston's generosity furnished the chapel at the new Lovett School and a room at Piedmont Hospital. William L. Blackett, retired foreign representative of Standard Oil and an Atlanta financier, died at his home. He was a member of the Piedmont Driving Club and the Capital City Club. Haygood Clarke, 68, a pioneer in investment banking and vice-president of Johnson, Lane, Space and Company, was a graduate of The Citadel. A guarantor of the annual appearance of Grand Opera in Atlanta, he was also a member of the Atlanta Art Association and the Piedmont Driving Club. Mrs. Treadwell R. Crown, 71, was well-known in gardening circles for her flower arranging and judging flower shows. She was also the garden consultant at Rich's. Beecher Duval, 39, was widely known to thousands of shoppers as "the whistling policeman of Forsyth Street." He had a natural whistle that kept the shoppers moving steadily in and out of Rich's.

Roy Drukenmiller, 63, Fulton County educator and musician, was the coordinator of instrumental music for Fulton County and was known thoughout the South for his work with the Shrine Band. Eldon Lee Edwards, 51, an automobile paint sprayer for General Motors, would be remembered as an organizer for the Ku Klux Klan in spite of the state's antimasking laws. Charles Crawford (Doc) Styron, 72, retired Atlanta Fire Chief, died after a heart attack at his home. At the time of his retirement June 1, 1959, he had been a fireman for fifty-one years, twenty of which he was chief. He left three sons following in his footsteps—all in the Atlanta Fire Department. Capt. Marvin L. Thomas, 54, described by associates as "one of the most popular and respected members of the police force," died the day after he had asked to be put on retirement. One of the organizers of the Atlanta School Patrol, he knew many of the children cooperating in this enterprise.

The legal profession lost another honored member in the death of Marvin E. Underwood, 83. In 1903 he was employed by King and Spalding and remained with that firm until he was appointed Assistant U.S. Attorney by President Woodrow Wilson. Resigning in 1917, he became chief counsel for the Seaboard Air Line Railroad. In 1933 President Herbert Hoover appointed him U.S. District Judge for the Northern District of Georgia, a post he held until retirement. He was a member of many legal societies, the Capital City Club, and the Cosmos Club in Washington, D.C.

NOTES

1. Atlanta Chamber of Commerce, "Metropolitan Atlanta—The First Million" (Atlanta, n.d.).

2. Atlanta Chamber of Commerce, Industrial Bureau, "Greater Atlanta" (Atlanta, n.d.).

3. Ivan Allen and Paul Hemphill, *Mayor: Notes on the Sixties* (New York: Simon & Schuster, 1971).

1961

ONE whose political intelligence told him that the years ahead would be fiercely challenging to any mayor of Atlanta was William B. Hartsfield. The arrival of the one-millionth metropolitan citizen, in Hartsfield's view, represented a challenge to the city that every new arrival would intensify. For all that had been done, one-fourth of Atlanta's million still lived in substandard housing, and though urban renewal was helping to make a dent in white and black slums alike, there was still a long way to go before wealthy owners of slum property could be persuaded to provide comfortable and affordable shelter for the city's poor. There was less tension between the races than in any other city in the South, but the school integration problem still festered. Unfortunately, there was no plan for the orderly development of the metro area across county lines. Old mistakes were being made over and over again and new slums created, though Fulton and DeKalb counties, through the Metropolitan Planning Commission, were engaged in some planning.

All these things were in Hartsfield's mind as he appeared before his Board of Aldermen to outline his plans for the sixties. The schools were closest to his heart, and he made an eloquent plea for open schools, publicly supported. The closing of the public schools, he argued, would bring Atlanta's progress to a halt.

"It will do little good," he argued, "to bring about more architecture and concrete while a shocked and amazed world looks at a hundred thousand innocent children roaming the streets." Another plan to which Atlanta's progress was deeply tied, he pointed out, was more urban renewal, to stop—or at least slow down—the flight to the suburbs, and to increase and improve living quarters for blacks and whites.

A new auditorium was needed, new stadiums, new parks and recreation facilities. In this talk, two decades before rapid rail transit became a reality in Atlanta, he foresaw and urged the creation of downtown traffic tunnels and the use of rail lines.[1]

From Hartsfield's manner and his tone of voice, it seemed as if he would try to stay in the mayor's office forever. But by now Hartsfield, for political as well as personal reasons, was already planning to return to private life. The next election was still a year away. But political patterns were changing. His friend and political analyst George Goodwin had discovered that in the mayor's race of 1957, in which Hartsfield had beaten Lester Maddox, the militant segregationist had gotten the major percentage of the white vote. To Hartsfield this meant that he could no longer be sure that the old alliance among city hall, the city's top business leaders, and the newspapers that had sent him into the mayor's office five times could prevail again. The prospect of trying one more time, and being beaten by some young newcomer, or some old enemy, did not appeal to him. It would be far preferable, he decided, to go out with his memories of 1959's M-Day and M-Week—Atlanta's celebration of its reaching the one-million population mark. That rejoicing had been converted at the last moment into tributes to Hartsfield. Messages poured in from mayors all over the world whom Hartsfield had met in his travels, and the city, at his urging, held a joyful celebration at the auditorium, with forty-four mayors and commissioners from surrounding counties joining in. The city also printed billions of dollars in simulated million-dollar Confederate bills and distributed them throughout the country as an expression of thanks for the real money that smart Yankees and westerners had poured into the city in recent years.

In an interview with Bill Emerson of *Newsweek* Hartsfield summed up the philosophy that had guided him:

We are a city too busy to hate. It's the pattern of modern Atlanta, set by Henry Grady. Our life blood is communication, contact with the balance of the nation. We seethe under the fact that we are not held in high regard by either political party. We strive to undo the damage that the South's demagogues do to the South and try to make an opposite impression from that created by the loud-mouthed clowns. Our aim in life is to make no business, no industry, no educational or social organization ashamed of the dateline "Atlanta."

Remember . . . the 14th Amendment guarantees Northern money equal treatment. The secret of our success—we roll a red carpet out for every damn Yankee who comes in here with two strong hands and some money. We break our necks to sell him.

Early in 1961 the town finally knew Mayor Hartsfield's plans for the future. Helen Bullard, who had been Hartsfield's political advisor for twenty years, came to him with the report that if Hartsfield was going to run again, Ivan Allen, Jr., would like to manage his campaign and would contribute $10,000 to it. If not, she said, Allen would like to know it, so he could make his own plans. She handed Hartsfield the money; he took it and went over to the window, looking out over Atlanta. When he turned back there were tears in his eyes as he handed her the money.

"Tell Ivan to come see me," he said.[2]

In his book *Mayor: Notes on the Sixties,* Ivan Allen describes that visit. Hartsfield kept him waiting for more than an hour, then when he was admitted to the office, Hartsfield talked for forty-five minutes of the difficulty of being mayor and working with aldermen who preferred playing golf to looking after the city's business. Then at last, Allen remembers, he got down to the real reason for his decision:

He went over to the window and stood there for a few minutes, mumbling to himself as the afternoon light played over his tired hulking frame and accented the wrinkles on his hands and neck. When he turned around he sounded like a very old, very tired man. "I've had this job for twenty-three years," he said. "I'm seventy-two years old, and I've been married for forty-eight of 'em, and now I'm in love with a very wonderful young lady and I want to marry her. I can't get a divorce and be re-elected mayor. If you'll send Helen Bullard over here tomorrow, I'll make my announcement and get out of the race so you boys can go on about your business. I've been around long enough."[3]

The next morning, June 7, 1961, at 10:00 A.M., he stepped out of his office to face the press and declared his retirement.

Editor Eugene Patterson was eloquent in his *Atlanta Constitution* editorial of June 8:

So long, Bill. You've done a great job. We know, you're still mayor and the hardest parts are yet to come. But just to hear your announcement, finally, that you don't intend to run forever makes us feel like saying "so long" in advance. That way we can say some nice things about you now.

About the nicest thing about you was the way you would come barging into the editor's office, sail your hat across the room and cuss us out with that fine, feigned fury that never quite concealed a cold, ordered mind. You were always at your best when you were wrong.

And, brother, could you be wrong!

But mainly, we have to admit, you were right. You were mighty right about this town. You understood her. She's not just a big brute of a concrete settlement. She has strength, heart, soul, honor and beauty. You gave her all of that. Plaza Park, the airport, a monkey house with sculpture on it, blossoms in pots in the middle of Marietta Street—little parts of a big beauty . . .

You made Atlanta something more than Marthasville, Bill. She believes in a decent regard for the opposite race and the opposite point of view. She believes in culture, in education, in compassion and vigor. She's a part of the world. You were a key man in making her what she is. You rode her streets alone at night to watch over her sleep. You sat at her political bedside on Saturdays and Sundays while the rest of us sat on our patios. You fought mighty battles for her, and gave her voice. . . .

So long, old tiger.

The "old tiger" had one more high moment before he stepped down from the mayor's office. On August 30, 1961, he and Chief Herbert Jenkins saw to it that the token integration of Atlanta schools was carried out peacefully and quietly. Hartsfield was determined that there would be no repetition in Atlanta of the howling mobs who had protested the integration of the schools in Little Rock and New Orleans and the admission of two black students to the University of Georgia. Atlanta, he felt, must stand out before the nation as a strong example of wisdom and tolerance in bringing about social change.

Hartsfield's and Jenkins's plans were simple. Four formerly all-white schools were to be integrated by the admission of nine black students, and a police task force was set up to guard each school, keeping away every white person not actually working there. In addition, a reserve force was held on standby at police stations, ready to move in a hurry to any school where trouble might break out. Hartsfield called a meeting of all the Atlanta newspapers and radio and television stations, and he laid down the ground rules. They could be in the vicinity of the school, to photograph or report anything they saw or heard, but they must stay out of the school buildings, and if riots broke out, they must stay out of the way of the police. At Hartsfield's urging, Dr. John Letson, who had succeeded Ira Jarrell as superintendent of schools, went on the air with Herbert Jenkins to urge parents and all Atlantans to accept the inevitable. Jenkins assured them that their children would come to school in safety, that his men could handle any problem that might arise. His officers, Jenkins told the parents, had studied the problem of segregation in seminars. They had read books and heard lectures on the history of the movement and the court decision they would be defending. Basically, he said, his officers would be answering one question: "Should a bunch of hoodlums be allowed to destroy the system of public education in Atlanta?"

The day came, the police took their places, and the children arrived. The cameras whirred; the reporters scribbled in their notebooks, recording the fact that the historic day was much like any other opening day of school in Atlanta.

With nearly three hundred out-of-town reporters in Atlanta, Hartsfield could not resist one last flourish of showmanship. He had the reporters drive from school to school looking for the violence that never happened. In the afternoon he chartered a bus and hauled around the city all the visiting journalists who wished to go. He drove them past some fine homes, calling out the names of the Negro businessmen, lawyers, bankers, and doctors who lived in them. He took them past more modest but still handsome houses where Negro teachers and smaller merchants lived.

That night he gave a cocktail party at the Biltmore Hotel for both black and white visiting journalists. He did not point out that this was in itself a landmark in the city's history.[4]

(The schools involved in the integration were Brown High, Henry Grady High, Northside High, and Murphy High. The children, accepted after stiff examinations, were Madelyn Nix and Thomas Welch, who were placed in Brown's 11th grade; Lawrence Jefferson and Mary McMullen went to 12th grade at Henry Grady; Donita Gaines made Northside's 11th grade, Arthur Simmons the 12th, and Willie Jean Black went into an accelerated group. Martha Ann Holmes made 12th grade at Murphy, but an 11th grader failed and another was accepted at Brown but did not attend.)[5]

Here was a beginning, a token truly, but walls had been breached that never could be built up again. In years to come there would be conflict over busing and pupil placement, teacher assignments and pay scales. But the action of the governor and the Georgia legislature and the Atlanta school board marked a turning point not only for Georgia but for all the Deep South. The ancient pattern of total defiance was ended.

To a great degree the quiet acceptance of desegregation in Atlanta was the result of the Sibley Report. Sibley found that most white people were against the action of the Supreme Court ordering the integration of the schools, but they recognized that the alternative—closing the schools—would be disastrous, a tragedy unthinkable. The quiet integration of the schools drew praise for Atlanta from the highest sources. Said President John F. Kennedy at a press conference in Washington on August 30, 1961:

> I want to take this opportunity to congratulate Governor Vandiver, Mayor Hartsfield of Atlanta, Chief of Police Jenkins, Superintendent of Schools Letson and all of the parents, students and citizens of Atlanta, Georgia, for the responsible law abiding manner in which four high schools were desegregated today.
>
> This was the result of vigorous efforts for months by the officials of Atlanta and by groups of citizens throughout the community.
>
> Their efforts have borne fruit in the orderly manner in which the desegregation was carried out with dignity and without violence and disrespect for law.
>
> I strongly urge the officials and citizens of all communities which face this difficult transition in the coming weeks and months to look closely at what Atlanta has done and to meet their responsibility, as the officials of Atlanta and Georgia have done, with courage, tolerance and above all, with respect for the law.

In 1961 a new element introduced itself into racial and business relationships in Atlanta. A black supremacy sect known as the Muslims developed a small but characteristically aggressive membership in the city. It was an extremist group that some observers considered potentially disruptive and even dangerous.

The sect, which was headquartered in Chicago, was headed by a Georgia-born Negro. The leader of the movement in Atlanta was known as Jeremiah X, or Jeremiah Habazz, whose original surname was Pugh. Muslims shed their old, or "slave" names, on entering the movement. In 1961 the Atlanta organization had a hard core of forty members with a total of seventy followers, investigators reported.

The Muslims were described by some as the Negro counterpart of the Ku Klux Klan because of similarities in devotion to ritual and commitment to supremacy of their race. Jeremiah X came to Atlanta around 1957 and was charged with organizing the group's activities throughout the Southeast. Malcolm X, Elijah Muhammad's chief assistant, made frequent trips to Atlanta.

With the announcement of Hartsfield's retirement, Ivan Allen, Jr., resigned from the Chamber of Commerce presidency and entered the mayoral race. He described the campaign in his biography. "Now," he wrote, "it was time to get into the sweaty business of campaigning. Thanks to the support of Mills Lane and the rest of the business community, not to mention a good stockpile of my own money, I had more than enough funds to run a professional campaign. I also had a ready-made organization, some 400 employees of the Ivan Allen Company who were loyal and ready to help wherever we needed a good crowd for a rally or help in a city-wide poll. And too, I had the best brains in Atlanta at my disposal. Helen Bullard as campaign manager, most of the leaders of the black and white business communities as unofficial aides and advisors."

It was obvious, said Allen, that he, the "silk stocking candidate," should run on a promise of continued prosperity, emphasizing his background as a business leader and a former president of the Chamber of Commerce, talking about Atlanta's future role as a national city, rather than merely as a regional distribution center.

Allen made the point that he had a clear edge over the other four candidates. None of them had the personal associations in the higher echelons of the city that he had (a distinction, it may be noted, handed down to him from a distinguished father), and none of them had the experience of doing big business, of dealing in terms of millions of dollars. However, before the first campaign rally, Allen had come to realize that this lofty Chamber of Commerce approach would not do. For there was one great issue concerning Atlanta and all the South that was more powerful than all other aspects of civic life. Said he:

"I could promise all I wanted to about Atlanta's bright, booming economic future, but none of it would come about if Atlanta failed to cope with the racial issue. That I knew was the *real* issue of this campaign."

Was Atlanta going to be another Little Rock, which literally died on the vine when it failed to face the school integration issue—or was it going to set the pace for the New South?

Allen knew that his most dangerous opponent would be the fierce segregationist Lester Maddox. So his decision was quickly made. He left the dinner table an hour before his first rally. He got on the phone to Helen Bullard, his political mentor.

"I'm going to jump on Maddox," he said.[6]

He did, and he won, but it was a bitter contest. The race issue was the crucial point. Various calls from angry segregationists came in, day and night, threatening bodily harm to Louise and Ivan and their sons. Finally, the situation became so tense that Allen, through Chief Jenkins, hired at his own expense two city detectives as bodyguards for his family, standing watch on alternate nights from 4:00 P.M. to 8:00 A.M.

As the race went down to the wire Allen realized that he was slipping. He was losing the conservative vote to Maddox and was not picking up enough strength in the black community to offset it. This was due in large degree to the activities of a third candidate, "Muggsy" Smith, a white insurance man who, in his appeal for the black vote, kept pounding away at the idea that Allen, after all, was the choice of the "white power structure." He pointed out also that, though Allen had done much to work out an agreement between whites and blacks on desegregation of department stores and theater restrooms and lunch counters, this desegregation had not yet taken place.

On the morning of the election Allen's pollster, Joe Heyman, vice-president of the Trust Company of Georgia, told him how the race would go. Allen, said Heyman, would get 38 percent of the vote; Maddox would get 24 percent, and "Muggsy" Smith would draw off enough of the important black vote to throw the race into a runoff between Allen and Maddox. This suited Allen fine, for he was sure that in a head-to-head confrontation with Maddox he would win handily.

And he did.

"In the runoff," he said in his book, "I received 65% of the vote—and in the Negro precincts I wiped him out, 21,611 votes to his 237."[7]

The election of Ivan Allen, Jr., to the office of mayor and the token integration of public schools had been landmark events in Atlanta in 1961. But another outstanding event took place this year in the field of civic journalism. Editor James L. Townsend on May 1 brought out for the Chamber of Commerce volume I, number 1 of *Atlanta*, a magazine that was to become far more than a typical Chamber of Commerce publication. In this first issue Opie Shelton, executive vice-president of the chamber, under then president Ivan Allen, Jr., outlined the need for such a magazine:

In the first place there is so much to tell about this dynamic, bustling, growing metropolitan area of ours, that all our existing communication media combined can't possibly tell the whole story. Then too, Atlanta must battle its friendly rivals if we are to maintain our position of leadership in the South. Other cities are constantly casting covetous eyes on Atlanta and try to whittle away our advantages.

But most important of all, perhaps, is that our own self-enlightenment in the tremendous growth we have had leaves many problems in its wake and the problems of today are nothing to compare with those which lie ahead.

Atlanta magazine became one of the outstanding civic publications in the nation. It did not accomplish this by blowing a triumphant bugle in issue after issue. As Shelton had promised, the picture of the city it presented was a warts-and-all portrait. An editorial in the first issue set the tone it would follow:

The famous old city of Atlanta is coming of age. This is the town which movies and books have long portrayed as the hub of Southern hospitality, and the Fried Chicken Capital of the World. But Atlanta is changing . . . has changed in fact. This booming nerve center of the South has turned a new face to the nation. And it's a broad-beamed face of fancy new skyscrapers, fast moving expressways, great wealth and plenty of hustle. This is Atlanta in the Sixties.

It might be said that Atlanta has seceded from the Confederacy. Rebel flags and Civil War relics came off the office walls years ago, and have been replaced with aerial photographs of the city's impressive new skyline. Stately white-columned mansions along Peachtree, once proud homes, are now filled to their antebellum attics with office workers.

Any visitor who comes looking for magnolias, mint juleps, or moonshine is bound to be disappointed; and any Atlantan will tell him that there are more peach trees in Pittsburgh than there are on Peachtree Street.

The boom of demolition rocks the city from stem to stern and nowhere can one escape the clacking of pile drivers. Broad new expressways are cutting through the city's heart; gleaming new shopping centers are drawing a new ring around the town; and towering new skyscrapers have come along to overshadow the Atlanta visitors once knew. . . .

In short, Atlanta has outgrown its reputation of charm and graciousness. It's still charming, and still gracious—but in a hustling, bustling, booming sort of way.

Atlanta's expressway system, designed to bring six major highways into and out of the city, was out of date almost before it got started. The Lochner Plan under which the highways were being built anticipated that the city proper would have a population of 400,000 in 1970, and that thirty-two miles of expressways would serve this number. But by 1960 the metropolitan population was well beyond projections. In addition, there were many more two-car families than expected. There were 421,590 cars and trucks in the metropolitan area in 1961, with 287,300 of them entering and leaving downtown every day.

The early expressways were built with money raised by a city-county bond issue, under a joint city-county bond commission, with W. O. DuVall as chairman.

In 1956 this city-county bond commission was discontinued when the Federal Highway Act, under consideration for thirty years, finally was passed. The highway bill provided for a 41,000-mile network of superhighways to be built across the United States; the federal government would pick up 90 percent of the cost from gasoline taxes. Georgia's share of an expanded program was nearly $650 million, of which Atlanta received $157,896,000 to build an expressway system now expanded to 119 miles in and around the city. The most costly segment of this was the downtown connector, giving entry and exit into downtown from any direction and costing when finished approximately

$23 million. Most state highway engineers believed that the expressway system visualized in the first year of the 1960s could be completely inadequate going into the 1970s.

Atlanta continued to grow in importance in air transportation. Statistics showed that between the hours of 11:30 A.M. and 1:30 P.M. Atlanta's new airport was the busiest in the world. More than 2.5 million people flew in and out every year. On June 2 Atlanta's leading political, civic, and business people welcomed one hundred of their counterparts from Los Angeles, San Diego, and Long Beach who flew in on Delta Air Lines' preinaugural transcontinental flight.

The convention bureau in the month of June brought in 18,690 conventioneers ranging from 10,000 Jaycees to 450 mobile home manufacturers, the Order of Rainbow Girls, and the Brotherhood of Locomotive Firemen and Engineers and their ladies. They left behind some $2.5 million with the hotelmen and merchants of the city. *Atlanta* magazine described the Jaycee gathering and explained the city's handicaps in attracting more conventions:

After the Jaycees convention had been committed to Atlanta, the fun really began. Joe Sheehan, young advertising manager of Retail Credit Company, became a full-time Jaycee Convention employee. His company, recognizing the value of such conventions, has given him a three-month leave of absence to serve as General Chairman of the affair. Sheehan is charged with the overall program and has several sub-chairmen to handle such things as housing, transportation, etc.

"We get a lot of pretty wild requests," says Sheehan, "but we try to take care of everybody."

The Mississippi and New York delegations have asked that they be allowed to re-stage the Civil War Battle of Kennesaw Mountain. Sheehan has arranged everything and is going to let them fight it out. The Texas delegation is planning a Texas-size chuck wagon barbecue; and Sheehan is building a mammoth barbecue pit near the auditorium. Another state delegation wants to have a full-blown breakfast meeting in the middle of Peachtree Street. As always, Sheehan has obliged. "Anything within reason," he says. Well, what's reasonable? "If it's not impossible, and not dangerous, it's reasonable," he adds.

The lack of auditorium facilities has been the negative factor in practically every major convention lost to Atlanta in the past few years.

Dallas, Texas, one of Atlanta's most formidable and frequent opponents, last year handled both the Rotarians (15,000) and the Kiwanians (15,000). The big factor was its beautiful new auditorium. Dallas can comfortably seat and feed 15,000 convention people. So can Miami Beach, Des Moines, Tulsa and Las Vegas.

More and more conventions are requiring space for their exhibitors, plus meeting rooms, plus large banquet facilities. And Atlanta is definitely minor league in the business of auditoriums.

What are the major factors unfavorable to Atlanta in getting more conventions?

The auditorium is the biggest factor.

Segregation is another factor. More and more conventions request that all the members be handled together. One hotel here has begun to handle limited numbers . . . that is, they will take a few Negroes into their private banquet rooms.

Limited hotel space is another factor. There are now 6,500 rooms available in Atlanta. That's 1,000 more than we had in 1955. . . .

There are now several motels under construction in the downtown area or near it. The Airtel—being added to the Heart of Atlanta—will handle 200 new rooms; the Riviera is adding another 110; the Airhost, out near the airport, will have 300 rooms; the Atlanta Americana, downtown, will have 340; and the new Holiday Inn will have 300 or more new rooms. And there are more on the way.[8]

Lockheed, operating the biggest aircraft plant in the country under one roof, gave Atlanta a lift when it was announced from the White House that it would build the newest Cold War transport, the new C-141 jet, under a contract that could reach $5 billion. The announcement of the C-141 contract kept Lockheed and its Atlanta-area facility in the forefront of winged aviation.[9]

By mid-1961 Atlanta was becoming well known around the world in the field of packaging. Mead Packaging, a gigantic firm with home offices in Atlanta employing 1,450 people, was now manufacturing paper cartons for soft drinks and bottled beverages that were being sold all over the world. Invented by the historic Atlanta Paper Company, the cartons became part of the Mead line when Mead bought that local company.

Founded shortly after the Civil War, the Atlanta Paper Company was originally the Elsas-May Company, paper jobbers. Atlantan Arthur Harris, active in many phases of local civic life, became the third generation of his family to serve as head of Atlanta Paper, becoming president of Mead Packaging when Atlanta Paper was taken over in the mid-1950s. Though his contributions to Mead were many, his sponsorship of the Mead "Painting of the Year" award gave special recognition to Atlanta's cultural achievements throughout the nation. Under this plan famous artists were hired to do original paintings with an Atlanta background; they were reproduced and sent out in thousands to Mead customers all over the United States and exhibited in dozens of cities.

The grand opening of an impressive addition to the Atlanta skyline took place on July 19–21, 1961, when Atlanta architect John Portman introduced to the city the new Atlanta Merchandise Mart, which he with his partner

H. Griffith Edwards had conceived and designed. Located at Peachtree and Harris streets, on a lot costing $1.8 million, the twenty-three-story skyscraper contained one million square feet of exhibit space, cost $15 million, and was built by Atlanta entrepreneur Ben Massell, who turned it over to Portman, as president of the Merchandise Mart Corporation, to operate on long-term lease. Hundreds of manufacturers, distributors, suppliers, and buyers would have office and display space in the vast new structure. To Atlanta business forecasters, this marked the beginning of a new era in merchandising in the Southeast, a prediction that seemed confirmed when some 15,000 of them from eleven states swarmed in to buy, sell, cheer, and gape at the opening exhibits.[10]

OBITUARIES

Ed L. Almand, 75, was a retired Fulton County commissioner who served for twelve years and held every chairmanship of every county committee. Before entering politics he was district manager of the National Life Insurance Company and had been coroner from November, 1946, until his retirement in 1956. He was active in civic and fraternal organizations. Dr. Peter Frederick Bahnsen, 90, Georgia's first state veterinarian, was born in Denmark and educated in Germany before coming to America in 1900. He was a founder and president of the first Veterinary Association in Georgia and responsible for the passage of the veterinary practice law in 1908. Under his direction great strides were made in enforcing the pure milk laws. Dr. Albert Edward Barnett, 66, was noted as a New Testament scholar and was a professor at Emory's Candler School of Theology. Esmond Brady, the son of Thomas M. Brady, a pioneer in developing the marble industry in Georgia, died while on vacation in Rome, Italy. His estate was divided between several Catholic institutions, including Sacred Heart Church, Our Lady of Perpetual Help Free Cancer Home, and Marist School. A considerable amount was left to St. Joseph's Hospital to build and equip a chapel in memory of his mother, Mrs. Elizabeth Burke Brady.

Cason Jewell Callaway, 66, died at his Blue Springs plantation. He inherited the presidency of Callaway Mills, established by his father, Fuller E. Callaway. After an early retirement at 43, Callaway turned his interests to agriculture, and his chief activity in recent years had been the development of the Ida Cason Callaway Gardens, a memorial to his mother. Long interested in education, for twenty-one years he served as a member of the Board of Regents of the University System. Mrs. Margaret Davis Cate, 73, was a historian widely known for her research into the colonial era of coastal Georgia. Charles Douville Coburn, who began his theatrical career at 14 and became known to millions of American movie and stage patrons for his distinguished face, gruff voice, and ready wit, died at 84. Channing Cope, 68, was known as "The Kudzu King." Noted for his efforts on behalf of soil conservation, the former newspaper columnist and radio announcer died at his Yellow River Farm. Robert L. Davis, 61, fell to his death from the addition to the Federal Reserve Bank, where he was employed on the construction job as iron-worker. Mrs. Raimundo de Ovies, the former Elizabeth Egleston DuBose, was the wife of the dean of St. Philip's Cathedral. Carling Dinkler, Sr., 66, was a hotel magnate and business and civic leader. He was an active supporter of the Atlanta Symphony and Sacred Heart Catholic Church.

A. J. Garing, 86, was bandmaster at Georgia Tech from 1928 until 1946. He was also the oldest remaining member of the John Philip Sousa Band, which he joined in 1904 and played with for sixteen years. He was affectionately known to thousands of Tech students as "Chief." Joseph M. Kruse, 55, manager of the Southeastern Division of Shell Oil Company, was known to his friends as "Beau." He was a popular member of the Atlanta Athletic Club and East Lake Country Club. Rev. J. W. O. McKibben, 73, was graduated from Emory at Oxford and Candler School of Theology. In recent years he had been a member of the North Georgia Methodist Conference and was associate pastor of the First Methodist Church of Decatur.

E. Warren Moise, 71, was an outstanding Atlanta attorney and civic leader. He attended Phillips Exeter Academy in 1906–1907 and then the University of Georgia. As a Rhodes Scholar at Oxford University he received a B.A. in jurisprudence and an M.A. and Bachelor of Civil Law Degree. He became a member of the Georgia Bar in 1915. He was on the board of many Atlanta firms, including the First National Bank, Atlanta Gas Light, Retail Credit, Draper-Owens, and Campbell Coal Company. He was chairman of the Bulow Campbell Foundation and a trustee for Berry Schools. His memberships included the Piedmont Driving Club, Old Warhorse Lawyers' Club, Phi Beta Kappa, and Chi Phi fraternities. Brooks Morgan, 86, had a varied career. At one time he was employed by the Southern Railway as manager in Atlanta. He then became vice-president of the A.B.&C. Railroad. For twenty years he was president of Brock Manufacturing Co. and for eight years was director of the Atlanta Chamber of Commerce. He was a member of the Rotary Club, the Piedmont Driving Club, and the Capital City Club. Leslie Joseph Moore, 63, was president of Atlanta's Tri-state Tractor Company and was widely known for the polled Hereford at his model Holly Springs Farm in Newton County. He was a member of the Capital City Club and the Atlanta Athletic Club.

Charles A. Shonesy, 58, was a veteran newspaperman and copy editor of the *Atlanta Journal*. His newspaper career began with the old *Georgian;* later he was on the staff of the *Constitution* and then copy editor at the *Journal*. Troy B. Stone, 61, former city alderman, was retired director of public relations for Fulton Industries, Inc. He had been chairman of the board of the Atlanta Public Library. Judge J. M. C. (Red) Townsend, 62, was the presiding judge of the Court of Appeals, Second Division, and known as "a champion of the Bill of Rights." Herman F. Weidman was a civil engineer and president of

Weidman & Singleton, consultants on waterworks and sewer system installations. His firm designed all the major waterworks and sewage disposal plants
presently in use in Atlanta. Joseph Bernard Wolfe, 84, civic and religious
leader, had been an employee of Union Life Insurance Co. since 1914. He had
been secretary at The Temple, past president of B'nai B'rith, and treasurer of
the Federation of Jewish Charities. He was a graduate of the Boys High class
of 1898.

NOTES

1. Harold H. Martin, *William B. Hartsfield, Mayor* (Athens: University of Georgia Press, 1978).

2. Ibid.

3. Ivan Allen and Paul Hemphill, *Mayor: Notes on the Sixties* (New York: Simon & Schuster, 1971).

4. Martin, *Hartsfield.*

5. Interview, Dr. Walter Bell, Aug., 1982.

6. Allen, *Mayor.*

7. Ibid.

8. *Atlanta,* July, 1961.

9. Sara Pacher, ibid., Aug., 1961.

10. Ibid.

1962

ON JANUARY 2, 1962, Mayor William B. Hartsfield made his last report to the Board of Aldermen, proudly announcing that once again the city had made a remarkable financial record, operating in this, his last year, on a cash basis. No money had been borrowed for operating expenses, all bills had been paid, and there was a cash carryover of $3,589,556.94, the largest in Atlanta's history. He listed other accomplishments with equal pride: the dedication of a new $20 million air terminal, the building of an observation tower at Grant Park, and the creation there of new bear pits and seal pools. "Most certainly," he said, "we have met the challenge of a growing and dynamic city. About all of these things, we can be truly proud." He went on:

We have tried to make our city attractive to those from other parts of the nation having both money to invest and plants to build. It has paid off, both with an influx of new citizens and investments. Atlanta's growing downtown is silent witness to the soundness of our effort to maintain a strong central city, and to attract here the kind of folks who will contribute to our future growth.

But the most important thing about our city, with its natural advantages, as the great southern regional capital and center of southeastern trade and commerce, is its good name and its image before the balance of the nation. In this electronic and jet age, no place, no people, and no set of officials can escape the eye and ear of the balance of the world. Nor can they escape their responsibilities as citizens of the world. . . .

Science has made all men neighbors, and as such they must find a way to live in peace and without hatred. Great decisions have been made in this field, decisions which have run counter to man of the habits and customs of the old South. Many sections of our Southland have tried to stop the inexorable clock of time and progress, but without success and at great cost to themselves.

Atlanta's mature and friendly approach to the problems of racial change has earned for us the respect of the nation. Our leadership has enabled others in the South to do likewise. As the great branch office and regional center of the South, Atlanta's nerves and blood vessels extend all over the nation. To have adopted any other course than racial progress and harmony would have been doubly tragic for us, and a serious blow to our national government in its fight to stave off world Communism.

Atlanta's peaceful school desegregation before the eyes of the whole nation was our finest hour. Our great airport terminal, which is our front door, and open to all regardless of race, color or creed, is evidence to the world of the fact that here is a city which means to be a proud part of the great nation which we must support. Regardless of our personal feelings or past habits, we are living in a changing world, and to progress Atlanta must be a part of that world.[1]

Though he knew his political sun had set, Hartsfield's pride in his own achievement and strong feeling for his city's future led him to prepare a memo for the guidance of his successor, Ivan Allen, Jr. It was blunt and to the point. The challenge he left to his successor was to protect the role of the City of Atlanta as the dynamic center of the metropolitan area. The outgoing mayor declared:

The worst thing that has happened to the friendly City and County relationship was the death of Carlyle Fraser. It was he who stopped the County from picking on the City, unfriendly legislation, etc. As you know, those now in charge of the County were bitter enemies of the Plan of Improvement. Now that Fraser is dead, I am afraid that they are going back into the business of City-hating, trying to introduce legislation putting the County back into the City business, insisting on unfair contracts, etc.

Believe me, Ivan, this business of protecting the corporate City from unfair impositions by the suburbs is the most important thing you can do, and it will require some fighting and making yourself occasionally unpopular with the suburban areas.

If I were asked to give the greatest service I rendered during my entire reign, I would say it was the general policy of protecting corporate Atlanta from unfair tax situations, unfair contracts, getting the County out of the City business, generally stopping the overall arrangement by which the suburbs seek to live off of revenue collected in downtown Atlanta, and also by stopping efforts to weaken Atlanta's sovereignty and to get it into activities which should be assumed by a broader tax base.

A Stadium is fine, but it should be financed in some way as not to put the burden on the corporate taxpayer. This expanding, dynamic city has too many other needs to be met out of its present bond capacity. Likewise, a start towards a new Transit System is fine, but the central City should dominate it. We do not want to get in the shape of Boston, which submitted to a Transit Authority dominated by the suburbs, who in turn kept low fares, with Boston paying the bill. Thus a city was forced to finance its own destruction. Incidentally, Boston is a classic example of a city completely hemmed in by dominant suburbs. When this happens, downtown will wither and die, and we want to avoid it in Atlanta.

The most important thing you can do in your four years is to preserve Atlanta as a dominant central City, keep the suburbs from running it or trying to live off of its central area taxes, and also in developing some form of revenue paid by all of the people who use Atlanta, instead of by those whose property lies within the corporate limits. . . .

Believe me, these things will require you to take firm stands and to be criticized for them, but they are basic to Atlanta's future prosperity.[2]

A month later, on February 20, 1962, Hartsfield's divorce decree became final. On July 11 he married Mrs. Tollie B. Tolan. Ex-mayor Hartsfield soon found himself on a comfortably generous retainer as counselor to the Coca-Cola Company, the Trust Company of Georgia, and the Georgia Power Company. With his $6,000-a-year pension from the city and a new $12,000-a-year job as head of the Southeastern Fair Association, plus income from investments, he had an income of some $60,000 a year, which was more than he had earned as mayor.

One area in which Hartsfield was to demonstrate an increasing irascibility as the years passed was racial relationships. Though the integration of the buses and lunch counters and the token integration of the public schools had taken place quietly during his administration, his concern that Atlanta remain a city with a white majority became an obsession. As mayor he had to deal somewhat indirectly with the fact that white flight to the suburbs was creating a black central city, where black political power was rising steadily. As mayor emeritus he could speak out more boldly, less concerned that he not wound the feelings of the blacks or lose their vote. He spoke unsuccessfully in favor of the annexation of Sandy Springs, north Atlanta, and Druid Hills, all white areas. While speaking before the North DeKalb Rotary Club he issued a blunt warning: If the exodus of moneyed whites to the suburbs continued, the central city would come under Negro domination, "and this would be bad for the Negro himself—for the worst element of his own race would rise up and take over."

He also had some kind words about the way his successor was handling the racial situation. Ivan Allen, Hartsfield said, realized what many merchants had not yet realized, that Atlanta could not be run under rules regarding race that were different from those applied to Kansas City or New York or any other place, and that the sooner the merchants, restaurateurs, and hotel men learned this fact of life—"the sooner we do it, desegregate and forget it, the better."

Almost immediately after taking office as mayor, Allen discovered that what Hartsfield had told him was true. Being mayor of Atlanta was no easy task, nor one that could be carried on by a man afraid of challenge.

Said Allen in his book: "When I moved into the mayor's office in January of 1962, it was obvious that Atlanta and Georgia and the rest of the South had come to the crossroads; that a time of dramatic change lay ahead of us and that we had to choose whether we wanted to fight change and drag along as we had always done in the South, or accept the opportunity to grow along with the rest of the country. At the bottom of everything at that time of course was the race issue."

Allen had inherited a competent staff of department heads from the Hartsfield administration, so his first move was to create for himself a reliable and loyal personal staff. He brought over from Ivan Allen Company as his secretary Ann Moses, a highly intelligent and articulate woman who was to be of invaluable help to him in the coming eight years.

As his right hand and troubleshooter, he picked Captain George Royal, who had served as bodyguard for the Allen family during the campaign, and finally after two years he persuaded Earl Landers to leave his job as city comptroller to come into the mayor's office as his administrative assistant.

"It was one of the smartest things I did as mayor," said Allen. "Landers had been the city comptroller for 34 years and had looked after the city's tax money with the same diligence most us looked after our private bank accounts. Probably the most liked and highly respected person in city government, he was totally dedicated, totally capable, totally committed to working behind the scenes, the perfect type of man a green mayor needs to help him pull the proper strings."

"I discovered very quickly," Allen wrote, "that running a city isn't as cut-and-dried as running an office equipment company; that it is one thing to make campaign promises and quite another thing to harness a massive city-government machine to make the promises come true."

The first of a series of delicate racial situations Allen would face as mayor came on opening night of the Southern Association Baseball Season at old Ponce de Leon Park. Allen was invited to throw out the first ball to launch the Atlanta Crackers' season. This was the first time that seating at "Poncey" had been integrated, and the first time Negro players would appear in a league game there. When Allen stood up to make his ceremonial pitch, there was a loud chorus of boos.

Allen soon learned that the best way to handle a racial problem was to handle it himself. Not long thereafter the opportunity, figuratively speaking, dropped in his lap. Prudence Herndon, wife of a prominent Negro lawyer, had gone into the City Hall cafeteria with nine Atlanta University Center students, both black and white, and had been refused service by the white waitress behind the counter. When George Royal brought word to Allen, he went immediately to the cafeteria and asked the waitress why she had refused service. Service, she said, was for City Hall employees only, or their guests.

"Very well," Allen said. "I'm the Mayor, a City Hall employee, and these are my guests. Please serve them." She still refused.

"Then," said Allen, "I'll serve them myself."

"If you put it that way," she said, "I will serve them." And she did, bringing them cool drinks as they sat at their tables.

At this moment every other diner in the cafeteria got up and went out. To Allen's surprise, they did not stay long. George Royal had stopped them in the hall outside and turned them back. "He swarmed over them like a mother hen," wrote Allen. "'You're a bunch of darned fools,' he said, 'giving up your cafeteria just because some young students want to cool off with a Coke.'"

"There is no doubt in my mind," wrote Allen in his book, "that I was turning a little more liberal every day as a reaction against the totally irrational and irresponsible acts of the white racists around me. I wasn't so all fired liberal when I first moved into City Hall, but when I saw what the race baiters were doing, or could do, to hold back the orderly growth of Atlanta, it infuriated me and eventually swung me to the extreme end opposite them. I reached the point that I had absolutely no compassion and no patience with these people."

His first year, Allen wrote, "was a time for me to learn how to be a mayor, a time for me to adjust to some of the fundamental facts of government life," and he learned one fact that startled him. As he took office, he learned that Atlanta's policemen were pitifully underpaid, their salaries far out of line with those of other cities. So he called a meeting of the finance committee and proposed a two-step pay raise for the policemen. But he soon learned that by tradition, if the police get a pay raise, so must the firemen. And if the firemen and policemen get a raise, all other city employees must get one, too. Finally, he recalled, "We had to finance a two-step raise for 7,000 or so people who work for the city, just to do something about the disgracefully low pay of 900 Atlanta policemen."

Allen recited that the worst setback he suffered during the difficult first year was the "resounding defeat" of the $80 million bond issue he was striving to pass, to provide money for schools, roads, sewers, a civic center and auditorium, even a million-dollar redevelopment plan that would turn Piedmont Park into "the most beautiful in-town municipal park in the South."

But, he recalled, he failed to convey to the general public and the Board of Aldermen his enthusiasm for the bonds. The whole Piedmont Park idea became a raging racial issue and blew up in his face—blowing up the bond issue with it. Allen reported in his book that the Woodruff Foundation had offered a gift of $4 million on the Piedmont beautification project but, as always, had asked that it be an anonymous gift. "The redneck elements started screaming that this was 'nigger money' and was really an effort to integrate the park (it had already been integrated but they failed to mention that). The bond issue was defeated by a 2 to 1 vote."

Allen blamed his own inexperience as a city administrator for this failure, in that he failed to convince the general public that the bond issue was needed. So he created a Citizens Bond Study Commission, headed by Edward D. Smith of the First National Bank, to look into the causes of defeat and make recommendations for another effort. Thus the following year, 1963, after the need for bonds had been in the news for several months, a bond issue of $39 million passed easily enough.

Allen at least temporarily lost his overwhelming support in the black community by mishandling another racial confrontation. Residents of Peyton Forest, a pleasant white neighborhood, came to the alarmed conclusion that a developer had plans to start building housing for Negroes in Peyton Forest, as well as nearby on Peyton Road. "A volatile situation began to build up," said Allen. "It was the classic situation of a neighborhood faced with racial transition. This took place in fifty-two separate situations in Atlanta in that one year of 1962."

Allen knew that over the years it had been a fairly common practice for aldermen to create a buffer by zoning a large area solely for commercial use. But to Allen, this was ridiculous for a city with a rapidly growing population desperately needing land for housing. The matter came to a head when the developer sold his own house in Peyton Forest to a black doctor—setting off a frenzy of alarm on the part of the white residents there.

Said Allen: "I promptly decided to close off the subdivision—entrenched whites on one side, encroaching blacks on the other—with a barrier on Peyton Road. I saw it as a way of accomplishing two things—calming white people in the neighborhood and focusing attention on the unused 800 acres so we could get it re-zoned and put to use for low or middle-priced housing. I saw it as a happy compromise." Unhappily, Allen concluded, "the people of Atlanta didn't understand all the subtleties of the situation. They only saw a crude barricade—'The Atlanta Wall' it came to be called—stretched across a road, making a dividing line between white and black."

The national press took up the story and questions began to arise about whether Atlanta really was "A City Too Busy to Hate." The feeling against Allen was understandably quite bitter in the Negro community.

Allen later admitted that he had been "completely in error in trying to solve the issue in such a crude way." He was saved when, after the barrier had stood for a couple of months, the courts ruled that the barrier was illegal.

Georgia politics changed profoundly in 1962. In late April ex-Mayor Hartsfield stood in a packed federal courtroom with his friend and fellow lawyer Morris Abram to hear young federal judge Griffin Bell read the death knell of the county-unit system. For Hartsfield and Abram it was the end of a battle that had begun for both of them nearly twenty years before. To Hartsfield, a city man to the core, it meant that the urban areas at last had come into their own. With the city man's vote no longer diluted in the Democratic primary, the state could draw from the great wells of political talent in the cities. Georgia could now go on to become a great state. The rural areas, he said, need not worry about Atlanta's dominating them. "Atlanta," he said, "has never been able to agree with itself."[3]

State Senator Carl Edward Sanders, thirty-seven, a moderate on racial issues, was the first Georgia governor to be elected under this "one man, one vote" rule. He defeated ex-Governor Marvin Griffin, fifty-five, who had been endorsed by the Klan and other white supremacist groups, and whose pledge was total resistance to desegregation.

On September 26, in a runoff primary in the Fifth Congressional District, Charles L. Weltner, thirty-four, another moderate in racial matters, beat eight-term Representative James C. Davis, an ardent segregationist. And in the general election in October, Leroy R. Johnson became the first Negro since Reconstruction elected to the Georgia State Senate. Another black candidate for the State Senate was defeated by a well-known white civic leader, Oby T. Brewer.

On April 30 the NAACP asked the Federal District Court in Atlanta for quicker and surer action in desegregating the city's public schools. Before the court could rule, the Most Reverend Paul J. Hallinan, Roman Catholic Archbishop of Atlanta, announced that beginning in September students would be admitted on a nonracial basis to eighteen elementary and five high schools in the archdiocese. And as autumn rolled around, seventeen Negroes were in parochial schools, and five more of Atlanta's public schools were quietly integrated.

Tasting victory in the fight for open schools, black leaders pressed for changes in other fields of black-white relationships. The U.S. District Court in Atlanta was asked to require Grady Memorial Hospital to end its segregation in the patient care and medical training program and its medical staff. The suit was filed by the NAACP in cooperation with Atlanta attorneys, who noted that the tax-supported hospital had received $6 million in public funds in 1960.

All-in-all, the race relations picture for 1962 was mixed. Much had been accomplished in Mayor Allen's first year in office. A beginning at least had been made toward the desegregation of the public schools, but black leaders held that the process was not fast enough, that it did not live up to the Supreme Court's order that it go ahead at "all deliberate speed." The Jim Crow signs at City Hall public rooms had been eliminated, City Hall cafeterias and lunch stands were serving blacks, black firemen were on the job along with white, and black policemen now could arrest white lawbreakers. And slowly, and at first reluctantly, Atlanta's good restaurants such as Herren's were opening their doors to Negro diners. Also, in its drive for jobs for blacks, Atlanta's Negro leadership was making noticeable progress. Downtown department stores and variety stores were beginning to hire Negroes in positions formerly reserved for whites. A bread manufacturer after only slight hesitation agreed to upgrade or employ Negroes in eighteen jobs formerly held by whites. A government contractor removed racial designations in his lunchroom and workshop restrooms, and public utilities were looking into the possibility of hiring black drivers. These changes had come about in a matter of months after years of fruitless negotiations.

Many changes, however, were setting the pattern for the future, in which blacks eventually would be found in all levels of employment in nearly every business and industry in the city. The changes would come slowly, and there would be many confrontations in the years just ahead. But the changes would come. The reasons were these, according to Fred Powledge of the *Journal:*

1. The Atlanta Negro has a great buying power, greater here than in most other places in the nation.

2. This dollar power can cause drastic changes in a business' economy as some department stores learned during the 1960 sit-ins and boycotts—if it is withheld.

3. The Negro in Atlanta enjoys a relatively high degree of organization.

There is no longer a crippling split here between "activists" and "gradu-alists," as there was before 1960.

4. The Atlanta Negro community, with its own banks, groceries and general merchandise stores, is capable of self-sufficiency. This is an important factor to consider in the event that a boycott—or "selective buying program," as it is sometimes called—is initiated.

There are several organizations at work to seek better employment op-portunities for Atlanta Negroes. Their methods differ slightly, but all hold the same ace in the hole—the power of the Negro dollar.

One such organization is an alliance of Negro ministers, which selects a pastoral "negotiating committee" to talk with businessmen. Another organi-zation seeks personal, verbal agreements with downtown merchants. A third is concerning its efforts in the area of federal defense contract holders, who are by law prohibited from engaging in discrimination.

Other organizations rely on subtle, gentlemanly conferences with busi-nessmen and employers. Still others are trying to obtain names of Negro specialists who are looking for jobs, so that a white businessman can no longer say, "there are no qualified applicants."

Although Dr. Ralph Abernathy in his Operation Bread Basket and a half-dozen other black organizations in Atlanta—including the Southern Christian Leadership Conference, the Committee on Appeal for Human Rights, and the NAACP—were making good progress, the fact remained that Negro employees in Atlanta still had a long way to go before their economic situation could be considered equitable.

Negro families in Atlanta had less than half the income of white families in the city. Government figures compiled in 1961 showed the average Negro family income was $3,307 before taxes. This was 48 percent of the white family's pretax income of $6,984. Fifty-seven percent of the white families owned their own homes, but only 19 percent of the Negro families were homeowners. Automobiles were owned by 78 percent of the white families, but only 31 percent of the Negro families. In 1960 the black family, after paying $98 in personal and income taxes, had money income of $3,209, all of which except one dollar went into current consumption. White families, after paying taxes of $889, were left with money income of $6,005, of which $5,633 was spent in current consumption.

During the decade of the city's most rapid growth, 1950–1960, the aver-age income of black families increased by less than one-third—31.86 percent or $799, from $2,508 in 1950 to $3,307 in 1960. The average income for white families increased by nearly one-half, 49.22 percent, from $4,620 in 1950 to $6,894 in 1960. At the same time, consumer prices were advancing by 22.8 percent, with the Negroes' capital income barely keeping up with the rise in the cost of living.

There were, of course, reasons for this discrimination other than race and color alone. In Atlanta in the 1950s, heads of white families had an average of eleven years of education. Among Negro families the average declined from eight years in 1950 to six years in 1960. This was explained in part by the fact that many Atlanta blacks had recently come in from rural areas, where they had not been encouraged to get an education.

The H. J. Russell Plastering Company, owned by Herman J. Russell, made history in early November when it became a member of the 3,000-member organization of the Chamber of Commerce. H. J. Russell was black, and the Chamber heretofore had been an all-white organization.

The Chamber of Commerce sent out form letters to prospective members, and the letters went to many business organizations in the city. The letter signed by Chamber president Ben S. Gilmer said: "This is your cordial invitation to membership in your Atlanta Chamber of Commerce. The addition of your support will add greatly to the effectiveness of our program." The person responsible for mailing the letters had not known that the Russell Company was owned by a black man. Russell accepted the invitation and paid his dues. Then the Chamber discovered that it had apparently broken an unwritten rule prohibiting Negro membership.

Ironically, just a week before the accidental invitation, the Greater Atlanta Council on Human Relations had asked Opie Shelton about the Chamber's policy toward Negro members, and he had answered: "Admission of Negroes to membership in the Atlanta Chamber of Commerce is a policy matter which I assume will come up for discussion in due time. Meanwhile, I believe that this organization's efforts in the area of human relations speak for themselves."

Early in May, 1962, Mayor Allen had said his official good-bye to a group of 106 Atlanta art lovers who were leaving for a tour of European galleries and museums under the sponsorship of the Atlanta Art Association. A month later, on June 3, tragic word reached Atlanta that their plane had crashed at Paris' Orly Airport and that all aboard except three stewardesses had perished.

"These were my lifelong friends," Allen wrote. "This was my generation. This was also the background of Atlanta's cultural society. The city's leading patrons of the arts. There was no precedent for this kind of agony."[4] The mayor decided to go to Paris to represent the families, to help identify the dead, and to bring the victims home as soon as possible. French officials were sympathetic and helpful.

"It was difficult to describe the feeling I had as we looked through the charred wreckage," Allen later wrote:

Only twenty-four hours earlier this huge droop-winged plane had roared down the runway, headed back to Atlanta with intimate friends of mine aboard. They had spent a month happily touring the art centers of Europe, had gathered valuable insights and ideas on what could be done to expand

Atlanta's culture, and had bought many expensive paintings, artifacts, and souvenirs to take back home for themselves or for friends. Trouble had developed as soon as the Boeing 707 was beginning to roll, and the pilot decided to abort takeoff by locking the wheels. The tires wore off, and then the rims. A tremendous amount of static electricity was building up as the plane slithered off the end of the runway. It clipped a couple of telephone poles, bounced across a narrow access road, slid another thousand feet on its belly and finally slammed into a small stone cottage, which spun it around and broke the tail section free, saving the lives of three stewardesses. Of the 127 persons aboard, those three were the only ones to live.[5]

Constitution editor Eugene Patterson expressed his sorrowful shock:

What can be said at this stunned moment, what words are there to measure this calamity in Paris? It is doubtful that any American city has ever lost, at a single stroke, so much of its fineness. None can be singled out. This was Atlanta; these were the caring men and the gentle women who contributed to more than the city's finance, politics, commerce. They lifted our eyes to the things that matter, to the meanings that history remembers when it has discarded the pettiness of wars and riches and little movements—to the arts, the culture that endures. These people were irreplaceable.

Long after the days of formal mourning were over, the Orly crash in all its grim details lived in the courts as survivors brought suits against Air France, charging that the crews had mishandled an overloaded plane. Finally, on July 7, 1969, seven years after the tragedy, what was described as the final settlement had been made. Said the *Atlanta Journal:*

The largest settlement in history for a single airplane disaster—$5.2 million—has been paid to the survivors of 62 persons who perished in an Air France plane crash in 1962 at Orly Airport in Paris. It was disclosed Friday that Air France completed the settlement last February when U.S. District Court Judge Edward T. Gignoux of Portland, Maine, signed an order dismissing 42 cases involving the 62 deaths which had been in litigation for more than six years.

In all 130 persons, including 106 Atlantans, died in the crash. However, survivors of about 60 others who were killed settled with the airline without litigation.

On a more positive note, the crash was the catalyst for the building of the $13 million Memorial Arts Center on Peachtree Street. The center (now named for Robert W. Woodruff) became the focal point of Atlanta's fine arts.

In 1962 Atlanta awarded its nineteenth Woman of the Year honors. Women were named in several categories, and one of them was chosen *the* Woman of the Year. A list of the distinguished winners up to 1961 follows: The first winner, in 1943, was Mrs. Francis L. Abreu, chosen for her wartime effort as volunteer director of the Red Cross. Abreu, Lucy Justus reported, now lived on Sea Island, devoting herself to her family and friends.

In 1944 Mrs. William G. Hamm was chosen because of her contribution to education, especially her founding of the Junior League Speech School. In 1962 she was still active in the school's operation.

In 1945 Mamie K. Taylor was recognized for civic service through the Georgia Home Economics Association. She was now chairman of the Georgia Commission on Children and Youth.

In 1946 Frances Craighead Dwyer, an attorney, was elected for her successful drive to bring about the enactment of a child labor law in that year. By 1962 she was retired.

In 1947 Ira Jarrell, superintendent of Atlanta City Schools, was nominated for her place in education. (Jarrell was nominated Woman of the Year in Civic Affairs in 1943, and is the only woman to have been nominated twice). Retired from the Atlanta schools, she was a director of the State Department of Education.

In 1948 Mrs. Howard C. Smith, a chairman of the Atlanta Music Club's education division, was honored for her efforts to bring music to the underprivileged. She remained active in Music Club activities and was choir director and organist at the Church of the Assumption.

In 1949 Dorothy Orr, historian, teacher, and school principal, was elected. At retirement in 1952 Orr celebrated forty-six years in her teaching career. She remained active in retirement, raising funds for scholarships to be used for teacher training.

In 1950 Mrs. C. Evans Joseph was known and loved by literally thousands of young Atlantans whom she had taught to dance when she was Margaret Bryan. The only winner from the field of business, Joseph in retirement had given up dancing but continued to teach the young.

In 1951 Evelyn Ewing, another winner from the field of education, helped to devise the curriculum revision made necessary when the Plan of Improvement brought many Fulton County schools into the Atlanta system. Ten years later Ewing was happily teaching high school English in Forest Park.

In 1952 Katherine Thomson was winner in the field of civic service. As a Motor Corps volunteer in the Red Cross she had more than 10,000 hours of driving to her credit. In addition to holding a full-time government job, "Miss Kitty" had added 8,000 more hours to her volunteer work.

In 1953 Dr. Leila Denmark, pediatrician, won recognition for her research in developing a single vaccine for whooping cough, tetanus, and diphtheria. For years she had given at least one day a week at the Central Presbyterian Church's Free Baby Clinic.

In 1954 Mrs. Mills B. Lane was honored for civic service as founder of Atlanta's Cerebral Palsy School, now one of the nation's outstanding schools for the palsied. Retired as chairman of the board, she remained active in the school, the Marian Howard School for brain-damaged children, and the Gatchell School.

In 1955 Ruth Blair was honored for her twenty years as a guiding spirit of the Atlanta Historical Society, where she was executive secretary. She retired shortly thereafter.

In 1956 Mrs. Rembert Marshall was saluted for her tireless effort on behalf of such civic projects as the Atlanta Symphony Guild, the Art Association, and the Atlanta Music Club. Marshall in 1962 was residing in Switzerland.

In 1957 Nora Belle Emerson was awarded the honors in education. She had developed a unique form of musical therapy that helped normal and handicapped children achieve their potential in music. She was now superintendent of the primary department of Westminster Presbyterian Church.

In 1958 Annie Sue Brown was named for her inspired work in the field of education. A science curriculum specialist, Brown had achieved national recognition for Atlanta schools in scientific participation. In 1962 her project was the introduction of new science programs in Atlanta schools.

In 1959 Mrs. Leon Frohsin was honored for civic service. In 1936 she had organized the Service Guild with sixteen friends. Their aim was to be useful wherever needed. Now numbering over 225 members, the guild had helped equip the obstetrical and gynecological clinic at Grady Hospital, where they also operated the gift shop. Still active in the guild in 1962, Frohsin for two years had been active in the Atlanta Association for Mental Health, which sponsored a program providing 50,000 Christmas presents for the patients at Milledgeville.

In 1960 Mrs. James N. Frazer won the honors for her civic service. "As chairman of the Cerebral Palsy Center's volunteer committee, she personally supervised the fund raising, planning and construction of the center." She was active, also, in the Junior League Speech School and the United Appeal Fund Raising Campaign.

On January 23, 1962, the Woman of the Year for 1961 was announced. It went, to no one's great surprise, to Adah Toombs, wife of the noted architect, for her labors in the interest of various civic enterprises.

DeKalb County Juvenile Court Judge Murphey Candler retired and recalled his thirty years of service to the county's troubled youth in an interview with reporter William Osborne, published in the *Atlanta Journal* on February 16. He had seen the court develop from the "stepchild" of the DeKalb judicial system with him as part-time judge and one probation officer handling some forty to fifty cases a year, to its present status as one of the county's important courts, handling 2,565 cases in 1961. At the bottom of each juvenile case, said the judge, there is deep tragedy, a lack of love and understanding between child and parents. The solution in juvenile cases depends on how deeply the probation officer and the judge comprehend the child's problems.

Robert F. Maddox celebrated his ninety-second birthday on April 4 by announcing a drastic change in the living pattern he had followed in one place for half a century. The Sunday paper reported: "After fifty years on West Paces Ferry Road Atlanta's grand old man is moving. The sale of his residence and surrounding 18 acres to the state will be completed this month, clearing the way for the construction of a new Governor's Mansion. . . . Maddox,·who was mayor more than fifty years ago, watched the city grow from 30,000 at his birth in 1870 to 150,000 when he was mayor in 1909–1910, to the 'City of a Million' in 1962—one of the South's great business, industrial and transportation centers."

Bright and alert of mind and body, vigorous for all his ninety-two years, Maddox on his birthday visited his downtown office in the morning and greeted guests at his home in the afternoon, receiving flowers, letters, and telegrams throughout the day. He seemed to enjoy reminiscing, talking about his years as chairman of the board of the First National Bank of which he was still a director, his experiences as director of several companies, including Georgia Power Company and Southern Bell Telephone and Telegraph Company. He was chairman of President Franklin D. Roosevelt's Bankers Advisory Committee, and was a former president of the Chamber of Commerce.

He had played no active role in city politics after he had left the mayor's office in 1910, though he had been a strong supporter of William B. Hartsfield as mayor and was now equally as strong in his support of Ivan Allen, Jr. Before he left the mayor's office he bought seventy-five acres of woods from his friend James J. Dickey, on which he had built his country estate, Woodhaven. As the city grew and began to surround this property, he sold off all but eighteen acres, the area he sold to the state for $250,000.

In mid-1962 John Paul Austin, forty-seven, Georgia born and Harvard educated, took over the presidency of the Coca-Cola Company, the phenomenal Atlanta business institution that in 110 countries around the world was selling about 70 million soft drinks every day. Salesmanship was nothing new to Paul Austin's experience. As a small boy in LaGrange, Georgia, he earned his spending money in the summer by selling light bulbs door-to-door for five cents apiece. He moved up from light bulbs to juke boxes. After meritorious service in the Pacific in World War II, Austin moved back to New York to practice law with his old firm there until 1949, when he joined the legal department of the Coca-Cola Company. He served in Chicago and in New York City, where he became assistant to the president of Coca-Cola Export Corporation. In 1954 he was elected a vice-president of the Export Corporation and was placed in charge of the African headquarters at Johannesburg. He rose to become president of the Export Corporation, and later he was promoted to executive vice-president of the Coca-Cola Company. On May 8, 1962, he was elected president.

He came to the top position at a time when the Coca-Cola Company was reaching new heights; 1961 had been the best year in the history of Coca-Cola. Sales totaled more than one-half billion dollars, most of which came from the soft drink syrups that it sold to 1,800 bottling plants around the world.

To chairman of the board Lee Talley, the Coca-Cola Company could have made no better choice for president than John Paul Austin. "He is immensely well-qualified for his new position by virtue of his character, experience and knowledge of the field. He is a young, able and vigorous leader, and he has had vast experience in all areas. Our company was founded in Georgia, and we are proud that our new president is a Georgian."

Austin commented that he did expect a continued expansion of the business that had started in Atlanta seventy-six years earlier, but he admitted that it was going to be hard to improve on the amazing record already set by the company. "I feel like that character in *Alice in Wonderland*," he said, "the one who said 'I'm going to have to run as fast as I can in order to stay in the same place.'"

Dr. Rudolph A. Bartholomew, seventy-six, was given the Hardman Award of the Medical Association of Georgia in 1962 for his outstanding work. He had practiced obstetrics in Atlanta for forty-five years, in which time he had delivered more than 12,000 babies. He was the author of the booklet called "Emergency Childbirth in Times of Disaster," which was distributed all over the world. The booklet, published by the Georgia Department of Public Health and the Georgia Civil Defense Organization, was only one of his contributions to knowledge in the field of obstetrics. For twenty-five years he was clinical professor of obstetrics at Emory University School of Medicine, retiring in 1955.

Another Atlanta doctor highly honored for his skills as both surgeon and physician was Dr. William Arthur Selman, who in 1962 celebrated his sixtieth year practicing medicine in Atlanta. During this long span he not only cared for multiple thousands of patients—right up until his retirement he was performing ten or more major surgical procedures a month—he also, according to *Journal* reporter Katherine Barnwell, "helped more young doctors develop into mature and skillful surgeons than anyone else in the city." When in January, 1962, he was honored for his sixty years of humanitarian service by the Georgia Baptist Hospital Medical Staff, Edwin Peel, administrator of the hospital, described him as a "wonderful doctor and a fine Christian gentleman," to which Dr. John S. Atwater, president of the Georgia Baptist medical staff, added: "We pay tribute to Dr. W. A. Selman, who has typified through more than half a century the finest image of the Good Physician."

The death of Mrs. Eleanor Roosevelt, widow of FDR, in her Manhattan apartment on November 7, 1962, brought sorrow to many Atlantans. Her visits to the city dated back to 1937. In March of that year, while on a speaking tour through the South, she spent the nearly three hours she had between trains to visit the city. Ever one to put her time to good use, she inspected the new city jail and took a look at government housing projects here. She made many visits to Georgia thereafter, going with her husband to the Little White House, his retreat at Warm Springs. In 1949 she attended a forum of 200 southern church-women in Atlanta at the Wesley Memorial Methodist Church, and to the surprise of her hearers she spoke somewhat in defense of the South in its handling of racial problems.

"I'm not one to feel that the South is the great offender," she said. "We in the North are as bad in many ways." At the same time she expressed her strong dislike for the Ku Klux Klan and its methods of armed and hooded intimidation. Her remark about the North grew out of violence erupting in Peekskill, New York, following a concert by a controversial Negro singer, Paul Robeson. On a visit to Atlanta in June of 1962, she was critical of southern law as it dealt with one black juvenile. At age fifteen, Preston Cobb, Jr., was convicted and sentenced to die for the murder of a seventy-year old white farmer. She took this occasion to protest the death penalty in her column and in a letter to Governor Vandiver, and as late as September she was still press-ing for clemency for young Cobb. Governor Vandiver assured her the Georgia Pardons and Paroles Board would review the case, as they did all criminal cases awaiting the death sentence. On her last visit to Atlanta, on June 25, she spoke in tribute to Israel. Mayor Ivan Allen welcomed her and said to her that Atlanta was created in the image of Franklin D. Roosevelt. "We believe we reflect the image you want Americans to have," he told her. Others who spoke in tribute to Mrs. Roosevelt in her visit here were Vice-Mayor Sam Massell—to whom she was "truly a great lady"—and Frank Allcorn, Jr., who was mayor of Warm Springs and who called her "a marvelous woman who was probably misunderstood by a lot of people." The Atlantan who knew her best of all perhaps was Charles F. Palmer, chairman of the Franklin D. Roosevelt Warm Springs Commission, and great friend of both the Roose-velts. She was, indeed, misunderstood by many people in the South, said Palmer, but she was above all a gracious lady and above all a "doer." It was at her urging that President Roosevelt, Palmer indicated, brought into being many of the laws that meant so much to the poor, the aged, the sick, and the lonely in the Depression years.

By meaningful coincidence, on the day after her death an announcement was made that would have pleased Mrs. Roosevelt very much. According to Dr. John H. Venable, director of the Georgia Department of Public Health, work on a $12 million Georgia Mental Health Center would get under way in December. Dr. Venable announced that word had come down from the U.S. Department of Health, Education, and Welfare that an original grant of $1,575,518 had been approved for the local facility to be built on the Georgian Clinic's Briarcliff Road property. A $6 million health center had originally been planned for the site, but this had been expanded. It would be, said Dr. Venable, the first of its kind in the United States, probably in the world. When completed the center would treat an estimated five hundred patients a day, with a large outpatient program supported along with the 200-bed hos-pital program.

As the hospital neared completion in late 1964, Emory University and the state agreed to its joint operation as a psychiatric teaching facility. Although it would be used both as an inpatient and outpatient hospital for Georgia's mentally ill, its primary objectives would be to supply the state with psychiatrists, psychologists, nurses, and social workers.

The creation of this little-publicized Mental Health Institute could be attributed in some considerable part at least to Atlantan Boisfeuillet Jones, who at the urging of President Kennedy had left his job as vice-president of Emory to come to Washington as the president's special assistant for health and medical affairs. While Jones was a student at Emory University he worked part time for the National Youth Administration, and on graduating he became assistant state administrator for the NYA. He soon was appointed head of the southeastern area. His career with NYA was interrupted by World War II, and he spent three years fretting at his desk job in Washington. At the war's end he took a job at Emory University, soon becoming dean of administration and then vice-president and administrator of health services.

In 1956 Jones, whose abilities had been noted in Washington, was named to the National Advisory Health Council. In 1960 he helped draw up the plank on health matters for the Democratic party platform, and on New Year's Eve, 1960, a personal telephone call from President Kennedy prompted the Jones family's move to Washington, D.C.

The firing of Marvin McDonald as concert manager of the Atlanta Music Club left Atlanta music lovers bewildered, dismayed, and, for a time at least, bitterly divided among themselves. McDonald, in his thirty years as concert manager, had made Atlanta one of the top concert cities in the nation, and the Atlanta Music Club was one of the strongest cultural influences in the city.

The decision to fire McDonald came only after months of deliberation, and it had nothing to do with McDonald's capacities as a promoter of top-flight concerts, both vocal and instrumental, but with his handling of club funds, under the incredibly loose and ineffective bookkeeping system that the club had employed over the years.

In his thirty years as concert manager he had taken the little Atlanta Music Club when it was just a small, select group and made it into an organization of national renown in the world of music. He had brought many of the great stars here for the first time—Galli-Curci, Lawrence Tibbett, Yehudi Menuhin, Fritz Kreisler, and Vladimir Horowitz among them. Leopold Stokowski was playing here when the banks closed in the Depression, and Atlantans eased their financial anguish by crowding into the auditorium. The Metropolitan Opera was absent from Atlanta from 1930 to 1940, but at McDonald's urging, and the Music Club's financial guarantees, it came back. Not only old stars but young and promising singers were introduced to Atlanta by McDonald—among them were Birgit Nilsson, Joan Sutherland, and

Maria Callas. McDonald in truth was a genius as a concert manager, but as a bookkeeper, a manager of the Music Club's money, he was completely inadequate.

Perhaps McDonald was fortunate at being dismissed when he was, for the Music Club was facing difficult times. McDonald had been able to fill the 5,000-seat Municipal Auditorium at bargain rates for season after season. But Atlanta's music lovers were finding it more and more difficult to drive into the heart of the city through heavy downtown traffic and find a place to park; and the auditorium's removable raised floor was not only considered a safety hazard, it gave forth disturbing grunts and groans during a concert. Moreover, whereas the All-Star Series had had little competition in the past, there now was a great deal—not only radio programs but many live musical events were competing with Music Club productions all over town.[6]

A reflection of the profound interest Atlantans were showing in real estate development in 1962 was the record-setting construction program that went on throughout the year. Chief Building Inspector William Wofford reported that the program, totaling $116,684,338, covered every type of construction and was the biggest in the city's history, rising well above the $113,756,000 set in 1959.

The year's total was taken from evaluations of all projects that received construction permits from the city. It included:

- —$440,000 worth of swimming pools;
- —a whopping $29,813,472 for new apartment buildings and $22,131,480 for one-family residences;
- —$14,647,962 for 47 office buildings;
- —$2 million for new churches;
- —$3.6 million for 62 stores and mercantile buildings;
- —$11,247,236 for 76 office-warehouse units;
- —$1,188,700 for 5 industrial plants.

Wofford said that eighteen projects cost more than a million dollars each, with an Atlanta Housing Authority undertaking the granddaddy of them all. Its 650-unit Negro development on Field Road, which included one hundred separate buildings, cost $8,401,673. The year also brought one of the first construction permits for a downtown theater in a decade. It was for the Rialto Theater reconstruction at Forsyth and Luckie streets. Wofford added that the city building inspection office already had about $5 million worth of plans on file for processing in 1963.

Among the churches dedicated in 1962 was one that stood out not only in its cost, which was more than $2.5 million, but in the splendor of its architecture and its status among houses of worship in Georgia:

The new Episcopal Cathedral of St. Philip, towering over Peachtree Road in Buckhead, was packed with clergy and laymen Sunday when it was dedicated as the Cathedral of the Diocese of Atlanta.

Acolytes with crosses and candles led a procession of 200 down the long aisle of the cathedral. Last in line was the Most Rev. Arthur C. Lichtenberger, 21st presiding bishop of the Protestant Episcopal Church in the U.S.A., who preached the sermon.

The great stone arches of the cathedral rang with the trumpet fanfare that began the procession. Brasses and timpani from the Georgia State College brass chamber ensemble joined the purple-robed combined choirs and the congregation in the processional hymn, "Hail Thee, Festival Day!" . . . Mayor and Mrs. Ivan Allen were among the more than 1,200 visitors attending the dedication of the $2.5 million cathedral. . . .

In the summer of 1962, in the Mediterranean off Sicily, artist George Beattie and Emory professor Immanuel Ben-Dor were lowered from the *Sea Diver*, a ship designed for photographing and examining and bringing up objects from beneath the sea. They lifted beautiful marbles, architectural items intended for a church 1,400 years earlier, and brought them to the museum at Syracuse. Fascinated by their first venture in the new art and skill of underwater archeology, Ben-Dor, Beattie, and the Edward Link Expedition visited other shipwreck sites in the Mediterranean and found 2,000-year-old Roman jars and Greek bowls that were even older. Working in the Sea of Galilee, they found thirty pottery jars and five anchors from a sunken ship. Two of the 1,900-year-old pottery jars are now in the museum at Emory University. The trip by Ben-Dor and Beattie was made possible by contributions from the Emory University Research Foundation, the Lucius Littaur Foundation of New York, Harry Elsas of Atlanta, and Mr. and Mrs. Sidney Wien, who had been among the Atlantans killed in the crash at Orly, France, in June.[7]

Beattie painted for the *Journal* magazine his view of the sea floor littered with the beautiful remnants of the past. In 1962 he also gained wide recognition for a painting called "Georgia Nocturne." It is an interpretation of Stone Mountain by moonlight, in which ghostly figures on horseback move in procession beside the blue lake in which lonely granite formations are reflected. Shafts of light illuminate the lake, the rock strata, and the figures of Lee, Jefferson Davis, and "Stonewall" Jackson. "Georgia Nocturne" became the official painting of Stone Mountain Memorial Association.

Thousands of Atlantans and visitors had the opportunity to purchase lithographs of Beattie's impression of Stone Mountain, but many thousands more in the years to come would get a closer look at its face from the red cable cars put in service there late in the year. A Swiss company had built the cable car and its airlift to the mountaintop, and it seemed appropriate to ask Dr. August Lindt, Swiss ambassador to the United States, to be present at the opening ceremony. Governor Ernest Vandiver broke a bottle of Swiss wine over one of the cars, naming it the "Helvetia," and Ambassador Lindt broke a bottle of a famous Atlanta soft drink over the other car, christening it the "Georgia."

Mayor Allen also said that the mountain was the "foundation stone" of the New South because "it is the only thing Sherman didn't burn in the War Between the States, or that the Yankee carpetbaggers couldn't cart away from this section."

Journalists and dignitaries rode the cable cars earlier in the week and found it a thrilling, spectacular experience. "The closeness of the cliff side of the mountain is a view that is new to everyone but a few daredevil airplane pilots who have swept down for a quick look and then back up again," wrote one, "and never has the granite hunk seemed so large as it does from the cable car swinging gently under its 2,000 foot span of cable. Never has the steep side seemed so steep." Full service for average Atlanta citizens and visiting tourists was still some months ahead.

One Atlanta institution was able to announce proudly that in this year for the first time it had exceeded its goals. The United Appeal, created in 1958 by combining the fund-raising campaigns of the Red Cross and the sixty-nine charitable agencies making up the old Community Chest, went over its $3,857,124 target by more than $10,000—and the money was still coming in on November 16.

In previous years the total received had never quite reached the estimated needs: in 1950, 97 percent; in 1960, 93 percent; and in 1961, 94 percent. The preliminary 1962 figure was $3,867,826, or 100.37 percent of the target. To John Sibley, chairman of the United Appeal Board of Trustees, this meant that Atlanta was at last "beginning to measure up to its social responsibility." Harold Brockey led the campaign in which 30,000 Atlantans took part in various aspects of the fund-raising, and received for his "great quarterbacking" in the campaign an autographed football helmet, presented by Frank Malone, who would be chairman of the 1963 fund drive.

At Decatur First Methodist Church ninety-one-year-old Rev. Walter Scott Robison recited the poetry of Alexander Pope as he finally retired from the ministry after sixty-four years. "Walk slowly off," he said, "lest some livelier age comes titteringly on and shoves you from the stage." Born when Ulysses Grant was president, Robison was the son of a Confederate chaplain who served with the 15th Georgia Regiment. He became a minister in 1898, rode the circuit for his first eight years, and retired first in 1940. With so many young preachers going into the military, he soon came back to the ministry as a supply pastor, and for another fifteen years had served the burgeoning Decatur church as associate.

Even more venerable in years and more widely known was Mrs. S. R. Dull, who in December of 1962 was still busy autographing her famous cookbook *Southern Cooking* and answering fan mail "as heavy as a movie star's" from lovers of her turnip greens and fried chicken. Still busy after retiring in 1942 as editor of the food section in the *Journal Magazine*, on December 7, 1962, she celebrated her ninety-ninth birthday.

Another newspaper veteran, of lesser years but equal authority in her field, was Margaret Shannon, who was appointed Washington correspondent of the *Atlanta Journal*. A prize-winning reporter, editorial writer, columnist, and a specialist in political news, she succeeded Douglas Kiker, who resigned from the Washington staff to become director of information for the Peace Corps.

On the night of December 19 sixty-five-year-old battalion chief C. V. Stewart, the city's oldest employee and the state's oldest fireman, was honored at a banquet at the Ben Hill Fire Station. The only remaining member of the department who had served in the old days of horse-drawn engines, he was feted at a fireman-cooked meal attended by Vice-Mayor Sam Massell and a number of city officials. Massell called him "an inspiration to all firemen," and battalion chief A. T. Hornsby presented him with a check "from the men of the Fourth Battalion as a token of love and respect."

Ground was broken for the new State Archives building by Archivist Mary Givens Bryan, using a golden pick, on June 7, 1962. Governor Vandiver started the digging, but Mrs. Bryan took the pick from him and continued the job herself when Secretary of State Ben Fortson warned the governor that President Kennedy had recently sprained his sacroiliac while breaking ground using a short-handled pick. The old repository—Rhodes Memorial Hall—had become inadequate, with papers going back to colonial days subject to leaky roofs and wintry winds. This could not occur in the new building, which would rise sixteen stories above the street, with four floors underground, and eight stories vaulted, humidified, and fireproofed to provide ideal conditions for the preservation of old documents.

Though many Atlantans were concerned with preserving the memorabilia of the past, others were more concerned with the shape of the future— with such subjects as rapid transit, expressways, vocational education, tax equality, and economy in government. On the night of December 4 Governor-elect Carl Sanders told the Atlanta Chamber of Commerce, gathered at the Dinkler Plaza Hotel for its 103rd annual meeting, that the state would strongly cooperate with the chamber on such projects. Outgoing governor Ernest Vandiver also spoke to the chamber, and for his cooperation in the past he was presented a plaque from the organization of businessmen, commending him for "imagination, enthusiasm, and personal participation" in strengthening Georgia's economy. Atlanta's economy, specifically, showed an upturn in 1962, according to outgoing president Ben S. Gilmer, with gains in factory employment, construction, use of industrial electric power, check payments, and sales tax collections. Edward D. Smith, president of the First National Bank and chairman of the chamber's "Forward Atlanta" Committee, was elected to succeed Gilmer.

Atlanta's efforts to provide services for the blind—counseling, job training, and remunerative employment—took on new and hopeful impetus with the creation in late 1962 of Community Services for the Blind, Inc., created by a blue-ribbon panel of citizens appointed by the Community Council of the

Atlanta Area, Inc. It was a nonprofit agency whose mission was to serve the approximately 4,000 blind persons in the Atlanta area "regardless of race, color, or creed." According to reports, fewer than half of these were receiving any help at all, and many of them were victimized by "unscrupulous people mainly to collect money and give no worthwhile service in return."

The new organization—Community Services—would ultimately offer social caseworkers for counseling, group work and recreation, information and referral services, home management, daily living programs, mobility orientation and home training, plus a workshop that would include legal training and job placement.

A glimpse of future teaching methods—and future problems—came late in 1962 when the Fulton County and Atlanta school systems began teaching Spanish to the first four grades by television. Twice weekly over Atlanta station WETV, Senorita Anna Marie Aviles (Senora Goolsby in real life) presented a program in Spanish vocabulary and pronunciation that was designed to have students speaking fluent Spanish by the time they reached high school. It was a unique program, the pride and joy of local school authorities, and was supposedly the only one then operating in the United States. Youngsters also seemed to love it, reading with Senorita Aviles as she pronounced the words on the screen as if she were really there in the classroom with them.

In mid-December of 1962 the *Journal-Constitution Magazine* announced the scheduled passing of what was described as "Atlanta's Ugliest Landmark"—a reference to the "Great Black Web" of trackless trolley wires, strung from one end of town to the other, lacing building and utility poles together like a great ramshackle machine tied up with baling wire. According to the Atlanta Transit Company, all the wires from Oglethorpe to College Park and from the Chattahoochee to Decatur would be down by Christmas, 1963, and Atlanta would be traveling by diesel bus.

The wires disfigured the sky above the city "like the angry scrawls of a bad boy in a library book," but they were "a gold mine in the sky" to the transit company. Once taken down and rolled on reels—a mile of line to a reel, 560 reels in all—the solid copper cables would be worth more than a million dollars. It was the final end of the line for the electric trolley in Atlanta. Atlanta's last rail-borne electric-powered streetcar had made its final run on the morning of April 11, 1949, and now the rubber-tired electric buses were to be abandoned, too.

The weather in the late fall of 1962 was the most miserable to strike the city in a generation. On the morning of November 21 slow but steady rains deluged the city under more than two and one-half inches in a matter of hours, making travel difficult and dangerous in Atlanta's streets and leading to considerable flooding along Peachtree Creek. Two weeks later it was teeth-rattling cold rather than rain that drove Atlantans indoors and rendered them in large degree immobilized. On December 12, early in the morning, the town awoke to a five-degree temperature that left its plumbing popping, its automobiles with frozen radiators, and car batteries unable to move the frozen engines. The cold did not diminish for three days. For three hours early Thursday morning the temperature was down to one degree, the coldest registered in thirty-five years. The coldest place in the state during this period was Blairsville, with an unofficial reading of 9 degrees below zero on the morning of Thursday, December 14.

For many Atlantans one of the highlights of the year was recognition that came to one of Atlanta's most famous citizens on his seventy-fifth birthday. Roland Hayes, the Georgia-born son of former slaves, celebrated with a concert in Carnegie Hall, marking not only his birthday but also the fiftieth anniversary of his musical debut. In the *Journal* Frank Daniel wrote his recollections of Hayes:

Mr. Hayes' tenor voice brought him international fame, and this in the days when no American concert manager would handle a Negro under any conditions. A triumphant European tour which helped introduce that continent to spirituals resulted in successes in this country, including and especially in the South. . . .

As I recall Hayes' first concert was at the Wesley Memorial Church, later at the Municipal Auditorium. The audiences were both white and Negro.

One side of the middle aisle was for whites, the other side for Negroes— and Marian Anderson's frequent Atlanta concerts were also presented like that. . . .

With typical Southern prejudice, I was startled when I first heard him sing Schubert and Brahms in the timbres characteristic of the Negro voice, but the art behind the performance quickly banished any preconception I might have harbored that Teutonic music should be sung by German voices.

His programs usually included a group of spirituals and one of them, "The Crucifixion," was unforgettable with its recurrent line, "He never said a mummerlin' word."

I expect it was singers like Mr. Hayes and Miss Anderson, appearing during the 1920s and 1930s with such poise and such vocal skill, that pioneered the change of attitude toward Negroes in the minds of a large percentage of the public.

They pointed the way to desegregation, and I was much impressed when last fall another singer, Atlanta's Mattiwilda Dobbs, appeared at the Atlanta Auditorium singing to a charmed audience, with no sheep-and-goats division along the aisles.

Though Roland Hayes's triumphant concert took place far away in New York's Carnegie Hall, there were many events cultural in nature that brought out the best in Atlanta's singers, dancers, actors, and artists. Mid-May brought the ninth annual Atlanta Arts Festival at Piedmont Park. There was something for just about everybody—from nudes to landscapes, mobiles to bold abstract splashes. There was even a booth set up where the children could create their own works of art. The Wit's End Players presented a satirical review on the festival stage.

Another landmark event in the field of the arts in Atlanta took place a month later, when on the night of June 12 the old Buckhead Theater closed its doors after thirty-four years at its site on Roswell Road, where it splits from Peachtree. After undergoing a $100,000 renovation it reopened as the Capri, a first-run house with *El Cid* as its "premiere" picture. The closing of the old Buckhead stirred nostalgia among some Atlanta moviegoers. It had opened in 1928 as a vaudeville and film house, and some of the nation's most famed entertainers, Gloria Swanson and Kay Kyser among them, appeared there. When Atlanta's downtown theaters banned Mae West's *She Done Him Wrong* in 1933, the Buckhead grabbed it. When the owners, John Carter and his wife Ruth, took over in 1933, the Buckhead was no longer a first-run house, but they did pull off one coup. They signed Andy Griffith of *No Time For Sergeants* to his first stage appearance in the United States.

The Atlanta Art Association took on new life this year. James V. Carmichael, president of the association, announced that Dr. Wilhelmus B. Bryan, director emeritus of the Minneapolis School of Art, would take over as director of the Atlanta Art Association. "His main job in Atlanta for the next few years," said Carmichael, "will be 'bringing into being the new School of Art the association will erect as a memorial to its members who died last June in the Orly Air Crash.'"

In 1962 downtown remained the retail center of the city despite the opening of Lenox Square, and an immense crowd, estimated at more than 100,000, massed beneath Rich's Crystal Bridge on Thanksgiving night to see "the lighting of the great tree"—a sixty-five-foot northern white pine. Spectators were jammed along nearly half a mile of Forsyth Street to get a look at the tree and hear the biblical Christmas story told in word and song. With the tree lighting, the Christmas shopping season in Atlanta got under way in earnest.

Atlanta, which in this year had done so much for the arts, for the dancers and the vocalists and the musicians, received in turn its own Christmas gift from them. The headline on Pat Watters's article in the *Journal* on the last day of December read: "No Better Way to End a Year Than in Exhibit of Our Very Best." He said: "The Gala Performance, a Christmas gift to Atlanta by the Atlanta Civic Ballet, the Choral Guild of Atlanta and the Atlanta Pops Orchestra, filled the city auditorium to its topmost perches, and many times more would have come if there had been room for them." Significantly, he noted, seating was desegregated, decently and with dignity.

Watters used the occasion to appeal for new facilities:

It was a great night for Atlanta, with much meaning.

That it was free, and that so many people came, grown-up and child alike, who ordinarily can't afford such theater out of even middle-class budgets, and that so very many wanted to come gave it meaning. We need to make such entertainment more accessible, and quit roping it off in dollar-marked, fasionable-dress snobbishness and selfishness.

That the auditorium was its usual jumble in intrusive noises and neck-craning seating, with a crowd still unseated after the first number because of the vastness and ambiguity of the auditorium, and that parking lot and street traffic before and afterward were a nerve-wracking tangle gave it meaning. We need a center, with adequate parking, for the performing arts. We need it badly; we need it now.

OBITUARIES

Dr. David Marx, rabbi emeritus of The Temple of the Hebrew Benevolent Congregation and a foremost Atlanta citizen for well over half a century, died at his residence. The words of Rabbi Jacob Rothschild were: "David Marx would have been ninety years old in March. He came to this pulpit in 1895—just twenty-eight years after the congregation was founded. His life spanned almost the entire life-span of our Temple. Such continuity of dedicated service is almost without parallel in the history of our Reform movement." Zach Griffin Haygood, builder of the National Library Bindery in Buckhead, also died. The old English style of the bindery building strongly influenced the design of neighboring homes and businesses. Benjamin Joseph Massell, the South's foremost Jewish philanthropist, leading Atlanta builder, and outstanding religious and civic leader, died in September. His death came unexpectedly at the age of 76, and his funeral was one of the largest ever held in Atlanta. Ernest Rogers, writing for the *Atlanta Journal*, said: "Bill Hartsfield, when Mayor, called him a 'one-man boom.' Ivan Allen, the elder, referred to him as 'the creator of Atlanta's skyline.' Having built more than a thousand buildings in Our Town and having had a part in countless other real estate transactions, it may be truly said that he has left monuments to his foresight and enterprise in all parts of our community. . . . Mr. Massell's success story is in the American tradition. Born in Lithuania and brought to this country by his parents at the age of 2, he became a resident of Our Town at an early age. He attended old Boys High School and as a teen-ager became a wage earner through necessity rather than choice."

Philip H. Alston, 81, prominent Atlanta attorney and civic leader, was senior partner in the law firm Alston, Miller and Gaines. He had served as president of the Atlanta Chamber of Commerce and had held that office in the Atlanta Bar Association. He was on the board of Davison-Paxon and the C&S Bank. His memberships included the Piedmont Driving Club, the Nine O'Clocks, the Capital City Club, and the Commerce Club. He was a communicant of St. Luke's Church and survived his wife by only two months. Allen C. Anthony, 55, was a well-known radio and television personality and personnel director of station WAGA. He had served as master of ceremonies and producer of the popular radio series "Dr. I.Q." Mrs. Walter Scott Askew, 78, was a civic and cultural leader and widow of an investment banker. A graduate of Bessie Tift College, she worked on the Atlanta Better Films Committee and the Northside Library Association. She had served as both state and local regent of the Daughters of the American Colonists and was a member of the DAR. Judge Luke Arnold, 64, died of a heart attack on his last day as chief justice of the Atlanta Municipal Court. Judge Arnold attended Lumpkin Law School at the University of Georgia and entered the firm of Key, McClelland & McClelland. He became executive secretary to Mayor James L. Key when that gentleman was elected. Judge Arnold served a total of twenty-eight years in Atlanta's city government. He was a Mason, a Shriner, and a member of the First Baptist Church.

William Mungo Brownlee, 82, was the retired president of five U.S. parent bottling companies of Coca-Cola, head of thirty bottling plants, and retired president of the Coca-Cola Bottling Company of Canada. Prior to joining Coca-Cola, he had served as president of Cable Piano Company when that firm was responsible for bringing the concert series to Atlanta. He was active in Masonic work and was a member of Rotary, the Piedmont Driving Club, the Capital City Club, and the Homosassa Fishing Club. Lt. Lewis T. Bullard, 54, a detective on the Atlanta police force, was the son of George Bullard, former superintendent of detectives. His mother served as a police woman until her retirement several years ago.

Raimundo de Ovies at his death at 85 was dean emeritus of the Episcopal Cathedral of St. Philip. A native of Liverpool, England, he came to America at a very young age and received his theological training at the University of the South, Sewanee. He came to Atlanta in 1928 as rector of St. Philip's, having served as chaplain at the University of the South. "Under his leadership the splendid Cathedral of St. Philip was acquired and from the pulpit of the humble temporary wood shingle building his eloquence moved man to greater vision and his words of counsel gave comfort and strength to the discouraged, weak and fallen." Thus spoke Bishop Randolph Claiborne of one of the city's most influential citizens. Edward F. Danforth died at 70. Before his retirement, Colonel Danforth was sports editor of the *Atlanta Journal*. Sam A. Goldberg, 60, was chairman of the board of Allan-Grayson Realty, a member of The Temple, the Standard Club, B'nai B'rith, and the Atlanta Real Estate Board. He was closely associated throughout his life with Ben Massell, and some friends attributed Goldberg's death to grief over the loss of his friend, who died two days earlier.

Malcolm E. Grant, 56, was president of Plantation Pipeline Company and was widely active in Atlanta's civic affairs. A former board member of the Chamber of Commerce, he also served as director of the Metropolitan Atlanta YMCA, the Metropolitan Atlanta Community Services, and the Rotary Club. He was a member of Trinity Presbyterian Church, the Capital City Club, and Peachtree Golf Club. Scott Hudson, 92, was one of Atlanta's great sports figures. The son of a Kentucky horse-trainer, Hudson was graduated from Centre College and began his career immediately as a trainer and driver of trotters and pacers. He moved to Atlanta in 1906 and soon joined the Atlanta Athletic Club. By 1915 he was elected to the board of directors and became president in 1919. He retired in 1945. Hudson was neighbor to and closely identified with the development of two young golfers, Bobby Jones and Alexa Stirling. Beside being instrumental in the development of East Lake Country Club, Hudson was the developer of one of the finest resorts in this area, Highlands, North Carolina—the retreat of many Atlantans. A founder of the Homasassa Fishing Club, he was also a member of the Piedmont Driving Club and the Capital City Club. Stiles A. Martin, retired state news editor of the *Atlanta Constitution,* was an authority on Georgia history. He was a longtime member of Druid Hills Methodist Church, of which he was historian.

Dr. Wallace Rogers, 86, had been the associate pastor of First Methodist Church. He at one time was district superintendent of the LaGrange and Decatur-Oxford districts and had been pastor in many small Georgia towns. He was the father of newsman Ernest Rogers and was an outstanding ornithologist and photographer. His collection of bird photographs was considered one of the finest in the nation. Milton Dargan, Jr., was a member of the firm of Dargan, Whitington and Conner. Milton Dargan, Sr., came to Atlanta in the early 1890s while Milton, Jr., was a toddler, to set up a branch office for a succession of British insurance firms located in Manchester and Liverpool. The elder Dargan not only became an outstanding insurance executive, he was a leader in many civic fields. He was one of the founders of the Piedmont Driving Club and a pillar in All Saints Episcopal Church. Young Milton, as tall and prepossessing as his father, followed him in the insurance business, and the two of them helped make Atlanta the insurance headquarters of the South. Mrs. Rix Stafford, the former Bessie Shaw, was woman's editor emeritus of the *Atlanta Constitution* and known to her newspaper friends as "Miss Bessie." She was the first parent-teacher editor and participated in the formation of the Garden Club of Georgia. She was a member of the First Baptist Church, the Atlanta Art Association, and Peachtree Garden Club. George Sargent, 79, was brought to East Lake Club by Bobby Jones in the 1930s to be golf pro. A native of England, he worked in Yorkshire and Canada before coming to Atlanta. Sargent won many fine tournaments, including the U.S. Open, and was head of the Professional Golfers' Association for many years.

Others passing in 1962 included Joseph H. Allen, former city councilman, who died at 53; Clarence Ernest Biggers, thirty-five-year employee of the State Highway Department and senior road design engineer; David H. Broome, Sr., police lieutenant in DeKalb County; Don J. Coffee, Sr., 76, owner and operator of the Buckhead Typewriter Service; Mrs. Daniel D. Dominey, Sr., 59, wife of the president of Universal Life Insurance Company and an active member of the Cathedral of Christ the King; Eugene H. Ellenby, 84, retired real estate salesman; Clarence Knowles, a representative of James Talcott, Inc. Mrs. Hugh M. Lokey, Sr., widow of a distinguished physician, was the former Rebecca C. Hamilton. She was a communicant of St. Luke's Episcopal Church and a member of the 1908 History Class and the Colonial Dames. Alfred T. Navarre, retired professor of geology at Georgia Tech, was 68; M. E. Peabody, 90, was a Presbyterian minister who was trained at Richmond Seminary; Mrs. William L. Roberts, 84, was the former Carrie Lee Nichols. She was a charter member of the Whitfield County Historical Society, the DAR, the UDC, and DAC. Charles H. Sanders, retired English professor at Boys High School and Murphy High School, died at 70; Alvis M. Weatherly, 74, was an employee of Southern Railway for fifty-two years. W. Stuart Witham, retired businessman, steward of St. Mark's Methodist Church, and trustee of Young Harris and LaGrange Colleges, died at 73; Bernard Yoepp, southeastern service representative of Sears, died at 55.

Those who died in the Orly Airport crash of Atlanta art patrons included: Mrs. C. A. Adair of Montclair Drive, Mr. and Mrs. Tom Chris Allen of Tuxedo Road, Mrs. Henrietta C. Ayer of West Paces Ferry Road, Paul Barnett of Piedmont Avenue, Mrs. Ralph J. Barry of Arden Road, Mrs. E. W. Bartholomai of Lenox Road, Mrs. W. P. Bealer of Colonial Homes Drive, Mr. and Mrs. George Beattie of E. Pine Valley Road, Mrs. Frances Beers of Peachtree Road, Mrs. Marion T. Benson of Habersham Road, Mr. and Mrs. Randolph Berry of Manor Ridge Drive, Mrs. E. Milton Bevington of Valley Green Drive, Mr. and Mrs. Roy Bixler of Mason Woods Drive, Mrs. David C. Black of Paces Valley Road, Katherine Bleckley of Piedmont Avenue, Dr. and Mrs. Harry Boon of Bolling Road, Mr. and Mrs. Morris Brandon, Jr., of W. Paces Ferry Road, Mrs. Fred Brine and Dorothy Brine of Peachtree Way, Mr. and Mrs. Fred W. Bull, Ellen and Betsy Bull, of Westover Drive, Mrs. Mary Bull of Ponce de Leon Apartments, Mrs. Ezekiel S. Candler of Club Drive, Mr. and Mrs. William A. Cartledge of Maddox Drive, W. D. Cogland of Vera Street, Mr. and Mrs. Reuben Crimm of Old Ivy Road, Mrs. L. W. Dilts of Timber Valley Road, Paul Doassans of 31 Lakeview Avenue (the Air France representative in Atlanta), Mr. and Mrs. Saul Gerson of Carol Lane, Mr. and Mrs. E. B. Glenn of Vernon Road, Mrs. J. M. Henson of Chatham Road, Mr. and Mrs. Redfern Hollins of Moores Mill Road, Mrs. Ewing Humphries of Downwood Circle, Mr. and Mrs. C. Baxter Jones, Jr., of Tuxedo Road, Mr. and Mrs. Arnold Kay of Douglas Road, Mr. and Mrs. Thomas H. Lanier of Howell Mill Road, Mr. and Mrs. Thomas G. Little of E. Beechwood Drive, Mrs. Hinton Longino of Habersham Road, Louise Loomis of Fifteenth Street, Dr. and Mrs. Allen P. McDonald of Peachtree Road, Dr. and Mrs. Christopher J. McLoughlin of Hillside Drive, Ruth McMillan of Beverly Road, Mrs. William Merritt of Peachtree Battle Avenue, Mrs. Lawton Miller of Argonne Drive, Mrs. Roy Minier of Walker Terrace, Mrs. Robert Emmett Mitchell of Peachtree Street, Ruth Morris of Peachtree Street, Mrs. Anna Mulcahy of Peachtree Road, Mr. and Mrs. David J. Murphy of E. Wesley Road, Robert S. Newcomb of Ponce de Leon Apartments, Margaret Nutting of Piedmont Avenue, Mr. and Mrs. Del R. Paige of Howell Mill Road, Mrs. Harvey Payne of Camden Road, Mr. and Mrs. Robert Pegram of Arden Road, Mrs. P. H. Perkins, Jr., of Peachtree-Dunwoody Road, Homer S. Prater, Jr., of Peachtree Road, Mrs. Marion Pruitt of Argonne Drive, Mrs. Clifford N. Ragsdale of Peachtree Road, Mrs. William Richardson of Peachtree Circle, Mr. and Mrs. Roby Robinson of Biltmore Apartments, Mr. and Mrs. W. J. Rooke of Tuxedo Road, Mrs. Helen Seydel of Lakeland Drive, Mr. and Mrs. Charles A. Shaw of Castle Falls Drive, Mrs. R. K. Stow of Emory Drive, Mrs. M. D. Therrel of West Paces Ferry Road, Mrs. T. L. Tidmore of Sheridan Drive, Mrs. Paul (Margaret) Turner of Montgomery Ferry Drive, Mrs. Frank Virgin of Vernon Road, Mr. and Mrs. Sidney Wien and Joan of N. Stratford Road, Mrs. Rosalind Williams of Club Drive, Mrs. Lysle Williamson of Twenty-fifth Street, Mrs. Walter Wilson of Piedmont Road, Vasser Woolley of Techwood Drive, Mr. and Mrs. Sykes Young of Knollwood,

Those not from Atlanta: Mrs. Theodosia L. Barnett of Tampa, Florida, Mrs. Leslie Blair of Marietta, Georgia, Dolly Brooks of Griffin, Georgia, Mr. and Mrs. Morgan Cantey of West Point, Georgia, Mrs. James R. Cowan of Marietta, Georgia, Mr. and Mrs. Forrest Cumming of Griffin, Georgia, Douglas Davis of Hapeville and Paris, Mrs. William I. Hill of Montgomery, Alabama, Mrs. Mary Ansley Howland of Decatur, Georgia, Marghretta B. Luty of Ridley Park, Pennsylvania, Mrs. Frank McPherson of Montgomery, Alabama, Mr. and Mrs. Louis Patz of Elberton, Georgia, Mrs. L. O. Rickey of Winter Park, Florida, Mrs. William King Self of Marks, Mississippi, Mrs. Fred Sorrow of Duluth, Georgia, Mr. and Mrs. Robert Turner of Marshallville, Georgia.

NOTES

1. Harold H. Martin, *William B. Hartsfield, Mayor* (Athens: University of Georgia Press, 1978).

2. Ivan Allen and Paul Hemphill, *Mayor: Notes on the Sixties* (New York: Simon & Schuster, 1971).

3. Martin, *Hartsfield*.

4. Allen, *Mayor*.

5. Ibid.

6. Atlanta Music Club, Minutes, Atlanta Historical Society.

7. Immanuel Ben-Dor and George Beattie, "Churches Found on the Bottom of the Sea," *Atlanta Journal-Constitution Magazine*, Dec. 9, 1962.

G OING into his second year as mayor, Ivan Allen, Jr., was aware of certain changes in his own attitudes. In his first year in office he had come to know many of the Negro leaders and to respect their desire for equal treatment under the law for their people. He also appreciated their willingness to let the white community work out the problems, slowly if need be, and without violence. He had also come to respect the goals of some white Atlanta businessmen who were well aware that Atlanta could never become one of the great cities of the nation and of the world so long as black men and women and their children were held in a state of economic, political, and educational subservience. Yet there were many other Atlantans who were unwilling to give even the slightest concession to the blacks. They did not want to live in the same neighborhoods, eat in the same restaurants, work on the assembly lines, ride side by side on a bus, or sit together in the same theaters.

The polarization of these two competing elements of Atlanta's citizens was reflected in the events both pro- and antiblack that made up the troubled twelve months of 1963. In mid-March it was announced that the exclusive private Lovett School had refused to consider for admission the five-year-old son of integration leader Rev. Martin Luther King, Jr. The early reaction from the bishop of Atlanta, the Rt. Rev. Randolph R. Claiborne, was that Lovett was "subject to no ecclesiastical control or supervision, by the Diocese or by the Bishop."

For two and a half months the bishop and the trustees of Lovett, two-thirds of whom were Episcopalian, brooded over this matter. Then, on June 5, the bishop issued a statement announcing the result of their deliberations. The trustees, he said, "adopted a definite policy in which they acknowledged their allegiance to the principles for which the Episcopal Church stands, specifically that segregation on the sole basis of race is inconsistent with the Christian religion." The bishop went on to declare, "If the Lovett School remains in effect segregated, it can no longer be considered in any way related to the Episcopal Church." In response the school changed its charter to disavow any ties with the Episcopal church.

The practice of segregation which threatened to create a schism in the ranks of Atlanta's Episcopalians did not long prevail. By the beginning of the school year in 1966, Lovett's trustees had made the decision to follow the teachings of the church. Black students were admitted, and have been since, with the school making vigorous efforts to recruit black athletes.[1]

Atlanta's Episcopalians were not the only religious group to have problems growing out of racial attitudes. On Wednesday night, May 1, 1963, fourteen white and Negro theological students were turned away from the prayer meeting at the First Baptist Church.

The Georgia Baptist Hospital held the same views as did the First Baptist Church. It did not admit Negroes as patients. Nor, as Atlanta moved on into spring, did Crawford Long, Emory, Egleston, Jesse Parker Williams, Scottish Rite, Piedmont, Ponce de Leon, Doctors, and Fulton hospitals. At St. Joseph's Infirmary the story was different. For some time, said an official, the Roman Catholic hospital had been accepting Negroes as inpatients, though there had been no public announcement of this policy. The only other Atlanta hospitals to accept them, according to a report by the Atlanta Council on Human Relations, were Grady, DeKalb General, and the Free Cancer hospitals. County-owned Grady Hospital at the end of May announced that beginning in June it would accept its first Negro intern and two student chaplain interns.

In another area of race relations Atlanta's Catholics moved out ahead of Protestants. At the Cathedral of Christ the King, the Most Rev. Paul J. Hallinan, archbishop of Atlanta, ordained two young black priests who had attended school in Atlanta.

One of Atlanta's and the nation's largest and most powerful Negro churches by 1963 was reaching beyond the pulpit and the sanctuary to serve its people. The *Journal* recorded:

The Church Homes project, sponsored by Wheat Street Baptist Church, Atlanta's largest Negro church, is reportedly the nation's largest relocation housing development and the first sponsored by a church and by Negroes. The 521-apartment project is for persons displaced as a result of urban renewal and civic improvement activities. . . .

Among the organizations who assisted in launching the project were the Atlanta Urban League, who discussed the idea with Rev. Mr. Borders and trustees of the Wheat Street Church, and worked out details with the FHA, which is providing complete financing on the project, and the Atlanta Life Insurance Company, which loaned the church $450,000 to buy 22 acres from the Atlanta Housing Authority.

A local Negro contracting firm, Jett, Banks and Russell, entered the low bid of $2,355,000 for the first 280 units. The church believes this is the largest contract ever handled by a Negro firm in Georgia and possibly in the nation.

In many other areas, slowly and quietly, white Atlantans took the short steps forward that gave blacks hope that their goal of equal opportunity might at last be met. In 1962 nine black students were enrolled in Atlanta's high schools; in 1963 there were forty-four. Twenty-four Negroes were attending Catholic schools; eight Negroes were at Georgia Tech, four of them in their second year. The Atlanta Art School opened its doors to two Negroes in January, and in February the Smith-Hughes Vocational School quietly integrated. The Atlanta Art Association took in two Negroes as members; the Fulton County Medical Society calmly integrated, and so did Alcoholics Anonymous.

The city and the county also took steps to ease tensions. On April 2 sixteen Negroes were added to Atlanta's previously all-white fire department, to serve at old Station 16 at Marietta and McMillan streets, until a new Station 16 was completed at Simpson Road and Flowers Place. And on the same date it was announced that a black engineer trainee had been hired at the city incinerator. There were many Negroes in the Sanitary Department as day laborers, and 8 of 212 truck drivers were black, but Green as an engineering trainee had the highest job rating of any Negro in the department.

The racial relationships that made the big headlines, of course, were not the reports of progress but of failure to progress. Day after day, week after week, the stories were repeated in dreary monotony as angry young blacks and their white supporters picketed restaurants that refused to serve them and stores that refused to hire them as clerks. The list went on and on, with every restaurant and cafeteria in the downtown area having had its confrontation with the picketers. On May 8 Chief Herbert Jenkins was asked to speak before a meeting of the Hungry Club, an organization of black businessmen who usually dealt with the white power structure on a friendly basis. On this day they were angry. The Rev. Martin Luther King, Sr., charged Jenkins's police with brutality in handling the sit-in demonstrators. And, he added, his people resented being called "nigger" and "boy" by the police.

The ninety or so blacks and whites assembled broke into loud applause. When it died down Jenkins answered good naturedly but seriously, "We're getting a new bunch of police officers who are starting their training next week." Then addressing Dr. King, he asked: "Can I depend on you coming up there and giving a 30-minute lecture on race relations?" He could, indeed, said Dr. King.

This meeting was a friendly interlude in what proved to be a continuing racial conflict in the streets. On May 24 seven persons, including a white minister, were arrested for trespassing when they refused to leave the Ship Ahoy Restaurant on Luckie Street. Two of the seven were black college students from Clark College and Morehouse, and four were white students from Emory, two of them female. These arrests brought to seventy-eight the number arrested since the sit-ins had resumed in downtown Atlanta on April 27.

The Rev. B. Ashton Jones was not discouraged by his arrest at the Ship Ahoy. Two weeks later he was seized bodily by restaurant owner Charlie Leb and forcibly ejected from Leb's restaurant at Forsyth and Luckie streets while a sizable crowd of passers-by looked on. Three times, when Leb grabbed Jones and tried to lead him out of the restaurant, Jones dropped to the floor. Finally, Leb grabbed the minister by the legs and dragged him across the floor, through a door, and out onto the sidewalk, where a policeman finally arrested him. The charge this time was more serious than trespass. He was charged with disorderly conduct—disturbance. Three of the four black students who entered with Jones and whom he tried to lead in song until Leb grabbed him, left when asked to do so, and no charges were filed against them. Another student, who refused to leave when asked to do so, was charged with violating the state antitrespass law. A third demonstrator was arrested and charged with trespass at Davis Fine Foods, when he joined a cafeteria line and refused to leave. Four others sat in at a Krystal at 32 Marietta Street but left after the manager called in a policeman, who asked them to go.

Up to this point white passers-by had stopped to look when demonstrators and police were in confrontation and had moved on quietly when ordered to do so. On the next day, Friday, June 6, the pattern changed. Some two hundred whites gathered in front of the S&W Cafeteria on Peachtree when eight demonstrators, four black and four white, sought to enter there, and another fifty or so whites gathered at Leb's. There they snarled, shouted, and heckled the demonstrators until the police arrived to arrest three of them, two of whom had to be carried bodily out the door. None of the heckling onlookers was arrested, but they were warned by police that it was illegal for them as well as for the demonstrators to congregate on the sidewalk so as to block doors.

So far, action on both sides had consisted mainly of shouting and occasionally shoving, but no blood had been spilled. As those guarding the restaurants grew more violent, the black demonstrators and their white supporters grew more passive. On Monday, June 17, fourteen Negro and white students were arrested and charged with trespass, offering only passive resistance. Again the scene was Leb's. The students fell to the pavement, locked arms, and blocked the entrance. When owner Charlie Leb asked them to move, they refused, and Leb employees tried to remove them by force. They punched and shoved the students, who continued to lie on the ground. In the process one student, a white girl, suffered a bloody nose and charged later that she was kicked and stomped, and another student was cut about the face. While this was going on, several hundred people gathered, shouting insults at the demonstrators, mainly at the five white men and the three white women among them. As tension mounted the police arrived and ordered the students to leave. When they did not, they were picked up bodily or dragged to the patrol wagon.

This "lie-in" was a variation of another tactic the protestors had begun to employ—the "hit and run" demonstration. Another small group had appeared first at the Krystal on Marietta Street, then Morrison's on Forsyth, and finally at Leb's. They left each place when the police ordered them to move on.

The degree to which the sit-ins were embarrassing Atlanta citizens, particularly the restaurant owners, was indicated by the fact that though many demonstrators had been arrested, charged, and bound over to state courts on trespass charges, none had been tried, for no restaurant owner so far had gone to court to press charges. Nor would there be any trials in the future, according to Fulton County Criminal Court solicitor John I. Kelley, unless the property owner was willing to make the complaint, rather than depending on the arresting officer. The property owners' reluctance, Solicitor Kelley intimated, seemed to stem from Supreme Court decisions, which on May 20 had struck down sit-in convictions in other states when it was argued by demonstrators' attorneys that the convictions were based on discriminatory laws.

On the day after the fracas at Leb's, an angry middle-sized white man took the law in his own hands. He stabbed a fifteen-year old Negro demonstrator who, along with another Negro and two whites, was trying to get service at Morrison's on Whitehall Street. It was the first use of a weapon since the demonstrations had begun in April, and the wound was not serious.

Earlier, on June 10, Julius Samstein, a white demonstrator, reported when he had attempted to enter Leb's he had been "manhandled" by a tall Bible-quoting white man who told Samstein he was being "obedient to Communism rather than Christianity." He grabbed Samstein by the throat and pushed him across the sidewalk in front of the restaurant, saying, "I've got Jesus in my heart and you ain't coming in here."

Another deeply religious white man found that his beliefs gave him a profound interest in peaceful integration—and in carrying out the belief, he discovered that racial discrimination was not an attribute of whites only. John Kermit Holland, a tall, gray-eyed man and former government employee turned voluntary missionary in his retirement years, sought to convey his philosophy by eating in black restaurants. Two of them—Paschal Brothers on Hunter Street and Henry's Cafe on Auburn Avenue, served him "graciously and without question." Others either ignored him until he got up and walked out, or served him and then told him not to come back again.

From the beginning of the sit-ins to the final confrontation that began in mid-summer, Mayor Ivan Allen kept a finger on the pulse of the town. His greatest concern was what might happen on June 12 when the city's swimming pools would open on a desegregated basis for the first time. It was no longer a matter of choice. In the fall of 1962 a federal judge had ordered the pools desegregated, after the city and Negro plaintiffs had signed a consent decree. Negroes went swimming at five previously all-white swimming pools as for the first time in the city's history the pools were opened to all its citizens. The only untoward event was a fistfight.

Shortly after the swimming pool landmark there was another, more important step. On June 23 a group of Atlanta restaurants, tired of fighting what seemed to be inevitable, opened their doors to blacks as well as whites. It was done without fanfare, without public announcement, and Edward Negri of Herren's on Luckie Street was the only restaurant owner who would comment on the results. He said that what restaurant owners had feared most, loss of business if blacks were admitted, had not come to pass. Negri honestly believed in blacks' right to eat where they pleased and in the restaurant's obligation to serve them, and he expressed these views. As a result, his place was picketed by whites protesting integration, and this did cost him some business. But the decision to serve blacks did not. A few white customers said they would not return, but many others said they would not dream of leaving Herren's—and some new customers said they came because they believed as did Negri, that "we've got two nations of people here, living on the same soil, and we've got to learn to get along together."

Negri had been "getting along" in the restaurant business in Atlanta since he was five years old. His parents, natives of Italy, came here then, and his father was maître d'hôtel at the Biltmore Hotel. Later, he was manager of the Piedmont Driving Club. In 1940 he became sole owner of Herren's, and passed the business on to his son, Ed.

The peaceful integration of the schools, the swimming pools, and more Atlanta restaurants smoothed in some degree the rocky path that Mayor Ivan Allen had been treading. However, the biggest challenge to his personal convictions lay ahead. Early in July of 1963 President John F. Kennedy began to push for a civil rights bill that would include a very strong public accommodations section. It would require that any private business involved, even remotely, in interstate commerce be forced to open its doors to anyone, regardless of color. The considerable racial progress that had been made in Atlanta so far had given the city and the mayor a liberal image. Atlanta had become a social oasis in a southern Sahara.

Word reached the mayor through Morris Abram that President Kennedy wanted him to come to Washington and speak before the appropriate committee in support of the bill. Allen told Abrams that he was in a political dilemma. Most of his powerful political friends and supporters, including the so-called liberals, were against the bill. He himself had not yet made up his mind about the bill. His testimony, he felt, would not have great influence on its passage, yet he believed that his support of it would cause him to be beaten in the race for mayor in 1965.

Allen asked Abrams to go back to Washington and tell the president how he felt. "Then," he added, "if he calls on me and still wants me to do it, if he recognized that I can't be re-elected and that my testimony isn't going to pass the bill, then I'll go." Soon after Abrams returned to Washington, the White House was on the phone to City Hall. Allen remembers the president's clipped Cape Cod voice: "You are right," he said. "Your testimony alone is not going to pass the bill. But I don't think your testimony will defeat you. I think there will be sufficient changes in the country by 1965 to where it not only will not defeat you, it will help you get re-elected."

So, still dubious and concerned, Allen went to Washington. With the help of Bill Howland, *Time-Life* reporter in Atlanta, Allen prepared his testimony. The thrust of it was that the public accommodations bill should be passed because desegregation would proceed no further on a voluntary basis, even in a city as solidly progressive as Atlanta.

The heart of his argument was that an American's citizenship could not be changed merely as a matter of convenience. If citizens could go into a bank to deposit money or borrow money, into a department store to buy a suit, into a supermarket to buy food, then how could they be turned away when they sought to register at a hotel or eat in a restaurant?

Up to the last moment Allen was worried about his trip. In Atlanta he confided in very few of his business friends, knowing how they felt and that they would try to dissuade him. But two people whose opinions he valued above all others, his wife Louise and Robert Woodruff, did urge him on.

Curiously, some of the black people whom Allen's testimony was designed to serve felt that he should not go. The day before he was to leave he called together twenty-four of Atlanta's top Negro leaders at a meeting at the Negro YMCA on Butler Street. Among them were men from whom Allen had learned much and whom he respected greatly—Martin Luther King, Sr., William Holmes Borders, Rufus Clement, Jesse Hill, Jr., A. T. Walden, and Benjamin Mays—men to whom Allen, and Hartsfield before him, had turned in times of crisis. He read his testimony aloud to them, and they were highly pleased. But a straw vote showed that only four or five out of the twenty-four believed he should go. Borders and Mays and King, Sr., wanted him to go. Those who disagreed felt that they did not want Allen sacrificed at the next election for testimony that was not necessarily going to pass the bill.

Allen was not sacrificed. He won handily in the 1965 election. And in 1964 the Civil Rights Act was passed. His testimony, presented with eloquence and conviction, may or may not have had a deciding influence—but his defense of his views under sharp attack from segregationist Senator Strom Thurmond drew high praise nationally. It began in the Senate Committee Room when Chairman John Pastore told him, "When a man like you [meaning a southerner] comes before this committee and states his story in such forthright manner, with such courage, I am proud to be here to listen to you, sir." Another senator, after Allen's testimony, said he "felt like the Senate had been visited by a man of quiet courage this morning." The *New York Times* in an editorial said, "On rare occasions the oratorical fog on Capitol Hill is pierced by a voice resonant with courage and dignity." Other northern and eastern newspapers joined in the praise.

In Atlanta and Georgia the reception was different. The *Albany Herald* criticized his "slick political moralizing," and the *Augusta Chronicle* said he had spoken for a bill "that would shackle private enterprise with one of the most restrictive burdens ever conceived in our free society."

His longtime friends on the *Constitution* took a middle ground. They could not join with him in supporting the bill, but they could praise him for standing courageously for what he believed in, and they reprinted the *New York Times* editorial. Personal reactions were angrier and more bitter. Vicious telegrams and letters poured in, but they were more than matched, 165 to 90, by letters from Negroes and the liberal community that were high in his praise. Gradually his business friends, who on the golf course and at the clubs had fallen silent at his approach, began to unbend a little. "Perhaps Ivan was right," they seemed to be saying. Mayor Emeritus Hartsfield said so, and so did Richard H. Rich. Gradually the hate mail dropped off to 35 percent—which Allen came to believe was "the percentage of haters we will always have to live with in the South."

Not long after his testimony and the public reaction to it Allen began to realize that the image of Atlanta and its mayor was brighter than it had been before, and instead of the Senate testimony's being an albatross around his neck, it became, as President Kennedy had predicted, a medal. In the 1965 campaign he carried a green leather-bound volume of the text of his testimony when he spoke before black audiences and he would read from it. His stand bound the black vote closer to him. The desegregation of hotels and restaurants he had urged had taken place quietly, and businessmen now looked upon him with approval.

More significant than this victory, though, was the change that had come over Ivan Allen in a personal way after his trip to Washington to testify. Up to that time his liberalism in racial matters, he said, "had been based in large degree on pragmatism." It was simply good business for Atlanta to be an open city—a "City Too Busy to Hate." His later feelings were based on belief that a city owes its services to all its citizens, that it must strive to raise the level of its poorest citizens and to get them off the relief rolls.

"I have finally crossed over and made my commitment on a purely personal basis," he wrote in *Mayor—Notes on the Sixties*. "And I think I took some of my friends with me."

The random hit-or miss sit-ins of 1961, 1962, and early 1963 were directed in the main against Atlanta restaurants and hotels that refused to serve Negroes. A vast network of behind-the-scenes activity had organized the students who were participating in the sit-in demonstrations. The headquarters of those involved was the Atlanta University Center and an organization called SNCC (Student Non-Violent Coordinating Committee), led by many active young blacks including Julian Bond.

All high school and university students interested in participating in the desegregation attempts at lunch counters, restaurants, cafeterias, and department store tearooms met together in groups to participate according to their particular interests and talents. Those people who felt they could not stand the verbal and sometimes physical abuse that would be directed at them could be involved, but at a level they could handle. Those who felt that prayer was the only safe and sure route were organized into prayer bands whose job it was to keep the other members spiritually fed and undergirded.[2]

In July, 1963, five Atlanta civil rights organizations reactivated the once-dominant Adult-Student Liaison Committee—its purpose to move against those Atlanta business houses that did not hire Negroes except in the most menial jobs. At a mass meeting on July 8, five hundred Negro leaders declared that there would be 5,000 new jobs for Negroes in Atlanta if discrimination in employment ended. In the future, they said, the desegregation movement would concentrate on this feature.

This revived group would be made up in considerable degree of adults, and demonstrations would be directed against such places as liquor stores and other small stores in black neighborhoods that had been hiring only white clerks. The big downtown stores and the public utilities also practiced discrimination in hiring, according to Rev. H. L. Bearden, general chairman of the Adult-Student Liaison Committee, and they too would come under scrutiny and, if necessary, be boycotted.

Myriad activities other than race concerned a growing, upward-surging Atlanta in 1963. In April, Mayor Allen announced happily that Atlanta would immediately begin construction of a runway parallel to the main runway at Atlanta airport. This would be able to handle planes carrying the heavy fuel loads needed for international flights and would double the acceptance rate for aircraft that had been stacking up over the city at peak hours. No tax funds would be used in constructing the new facilities, the mayor said. Revenue from the airport itself, based on the increased business generated by the new runways, would retire the revenue certificates.

With the new runway still in the planning stage, the new terminal building celebrated its second birthday without fanfare but with 10,000 persons passing through the still sparkling building on May 3. In 1962 a total of 4,109,549 passengers had used the facilities, making the Atlanta airport the fifth-busiest passenger airport in the nation. During the peak noon and 5:00 P.M. periods it was said to be the busiest in the world. Ten thousand employees now served the airport, for an annual payroll of $50 million, making the airport the second largest employer next to Lockheed in the Atlanta area.

After years of planning and sporadic fund-raising, 100,000 citizens of East Point and Hapeville, the Tri-Cities area, finally got a hospital of their own. The *Journal* explained:

The hospital, located on East Cleveland Avenue, resulted from an intensive fund-raising campaign in the Tri-City area. Local citizens raised $1,270,000. . . .

The [Tri-City Hospital] authority was created in 1956 jointly by the governing bodies of the cities of East Point, College Park and Hapeville to study and plan for construction of the hospital. It is the outgrowth of three previous authorities, the first of which was created in 1952. The authority at first planned only a 100-bed hospital, but then upped the size to 150 beds when a study revealed this was the minimum need for the South Fulton area. Officials said the hospital will be operated on a nonprofit basis with surplus poured back into future expansion. It will be a general community-type hospital with rates for private patients comparable with neighboring hospitals. Indigent patients will also be accepted and compensated for by the Fulton-

DeKalb Hospital Authority at a rate now being paid to Grady Hospital for performing identical services. . . .

The facility, with one of the most modern surgical suites in the nation, was financed by state and county funds and a federal Hill-Burton grant, totaling $1,271,925. Revenue bonds in the amount of $500,000 were also issued and sold.

Despite the rush to suburban retailing in 1963, Davison's downtown department store got a multimillion-dollar floor-by-floor refurbishing, and a new 700-car parking garage would be built, covering the entire block back of the store, bounded by Carnegie Way, Cone, Williams and Fairlie streets. W. W. Dreyfoos, president of Davison's, said the modernization program would include high-speed elevators, special lighting effects, and architectural designs through the store's 588,000-square-foot structure that would dramatize its beauty—particularly the first floor, with its 35-foot ceilings. Davison's already had a suburban store at Lenox Square and was considering three other locations. The downtown location on Peachtree Street was leased from Emory University and a new thirty-year lease was negotiated with Emory. Davison's first opened its doors in Atlanta in 1891 and since 1925 had been a division of R. H. Macy and Company, Inc., of New York.

While Davison's was extending the lease on its downtown store, another venerable Atlanta institution was calling it quits. Jacobs Drug Store No. 1, a Five Points institution since 1879, announced that it had not renewed its lease on its Peachtree-Marietta Street corner and would close its doors on June 1. It was on this site, though not in the same building, that in 1886 the first glass of Coca-Cola was served to a customer. Though the downtown store was closing, the firm would still be operating eighteen drugstores in the Atlanta area.

"We had to move," said Addison Smith. "The move of drugstores is to the suburbs. We advertise things in the paper that we just can't carry in a downtown store. For instance, our newest stores contain 10,000 square feet, the downtown store at Five Points contains 1,000." Smith agreed that the move marked for Jacobs, and many another downtown business, the end of an era, an era that saw Atlanta grow from a small town to a metropolis of more than a million people.

Atlanta's surging growth to a population of a million had its effect on the city's public golf courses. In the ten years from 1953 to 1963, paid rounds had increased from 178,826 to 247,605 on the city's six city courses, and City Parks Department manager George Simons was pushing for the construction of another eighteen-hole course. A new course seemed sorely needed, for Candler Park, on which 47,747 paying golfers played in 1962, lay in the path of an oncoming expressway and would have to be closed. Despite the huge increase in the number of paying players, Atlanta was losing money in its efforts to keep the courses in top condition. It had put $260,000 directly into the operation of its six courses in 1961 and faced a deficit of $54,360.

In July DeKalb Federal Savings and Loan became the fifty-seventh federally insured financial institution to be robbed in two and a half years. A total of $622,021 had been reported taken and arrests had been made in only twenty-seven cases. Stirred to action perhaps by this wave of robberies, the state decided that not only Atlanta but all of Georgia needed to increase the knowledge and effectiveness of its police. Therefore, with Governor Carl Sanders providing the money from surplus funds, work moved forward on the construction of a $550,000 police training facility.

A forty-five-acre tract of land on Confederate Avenue next to the Department of Public Safety was chosen because it was already owned by the state and because its proximity to Atlanta gave it accessibility to specialized teaching talent and to specialized supplies. The building would include sleeping quarters for seventy-six men, a minimum of three classrooms, and full training facilities for use by a staff of six to ten.

To most Atlantans, robbery and murder were tragic events that happened only to other people, in other parts of town. They flared in the headlines for a day and then were forgotten by all except their victims. Far more frequent and far more distressing to whole neighborhoods at once were the torrential rains that in this cloud-heavy year buried large areas of the town under flood waters.

At dawn on April 30 Woodward Way, again in 1963 as in 1962, was deep under water. The road, the front yards, even porches that had not been raised since the floods of the year before, were drowned under the rushing waters of Peachtree Creek, East Indian Creek, and Nancy Creek. Civil Defense Reserve units from Marietta, Red Oak, Forest Park, and elsewhere launched boats on flooded Peachtree Battle Avenue and Peachtree Battle Circle, Bohler Road, and Woodward Way, to bring an estimated fifty families out of the path of the flood. Nancy Creek-siders in Decatur were flooded and many streets collapsed there, as in Atlanta, but danger was greatest in flooded basements. When the water had receded, however, and the damage had been assessed, it was somewhat less than the $500,000 that had been predicted.

In certain low-lying areas the floods in the long run had a beneficial effect, for they stirred the city to action. For example, the heavy rains falling in the Buttermilk Bottom area made it necessary to move thirty families from flood-plagued Chestnut Way and Butler Street NE. Half of these, at least, would be moved to seventeen units in city-owned urban renewal projects, while the city hunted housing for the others.

The flooding of residential areas seemed to stir the city's leaders to take action in projects long needed but delayed. It was lack of adequate sewer lines and drainage ditches in Buttermilk Bottom that had led to the flooded homes, mud-stained clothing, spoiled food, and dangerous sanitary conditions there.

Therefore the city decided to build an $800,000 sewer line from Piedmont Park to just south of Butler Street.

In contrast Atlanta in this spring of 1963 achieved an educational record of which it could be proud. Commencement exercises at the Atlanta public school system's twenty-three regular high schools would begin graduation exercises on May 22 and continue through the first week in June. The 4,132 graduates would be the greatest number in Atlanta's history, 600 more than had graduated in 1962. The biggest classes would be Washington High School with 385 graduates; Henry Grady was the second largest class with 288 seniors. Atlanta's growing school population was now about to exceed its classrooms.

There were more than 77,000 students in 114 elementary schools and more than 32,000 in high schools. An additional 8,000 attended vocational schools or schools for handicapped children. Of Atlanta's twenty-three high schools, seventeen were predominantly white and six were Negro. Nine previously all-white schools now had some Negro students.

DeKalb County, where voters had recently approved a $12 million school building program, had the second largest high school graduating class, with 1,900 expected to receive diplomas. Fulton County schools ranked third, with 1,091 expected to graduate. Graduates statewide numbered 35,057, slightly down from the record high of 1961.

In the spring it was announced that Trinity School, a 200-student private elementary school of the Presbyterian church, had accepted a Negro child for enrollment in the first grade. The six-year-old child, a girl, had completed the required admission tests, met the standards of the school, and was accepted in a routine manner.

The Westminster School, under the direction of Dr. William L. Pressly, was the first non-church-related private school to accept a black child; in 1965 the board of trustees voted to open the school to students of all races.

On June 6 the Coca-Cola Company announced that it had just turned out its four-billionth gallon of syrup—enough, when mixed, to fill 512 billion bottles of Coke. It had taken seventy-seven years to turn out this amount. The first billion gallons had taken fifty-eight years to make and market, the second billion took nine years, the third billion took six years, and the fourth billion was sold in four years. Lee Talley, chairman of the board, Paul Austin, president, and John Staton, vice-president of manufacturing, had themselves photographed smiling happily as Staton handed the four-billionth gallon jug to Talley.

Early in July a downtown landmark changed hands when the ten-story Grant Building on Walton Street between Broad and Forsyth was sold to the Standard Federal Savings and Loan Association. The price was thought to be $1.2 million.

The building had been constructed in 1898 on a site already rich in history. On this spot had been built the first St. Luke's Episcopal Church, and the funeral of Gen. Leonidas Polk, Episcopal bishop of Louisiana, who was killed at Kennesaw Mountain in 1864, was held there. The church building withstood the bombardment that summer but was destroyed when Sherman burned Atlanta later that year. After the war Capt. William D. Grant played a prominent part in the rebuilding of Atlanta, and he and his son, John W. Grant, erected the Grant Building on the Walton Street site. It was originally called the Prudential Building and was one of the city's first steel-framed buildings.

The Grant Building sale came at a significant time in the history of the title insurance business in Atlanta. The voluminous title records, some of them going back to 1825, were transferred at the end of March from the Atlanta Title Insurance Company's old building at Pryor Street and Auburn Avenue to new and safer quarters in the company's new headquarters, the Title Building at Pryor and Decatur streets. Pearce Matthews remembered dramatic scenes as he worked with families in such cases as these: "We have seen husbands and wives cry and quarrel as old homes went and new homes were acquired. . . . We have seen people sit at our desks with flushed cheeks and glistening eyes as they accepted fabulous prices for property as big money flowed south in the national urge to own property in Atlanta."

Pearce Matthews was Lawyers Title Corporation's first Georgia manager, and he was elected a vice-president in 1943 when the national firm acquired ownership of Atlanta Title and Trust Company.

Matthews, his son John, and their associates had closed title deals for some of the largest and most important real estate transactions not only in Atlanta, but in Georgia. Included were most of the large apartment complexes, hotels, office buildings, and bank buildings erected in Atlanta in the past twenty years. Examples were the W&A Railroad right-of-way for the state, to determine if Georgia had clear title to railroad air rights, and sale of the 70,000 acre farm of the late Henry Ford in Bryan and Chatham counties, which was bought by the International Paper Company. For the simultaneous closing of sales and loans on fifty Atlanta apartment houses, Lawyers Title and Draper-Owens, the realty brokers, received national awards.

One Atlanta firm made up of a father and his two sons had grown steadily over the years and had reached landmarks in 1963. George W. West, "a tall silver-haired man with the look and bearing of a senator," according to George Erwin, shared with his sons, George Jr. and Charles, and Herbert West, a nephew, the management of not one but three successful companies. The elder West was chairman of the board of all three: the West Lumber Company, founded by his father J. J. West in 1887; the First Federal Savings and Loan Association of Atlanta, which George, Sr., founded, and Home Owners Co., a real estate firm organized after World War II. George West, Jr., was president of First Federal; Charles West was president of West Lumber Company; and Herbert West was president of Home Owners Company.

The lumber company had only eight or ten employees at the start. By

1963 they had increased to 350, and the company was selling "cash and carry" building materials at fourteen places in three states—five of them in the Atlanta area.

First Federal Savings and Loan opened in the Healey Building in 1924, with original assets of $1,436. In 1963 its assets were $66 million, its offices were overcrowded, and a new and modern seventeen-story building was being erected at the southeast corner of Marietta and Forsyth streets, in the heart of downtown. The new building would occupy the site of the old Ivan Allen–Marshall Building, an ornate structure built in 1876. Before it was demolished it was the oldest "tall building"—three stories—in the area, and it contained the late President Woodrow Wilson's first law office.

Besides holding many high offices in the national savings and loan organization, George West had served his city long and well. He was president of the Atlanta Chamber of Commerce in 1929, served on the board of the U.S. Chamber for sixteen years, and was active in the first Forward Atlanta Campaign, which brought much new business to Atlanta in the days before the Depression.

Not all Atlanta's old firms kept their identity in this year of economic shift and change. In mid-April it was announced that Foote and Davies, Atlanta's seventy-three-year old printer of books, magazines, and catalogues, was being bought by the New York firm that published *McCall's* magazine. Plans to merge were announced by Herbert R. Mays, president of McCall Corporation, and Albert I. Love, president of Foote and Davies, at a meeting of the Foote and Davies directors. Total money involved in a transfer of stock was said to be $6.4 million.

Not a sale, but national honors came to an Atlanta magazine. The National Headliners Club, comprised of leaders in all fields of news dissemination, had awarded the *Atlanta Journal-Constitution Sunday Magazine* a Special Headliner Citation. The magazine, edited by George Hatcher, was honored for its Golden Anniversary issue, which included outstanding pictures and stories from the magazine's fifty-year history. Angus Perkerson, editor of the magazine for many of these years, was also a Headliner award winner for "general excellence in editing a locally produced Sunday magazine." The 1962 anniversary edition, which Hatcher produced, had contained bylines of famous authors published by Perkerson. They included Margaret Mitchell, Will Rogers, Ward Greene, William Seabrook, and Don Marquis.

Two other Atlanta journalists received Headliner awards. They were *Newsweek* magazine's Atlanta bureau chief Joseph Cumming, Jr., and staffer Karl Fleming for the contributions to *Newsweek's* article "The Sound and the Fury," written by national affairs editor Peter Goldman, describing the Oxford, Mississippi, race riots.

Three Atlantans were presented Brotherhood Awards by the Atlanta Chapter of the National Conference of Christians and Jews—an indication that in this sometimes troubled area of race relations Atlanta was in truth a city of tolerance and understanding. Those honored were Richard H. Rich, chairman of the board of Rich's, Inc.; Edgar J. Forio, senior vice-president of the Coca-Cola Company; and John A. Sibley, honorary chairman of the board of directors of the Trust Company of Georgia. Several hundred Atlantans attended the black-tie dinner to hear Dr. Herman L. Turner present the award to the three "for distinguished service in the field of human rights and brotherhood."

Considerable concern for his fellow men and women was shown by New York philanthropist Charles Anderson Dana, whose gift of $350,000 to Agnes Scott College was the largest ever received by that institution from a living donor. The record gift up to 1963 was $4.25 million from the will of Mrs. Frances Winship Walters in 1954. Dana's gift would enable Agnes Scott to proceed with the construction of a $900,000 Fine Arts Building, said Dr. Wallace M. Alston, president of the college. Dana, an eighty-two-year old retired lawyer and industrialist, had no known connection with Agnes Scott, said Dr. Alston. "He's a new friend." The gift came as part of the college's seventy-fifth anniversary development campaign that sought to raise $10.5 million by 1964.

A learning institution of another sort—Georgia Baptist Hospital—received a towering new thirteen-story dormitory for student nurses in 1963. The Warren P. and Ava F. Sewell Foundation donated $500,000 to help finance the cost of construction. To Edwin Peel, administrator of the hospital, "the difference between this new dormitory and our old facilities is about like the difference between daylight and dark. Our students were housed in three different old buildings which were very, very crowded." The new dormitory cost $2.75 million and housed 371 students but had facilities to accommodate 502. Enrollment would be increased gradually to that point.

In mid-June the Georgia Hall of Fame announced that Governor Carl Sanders had allocated funds to erect a memorial in honor of Georgians who fought in the Battle of Kennesaw Mountain.

Two other Kennesaw "relics," one a locomotive, the other an ancient hotel, were much in the news in the spring of 1963. On April 12 Governor Sanders rode the "General," which had hauled supplies to the troops around Kennesaw and brought the wounded out, to the historic old Lacey Hotel in Kennesaw, where the train crew had stopped for breakfast on April 12, 1862. This was the date on which James J. Andrews, a Union spy, and nineteen men in civilian clothes who had boarded the train in Marietta seized the "General." Their idea was to shorten the war by tearing up the rail line between Atlanta and Chattanooga, but the attempt ended in failure when the "General" ran out of steam near Graysville and the raiders abandoned her and fled into the woods. All were captured. Eight of them, including Andrews, were hanged in Atlanta in June. Eight others were jailed but escaped from prison and made their way back to Union lines, and four were pardoned. In time, all were given the Congressional Medal of Honor, the first time it was ever awarded.

As for the "General," many a mile of iron track was to flow under its steam-driven wheels in the years to come. It was repaired and put back into service. In 1895 it had steamed into Atlanta to go on display at the Cotton States and International Exposition, and not long thereafter it was put on a siding at Vinings, destined for the scrapheap. But the old Nashville, Chattanooga and St. Louis Railroad decided to restore the engine and put it on display. And on display it stood for years, in the L&N station at Chattanooga, as a museum piece. Then in 1961 it was pulled out, completely overhauled, and sent on a two-year tour of most of the states east of the Mississippi and a few in the West. Its first journey, begun on the hundredth anniversary of the Andrews Raid, was over the road it had traveled so long before, from Atlanta to Big Shanty (Kennesaw). It visited twelve states in 1962 and eleven in 1963. Only twice in 11,200 miles of travel under its own steam did it break down and have to be laid up for repairs. It was one of the most important historic exhibits at the World's Fair in New York.

Considerable controversy arose as to where the "General" would go on permanent display. As far back as 1939 the Georgia legislature had passed a resolution that the "General" be removed from Chattanooga and returned to Georgia. In 1959 there was strong pressure for it to be placed in a proposed museum at Stone Mountain. But Chattanooga demanded it be returned there, and in a series of court battles over a decade Atlanta demanded it be returned here. No agreement was reached.

In 1967 Chattanooga seized the engine and moved it to the L&N railroad yards in Louisville, Kentucky, and there it remained until 1976 when a Supreme Court decision approved its return to the State of Georgia, to be placed in a specially built museum at Kennesaw.

Two important Atlanta institutions received new leaders in 1963. In July Dr. Sanford S. Atwood, the fifty-year old provost of Cornell University, was chosen as the sixteenth president of Emory University—succeeding Dr. Walter Martin, who resigned to become the chancellor of the University System of Georgia. Dr. Atwood, a Presbyterian, was the first non-Methodist to head Emory University in its 126-year history.

In May, Gudmund Vigtel, until recently assistant director of the Corcoran Gallery of Art in Washington, took over his duties in the newly created post of dean of the art museum of the Atlanta Art Association. Born in Norway in 1925, he had lived in Norway, Sweden, and Austria before coming to Atlanta in 1946. During the war he had served in the Free Norwegian Air Force. After the war he attended Piedmont College and studied at the Atlanta Art Institute. In 1952 he received a bachelor of fine arts degree from the University of Georgia and a master of fine arts degree the following year. Atlanta Art Association director Dr. Wilhelmus B. Bryan saw Vigtel's duties as museum dean "encompassing selections of art exhibits, and planning of related activities, and [he] would also oversee the museum staff and 'take charge of publications.'"

Less than a month after Vigtel's arrival in early May, Atlanta marked the first anniversary of the greatest tragedy the city had suffered since the Civil War. On June 3, 1962, a plane chartered by the Atlanta Art Association had crashed on takeoff at Orly Field, Paris, killing 130 people, 115 of them Georgians and nearly all from Atlanta. Several churches held memorial services and many memorial contributions, notably toward an arts center, had been made or were in progress.

In June George W. Woodruff was awarded Georgia Tech's highest alumni honor—the Distinguished Service Award—at Tech's seventy-fifth anniversary commencement. The accolade, read by Tech's President Edwin D. Harrison, cited Woodruff's long and dedicated record of devotion to the cause of higher education in Georgia, exemplified by his service as a trustee of the Georgia Tech Foundation, Agnes Scott College and Emory University:

That business and civic career began in 1917, when Mr. Woodruff finished his studies at Tech, and took a job as draftsman with Atlantic Steel Company in 1918, rising from this to become chairman of the board of the Continental Gin Company by 1934—a position he held until his retirement in 1959. Currently he is a director of ten corporations, including Atlantic Steel and The Coca-Cola Company. In the field of public service he has carried heavy responsibilities. He is chairman of the board of Rabun Gap-Nacoochee School, a commissioner of the Franklin D. Roosevelt Warm Springs Foundation, a trustee of the Emily and Ernest Woodruff Foundation.

In 1963 Georgia Tech also honored the late William A. (Bill) Alexander, one of the most beloved coaches known to collegiate football, by installing him in the Tech Hall of Fame. "Coach Alex" took over in 1917 after the great John Heisman left to take the head coaching job at Pennsylvania. From then through 1944, Alexander's teams won 134 games, lost 95, and tied 15. His first year Tech won 8 and lost 1 game, and in his last year he led Tech to the Orange Bowl. In between there were bowl games galore. In 1944 he was awarded the Amos A. Stagg Award by the American Coaches Association for his "contribution to football."

Longtime Fulton County Manager A. E. Fuller and two veteran judges retired in 1963. Fuller had been manager for about sixteen years. W. Frank White, presiding judge of the Municipal Traffic Court, retired after ten years on the grueling job. Judge W. W. Woolfolk, for sixteen years judge of Fulton County Juvenile Court, retired at the end of his term in October. Said he: "I've given 34 years, perhaps the best years of my life, to service of other people, particularly other people's children. I think it's time now that I give some serious consideration to making plans for my own family's future." Before going on the bench he had served nine years as a probation officer, and it was in this period that he developed theories on juvenile delinquency and the handling of young offenders that gained him national recognition. He was active for many years in youth work before assuming his duties as judge. He had served as executive director of the Atlanta Boys Club for several years. A native of Russell County, Alabama, Woolfolk was a graduate of Emory University and the Woodrow Wilson Law School.

In mid-June word came down from Washington that Erle Cocke, Sr., of Atlanta would soon retire as chairman of the Federal Deposit Insurance Corporation. The board had three members who handled the $2.5 billion deposit insurance fund. Cocke, sixty-eight, a former president of Fulton National Bank in Atlanta, planned to return to Atlanta.

The Shining Light Award was presented in the name of the late Dr. George M. Sparks, who had built the school now in 1963 known as Georgia State College. The memorial gas light, and the plaque that bore the record of his services, would be kept permanently at the college in Sparks Hall, which was named in his honor. Mayor Ivan Allen made the presentation to Dr. Noah Langdale, president of the college. A native of Quitman, Dr. Sparks had been a newspaperman before becoming an educator. In 1928 he had become director of the Georgia Tech Evening School of Commerce, and from it he had developed Georgia State. He became president of the new school in 1955, retired in 1957, and died a year later at the age of 68.

As of 1963, under Dr. Langdale, Georgia State was already one of the university system's largest units and was growing larger. On May 17, five days after the presentation of the Shining Light Award in memory of Dr. Sparks, Dr. Langdale was wielding the shovel at ground-breaking ceremonies for the college's new $1.75 million all-purpose building. It would stand at the northeast corner of Decatur Street and Collins Street SE, at the Courtland Street viaduct. The first two floors would be all parking, the upper two would contain a cafeteria, offices, a student cafeteria, and bookstore, and there would be a penthouse at the top. The main entrance would be at the third-floor level from Courtland Street across from Sparks Hall.

As the educational pulse beat stronger in Atlanta with the growth of Georgia State so did the industrial and economic pulse beat more strongly in the vicinity of Stone Mountain. There, in a pouring rain on June 17, Governor Carl Sanders cut the ribbon that would open the new Stone Mountain Industrial Park, where twenty-one industrial plants in the fields of research, development, testing, and evaluation were working, under construction, or planned. H. G. (Pat) Patillo was builder of the complex with the support of DeKalb County and its commission chairman, C. O. (Charles) Emmerich, Sr.

In May Piedmont Park hosted the tenth annual Atlanta Arts Festival. As a sign of the week-long event's steadily growing popularity, on its opening night some 25,000 people ignored cloudy skies to stream into the park, examining panels of painting and gardens of sculpture, listening to music and cho-

In the 1960s Atlanta's convention industry was boosted by the opening of the Civic Center with a 4,500-seat auditorium and an adjacent exhibit hall. John Portman's Regency-Hyatt House hotel with its flying-saucer-like, roof-top restaurant and twenty-story-high atrium revitalized Atlanta's hotel industry and set a trend for hotel architecture nationwide.

Mayor Ivan Allen and C & S banker Mills B. Lane, Jr., were the driving forces in building the Atlanta–Fulton County Stadium and in bringing major-league sports to Atlanta in 1966. Allen and Lane regarded the downtown site adjacent to the interchange of Interstates 20, 85, and 75 as the crossroads of the South.

Atlanta boosters, especially Mayor William B. Hartsfield, were dedicated to making the city a crossroads of the air as well as a rail and highway center. In 1948 when the city opened this new terminal, Atlanta ranked seventh nationally in airline activity. The facility was built mostly of war-surplus materials and cost only $270,000.

A modern air terminal, with distinctive turquoise wall panels, went into operation in 1961 and served for about twenty years until it was replaced by a midfield facility. During this period the airport rose to number two nationally and was renamed in honor of the late Mayor William B. Hartsfield, who had tirelessly promoted aviation in Atlanta.

Heavily endowed with Coca-Cola money from the Candler and Woodruff families, Emory University is Atlanta's largest private institution of higher education. The library in the center of this view opened in 1969.

This 1967 photograph was taken to help Georgia State College (now Georgia State University) plan its expansion. The campus was then composed of the buildings immediately south of Hurt Park and the light-colored building in the lower right.

The Atlanta skyline added impressive new buildings between the mid 1950s (top photo) and the beginning of the 1970s (bottom photo). The most dramatic change was the addition of the Peachtree Center complex (lower right).

LEFT: Martin Luther King, Jr., grew up in Atlanta and attended Morehouse College before completing his graduate studies in the North. Soon after leading the successful bus boycott in Montgomery, King returned to Atlanta to head the Southern Christian Leadership Conference.

BELOW: Martin Luther King, Sr., and Coretta Scott King carried on much of the work Martin Luther King, Jr., had begun before his assassination in 1968. Here they hold a press conference (circa 1970) inside Ebenezer Baptist Church, where the younger King had been copastor with his father.

ABOVE: Around 1970, when this photograph was made, the Atlanta City Council was still predominately white.

LEFT: Mayor Sam Massell (left) visited with Mayor Kenneth Gibson of Newark during the National Conference of Mayors in Atlanta in 1971.

LEFT: Herman Russell (left) became one of Atlanta's wealthiest and most influential black citizens by turning a modest plastering business into a large construction firm.

BELOW: In 1973 Vice-Mayor Maynard Jackson announced his candidacy for the top spot, which he subsequently won, becoming Atlanta's first black mayor.

ral singing, and hearing Mayor Ivan Allen inaugurate the festivities. As the week progressed the program broadened to include folk singing, dancing children, and a review of the arts in pantomime by the Wit's End Players.

While local critics in the field of music deplored Atlanta's failure to provide proper facilities for orchestras and their soloists, two observers from afar came to look closely at the town in all its aspects. One was Jerry Hulse, travel editor of the *Los Angeles Times,* whose lighthearted survey titled "On the Go— Atlanta's Whistling Dixie Over Gains," was published in the *Times* on April 21, 1963. In the same month Perle Mesta, Washington's famous "Hostess with the Mostes'," advisor to presidents on social matters, presented in *Mc-Call's* magazine her story: "Atlanta Adventure, The New Southern Society." Between Hulse's brief irreverent summation and Mesta's warmly favorable reaction to the things she saw and the people she met, a balanced picture comes through that accurately presents Atlanta and its people as they moved on into the mid-sixties. Mesta's article was conversational in tone:

Naturally, I didn't expect to find crinolines and hoops. But if you haven't been to Atlanta, you do find yourself thinking of the city in terms of Scarlett O'Hara and her contemporaries. But, believe me, there is a *new* Atlanta. Not just new with the newness of four-lane expressways or a changing skyline of modern million-dollar buildings. It also has a new expanding outlook that is reaching out to include fresh ideas—in industry, culture, and social life.

Atlanta is a city of a million plus. Its social life has naturally undergone changes since the days when a few *grandes dames* (in particular, the famous Mrs. William Lawson Peel) were the unquestioned social arbiters and "society" was rigidly fenced in to keep out any but the oldest, best, and most affluent families. Being from the right family is still important, and there's an aura of conservatism that might seem somewhat reserved to those accustomed to the more relaxed internationalism found in Washington and New York social circles.

But within its own framework, Atlanta society is welcoming newcomers. Where once there were just two clubs for anyone who really "belonged," there are now many fine social town and country clubs. The Nine O'Clocks, formerly the only club for young male fashionables, now has rivals: the Gentry Club and the Benedicts, which is a very selective group of young married men. There are also several Junior Cotillions instead of one.

BUT EVERYWHERE, CULTURE. Throughout Atlanta, I found a tremendous interest in cultural activities. The city is the home of Georgia Tech and ten other colleges and universities. It boasts a great old Art Association, has three ballet groups, both symphony and "pops" orchestras, and no fewer than 200 garden clubs. Every spring, with fervor and fanfare, it bids welcome for a full week to the Metropolitan Opera.

My visit to Atlanta really started 'way cross the country, in California. There recently I ran into Georgia's governor and forty-six fellow Georgians, selling the advantages of living and doing business in their state. Georgia is on the move, they said. So I went to see for myself.

Mesta was given a tour of the best of Atlanta society. She attended a mayor's luncheon at the Capital City Club. She had tea and pecan pie with Betty Talmadge at Senator and Mrs. Talmadge's 150-year-old plantation home in Lovejoy. She took in a debutante ball at the Piedmont Driving Club. Richard Rich hosted Mesta at a cocktail-buffet preceding the Atlanta Civic Ballet's performance of the "Nutcracker." A ladies' luncheon at the Piedmont Driving Club, a trip to the art museum, and another dinner at an antebellum mansion known as Mimosa Hall rounded out her visit. She had met most of the city's high society, and went away impressed.

"We hold on to what is good of the old here," Mrs. Albert Thornton told Mesta. "We are a Southern people. But we are not sluggish." Mesta agreed: "I think that about sums it up. Like most people's, Mrs. Thornton's world prefers the companionship of old friends. But it does not close its eyes to the need for growth and expansion on many fronts, and its vitality keeps moving it forward."

Whereas Mesta focused on society, in his flippant survey for the *Los Angeles Times* Jerry Hulse looked to the outward signs of growth and vitality:

Few here have fiddled since Atlanta burned and General Sherman stormed through to the sea.

On the contrary, Atlanta is on the move, with skyscrapers cluttering the horizon.

Only recently Atlantans previewed the world's only double decker drive-in restaurant. At the same time, city fathers sang their praises of Dixie's newest airport outside town. And now they've nipped the ribbon on the newest and biggest shopping center in the whole South, a massive pile of concrete they call Lenox Square.

The more than half-hundred shops in Lenox Square have on hand items ranging from white mice to full grown mink. Besides mink and white mice, a pet store sells rattlesnakes, ocelots, jeweled dog collars and such foul-weather Fido gear as rain boots, raincoats initialed if you please.

In this day when airports are being placed so far outside town they are sometimes claimed by the next state, someone in Atlanta pulled an unforgiveable faux pas and placed theirs 8½ miles from the center of town.

A rather curious institution is the equally new airport hotel, the Air Host. Here guests get the impression they've been whisked away by flying saucer and deposited on some unknown planet.

Bellboys dressed like space cadets tote luggage through the hallways, the restaurant serves heavenly hamburgers up on Cloud 9, and when one picks up the phone in his room a small voice at the other end answers, "Control tower."

Atlanta is the home of the famed Ramblin' Recks of Georgia Tech, a night club where cancan girls do the twist, and a large chunk of gravel known as Stone Mountain Memorial Park. It is here that you will find the world's "biggest park railroad" and an aerial tramway running to the 783-foot summit. In the construction state are a Civil War Muesum, outdoor theater, motels, trailer parks, plus beaches beside a lake, the color of cafe au lait.

Cut into the face of Stone Mountain—Georgians call the granite mound the eighth wonder of the world—are still unfinished carvings of Generals Robert E. Lee and Stonewall Jackson and Confederacy President Jefferson Davis. It is, if you please, the Mt. Rushmore of Dixie. The efforts of Augustus Lukeman are bannered by Atlantans as the largest sculptured figures, modern or ancient, in the world. Backing up the claim, the park's publicity pundit declares that the 58-foot sword worn by Lee, if cut from the figure would weigh in excess of 100 tons.

Across the freeway from Georgia Tech, near downtown Atlanta, Frank Gordy's double-decker drive-in is swathed in mustard and buns, dispensing nearly three million hot dogs a year at the pre-war price of 15¢ each. Only recently, when traffic became unreasonable, he added the top deck, which he refers to as the Lunching Pad. Here car hops relay orders by walkie talkie radio to a tower not unlike that found at an airport.

Among other things, Atlanta is the home of Coca-Cola, Delta Airlines, elegant old antebellum mansions and a gas lamp that's been burning at Alabama and Whitehall Streets since the War Between the States.

The Civil War is the subject of the city's foremost tourist attraction, the fifty-foot high Cyclorama in Grant Park. The world's largest painting, it portrays with lifelike effect the bloody beginning of the Battle of Atlanta.

In the early months of 1864, Union troops moved toward Atlanta through Ringgold, Tunnel Hill, Dalton, Adairsville, Kingston, Allatoona, Big Shanty, Marietta, Peachtree. Atlanta was the key city in Sherman's march to the sea, and it was there that the doom of the Confederacy was sealed in immense bloodshed on July 22. In that single day, more than 5,000 men died.

Besieged, occupied, and burned to the ground, Atlanta took root again.

Neither Hulse nor Mesta met or mentioned Maggie Davis, whose novel, *The Far Side of Home,* came out shortly after they had left and caused considerable excitement in Atlanta literary circles. Davis, born and reared in the Bronx, had adopted Atlanta and Jonesboro, Georgia, as her home, and in this book the Civil War and the men who fought in it was her theme. The Literary Guild chose it as the book of the month for July, 1963, and Atlanta's observers of the literary scene greeted it with high praise. To Pat Watters, the *Journal-Constitution* book editor, the book was the work of a "sensitive, devoted talent" who in this novel had produced "a work of lasting value." The Macmillan Company, who had also published Margaret Mitchell's epic novel, described *The Far Side of Home* as being "the other side of *Gone with the Wind.*" This was in some degree true, for it brought to life something other than the romantic picture of an Old South and lovely ladies dancing in ballrooms or columned mansions with gallant officers in gray who owned broad plantations worked by slaves.

There were other Atlanta writers who produced outstanding books in this same year. *Atlanta* magazine wondered "how on earth to reach down and dip out a bucketful of the best from that vast river of books published in 1963." Ralph McGill, publisher of the *Constitution,* wrote a book, *The South and the Southerner,* that was one of the distinguished books of the year. His fellow staffer Celestine Sibley turned out *Peachtree Street, U.S.A.* Two other nonfiction works worthy of note were Robert Wallace's history of Georgia Tech, *Dress Her in White and Gold,* and Emory professor Floyd Watkins's book *Yesterday in the Hills,* which he wrote with his father, Charles H. Watkins.

Another literary event of this year was the presentation to Emory University of the private papers of the late Julian LaRose Harris, noted reporter, editor, and foreign correspondent and the oldest son of Joel Chandler Harris, creator of Uncle Remus. Born in Atlanta in 1874, Julian Harris began his career as a reporter with the *Constitution* in 1892 and by 1900 was made managing editor. From 1905 to 1913 he was editor of *Uncle Remus* magazine, which he and his father founded, and it was in this period that he became dedicated to the effort to bring about the overthrow of the Ku Klux Klan, which he knew to be the source of much social, political, and economic injustice toward blacks in the South. After he and his wife, Julia Collier Harris, covered World War I, he as editor of the Paris edition of the *New York Herald,* she as reporter representing the Herald Syndicate, they came back to Georgia where they bought into the Columbus *Enquirer-Sun* in 1922 and became sole owners and editors four years later, in 1926. The paper was awarded the Pulitzer Prize "for the most distinguished and meritorious public service rendered by an American newspaper during 1925," and specifically noted was the paper's brave and energetic fight against the Ku Klux Klan, against enactment of a law barring the teaching of evolution, against dishonest and corrupt public officials (some of whom he named), and for justice to the Negro and against lynching.

Julian LaRose Harris died on February 9, 1963, at the age of eighty-nine, and at last was stilled one of the boldest and most powerful editorial voices ever heard in the South. The papers, given to Emory by his widow Julia, would become part of the Harris Collection started at Emory by Thomas H. English more than a generation before.

Notable among the happenings that would be long remembered in Atlanta and the nation was the final decision, long deferred by nearly fifty years of wrangling, to choose at last the sculptor who would finally complete the Stone Mountain Memorial. Chairman Matt McWhorter of the Memorial Commission announced that the choice was Walker Kirtland Hancock from Gloucester, Massachusetts, grandson of two Confederate veterans. Hancock was one of the nation's outstanding sculptors, having won many top awards both in the United States and in international competition, including the Prix de Rome, and he had done several war memorials.

The carving as it stood in 1963 was the result of many years of controversy, artistic, political, and financial. It was, in fact, a monument to anger, stubbornness, frailty, and jealousy, rather than to the nobility of the Confederate cause. In 1906 Helen C. Plane, first president of the Atlanta chapter of the United Daughters of the Confederacy (UDC), conceived the idea for the memorial. Ten years later S. H. Venable, whose family owned the mountain, gave it to the UDC, provided it be used as a memorial. In 1924 the still incomplete head of Robert E. Lee as carved by the famous sculptor Gutzon Borglum was unveiled there, but in 1925 Borglum's contract was cancelled and in anger and frustration he destroyed his models and left. He was replaced by Augustus Lukeman, who destroyed Borglum's completed head of Lee and replaced it with his own model.

This led Venable, who had believed in Borglum, to reclaim the mountain, as the original deed to the UDC entitled him to do. Thus, for a period of thirty years the project was in a state of suspension. Finally, in 1958, the state bought the mountain and the 38,000 acres around it for a Stone Mountain Memorial Park, and in 1963, with state funds available, Walker Hancock was hired to complete the carving—not the marching army with Lee at its head that Borglum had envisioned, but the three leaders, Lee, Jeff Davis, and Stonewall Jackson, on horseback. Lukeman died in 1935. But Borglum went on to other grand scale works, including the carvings on Mount Rushmore, before he died in 1941.

In 1970 the Hancock carving was dedicated. It had taken fifty-five years from concept to completion.

OBITUARIES

Roy M. Avey, 69, an official with Lucas and Jenkins Theatres, was Atlanta manager for MGM in charge of distribution of *Gone with the Wind* throughout the Southeast, after its gala premiere at Loew's Grand Theatre. Jake Abel, born Abelson in Russia, came to Atlanta as a youngster and became well known as a boxer, being a ranking welterweight by the time he was 20. Dr. Lon Woodfin Grove, 73, retired associate professor of clinical surgery, had been chief of surgical services at Egleston Hospital. He was a graduate of the University of Alabama Medical School, the University of Pennsylvania, and Harvard. He came to Atlanta in 1919 after serving in France. His colleagues credited him with "firsts" in nearly all abdominal and gastric surgeries at Emory Hospital. He was a member of many medical societies and the Piedmont Driving Club, the Capital City Club, the Atlanta Art Association, and the Symphony Guild. The medical profession lost another staunch member in the death of Dr. Hugh Edward Hailey, 53, who died when his sports car crashed into a tree. A graduate of the University of Georgia, Emory University Medical School, and Vanderbilt, he was also a veteran of World War II. After the war he established his practice in dermatology in Atlanta and became associate clinical professor of dermatology at Emory. He was a member of the Piedmont Driving Club, the Capital City Club, and the Nine O'Clocks.

James Gilbert Ison, 79, enjoyed the reputation of being one of Georgia Tech's first nationally famous athletes, being first baseman of the baseball team. With his brother R. D. Ison and Lindsey Hopkins, Sr., he organized the Ison Finance Company. William Cole Jones was chief editorial writer and associate editor of the *Atlanta Journal* until his retirement in 1951. A graduate of Mercer University, he had specialized in English and Greek, and for a few years he taught both subjects there before beginning his newspaper career. He served as senior warden of St. Luke's Church. Sister Henrietta Keel was the founder of the Savannah Street Mission. For years Keel was touched by the plight of the children in the section of Atlanta known as Cabbage Town and Picketts Alley. They had no place to go and nothing to do. Gathering them around her in a vacant lot, she told Bible stories and taught them games. Soon Atlanta club women became interested in her work and through many campaigns sufficient funds were raised to build the Savannah Street Mission and, after its success, the Fellowship Mission on Kelley Street.

H. O. Smith died at 83. He was former principal of Boys High School. A magna cum laude graduate of Harvard in 1903, he came to Atlanta to Boys High in 1909. He earned an M.A. from Emory in 1927 and an honorary doctorate of humane letters. Boys High alumni honored him, too, creating the H. O. Smith Excellency of Scholarship Fund. He was a member of the First Presbyterian Church. Jack Savage, 67, Atlanta's city attorney for almost thirty years, had been elected to City Council after graduation from Atlanta Law School. He resigned to become assistant city attorney at the death of James L. Mason in 1935. He was a Mason, a Shriner, and communicant of Druid Hills Methodist Church. George C. Biggers, Sr., former president and general manager of Atlanta Newspapers, Inc., died at 70. He was past president of the Southern Newspaper Publishers Association and American Newspaper Publishers Association.

NOTES

1. Interviews, school and church officials, 1982.
2. Interview, H. Eugene Craig.

1964

GOING into 1964 Atlantans looked back upon the year just past and realized that their city was indeed on the move, not only in the economic, social, and educational sense but also in the basic meaning of the word—moving from one location to another. In its January, 1964, issue *Atlanta* magazine interviewed John Sloan Smith, president of the Aero Mayflower Transit Company of Indianapolis, one of the nation's largest household moving firms. He said that in 1963 more than 200,000 people changed addresses in the Atlanta metropolitan area—meaning roughly that one in every five Atlantans switched living quarters in the span of a single year. And of these, 170,000 simply moved from one place to another in the five-county metropolitan area.

"And though we can't prove it," the magazine commented, "we suspect that most of these moves come about because of economic gains that enabled individuals and families to upgrade their residential accommodations." Smith pointed out that for every seven people who moved out of the Atlanta area, eight moved in from other areas of the state and nation, leaving a healthy net immigration.

One prospective incoming group in 1964 was a symbol of Atlanta's increasingly cosmopolitan atmosphere. Early in January a representative of *Playboy* announced that a new Playboy Club would open that fall in the Dinkler Plaza Hotel at Fairlie and Spring streets. The Atlanta club would employ eighty-two people, including forty "Bunnies," some of whom would be recruited locally. The starting salary for young "Bunnies" would be $200 a week—"a lot of carrots," observed *Atlanta* magazine.

In February, March, and April "Sabin Oral Sundays" were held in an effort to give to at least 80 percent of all those living in the Atlanta area the vaccine that would finally stamp out poliomyelitis. The Fulton County Medical Society sponsored the effort. Older children and adults received their doses on sugar cubes, and babies were dosed with a dropper. A voluntary donation of 25¢ was asked to help defray expense, but all were to receive the vaccine regardless of ability to pay. At least 800,000 of the 1.2 million residents of the eighteen-county Atlanta area were immunized.

Furniture dealer Rawson Haverty was named president of the Atlanta Chamber of Commerce for 1964, and Edward D. Smith, president of the First National Bank of Atlanta and immediate past president of the chamber, continued as chairman of the Forward Atlanta Committee, which directed the $1.6 million program of research and advertising begun three years earlier. Individual Atlanta companies joined with the Chamber of Commerce in a program of cooperative advertising that brought the city's Forward Atlanta program to the attention of *Wall Street Journal* readers throughout the East. The chamber and individual companies shared the costs equally. Delta Air

Lines was the first, plugging Atlanta as the sixth-largest scheduled airline operation center in the United States and Delta as the fifth-largest domestic air carrier. Eastern was the next, its full-page ads showing a map of the nation with Eastern's routes outlined and the message "Atlanta Invites Business to the Heart of the South." Patillo Construction Company and McDonough Construction Company, two local industrial developers, each took a full page, and soon the requests were beginning to pour in for more information about the city and from local business firms asking how they might join the ad program.

All in all, the Forward Atlanta campaign was advertising heavily in business publications, pointing out Atlanta's rapidly expanding economic development. Its theme: new jobs, 40,000 of them in two years. And new housing—only five cities in the United States were ahead of Atlanta in housing starts, with 26,539 new homes and apartments being built in two years. In 1960 Atlanta was twenty-first in new housing starts. In 1963—sixth. The ads appeared in the *Wall Street Journal, Business Week, Business Management, Dun's Review,* and *Industrial Development* in May, and would be in the June issue of *Fortune.* Paralleling the ads was a series of ads in the *New Yorker* telling how people loved life in Atlanta.

The analysis and profile of Atlanta business prepared in *Atlanta* magazine by Dr. Willys R. Knight, director of the Bureau of Business and Economic Research at the School of Business Administration at Georgia State College, was a forecast of another fortuitous year. The Georgia Department of Labor showed that more than 21,000 persons had been added to the Atlanta area's civilian labor force in the preceding year. The latest unemployment figures showed jobless ranks down by 400, and of a total labor force of 423,500, only 2.6 percent were unemployed. The national rate was 4.8 percent.[1]

Every cheerful Chamber of Commerce statistic has its "on the other hand," and in Atlanta the increase in population created a growing problem. An article by Bruce Galphin announced, "If you've inched bumper-to-bumper through freeway traffic, if you've watched congestion grow more severe year by year, and decided Atlanta's traffic has reached the intolerable stage, brace yourself; things are going to get worse!" The problem, wrote Galphin under the title "Ominous Rumblings Along the Freeway," boiled down to a cold proposition in Malthusian mathematics:

The number of automobiles in the five-county metropolitan area has been almost doubling every ten years since 1942, and the estimates suggest another doubling by 1972. The number and size of downtown streets is relatively stable. More and more vehicles, then, are competing for more or less unchanging street space.

The central city literally is in danger of strangulation by the very traffic that has been a reflection of its progress. In time, some radical changes in Atlanta's traffic habits are going to be necessary if the center of the city is to retain its vital pacing of the area's economic growth. But even the most promising proposal—rapid transit—is a critical decade away.

Galphin saw the problem clearly:

Take expressways, for instance. Once they were some dreamed-of, twentieth century marvel that would get you home in fifteen minutes, or to the airport in twenty. That they have done—provided you don't have to ride them during the rush hours. But look what else they have done:

By slashing travel time to the central city, they have turned farm land into split levels, opening up vast, far-flung new suburban areas. The more widely scattered the residential sections, the more difficult it is for transit facilities to serve the public. The poorer the transit service, the more necessary for the family to operate two or more automobiles, and to drive at least one of them daily to work. For the transit system, this can turn into a vicious cycle of fewer passengers, higher costs, increased fares, and even fewer passengers.

Galphin's study named those freeway junctions at which impatient motorists had suffered the most accidents in the previous nine months and the most fatal accidents in the past decade. Worst was the northeast-northwest freeway junction where traffic from Marietta and Gainesville merged. One hundred and nine accidents were reported there in the preceding nine months, and twelve people had lost their lives in four accidents in the previous ten years. Number two on the list was the south freeway–Cleveland Avenue ramp onto the freeway junction, where fifty-eight accidents were reported in nine months and one death in the preceding ten years. Third was the north freeway at the North Avenue–Williams Street exit, where seventy-four accidents occurred in nine months and one death in the past decade, and fourth on the list of killers was the northeast freeway–Peachtree Street intersection, where fifty-three accidents were reported in nine months. The fifth most dangerous spot was the on-ramp at Brookwood Station.

Thus, in 1964 Galphin analyzed the problem and foresaw the changes that were inevitable if downtown Atlanta was to survive as a central urban core. "The price of progress, in short," he concluded, "is money and patience."[2]

Another knowledgeable observer of Atlanta traffic, its threat and its promise, was Ed Hughes, managing director of the Atlanta Traffic and Safety Council since 1962. Before that he was the city hall reporter for the *Atlanta Journal* in which post he learned that in Atlanta, as in the nation, traffic was the most lethal force facing Americans under twenty-five—and one of the most deadly for all Americans. In Hughes's Traffic Control Office on the eleventh floor of the Commerce Building, maps showed the pattern of zig-zag streets, the on-and-off ramps, and the spots where deaths had occurred. Hughes, in an interview with reporter Reese Cleghorn in the January *Atlanta* magazine, agreed with Bruce Galphin's analysis. In Atlanta, so far as traffic was concerned, "things are almost certain to get worse." And, "while downtown traffic grows more complex and more dangerous, we are duplicating in the suburbs the problems we have created downtown."

The organization of which Hughes was chairman was a nonpolitical aggregation of volunteers—business and professional leaders whose hearts, minds, and common goals were wrapped up in the growth and progress of Atlanta. It had no ties with government and received no political funds. It was dependent upon the support of downtown business and sometimes had to take issue with certain elements of the business membership. Since its organization in 1952 when the Traffic and Safety Council was formed by merging two older organizations, the Greater Atlanta Safety Council and the Greater Atlanta Traffic Improvement Association, much had been accomplished. In 1964 the budget was about $60,000, and the financial supporters of the council were department stores, banks, and insurance companies, who were aware that the city, through automobile accidents, was losing as much as $19 million a year in the high cost of hospital emergency facilities, funerals, lost earning power, vehicle repair, and insurance.

In the wake of the ruling in 1962 that opened Atlanta's public swimming pools to blacks and whites alike, pool builders swarmed into the city seeking contracts to build private pools for affluent homeowners. Some of the builders, it was discovered, were not as honest as they could be, and the pools they built were poorly constructed. In response, eighteen Atlanta companies whose specialty was building, equipping, and servicing swimming pools formed themselves into a group called GASPA—Greater Atlanta Swimming Pool Association, Inc. By governing themselves under a strict code of ethics, they hoped to make life hard on the ones who soaked the unwary. According to Ed Wait, GASPA president, pool building had grown at such a rate that whereas in the early 1950s in Atlanta only twenty pools a year were built, in 1963 about three hundred were installed.

The year that came in with flooding rains that put acres of Atlanta and Decatur residential property under water was marked throughout by spectacular blazes. Firemen could well have used a drenching downpour on two fires, both "suspicious." One destroyed the old North Building at Decatur High School on May 17, and the other, the empty Ponce de Leon Theater on June 6. But the most spectacular conflagration came late in the year, on December 4, when the Mayfair Club was destroyed by flames that fire companies could not control. Headwaiter Charles Frey died of smoke inhalation when trapped in the basement. Some one hundred people, including eighty-five women who were playing Canasta, were evacuated safely. It was they who first discovered the fire about 3:00 P.M., when smoke started seeping through the floor of the ballroom in which they were playing.

The clubhouse sat at the top of a sloping lawn at 1456 Spring Street. A "quietly unpretentious" two-story building, it had been a focal point of Jewish civic and social activity, though its membership was not restricted to the Jewish people. It had been founded in 1930 by thirteen prominent Atlantans who met at the Biltmore Hotel until it built the clubhouse in 1938; only recently had it been expanded and remodeled. Through the doors of this building had passed such celebrities as Eleanor Roosevelt, Israeli Prime Minister Golda Meir, comic Jack Leonard, Senators Herman Talmadge and Richard Russell, Governor Carl Sanders and many of his predecessors, Mayors Ivan Allen and William B. Hartsfield and countless others. "Almost every candidate for major office in Atlanta or Georgia has found the time to say his piece at the Mayfair Club, perhaps largely through the influence of its politically minded hierarchy, especially Abe Goldstein . . ." Mendel Romm, Sr., one of the thirteen founders and the club's second president, remembered that not only politicians and statesmen but all the nation's top entertainers—singers, ventriloquists and standup comics—had been at the club, either as guests or performers.

The Mayfair went down in a blaze worthy of its status. The fire had been burning for some time when flames burst through the roof, shooting fifty feet into the air, and the black smoke was visible across town. Homegoing traffic slowed to a crawl on the expressway, and thousands watched from vantage points along Spring Street. The electric clock on the side of the building near the swimming pool had stopped at 3:08 P.M. It was after 5:00 P.M. before three aerial companies, twelve engines, and a rescue company, totaling eighty-five men under the direction of Chief C. H. Hilderbrand, finally brought the last flame under control. Only the white brick walls and a small section of the roof were left standing. As to what caused the fire? "We have no idea," said Lt. M. H. Sullivan of the arson squad.

The business and construction upsurge of the early 1960s continued in 1964. Not a single major hotel had been built in Atlanta since the banner year of 1924. That year the elegant Atlanta Biltmore with its 600 rooms opened in the spring, the Robert Fulton followed in the summer with 250 rooms, and in the fall the old governor's mansion gave way to the elegant new Henry Grady Hotel with its 465 rooms. But no new hotel graced the downtown horizon in the intervening years, though motels and motor hotels had moved into the center of the city from the outskirts.

Now, though, a grand new downtown hotel was on the drawing board, to be located in the Peachtree Center development. The announcement was made jointly by Granger Hansell for Phoenix Investment Company, Charles Massell of the Massell Companies, and architect-developer John Portman for himself and Texas developer Trammell Crowe. The new building, which was being financed largely by Atlanta money, would cost $5 million, would have 800 guest rooms and would be one of the largest hotels in the South. It would be on the east side of Peachtree in the block bounded by Peachtree, Baker, Ivy, and Harris, and it would contain an exhibition hall of 24,000 square feet and a grand ballroom to accommodate 3,000 people.

An unusual feature of this new hotel, to be known later as the Regency-Hyatt House, would be a garden court, roofed with glass domes. Rising twenty-one stories, this court would be kept at a springtime temperature, and open balconies on each floor would extend into this atmosphere of springtime. September, 1965, was the predicted opening date.

Plans for other significant buildings continued. Latest on the skyscraper bandwagon was the Trust Company of Georgia, which revealed long-developing plans for a new structure of twenty stories or more at its present main office site, to be started in another year. A new site was A&P's $5 million food storage and distribution center in southwest Atlanta, which would serve company supermarkets in Georgia, Alabama, and Tennessee. Starting under construction in February of 1964 was still another expansion of Rich's, this time an 87,000-square-foot service building rising behind and connected with the downtown Store for Homes. The Mead Packaging Division of the Mead Corporation of Dayton, Ohio, would invest $1 million in an addition of 200,000 square feet to its main plant in Atlanta. International Harvester continued to expand its Atlanta facility with the purchase of a 9.3 acre site to be a new motor truck sales and service branch. (This would be the company's fourth expansion project in Atlanta in less than a year.) Also announced in February was the schedule of completion of Miss Georgia Dairies, Inc., of their new $2.5 million processing plant and headquarters.

One Atlanta landmark was destined to vanish in the mid-sixties. The First National Bank announced its plan to pull down the old Peachtree Arcade and replace it with a forty-story addition to its present headquarters at Five Points. Frank Daniel in the *Journal-Constitution* of January 19, 1964, told the story of the Arcade building, erected during World War I, and of the Concert Hall that had stood on the site during the Civil War. It was used as Confederate barracks and as a prison for James J. Andrews of Andrews's Raiders, until he was hanged. In the days after the war the old barracks was torn down, and the National Hotel, the biggest in Atlanta until the Kimball House, was built. The National burned in 1906 and was followed by the Emery Steiner Building, and part of its structure was included in the roofed-over Arcade, which housed many shops and offices and provided dry passage from Peachtree to Broad Street.

Another major project of 1964 was the ten-story addition, costing $6 million, being built behind the Southern Bell Telephone Central Switching and Equipment Center on Ivy Street. Extra height and strength were added to each floor in the 177,000-square-foot addition to accommodate massive new equipment.

This construction boom, planned and under way, made Atlanta outstanding in the South. The value of private construction in Atlanta in 1963 was greater than for the entire states of Tennessee or Louisiana or North Carolina. The building figures for Greater Atlanta exceeded in value new construction in the combined states of Montana, Wyoming, North Dakota,

South Dakota, Mississippi, Vermont, and West Virginia. To house Atlanta's growing population, an average of 1,800 units per month were being built, according to Willys Knight of Georgia State University's Bureau of Business and Economic Research.

The mid-sixties saw the beginning of a revived interest in close-in areas such as Ansley Park, Druid Hills, and Midtown. One group of young developers was doing something about this need for "in-town" living. Promoting their development as "just five minutes from Five Points" and christening it with the elegant sounding name "Westchester Square," they were building a townhouse community in uptown Atlanta.

The idea was the brainchild of A. A. Huber, whose team included realtor Spencer Smith, developer Tom Cousins, and architect Henri Jova of Abreu and Robeson. The uptown location they purchased was the former site of the home of Ben Massell, and before that, it was the home of Mr. and Mrs. Edward H. Inman. Where one family once lived, now twenty-five families would dwell comfortably in units containing from 1,700 to more than 3,000 square feet and costing from $35,000 to $100,000.

Though interest in townhouses and inner-city locations appealed to many Atlantans, to many others, particularly the sports-minded, acreage in the rolling hills around the city still was highly desirable. The purchase of 952 acres in northwest Fulton County for $1,428,000 ($1,500 an acre) was announced on March 29 by Atlanta Country Club, Inc. The extensive tract was to be used for a golf course with surrounding home sites for members of the club and others.

Comprising a portion of the John Sibley estate (280 acres) and the old Hughes Spalding estate, the land was bounded by the Chattahoochee River, Sope Creek, Paper Mill Road, and Johnson Ferry Road.

"The club's facilities are being designed to provide for a national golf tournament on a major scale as an annual event," a descriptive brochure stated. "Both the PGA and the citizenry of Atlanta have long coveted such a tournament, but until now no facility existed to host such an event. The club has received firm assurances of major sponsors for prize money, and the unique suitability of the club from a player, spectator and TV standpoint will assure it a prime position on the professional circuit."

In April of 1964 Atlanta's two venerable daily newspapers, the *Constitution* and the *Journal*, would find themselves confronted with a confident and highly conservative competitor in the afternoon newspaper field. Said former Congressman James C. Davis, promoter of the new *Atlanta Times*, as he announced his plans in an interview published in *Atlanta* magazine, "The sensible, right-thinking people of Atlanta have waited a long time for a newspaper to express their views—the support of freedom of religion, freedom of speech, the press, and individual rights and private property."

"Atlanta," continued ex-Congressman Davis, "has newspapers with out-of-state ownership that promote radicalism in every form, the New Deal, the Fair Deal, Modern Republicanism, and have completely disregarded the right-thinking, sound-thinking people of Atlanta and Georgia. There is a tremendous need for a paper that will present the news factually, without bias." Since 1961 the corporation, which Davis headed without pay, had been raising money by public subscription. The goal was $3.5 million. At the time of his announcement, Davis had raised $1 million.

In early February the administrative staff moved into a 60,000-square-foot building on Forrest Road (now Ralph McGill Boulevard). The presses from the old *New York World-Telegram* were being readied in the facility. Over 70,000 subscriptions had already been sold, and many potential advertisers had indicated their interest. Unfortunately, the *Times* itself did not long survive. Its first edition hit the streets, not in April but on June 12. Its welcome was mixed. At 9:00 A.M. on the first day, a male voice on the telephone growled at the switchboard operator: "At 11:00 this morning a bomb will explode at your plant and the *Atlanta Times* will be blown to Hell!" Judge Davis was advised, and he passed the word to I. M. (Mel) Orner, the business manager, and editor Luke Green. The decision was made not to close the plant, but to press on with the day's program. The FBI was called; they came and searched and found no bomb. The trucks hit the streets with the papers.

Robert Carney, in his book *What Happened at the Atlanta Times?* published five years later, told the story of the paper's warm welcome but quick demise.

"The first issue was a giant success but the big press run [128 pages], traffic, etc. made it costly for the circulation department. Carrier boys waited and waited for late papers. Many were drenched and parents forced them to return home. It took days and weeks in some areas to get re-organized, and though the paper carried a good assortment of local, national, and international news, along with good sports coverage and other features—it soon became clear that the newcomer did not have many weeks to live."

The reasons for the *Times'* ultimate failure were many and varied, and Carney details them in his book. They boil down to the fact that the paper tried to expand too far, too fast. Many Atlantans and Georgians responded favorably to its conservative editorial message and were angry when an overburdened circulation department could not get their papers to them on time.

In circulation and in advertising and the business offices—and in the press room—there was "too much to do, too quick, with untrained people," Carney wrote. The crisis came when the paper's board of directors ordered it to expand its circulation statewide. This was done, and circulation increased from 93,288 daily and 92,875 Sunday in September, to October figures of 116,603 daily and 119,134 Sunday. But, as had been predicted, the extra circulation, to areas as far from Atlanta as Macon, Augusta, Columbus, Savannah, and points between, cost the paper an extra $60,000 a month. This increased circulation over a wider area also stimulated a need for bigger and faster presses, and these were bought for a down payment of $500,000.

Ineffective operation by an overworked circulation department delayed the official publication of the October circulation of the *Times* until February, 1965. This, Carney indicated, was the final blow. Big advertisers such as Rich's and Davison's could not write their advertising contracts with the paper until these official circulation figures were in hand, and this penalized the paper beyond measure. National advertisers, such as the big automobile companies, could not make up their advertising schedules, either. As a result, with expenses rising and income falling below expectations, strong differences arose between members of top management. Judge Davis was replaced as chairman by I. M. Orner, executive vice-president and general manager. Then Orner went on vacation—and died. Judge Davis resumed the title of chairman, but the board took over the managing of the papers. They reduced the size of the paper, cut out the TV weekly magazine, and pulled the circulation area back to within a fifty-mile radius of Atlanta.

Efforts were made to bail out the paper by selling stock to owners of papers in other towns, and to big conglomerates such as DuPont, but nothing worked. The payroll checks for Christmas bounced and, going into 1965, the annual figures showed that the *Times'* loss in 1964 was $2,013,000—and its liabilities totaled $1,237,000. Earlier, on January 29, 1965, Lamont DuPont Copeland, Jr., son of the president of the DuPont financial empire and owner of two conservative California dailies, had offered $1 million for a 60 percent share of the Atlanta Times Company. He had paid in $100,000 when, in March, he unexpectedly withdrew his offer. He had learned, he said, that the *Times'* finances were in worse shape than he had thought. With Copeland and DuPont out of the picture, Roscoe Pickett, controversial lawyer in Atlanta and a strong Goldwater supporter who had been soundly beaten by James Mackay in the race for Congress, was called in as the president. Along with Judge Davis, he was a founding stockholder in the *Times* and was the company's first treasurer. His first move was to ask the employees to "loan" the company a week's salary. Many did and never were repaid.

"August 31, 1965, was the last day," wrote Robert Carney. "In many ways it was anticlimactic. When about 300 people have gone through so much for so long, they become numb to reality. They work. They see. They go through the motions almost automatically. That is the way the last day was."[3]

While the *Times* was struggling to survive, various Atlanta enterprises were surging forward. On March 19, 1964, Gov. Carl Sanders formally opened a $3.5 million refrigerated warehouse and frozen-food handling space on the south expressway. This was the brainchild of B. C. Simpson, who called himself "a self-made Atlanta entrepreneur." Simpson spent the first part of his life developing a highly successful trucking business. When he sold the trucking firm, he organized a new business, the first commercial cold storage warehouse built in Atlanta in twenty-five years. His first building contained 520,000 cubic feet, and each year it had expanded until it reached

2.1 million cubic feet. The new building dedicated by Governor Sanders was on a 52-acre tract and contained 4.16 million cubic feet of refrigerated space.

In another area of business Atlanta had grown surprisingly. In the spring of 1964, according to *Atlanta* magazine, there were thirteen firms in Atlanta supplying temporary talent to firms needing to boost their regular staffs for a month or so, either because of absenteeism or work overload. Twenty years earlier, Atlanta had no temporary talent service.

Another name would join the ranks of Atlanta's "big business" circles in this year of 1964. The newcomer was Oxford Manufacturing Company. Barely twenty years old, this apparel manufacturing firm would hit the $70 million sales mark for the fiscal year ending in August. It was a new entry in the very select circle of Atlanta-based business enterprises listed on the New York Stock Exchange. The only other local corporations quoted on the Big Board were Coca-Cola, Delta Air Lines, National Linen Service, and the Southern Company.

Visitors to Atlanta often noted that it was truly a "city in the trees." Heavily forested surrounding areas were making Atlanta a center of tree-related industries. Gray Hodges, southern editor of *Pulp and Paper Magazine*, reported that in the five counties of the Atlanta metropolitan area more than 4,200 people earned their living in wood-using industries—earning $16.5 million in 1963. There were 685,000 acres of forest lands in the five counties, and 205,000 of these were in Fulton County. Within a fifty-mile radius of Atlanta there were 3,623,000 acres of forests.

Growing even faster than the wood products industry was the poultry industry, producing more than a billion dollars a year in gross farm income. The center of this industry, located less than fifty miles north of Atlanta, was spurred on by Charles J. Thurmond, president of Jesse Jewell, Inc., the leading processors. Broiler production, said Thurmond, was up from 50 million birds in 1956 to 2 billion in 1963. Advanced feeding technology now made it possible to bring a chick to a 3½-pound market bird in eight weeks on seven pounds of food. Twenty years earlier it had taken sixteen weeks and twelve pounds of food to produce a 2½-pound chicken.

One of the most important developments of 1963–64 was the commencement of the action that would make Atlanta a major-league city in sports. Mayor Ivan Allen made clear his desire to build a great Atlanta stadium that would be the home in future years of big-league teams in all fields of sports. Banker Mills B. Lane told Allen that he would be glad to back Mayor Allen's stadium ideas with the resources of his Citizens and Southern National Bank. Mayor Allen and Paul Hemphill tell the story of what happened in the mayor's book *Mayor: Notes on the Sixties*. Allen took Mills out to the place he visualized as the site for the new stadium—a large acreage in the Washington-Rawson area, just south of the capitol. Once one of Atlanta's nicest neighborhoods with majestic trees and beautiful old homes surrounded by stone walls, it had deteriorated into one of the city's worst slums. The area was being cleared under urban renewal. This place—where four interstate highways come together—was an ideal site for a stadium. Recalled Allen:

When Mills Lane commits himself to something like that, I had learned, you can count on its being accomplished. I finally had found somebody who was going to build Atlanta a stadium, and fortunately it was the one man in town who had the enthusiasm and the resources, plus an understanding of the risks involved, to do it. We were ready to go now. I began carrying out a calculated plan of bringing twenty or twenty-five of our most prominent citizens—press executives, bank presidents, heads of the major companies—to the site, giving them the grand tour of the building site, so I could get them excited over the idea of the stadium. News of what was going on broke in the newspapers. The Stadium Authority started holding meetings. Major-league fever was catching on all over town.

A delegation went to Cleveland, where the American League was having its annual meeting in connection with the All-Star Game, but Joe Cronin, president of the league, told them that Charlie Finley did not have enough votes from the other owners to move his club out of Kansas City. (Finley had seen the site earlier and had expressed interest in moving his Kansas City Athletics to Atlanta.) Wrote Ivan Allen:

The next day, however, we were in business again. Arthur Montgomery had arranged a lunch for us with a group of Milwaukee Braves' major stockholders. . . . There were no specific arrangements made during the long luncheon we had that day, but we did begin to talk about the possibility of moving the Braves from Milwaukee to Atlanta. The courtship was on.

Immediately, Mills Lane began his moves. He brought together two architectural firms, gave them a contract and put up the money for them to draw up plans for an ideal stadium. . . . I was, frankly, beginning to get cold feet. We had no specific agreement with the Braves, we had never met with the county commissioners, we had never met with the board of aldermen. There was just Lane and the members of the Stadium Authority, Arthur Montgomery, and myself. Lane showed me the plans that had been drawn while I was gone [on an African safari], and it was then that I realized the size of this project and the speed in which it was moving. "Mills, you have no security on this thing," I said. "You're in awfully deep, and I think it's time you took some steps to protect yourself and the bank." He simply told me, "You go back over to City Hall and run the city's business, and let me run this show."

The plans for the stadium were completed toward the end of the year and sent to the Braves management, which made certain necessary changes, and then in February of 1964 Lane and Bob Richardson and I arranged for a secret meeting in Chicago with their top officials. This is when we made our agreement that the Braves would come to Atlanta. We couldn't draw up a full contract, which would have been premature, but instead came to a verbal understanding that we would immediately begin work on the stadium, and the Braves would come to Atlanta for the 1965 season. We sealed it with a handshake and went back home to make the announcement and start work on construction of the stadium.

I can't imagine a more ambitious idea than trying to build something of this magnitude in twelve months, which is what we had to do if the stadium were to be ready for the opening game of the 1965–66 National League season. Outside of Grady Hospital, this was the largest construction project that had ever been undertaken in Atlanta. The usual time allotted to something like this would be two or even three years, but we were paying a $600,000 premium to the contractors to finish it in one year. In the long run, though, building it in a hurry was probably the most economical thing to do because we got our money at three per cent interest and started construction before building costs began to escalate. How we ever built something that large without a strike or some other slowdown, I'll never know. But all during the summer of 1964 this magnificent structure was slowly rising out of the ground, like another phoenix from the ashes, and the construction of the stadium—right there at the interchange, for everybody to see—had baseball fever running high in Atlanta. It was the symbol that we had broken away from the old small-town attitudes and were moving up a notch to join the very biggest cities in the United States. . . .

We went to New York early in 1965 to sign the final contracts and make it official that the Braves would move to Atlanta in time to open the season there, but we wound up in court with the city of Milwaukee. After half a century in Boston the Braves had moved to Milwaukee in 1953 and had gone over the million mark in attendance five different seasons and the two million mark four times. But for three consecutive years now (1962, '63, '64) the club had not reached one million, which was the main reason it wanted to move. The city of Milwaukee suddenly cared about their Braves, and the legal hassle that exploded became the top story on sports pages all over the country for several months and wound up costing both cities a considerable amount of money in legal fees (in Atlanta's case, $800,000). It was eventually ruled that the Braves would have to play out their contract in Milwaukee (where they drew only 555,584 fans during the '65 season) before being allowed to transfer to Atlanta. It had cost us a premium of $600,000 to have Atlanta Stadium completed in fifty-one weeks, and now all we had to show for it was one final summer of watching the Atlanta Crackers. That became an issue during my campaign for re-election in late '65 ("Allen's Coffin," some called the stadium), but all was forgiven on the night of April 12, 1966, when 50,671 jammed the place for the regular-season opener for the new Atlanta Braves. I had spent many hours lying awake in the middle of the night, thinking about that empty stadium and how I had led Mills Lane into building it, and being there that night to throw out the first ball for the first Braves game had to be one of the greatest thrills of my life.

Though Allen, moving on through his first term as mayor, had much to encourage him, there was much going on that caused him grave concern. In the ten years from 1953 to 1964, major crime in Atlanta had increased by 142 percent. This was fifteen times faster than the population growth, making Atlanta's crime rate higher in almost every category than in other U.S. cities of comparable size.

So far as Allen's police and the U.S. Justice Department could tell, this was not "syndicate" crime—managed by professional mobsters pulling strings from New York, Chicago, or Miami. It was locally managed, by a "Dixie Mafia" of "good ol' boys" interested in such "minor" crimes as gambling, illegal liquor making, prostitution, and a traffic in drugs.

Atlanta also was, as in the past, the non-tax-paid liquor capital of the world, providing a market for 90 percent of the 50,000 gallons of moonshine produced each week in some 650 stills operating daily in the Georgia hills. The city's auto theft rates were three and a half times the national average— 4,210 stolen cars in 1964 totaling $3 million in losses. The "Bug"—a lottery operation—also was thriving. One of the dozen known "bug" operations, which was broken up in 1965, was doing $2,000 a day in bets, and the usual wager was less than a dollar. The newly created Atlanta Commission on Crime and Delinquency learned that fifteen Atlanta hotels were considered excellent "hustling places" by the city's small army of prostitutes, and narcotics users indicted by the Fulton County Grand Jury rose from thirty in 1964 to eighty in the next year. By then, the mayor pointed out, the city had acquired a sizable "hippie" community.

For a year or more, Mayor Allen was convinced that Atlanta had no need to be concerned with the Mafia's moving in to take over from the local "good ol' boys," who had grown up in the city's white slums and the small dusty towns in the Georgia hinterlands. They might be moonshine distributors on a large scale, lottery kings, bookies, or organizers of auto theft rings. But, to Allen, it seemed obvious that the cultural gap between the local Bible Belt thieves and the Mafioso was so wide that they never could be civil to each other, much less become partners in crime.

"To worm its way into a city," Allen wrote, "the Mafia needs three basic things, a public apathy, protection from high officials inside the city government, and some contact with the local machine. But that civic pride which had been the catalyst for the tremendous growth of Atlanta in recent years was an assurance that Atlanta's citizens would care a hell of a lot if big-time crime moved in."

There had not been a scandal in city hall in thirty-odd years, Allen recalled, and he had complete faith that Police Chief Herbert Jenkins and the key men in other city departments would not break that streak. Also, the town had a built-in "fifth column" in the local criminals, the "good ol' boys" who, Allen believed, could be depended upon to keep the doors shut against the incoming Mafioso. However, Allen admitted later that by the late 1960s the Mafia had begun to arrive in Atlanta.

Racial tension, as in the past, marked the year's activities from the start. Early in January, 1964, Negro action groups had met in the Atlanta offices of the NAACP and had laid out a detailed battle plan in which the Southern Christian Leadership Conference (SCLC), SNCC, the Committee on Appeal for Human Rights, and Operation Breadbasket all would take a part. The tactics, as outlined by the Rev. Wyatt Tee Walker, close aide to the Rev. Martin Luther King, Jr., would be nonviolent, but stubbornly carried out. The idea was that the students would demonstrate clearly what the issues were—and the leaders in the black community would then negotiate these issues with the leaders in the white community.

The year of confrontation began on January 7 when high school students began "playing hookey for freedom" and taking to the downtown streets after a brief, short course in nonviolent active techniques put on at Rush Memorial Congregational Church on Chestnut Street. There were some 150 of them in the line of march as they crossed Hunter and Forsyth streets, headed for City Hall. There, when Mayor Allen told them that he did not intend to "recognize a group of school children who demonstrated during school hours without the authorization of school authorities," they stormed up the steps to his second-floor office where they took off their coats and sat down on the floor of his reception room.

There, two school officials attempted to calm the students and persuade them to leave quietly. Dr. Raul Stephens, deputy superintendent of schools, began by addressing them as "Boys and Girls" but they shouted him down. "We want to be called 'citizens,'" they shouted. Finally they let him speak; he told them that they were out of school illegally and must return. Next, Dr. J. Y. Moreland, principal of Washington High School, from which many of the students were playing hookey, made his pitch. "I am here because I love you," he began—and they shouted with derisive laughter. Then they began to voice their own complaints—about triple shifts and overcrowded classrooms. Finally persuaded by school officials to leave, they marched from the mayor's office to a hamburger stand several blocks away. They were refused service, but they remained inside and on the sidewalks near the door while city police conferred with the management. No arrests were made, and after a time they left, going to a short-order restaurant nearby. There the doors were closed and locked, and finally, after being ordered to clear the sidewalks, they headed for home. It was a tense beginning to a tense year.

Though Mayor Allen was stern in his attitude toward the students who played hookey from school on January 7, two days later, in an address to the Hungry Club, he announced his support of a bill, sponsored by state senator Leroy Johnson, which would pave the way for a public accommodations law that would cure many of the ills the students had played hookey to protest. The amendment to the city charter proposed by Senator Johnson, the only black member of the legislature, would permit city aldermen to pass a bill that would forbid discrimination in restaurants and hotels in Atlanta because of race.

Allen challenged the surrounding areas outside the city limits to pass similar legislation. The forty-six separate authorities that governed the 700,000 persons living in metropolitan Atlanta outside the city limits had not matched the steps already taken by Atlanta in desegregating police and private facilities, and in offering equal opportunity for employment to all people, regardless of race. The mayor also praised "the responsible Negro leadership of Atlanta, and urged Negroes of Atlanta not to turn leadership over to groups that have no responsibility other than to create an incident."

Actually, in Atlanta over a period of months much of the desegregation that the Negro community was demanding had been taking place. However, many institutions that were opening their doors to blacks were doing so only if it was agreed that they not be publicly identified. Therefore, it came as some surprise when Mayor Allen, on January 10, announced that fourteen Atlanta hotels and motels would "honor all room reservations, including those made by Negroes." This was the first time that public accommodations involved in desegregation had agreed to the public disclosure of their names, and it came about after a series of meetings between the operators, Mayor Allen, and civic leaders. Thirty-five hotel and motel operators and one hundred restaurant operators took part in the sessions, but the restaurant operators took no action. "However," Allen said, "the Restaurant Association has urged its members to consider the facts that were brought out yesterday and to search their hearts, minds and consciences and make their own decision as to what their future course of action will be."

The hotels and motels named by Allen were the Air Host Inn, Atlanta Americana Motel Hotel, Atlantan Hotel, Atlanta Biltmore, Atlanta Cabana, Dinkler Plaza, Hilton Inn, Peachtree Manor, Piedmont Hotel, Riviera Hotel, Howard Johnson's South Expressway, Howard Johnson's Northeast Expressway, Howard Johnson's Northwest Expressway, and the Marriott Motor Hotel, still under construction. Before the week was out, the Holiday Inns on the Northwest Expressway and on Piedmont Avenue also desegregated.

Other doors than those of hotels and motels were being opened to Negroes in the early months of 1964. On January 15 Mayor Allen nominated Dr. P. Q. Yancey to the Fulton County Board of Health for a four-year term. His nomination, believed to be the first for a Negro physician, went to the Board of Aldermen for election. Dr. Yancey, a graduate of Meharry Medical College in Nashville, was a member of the Atlanta Medical Society and was the brother of Dr. Asa Yancey, chief of surgery at Hughes Spalding Pavilion at Grady Memorial Hospital.

Allen, toward the end of January, planned to name Negro attorney A. T. Walden as traffic court solicitor, the first time a black man would hold such a position in Atlanta. As it turned out, however, Walden, who had retired from his legal practice, did not want the heavy duties of a solicitor. Instead, he agreed to be named to a pro hoc vice—meaning "for this term"—judgeship. He would serve on a temporary basis when other traffic judges were ill or on vacation, or for any reason were off duty.

Clayton R. Yates, another Negro businessman and civic leader, was to be named to the Fulton–DeKalb County Hospital Authority at a meeting of the Fulton County Commission on January 22. He was the first Negro to be appointed to this board. Yates, sixty-seven, was chairman of the board of the Citizens Trust Company, president of the South View Cemetery Association, Inc., and the Southeastern Fire Insurance Company, and was vice-president of Mutual Federal Savings and Loan Association of Atlanta. In civic activities he was chairman of the board of the First Congregational Church, treasurer of the Hunter Street YMCA, a member of the executive committee of the Republican party in Georgia, and a trustee of Morehouse College, from which he graduated, and of Atlanta University.

In the appointment of black specialists to important civic jobs, in the hiring of more Negroes on jobs hitherto closed to them, in the opening of more restaurant doors to black diners, in the acceptance of eight black business firms into membership in the Chamber of Commerce, in the drive in Fulton County to register more voters, including the appointment of Negro registrars to "get out the vote" in black communities, it seemed clear that at last white and Negro populations were slowly lowering the barriers that had stood between them down through the years. This did not mean that loud and angry demonstrations were ended; they were not—and the danger of bloody street fighting grew more likely as the Ku Klux Klan began to demand the right to hold mass rallies in the public parks. Yet, even here, when there was actual combat, there was an element of restraint that had not existed before.

Paul Valentine in the *Atlanta Journal* of January 29 told of a confrontation the previous Saturday night:

Veteran police officers described the eight hours of student-led demonstrations and Klan-led counter-demonstrations Saturday night as one of the most explosive situations in their memory.

Late Saturday night, in front of the Downtown Motel on West Peachtree Street, a fist-swinging melee broke out directly involving at least 50 whites and Negroes. On the sidewalks were some 200 Negroes and about 100 Klansmen and their sympathizers. . . .

How did the street fight in front of the motel develop? SNCC picketers arrived and formed two lines on the sidewalk with a narrow path between them. They sang, chanted, clapped. Soon the Klansmen arrived and formed a march line on the sidewalk. Grand Dragon Calvin Craig exhorted the white crowd: "Show 'em we got the same rights they have! Show 'em we can walk this sidewalk, too!"

Craig then ordered the whites, many of them robed, to walk between the two lines of jeering, chanting Negroes. As Klansmen ran the gauntlet, Negroes and whites alike yelled, cursed and gestured at each other in an almost nose-to-nose confrontation.

The Klan line marched through once, then turned around and started through again. The din of cursing and yelling rose. The double line of SNCC demonstrators weaved unevenly. Then, suddenly, one of the lines brushed against a robed Klansman. He was shoved off balance and turned toward the line of Negroes.

In an instant, the lines disintegrated into a confusion of twisting bodies, flying fists and certified bedlam. Police moved in. People on the periphery moved in, pulling and tugging. The din grew, but above it could be heard voices of a few Negroes imploring the demonstrators to retreat. . . .

The violence culminated some eight hours of unrelenting demonstrations and counter-demonstrations. With the police now in control again, the SNCC faction turned and headed back toward center city. The Klan headed the other way. A few minutes later, quiet returned to the streets.

The streets, of course, did not remain quiet. On Monday night after the weekend of riots, hundreds of marching, singing black demonstrators swarmed through downtown Atlanta and followed a sound truck through black residential neighborhoods, calling on their leaders to plan more massive segregation protests. There were 116 arrests, and some of the protestors were injured when they fell on the sidewalk and had to be dragged by police to the patrol wagons. Some injuries, police claimed, occurred when those arrested started breaking up furniture in the jail.

Among those arrested, and who went quietly without protest, was black comedian Dick Gregory. Those who did block streets and restaurant doorways, and had to be dragged to police cars, and who then smashed furniture in jail, had not had the opportunity to be trained in the Gandhian tactic of nonviolent protest, according to Debbie Ames, field secretary of SNCC.

Mayor Allen's reaction to the weekend of violence was to call together some three hundred of Atlanta's top leaders, both black and white, in business, the professions, the churches, and civic organizations. Allen, in his speech to the group, said that he intended to use "all the forces of the city, including my own best efforts, to guarantee racial harmony." Then he added: "Between the white and Negro community there is a sharp difference in the definition of the term, 'racial harmony.' The white community as a whole tends to define racial harmony as the absence of disturbance. The Negro community—to a man—defines it as the establishment of their full rights as American citizens. I am determined to use all of the authority I have to see that in Atlanta both definitions are fulfilled."

He urged the Atlanta Negro community to adopt a cooling-off period in their demonstrations against the Atlanta restaurants, for "further demonstrations of this kind endanger the law and order of our city." The mayor had announced that he planned to set up in the mayor's office a Civil Rights Section "to insure the Negro community full rights in the matter of public facilities, jobs, job training, and housing."

One who knew that he would never offer the Negro community "full rights" to eat in his restaurant was segregationist Lester Maddox, ax-handle-waving owner of the Pickrick. So, near the passage of the Civil Rights Act in July of 1964, he closed the restaurant rather than obey what the act demanded—that he open his doors to blacks as well as whites. It proved to be a highly productive political move. In 1966 his opposition to integration propelled him into the governorship, in what was called "Probably the most hectic and confusing election in the history of the state."

In the year 1964, when Lester Maddox was battling the government's order that he serve Negroes or close his Pickrick Restaurant, the man he contemptuously called Martin Luther "Coon" was awarded one of the highest honors a citizen of the world can receive. Martin Luther King, Jr., was chosen to receive the Nobel Peace Prize for his ten-year struggle for the rights of men and women, black and white, to live and work side by side in a world of equal opportunity. And though King himself had been cursed, spat on, jailed, and his life threatened, he had carried on his campaign peacefully, completely dedicated to nonviolence.

To Mayor Ivan Allen, Jr., this meant that Atlanta had a chance to cross the last social barrier, to cast aside "the remnants of our old bigotry." He would give a dinner honoring Dr. King—a biracial banquet to which the city's leaders in all fields would be invited. It took some pushing on Allen's part, for not only were the blue-collar followers of Lester Maddox opposed to King and all he stood for, but many prominent members of the business community were angry at Dr. King's success at desegregating public facilities.

Allen found himself a half-step ahead of his business friends. The award had been announced on October 14, 1964. For several weeks, in private talks he kept up the argument—how would Atlanta, struggling to become one of the leading cities of the nation, look if Martin Luther King, Jr., recipient of this great honor, were not even recognized in his own city? Finally with endorsement from Paul Austin, president of the Coca-Cola Company (and indirectly from Robert Woodruff himself), the dinner plans took shape.

Allen, in his book, recalled that evening late in January of 1965 when the dinner was held—three months after the announcement of the award:

Almost every major white business leader in Atlanta was in attendance the night more than fifteen hundred blacks and whites gathered at the old Dinkler Hotel in the very center of downtown Atlanta to honor Dr. Martin Luther King, Jr. Understandably, there was tension in the hall where the banquet was being held. Out front, on the sidewalk, some members of the Ku Klux Klan were picketing. There had been a raft of bomb threats, and we had some two hundred plainclothesmen planted in the audience. Then, too, there was the natural uneasiness that would come at a first biracial gathering such as this. I had an opportunity to put everyone at ease, which I felt was my job, when those of us who would be at the head table were waiting in another room before entering the main dining hall. Somebody came up to the Reverend Sam Williams and me and apologized to us that the dinner was going to run about forty-five minutes late because of the unexpectedly large turnout. "Don't worry about that," I said. "My friend Sam Williams has been waiting for a hundred years to get in that ballroom, and forty-five minutes one way or the other isn't going to bother him much."

It was a wonderful occasion. The King children were in the peak of their youth, climbing on top of the table and under the table, getting all of the attention they could. I was seated next to Mrs. King, and as I talked to her I began to see the great depth and patience she had. Dr. King made a magnificent address, and I gave him a proclamation bound in a beautiful lavender velvet portfolio, probably the most handsome official gift the city presented while I was in office. The evening was also another chance for me to get to know Martin Luther King, Jr., a little better. Here he was, winner of the Nobel Prize, giving him every reason in the world to be somewhat bitter or pompous toward people who had spent much of their past lives fighting what he had dedicated his life to do. But he was a big man, a great man.

Mrs. Coretta Scott King also remembers that evening: It was to her "the most surprising of all the tributes" that her husband received in connection with his Nobel award. There was, she knew, a strong mixture of feeling in Atlanta's white community. Wrote Mrs. King:

When we arrived at the hotel that night we beheld a beautiful sight. The big ballroom was filled with fifteen hundred people, and several hundred had to be turned away. There were Negroes and whites from all levels. Judges and top-ranking industrialists were sitting at the same tables with cooks and porters, all mixed up deliberately. The audience was about sixty-five percent white and thirty-five percent black. It seemed as though everybody in Atlanta was there—completely integrated. Ten years, five years, even one year before, such a sight would have been unthinkable in a southern city. . . .

At the end of the ceremonies, after all the beautiful tributes had been paid, we all joined hands and sang, "We Shall Overcome." It was tremendously moving—the spirit of it. We *had* overcome a major barrier for a southern city. We felt, for that night at least, it was really "black and white together" in Atlanta.[4]

Not only Martin Luther King, Jr., but many others were seeking some solution to the growing racial tension. Even Calvin Craig, grand dragon of the

Ku Klux Klan in Georgia, in 1964 had come forward with a proposal which he considered would keep peace between the races. He asked that Atlanta establish a new biracial group, made up of an equal number of black integrationists and white segregationists. This group would probe any civil rights dispute that might arise. His view was that there should be no law either upholding integration or imposing segregation in public accommodations. The owner of the store or restaurant, or any other agency serving the public, should be permitted to make a private decision without fear of reprisal as to whether to serve whites only, or Negroes and whites, or Negroes only.

Once the business owner had decided, a list of segregated and integrated establishments would be made up and announced publicly, and each establishment would have a sign in the window announcing which people it would serve. Craig pointed out that this would prevent sudden racial flare-ups—for "white segregationists are confused, embarrassed and enraged when they walk unwittingly into an integrated establishment. Negroes are embarrassed or enraged if they go by mistake into a segregated restaurant and are asked to leave."

The Ku Klux Klan leader's proposal was similar in mood and message to a Fulton County Grand Jury special presentment adopted on January 29, 1964. The grand jury deplored the violence of racial demonstrations and asked whites and Negroes to mediate their problems. In a special presentment the jury deplored "recent and continued demonstrations that involve violations of the law, which are now being fanned to the near-kindling point of open violence by irresponsible elements among both white and Negro." The presentment called upon the Atlanta Police Department and the sheriff of Fulton County to "take such measures as are necessary to see that law and order is maintained." "We are deeply concerned at the prospect of further violence, even bloodshed," the jurors wrote. "We therefore call upon all citizens of this county, regardless of their sympathies or connection with the issue, to respect law and order. Without permanently abrogating any of their basic rights, we call upon them to invoke mutual respect, understanding and trust, and to rise above the heat of the present situation."

For a number of distinguished Atlantans 1964 was the time for retirement, for laying their burdens down by a trout stream, or a golf course, or a friendly rocking chair.

Among them was Dewey L. Johnson, age sixty-five, who for thirty-five years had been serving the city's electrical department—first as electrical inspector, and then for thirty-one years as superintendent for electrical affairs. Another Atlantan going into retirement in 1964 after years of service to the city was George Simons, head of the Atlanta Parks Department since 1931. Since then Simons, who had been a printer on the old *Atlanta Georgian* and on the *Journal-Constitution* when the *Georgian* closed, had seen the Parks Department grow from 70 employees to 450 (600 in the summer), and its budget had increased from $100,000 in 1931 to about $3 million in 1964.

Much of the growth had been the result of the city's expanding its boundaries. Old areas, however, had not been neglected. The biggest Parks Department accomplishments were the new zoo in Grant Park and the remodeling of the Cyclorama there. Another retiree in this year was a national, not just a local, figure—Representative Carl Vinson, dean of the House of Representatives in Washington. Six hundred government, civic, and business leaders gathered at the Dinkler Plaza Hotel on the night of January 22 to honor the venerable congressman as he accepted the Georgia Medal for Distinguished Public Service. Their applause was loudest when Dr. Rufus Harris, president of Mercer University, said in presenting the medal: "Countless Georgians tonight carry in their hearts a lingering hope that he may 'carry on' in Congress." Vinson's answer: "When a man reaches 80 years old and 50 years in Congress, it's time to go home."

Honors fell thick and fast on other Atlantans and Georgians. On Saturday night, February 15, three great sports figures, golfer Bobby Jones, baseball star Ty Cobb, and footall coach William A. Alexander, were inducted as charter members of the Georgia State Athletic Hall of Fame at a huge sportsman's banquet at the Dinkler Plaza Hotel. The induction address was made by Gov. Carl Sanders, who said in part: "I doubt if any state in the union can boast of such sports Gargantuas as we have chosen for our initial Hall of Fame induction: Bobby Jones, the first and only undisputed golf champion; Ty Cobb, voted in every poll the greatest baseball player who ever lived, and Bill Alexander, who firmly established Georgia Tech as a national football power, a position which she so pre-eminently still occupies."

An eloquent expression of Atlanta's and Georgia Tech's affection for longtime Dean of Men George Griffin came on his retirement in May of 1964. Griffin retired after forty years of service to Georgia Tech that ranged in nature from scrub football player and coach to dean of students. He had served thirteen years as assistant to the late Dean Floyd Field and eighteen years as successor to Field.

A man somewhat more venerable than the recent honorees and retirees had his day of retirement in March. Robert F. Maddox had started to work as a very young man in 1889, and his career had been a busy one. Along the way he had been president of the American Bankers Association, president of the Georgia Bankers Association, mayor of Atlanta, and sixty years earlier had been president of the Atlanta Chamber of Commerce. Maddox was retiring after seventy-two years of continuous service on the board of the First National Bank of Atlanta. "As he approaches his 94th birthday," said *Atlanta* magazine, "Mr. Maddox is without peer in distinguished service."

One Atlantan received a knighthood in this year of honor. King Boudouin of Belgium awarded Henry L. DeGive, his honorary consul in Atlanta, the title of Chevalier de L'Order de la Couronne—the Order of the Crown. DeGive was the third member of his family to hold the Belgian consulship in Atlanta. His grandfather had been the first consul more than a century earlier; he succeeded his father, Henry L. DeGive, Sr., at his death in 1948, and since had been busy promoting trade relations between Belgium and the United States. The DeGives had left their family name on several Atlanta landmarks, among them the DeGive Opera House, located first on Marietta Street, then on Peachtree, later the site of Loew's Grand Theater. This latest consul, an Atlanta native, was an alumnus of Princeton University, Harvard Law School, and the Sorbonne in Paris.

John F. Still, Fulton County's nationally recognized comptroller, had been named the outstanding local government money-manager of 1963. Still, at age fifty-four, had been an employee of the county since 1933 and was awarded the Good Government Award of the Atlanta Junior Chamber of Commerce in a field of five finalists. One of his achievements was his publication the previous year of a budgeting manual that would be used statewide. He traveled over Georgia, teaching other financial officers from his book.

In the twenty-first year of the Woman of the Year awards Mrs. A. Thornton Kennedy was selected as the winner in the arts. She had worked for many years as a volunteer for the Art Association and the Atlanta Symphony. Mrs. Mark L. Trammell was the honored businesswoman. Deaf and dumb until she was twelve, she completed her education after she was an adult; she flew with the Women's Airforce Service Pilots during the war and ultimately turned a failing marine parts supply business into a million-dollar annual gross. Mrs. Trammell attributed her success to her husband's constant support and encouragement. Florene (Mrs. Edgar M.) Dunstan was Woman of the Year in education. Dr. Dunstan was an Agnes Scott Spanish teacher and a devoted teacher in her Baptist church. In 1963 she had served as president of the Atlanta Branch of the American Association of University Women. Lydia McKee, the founder and executive director of Atlanta's Visiting Nurse Association (a Community Chest agency), won in the public health field.

The overall Woman of the Year was the winner in civic service, Mrs. Henry Toombs. Adah Toombs had led a twelve-year fight to get Georgia children out of jails, and it paid off in 1963 when the legislature finally passed a bill she had been advocating.

Though not listed among the 1964 Women of the Year in Atlanta for her achievements in 1963, Mrs. Harry M. Thweatt did achieve one distinction. She became the first woman member of BOMA—the Building Owners and Managers Association—when she was appointed manager of the Medical Arts Building. She had gone to work there in 1927 as a "Girl Friday" and "general flunky" for the new building's owner and builder, Harry M. Thweatt, who taught her the business of managing a big downtown office building. Thweatt's wife died in 1956, and he and his Girl Friday were married in 1960. In October of 1963 Mr. Thweatt died, and the building's board of directors named her the new manager and secretary-treasurer. Ten tenants then in the building were there when she first came to work in 1927.[5]

Another important local woman also reached a milestone in 1964.

Christine Smith Gilliam had served the city for almost two decades as Atlanta's official movie censor. *Atlanta* magazine commented:

Ever since 1945 when she began a stormy, tough-skinned tenure as the city's movie censor, she has waited for the last reel to unwind. When it finally did, it was at her request. She resigned her $7,202 a year job, suggesting to Mayor Ivan Allen that the position end up on the cutting room floor.

Some 5,500 movies ago, Mrs. Gilliam started her marathon, pungently rating what she saw. But in recent years court decisions have blunted her effectiveness, curtailing her authority to grade films publicly as suitable for "adults" or "youths." The courts ruled the grading system "prior restraint."

In reflection, she singled out *Red Shoes* for praise. "From the standpoint of artistry, no movie topped it." In other categories, she lauded *Henry V* and *Richard III* (Laurence Olivier) as "extremely well done." As to movies with themes about psychopaths, she singled out *The Seventh Veil* as "an excellent movie," and in comedy *Please Don't Eat The Daisies*, *Room for One More*, and *Cheaper by the Dozen* were remembered as among the best.

Mrs. Gilliam's reign was dotted with court actions and debate. For her, this is past. What now, Mrs. Gilliam?

"I may cultivate my garden, return to my music and cooking," she said.[6]

Dignitaries of various ranks and stations were coming and going in Atlanta throughout 1964. One was Billy Graham, the famed evangelist, who arrived to speak at a prayer breakfast hosted by Gov. and Mrs. Carl Sanders on the morning of January 14 and later in the day at a joint session of the General Assembly. From it he drew a shouted chorus of "Amens" as he prayed and preached for more moral and religious strength in government.

Graham's visit was the top religious news for the moment, but much was going on in the Georgia field of religion. In the Presbyterian Church in the United States, for example, there were about nine hundred churches with vacant pulpits, because of normal rates of death and retirement, and though the historic Columbia Theological Seminary in Decatur was the largest Presbyterian seminary in the United States, it graduated each year only about a third of the young ministers that the church needed. So that it could expand, Columbia Seminary was looking for funds with which to build a chapel, a gymnasium, and other church-affiliated buildings.

Peachtree Christian Church (Disciples of Christ) dedicated a new $600,000 multiple-use building for its 2,079 members. It was the first big addition since the church had been built in 1928 where Peachtree and West Peachtree split. Principal speaker at the dedication, which took place on Sunday, January 5, was Sen. Richard B. Russell, whose theme was that Americans have more material wealth than the rest of the world, but have not equalled the spiritual life of the nation's founders.

The migration of downtown population to outlying areas plus the need for intown commercial building sites had its effect on many of the older downtown Atlanta churches. Going into 1964 the site where Westminster Presbyterian Church had stood, at Ponce de Leon and Boulevard, was only a pile of rubble. It had been sold in 1961 to Ponce de Leon Investment Company, Inc., which had plans to build a twelve-story building there. Westminster Presbyterian had moved on to its new site at 1438 Sheridan Road NE, reported to be a more central location for its membership. The late Peter Marshall had been the noted pastor of Westminster at its old site, in the 1930s.

In March it was announced that another old church, in the heart of Atlanta, would go under the wrecking ball, to be replaced by a commercial structure. A twenty-three-story office building would be erected on the site of Wesley Memorial Church, at the southeast corner of Ivy Street and Auburn Avenue.

While some old Atlanta churches were making way for commercial buildings or taking on new life and dimensions through fund drives, one of the oldest of them all, St. Luke's Episcopal, was celebrating its one-hundredth anniversary. Its earliest ministry was to the thousands of Confederate soldiers and refugees pouring into Atlanta before the advancing troops of General Sherman. In August of 1864 the little wooden church, built at a cost of 1,200 Confederate dollars, was shelled, and in November it was burned in the burning of Atlanta. After the burning, its communicants scattered, and for six years St. Luke's did not exist. Then in 1870 a small group of five survivors of the original congregation assembled and began holding regular services.

One project marking its one hundred years of service was the Centennial Memorial Window, "Peter's Confession," to bring color, beauty, and a spiritual message to the north side of the balcony. The congregation was raising a centennial Thanks Offering—$100,000—to be used in a scholarship fund for the education of the clergy and for the support of the Episcopal church seminaries and training schools throughout the world. The theme of the centennial observation was "God Speaks to the World through Men, not Bricks and Mortar."

Meanwhile, one man proposed to speak by providing money for bricks and mortar. A local philanthropist who preferred to remain anonymous offered to give the city $4 million toward the construction of a cultural center, provided another $2 million could be raised by public subscription. The donor, of course, was Robert W. Woodruff of the Coca-Cola Company, who was not yet willing to acknowledge publicly his fabulous contributions to education and the arts in Atlanta. The center was to be developed on Art Association property at Peachtree and Fifteenth streets, and was to consist of a single structure, unifying the existing Art Association Museum Building with a symphony hall, a repertory theater, and quarters for the Atlanta School of Art.

The Metropolitan Foundation of Atlanta, established in 1953 by five Atlanta banks, gave Atlantans an opportunity to distribute funds to dozens of worthwhile charitable organizations dealing with youth and child welfare, education, health, intergroup relations, care of the aged, and religious and cultural activities. The banks, which were the foundation's trustees for the fund, would hold and invest the funds as the donors designated—or at their own discretion if no designation were made. In the eleven years since 1953 the foundation had distributed more than $1.5 million to groups that ran the gamut of worthy causes. In 1963 it gave over $250,000 to charitable, educational, religious, and cultural activities. These went to such diverse recipients as Northside Alcoholics Benevolent Association; the Community Council of the Atlanta Area, to help finance a neighborhood improvement program; the Atlanta Legal Aid Society; Recordings for the Blind, Inc., to provide new recording facilities for blind students; the Carrie Steele Pitts Home for Negro children; and the Atlanta Symphony Guild.

Atlantans had the chance to see lots of big-time entertainment in the summer of 1964. One of the highlights occurred when Dorothy Kirsten, Robert Merrill, and Richard Tucker sang in a program titled "Grand Opera at the Park." This performance followed by one week the usual summer season of Theater Under the Stars, which began July 14 and ran through August 23. The program included Van Johnson in *Bye-Bye, Birdie*, Julius LaRosa in *West Side Story*, Ann Blyth in *Sound of Music*, Jane Morgan in *Gypsy*, Michael Allinson in *My Fair Lady*, and Ginger Rogers in *Tovarich*.

For all its confidence in the future, Atlanta in 1964 was still proud of its past and joined eagerly with the State of Georgia, through the Civil War Centennial Commission, in laying plans for the most intensive commemoration yet observed of the part Georgia played in the war of 1861–65. Atlantan Beverly DuBose, chairman of the commission, announced that the week of June 8 through 12 would be Georgia Civil War Centennial Week, and Civil War Centennial commissions from throughout the nation would come to Atlanta for their annual meeting. This event would bring to the city leading historians for talks and lectures and other events open to the public, and the week would conclude with the National Conclave of Civil War Round Tables. The Centennial Commission was also working through state, county, and city officials to provide more adequate marking of battlefields, army routes, and other interesting data of the Civil War.

OBITUARIES

Bona Allen, Jr., prominent Gwinnett County industrialist and philanthropist, died at 87. He was president and board chairman of Bona Allen, Inc., a Buford leather products company employing over 500 people. A graduate of Emory at Oxford, he joined his father's company in 1897 and became president in 1925. Allen's company donated the land for Buford's high school and he was a trustee of Young Harris College. He was a member of the Savannah Yacht Club, Yaarab Temple, Masons, and the Capital City Club. Harold William Beers, Sr., was the founder of Beers Construction Company. A graduate of MIT, he came to Atlanta in 1907 to join Southern Ferrow Concrete Co. He became president in 1925, and ten years later he and his son formed their own construction company. His memberships included the Piedmont Driving Club, the Capital City Club, the Commerce Club, Atlanta Historical Society, English Speaking Union, and Farmington Country Club in Charlottesville, Virginia. Dr. Joseph Z. Biegeleisen, 41, was a bacteriologist at CDC responsible for research projects concerning rapid diagnosis of bacteria-caused diseases. L. M. (Rip) Blair, 69, was a five-term mayor of Marietta and one of those responsible for bringing Lockheed to Georgia. A graduate of Emory at Oxford, he served in World War I and then opened a law practice in 1919. He was a member of the Capital City Club and Marietta Country Club, a former president of Rotary, and a member of the First Methodist Church.

Dr. L. Minor Blackford was a distinguished heart specialist and medical writer. He was an authority on the Civil War and had published several books on the subject. Dr. Alfred Blalock, 65, pioneer heart surgeon who helped perfect the "blue baby" operation, was a graduate of the University of Georgia and Johns Hopkins. He received the American Medical Association's Distinguished Service Award in 1953. William H. Boring, Jr., 52, was editor at the Coca-Cola Company. He began his writing career on the staff of the *Constitution* and joined Coca-Cola in 1952. He was editor of *The Refresher* magazine and later *The Coca-Cola Bottler*. He was a graduate of Emory and a member of St. James Methodist Church.

Mary Givens Bryan, 53, was director of the Georgia Department of Archives and History. She had thirty years of experience as an archivist and was a pioneer in the microfilming of important documents. She attended Emory and Women's College of Georgia at Milledgeville. Ben Fortson, secretary of state, said she made all the plans for the handsome new archives building, one of the finest in America, which she did not live to see completed. John L. Conner, 60, founder and chairman of the board of Southern Federal Savings and Loan, was national director of the Navy League and had served as lieutenant colonel on the staffs of three Georgia governors. He was a member of the Atlanta Athletic Club, the East Lake Country Club, the Buckhead Fifty, and the Thirteen Club. He was a Mason and member of the First Presbyterian Church. Dudley Dorch, Sr., founder of the Dorch Baking Company and devoted member of the Seventh Day Adventist Church, died at 86. J. Lyon Duckworth, 65, was vice-president and general counsel of the Life Insurance Company of Georgia. He was a graduate of Young Harris College and Lamar School of Law at Emory University. He was associated with the firm of McElreath, Scott, Duckworth and Riley before becoming general counsel for Life of Georgia. He was active in Kiwanis and Druid Hills Baptist Church.

Mrs. Samuel R. Dull, one of the world's leading cooking authorities, died at 100. She was the author of *Southern Cooking*, which had been steadily reprinted since 1928. She started a column on cooking in the *Atlanta Journal* in

1920 that continued for many years. She was proud to be the oldest member of First Baptist Church, where she was active for seventy-five years. Dr. Murdock S. Equen was the founder and chief of staff of the Ponce de Leon Eye, Ear, Nose and Throat Infirmary and one of Georgia's best-known medical men. For his specialized work in throat surgery he received the Thomas A. Edison Gold Award in 1944. A graduate of Vanderbilt, Emory, and the University of Pennsylvania, he was a member of many medical associations, the Kiwanis Club, the Piedmont Driving Club, the Capital City Club, and St. Philip's Cathedral. Edgar Ivan Hilderbrand, veteran of thirty-six years' service with the Atlanta Police Department, died at 67. Among other assignments, he had been superintendent of detectives.

Dr. G. Ray Jordan, a leading Methodist instructor in preaching techniques and professor of homiletics at Emory's Candler School of Theology, died at 68. He was the author of twenty books and more than 200 articles. Dr. Jordan was a graduate of Duke, Emory, and Yale. He was a member of Rotary, Kiwanis, the Atlanta Athletic Club, and the East Lake Country Club. Phillips C. McDuffie, Sr., prominent in Atlanta business, legal, and civic circles, died at 80. He was retired from the law firm of Wimbash, Watkins and Ellis. McDuffie was the developer of Garden Hills and was instrumental in the establishment of North Fulton High School. He was a life member of the Capital City Club and the Piedmont Driving Club. He also belonged to the Atlanta Lawyers' Club and the Atlanta, Georgia, and American Bar Associations. He attended Second Ponce de Leon Baptist Church. Dr. Earl Rasmussen, Atlanta surgeon, his wife Jean, and their thirteen-year-old daughter Lauren died in an automobile accident. Dr. Rasmussen was an assistant professor of surgery at Emory University and was formerly assistant to Dr. Lon Grove. He was a graduate of the University of Virginia and served with the Emory Unit in World War II. Mrs. James A. Rounsaville, president general of the UDC in 1901–1903 and one-time Georgia regent of the DAR, died at 99. Daniel Sinkler, 57, was community relations director for Eastern Airlines and director of the Atlanta Convention Bureau. He was a member of the Piedmont Driving Club, the Commerce Club, the Capital City Club, the Atlanta Athletic Club, Racquet Club, Rotary, and St. Philip's Cathedral.

Charles E. Thwaite, Jr., chairman of the board and chief executive officer of the Trust Company of Georgia, died at 52. He attended Georgia Tech and served eighteen months in Europe in World War II. He was a director or trustee of many organizations and held memberships at Augusta National Golf Club, the Capital City Club, the Commerce Club, the Peachtree Golf Club, and the Piedmont Driving Club. He was on the official board of Northside Methodist Church. B. E. Thrasher, Jr., state auditor and employee of the state since 1927, died at 59. He was a graduate of Georgia Tech. Frank Wilson, superintendent of Grady Hospital and president of the Georgia Hospital Association, died at 62. He was a native Atlantan and graduate of the University of Georgia. Before going into hospital work he had been vice-president of Randall Brothers Lumber Company. Mr. and Mrs. J. Warner Morgan (she was the former Jean McIntosh) died in a plane crash in Louisiana. They were members of First Presbyterian Church, and he was active in the Rotary Club and the Capital City Club. John L. Zachry, 94, was Georgia Tech's oldest alumnus and had been a real estate operator for fifty years. He was chairman of the board of Capri Motel.

Clarence Calhoun, practicing attorney for forty-three years and a founder of Gordon Foods, died at 75. Alvin Bingham (Bing) Cates, veteran Atlanta realtor and chairman of the board of Adams-Cates, died at 77. Mrs. H. L. Davidson, Jr., 52, was the former Helen Candler, daughter of Asa, Jr. She was a member of the Junior League and Dunwoody Methodist Church. Wilmer Crouch Davis, owner of the Hampton Hotel and twice president of the Atlanta Hotel-Motel Association, was a member of the Piedmont Driving Club, the Nine O'Clocks, the Atlanta Athletic Club, and Second Ponce de Leon Baptist Church. Lowell Dowdell, president of Northside Building Supply Company in Doraville, president of Fulghum Sales & Engineering, and president of Fulghum Industries, died at 62.

Howard B. Harmon, vice-president of Retail Credit Company with thirty-seven years' service, died at 70. He was a vestryman at St. Luke's Episcopal Church, a member of Kiwanis, the Capital City Club, and the Piedmont Driving Club and was a Mason and a Shriner. Bessie Jordan, personal maid and devoted friend of Margaret Mitchell, died at 64. She had written a book, *My Dear Miss Peggy.*

NOTES

1. *Atlanta,* Jan., 1964.
2. Ibid.
3. Robert Carney, *What Happened at the Atlanta Times?* (Atlanta: Business Press, 1969).
4. Coretta Scott King, *My Life with Martin Luther King, Jr.* (New York: Avon Books, 1970).
5. *Atlanta,* Aug., 1964.
6. Ibid.

1965

THE facts were plain to see; Atlanta in the half-decade from 1960 to 1965 had become one of the busiest, most exciting progressive cities in the country. Not only in the acquisition of major league sports teams, but in construction in all its forms, the metropolitan area had boomed. Opie Shelton, in his column in the August 1964 issue of *Atlanta* magazine, told the story of what had been built and where. The list included 70 new office buildings (22 downtown) containing 12 million square feet; 84 new manufacturing plants of more than 6 million square feet; 116 new warehouses of 7 million, excluding 7.5 million feet of cold storage space that was built; 32 other installations, such as the Georgia Department of Archives and History with over 3.5 million feet; 22 motels or motor hotels built with 3,737 rooms, one hotel with 800 rooms; 15 movie theaters with 13,500 seats; 5 hospitals with 1,750 beds. "We are building a cultural center to cost over $8,000,000; we are building a $9,000,000 auditorium; we have built a stadium costing $18,000,000, already as active as a beehive; a new trade center of over a million square feet, an industrial city of 1,500,000 feet."

This surging, growing metropolis was the headquarters city of a vast sprawling complex of varied communications facilities, which made Atlanta the undisputed hot-line for the Southeast and tied the city to the nation and the world.

To Southern Bell, this world is 4,500,000 local telephone calls a day, 100,000 long distance calls. Atlanta's twenty-eight communities tied together by 650,000 telephones is the largest toll-free dialing area in the world.

To three large daily newspapers, it is 477,187 papers sold daily, nearly a million readers if just two people read each paper.

To the three commercial television stations in Atlanta, it is 756,700 homes with television sets, which, by the national average, watch five hours and twenty-one minutes of T.V. a day.

For Western Union in Atlanta, it is sending or receiving two million telegrams a month—and delivering them in a variety of ways on a variety of different machines . . . Telex, Desfax, Teleprinter, Broadband Switching.

For educational television stations, like WETV, it means beaming twenty daily programs a week into 1,833 television receivers in fifty classrooms in Atlanta and Fulton County schools alone.

To the Interdenominational Protestant Radio and Television Center near Emory, it means writing, producing, filming, and distributing films to 2,200 radio and television stations throughout the nation.

To the United States Public Health Service, it is the largest audiovisual communications facility devoted to health in the world.

And it is more; it is the National Archives of Medical Motion Pictures, moved last year from Washington, D.C., to Atlanta with its collection of 700 films ranging in subject from African Sleeping Sickness photographed by a medical missionary over a period of 33 years to on-the-spot movies of battlefield surgery in World War II; twenty-seven radio stations with rock and roll and folk and jazz and popular music and "eyes in the sky" and newsmen on the go with portable tape recorders; it is laboratories turning out color slides and 8 mm color movies and advertising agencies turning out brochures and publicity releases; it is the Associated Press and United Press International with Western Union fingers to every remote, lost, forgotten hamlet in the world, and news bureaus for *Time, Life,* the *Wall Street Journal* and the *Los Angeles Times* covering Atlanta on the spot; and it is the aspect of pay television beaming first-run movies, sports events, and Broadway hits into the living room.

In Atlanta, it is bread and butter, livelihood, and profession of 17,000 people. That's what the world of communications is.[1]

When he ran for mayor in 1961, Ivan Allen, Jr., had planned to step down after one term and pass the job on to some other young member of the business community. But this was not to be. The black citizens urged him to stay on because of his testimony for the Kennedy public accommodations bill and his handling of the Martin Luther King, Jr., Nobel Prize dinner. He had the business leaders on his side because desegregating the schools and restaurants and business houses in 1962, 1963, and 1964 had been relatively painless. And even the folks who did not like the way he seemed to favor the blacks liked him because they loved sports—and he had built the stadium.

The city had made great progress in all areas in his first four years—and there was every prospect that this growth would continue. If the gross national product continued its upward surge and unemployment continued its decline, Atlanta, sharing in this prosperity, would grow into a regional and national giant. And there was no reason why he, with his experience, should not lead this progress for at least one more four-year term. So, he ran against Lester Maddox and Muggsy Smith and won.

In his State of the City Address in January of 1966, he told his aldermanic board of his confidence. Atlanta, he told them, had not spent the past one hundred years rebuilding from the ashes to fall prey now to corrosion, corruption, and community disease. "We have the means, the moral determination and the motivation to become, perhaps not America's largest city—we can wait awhile on that—but her finest city. . . . Perhaps we will set a pattern for other cities to follow and thereby create a better way of life for the more than one hundred and thirty million Americans who have cast their lot with the cities. . . . This is indeed a time for decision for our beloved city, and I am confident that her five hundred and four thousand citizens will move in behind this bold effort to make Atlanta truly America's finest city within your lifetime and mine."

However, he continued, in the second half of the sixties, Atlanta was going to have to cope with an entirely new set of problems—problems that had resulted from growing from a sedate regional center to a booming, national city. "Atlanta," he said, "will have to come up with more ways to find money to finance rapid transit, and urban renewal and pollution control."

Speaking to business leaders in Charleston, South Carolina, in December of 1965, Mayor Allen said that Atlanta had enjoyed a four-year economic boom. Much of it was based on the effort to restore old and fading areas of the city to the status they once knew. "It is my considered opinion," said Allen, "based on my experience of many years as a businessman and my first four years as mayor, that one of the most potent factors in boosting our Atlanta economy to its all-time high is our urban renewal program. . . . Two basic indices, construction and employment, show how solid is this surge of success," he added. "Building permits for the past four years should reach half a billion dollars in Atlanta by December 31. . . . The total for the past four years now stands at $492,052,000 as of December 3."

"In employment, the record is equally impressive," the mayor said. "In 1961, when I was president of the Chamber of Commerce, we set 10,000 new jobs a year as our goal for our Forward Atlanta Campaign in the Atlanta metropolitan area. We thought that was a high target. But for each year since then, new jobs created in our metropolitan area have more than doubled that goal. Correspondingly," he said, "unemployment, already less than half the national average, has dropped to a new low of 2.1%." The mayor concluded, "The dollars urban renewal invests in rebuilding and restoring blighted areas put people to work. They bring new businesses into being. They reach out far and wide. As they restore and develop property, they build up the value of our most important resource, our people."

And, though Allen pushed Atlanta forward in these areas throughout 1965 and thereafter, it was Decatur and DeKalb County that would produce the earliest and most spectacular results. A major urban renewal program got under way there in January, 1965, when the Decatur Housing Authority contracted to raze about a dozen old store and office buildings, plus a couple of dozen ancient dwelling houses. These were replaced with the new ten-story DeKalb County Building, which could house most of the county offices.[2]

Other construction in the direction of Decatur was under way early in 1965. Wesley Woods, the new Methodist retirement center on Clifton Road near Emory, was scheduled to open for public inspection on February 19. This facility consisted of 200 rooms and apartments in two towers of ultra-modern design standing ten and thirteen stories high.[3]

Atlanta and Fulton County's population was pushing upward in 1965 at such a pace that thirty-eight new precincts were added in an effort to avoid crowding at the polls. Thirty of the precincts were in Atlanta and eight were outside the city, and each polling place could accommodate no more than 2,500 voters.

Many of the new county residents were coming into the area to work in new business establishments that were being put up beyond the city limits. At Sandy Springs, for instance, Western Electric broke ground for a new $2 million building which would turn a thirty-acre cow pasture into a regional headquarters office site for 1,350 engineers, administrators, and clerical help.

Breaking ground for new buildings kept Gov. Carl Sanders busy throughout the year. On April 7 he crossed spades with four distinguished Atlantans as they took the first step in the construction of a 260,000-square-foot Sears store and a First National Bank branch in Buckhead at Peachtree Road and West Paces Ferry. Taking part in the ceremony were the governor, Mayor Ivan Allen, Jr., James D. Robinson, Jr., chairman of the board of the First National Bank, L. E. Oliver, Sears vice-president, and Luke Surensson, general manager of Sears in the Atlanta area.

Two big northern companies, aware of Atlanta's special status in these changing times, announced in May their plans to expand their operations in the Atlanta area. On May 19 Curtis 1,000, Inc., a business envelope firm, said it would complete transfer of its corporate headquarters from St. Paul, Minnesota, to Atlanta later in 1965, probably in September. And Sinclair Refining Co. said it would consolidate some of its New York offices into a new Atlanta-based Eastern Marketing Region headquarters that would occupy a new $3.5 million 135,000-square-foot building to be erected in Executive Park on the Northeast Expressway at North Druid Hills Road.

In June of 1965 the Hartford Fire Insurance Company and the Hartford Accident and Indemnity Company were saluted at a luncheon when Mayor Allen and Harllee Branch, president of the Southern Company, paid tribute to the Hartford companies at the dedication of a new eighteen-story building facing Hurt Park. It was the first time ever in the South and only the third time in its 160-year history that the Hartford Company had held a board meeting outside the home offices in Hartford, Connecticut. At the Southern Company luncheon John H. Ledbetter, retiring manager of Hartford's southern department, received an inscribed silver platter. Ledbetter, a native Georgian, had been with Hartford for fifty years. Ivan Allen presented Hartford chairman Manning W. Heard the silver-plated shovel Allen had used to break ground for the new building in July of 1963.

In July, Governor Sanders, along with a Dallas, Texas, industrial development firm and many Atlantans high on the financial levels, jointly announced a plan designed to offer economic opportunity to thousands of local citizens. A 3,000-acre tract along the Chattahoochee River was to be transformed into the largest industrial development park in the Southeast, and the second largest one in the nation. It would include an amusement center similar to "Six Flags Over Texas," which the development firm, the Great Southwestern Company, operated between Dallas and Fort Worth. The Atlanta project would be built at a cost of about $7 million and would cover a 100-acre site, with that many more acres set aside for parking and landscaping, as a buffer zone between the play area and the industrial complex.

Ewell Pope and Frank Carter, partners in the Pope and Carter Company of Atlanta, specialists in the development of commercial and industrial properties, worked for five years putting together the 3,000-acre site, for which they earned a brokerage fee of $400,000, the largest ever paid in Atlanta for a single industrial tract. The holding group that purchased the property was made up, among others, of Winthrop Rockefeller; Maurice Moore, president of Continental Trailways in Dallas; and Dallas financier Trammell Crowe, already known in Atlanta for his investment in the Merchandise Mart and the Regency Hotel.

Mayor Allen expressed the "grateful appreciation" of Atlanta for the selection of Atlanta as the site of the new park. The *Journal* described the prominent Atlantans' day in Dallas. "During the day the Atlanta visitors were given a fun-filled tour of the Dallas Amusement Park, where there is a history of Texas since Indian days, and a businessman's tour of the industrial park. Making the trip as guests of the Great Southwest were Pollard Turman, president of the Atlanta Chamber of Commerce; Drs. O. C. Aderhold and Sanford S. Atwood, presidents, respectively, of the University of Georgia and Emory University; James V. Carmichael, chairman of Scripto, Inc., and John J. McDonough, chairman of the Georgia Power Company."

Thus, through a combination of Georgia ambition and ingenuity, and Texas know-how, plus money, the "Six Flags Over Georgia" family entertainment center was opened less than two years after the Dallas planning session, on 276 acres of landscaped parkland just off the I-20 highway, twenty minutes west of downtown Atlanta. Soon after the opening on June 16, 1967, it was attracting thousands of tourists daily from all over the United States, to an Atlanta bearing little resemblance to the past.

Atlanta, nearing 1966, already was beginning to think of itself as an "international city," although there was as yet no direct transport by air from Atlanta to the cities of Europe or Asia and the airport was not yet an "international" airport. It was definitely, however, an "inland port," and the U.S. Customs House at Third Street and Piedmont Avenue was a very busy place handling goods from everywhere. As the *Journal-Constitution* explained:

The U.S. Customs House for the "inland port" of Atlanta does a booming business in the metropolitan area.

Receipts for this particular port of entry for imported goods have skyrocketed from $500,000 in 1958 to more than $2,000,000 a year.

And, according to Newton Medford, Jr., deputy collector in charge of the Atlanta office, "it's continuing to rise. We don't see any limitation in the future."

A customhouse, particularly a thriving one, seems a bit unusual for inland Atlanta.

Nonetheless, its 12 employees:

—Clear thousands of dollars of merchandise imported to Atlanta from foreign countries.

—Inspect foreign-sent packages bound for destinations in the southeast United States.

—Enforce regulations on goods imported to Atlanta such as requiring licenses for certain types of firearms.

—Work with other government agencies, such as the U.S. Food and Drug Administration, on inspection of such imported goods as cosmetics, drugs and food.

—Inspect purchases of tourists coming straight into Atlanta on chartered flights.

—Collect fines for the Immigration Service.

—Collect taxes on alcoholic beverages for the Internal Revenue Service.

—Inform out-going tourists of rules and regulations on their overseas purchases.

There are other duties, said Mr. Medford, ranging from providing for auctions for unclaimed and seized goods to intercepting tablecloths sent from Red China.

The Atlanta office comes under the jurisdiction of Mrs. Marion F. Baker, current collector of customs in Savannah. Mr. Medford heads the Atlanta office.

"Primarily," Mr. Medford said, "we perform the same function as a sea port. Only we clear merchandise that comes by trucks, by rail or by air."

Imports bound for Atlanta are sent by bonded carriers directly from a seaport to Atlanta where it is inspected, as it would be in Savannah or Mobile.

Movement into Atlanta of new people from East and West had a stimulating effect on old firms long in business here. For example, "The John H. Harland Company of Atlanta, the largest independent bank check producer in the South and the third largest in the country, . . . reported record sales and earnings for 1964. . . . Commenting on his firm's business activities, the president said he expects that the company during 1965 will equal its performance in the previous years by showing another 15% increase in sales. He said Harland at present has new manufacturing units under construction in Richmond, Virginia and New Orleans, Louisiana and recently opened a retail office supply division in Atlanta at 470 Armour Drive, N.E. The company was founded in 1923 by Mr. Harland, and now operates branch plants in Miami, Orlando and St. Petersburg, Florida and in New Orleans, Nashville, Greensboro and Richmond."

As Atlanta expanded toward the north, Lake Lanier became more important as a vacation and recreation spot for the summer months—and even in the dead of winter it had a singular beauty that attracted the wayfarer.

A *Journal-Constitution* account explained:

By actual statistics Lanier is the most popular hydro-electric reservoir in America. Last year Army Engineers counted 7,738,000 visitors. The reservoir stretches from the dam near Buford 40 miles northeastward up the Chattahoochee Valley past Gainesville to Lula, and spreads northwestward up the Chestatee to the gold regions, almost to Dahlonega.

Besides serving as the nation's Number One recreation area and producing electric power, Lake Lanier assures Atlanta of an adequate supply of water through all four seasons of the year. It is a much more beautiful and spectacular thing than the poet Sidney Lanier could ever have dreamed of when he was writing about his favorite river.

There was, of course, another facet to Lanier—its danger. Since the huge reservoir began filling in 1956, the lake had claimed the lives of sixty persons. Forty-eight of these were in, or on, the lake—swimming, fishing, boating, wading, skin diving, skiing, or trying to save someone else who was in trouble. Twelve others were killed in nonrecreational actions, some when motor vehicles in which they were riding plunged into the lake; some committed suicide; one fell off a pier and was drowned. The rough bottom of the lake near shore was particularly dangerous for youngsters under twelve; while wading they could step in a hole and go under quickly. More than half the swimmers who drowned were aged thirteen through twenty, and 27 percent more were twenty-one to thirty-five. Many accidents were caused by the victims themselves. They wore ineffectual life preservers, or skied without a ski belt—and some were reckless, careless, or intoxicated boat operators.

In October the Atlanta area saw one of the most dramatic trials in many years. On April 17, 1964, three Gwinnett County policemen, Jerry R. Everett, Ralph K. Davis, and Jesse Gravitt, were lined up side by side, handcuffed, and shot to death on lonely Arc Road near Lawrenceville. They were shot in the back of the head with their own guns. Then began the most intensive investigation of a crime in the recent history of Georgia, but it was only after fourteen months that the GBI, aided by the DeKalb County Police Department and the DeKalb County Sheriff's office and Solicitor's office, had solved the triple murder.

At the trial on October 6, 1965, one of the three accused men, Wade Levi Truett, was granted immunity in exchange for his testimony about how the horrifying killings took place. He and the two others accused, Venson Eugene Williams and Alec Evans, a former Gwinnett County deputy sheriff, were stripping a stolen automobile for parts. The policemen came upon them unexpectedly, were seized, and shot. Truett claimed that he had not actually done any shooting. But he had manacled the officers together with their own handcuffs. He told how the first shots had failed to kill all the men, so Williams reloaded and shot them again. The headline in the *Constitution* of October 8 summed up the story in an eight-column headline across page 1. "WILLIAMS CONVICTED . . . NO MERCY RECOMMENDED . . . DEATH SENTENCE MANDATORY."

Month after month in 1965 the headlines in the Atlanta newspapers had headings of crime: March 18, "WOMAN, 77, RAPED, PRAYS FOR YOUTH"; April 7, "BANDITS USE KNIVES TO ROB BUS DRIVERS"; April 8, "LIQUOR STORE 'CUSTOMER' GRABS $5,000"; April 28, "WOMAN IS BEATEN, $4,600 TAKEN"; April 23, "CLERK IS SLAIN BY BANDIT WITH SHOTGUN."

Crime sometimes turned out to be a family matter. A family of three generations was involved in a burglary ring that "has plagued Atlanta like a gang of wolves." The family, made up of a grandmother, her son, and her grandson, committed twenty-four house burglaries and eighteen car thefts in the northwest section of Atlanta.

The gambling process called "The Bug" was still active in Atlanta, and in mid-March a lottery combine doing more than $1 million a year was smashed in simultaneous operations by teams of U.S. Treasury agents and representatives from the Fulton and DeKalb County solicitors' offices.

As the year moved on to hot midsummer, when crime in the Atlanta area always shows an increase, law enforcement officials of the metropolitan area laid plans for tighter policing and more effective identification and chasing down of suspects. "Atlanta Metropol," the new six-country agency, was to set up a network of teletype stations and organize a Metropol institute, to conduct 100-hour police training courses in the metropolitan areas. The prime criminal target, according to College Park Chief T. Owen Smith, Metropol chairman, was the night prowler. "He is the most persistent and dangerous criminal to come in contact with the police. He is the cat of the criminal jungle. He may start as a Peeping Tom and end up a murderer."

Mayor Allen's concern with crime in Atlanta, which had increased by 142 percent from 1954 to 1965—or fifteen times the population growth—led to his naming a group of topflight citizens to an Atlanta Commission on Crime and Juvenile Delinquency. The organization opened its office on the second floor in City Hall and scheduled its first meeting for July 16, 1965. Thereafter, it was deeply enmeshed in the study of crime in Atlanta in all its manifestations. Hugh Peterson, Jr., a young attorney, was retained as associate general counsel to the commission and—for the time being—its only full-time employee.

The most mysterious and in some ways the most fearful tragedy of the year began not at the lake but in the parking lot at the shopping mall at Lenox Square. There, Mary Shotwell Little, age twenty-five, secretary to the personnel manager of the Mitchell Street branch of the Citizens and Southern National Bank, was last seen after shopping with a friend. Her car was found the next day containing blood-stained articles of her clothing. The C&S put up a

$1,000 reward, and the investigation went on for months as Atlanta detectives traveled the South checking out leads. But her body was never found and no suspect was ever identified.

As many Atlantans knew, particularly the police, the greatest stimulus to crime in Atlanta—and in any city—is poverty and illiteracy. And in Atlanta these two civic evils were being attacked from many directions. Many Atlanta ministers felt their obligation to serve not only their congregations, but all the people of the inner city, "where thousands live in poverty and despair." Three of them, Dr. L. Bevel Jones, pastor of St. Mark Methodist Church; Dr. Fred R. Stair, pastor of Central Presbyterian; and Dr. Charles E. Wilson, Methodist minister to the inner city, spoke to the Atlanta Kiwanis Club on the subject "Our Changing City Challenges the Church." They described their projects, including a baby clinic, ministers in housing projects, and grocery buses to take people shopping.

Other churches and ministers were also active in areas of the city that were changing from white and fairly prosperous to black and poor. Atlanta's Presbyterians and Episcopalians, for example, had begun a joint ministry in a traditional community where many of the churches had moved out in recent years. The Kirkwood community of some 25,000 persons was once predominantly white. When the white population dropped to 25 percent, the Kirkwood Presbyterian Church decided to move out. The Atlanta Presbytery, though, decided to stay in the community and began to push for the formation of Kirkwood Christian Center, which would "serve all the people in Christ's name." The Episcopal Diocese of Atlanta voted to join in, too. Their purpose was not to develop a new church, but to serve a community—to provide its older people with counseling, to provide community members with instruction in economics, child care, planned parenthood, reading for adults and children, and shop skills. For the children, play rooms and playgrounds would be provided, even baby sitters when needed. The center, of course, would offer both church and Sunday school services, patterned after general Protestant services conducted in the armed forces.

In 1961 the Protestant Welfare Service was established. Its duty was to direct the needy person or family to the welfare agency, church or civic, state or federal, that could handle their particular needs. The agency also sought to discover and weed out the fakers and phonies. In 1965 the newspapers told how the service had grown under the direction of Lillian Rowland:

Last year, the Protestant Welfare Service had 4,200 requests for help, more than twice its first-year total in 1961.

It paid 181 rents during the year, put groceries on the table for 283 families, got new jobs for 401 people, provided new living facilities and furniture for 51 families, bought clothing for 357 families and counseled and provided other social services for 721 other people.

The service also referred 603 other people to individual churches for help. The Protestant churches of Atlanta organized and support the service and it's to these churches that most of the referral cases go.

"In Atlanta, there is an agency to serve almost every need you can think of," [Rowland] said. "And we know where it is."

The poverty of the inner city and how it could be alleviated was of deep concern to many others than the ministers. C. O. Emmerich, Sr., head of Opportunity Atlanta, Inc., the city's antipoverty agency, told a group of local planners that they must combine their efforts to size up "the scope and intensity of the local poverty situation" and come up with a complete long-range program of action. Listening to his plea for a workable program were representatives of the Metropolitan Planning Commission, the Atlanta Community Council, the United Appeal, the Atlanta Housing Authority, and the Planning Department of the city government.

One helping agency that was able to expand in 1965 was the Atlanta Mental Health Association, which opened Georgia's first rehabilitation house for male mental patients whom the state considered capable of being restored to adequate social and vocational functions. The facility would house fifteen men. A house for women thought to be capable of rehabilitation had been opened late in 1964.

Meanwhile, reported the *Journal-Constitution:*

The first buildings of the little-publicized Georgia Mental Health Institute, called by mental health officials "the foundation stone of Georgia's new mental health program," are scheduled to open in early July.

The $12,500,000 complex—a four story building and eight cottages—has been growing steadily on its site on Briarcliff Road. Many of its personnel have been obtained; plans have been made.

The Institute, which will be administered by the state Health Department's Division of Mental Health, will be jointly operated by the state and Emory University. It is composed of features found in the best mental health facilities in this country and Europe.

Two years in the planning, the institute is one of the very few buildings designed for the purposes outlined for it—teaching and research.

Although it will be used as both an in-patient and out-patient hospital for Georgia's mentally ill, the institute's primary objectives are to supply the state with psychiatrists, psychologists, psychiatric nurses and social workers.

Atlanta in these middle years of the sixties was still working to find an answer to its most important problem—that of racial relationships. While the conflicts growing out of the Civil Rights Act of 1964 brought a certain amount of confrontation between whites and blacks, compared with the violence loosed in other southern cities Atlanta was a relative oasis of civility and tolerance. In 1965, after the Voting Rights Act became law, several more blacks were elected to the Atlanta City Council, the Atlanta Board of Education, and the state legislature.

The dinner given Martin Luther King, Jr., after King had been awarded the Nobel Peace Prize, as described earlier, was the highlight of the racial news of 1965. There were many other areas, though, in which relationships between black and white were also making progress. In January a number of white Fulton County and City of Atlanta officials were guests at a men's cocktail party given at the home of black state senator Leroy Johnson. In the same month the all-white Georgia Dental Association announced that it had amended its bylaws to permit Negro dentists to participate in nominating dentists to various state boards, such as the Board of Health, Hospital Advisory Council, Board of Dental Examiners, and Radiation Control Council. The amended bylaws now said that "any" registered dentist could submit nominations. However, Negro dentists were still excluded from membership in the white Northern District Dental Society. And without membership in a local dental society black dentists were excluded from the Georgia Dental Association and the American Dental Association. These organizations did not recognize the black dentists' organization in the Atlanta area—called the North Georgia Dental Society. Black dentist Dr. R. C. Bell brought suit in federal court to get the exclusion removed completely, and before the year was out it was done.

Black teachers saw a brighter picture. Delegates to the annual Assembly of the Georgia Education Association, made up of the leaders of Georgia's 20,000 white school teachers, on January 9 voted to admit 10,000 black school teachers to membership in the GEA. The teachers of the state still had to vote to approve or disapprove their delegates' action urging the admission of black teachers to GEA.

In mid-February the NAACP went into court seeking to speed up Atlanta's school desegregation plan, arguing that the present grade-a-year plan was not only too slow but it was also rigged to allow white pupils to escape desegregating schools. Dr. John Letson, superintendent of Atlanta schools, argued that white pupils had the same right to attend the school of their choice as did the Negro students. The black community not only felt that integration should be stepped up to at least two grades per year, it also felt that some of the school buildings to which black students were being transferred were less desirable than those in the segregated areas they were leaving. For example, they pointed to the transfer of black students from C. W. Hill School to the Howard Annex, which was made up of 200 mobile classrooms. Jesse Hill, Jr., a Negro insurance executive and publisher of the *Atlanta Inquirer,* protested this policy before the Atlanta school board, and entered a heated argument with school board president Oby Brewer, Jr. In the course of argument, in which the black group threatened to resume protest marches, Brewer accused Hill of making a "grand stand play" when he said that Negroes were ready to begin demonstrations again. Dr. Samuel Williams, president of the Atlanta Chapter of the NAACP, joined with other black leaders in protesting putting black children in buildings such as Central High and the Howard Annex, which had been judged unfit for use as a school. Williams declared that despite some "good officials" in Atlanta, "the Negroes are still getting the short end of the stick." The black children, he said, were not getting equal treatment under the law. The basic reason for moving the children from C. W. Hill School to the Howard Annex was so that the Hill School could be demolished to make way for the new city auditorium.

In early April of 1965 Judge Frank Hooper of the U.S. District Court had ordered Atlanta's schools to be desegregated at two grades a year instead of one, thus doubling the original pace, and at the request of the school board had ordered that, beginning in Spetember, integration must be stepped up to begin in the elementary grades from kindergarten and first grade, up to the seventh. At this accelerated pace, all Atlanta schools would be integrated by September of 1968.

NAACP plantiffs, however, were not content with this decision. "The Atlanta plan is inadequate to achieve complete integration of Atlanta's public schools because it fails to provide for the desegregation of teachers, supervisors and other professional personnel," they claimed. They filed a plan with the Fifth Circuit Court of Appeals which, they hoped, would result in "immediate desegregation of all Atlanta schools and their activities, functions and facilities."

By early July, however, the Atlanta school board had decided it could desegregate all grades in the city schools in this year, and the NAACP protest dwindled to a minimum. Jesse Hill, Jr., representing the C. W. Hill School PTA, said at a press conference: "Assuming that the Board of Education follows through immediately with desegregation of all grades as indicated, Negro leaders will remove what could have been serious hurdles for the board financially, and for the City of Atlanta, in development of the new auditorium complex."

"The board action," the press reported, "also headed off another strong protest from the Negro community of the West Manor School area, where in recent weeks Negroes have purchased many of the homes surrounding the West Manor School. . . . Hill's endorsement of the board's sweeping desegregation plan was seconded by the Rev. Samuel Williams, head of the Atlanta NAACP, and by state senator Leroy Johnson. The desegregation decision was preceded by lengthy negotiations between school officials and Negro leaders over relocation of the C. W. Hill School, which is being demolished to make way for the new auditorium in the Buttermilk Bottom Urban Renewal area."

The desegregation of all grades for all schools proceeded as planned in September, and in late November Al Kuettner, UPI reporter, interviewed some white Atlanta teachers as to what had happened. Interviews with six of the teachers gave a fascinating picture of the subtle changes in human relationships that take place when white and black, male and female are first put together in the classrooms and on the playgrounds. (It is interesting to note that Kuettner in his questions uses the word "Negro," but the teachers in reply generally used the word "colored." The word "black" was not often used in the sixties. In Atlanta and the South in general in the sixties the supposedly more acceptable word "colored" was frequently used instead of "Negro," which in southern speech came out "Nigra," nearly as offensive to the black population as "Nigger.")

Excerpts from the tape recordings of Kuettner's conversation with the teachers follow:

Q. What reaction did you get from white children when Negroes first came into your class?

A. (High School) A small percentage were belligerent. . . . A small percentage comical, laughing about it. . . . Whenever there were just a few Negro students, there were a few brave souls who tried to help them. But then they lost some of their white friends.

A. In my elementary school the situation was different. I was delighted to see how well they got along. They acted just like children. We went out to recess and I said, "Form a circle." I didn't tell them how to form it. But there would be white children dotted along with Negroes. They would be holding hands and they didn't see any difference. There was more the reaction of curiosity. The first week I would see them feeling each other's hair.

Q. Do you find cases where a white boy stands up for a Negro boy and vice versa?

A. I had that happen in the cafeteria just the other day. A white boy was chasing a colored boy and a colored boy turned around and said the other colored boy had been wrong. He had called him a pig or something like that and the colored boys all said, yes I heard Fred say it. They were looking more to be honest than whether this one was white or not.

Q. Do the Negro students have leadership qualities?

A. Very definitely. My sixth grade class elected a Negro girl president and a white girl vice president. The whites are outnumbered (9 to 20), but each girl was very well qualified.

Q. Do you find them more, or less, eager to learn?

A. Less eager.

A. But very responsive.

A. When you discuss something, they are very eager and just jump out of their seats to talk about it, their little hands leaping into the air. But they have a very hard time getting down to that systematic format where you can really learn. They are not organized. It's their home life, I think.

A. But when they respond, it's like any other child except with a little more enthusiasm.

A. They are bubbling all the time.

A. They don't walk down the hall . . . they bounce.

A. The first week of school, I spent the whole time trying to get them to raise their hands, not to speak out . . . just to get them to sit down, stay in their seats . . . not to go to the pencil sharpener. . . . I have sixth grade. . . . they should have learned it by now.

Q. Do you still find this same thing in high school?

A. The same thing. . . . they are still responsive, very eager but not to learn . . . they still don't want to stay in their seats.

Q. How about discipline?

A. The colored children are so far behind . . . even the bigger ones . . . so far behind in education, it's obvious they never had the discipline of fast learning in class. . . . they are not exposed to this at home and I don't think they have been exposed in their schools.

A. We speak two different languages. . . .

A. You try to use something that you assume the child has already experienced and, unless it is Popeye or Bugs Bunny or something he has seen on TV, he can't understand.

Q. Do you find Negro pupils belligerent at you when you lay down a firm rule? Do they blast out at you?

A. Not so much belligerent. But they'll haggle with you. If you'll argue with them, they're not being vicious. They just like to haggle. They have a way of beating you on discipline. They drag.

Q. What's the reaction of the few white pupils you have to all this?

A. They are very quick to blame the Negro children. I had a note from a parent of a white child who said she was keeping her daughter home because the "niggers" were beating her up. Well it turned out this child made up that story. They're quick to do that.

A. And the white kids expect us to back them, right or wrong.

A. Last year we were supposed to have a 700 to 300 ratio (in a high school). They ran in 400 more. And the white kids began to look around and they felt outnumbered. They got scared and on Friday after school opened, 400 withdrew.

Those whites were together. They had started at the school and they were going to finish, come hell or high water. Most of them were juniors and on the football team. These whites protected each other. The boys got together and made sure the girls got safely down the halls. I will say, the Negro boys have not gotten out of line with white girls so far, and so far as I know, no white boy has said anything out of line to a Negro girl.

By the way, one good thing happened this year. We had three white boys on the baseball team. The rest were Negroes. Last year, it was totally white. And they elected a white boy captain this year.

Q. Have you run into cases where Negroes have joined in extracurricular activities?

A. Yes, and another strange thing. Many times, when the Negroes are in the majority they will elect whites but you don't find whites electing Negroes.

Q. Are you able to tell how many years behind these Negro children are?

A. In reading the eighth grader reads at third grade silent and second grade oral level.

Q. Wouldn't you say this is the major contributing factor to the loss of interest?

A. They can't do it so they give up. It's not that they are not interested. It's just frustrating.

A. Small classes are the answer. I have 40 in my third grade class. If I had 20, I could do miracles.

A. If they started integration in kindergarten instead of high school, the problems would not have been nearly so bad. When these Negro children we now have in kindergarten get to you in eighth grade, they will be much more prepared. The kindergarten child most of the time doesn't know the difference between colored and white. They play together.

Q. Can the situation about the Negro children be changed?

A. When these children learn they are going to make better homes . . . somehow the school today must find a way to reach the home.

While the controversy raged on the city school level, Georgia Tech had more pleasant news. John Gill, a Negro sophomore, was elected managing editor of the college newspaper, *The Technique*—the first major office to be held by a Negro student at Tech. Gill of Atlanta was named to the post by Tech's Publications Board made up of editors, business managers, and faculty advisors of all Tech student publications. *The Technique,* in an editorial, praised Gill's selection. "Negro students," the editorial pointed out, have attended Tech since 1961, "but most campus activities have remained, in effect, closed to non-white students." Georgia Tech's student body should be "proud" of Gill's election, the editors said, "for he is well qualified for the post. He is a Dean's List student and a member of the Tech band and Glee Club."

In other areas of human relationships integration was going ahead swiftly and peacefully. At the 121st annual session of the Synod of Georgia in Savannah on May 19, Georgia Presbyterians voted to end all racial segregation among Presbyterians. The Presbyterian Church had never been officially segregated, according to Dr. James G. Patton, the outgoing moderator. But the geographical location of certain churches resulted in the formation of all-Negro Presbyteries. Only two of them in the Synod of Georgia were in the all-black Georgia-Carolina Presbytery, and at the meeting on May 19 they joined the Southwest Georgia Presbytery. This left only North and South Carolina churches in the all-Negro Presbytery.

One incident early in 1965 showed that the relations between the races had mellowed somewhat. In May of 1964 the Rev. Ashton Bryan, an elderly white minister, had been arrested in Atlanta for the crime of "disturbing public worship" when he came to a white church service, bringing two Negroes with him. He was tried and sentenced to eighteen months in jail. He served eight months and one day. Upon his release the *Atlanta-Constitution* commented:

> The people cannot give him back the eight months and one day he spent in a cell. But he has given the people something—a look inward. And what the people at last found there was good.

The State Board of Pardons and Paroles extended the clemency that remitted his $1,000 fine and spared him the rest of the 18 months' imprisonment to which he had been sentenced. But the Board acted at the urging of many and in the name, we think, of the general society.

Eight of the 12 jurors who convicted the old man of disturbing public worship wound up advocating his release. None of the 12 dissented.

The Rev. Roy McClain, whose church the Rev. Jones was seeking to desegregate, urged the Board to free the man. The church had long since desegregated. But Mr. Jones, nearly 70, was still in jail. In what the imprisoned man's wife called a "beautiful appeal," Dr. McClain spoke to the heart of the white South, as well as to the Board:

"I want all I say and do, so help me God, to be a part of the solution to this human knot of which this is a tiny thing. This is one grain of grit on a beach of sand that's a billion miles wide. I want everything I say and do to be a part of the solution and no part of the problem."

The late Sol. Gen. William Boyd advocated, before he died, the release of the man he had prosecuted.

Judge Durwood Pye, who passed the sentence originally, opposed clemency.

The *Constitution* editorial was accurate in that the freeing of Dr. Jones, the opening of the white churches to black men and women, the melding of black and white dental societies, the election of blacks to public office (at least seven blacks would take office in Georgia's House of Representatives in January of 1966—and one of them, Grace Hamilton, was a woman), and the speed-up of school desegregation, all gave testimony to the fact that indeed, in Atlanta and Georgia, things were changing.

At Atlanta University commencement exercises five people who had done much to bring about these changes were granted honorary degrees. One was Roy Wilkins, executive secretary of the NAACP, who received a Doctor of Laws degree for his "distinguished and outstanding contribution to the achievement of human dignity and justice for all men." Another was Ralph McGill, publisher of the *Atlanta Constitution*, who was awarded a Doctor of Humanities for being "a man of keen insight, great moral courage and force, lover of people, prophet, and conscience of 'The New South.'" These were fitting tributes to McGill and to Wilkins. The third man to receive his honorary doctorate was Carl T. Rowan, distinguished journalist and director of the U.S. Information Agency. In the main address Rowan told the audience of young Negroes what the future held for them:

"The Negro's battle has just begun," said Rowan, "and he will need all the brainpower, all the charm, all the social grace, all the instruments of moral suasion he can muster to win it.

"We have just about succeeded in knocking down the legal barrier to first-class citizenships," Rowan continued. "Now begins the tougher, more complex task of surmounting the social, educational, cultural and other obstacles that can be as circumscribing as any slave ship in 1619 or any segregation statute in 1916.

"To complete the task," he said, "will require much more than 'those legislative tools being fashioned in Washington.'

"The battle for human dignity is complex, and always has been, and must be fought on many levels."

Two others honored in addition to McGill, Wilkins, and Rowan were Georgia Douglas Johnson, pioneer Negro writer, who received the Doctor of Literature degree "for being a credit to her native city, Atlanta, her Alma Mater, Atlanta University, her race, and humanity," and Dr. Cornelius V. Troup, president of Fort Valley State College, who was awarded the Doctor of Laws degree for his service to local and national social and religious communities.

With a Head Start Program under way, busily preparing small black children for school, and black students in all the public schools from kindergarten to high school observing, or at least being exposed to, the same education as the white students, the black leaders of Atlanta raised their sights. They had achieved much. They wanted more. In order that the oncoming generation of young blacks would be sure of finding a place in which they could employ their newly developed talents, representatives of the Atlanta Summit Leadership Conference and the Negro Voters League began a push for "more than token" appointments for their people in city government posts.

A delegation of prominent Negro spokesmen presented Mayor Ivan Allen, Jr., with an eight-point program. It included (1) the naming of Negro Traffic Court and Criminal Court judges; (2) the appointment of a Negro as an assistant city attorney; (3) the inclusion of Negroes in representative numbers on all boards and agencies appointed by the mayor and Board of Aldermen; (4) desegregation of administration in the public housing program; (5) employment of more Negroes in responsible city government jobs. Attending the session with Mayor Allen were Fulton Senator Leroy Johnson, Dr. Martin Luther King, Sr., Alderman-nominee Q. V. Williamson, Donald L. Hollowell, the Rev. Samuel Williams, and Jesse Hill. One of the points reportedly stressed with the mayor was a strong feeling that Negroes should have more say in direction of the local poverty war agency, Economic Opportunity Atlanta, Inc. (EOA).

Two Atlantans symbolized the racial situation in the South in the mid-1960s. Longtime civil rights activist A. T. Walden died in July, and long-time segregationist Lester Maddox was beginning the effort that would ride him to the governorship on a wave of white backlash. Maddox had long mixed political commentary with his advertisements for his Pickrick Restaurant. On January 2 he ran a long notice in the *Constitution*. In April he was to go on trial in Fulton Criminal Court for driving three Negroes from his segregated restaurant at pistol point in July of 1964.

In his angry and eloquent diatribe, Maddox expressed the attitude of thousands of Atlantans and Georgians who shared his views. Excerpts follow:

LESTER MADDOX SAYS:

As we go into another year that God has blessed me with being a part of, I thank Him for those of you, our customers and friends, who, because of your prayers, patronage and support, have helped us to pass beyond the year of 1964 that threatened our life, liberty and property. We were able to make it through 1964 because of God and because of you whom He sent our way.

WE STILL FACE

the threat that was ours during 1964, that of losing our freedom, liberty, property rights and constitutional government . . . as demanded by the Communists, their Civil Rights Act of 1964 and the lawless racial (black and white) agitators, but we are still fighting for our survival as a civilization and as a free people. We promise never to forsake this fight.

MUCH OF 1965

will require my presence in court, but more important, freedom, liberty, private property rights, the American Free Enterprise System, constitutional government and all that we love will be on trial. We must win because Americans of every race, creed, color and national origin cannot afford to lose.

YES, I AM GUILTY—

guilty of obedience to God; guilty of loyalty to my country; allegiance to the American Flag; guilty of demanding my God-given and U.S. Constitution-given rights, and, yes, guilty of being ready and willing to let others take my life if it becomes necessary . . . BUT NEVER TO TAKE MY LIBERTY. And I am guilty of believing the U.S. Constitution means what it says and, therefore, I must take my stand and fight to protect my life, liberty and property. . . .

I take my stand because the Civil Rights Act of 1964 prohibits the free exercise of my religion as guaranteed in the U.S. Constitution. Jesus said in Matthew 20, verse 15, "Is it not lawful for me to do what I will with mine own?" Yet the Civil Rights Act of 1964 denies me this right. The unGodly and Communistic Civil Rights Act teaches and legalizes sins against God and crimes against man when it leads others to KILL, STEAL and COVET that which belongs to other Americans.

And the stand I take is the same as it would be if all Americans were

Negroes, or if all were Whites. My stand is for liberty, freedom and constitutional government and race has nothing to do with it. The government does not own my property, pay me any subsidies and has not offered to buy my property. . . .

THE CIVIL RIGHTS ACT

of 1964 had the full support of the Communists. It was their pet project and has been for many years. They were determined that it should pass even though it was unConstitutional, because they knew that through such legislation they could wipe out private property rights and in so doing it was their sure way to destroy freedom and liberty in America. . . .

OUR SUNDAY MENU:
ROAST YOUNG TURKEY with dressing,
Giblet Gravy and Cranberry Sauce . . . . 55¢
BAKED SPANISH MACKEREL. . . . . 50¢
BREADED VEAL CUTLET. . . . . 55¢
ROAST ROUND OF BEEF . . . . 70¢
LESTER'S MEAT LOAF . . . . 50¢
SKILLET FRIED CHICKEN . . . . 50¢
Choice of vegetables, fruit and vegetable salads at 10¢, 15¢ and 20¢

Atlanta police chief Herbert Jenkins recalls that Lester Maddox in 1965 became the first person in America to be prosecuted for violating the Civil Rights Act of 1964. Burke Marshall, assistant attorney general in charge of civil rights, came to Atlanta to prosecute and convict Maddox in federal court. "This was the end of The Pickrick," wrote Chief Jenkins, "and the beginning of Lester Maddox who went on to become Governor and Lieutenant Governor of Georgia."[4]

In his campaign speeches Maddox used the same political arguments he had used in his "advertisement" in the paper, believing correctly that thousands in Georgia shared the same views. In his speeches he also expressed the idea that fluoridation of the Atlanta city water supply was "Communistic inspired forced medication," a "socialist plot."

The death of black leader A. T. Walden inspired a *Constitution* editorial entitled "His Life a Monument":

Like the rings on a great oak tree, the life of Austin T. Walden was both a history and a monument.

The child of former slaves, reared in material poverty but spiritual richness near Fort Valley, he trod ground never before touched by his race, heard himself denounced as an agent of radicalism, and lived to see the struggles he had begun so successful that younger Negroes thought him soft and slow.

There was indeed great patience in A. T. Walden; there had to be for him to master the long struggle to work his way through Atlanta University and on to a law degree from the University of Michigan in 1911 and then head back home to Georgia where everyone told him there was no place for a Negro lawyer.

He practiced for a time in Macon, but moved in 1919 to Atlanta. His firm prospered, and his work in the courts was varied; but it was civil rights that drew the headlines and the displeasure of the mighty. Here he showed the other side of his nature; the unflinching, steel-nerved devotion to equal justice.

Mr. Walden led the fight to open the Democratic primary in Georgia to Negroes, then pushed a registration drive that placed some 50,000 of his race on the books.

He won equal pay for Negro teachers after a six-year-long fight. He was the first Negro in Georgia to aid in prosecution of white men: two members of the "Blackshirts" hate group who drew prison terms for killing a student near Clark College. And he took part in prosecuting the Columbians on incitement-to-riot charges.

One of his unsuccessful efforts was trying to win admission of Horace Ward to the University of Georgia Law School, but he had the satisfaction of Mr. Ward's later winning a seat in the Georgia Senate.

When the students who were beginning to think of him as an "Uncle Tom" were deeply embroiled in demonstrations for open accommodations in Atlanta, it was the steadying hand of Mr. Walden and his respect among the white leadership that won victory at the conference table in 1961.

Nearly 30 years ago, University of Michigan Law School alumni chose Mr. Walden as the man who had achieved the greatest distinction in his profession in the face of the obstacles of his race. But it was not until the shackles of racism began to fall that he received honors at home: membership on [the] City [Democratic] Executive Committee, one of the first Negro delegates to a Democratic National Convention, [and] a municipal judgeship.

The honors came late, but they were really not all that important. Austin T. Walden was already his own monument.

Atlanta and Georgia are better today for the gentleness and the steel of Austin T. Walden. He will be deeply missed.

(The editorial in all probability was written by editor Eugene Patterson, who was Walden's friend.)

The Negro Summit Leadership Conference, made up of the leaders in NAACP and other black organizations, kept pressure on the white power structure in many ways. For example, they presented a letter to Boisfeuillet Jones, chairman of Economic Opportunity Atlanta, Inc., complaining that a black member of EOA was not being given enough authority in the War on Poverty program. Three weeks later after the letter incident a development in EOA pleased the black leadership. It was announced that President Lyndon Johnson was going to appoint attorney Donald Hollowell, a longtime Atlanta civil rights leader and chairman of the Atlanta Negro Voters League, as southeast regional director of the Equal Opportunity Employment Commission, which was set up to administer the fair employment aspects of the 1964 Civil Rights Act. Said the *Journal*, "Franklin D. Roosevelt, Jr., director of the commission, said in Atlanta Friday that the agency has received 3,000 complaints of discrimination. Four hundred of the complaints came from women, Mr. Roosevelt told a group of Fulton County Democrats."

The dialogue between the Black Summit Conference leaders and the EOA board set a pattern that would be followed for many years to come: The blacks asking for more and more recognition, more and more participation in government at all levels, and the white leaders agreeing—but demanding that the blacks accept responsibility for what they did with their new-found power.

Several innovations in education provided opportunities for Atlanta's youth and older learners in 1965. With a $3.1 million grant from the Ford Foundation, the Atlanta public school system and Emory University were to open an experimental school to aid disadvantaged children. This "urban laboratory in education" would begin for four-year-olds at Grant Park and E. A. Ware schools under the direction of Dr. Arthur Parkllan, former director of a school-community planning project in Detroit. Disadvantaged children he described as those who had been denied normal relationships with their family and with other children, and who had had no contact with such learning sources as newspapers, books, or vacation travel.

The Ford grant for the Atlanta project was one of six made to southern groups interested in improving education for disadvantaged children. Similar grants were made in New Orleans; Huntsville, Alabama; Durham, North Carolina; Houston, Texas; and Nashville, Tennessee.

While plans for the Experimental School for Disadvantaged Children moved ahead, ground was broken for the Atlanta Area Vocational Technical School that would be the largest of its type in the country. Located on Stewart Avenue SW, the school was designed for an enrollment of 4,000 day and night students and would offer more than forty-five educational programs. "Governor Sanders, who presided at the groundbreaking, said the school will form another unit in a string of 29 such schools expected to enroll more than 30,000 students throughout the state. 'Georgia leads the nation in vocational education programs and our schools have become the model for the entire country,' he said."

While the state was pressing on with its vocational school, the Atlanta Board of Education was seeking $50.5 million to support the city school system in 1966–67. More than half, or $29 million, would come from the city; about a third, or $16 million, would be the state's contribution; and the remainder of roughly $5 million would come from federal or other revenues. Atlanta had already voted a $200-a-year salary increase to each of its 4,500 teachers. The American Federation of State, County and Municipal Employees was seeking a raise of from 20 to 40 percent for eight hundred custodians, laborers, and other nonteaching employees in the school system.

Atlanta in this year not only needed more money for teachers and janitors, it needed new schools, according to Ed S. Cook of First Ward, who had been on the Board of Education for over thirty-two years. In January Cook was unanimously elected president of the board, and he immediately called for a $20 million bond election to build new schools. The need, he said, was as great in Atlanta in 1965 as it had been in 1949, when he was rounding out a fifteen-year term as president of the board.

An innovative teaching program for youngsters reached Atlanta in 1965. The Montessori system, created by an Italian woman, Dr. Maria Montessori, had as its watchwords LOVE, WATCH and WAIT. The Montessori method was now being employed at Ashdun Hall. Hal R. Lee was administrator and the facility was used as a training center for Oglethorpe University, where British educator Claude A. Claremine and his wife Frances taught the Montessori method to teachers in classes and supervised their on-the-job practice in Ashdun Hall classrooms. "In the Montessori classrooms the teachers' task is not to dominate, but to 'draw out' the minds of the three and four and five year olds, to teach them to learn reading, writing, mathematics, music and manners, by the use of dozens of different playthings—toys which really are tools to be used to awaken thought, logic, personal relationships and abstract conception."

Six months before city schools opened in August, a new type school in downtown Atlanta had turned out seventeen Negro women graduates in an occupation hitherto closed to them. They had spent two weeks in a course that trained them to be cashiers. It was the first time that most of them, ranging in age from twenty-two to over thirty-five, had any professional training at all. Up until they started school, they were on the welfare rolls.

The school, which taught six other courses requiring both mental and manual skills, was the Manpower Training Center. As part of the federal antipoverty program it had 119 students in its training program, 80% of whom were be hired almost immediately upon graduation.

Many Atlanta children from both black and white, poor or well-to-do families were difficult to motivate, and there were teachers who were dedicated to this service. A private school had been created in Atlanta especially designed to serve them.

"What does a parent do when she comes face to face with the realization that her child is a 'slow learner,' one of the three out of 100 who has suffered some brain damage or mental retardation, or has some emotional difficulty? Where can she turn for help?"

Northside School, Inc., on Mathieson Drive NE, was the answer for many. It was a nonprofit, nonsectarian school for boys and girls between six and sixteen with a program tailored to meet the needs of slow learners who were educable. The flexible curriculum closely paralleled that of public schools but was paced to the educable level of each child. Tuition at the school was $900 per year, including books and supplies. Scholarships were available.

The Fulton County school board was also pushing for more money after raising the salaries of its teachers by $200 a year. The board by unanimous vote adopted a budget of $13,891,186 for 1965–66, which was $1.5 million more than the budget for 1964–65. Fulton's taxpayers would contribute more than $7 million of the total, the remainder coming from the state and federal sources.

All government agencies found it necessary to raise more money during and after 1965. Fulton County went into the year with a revised budget of $28,825,631, which was $2,632,372 over 1964. As the year drew to an end, the Fulton County Commission met in special session and approved a 1966 budget of $34.2 million, which according to Comptroller John Still would leave a cash surplus of $300,000 at the end of 1966. Largest item in the 1966 budget was for the operation of Grady Memorial Hospital. The county's contribution in 1966 was $7,567,480—nearly a million dollars more than was budgeted in 1965. Fulton's 1,400 employees would receive raises in 1966, which meant an additional $811,000 would be appropriated. The county would also make its first payment of $322,490 on the new $18 million Atlanta Stadium.

The finance committee of the City of Atlanta's aldermanic board voted late in December, 1965, to give the 6,149 city general workers more than $2 million in pay raises and salary adjustments in 1966. Mayor Ivan Allen, Jr., and Alderman John A. White, finance committee chairman, said the pay boosts could be financed without an increase in taxes, except on beer and wine package stores and places where beer and wine were served.

The State of Georgia was far less generous with funds for its capital city than were other states, which, according to Mayor Allen, were aiding their large cities with nearly nine times as much support as Georgia was giving Atlanta. In a speech to the Airport Rotary Club on October 3, the mayor said that Atlanta's share of the recent $6 million state-aid package was $2.66 per capita. Cities of comparable size were averaging $23.28 per capita in other states. "To put the problem simply," Allen said, "we are getting less state financial assistance as we get more of the state's population." He also said the city was restricted in the types of revenues which were directly available to it. Other cities of comparable size to Atlanta were averaging around $137 in revenues per capita while Atlanta only averaged $88. "Only by skillful management and the bulwark of an expanding economy have we been able to do as well as we have done," he said.

Mayor Allen, like Hartsfield before him, believed that annexation offered the city a chance to obtain needed revenue. "When a municipality needs elbow room for balanced growth and when people in unincorporated areas desire municipal services available at a reasonable cost, then the mutual solution lies in annexation of these people and their property. . . . Gentlemen, we are looking to the mushrooming residential suburbs, mostly to the north of Atlanta. And we are in a position to offer fine municipal services to our neighbors in these outlying unincorporated areas at a price they are willing to pay."

Honors of various kinds came to Atlantans and former Atlantans in this year of 1965. In January, Charles H. Jagels, one of Atlanta's favorite adopted sons, and his wife came back to the city after an absence of five years in Washington, D.C. Jagels came back at the request of Richard H. Rich, of the Atlanta Arts Alliance, who invited him to become president of that organization, in association with four vice-chairmen. They were James V. Carmichael of the Atlanta Art School (and member of the Georgia Board of Regents), Lucien E. Oliver of the Atlanta Symphony Orchestra, Granger Hansell of the Atlanta Art Association, and Willian Bowdoin in charge of administration.

The *Journal* told of Jagels's many activities:

New York born, Mr. Jagels is a graduate of Lehigh University. He became associated with R. H. Macy in New York in 1924, and was executive vice president when transferred to the Atlanta affiliate, Davison-Paxon Co., in 1940.

He became president of Davison's in 1941 and later chairman of the board. In 1960 he chose early retirement and went to the national capital as president of Lansburgh's, Washington's oldest department store. . . .

In Washington Mr. Jagels was on the executive board of the Washington Symphony; chairman of the retail bureau of the Washington Board of Trade, director of the First National Bank there, and director of the National Retail Merchants Association, among other activities. . . .

The Jagels have throughout the last 25 years been prominently identified with the civic and cultural life of Atlanta. As a member of the Atlanta Music Festival Association, Mr. Jagels saw the Atlanta opera season extended from four to seven performances. He was president of the Music Festival Association when he left for Washington. For three terms he was president of the Atlanta Symphony Orchestra, on the executive committee of the Atlanta Art Institute, and founded Atlanta's Woman of the Year program. He created the Southern Annual Art Exhibition, in cooperation with the Junior League of Atlanta, which displays about 1,000 paintings each year.

He was a director of Fulton National Bank; on Mayor Hartsfield's Crime Commission, 1958–60, co-chairman of the Red Cross Campaign and the United War Fund.

John J. (Jack) Williams, executive secretary of the Georgia Association of Broadcasters and assistant professor of journalism at Georgia State College, was named by Atlanta's Jaycees as the Outstanding Young Man of the Year in Atlanta for his work in broadcasting. Four other outstanding young men were also honored. They were the Rev. Paul L. Walker, religion; Dr. Robert

K. Brown, education; John W. Shrever, Jr., community service; and William W. O'Neill, business.

Another representative of the communications media received a national honor in the spring of 1965. Margaret Shannon, Washington correspondent for the *Atlanta Journal,* received the Brenda Award for her "reporting of Washington affairs," notably her in-depth reporting of the political scene in Georgia during the recent national election. The Brenda was awarded by the Atlanta Chapter of Theta Sigma Phi, national professional fraternity for women in journalism. Also honored by the Atlanta Chapter was Lt. Col. Lillian Hansen of the Salvation Army, editor-in-chief of the Salvation Army publications and the first person to wear a Salvation Army uniform into Russia after the Army was ejected by the Soviets following the Revolution.

For the first time in its history the city itself paid tribute to people and organizations who had helped in some way to make the place more beautiful. The Atlanta Beautiful Commission, created by Mayor Allen and headed by Mrs. Mamie K. Jones as chairman, selected the one hundred recipients of awards. Ouida Canaday, Atlanta artist, who was one of them, designed the specially framed certificates that Mayor Allen presented.

Honors came to I. Heiman as he lay in his hospital bed. For sixteen years he had served as Blood Drive Chairman for the American Legion and Masons in Atlanta, preaching that "the best charity is anonymous charity," and urging them to go to the Red Cross and give blood. They responded with an estimated 10,000 pints—five gallons of which he gave himself. Now, in the hospital with a spinal infection, Heiman's friends decided that his anonymity should be broken. On Sunday, May 2, they would have a blood drive at the Red Cross Center at 848 Peachtree Street, which they had named for him.

Another individual honored for a special service to mankind was Carol Joe Bishop of East Point, who organized The Little Red School House for mentally retarded children in 1951. For this she was named to receive the Service to Mankind Award of the local Sertoma Club. Mrs. Bishop started the school in a borrowed portable building, with six students. The school now owned its own building and land and had forty-three students.

A list of individuals reading like an Atlanta "Who's Who" planned to pay their tribute to James F. Crist, executive vice-president of the Southern Company, after forty years of distinguished service.

A native of Montgomery, Alabama, Crist had graduated in 1921 from Virginia Military Institute and in 1924 from Massachusetts Institute of Technology. After service with the Alabama Power Company and the South Carolina Power Company, he joined the Southern Company in 1947 as vice-president after the company was established to take over the ownership and operation of four electric companies.

Another notable retiree was Captain William E. Waters, known wherever Eastern Airlines flew as "Muddy" Waters. He had been a pilot since he was seventeen and now after twenty-nine years and millions of miles in the air with Eastern, and many miles more with Jennies in the 1920s and bombers in World War II, he was retiring. Waters was only the second pilot out of Atlanta to make it to the mandatory retirement age of sixty.

Notables in various fields came into Atlanta during this busy year. One was Erskine Caldwell, a Georgia writer, author of forty-eight books that had sold more than 67 million copies. He came in on February 9 to speak at the third annual Creative Arts Festival at Emory University. With his wife, Virginia, he visited the *Journal*, where he was formerly a reporter. Born at Moreland, in Coweta County, he attended high school at Wrens, Georgia, played football at Erskine College in South Carolina and attended the University of Virginia and the University of Pennsylvania, by alternately working a year and studying a year.

He told Frank Daniel, who interviewed him for the *Journal*, that he served a ten-year apprenticeship before any of his stories were published. During this decade he was a reporter on the *Journal*, though he was writing short stories all the time. These attracted the attention of Maxwell Perkins of Scribner's, who became his editor, as he had been for Ernest Hemingway and Thomas Wolfe. After a first volume of short stories called *American Earth*, he moved on to the novel, and two of his most widely acclaimed ones, *Tobacco Road* and *God's Little Acre*, appeared. His newest book, *In Search of Bisco*, about his experiences in Coweta County would appear in April, 1965.

Four even more famous people came to Atlanta in August of 1965 for a visit that was heralded for weeks in advance and had Atlanta youngsters excited to fever pitch. The much adulated musical Beatles had left Liverpool for a tour of America, which included a one-night stand in Atlanta. On Wednesday night of August 18 the Fulton County Stadium was filled to capacity with screaming thousands of teenagers.

A highly disturbing point of view by a thirty-eight-year-old professor of Bible at Emory marked the closing days of 1965. Dr. Thomas J. J. Altizer, the spokesman for a new creed called "Christian Atheism," announced in the October issue of *Theology Today* that God is dead! This set off a national furor in religious and educational circles. Altizer, who described himself as being a "relatively inactive Episcopalian," was labeled a "Godless Communist" by a Methodist bishop, and herds of Emory alumni demanded that he be fired. But, with theological seminaries all over the country clamoring to hire him, Emory refused to dismiss him—thus earning for itself, said Betsy Fancher in *Atlanta* magazine, a lasting image as a symbol of academic freedom. And Altizer, seemingly content, stayed on, publishing with his friend, William Hamilton, a book called *Radical Theology and the Death of God*. He also tried to explain to Fancher what he meant to convey to the world. She had asked if God is dead, when did He die? Altizer's answer was clear, perhaps, only to another theologian. But, one sentence seemed to sum up what he was trying to say: "With the Crucifixion God emptied Himself of glory, power and being and became truly, finally and actually real. This is all there is."

Altizer stayed on at Emory, quietly teaching and lecturing until 1968, when he became a professor of English at the State University of New York at Stony Brook. There, he continued to teach and write (*Descent into Hell*, 1970, and *The Self-Embodiment of God*, 1977).[5]

OBITUARIES

Mrs. George W. Adair, Sr., the former Thomas Howell McBride, granddaughter of Thomas Howell Cobb, Confederate general, was affectionately known as "Mrs. T. H." She was the widow of a prominent Atlanta realtor. William T. (Bill) Boyd, 44, was solicitor general of the Atlanta Judicial Circuit. A graduate of Atlanta Law School and in the Army Air Corps in World War II, he was a Mason, Elk, Kiwanian, and Cherokee Country Club member. Dr. Montague L. Boyd, Sr., 82, was a well-known Atlanta urologist and head of the Urology Department at Emory University. That same department at Piedmont Hospital is named in his honor. He was a graduate of Emory at Oxford and Johns Hopkins Medical School. He served in World War I and was a member of the Piedmont Driving Club and Savannah Yacht Club.

Gen. William E. Brougher, 76, was widely known as a lecturer on his experiences in World War II. He was a prisoner of the Japanese on the Bataan Death March and in nine prison camps. General Brougher was in the first group of prisoners to be flown home from the Far East and arrived in Atlanta with Gen. E. P. King. They were greeted with a parade. Dr. Ferdinand Phinizy Calhoun, 85, was a distinguished ophthalmologist and the son of a pioneer Atlanta ophthalmologist, Dr. Abner Calhoun. He graduated from the University of Georgia and attended Harvard and Emory Medical School. Dr. Calhoun had received numerous honors in the medical world and established a lectureship at the University of Georgia in honor of Ferdinand Phinizy, his grandfather. With family members he established and endowed the medical library at Emory as a memorial to his father. The Chair of Ophthalmology at Emory was established in his honor in 1960. William Candler, Jr., 46, the son of prominent Atlantans, was vice-president and assistant treasurer of the Biltmore Hotel and operated a cattle ranch near Orlando, Florida. Fred L. Cannon, 68, president of the Red Rock Corporation, was a former manager of the Atlanta Dr. Pepper Bottling Company. He had been president of the DeKalb County Chamber of Commerce and the Fulton-DeKalb Charity Horse Show. He was a member of the Atlanta Athletic Club, the Commerce Club, and the Atlanta Chamber of Commerce.

J. S. Childers, 66, president of the publishing firm of Tupper and Love, was a former editor for the *Atlanta Journal*. He was a graduate of Oberlin College and a Rhodes Scholar specializing in history and literature. He served as a naval aviator in World Wars I and II and had written six novels and four travel volumes. Wylie Owen (Skipper) Cheney, principal of old Tech High

School for twenty-six years, died at 81. He was a graduate of the University of Georgia, where he was a Phi Beta Kappa, and of the Atlanta Law School; his memberships included Ansley Park Golf Club and the Druid Hills Baptist Church. Dr. Frank Cunningham, 53, was born the son of a sharecropper and became the president of Morris Brown College in 1958. He had joined the school as dean of the seminary and head of the division of philosophy. Roy Lance (Shorty) Doyal, 66, one of Atlanta's best-known football figures, had at one time been Fulton County commissioner. A graduate of Georgia Tech, he played football under John Heisman and W. A. Alexander. As football coach at Marist he led his teams to a 232–61–12 record, and at Boys High his record was 200–41–12. This was one of the greatest high school coaching records in America. He was voted Most Popular Teacher at Boys High five times. Clarence R. Garrett, manufacturers' representative and active in Masonic affairs, was the father of historian Franklin M. Garrett.

Herman Hancock, reporter for the *Atlanta Constitution*, won a Pulitzer Prize in 1931. He was 67 and a graduate of Emory University. The Very Rev. Alfred Hardman, 63, dean of the Cathedral of St. Philip, was a native of England and a graduate of the University of the South, Sewanee. He was chairman of the board of Lovett School in 1963. Judge Thomas Grady Head, 67, was elected to the House of Representatives in 1935. He became attorney general in 1943, and in 1945 he took a seat on the Supreme Court. Charles Thomas Hicks, chairman of the board of Bowater Paper Company, was a member of Rotary, the Piedmont Driving Club, the Capital City Club, and Peachtree Golf Club.

Dr. Walt Holcomb, 87, had been a preacher since he was 17. For five years he had conducted revivals with Sam Jones, the great evangelist. He was graduated from Emory at Oxford and Randolph-Macon. He had been pastor of Decatur First Methodist, Calvary, and Wesley Memorial churches. Fred Lanoue, 57, swimming coach at Georgia Tech since 1936, was noted for his survival technique called "Drownproofing" and had written a book about it. His death occurred while he was teaching this method to Marine recruits at Parris Island. William Monroe, 70, was a nurseryman who designed and planted many gardens in Druid Hills, Ansley Park, and the Buckhead area. The parks he planted included the amphitheater at Chastain Park. William Chenault Munday, the last survivor of the "Big Three" in sportscasting— Ted Husing, Graham McNamee, and Bill Munday—died at 61. He joined the staff of the *Atlanta Journal* and after broadcasting some Atlanta Crackers baseball games for WSB, he was on his way. He was the first to broadcast a college basketball game in the South, and in 1929 he did the first football game when WSB ran a telephone line to Athens for the Georgia-Oglethorpe game.

Guy H. Rutland, 72, prominent Decatur businessman and civic leader, was associated with many church projects and was chairman of the board of deacons of Decatur's First Baptist Church. He donated $200,000 for the building of a gymnasium for the Decatur-DeKalb YMCA. He had been on the board of directors at Decatur Federal. Austin Thomas Walden, 80, born the son of slaves, was a fighter for equal rights. He attended Atlanta University and received his law degree from the University of Michigan. A special award from Michigan in 1964 said: "He involved himself deeply with the drive of his race for equal rights under the law. He has lent direction and spirit to the NAACP . . . and has become the beloved elder statesman of the Negro community in Atlanta and has won the confidence of the city as a whole." He practiced law forty-nine years. William B. Hartsfield said, "Much of Atlanta's outstanding pioneer progress and better race relations was due to the effective leadership of Colonel Walden." Dr. Jesse Hardman York, specialist and authority on vein surgery, was also a great sportsman and active in organizing gun clubs throughout the state. He was a graduate of Mercer and Emory Medical School and was a member of Druid Hills Baptist Church, the Capital City Club, the Atlanta Athletic Club, and the Riverbend Gun Club.

NOTES

1. *Atlanta*, Aug., 1964.

2. *Atlanta Times*, Jan. 28, 1965.

3. *DeKalb New Era*, Jan. 28, 1965.

4. Herbert T. Jenkins, *My Forty Years on the Force, 1932–1972* (Atlanta: Center for Research in Social Change, Emory University, 1973).

5. *Who's Who in America, 1980–1981* (Chicago: Marquis, 1982).

BRUCE GALPHIN portrayed Atlanta of 1966 as one massive traffic jam. "In a red-hot, deep-dish, high-rise city, mix: Too many automobiles, narrow, rambling streets, antiquated planning and engineering, add just a fraction of necessary funds, season liberally with public apathy, simmer until it comes to a boil and you've got Traffic Jam."

In a tongue-in-cheek collection of "notes made while waiting on a rapid transit train" Galphin pointed out that with the cars and trucks in metropolitan Atlanta doubling every ten years, Atlanta must push on at once, widening some streets, creating reversible lanes in others, abolishing left-hand turns at any time and not only in rush hours, forbidding street side parking on certain areas. But, he noted, none of these things, many of which were already in operation, would carry the city through until the future date when rapid transit by rail could take the burden off the surface streets. But the main challenge at the moment was new construction of east-west and north-south throughways through the city, with an outer loop and inner loop around the city. Some of this had already been done, but there were gaps that needed to be filled in. These included expanding and modifying interchanges in the north freeway from downtown to Brookwood; completion of the perimeter road, I-285; completion of I-20, the west freeway; and completion of the Stone Mountain freeway, from Boulevard to the perimeter; and building I-485, the highly controversial "inner loop" connecting Lakewood Freeway with other parts of the expressway system; and finally a north link of the "inner loop," generally following Peachtree Creek.

Wrote Galphin: "Some of these are near realization. The West Freeway, for instance, should be finished this year, and Governor Sanders has promised to let the remaining portions of the 'Outer Loop' to contract before the end of the year. The North link is the farthest away: No specific route has ever been planned." He saw problems ahead:

Just as each bottleneck must be analyzed individually, so Atlanta's overall traffic flow must be continually examined and treated. Changing land use or driver habits will create problems at points unforeseen today. What is now a "solved" problem may grow thorny again. An especially valuable means of keeping tabs on the continually shifting problem is an unofficial interagency committee which meets on the first Thursday of every month. Represented are the City's police, Traffic Engineer, Traffic Judges, Construction Director, School Superintendent, Planning Chief, City Attorney, State Highway Department, Atlanta Transit Company, Trucking Lines and, frequently, comparable officials of DeKalb and Clayton counties. Where once there was little or no liaison, and where action was often taken at cross purposes, there is now co-ordination and mutual appreciation of others' problems. Ed Hughes of the

Traffic and Safety Council describes the meetings as "Let-your-hair-down sessions" and says they are "more effective than anything else I've seen around here" in pin-pointing and treating traffic problems.

So, if you can't see the Rapid Transit Train down the track yet, have courage.[1]

Galphin concluded this article on a note of hope and confidence. The attitude of many Atlantans, however, was probably best expressed by Carleton Palmer and Jack Kaplin in a song they wrote for Lowery Music Company in 1965. The title was "They Are Tearin' Up Peachtree, Again."

As highways stretched out, the people followed, but the city limits did not follow.

Ever since 1947 when the "General Assembly granted municipal powers to Atlanta, and set its boundaries as a circle of one mile from the Zero-milepost in the railroad depot at what is now Plaza Park," the city had been pushing out. Expanding jaggedly and intermittently in all directions around the town, it had increased more than thirty-fold. And in the spring of 1966, the battle was still going on. In the Boulder Park area, west of town, with many black residents, state senator Leroy Johnson proposed giving residents options to come into the city if they wished but nobody seemed particularly excited about the prospect.

In Sandy Springs, however, with the increasing white population seeking living space and quietness and a refuge from the inner city that was growing rapidly more noisy and crowded, door-to-door polls showed a two-to-one opposition to the idea of joining up with the city. The opponents, in the main, were old Sandy Springs residents who had been there since the time when it was remote and rural, and who wanted it to stay that way. Others opposing were those who fled the city to escape rising taxes, even though they soon discovered that police protection, water, lights, sewage, and street lighting cost as much in Sandy Springs as they did in the city, whether provided by the county government or by extension of Atlanta's service in the area. However that might be, residents of Atlanta's richest and most independent suburb decided to retain their separation from the city—to remain an unincorporated area under Fulton County police and fire protection, while Atlanta provided water, at what it cost within the city, and garbage pick-up that was none too satisfactory.[2]

The Atlanta Chamber of Commerce, under the direction of President W. Lee Burge, sent into Sandy Springs a most eloquent and persuasive plea prepared by the Sandy Springs–Atlanta Team for Tomorrow. It touched on every question and issue between the city and the suburb, and the answers were designed to prove factually that Sandy Springs would be better off overall, as to taxes, fees paid for police, fire, garbage and water services, the quality of the service, and the added voice of Sandy Springs residents governing the city as a whole. But the big question, the brochure said, was this: "How can Sandy Springs take full advantage of, and get its share of the results of the tremendous economic, cultural and industrial boom now gripping Atlanta? And the answer is—by becoming an integral part of the city. By participating in the leadership. By seeing the vision of a great and continually growing Atlanta. By joining in the grand enterprise of full participation in the invigorating present and the stimulating future of *one great* city. 'Atlanta is an attitude, not an area.' "[3]

The eloquent article did not prevail. At the May 11 referendum, by a three-to-one vote, Sandy Springs stayed Sandy Springs.

In an *Atlanta* magazine article analyzing Atlanta's growing skyline, Richard Hammock gave a step-by-step account of the great office building boom of the previous ten years. Wrote Hammock, under the title "Chronology of a Skyline":

In the first six years of the Sixties, Atlanta's construction boom has touched every quadrant of the Metropolitan area, generating better than fifty million square feet of new commercial and industrial space alone and producing such works as the Stadium, warehouses, high-rise apartments, and the increasingly taller office buildings that are ridding the city of its "snaggle-tooth" skyline.

Altogether, the construction activity, plus another $1,016,000,000 in residential housing and apartments, has placed Atlanta, which has only the 23rd largest population of any such center in the country, in tenth place nationally, in the amount of general contracting work done.

Moreover, the boom has caused a 55% enlargement of the total contract construction labor force—it now stands at about 36,000 and has provided opportunities for industrial general contractors, whether old or new, locally headquartered or branch operation, to increase greatly their contract portfolios and profitable operations.

But the use of that word "Boom" to describe so much building doesn't please all the men doing it. "The word can be thought of as like a balloon—full of air," said Ira H. Hardin, one of the city's more prominent industrial general contractors and immediate past president of the 8,000-member associated general contractors of America. "We think there is solid growth there," he said. . . .

Until 1955, the year Atlanta's Phoenix took to wing with the completion of the 22-story Fulton National Bank building, downtown on Marietta Street, the city had gone 25 years without a major office building (the last was the William-Oliver Building at Five Points), and had seen only lacklustre efforts in other directions in industrial and commercial work, probably the best known being the 7-story addition of Rich's Store for Homes.

There had been aspiration before 1955. For example, H. T. Dobbs, Sr., in 1941 announced plans for a 26-story ultra-modern office building at the northwest corner of Peachtree and Linden Streets. A year later there was an announcement that an addition to the Henry Grady Hotel would be made, at the rear of the present structure, that would be 32-stories. Both would have topped the city's then tallest structure, the 21-story Rhodes-Haverty building. Neither plan materialized, perhaps because of the War, but both illustrate that Atlantans, long before the magic year of 1955, were looking toward spectacular growth for their city.

Tallest among these finished or under construction in 1966 is the forty-one-story First National Bank Building, nearing completion on Peachtree at Five Points. . . . An Atlanta architectural firm, Finch-Alexander-Barnes-Rothschild-Paschal, designed the $19,000,000 structure which is the tallest south of Baltimore and east of New Orleans. The Henry C. Beck Company is building it.

Atlanta's second tallest is the National Bank of Georgia Building, also on Peachtree at Five Points. Completed in April of 1961 at a cost of $10,000,000, the 31-story structure is 432 feet tall and contains 350,000 square feet of space. It was designed by Hedrick and Stanley of Dallas and was also built by the Henry C. Beck Company.

Two other major developments under way highlight Atlanta's office building projects, the downtown Peachtree Center Complex being evolved by Atlanta architect John Portman and Dallas financier Trammell Crow and the Executive Park being located in North Atlanta, where the Northeast Expressway is intersected by North Druid Hills Road.

Peachtree Center is a long-term development requiring careful study and planning. In effect it is a redevelopment in a four block area of Peachtree popularly called "the corridor," which extends from the Pryor Street intersection to Baker Street. As Mr. Portman envisages the Center, seven buildings will be constructed, including office units, parking decks, a hotel and a new bus terminal.

Two of the office structures are completed, the million square foot Merchandise Mart Building, at a cost of $15 million, and the 30-story, 500,000 square foot Peachtree Center Tower that was built at a cost of $10 million. Both contributed to the building boom of the last few years, the Mart having been completed in 1961 and the Center Tower in the summer of last year [1965].

Under construction and expected to be completed this fall as part of the Center complex is the 22-story, 850-room Regency Hotel. The $15 million structure surrounds an open air court, with community balconies overlooking the court from every floor.

[Another] major development, Executive Park, is one that has received much less public attention than it merits. This 103 acre site, under development for a year, is being transformed into what is perhaps the nation's first all-office building park which plans to design architecturally the interior of each building to fit the needs of the tenant, to style architecturally the very modern exterior of each building to fit the "image" of the tenants, and to coordinate the entire project into an aesthetic whole through careful use of landscaping. . . .

In mid-1966 Amoco Oil started a building in Executive Park to house its marketing activities for ten southeastern states. About nine hundred people would be employed there, over one hundred more than at its previous location on West Peachtree.[4]

In his *Atlanta* article, Hammock continued:

Shopping centers, for example, are part of the significant contribution. Besides Lenox and Greenbriar, other large ones completed during the boom are North DeKalb, Columbia Mall, Ansley Mall, and Cobb County. North DeKalb, which like Greenbriar has an enclosed mall, is an $8,500,000 development of 420,000 square feet with 53 retail stores; Columbia Mall is a 25-store center of 400,000 square feet built at a cost of $6,000,000. Ansley Mall is a $3,200,000 development of about 201,420 square feet with 26 leased (32 projected) stores.

Urban renewal areas have become the sites of other especially prominent projects, among them the 880,000 square foot Atlanta Stadium near the Southeast Expressway, built by Thompson-Street Company, general contractor, at a cost of $18,000,000. Another urban renewal site being given a comparable development is at the corner of Piedmont and Forrest Avenues, where the city's 171,000 square foot auditorium is being built by Warrior Constructors, Inc., of Houston.

In fact, that urban renewal area, from the site of the auditorium south a few blocks, has become the scene in the past four years of a very substantial part of Atlanta's building boom. Some 800,000 square feet of office, high-rise apartment and motel space is in place and completed in the area, and the total does not include smaller structures, parking decks, or non-high-rise, garden-type apartments. This finished work represents an investment of better than $16,000,000. Additionally, 350,000 square feet are in the planning stages for this urban renewal area in office buildings alone, worth an aggregate $8 million.

"Uptown," the vicinity of West Peachtree and North Avenue, is yet another boom area in the city. Life of Georgia at the southwest corner of the two streets has work coming along smoothly on its 29-story, 410,000 square foot tower. The $13.5 million structure, designed by Atlanta architects Bodin & Lamberson, is being built by Daniel Construction Company of Georgia on a 3.1 acre site that will be carefully landscaped.

Across the street from the Life of Georgia Tower, on the southeast corner, is the site where The Citizens & Southern National Bank plans a $6 million 15-story, 160,000 square foot building that will be cylindrical in shape. Designer of the unusual—for Atlanta—building is Richard Aeck, AIA here, who said the unit "is as much sculpture as architecture."

One block east, at the corner of Peachtree and North Avenue, is the site of the recently completed Peachtree North Avenue high-rise apartments that typify a half dozen others built in the city in the past five years or so, among them the Landmark. Peachtree North Avenue has 256 units and is 20 stories tall.

Atlanta's construction boom likely will remain strong throughout the remaining years of this decade. Projects announced, but not yet started, give a good picture of what to expect. The Equitable Life Assurance Society of the U.S. soon will begin work on its 34-story, $20 million building downtown that will replace the Piedmont Hotel, now being razed to make room. Equitable's building, at 453 feet tall, will become the city's second tallest when completed and will help fill the snaggle-toothed gap between the island of tall structures at Five Points and a second island around the Merchandise Mart on Peachtree.

Another high-rise office built there will be a beautiful addition to the skyline to help close the "gap" is the 28-story 530,000 square foot unit announced by the Trust Company of Georgia, a $15,000,000 structure that will be erected in the downtown block edged by Edgewood, Pryor, Auburn, and Equitable Place. Architects for the building are Carson, Lundin & Shaw, Inc., of New York.

That second island itself is growing. The William Summerling Company has announced plans by a group of local investors to begin a 27-story building on Peachtree next to the Georgia Power Company's Electric Building, the new unit to contain 350,000 square feet and to cost an estimated $9,600,000.

Also, Great Southwest Atlanta Corporation is settling into the work of developing the Great Southwest Industrial Atlanta Park, near the Chattahoochee River and the I-20 Expressway, a three-thousand acre project called the nation's second largest of its kind. The Industrial Park will provide sites for warehouses, offices and factories and is expected to represent $40,000,000 in investments when completed.[5]

The story of building in Atlanta was not only the record handed down by architects, designers of business suites and offices, and those able to finance these million-dollar projects. It was the story of men in hard hats walking the high steel.

The men seemed to sense that Bill Diehl (who later was to make a national reputation as a novelist and movie writer with his book *Sharkey's Machine*) was a kindred spirit, as he climbed high in the sky to walk the girders with them, watch them walk, and listen to them talk. The combination made a fascinating character study of men at work on jobs of which the average man knew absolutely nothing. The following is part of Diehl's story:

Below [worker Glenn Bailey] was the gold dome of the capitol building and behind it, looking like a cupcake, the new stadium. Over there, twenty miles or so away, was Stone Mountain, and to the north, way up yonder, along the horizon, was the edge of the north Georgia mountain range. It was, he conceded, one helluva sight and one to which he had paid little mind before. The pusher, a busy man, does his sight-seeing last. But now it was almost over. In a few more days the raising gang would be finished, and the iron workers would be packing up their worn tools, turning in their safety helmets and safety belts, and drawing their last paychecks. The last column would be in place, the last members hooked in, connected, bolted down, welded off, and plumbed straight. The iron workers would be moving on to another job, and "finishing" on the historic building would begin. But, on this day, under a blazing sun with the temperature hovering around fifteen degrees, twenty degrees colder than down on the street, there was still work to be done.

The iron workers wore bunched-up shaggy clothing, most of it work-shiny and patched. They wore thermal underwear, long johns, dungarees, hooded sweaters, hunting jackets with the red flannel patches still tacked to the back, and the heavy canvas work gloves with names like "Red Ram" and "Big Hank" and "Lucky Harry." Their fiberglass safety helmets had tuck-in linings that wrapped around their ears and tucked down under their collars and had "AB" for American Bridge, stenciled across the front. Whether they work on bridges or high buildings or a one-story warehouse, they are known as "bridgemen," and their jobs are described in simple, Spartan terms: the "hook-ons," the "connectors," the "pusher," the "flyer," the "bolt-ons," the "swing-men," the "welders." These are the men of the raising gang who hook the cables around the heavy steel members, swing them into place from the derrick, connect them one to the other, bolt them in, fly from one joint to the next making the temporary welds, and, finally, move in and weld them down permanently. They all worked with a steady, unbroken rhythm, and if the wind and cold bothered them, it didn't show. They worked with cigarettes and cigars hanging from ragged lips, with pencils jammed up inside the linings of their safety helmets, with tobacco and chewing gum tucked in their cheeks, and they moved with grace and ease among the steel members with the nonchalance of a man walking down the boardwalk rather than across a six-inch wide piece of steel thrown across the edge of the sky. Most of them were old hands who had been around a long time and had seen a lot of iron put together. Four of them were over sixty years old and, adding up their time, had spent more than two hundred years on high iron all over the world.[6]

The nation's two leading retail chains participated in Atlanta's 1960s expansion. J. C. Penney would bring jobs to the south metro area at its multi-million-dollar catalogue distribution center being constructed on 270 acres of land in Clayton County along the south expressway. The building would have 2,050,000 square feet and employ two to three thousand people. There were 1,669 Penney stores in the world, and 23 in Georgia. Five of them were in the Atlanta area, the newest at Greenbriar Shopping Center.

Not to be outdone by its competitor, Sears Roebuck in 1966 opened its new retail store in Buckhead. This glamorous new marble-faced store became the largest suburban department store in Atlanta, surpassed only by the downtown Rich's and Davison's. The largest Sears in the Southeast, it was one of the most elaborate in the nation, carrying more than 80,000 items in its fifty-two departments. The facade was made of 3,360 pieces of marble cut to let the dramatic back-lighting shine through. The new store brought the total Atlanta area stores to five, with seventeen catalogue outlets. (In 1985 the Buckhead Sears was demolished to make room for a high-rise office complex. The marble facade could not be saved.)

Another unusual achievement in the construction field, in the design and construction of a 300,000-square-foot building that was ready for occupancy in 180 days, was reported in April. The new structure was Lockheed Georgia's Engineering Office Building, one of the largest in the nation, where 4,000 members of the Lockhead Company's staff were to occupy several acres of enclosed space.

Architects and engineers for the building were the Atlanta firm of Heery and Heery, who used a new design principle that cut a year off the normal design and construction schedule, a speed-up made necessary when Lockheed Georgia received a $2.4 billion C-5A contract from the Air Force. The first 50,000 square feet of the new building were ready in January.

The speed-up in construction was made possible by a process called the Schools Construction Systems Development Design (SCSD), developed in California in 1964. It featured five-foot-square modules, pre-engineered to fit compatibly in a number of different building designs. The development of the system was financed by the Ford Foundation and was a revolutionary approach to school construction.

The system, Atlanta architect-engineer George Heery pointed out, brought industrialization into the building trade, with resulting lower costs. The pre-engineered compartments included structural, frame, roof, lighting and ceiling systems, internal painting and heating and air conditioning systems. Costs were drastically lowered. The Lockheed building, for example, was to cost approximately $4.6 million, or less than $16 a square foot.[7]

In addition to making progress in the field of construction, Atlanta in 1966 was rapidly becoming one of the leading insurance towns of the country, and two Georgians were becoming widely known in the trade as experts in forecasting the growth of insurance. One was a teacher, Dr. Kenneth Black, Jr., chairman of the Georgia State College Department of Insurance, whose curriculum probed new frontiers. The other was James L. Bentley, Georgia State Insurance commissioner, who early in the year was named Chairman of the Executive Committee of the National Association of Insurance Commissioners, one of the two top posts in the organization of fifty state concerns who regulate the industry. Georgians purchased $1.7 billion dollars in life insurance in 1964, 15 percent over 1963, and preliminary figures indicated growth was at an equal rate in 1965 and into 1966. The average family in Georgia increased its insurance holdings from $5,800 to $13,400 over the past decade.

More than 40,000 Georgians were employed in the insurance business, and more than 24,000 of them were in Atlanta. One hundred twenty-four underwriters were members of the Million Dollar Round Table, an affiliation of top salesmen each of whom sold $1 million worth of insurance in 1965. Of the 124, 83 were Atlantans.

Forty-seven of the fifty largest life insurance companies had operations in Atlanta, and nearly 8,050 firms maintained home offices, regional headquarters, or principal sales offices here. These national insurers accounted for about 90 percent of all premiums written in the United States, and they owned almost 95 percent of all insurance assets. Many of these assets were visible in Atlanta, where many new office buildings, motels, and apartment projects were financed with insurance funds.

Life Insurance Company of Georgia had 47 percent of its assets invested in the South in the mid-1960s. Equitable Life Assurance Society of the United States had $67 million in Georgia mortgages and real estate on December 31, 1964; New York Life as of the same date had $27 million in nearly 2,000 mortgages in metropolitan Atlanta, five of them on apartment buildings totaling $20.5 million. The $8.5 million mortgage commitment of the Regency Hotel in November, 1964, by Massachusetts Mutual Life Insurance Company was the second largest in the company's history to that time.

Between 1960 and 1965 insurance companies built or planned for themselves enough office space in Atlanta for a building more than 135 stories high. Already completed were the buildings by Hartford Insurance Group, seventeen stories; John Hancock Mutual Life Insurance Company, eight stories; Bankers' Fidelity Life, ten stories; Foundation Life, five stories; MONY, eleven stories; Continental Insurance, twelve stories. The two biggest were still to come—a twenty-nine-story Life of Georgia Tower at West Peachtree Street and North Avenue, and a thirty-four-story building for Equitable on the site of the sixty-three-year-old, eleven-story Piedmont Hotel on Peachtree Street.

After the closing of the Piedmont on May 3, 1965, the *Constitution* ran a sentimental editorial:

For more than 60 years the Piedmont has been an Atlanta landmark, a piece of its skyline, a vital factor in the lives of those who came and went in the Gate City of the South. It has been regarded as a second home for many a traveler. Its good reputation as a hostelry of quality was jealously guarded by those employed there.

And now, at the age of 62, the Piedmont has quietly died.

It will give way to the wrecking crews who will demolish it. And they, in turn, will give way to the construction crews who will erect on the site a soaring edifice which will become a vital part of Atlanta.

Equitable's new building will be one of the tallest in the city and thereby will alter Atlanta's constantly changing skyline.

It is with regret that we see an old friend, the Piedmont, depart.

But a static city is a stagnant city and Alanta is far from that. And so, with justifiable pride, we look forward to the addition of the new Equitable building as a part of the city's central business section.

In the arts as well as in skyscraper building 1966 was a landmark year for Atlanta. Henry Sopkin, maestro of the Atlanta Symphony for twenty-one years, was to retire at the end of the year, to be replaced by Robert Shaw (whose genius with the baton proved to be as enduring as Mr. Sopkin's had been).

Said Charles Jagels, president of the Atlanta Art Alliance: "Henry Sopkin has served Atlanta well during his two decades as maestro of the Atlanta Symphony." Devereaux McClatchey, a music-loving Atlanta attorney, characterized Sopkin's accomplishments. "Henry Sopkin personifies the ideal of growing. He took the small seed with which the Atlanta Symphony began and developed it until it became a modern orchestra. He is to be admired because of what he is and what he has done, and all Atlanta should be proud of him and the Symphony."

Leslie C. White, manager of the Atlanta Symphony, remembered him in his first days as maestro. "What boundless energy! He did literally everything necessary to the presentation of a symphony concert. He set up music stands, he distributed music, he cajoled his young musicians through difficult rehearsals. He was conductor, teacher, and father confessor. It all had just one goal, to give Atlanta a fine symphony orchestra. The degree of his success and the hardships involved in achieving it will only be known by those of us who have had the privilege of working closely with this man of vision and absolute dedication."[8]

Atlantans soon were to learn that in Sopkin's successor, Robert Shaw, the Atlanta Symphony had acquired another "totally committed man." "I can only say he understands me better than myself," said famous composer Francis Poulenc. "He divines my intuitions. It is as though my work were being performed fifty years after my death. Never in my lifetime did I expect to hear any composition of mine played with such calm and perfection. . . . He is, of course, a genius!"

Also making music at this time was a group who later would do a tremendous job for Robert Shaw for the mutual benefit of music loving Atlantans. The Atlanta Choral Guild, a group of 275 amateur members who perform great choral works for the sheer joy of singing, was prospering in 1966. The club was born in 1939.

Atlantans interested in art welcomed a new painter on March 6, 1966. On that day, Betty Foy Sanders, wife of the governor, showed her paintings to the public for the first time in an exhibit at the High Museum of Art. Her goal was to raise $15,000 to build a fountain at the entrance to the new executive mansion on West Paces Ferry Road.[9]

Atlanta long had looked upon itself as a big-league city in many ways, and it finally became a real big-league city in both baseball and football in the same year, something, according to Furman Bisher in the *Journal,* that had never happened before. Forsaking the cold of Milwaukee, the Braves became a reality on the Atlanta sports scene with the arrival of the 1966 season. For openers, there were exhibitions versus the World Champion Dodgers and the New York Yankees. Then, at last, on April 12 came the official beginning of big-league play in Dixie. The Braves faced the Pittsburgh Pirates, managed by a former Atlanta Cracker manager named Harry Walker. The Braves lost 2–3, in extra innings, before a crowd of 50,671.

Milo Hamilton, formerly with the Chicago White Sox, was brought to Atlanta by Don Elliot Heald, general manager of WSB, to broadcast the Braves play-by-play with Ernie Johnson. Bobby Bragan, the Braves' manager, was a man famed less for his genius as a manager than his hatred of umpires and all the hierarchy of baseball ownership. By the time he had reached Atlanta he had been thrown out of more ball games than any other player. He lasted slightly less than a year in Atlanta before being replaced as manager by Coach Billy Hitchcock.

Atlanta in 1966 had lured the Braves by building a big-league stadium in a minimum of time—51 weeks to be specific—and for minimum cost—$18 million. By the end of the first season, the Braves had played before a total of 1,539,000 in seventy-five home games. They won eighty-five games and lost seventy-seven and finished ten games behind Los Angeles.

The first official appearance of the Braves in Atlanta brought to an end nearly three years of agonized negotiations by the Atlanta–Fulton County Recreation Authority, headed by Arthur Montgomery. He had met first with the owners of the Kansas City Athletics and later with the owners of the Milwaukee Braves, both of whom desperately wished to move their teams to new surroundings—preferably to Atlanta.

Credit for bringing the stadium to Atlanta is most often attributed to Ivan Allen, Jr., and its financial backer and advisor, Mills B. Lane of the C&S Bank. It is also true that the structure probably would never have been built if it had not been for the strong backing of Fulton County Commissioners Harold McCart, James H. Aldredge, and Archie Lindsey. With Chairman Arthur Montgomery, Earl Mann, Henry Dorsey, Edgar Forio, Earl Landers, and Opie Shelton, they made up the Atlanta–Fulton County Recreation Authority, and they backed not only the building of the stadium and the Braves' transfer, but the establishment of Atlanta as a big-league football town. Each was chairman of the Recreation Commission at a crucial time from 1964 through 1966, and each helped to work out an arrangement whereby the city and county governments agreed to underwrite the purchase of a big-league franchise, the city carrying two-thirds of the obligation to finance the endeavor if gate and concession income should fall short, with the county contributing one-third.

For a while it seemed that the Bidwell brothers, Charles and William, would move their NFL St. Louis Cardinals to Atlanta to play in the new stadium under construction. But St. Louis citizens stepped in and smoothed the way for the Cards to play in a modern stadium on the banks of the Mississippi, and the Atlanta deal was off. When this happened, Pete Rozelle, the NFL commissioner, held out little hope that any NFL team could be moved to Atlanta. But Atlanta businessman James Clay and his associates applied for a franchise both to the NFL and the AFL, and Charles Leachman announced he had picked up earnest money for an AFL franchise. However, they were working at cross-purposes, and it was a relatively little-known Atlanta businessman, Rankin Smith, who finally scored.

One observer described the construction methods:

The accomplishment by Thompson and Street [general contractors] has been hailed not only by proud stadium authorities and the Atlanta populace, it has been recognized (and studied for excellence) throughout the construction industry. The job was done on driving dedication and perseverance—and on the basis of rigid requirements written into the contract by the architects. These were 1: That construction follow the "Critical Path Method"—that is, every major phase of construction had to be previously scheduled in logical order and followed. 2. Construction progress had to be monitored every two weeks by computer. (This was one of the earliest instances of the use of the computer in construction.) The computer considered progress and reported on jobs that were behind and, more important, jobs that were potentially behind.

Because of the rigid requirements and unprecedented schedule required by the architect to build the stadium in twelve months, only two contractors competed to do it. To build the stadium in record time, Thompson and Street got an additional sum of approximately $700,000, most of which went for overtime and other hurry-up expenses. (The contractor was paid a total of $13,827,500. The remainder of the total stadium figure of $18,000,000 was for land cost, architect and engineers fees and other costs.)

At one point, the company had double ten-hour and eight-hour shifts working six days a week.

The local architects who designed the stadium had scored quite a coup. The tandem firms of Heery & Heery and Finch, Alexander, Rothschild, Barnes & Paschal were awarded a contract to duplicate their Atlanta feat in Cincinnati. The Cincinnati stadium would cost $25 million to $30 million and would employ basically the same design and construction techniques. Cincinnati officials visited Atlanta for the Braves' opening game and, after touring the stadium and talking with officials, awarded the contract.[10]

The stadium was well used even before the Braves opened. Sidney Scarborough, stadium manager, pointed out that more than 536,065 fans came in between April, 1965, and April, 1966, for various events. The Atlanta Crackers drew 161,265; Braves exhibition games drew 180,000; Boy Scouts, 20,000; the Beatles' show, 30,000; the Vikings-Steelers football game, 39,000; and the Colts-Steelers football game, 47,000. The last event before the dedication day in April, 1966, was the Affirmation Vietnam Rally that drew 15,000. The big attendance at the Colts-Steelers and Vikings-Steelers football games indicated that Atlantans were truly ready to welcome a professional football team. A booklet, *The Atlanta Stadium—Special Dedication Edition,* written by an unidentified author, told the story:

With everyone running in all directions certain influential business and political leaders enlisted J. Leonard Reinsch, president of Cox Broadcasting Corporation, for help. Cox has television, radio and newspaper holdings in several states, including Georgia. Reinsch did his job well. It was he who nearly purchased the Denver Broncos, only to have a stock squabble among the several team owners stymie the transaction. But on June 7, 1965, he got results. The AFL awarded its Atlanta franchise to Cox for $7,500,000 contingent upon acquiring exclusive stadium rights.

Pete Rozelle [of the NFL], who had been moving deliberately in Atlanta matters, suddenly caught fire and hopped the next plane south to protect his league's claim on one of the most progressive metropolitan centers in the country. He promised expansion by 1966, a year earlier than his original plan. Stadium Authority and city officials were impressed. They found themselves in what Arthur Montgomery called "the catbird seat," choosing between two leagues.

The problem for Rozelle was to find the right man to own the NFL team. Through Governor Carl Sanders, he met Rankin Smith. There was rapport between the young commissioner and the young insurance executive from the beginning. Two other affluent franchise-seekers were in the picture, Lindsey Hopkins of Atlanta and Miami and William G. Reynolds of the Reynolds Metals Co., Richmond, Virginia. Hopkins, a multi-millionaire sportsman who lived down the street from Smith in a fashionable Northwest Atlanta section, was several years older. He also represented many wealthy non-Georgians in the deal. Reynolds, of course, maintained his residence out of state.

When Smith, an Atlanta native and deeply rooted there, was chosen, there was no ill feeling among the others. He made Hopkins a minor stockholder, and after the Stadium Authority had picked the NFL over the AFL, he publicly applauded J. Leonard Reinsch of Cox for what really amounted to being a catalyst in the NFL's swift action. . . .[11]

As yet, no team existed, even by name. Smith had to find and hire a coaching staff and organize a scouting crew to roam the country, checking on prospective players. He named Gene Cronin, a former NFL player and scout for the Detroit Lions, as his director of player personnel. He named E. M.

(Bud) Erickson his administrative assistant. Formerly general manager with the Lions, Erickson took over many other duties as well.

A contest was held to select a name. "Falcons" was suggested by forty persons, but the winner was Miss Julia Elliott from Griffin, Georgia, for the reason she gave for her choice. "The Falcon is dignified, with great courage and fight. It never drops its prey. It is deadly and has a great sporting tradition."

Next came the choice of a coach—Norm Hecker, former assistant to Vince Lombardi. The Falcons' first draft choice was Tommy Nobis, the great University of Texas linebacker who signed with Smith for an "undisclosed sum," though a Texas millionaire named K. S. (Bud) Adams, owner of the Oilers in Houston, said he would be willing to pay $400,000 for the huge red-head.

Evidence of how Atlantans felt about Smith's new team and Atlanta's new stadium was obvious from the moment it was announced in late June that Smith had bought the franchise for the highest price ever paid for a team, between eight and nine million dollars. By Christmas of 1965, 45,000 season tickets had been sold.

In February, 1966, at the annual NFL meeting in Palm Beach, the Falcons were officially voted into the league, and at that meeting Hecker, Cronin, and their scouting staffs had forty-two veteran players in an expansion draft, which many believed gave the Falcons a better start than any of the other expansion teams before it.

During all the furor over the building of the stadium, the coming of the Braves and the buying of the Falcons by Rankin Smith, Atlantans had said good-bye to the venerable structure called "The dowager contessa of Ponce de Leon Avenue." "Poncey" Park had been the home of Atlanta baseball from 1907 to 1964, and it had been a recreation spot since the 1870s. On October 26, 1965, it went under the auctioneer's hammer. The ten-acre ball park and the Zachry Estate beside it brought a total of $1.25 million. Earl Mann owned the ball park under the name of the Atlanta Crackers, Inc. "Colonel" Pierce Smith, the auctioneer, bellowed for bids for five hours from a tent pitched over the pitcher's mound in front of the partially dismantled grandstands. Looking on were several hundred lawyers, real estate men, baseball men, bankers, and just plain folks, who joined in singing "Take Me Out to the Ball Game" with organist Dale Sloan. At the request of the auctioneer they also sang "The Star-Spangled Banner" because Earl Mann wanted to hear it just one more time here in the ball park.

Mann, perhaps more than any other Atlantan, would miss the old park, for here, in the prettiest minor-league park in the country, was the home of seventeen pennant winning teams in a span of twenty-five years, the best record of any other team in the history of organized baseball, except for the New York Yankees.

One major accomplishment of 1966 was the creation of a Civic Design Commission to advise the city government in its efforts to further the artistic, cultural, and environmental development and the redevelopment of Atlanta. The fifteen-member commission, whose members would serve without pay, included three lay members and two members each from the fields of architecture, painting, sculpture, engineering, and planning. There were also two members chosen for their knowledge of the historical and architectural traditions of the city.

In the months following the founding of the commission in 1966, many meetings resulted in the approval by the aldermen of an amendment to the old zoning ordinances of 1954. It read in part, as follows: "The intent of this Article in establishing the Historical Atlanta District is . . . To promote the educational, cultural, economic and general welfare of the public through the preservation and protection of the old, historic or architecturally worthy structures in quaint areas or neighborhoods which impart a distinct aspect to the City of Atlanta and which serve as visible reminders of the history and cultural heritage of the City, the State and the Nation."

The commission in its beginning days did not confine itself simply to preserving the appearance of historic buildings and houses. It looked about for historic areas that might be restored. And out of this interest came Underground Atlanta, bringing to life the old store fronts beside the railroad tracks in the heart of town. The following resolution was drawn up:

WHEREAS: The Atlanta Civic Design Commission believes in the general proposition that it is desirable to preserve some of Atlanta's all too few existing landmarks and

WHEREAS: The footings and ground floors of a number of business buildings dating from the 1870's, 1880's and 1890's presently exist beneath the Pryor Street, Alabama Street and Central Avenue viaducts, constituting interesting examples of architecture of the period and

WHEREAS: The Commission further believes that it would be historically desirable and commercially feasible to clean up the area and restore certain of those buildings and lease them to desirable tenants. Therefore it is hereby

RESOLVED: That the Aldermanic Board be requested to give consideration to designating the ground level intersection of Pryor and Alabama Streets for one block in each direction as an historic site.

And Underground Atlanta did come alive, with old buildings restored beneath the viaducts, old paint removed to show the names of ancient stores and shops of the 1870s and the 1880s, and new merchants of all types coming in to bring the sound of music and of clinking cash registers to the area.

But throughout 1966 and on into 1967 this was only a dream, a goal, of Paul Muldawer and Joseph Perrin and their associates of the Civic Design Commission. By December of 1967, however, the idea had caught on, and a number of persons were showing an interest in some sort of restoration that would not only be an historic monument, but a place for profit making comparable to New Orleans' French Quarter or Saint Louis' Gas Light Square.

The brief boom and then the failure of Underground Atlanta in the 1970s and later the prospect of its revival in the 1980s were far in the future for the Atlantans of 1966–67. Their interest was in the erection, in Grant Park near the zoo, of a famous merry-go-round. A bit of history was brought to the park with an antique merry-go-round. The August issue of *Atlanta* magazine explained: "Atlanta has been getting back at the North since Sherman set fire to the place," jests a Rochester, New York, businessman. After stealing the Braves from Milwaukee, Atlantans absconded with Rochester's merry-go-round. This carousel, one of the few remaining antique carved ones in the country, operated at Genesee Valley Park for fifteen years. It is one of the ninety remaining in the United States. The twenty-ton carousel, which cost about $20,000, was built by German-born Gustav A. Dentzel in 1885. It was the first to feature hand-carved zoo animals. Dentzel brought skilled woodcarvers from Germany, and several companies were formed to produce the lavishly decorated, finely carved animals. Gradually the skill vanished in America and Europe. Modern merry-go-rounds consist of aluminum horses that do not hold a candle to the magnificent relics of yesteryear. As dry rot and fire destroyed carousels, those remaining were becoming valuable museum pieces. The Dentzel animals had been repaired and freshly painted for the trip to Grant Park, where they were to give countless hours of pleasure to children for many years to come.

Not long after Mayor Emeritus William B. Hartsfield brought the fine antique to Atlanta in 1966, it became clear that neither fire nor dry rot, but Grant Park's pigeons and zoo visitors were the greatest threat to its beauty and its operation. In a period of twelve years from 1966 to 1978, approximately one and a quarter million people rode it. But over this span of years vandals, prowling the park by night, had gouged out the eyes of many of the animals, had broken their legs and chopped off their tails. By 1978 these depredations had increased. So the decision was made, with greatest reluctance, according to Tollie Hartsfield, to sell the wooden animals, which were still highly valuable as antiques, to collectors who wanted to display this type of folk art in their homes. They would be replaced by far less valuable but more durable animals made of fiberglass or aluminum. The Dentzel genius in carving spectacular animal shapes would not be lost, for the new animals would be molded on the old forms.

(In the summer of 1982, at the request of Mrs. Hartsfield, three months of research into the process of restoration and renovation of the Grant Park carousel was conducted, and out of this came a blueprint for restoration. To carry out the plan, Atlanta Zoo Carousel, Inc., a nonprofit corporation, was started.)

While the newly organized Atlanta Civic Design Commission in 1966 was promoting the preservation of historic places such as Underground and seeking projects that would enhance the beauty and effective functioning of the city's streets and buildings, a more venerable city organization was striving to create and coordinate agencies whose purpose was to improve the health, housing, and general social welfare of Atlanta's people. Ever since its formation in 1923, the Atlanta Community Planning Council had been at work. It had a remarkable record, working on the theory that "Helping to build the city is helping to build the world."

An editorial in the *Constitution* praised one of the council's mid-1960s efforts: "Faced with a certainty of increasing need, it is good to note that hospitals in the Atlanta area are planning additional facilities. According to a survey by the Community Council, 18 of the city's 27 hospitals are planning major additions before 1975. An estimated 2,544 beds will be added in the 18 facilities, supplementing a total of 3,279 now. . . . The Community Council deserves thanks for inventorying existing and planned medical facilities in the area. From their report should come an awareness of need and a boost to planning other needed facilities."

While company presidents and boards of directors were gazing happily at rising incomes and bulging coffers, the United Appeal in the year 1966 also had reason to rejoice. Its recently completed 1965 fund drive brought in $5.2 million, a new record, while campaign costs were held to an all-time low of 5 percent. Edwin L. Hatch, chairman of the trustees, pointed out that the low cost of making the drive meant that 95¢ of every dollar collected could be used by the some 400,000 local citizens who would be helped by the United Appeal Agencies.

As Atlanta's private citizens were taking to the streets to raise $5,000,000 for the local needy, the Atlanta city government was pushing hard for gifts under the federal aid-to-cities programs. The result was that by May, $43 million in federal grants had been set aside. These did not include separate grants obtained by the Atlanta public school system or by Economic Opportunity Atlanta, the local antipoverty agency. A report on these funds was prepared by Dan Sweat of Mayor Ivan Allen's office, whose chief responsibility was to see to it that Atlanta capitalized fully on federal aid programs.

Economic Opportunity Atlanta used federal funds for several projects at low-income housing areas including the West End Apartments, the New Palmer Building on Techwood Drive, and the Hilliard Street Antoine Graves Apartments. Planned were several health and recreational services plus a day-care center for the elderly, where low-income working families could leave their elderly parents while they go to their jobs. Old people, however, would not only be recipients of attentive care. Those able to do so would employ their talents as foster grandparents. Under another EOA grant totaling $100,000, low-income elderly could be trained to provide extra care for children in hospitals and detention homes.

Just how well the "Grandparents" program was working was described by Celestine Sibley. She visited the Carrie Steele Pitts Children's Home and heard from Mrs. Mae Yates, director of the home, of the amazing qualities of Mrs. Josephine Glass, one of the volunteer grandmothers:

Mrs. Josephine Glass, 77 years old, a slender, brown-skinned woman with gray hair, went to Carrie Steele Pitts home from the EOA or Poverty Program's first grandmothers' class in the Atlanta area. She had reared a family of her own and she had more time and energy on her hands than she had money to live on. Today she works four hours a day at the home for a total of $25 a week in money and immeasurable love and gratitude.

Mrs. Yates contends that Mrs. Glass is "the best grandmother in town," voluntary or involuntary. She is a relaxed, easy-going woman with abundant humor and an understanding heart. Lonely and shy children are her specialty but she seems to have time for walks and stories and rainy day handicraft sessions with all of them.

"Pleasure in the out-of-doors is something a slum child has to learn. And all of us, I suppose, have to cultivate the skill of seeing the world around us."

"Grandmamma" Glass, as the children call her, knows about trees and flowers and birds and she has the children interested in knowing about them. She is an indefatigable storyteller and when the weather is bad she reads aloud, conducts crayon coloring sessions, and helps the young ones with handwork.

It seems a sad commentary on our times that there are so few natural grandmothers on deck to take a hand in rearing children. But Mrs. Yates, an intensely practical woman, doesn't waste time with any repining over that.

"I'm just glad the government has taken a hand to make up the lack," Mrs. Yates said. "When a new class graduates we hope to get at least two more grandmothers and a couple of grandfathers."

The grandparents will have time for the individual attention that house parents can't always give. Among other things Mrs. Yates has noticed an improvement in the children's manners and a general "gentling" of the young.

The Fulton County Department of Family and Children's Services was another beneficiary of federal largesse. Wellborn Ellis, department director, announced that it had received $1,134,647 for the operation of Project Uplift in 1966, which was $300,000 more than had been spent on the Economic Opportunity Project in 1965, its first year. The program was designed to provide training and work experience for unemployed heads of households. In 1965, 556 persons were given a basic course in reading and placed in jobs as trainees.

The federal government indicated its continued interest in serving Atlanta and Georgia by opening two Federal Information Centers in Atlanta. One provided information about jobs available in federal offices throughout north Georgia. The other answered questions about federal programs and services available to individuals in the Atlanta area. Both centers were located in the Federal Office Building on Peachtree Street.[12]

The marches, the sit-ins, the arrests and demonstrations that had made 1965 a year of racial violence in Atlanta and the South seemed to have about run their course as 1966 began. Nationally, the civil rights drive had been substantially successful. The marches and the sit-ins and the demonstrations had accomplished much of what they had been intended to do. The federal laws had been passed.

Now a new element was injected—the implication, at least, that a rift was growing between the three main civil rights organizations in Atlanta—SNCC, NAACP, and SCLC. The situation arose out of statements made by SNCC leader Julian Bond on a nationwide TV program shortly after his election to the Georgia House of Representatives and before his swearing in. On this program he said that he agreed with a SNCC statement in which the United States was called the aggressor in the Vietnam War and in which it was stated that "women and children are being murdered." He also expressed sympathy with the draft-card burners, though he said he had no intention of burning his own.

These statements outraged many members of the Georgia legislature, so four days later, on January 10, when the newly elected members were to be sworn in, Bond was told to remain seated while the other 204 stood up to take the oath. Bond, determined to stand fast on his right to speak out in a free society, refused to recant or apologize. Instead, he brought suit in federal district court, and on February 18 a three-judge panel voted 2 to 1 that the state was within its right in refusing Bond his seat in the legislature. The dissenting vote came from Judge Elbert Tuttle, chief justice of the Fifth Circuit Court of Appeals. Bond's attorneys appealed to the Supreme Court, and on December 2 the verdict came down: Bond had been properly elected and should be allowed to take his seat in the Georgia House of Representatives. He did, and served there until 1975, when he was elected to the State Senate.

As Bond took his case to the courts, his friends in SNCC, SCLC, and NAACP, including Martin Luther King, Jr., took to the streets to protest Bond's treatment. Marchers surrounded the capitol and heard King declare that there was "no legal or moral way to justify the state Legislature's refusal to seat Julian Bond." After King left the scene more violent confrontations resulted in some minor injuries.

For Bond, the controversy over his legislative seat was the beginning of a career in the field of civil rights that brought him national attention. In 1968, at the Democratic National Convention in Chicago, he became the only black man in history to be nominated for vice-president of the United States. He had to refuse, because he was only twenty-eight years old. In 1966 he had resigned from SNCC, and he later became president of the Atlanta branch of the NAACP. His fame led to a career speaking to college groups across the country.

Martin Luther King, Jr., and Julian Bond followed peaceful avenues of protest, but a violence-prone Negro leader named Stokely Carmichael stirred a riot in Atlanta that had Mayor Allen facing a howling mob. The time was September of 1966 after a sweltering hot summer. The scene, a festering black slum called Summerhill. Allen had achieved high status in the black community through his support of the public accommodations clause in the newly passed Civil Rights Act of 1964. And Atlanta slums were gradually becoming cleaner, safer, more decent places to live.

But Summerhill's 354 acres, which once had been one of Atlanta's most pleasant downtown white neighborhoods, now was a teeming slum, with some 10,000 Negroes crammed into the crumbling, unpainted houses. The newly created Atlanta Commission on Crime reported that Summerhill ranked tops in every category—juvenile delinquency, rape, robbery, murders, everything. Here in the shadow of Mayor Allen's proudest creation— the Atlanta Stadium—was a tinderbox of poverty, disease, crime, frustrations, and unrest. The place was ripe for a riot—and on the day after Labor Day it came.

It began in the morning when Stokely Carmichael came to Allen's office at City Hall to protest the mass arrest of a black antiwar group that some days earlier had tried to break into the Army Induction Center. He refused to shake hands with Allen, raged about police brutality, and tried to block the doorway to the mayor's office. Finally he left. But this was just the beginning of the day for both Carmichael and Allen. Soon, word came in that a young black man wanted for car theft was spotted by Atlanta detectives cruising through Summerhill. When arrested, he broke away and ran, and the arresting officer shot him in the leg. Carmichael learned about this immediately— and soon was cruising through Summerhill in a SNCC sound truck stirring the residents up, claiming that the young man had been "murdered on his mother's front porch" and that the people of Summerhill must rise up in revolt before "Whitey kills us all."

Allen knew what he must do. He asked his secretary to send for the twenty-five Negro ministers Allen had asked to help him when an occasion such as this should arise. And he asked her to advise Governor Carl Sanders that he would need at least two hundred state troopers to back up the Atlanta police.

But Allen knew that, in the last analysis, he had to go to Summerhill and show himself to the gathering mob, and somehow persuade them to quiet down and keep the peace. When he and George Royal got there, cars were overturned and burning and, where Capitol Avenue intersected with Ormond, a crowd of more than a thousand people was swirling aimlessly around. The few policemen who had arrived had been forced to pull back from the center of the area. And it was into this whirling mass that the mayor and George Royal, in their conservative business suits, and a young police officer named Morris Redding, in uniform, moved until they were surrounded. Their purpose was to avoid a show of force, to buy time, to find the riot's leaders, to talk to them, or to bring in the ministers to talk to them when and if the ministers should arrive. Back and forth through the crowd the three marched, buying time, trying to keep the trouble confined to the Summerhill area, while the police, now arriving in force, set up roadblocks on the streets leading out of the area.

As Allen, Royal, and Redding marched, most of the rioters moved back to clear a path; others cursed them and spat at them—these well-fed white men striding down the street in business suits into a hooting mob of disenchanted and confused black people.

Said Allen in *Mayor:* "I don't think I can ever relate my exact feelings. I knew a knife could be stuck into me and nobody would ever know who did it. I knew I could be pounced upon and trampled. I knew I could be hit by a brickbat flying from a hedge. I knew I could be shot from a second story window. With every step I became less confident that I was going to be able to do any good."

But he, and the others, kept trying, kept walking—soon they were aware that the word was spreading about who he was. "It's the Mayor. It's the Mayor," would ripple through the crowd. Finally, as he tried to address them, they fell silent. He told them to select their leaders—their spokesmen—and they all would go over to the stadium and talk over their problems. They seemed to agree, and soon Allen, feeling like the Pied Piper, was leading hundreds toward the stadium, waving for the police to move a blockade out of the way. The sight of the police seemed to set off ancient fears and rages—somebody shouted, "We ain't going to no white man's goddam stadium. They'll get you in there and the po-leeses will shoot you down. . . . Get the white honkey bastards before they get you." They turned and followed him no further. "All our efforts at reasoning with the crowd went downhill from that point," Allen recalled. Then, somehow, a police car had gotten right into the middle of the intersection at Capitol and the car became the very center of everything. There were about 2,000 people around the car, and bricks were being thrown. There was a pulsation, a fever in the mob that had not been there before. "We knew we had to do something fast. So far we had been able to keep them moving, keep them divided, but now they were together and it was a dangerous situation."

Somebody, Allen recalls, handed him a bull-horn and told him to get on top of the police car and try to talk to the mob from there. He took the bull-horn, was boosted up on the hood, and from there climbed on to the car top, while the crowd alternately cheered and jeered.

"I knew I had made a serious tactical mistake the minute I stood on the top of that car, alone, vulnerable and exposed, looking down at a mob of 2,000 people, taunting me."

Although Allen realized he was doing no good, he asked a "responsible looking black man" in a clerical collar to come up on the car top and pray. But when Allen helped him up to the top of the car and handed him the bull-horn, the man began a wild harangue, mocking Allen's pleas for peaceful relationships. Then a young SNCC follower grabbed the bull-horn and began bellowing, "Black Power, Black Power, Black Power."

With this, wrote Allen, "the crowd began rocking the car and the crescendo was shattering. People were yelling 'Black Power' and I was alone atop the police car, and the crowd was surging in on me and bricks began to fly and just as I was jitter bugging, trying to keep my balance, I dived off the car and into the arms of Morris Redding and George Royal."

With Allen safely on the ground and out of reach of the crowd, the police—who under his orders had done little other than to set up roadblocks leading away from the riot scene—now began releasing tear gas in such clouds that Allen himself was choked by it, along with the mob and the people who had taken refuge in the ragged houses. With the tear gas the crowd broke up. The riot was over, no one had been killed or gravely injured. Chief Herbert Jenkins picked up the mayor and whisked him back to City Hall, where he stripped off his soaking wet clothes, took a shower, calmed down a bit, and sat for a while talking to Louise, his wife, who had spent a day of agony watching the event on television. Allen's account continued:

Then I got back in the car and returned to Summerhill, to stand on the corners with the police and press at nightfall. Everything was quiet now. Whiffs of tear gas still could be smelled in the low areas. The lights of police cruisers picked up glints from the bits of shattered glass littering the streets. I could see the blue-white lights coming from television sets inside most of the houses and shabby rooms, and knew the people of Summerhill were going through the eerie experience of watching themselves on the network news shows, watching the tragic play of brick-throwing and gun-firing, watching their mayor as he was shaken off the top of an automobile, watching their neighborhood as it was turned into a battleground—and I hoped it would have as sobering an effect on all of those frustrated people inside those ragged houses as it had on me. On the streets of Summerhill that night I was button-holed for interviews by the national news media, wanting to know if there was any way this could have been prevented. "Yes," I said, "had we started a hundred years ago making the necessary corrections, and had the wisdom in America then not to let these slums become the places they are. . . ." We had said it many times before, and we had meant it, but never with the conviction that we had that night as Summerhill and the rest of Atlanta drifted off into a fitful sleep.[13]

Many problems other than those arising out of civil rights beset Atlanta and the metro area in this sometimes tranquil, more often troubled year of

1966. Fires of undetermined origin harassed a fire department already restive and unhappy over a salary scale in which a "base private" in the department with a wife and three children would get more money if he went on welfare than if he stayed on to fight fires.

Atlanta's fire losses, thanks to improvement in the equipment and skill of personnel, were dropping each year, from $6 million in 1963 to $4.7 million in 1964 and $3.2 million in 1965. But fatalities were increasing. There were twenty-two persons killed by fire in 1964, twelve of them in fires caused by smoking in bed. There were thirty fire fatalities in 1965. No firemen were killed in either year, though there were 145 injuries.

Many spectacular blazes made the headlines. On February 3 a blaze of unknown origin destroyed the Thompson Industries plant, which manufactured plastic cups in Stone Mountain Industrial Park. Arson was suspected in a four-alarm fire that roared through the unoccupied Miss Georgia Dairies Co-operative building on Whitehall Street. About fifty legislators were among the ones who fled their rooms in varying stages of undress when fire broke out in a freight elevator in the Georgia Hotel. The blaze was confined to a basket of soiled linen.

While Atlanta's firemen fought recurring blazes with skill and valor, as in the past, they were still stubbornly and sometimes angrily demonstrating. In early 1966 they formed a union, called the Atlanta Firefighters Union Independent, an offshoot of the older Local 1347, the International Association of Firefighters of the AFL-CIO. On June 4 they issued the ultimatum: five hundred of them were ready to walk off their jobs if the City of Atlanta did not listen to their requests for "shorter hours and more compensation." (They worked a sixty-hour a week shift and wanted this reduced to fifty-six hours.)

By June 8 they had walked off the job, and when Mayor Allen arrived at the huge Lakewood Avenue Union Hall, they booed him and several times shouted him down. Allen's persuasive eloquence finally calmed them, and after three days they went back to work, though still insisting on their claim to more pay and shorter hours. By July 7 Georgia Tech President Edwin D. Harrison had agreed to act as mediator between City Attorney Henry L. Bowden, representing Atlanta, and Robert Mitchell, attorney for the fire fighters union, but to no avail. On September 3 they walked out again and only eighteen engines were in service, scattered among the city's thirty-three fire stations. Chief Herbert Jenkins instructed his off-duty policemen and detectives to man the stations and the fire engines.

On October 2, 1966, the City of Atlanta put a full-page ad in the Sunday *Journal-Constitution*. Beside the picture of a handsome fireman in a gold-encrusted military type dress cap was the plea, "THE CITY OF ATLANTA WANTS YOU. . . .—Choose a Career as a Firefighter. Enjoy the benefits and privileges in being one of the 750 who protect lives and property of our great country." The ad explained the pay and perquisites (hours of work, it may be noted, were not mentioned).

* Age 18–35 (Up to 40 with previous fire fighting experience.)
* Starting salary $4,836 a year with automatic increase on January 1, to $5,256.
* Free Uniforms
* Additional increases each year for five years and then longevity increases.
* Excellent opportunity for promotion—with salaries of more than $10,000 in key positions.
* 20 days vacation with pay—30 days sick leave annually.
* Paid annual military leave for reservists.
* Retire at 55 on $350 or more a month.
* Hospitalization and life insurance at low rates.
* You do not have to be a resident of Atlanta.

And so, it seems, that after more than a year of smoldering conflict between the city and the firemen, the firemen, through their stubbornness, had gained much of what they had asked for in the first place.

Not only the firemen but the city carpenters and sheet-metal workers went on strike in 1966. Both walked off their jobs on July 1, bringing Atlanta's previously booming construction industry virtually to a standstill. The carpenters, who before the strike were earning $4.00 an hour, were asking for an increase to $5.05 in a period of a year, plus the establishment of health and welfare, vacation, and pension funds. The contractors offered a 45¢-an-hour increase over a period of three years. The sheet-metal workers, who worked heating and air conditioning, earned $4.25 an hour and were asking for a $1.05 increase in two years with fringe benefits. The contractors offered a 45¢ raise. The debate went on throughout the summer.

Hundreds of workers left Atlanta, finding work in other towns as the sometimes acrimonious negotiations were going on throughout the summer. During this time twenty-seven Atlanta building projects, costing more than a million dollars each, were halted. By late September, however, the International Carpenters Union proposed a contract that Atlanta management could accept. It provided an increase of $1.05 plus benefits, over a period of three years, instead of the $2 increase over two years, which the carpenters had asked for. As the word got around that their contract war was over, carpenters by the hundreds began coming home to Atlanta, and work was immediately begun on the largest of the unfinished buildings. Among these were the Massey Junior College, the forty-one-story First National Bank, the Regency Hotel, and the court house and several schools in DeKalb County.

Despite labor problems that halted construction on many buildings, after almost five years of planning and twelve months of construction, WAGA-TV was at last settled in its new million-dollar, five-level, white brick building on Briarcliff Road. The 52,000-square-foot structure housed more than $1 million worth of technical equipment, including one of the most modern color systems in the country. Constructed on twenty-eight acres in DeKalb County, the complex, built around a 1,100-foot transmission tower constructed in 1955, was located on a historical spot earlier inhabited by Creek Indians (Indian mounds, arrowheads and a corn grinding stone were found on the property), and later, during the Civil War, it was a camp area for Cox's Division of Schofield's 23rd Union Corps as they pressed to take Atlanta.[14]

Many records, some good, some bad, were set in these busy years of 1965–66. The Atlanta Post Office canceled more than 165 million pieces of mail during the holiday period from December 4 to December 30, making it one of the ten busiest post offices in the nation. The Atlanta facility set new records both for the total year and for a single day, when on December 17, 1965, some 9,964,000 pieces were handled. The Atlanta Post Office, officials said, had been running about 20 percent above the preceding year's average all year, which was considerably higher than the national average.

In the field of business the venerable Southern Bed Company reported the highest sales and net increase in its eighty-three-year history. President W. P. Rooker said that sales in 1965 totaled $13,922,586, a 24 percent gain over 1964, while net profit jumped 21.5 percent from $501,405 to $607,434. The company had subsidiary plants in San Antonio and Tampa, and both contributed substantially to the overall sales picture. The San Antonio plant specialized in furniture for dormitory rooms, and it complemented the bedding manufactured in Atlanta and Tampa. These products were manufactured under the brand name Southern Cross. Chairman Richard Schwab announced that, effective March 15, the old corporate name of Southern Spring Bed Company would be changed to Southern Cross Industries, Inc.

Another record breaker in the field of finance was the Atlanta Federal Savings and Loan Association, whose assets at the end of 1965 topped $300 million for the first time in its history. The firm's assets grew by $28 million during 1965 alone.

At the beginning of 1966 Georgia's electric chair had gone unused for a full twelve months. For the first year since 1924, when the state switched from hanging to electrocution, not a single person had been put to death in the chair. Though the state traditionally had led the nation in executions, some four hundred since 1924, there had been a steady dwindling in number for several years past. This, evidently, was the result of a growing reluctance on the part of juries to demand a life for a life. For many years executions at Reidsville ran from fifteen to twenty a year, but there had only been fourteen since 1960.

Knowing that many Atlantans, particularly those in the lower economic echelon, looked upon policemen as mortal enemies, Chief Herbert Jenkins and police captain Morris Redding in mid-1966 worked out a program designed to change that attitude.

"By detailing police officers to do what can only be called social work,

Atlanta has set out to convince residents of slum communities here that cops can be good guys," reported Raleigh Bryans in the *Journal-Constitution*.

"In the view of the man in charge, police Capt. Morris Redding, the effort is paying off, not only in a better image for policemen, but in broadened services to the citizens affected. What the city has done so far is assign a policeman in each of six slum communities to function not as an enforcer of the law, but as a 'counselor.' These men operate out of the neighborhood service centers established by the local antipoverty agency, Economic Opportunity Atlanta, Inc."

Captain Redding explained the program:

"We are helping people get to the EOA (the antipoverty agency). We explain to them exactly what the EOA has to offer. We try to get young people interested in the youth corps (an EOA program).

"We counsel people on the necessity of their staying in school and in fact it looks like we have persuaded about 140 kids to go back to school, after they had become dropouts.

"We go to people in the communities and we say, 'What can police officers do to help you?' This is important, because we find that a lot of people just aren't familiar with what the law is. They just don't know what a lawful arrest is.

"To reach people, we are going to civic, church and PTA meetings and we ask them to discuss all their problems. I figure that we have reached 18,000 people by now."

Bryans continued his account:

The program Capt. Redding heads is an outgrowth of one of the recommendations made last year by Mayor Ivan Allen's Commission on Crime and Juvenile Delinquency.

The members of that commission, in their report, concluded that slum dwellers here, as elsewhere (in, say, Los Angeles' Watts community) tended to look upon policemen as ever-present foes.

They said in their report:

"For most of the residents (in local slum areas), the only contacts with policemen are unpleasant ones, arising out of their own scrapes with the law or those of their family or neighbors.

"Their own lack of education and general distrust for authority in many instances prevent them from relating in any positive manner to law enforcement officials.

"They often regard the police as outsiders who have no knowledge or appreciation of their problems. General apathy and dislike of involvement contribute further to reducing voluntary cooperation with the police force or even reliance on the police for protection and maintenance of the peace."

The crime commission members also made it clear there was another side to the coin—that policemen were subject to attitudes which could contribute to the hostility they so often encountered.

"It seems reasonable to conclude," said the crime commission, "that most policemen deal primarily with disruptive and law-breaking members of society and that it would be difficult for them to refrain from developing a somewhat negative attitude toward high-crime areas."

In one more step, Bryans reported:

Captain Redding and police Chief Herbert Jenkins now are preparing to expand their program . . . by instituting footbeat patrols in the slum communities involved.

The idea is that pairs of policemen by patrolling the communities day in and day out will become familiar men in the communities and—hopefully— welcomed enforcers of the law.

In the past, most officers have patrolled the communities in automobiles, or perhaps have been dispatched in to make an arrest. Thus, officer-citizen contacts have been scant.

Capt. Redding believes that in instituting the footbeat patrols, he will find it beneficial to team one white officer with one Negro officer. His idea is that something can be done this way to overcome some Negro area antipathy and distrust for white officers.

In an uplifting mood C&S National Bank in 1966 inaugurated daily helicopter flights between C&S branches in Atlanta and as far away as Newnan. The helicopter's home port was located atop the Mitchell Street office, and specially adapted flagpoles were placed outside the branches so that the helicopter could pick up the bags without landing. C&S officials believed this was the first interoffice transport service of its kind in the country and were optimistic about its possibilities.

For the first time in its forty-two-year history, the Atlanta Legal Aid Society elected a woman president of its board of directors. Margaret H. Fairleigh, partner in Poole, Pearce and Cooper, had practiced law in Atlanta since 1942. Another first for Legal Aid this year was the election of three blacks. Senator Leroy Johnson was named to the board of directors, and William H. Alexander and Horace T. Ward, to the advisory board. The society now had seven full-time attorneys, and in the past year had handled 8,000 cases— nearly 700 per month—of which 1,000 were litigated in the courts. Legal Aid is empowered to handle only civil cases, which are divided about equally between domestic and economic problems.

The new stadium lent itself to more than athletic events, and one of the most exciting was Atlanta's first annual Jazz Festival, which drew 4,000 fans the first night and double that number the second night. The fans really "dug it"—listening to the greatest aggregation of jazz names ever assembled in the

South. Among them were Louis "Satchmo" Armstrong, Stan Getz, Count Basie, Dave Brubeck, Art Blakey, Thelonius Monk, and Nina Simone. George Wein, the producer, felt it went well, and Rod Kimble, in charge of Stadium Productions, hoped that by 1968 the occasion would be the second largest festival in the country.[15]

Atlanta continued to grow in stature as an insurance capital. Connecticut Mutual Life Insurance Company celebrated its centennial in Georgia in 1966. The company started service in Atlanta in 1866 and had over 20,000 Georgia policy holders. In 1910 the Georgia operations were centralized in Atlanta. The Atlanta agent in 1869 had trouble getting policies accepted by the home office because of the high incidence of yellow fever and malaria here, and the majority of his policies were for marine and fire insurance. But by 1966 P. L. Bealy Smith was Georgia general agent, and Connecticut Mutual had $150 million worth of policies in force in Georgia.

Many of Atlanta's traveling socialites also became airborne with the city's most novel organization—a clubhouse in the sky. For a fee of $150 and dues of $8 per month, they could join the Atlanta Skylarks and own a part of a DC-7. The purpose was to afford group travel at a very low rate. Two young lawyers in Washington, D.C., conceived the idea two years earlier when airlines were converting to jet, and they were able to purchase a $2.5 million plane for $100,000. The idea of a flying "country club" soon spread across the country. The inaugural flight of the Atlanta group was to Nassau. The DC-7 seated seventy-seven people but the club hoped to attract 1,000 members. About thirty trips a year were planned, mostly week-end hops.[16]

An acute labor shortage had Atlanta for the first time in its grip. According to the Department of Labor, the number of employable unemployed in Atlanta was under 1 percent, and for the first time the Sanitation Department was picking up trash collectors daily from the "drifters and laborers" pool downtown.

One of the businesses flourishing in Atlanta in 1966 was the home-building industry.

The vast estates that long ago had made Atlanta the City of Homes were being complemented by "bold new concepts" in living. Townhouses, factory-manufactured houses, and close-in country-type homes were transforming the ever-expanding Atlanta residential landscape. In the first six years of the decade more than $1 billion was spent on houses in the expanding urban area. The increase in the number of houses built reflected an increase in the population in the metro area from 1,050,000 in 1960 to 1,300,000 in 1966. The increase in size of houses, from two bedrooms and a bath with a one-car garage to four bedrooms and two and one-half baths and a two-car shelter reflected an increase in the median income from $5,500 in 1960 to $7,050 in 1966. The more elegant homes and apartments, of course, were being bought with incomes well beyond the median. For instance, the typical loan customer seen by the savings and loan companies was thirty-three, married, had two children, and had an income of approximately $10,000 a year. His wife might work, but probably did not. The customer was a skilled technician or a white-collar worker with executive potential and had reached what could be called a "first plateau of success." He was making a good living, had a good future, and was buying a $26,000 to $27,000 house on which there was a mortgage of $21,000. The house was probably his second, and if so was larger and more expensive than his first.

The statistical picture the Federal Housing Administration had of the average person who used its mortgage loan insurance program in metropolitan Atlanta was similar:

He is just over thirty-one years of age, has a family income of $9,000 annually, bought a house for $16,562 (closing costs brought the total to $17,033). He paid part of that amount himself and made a loan of $16,006 on a mortgaged term of thirty years.

The house itself, on an average compiled from FHA insured houses, had 1,219 square feet of living area (FHA and VA houses usually reflect smaller floor areas than do conventionally financed houses, which constitute the largest part of the Atlanta housing market). It also had three bedrooms, and most (61%) had more than one bath.

Carl Nix of Spratlin Associates, Inc., metropolitan Atlanta's largest developer of residential subdivisions, a firm that had some six thousand lots in various stages of completion in twenty-seven north Atlanta area subdivisions, described the typical suburban residential development with conventionally financed homes starting at about $25,000. His comments were in general agreement with an informal poll taken of members of the Homes Builders Association of Metropolitan Atlanta:

In styling, or "front elevations," the buyer is looking for Georgian Colonial, Colonial ranch, Williamsburg, Cape Cod, New England Farm, New England Colonial, Garrison Colonial, French Colonial, French Provincial, French Regency, Southern Colonial, and clean, modified contemporary, not necessarily in that order. Styles that are described as "poor" in popularity at the moment are plain ranch, far-out contemporary, split foyers, and T-split levels.

Another point the poll showed is that brick is still the most popular building material, but customers are "not as sold on it as they used to be," and cedar and redwood shingles are returning to popularity.

Though these outside styles are first to attract the buyer's attention, the really significant changes made in the past few years have occurred in the interiors. Kitchens are larger, contain built-in appliances, vent-hoods, garbage disposals, dishwashers, often a desk, more cabinet space, a dinette area, and plumbing and electrical connections for a clothes washer and a clothes dryer, with the latter usually in a separate room.

Bathrooms are larger and more heavily tiled, feature glass doors in lieu of the old shower curtains, have finished vanities, often with two lavatories, are better lighted, and are equipped with more handsomely designed fixtures. Bedrooms, too, are larger, and the master bedroom usually has its own private bath. Where possible, basements are semifinished, if not fully finished, and frequently feature enough room for both a rumpus area and a bar. . . .

Such significant changes sound expensive, and of course they are, but statistics show that the house purchaser now is getting more per dollar than did his counterpart of the mid-1950s. For example, a division of the F. W. Dodge Co., a market analysis firm, recently made a study of architect-designed houses built in fourteen cities across the nation. They then compared those costs (land excluded) with the costs that would have been met had the houses been built in the other major American cities, among them Atlanta. The results of the study showed that of all of these cities, Atlanta's costs were the least expensive, in many instances by amounts of up to 25 and 30%.

Atlanta magazine explained a change in the housing market: "As Atlantans' taste in housing has become more worldly, it has become more 'old worldly.' The city has shown an eager acceptance of the townhouse, two clusters of which are nearing completion and are the first such developments in the state in several decades. The two are Westchester Square [in Ansley Park] and Paces Place [in Buckhead]."[17]

In a year when new permanent residents were crowding into Atlanta, a run of visitors made necessary the expansion of Atlanta's Convention Bureau. James Hurst headed a staff of seven in new quarters at Peachtree Center, chosen for proximity to convention activities, readily available to the major motels, hotels, and the new auditorium. Atlanta was host in 1965 to 316 conventions and trade shows whose visitors spent some $45 million. The Convention Bureau snagged some good groups for the future, including the American Legion National Convention and Rotary International.

In mid-1966 the Fernbank Science Center contracted to build the main building of one of Atlanta's most valuable resources. Fernbank Forest, the home of the center, lies in Druid Hills in DeKalb County, and for fifty years it was owned by Z. D. Harrison. He built his home there and laid out and planted marvelous gardens of flowers. Fernbank was a deep, tangled wildwood that gave giant beeches, tulip poplars, hickories, pines, oaks, and sweet gums safe haven, as well as fern, jack-in-the-pulpit, trilliums, and a myriad of wild flowers.

Harrison felt that such a wealth of beauty should be shared, and Fernbank soon became a bird, tree, and wild-flower sanctuary, the happy hunting ground for bird lovers and children. By 1938, fifteen persons had acquired the property, organized it as Fernbank, Inc., and after some debate, turned it into a nonprofit educational corporation without capital stock. Out of this came the Fernbank Science Center, which was to become with time an important educational resource for nature students throughout the nation.

In the late 1950s the board of trustees began to negotiate with Emory University and the DeKalb County school system about the use of Fernbank. Ultimately, Superintendent Jim Cherry, who had long seen the possibilities of Fernbank, appointed a committee of science teachers to make a study of the property and suggest how it could best be put to use. DeKalb County was able to obtain a forty-eight-year lease on the property in March of 1964. In 1965 DeKalb's citizens voted overwhelming approval of the $18.5 million school bond issue that included $300,000 for use at Fernbank, and the United States Office of Education chipped in with $190,549 for the salaries of personnel, the development of nature trails and observation stations, and the restoration of native shrubs and flowers.

D. W. Williams's history of the center declared, "It was during the period of 1959–66, under the chairmanship of W. A. Horne, Jr., that the details of the arrangement between the Fernbank Forest Board of Trustees and the DeKalb Board of Education were formulated into a working reality for the Fernbank Science Center. This lease agreement ensured that the primary objectives of the Fernbank Forest, Inc., charter were fulfilled, and also spelled out the guide lines which control the use of the Forest."[18]

In the summer of 1966, Jim Cherry at last found time to sum up his view of Fernbank's future. He signed a contract to construct the $711,000 main building and said, "Fernbank Science Center will be unique. . . . It will provide a bridge for children, for students at Georgia Tech, Emory University, Agnes Scott and other institutions . . . a bridge for the outside world into the world of one-cell animal life, where a thousand protozoa live in splendid isolation within a droplet of water. Over this bridge they can travel into the primeval forest and into the world of space—where planets and suns live in galaxies, and where it is only fifty light years to the nearest neighbor. Over this bridge students can travel to knowledge, to understanding, to beauty, and to a new love of Nature and the natural sciences."[19] Jim Cherry's optimistic forecast about the role Fernbank would play as site of a great science center proved to have been a modest understatement.

The Atlanta Junior League served the city in many ways, and in 1966 the 1,400 members of the league celebrated its fiftieth anniversary. The half-century mark found them one of the largest of the 211 Junior Leagues in America, with 3 million volunteer hours and more than $825,000 in contributions to their credit. "Perhaps their most important contribution in time, money and effort," declared *Atlanta* magazine, was the Atlanta Speech School:

From its beginning in 1938 it has grown into one of the three best schools of its kind in America. The Speech School serves as an elementary school for deaf children, and there are clinics for the deaf of all ages. More than $434,000 has been contributed to this one project. . . .

The League has been active in almost every phase of Atlanta's life including hospitals, education, child care, theatre, art, music and legal aid. In 1962 they established the International Student Bureau and recently donated $10,000 toward the building of the Atlanta Memorial Cultural Center. The next fifty years will no doubt equal, and perhaps surpass, the productiveness of the Atlanta Junior League's first half-century of community service.[20]

While the Junior League celebrated a half-century of service, another Atlanta-area institution was changing its approach, although educating youth remained its mission. For sixty-five years the massive red brick buildings on the campus of Georgia Military Academy in College Park had looked out on the comings and goings of a seemingly endless long gray line of cadets. In August of 1966, however, Georgia Military Academy became Woodward Academy, a private, coeducational, college-oriented preparatory school. Named for Col. John Charles Woodward, founder of GMA, the school gave up its military program. The change was not an abrupt one, but it took place over a period of three years, enabling students who enrolled for ROTC training to complete their course. Thereafter, all emphasis was on liberal arts and college-required courses. In addition to the traditional math, science, English, history, and social studies, students would have access to practical applied subjects such as speech, typing, driver education, and mechanical drawing. Also, art, music, dramatics, and Bible studies were to be emphasized, and a stronger athletic and players' education program would be stressed. "As things are shaping up now," an article in *Atlanta* magazine stated, "Woodward Academy has the makings of a first-rate college preparatory school."[21]

In December of 1966 the Salvation Army was struggling to raise at least $125,000 to spend for Atlanta's poor in 1967. In Atlanta, the army's program encompassed almost every area of human life. Emergency relief was offered to any deserving area in the region and on an individual basis to families stricken by tragedies ranging from eviction to sudden illness. It operated a Women's and Children's Emergency Home on Boulevard. Across town on Luckie Street it provided a hotel for transients. A few blocks away was the Men's Social Center, for men who checked in on a voluntary basis to find help in their struggle against alcoholism. There seventy-five men from all walks of life earned room and board and $2.00 per week allowance by collecting and repairing toys, electrical appliances, and household goods for the Salvation Army Thrift Shops in Atlanta. The army's League of Mercy ministered to the sick in the Atlanta hospitals, and there were six Corps Centers in the Atlanta area that served as churches to the surrounding neighborhoods as well as to corps members.[22]

A very special need got special attention in 1966. In 1965 there were 466 suicides reported in Georgia; an estimated 1,000 more went unreported or were disregarded or were disguised as accidents, and at least a third of these took place in the Atlanta area. Even in the nation where one suicide was attempted every minute of the day and one succeeded every half hour, Atlanta's rates were light but growing higher. The national average was 10.3 suicides per year for 100,000 population, and both Clayton and Cobb counties almost doubled that average, and both Fulton and Cobb counties exceeded it. The Suicide Prevention Center, housed in a bleak room on the third floor of the Fulton County Health Department, was established by Fulton County Mental Health Associates in August of 1966 and was the first such center in the country to have been financed by local funds. Help was available around the clock. The telephones at the center were handled by six women, ranging from a graduate psychologist to a middle-aged housewife. All were trained in suicide prevention techniques.

Atlantans could say good-bye to 1966 with the sound of very special music. Beginning on Christmas Day, the Atlanta Civic Ballet and Atlanta Symphony Orchestra presented the first of a week-long series of performances of Tschaikovsky's *The Nutcracker* at the Municipal Auditorium. Nothing in scope or size had been attempted to match the 1966 production for sheer size, staging, and impact. It was the production of New York City Ballet's fabled George Balanchine and was a rare full-length production that had never been performed by any company other than the New York Symphony. Most times, the production of *Nutcracker* is limited to the lovely, familiar second act, but this time the full eighty-five-piece Atlanta Symphony Orchestra accompanied the entire ballet and performed over and over for a full week. This occasion marked the first full-scale cooperative effort among the members of the Atlanta Arts Alliance who would make up the permanent resident companies of the new cultural center.

OBITUARIES

Mrs. George Baldowski, mother of cartoonist Clifford "Baldy" Baldowski, died at 70. She was the former Marian Tutt of Wilkes County and the widow of the former advertising manager of the *Augusta Herald*. She had been active in PTA work and was especially interested in service clubs for those in the military. For many years she had been receptionist at the information desk in the State Capitol. Dr. Herschel C. Crawford was former president of the Georgia Medical Association and an Atlanta physician for forty-six years. He was a graduate of Emory and had done postgraduate work in Vienna and New York. He was at one time president of Georgia Baptist and Piedmont hospital staffs and of the Fulton County Medical Society, and he was assistant professor of ophthalmology at Emory. Dr. Frank L. Lamons, prominent orthodontist and president of the Georgia Dental Association, died at 66. For fifteen years he had been professor of orthodontics and chairman of the department at Emory. He was graduated from Emory School of Dentistry in 1924 and became associated with Dr. Thomas B. Hinman.

Allie B. Mann, who had spent forty-three years in Atlanta teaching circles, died at 85. She graduated from Girls High and Goucher College and received an M.S. from Emory. She taught at Girls High for thirty-one years and served as head of the Science Department from 1914 to 1934. She later became principal at Grant Park School. Harold F. McCart died at 58. He was Fulton County commissioner and active in insurance circles. He was a graduate of Mercer and a member of Ansley Park Golf Club, the Capital City Club, the Commerce Club, Shrine, Elks, and Kiwanis. He headed the board of stewards at Peachtree Road Methodist Church. Dr. J. Elliott Scarborough, Jr., one of the nation's outstanding cancer specialists, died at 58. He came to Atlanta in 1937 to direct and develop Emory's Medical Center and Clinic and headed the Emory University Cancer Clinic; its distinguished reputation in American medicine brought him the highest honors. He was an elder at First Presbyterian Church and member of the Piedmont Driving Club and the Capital City Club. Ernest L. Sikes was police chief of DeKalb County and a veteran of twenty years of public work. For sixteen years he served on the Atlanta force, achieving the rank of captain.

Miss Tullie Smith died after a long and useful life. She worked with drives for the Red Cross, the American Cancer Society, and the Community Chest. Her two-story antebellum farm house on North Druid Hills Road was later moved to the grounds of the Atlanta Historical Society. George Z. Vance, Jr., make-up editor of the *Atlanta Constitution*, died at 44. He was a graduate of Emory and a member of North Avenue Presbyterian Church.

John A. White—"Atlanta has lost one of its finest citizens in the passing of John A. White, veteran public figure and civic-minded citizen" wrote the *Constitution*. His death of a heart attack "removes one of our most colorful individuals from the political scene. Mr. White, who made his home in Atlanta for more than fifty years, lived forty-four of those on the city's legislative body. He was leader of the board of aldermen, often pioneering in fields in which others feared. His splendid service was rewarded by uninterrupted membership on the board since 1923, years that can be classified as dedicated and marked by distinguished service."

NOTES

1. Bruce Galphin, *Atlanta*, Mar., 1966.
2. Bruce Galphin, ibid., Apr., 1966.
3. Atlanta Chamber of Commerce, "Atlanta—Sandy Springs—Town for Tomorrow" (Atlanta, 1966).
4. *Securities News*, Aug. 18, 1966.
5. *Atlanta*, July, 1966.
6. Bill Diehl, "The Iron Men," *Atlanta*, Apr., 1966.
7. *Atlanta*, April, 1966.

8. Ibid., May, 1966.

9. Ibid., Mar., 1966.

10. Ibid., July, 1966.

11. Atlanta-Fulton County Recreation Authority, "Atlanta Stadium—Special Dedication Edition" (Atlanta, 1966).

12. *Securities News,* Aug. 18, 1966.

13. Ivan Allen and Paul Hemphill, *Mayor: Notes on the Sixties* (New York: Simon & Schuster, 1971).

14. *Atlanta,* Dec., 1966.

15. Ibid., July, 1966.

16. Ibid.

17. Ibid.

18. On Fernbank, see Bill Shipp, *Atlanta,* Sept., 1966; D. W. Williams, *History and Development of Fernbank Science Center* (n.p., n.d.); and "Fernbank" folder, Atlanta Historical Society.

19. "Fernbank" folder.

20. *Atlanta,* Sept., 1966.

21. Ibid., Oct., 1966.

22. Ibid., Dec., 1966.

T HE year 1966 was characterized by strikes that brought vast Atlanta construction projects to a temporary halt, by crime, by confrontations in the streets between civil rights advocates and defenders of the old patterns of racial relationships. Optimists hoped that at last the worst was over; but when Atlantans moved on into the year 1967, they would be shocked at continuing violence, unrest, and divergence from the norm in many areas of life.

Many Atlantans joined their fellow Americans in the increasing antiwar sentiment as more troops were shipped to Vietnam and casualties continued to mount. In February, Martin Luther King, Jr., spoke out against the war. Antiwar demonstrators marched on the Pentagon October 21, and 647 of 150,000 were arrested. Similar demonstrations had occurred in Chicago, Philadelphia, and Los Angeles. In Oakland police arrested 125, including singer Joan Baez.

And, while the war was being vigorously protested, blacks were continuing their demands for civil rights and were showing an increasing militancy. Race riots rocked 127 American cities, killing 77 and injuring 4,000. In June there were riots in Boston, Buffalo, Cincinnati, Tampa, and in Atlanta. As the weather got hotter, so did tempers. In July there were further riots in Birmingham, Chicago, Detroit, New York, Milwaukee, Newark, and Rochester. The most violent areas were Detroit and Newark. Federal troops were used in Detroit, the first use of federal forces to quell a civil disturbance since 1942. A Black Power Conference in Newark had adopted an antiwhite, anti-Christian, and antidraft resolution; and black militant H. "Rap" Brown of SNCC had cried "Burn this town down" on July 25 in Cambridge, Maryland. Police arrested him for inciting a riot. Another SNCC leader, Stokely Carmichael, urged blacks on August 17 to arm for "total revolution."

In Atlanta Martin Luther King, Jr., firmly rejected Carmichael's Black Power movement. However, in April King had called the U.S. government "the greatest purveyor of violence in the world," and had encouraged draft evasion and a merger of the civil rights movement and antiwar movement.

The unrest in the black community was in some degree allayed by President Lyndon Johnson's appointment of Thurgood Marshall to become the first black Supreme Court Justice on the resignation of Mr. Justice Clark.

And a black movie star brought pride to his race by starring in three of the year's top movies. Sidney Poitier had the leading role in *To Sir, With Love*, *In the Heat of the Night*, and *Guess Who's Coming to Dinner?* All three of these movies ran for extended engagements in Atlanta's theaters. Two decades earlier the city had banned movies that even hinted at interracial contact.

To learn more about the counterculture that was becoming so manifest, Atlanta readers would buy a rock and roll publication called *Rolling Stone* and try to understand what they were seeing as they rode through the section of town surrounding Tenth Street—which had been taken over completely by a new look of youth: long-haired, bearded young men and their long-skirted, barefooted girl friends—the "flower children" or "hippies"—the product of the years of unrest and drug abuse. There would soon be a local counter-culture newspaper called *The Great Speckled Bird*.

The hippie colony in Atlanta soon became famous far beyond its borders. *Summer of Love* was the title of a movie made about the hippie community in Atlanta in 1967. And a summer of love it was among the flower children; but it was a summer and ensuing years of worry and frustration for landowners and shopkeepers along Peachtree from Tenth to Fourteenth Street. The community, once a nice shopping area for in-town residents, began to deteriorate.

According to Bruce Donnelly, a young Methodist minister who at the urging of Atlanta's church and business groups had opened the Twelfth Gate Coffee House for artists and hippie types, there were about 1,500 members of the community in the Fourteenth Street area off Peachtree in the summer of 1967. They ranged in age from thirteen to the early twenties, and among them were many missing children. Soon a new and larger hippie coffee shop, called the Fourteenth Gate, was opened on the main floor of the old building whose basement, called the Catacombs, was the original hippie hangout.

Reporter Dick Herbert wrote an insightful description of the Fourteenth Gate as it seemed to him on a visit that lasted two nights and a day:

An infant is curled asleep on the drab carpet of the Fourteenth Gate, a milk bottle's nozzle tucked at his mouth. A boy with long hair and a girl in raggedy-edged bermudas sit Indian style not far away, browsing through magazines.

The walls are papered with posters of old B-grade movies and in the kitchen is a table at which a frazzled red-head named Alfie and other shaggy-haired youths sell hot dogs in plain bread for 15¢ a piece, Kool-Aid and coffee for nickles, soda pop and chips for a dime.

In the front room is a juke-box blaring. Youths are at oil-cloth covered tables reading quietly or talking. Some have beards, some shaggy or teased but uncombed hair, some sandals, some with beads, but also some in sports clothes with combed hair and shaved faces.

Among the posters on the wall over the sleeping infant is another message: "Sorry, no crashing. It's the law."

"Crashing" is a Hippy word for bedding down. Hippies used to gather in "crash pads," as many as 20 or more in one apartment, sleeping on news-papers or pallets, but police applied heat and have pretty well broken up the practice.

Dick Herbert pointed out that there were at least three types of hippies: honest hippies, plastic hippies, and hippie types. The plastics were described by the Reverend Donnelly as "usually younger, more irresponsible, thrill-seeking teen-agers who come to the area in an indiscriminate search for drugs and sex, usually finding both and usually ending up as an arrest statistic."

By 1968 Atlanta's once "gung-ho" hippie colony was dead, except for a small core still hanging on. There had been some 1,500 hippies in the Peachtree-Fourteenth Street area in the summer of 1967, but two years later only about 300 remained. The others had moved on to other cities, or more likely had decided they had had their fling and, as Reverend Donnelly wrote, "had gone back home with a new lease on life."

Crime and racial violence in Atlanta seemed to be relatively mild as 1967 moved on into its long, hot summer. The calm broke in the small and previously tranquil section of Dixie Hills in west Atlanta on June 21. There violence broke out, and a forty-six-year old man was killed and a nine-year-old child was critically wounded. Witnesses said a black youth had thrown a Molotov cocktail at a policeman, and the policeman had fired his hand gun into a crowd sitting on the steps of their apartment building. The man, Willie B. Ross, was killed and the small boy, Reginald Rivers, was shot in the stomach.

The shooting ended the second day and night of rock throwing and gun-firing that had begun on Monday night June 19, around Dixie Hills Shopping Center. On Tuesday afternoon Senator Leroy Johnson had formed a "Youth Corps," which he hoped would help prevent a repetition of Monday night's rock throwing and arrests. The meeting was also attended by members of SNCC.

"Later," the *Journal* reported, "word was passed in the community that SNCC was planning to 'tear the place up.' A crowd of about 100 Negroes, mostly in their 20s, had gathered by 9:00 P.M., as dusk began to set in."

An initial force of about 25 policemen wearing riot helmets and armed with shotguns and carbines in addition to their pistols waited around their vehicles at the shopping center. Only the Neighborhood Service Center was open at the center, and here newsmen and Dixie Hills community leaders congregated.

As darkness fell, three shots were heard. A few rocks were thrown, at least one of which crashed into a police wagon window. Suddenly, the crowd lining the streets around the shopping center had vanished.

Police waded into the darkness outside the dim lights of the shopping center. There was a fusillade of between five and 15 shots, all apparently fired into the air, as the officers attempted to drive several youths from behind a nearby apartment house. . . .

It was not long after the first shots were fired—not by police, the superintendent said—that the fatal shooting occurred.

For such violence to break out in this area was a surprise. Two investigative reporters, John Askins and David Nordon, moved into Dixie Hills to a job of research. When asked why violence had broken out in such a seemingly quiet neighborhood as Dixie Hills, they indicated in their report that Dixie Hills was not and had not been as tranquil as it appeared on the surface. The lengthy study also made clear the dark angers and the fears that dominated the mood and attitude so little understood by white Atlanta:

Until last weekend, most of Atlanta had never heard of Dixie Hills.

It is small, as such areas go; certainly smaller than some of the better known Negro sections like Summerhill, where riots broke out last summer.

And, like other trouble spots of the past, it is not a slum—yet.

Most of the area is filled with small, neat, middle-class Negro homes. Near the edge lies a large, low-rent, privately owned apartment complex which curves around a small shopping center.

Here, all the things that make a racial disturbance stewed together for three days and then boiled over into violence Monday and Tuesday nights. Here, Atlanta's oft-predicted long hot summer may have begun in 1967.

Row after row of the multi-story apartments sit atop a parched concrete and clay desert. The absence of trees and grass stuns the eye; the vista is stark, sullen, oppressive.

The apartments are extremely hot even at night. By day, they are nearly unbearable. And their windows are so constructed as to make air conditioning impossible.

There is no swimming pool in Dixie Hills, no shade trees. Nor are there any recreation areas—no pool halls or gyms or movie houses or bars or playgrounds or parks.

Tuesday morning, after a violent night, a bulldozer was leveling a vacant lot to lay the groundwork for a play area.

Q. V. Williamson, the Negro real estate man who represents the district on the Atlanta Board of Aldermen, was explaining that a pathway would be opened from the apartments as well, leading to nearby Anderson Park, which has been difficult to reach.

A baseball diamond will be provided in the park, he said, and shower stalls erected in the new play area.

"These things have all been on the schedule," he plaintively told a few constituents. "We just haven't had enough personnel, or enough money to do them."

Suddenly, the city has enough personnel and money. Tuesday, the people who make Dixie Hills their home were asking each other the same question: "Does it take a riot to get things done around here?" Their petitions, they said, have gone unanswered.

"What they're doing now are some of the things we have worked so hard for," resident Howard Watson said. "They always told us we were not depressed enough." . . .

"Police are wont to blame Carmichael whenever a riot occurs and he is anywhere nearby. But Dixie Hills residents are skeptical. "Stokely didn't start this riot," a tan-skinned youth volunteered. "The police did."

What makes Stokely Carmichael "big" in the Negro world, he continued, "is that everywhere he goes, he gets arrested. The man could just walk into a place and they'd pick him up. And every time they do, he grows another 10 feet."

Those who live in Dixie Hills are for the most part hopeful that the recent violence will not be repeated. But they doubt either the new-found play areas or the "Youth Corps" proposed by Sen. Leroy Johnson will be more than shaky stopgaps.

Not all the racial news at this time, of course, was of riots, rock throwing, and sudden death. North Georgia Methodists in conference at East Lake Methodist Church on the day after the Dixie Hills troubles took action leading toward deeper understanding between white and black. *The Journal* explained:

North Georgia Methodists created their first fully integrated church program Wednesday with the adoption of a resolution from East Lake Methodist Church.

The annual conference has agreed to help underwrite operational expenses of the church, located near Decatur.

The church is in a transitional area and numerous white families have moved out of the community as Negroes have moved in.

A group of about 75 white members of the church have agreed, however, to stay at East Lake, and develop a ministry to all people there.

Negroes have attended several white Methodist churches in the Atlanta metropolitan area for the past five years, but the East Lake project will be the first racially integrated church program.

This means membership in all activities of the church would be open to all races.

The inauguration of Lester Maddox as governor in January worried some Atlantans. Reginald Murphy of the *Constitution* responded to a New York editor who called to ask, "What's going to happen to your state now that Maddox is Governor?" Murphy's answer was to the point. "We have survived, as we will survive. We may be surprised. Have you seen his inaugural speech? Let me read you a couple of sentences: 'There will be no place in Georgia during the next four years for those who advocate extremism or violence . . . Those Georgians who cannot help themselves will have a friend in the governor's chair for the next four years.'" Indeed, Maddox's actions as governor proved to be more circumspect than many had feared.

In 1967 a number of metro Atlantans of some financial and social standing were carrying on a campaign begun in 1964—a campaign to make betting on race horses legal in Georgia. Pari-mutuel betting, meaning gambling on the horses under strict state supervision, was already legal in twenty-eight states. The new interest in Georgia was created by three conditions—the creation in 1964 of the Georgia Thoroughbred Breeders' Association, the success of major league sports in Georgia, and the state's constant search for sources of revenue.

John A. Wayt, Jr., an "egg farmer" from Roswell, was one of the founders of the Georgia Thoroughbred Breeders Association and was its most persistent spokesmen. A solid citizen and a Rotarian, Wayt said,

The Georgia Thoroughbred Breeders Association was not organized to bring horse racing to the state, but it was organized to build a firm foundation of reputable people for the sport if and when pari-mutuel betting is legalized. My contention is this: Gambling is best kept under control and in the right hands if legalized and strictly supervised. Now it is being done in what we call "horse parlors" and by greasy bookies. Pari-mutuel wagering keeps it on the track and under severe scrutiny. . . .

The way we look at it, horse racing can become an instrument of vast improvement in our state's tax structure. The politicians speak of needing new revenue to raise teachers' pay and school standards, speed up highway construction, and increase benefits for the aged. Within three or four years, legalized pari-mutuels could be bringing in $5,000,000 with no burden on the public at all. What these people must be brought to realize is that a race track becomes a tourist attraction, that most of the money wagered is the money of visitors, and that it doesn't necessarily follow that legalizing racing brings in a flood of sin and corruption.

Many of Georgia's Baptists, Presbyterians, Methodists, Lutherans, and others formed a hard core of resistance which, according to Furman Bisher, kept the state legislature cowering in fear. Jack Harwell, editor of *The Christian Index*, attacked the pro-betting argument: "When the advocates of gambling say there is going to be gambling anyway, let's legalize it and control it, it is the age-old argument that wrong is inevitable, so let's give in and legalize wrong. Follow this line of thinking, and you have no morals at all. Prostitution is inevitable, so legalize prostitution. Dope usage is inevitable, so legalize the open sale of dope, and so on. This is a line of argument that will never stand up."

In some of the hungry years that lay ahead many Atlantans would look back on the mid-sixties as a truly golden age, notably for graduates of the city's colleges. An army of recruiters 2,400 strong had descended on Georgia Tech in one nine-month period ending in May of 1966 bringing with them 1,000 job offers from 740 business houses around the nation. Each of Tech's 1,300 graduating seniors, master's candidates, and would-be Ph.D.s were interviewed at least fifteen times. "The army of recruiters," said Neil DeRossa, director of Tech's Placement Service, "was the largest in the history of Tech, and probably one of the largest programs of recruitment in the United States. The reason is this: Non-defense industries were at the peak of their expansion, employment was at the pinnacle, and so was industrial construction."[1]

Throughout nearly all the decade, James L. Townsend, from his editor's chair at *Atlanta* magazine, told, through the town's top writers and his own column, the story of the surging growth by which Atlanta became a new kind of city. He was leaving the magazine he launched, and the son of a Lanett, Alabama, textile worker, wrote,

This city is sort of the national hero of the sixties, and we are in what is undoubtedly Atlanta's decade. (More than 150,000 persons have moved here during these few years, surpassing the entire population of such cities as Topeka, Kansas, and Green Bay, Wisconsin and Daytona Beach.) And we've done all the things a city ought to do to become a national hero in its time: We've built tall buildings, added such sophisticated highway tools as the downtown connector and the quick access route to the airport, built an auditorium, raised the money for a cultural center, and brought in big league sports. We've got good notices in all the national newspapers, big stories in the magazines, and NBC has for years treated us like second cousins. Our mayor has become famous; the Braves drew well in a losing season; the stadium was full when the Falcons beat the Vikings, was equally as full when the Packers beat us by more than fifty points, and the highlight of the season was when 56,000 fans gave the Falcons a standing ovation merely for leading the Baltimore Colts at half time. We've done all these things and more; we've been the Willie Mays of American cities.

My question now is: Where do we go from here?

The fact is, we are ripe now for error, ripe for the role of fallen heroes like New York and Los Angeles and Chicago, and the surest way to that graveyard is contentment and satisfaction with what we have done. Lee Burge said it well, I think. In the most brilliant and meaningful speech of 1966, Mr. Burge, in his final speech as president of the Atlanta Chamber of Commerce, called Atlanta a new kind of city—geographically, economically, politically, and spiritually. But, in closing, he observed that Atlanta is, and must be, a discontented city, one which admits to and plans for the problems of the future.

Those distant seventies and eighties are very near. By 1980 we'll have more than two million citizens, and another million will join them by the turn of the century, which means that Atlanta is moving, for real, into the big leagues, and simple multiplication will tell you what that means. It means that many more cars will jam the streets, that much more disease and poverty will have to be dealt with, that much more housing will have to be planned, and much more financing will be needed for an already underfinanced city. It's going to be a big and, perhaps, telling load.

To me, this is the finest city in the country, the best place in the world today for a young man, and I don't want us to get caught short in the crush of success. It's happened before.

We're going to be a very big city, but it's all for nothing unless we're also a good city, because only that is worth the effort.

Townsend, who then left for reasons of health, had built *Atlanta* magazine into a model for Chamber of Commerce publications all around the country. Later the chamber relinquished control of the magazine. Townsend returned and served as associate editor of *Atlanta Weekly* until he succumbed to cancer in 1981.

In the issue of *Atlanta* magazine after he left the editorship Townsend wrote "Profile of a Patriach"—the story of Richard H. Rich and what he had meant to Atlanta. The occasion was Rich's reaching age sixty-five.

Richard Rich, chairman of the board, grandson of the founder, and, therefore, keeper of the traditions, is probably better at his trade than even M. Rich was. He would never admit to—or, for that matter, even discuss— such heresy, but it is nevertheless true. At sixty-five, he is at the pinnacle of a career that has no equal in retailing, and he has received every accolade his industry offers including the Gold Medal as the nation's outstanding retailer.

So it can be said with certainty that R. Rich has kept the M. Rich traditions—service, quality, leadership, profits—in a fashion that would have pleased, and probably astounded, the founder. As a result, the store—there are six of them now—will do more than $150,000,000 in business this year. . . .

He worked in the stockroom as a boy, matriculated at the Wharton School of Business, where he was near the top of his class, and later studied in graduate school at Harvard. From there he began the process of preparation in earnest, working in the garment district of New York, in the silk mills of New England, and in a score of departments at Rich's. . . . [He] became one of the firm's vice-presidents just before the beginning of World War II. . . .

Returning to Rich's after the war, he was, at forty-three, neither young nor old, and he was in no wise assured of his future there. The store had done good business during the war but suffered somewhat, as all similar businesses did, from the excess profits tax. Employees were returning, an economic boom was on the horizon, and Major Rich was eager to get his feet wet again. Frank Neely and Walter Rich were the chief executives of the store, and Dick had been away for several years. He had a proposal. He said he would like to free-lance for a few months before accepting a specific assignment, doing a bone-deep survey of the whole operation, looking for weak spots, and returning with recommendations for correcting them. . . . His study was a marvel of efficiency. He suggested a new credit manager and several other key person-nel changes in the control division. He was named vice president and trea-surer.

In 1949 he was elected president of Rich's, a choice that was popular with everyone—stockholders, employees, colleagues—and the store has grown steadily under his management. Among the more important decisions made by Rich in his period of major management was one concerning the boom in branch stores. In the Fifties it was commonplace for major department stores to begin opening branches in a ring around their cities, but Rich advised caution and began his customary study of the situation, which included visits to many major department stores who had expanded to the suburbs.

"The thing that troubled me most was that too many of them were building bright new stores in the shopping centers and were letting the downtown store go to hell. I didn't want that to happen to us. We had faith in downtown Atlanta."

So, while some of the other major retailers around the country were jumping full force into the suburbs, Rich went to his own board of directors with a set of ground rules. Before moving into the new suburbs, he said, Rich's should spend $10,000,000 in improvements to the downtown store. Then, he wanted to meet the problem of parking downtown, which is one of the major attractions of a shopping center, and Rich's did, building several new facilities. Third, he thought Atlanta's metropolitan population should reach and exceed a million before the move was made. The board bought the whole program, and, by the time the magnificent new facility had been built at Lenox Square, all the conditions had been met. . . .

Today, as chairman of the board, he is not charged with the active management of Rich's, but rather with policy. He presides, of course, at directors' meetings and participates in major decisions, but the operating management is in the hands of his good friend, Harold Brockey, who was elected president in 1961 when Rich stepped up to chairman. . . .

What makes the public service background of Dick Rich so astonishing is the fact that it is so endless, that it runs so far beyond what is expected, and that the results have been so consistently meaningful. It is considered good form for an executive to return the loyalty of his city and profession by good works and public-service, and men who rise to the top of their field in a city like Atlanta usually have a background of such work, but it is extremely doubtful that anyone has a track record to match his. Two of his most significant roles are still playing currently—that of chairman of the Atlanta Arts Alliance and the key role as chairman of the Metropolitan Rapid Transit System.

The Arts Alliance may prove to be his most satisfying achievement. While Rich is unemotional when he speaks of it now, a close friend says that the crash at Orly which claimed the lives of 105 Atlantans struck him a deep blow. The Arts Alliance, with Rich in a leading role, was formed to build a memorial to those who died, and, though it may not have affected his thinking, it is known that Rich had more than eighty friends die in the fiery crash. His leadership is credited with bringing about construction next year of one of the country's most elegant cultural centers, a $13,000,000 memorial. . . .

The list of services behind him is very long, too long even to contemplate, and to name only a few important ones is to omit many others, but he has been president of the National Retail Merchants Association, the Atlanta Retail Merchants Association, the Atlanta Chamber of Commerce, the Atlanta Rotary Club and has headed a half dozen major charities. His honors include Georgian of the Year, the Armin Maier Cup from Rotary, an honorary doctor of laws degree from Emory, and a score of other distinguished awards.[2]

Echoes of the Atlanta firemen's strike in the fall of 1966 were heard in the spring of 1967 though the time of crisis was over. By June of 1967 the total firefighting force was up to 811 men, 28 more than were on the force when the strike began in September. The Fire Department still had 85 vacancies to fill, for one by-product of the strike was the realization that the city needed to open a new fire station, move in a new battalion, and increase the work week to fifty-six hours. Of the 541 firemen who went on strike in September, 330 were rehired. In early July a number of the firemen who were not rehired following the strike, acting as members of the Atlanta Fire Fighters Independent Association, brought suit against the city in federal court. They claimed that their suspension and the failure later to rehire them was a lack of due process and a violation of their Constitutional rights. U.S. Judge Lewis R. Morgan ruled against them in the case that would have restored their old jobs and seniority.

While some Atlanta firemen were fighting against retirement, a distinguished Atlanta educator was looking forward to the day when he would step down. Dr. Benjamin Mays retired on June 30 after twenty-seven years as president of Morehouse College. A dinner was held in the grand ballroom of the Marriott Motor Hotel, sponsored by the Morehouse College Alumni Club of Atlanta. When Dr. Mays took office in 1949, the college had two faculty members with doctoral degrees. Now thirty-five members had Ph.D.s and enrollment at the college had doubled. He hoped the school would attract more white students in the future.[3]

Alan F. Kiepper, who became Fulton County manager in October, 1963, left to accept the job as city manager of Richmond, Virginia. Carl Johnson, manager of Guilford County, North Carolina, was chosen to succeed Kiepper.

Before departing for his new post Kiepper was the first recipient of the annual award for distinguished services to the local government presented by the Atlanta Regional Metropolitan Association. Kiepper expressed his views on local government management, and they became the basis for a *Constitution* editorial on May 28, 1967: "Now that [Kiepper] is leaving he can speak his mind somewhat more freely than in the past. He tells us that the big thing we must do here is work for one government for city and county. . . . He observes that the Plan of Improvement, which has been in effect for approximately 15 years and which is a partial blend of the two governments, still upsets some people, but that nevertheless we must pursue the ideal of providing service on a countywide basis. There is cool logic in all Mr. Kiepper says, and the only thing between the idea and its consummation is human nature. We have the routine jealousies and protective gestures of the small empire builders to overcome, but the idea is right and the time for it is now."

Kiepper departed for Richmond, but he did not forget Atlanta, for he came back in 1972 to take over MARTA and guide it through its first decade, creating the basis for one of the finest bus and rail transit systems in the country. In 1982 he left again, this time to take a high-paying job as chief executive officer of Houston's rapid transit system.

Carl P. Reith, who was resigning from the presidency of Colonial Stores, Inc., a grocery-store chain, was relinquishing one of the highest salaries in Atlanta—$100,000—as indicated by a published list of Atlanta business executives annually earning $20,000 a year or more. The complete list filled four columns; salaries ranged from $20,256 for an insurance company vice-president to a select group making $100,000 or more. Rich's top officials, chairman Richard H. Rich and president Harold Brockey, led this line, each with a stipend of $150,500, and executive committee chairman Frank Neely followed closely with $150,400. Next came Paul Austin, president of Coca-Cola, at $141,800, and chairman Lee Talley at $141,600. Delta paid its president C. E. Woolman $130,000; the Southern Co. gave president Harllee Branch, Jr., $125,000; chairman Joseph Lanier received $101,400 from West Point-Pepperell; and president J. Leonard Reinsch of Cox Broadcasting shared the $100,000 spotlight with Carl Reith of Colonial.

These, of course, were salaries of top executives, board chairmen and company presidents. Just below them were vice-presidents, treasurers, and other specialists at $90,000, $80,000, or $70,000. Also, it must be noted here that the figures cited were in many cases the lesser part of the official's income. Bonuses and stock options added greatly to these figures.

Such salaries were truly impressive when measured against a "moderate" standard of living.

Government figures showed that "it cost $8,434 a year, or about $162 a week, for a well-established family of four persons to maintain a 'moderate' standard of living in Atlanta. The figures are based on autumn 1966 price levels. The Atlanta cost is 8% below the national urban average of $9,191 and 17% under New York city's $10,195, according to the Bureau of Labor Statistics." However, Atlanta's new cost level was nearly 50 percent higher than the $5,642 of 1959 and double the $4,315 of 1951. Well over half the increase in costs was attributed to more elegance in manner of living, and less than half to price increases, according to the Bureau of Labor Statistics.

The Fulton County budget recommendation for 1967 was $38,147,260, an increase of less than $1 million, which would not necessitate an increase in county taxes. The biggest items were a planned expenditure of $9.5 million to modernize Grady Hospital and $7.5 million to improve law enforcement. County employees including judges and commissioners had been granted raises.

Beginning in 1968 Fulton County's public defender would be paid a starting salary of $15,000, a wage comparable to senior trial lawyers in Solicitor General Lewis R. Slaton's office. The defender system, the first in Georgia's history, replaced the old court-appointed method of handling the defense of people too poor to employ a lawyer. More than a dozen Atlanta lawyers applied for the position, made available by 1967 legislative action.

In 1967 Atlanta businessmen took a close look at the Forward Atlanta program, which they had begun and which now was finishing its sixth year of shouting Atlanta's virtues to the world. The *Journal* explained the program's success.

In 1960, when the Forward Atlanta idea became a fact, Atlanta was a nice town, with a number of natural advantages but it was not growing as rapidly as it might. There were well-based fears that aggressive promotion by places on the order of Charlotte and Jacksonville might push Atlanta from the top of the Southern heap and make of us a second class city.

What happened? Figures for the last six years show that:

Population is up 22%.

Bank deposits are up 77%.

Retail sales are up 63% and per capita income is up 44%.

Worth it? Easily.

On Sunday, June 4, the Chamber of Commerce announced that funds would be sought to continue the Forward Atlanta program through 1970.

Fine. We have momentum, and another push should be very productive.

This time the Chamber has in mind promoting us as a national city, the idea being that our dominant position in the South is assured. This time Atlanta will emerge as a competitor of New York, Chicago, Boston and the like.

Why settle for regional offices when you can have national headquarters?

Forward Atlanta. Money invested in this program should be returned a thousand fold.

Atlanta's confidence in its future was expressed in several ways in these waning years of the decade.

Only eighteen months after the new 500-room Marriott Motor Hotel opened its doors, it had attracted nearly a million registered guests, plus a vast number of diners, cocktail hour droppers-in, and conventioneers. To Marriott president Willard Marriott, Jr., this meant only one thing—many people who had been spending their tourist dollars in Miami, Dallas, or New Orleans were now looking to Atlanta—and he meant to encourage that changing travel pattern. So he announced that the Marriott chain would begin construction on a new 300-room addition to the original motor hotel. The new addition would include a 500-car parking garage, a specialty restaurant seating 150, a 50-seat cocktail lounge, and a thatched-roof cabana bar located beside its swimming pool. The 300-room addition would make it the largest motor hotel in the world—and as a luxury touch, each suite and bedroom would contain a color television set.[4]

While Marriott's Tower rose skyward, not far away Georgia State University was taking on a new look and a startling new dimension on a ten-acre plot in the heart of the city. There Andrew Steiner, architect of Robert and Company, was transforming the old city blocks, crisscrossed by busily traveled streets, into a split-level campus providing space for 32,000 students and teaching staff, on forty-four acres of classrooms, art galleries, libraries, and administration buildings. Vehicle travel would move only on the lowest level. Under the Steiner plan, which should be completed by 1975, no classes on the upper levels would be more than a ten-minute walk apart. The transformation was already well under way in 1967. A few years earlier the school's home had been a converted six-story garage, and before that it had occupied at least eight other sites in Atlanta under eight different names. "Since it was founded in 1913, it had occupied space at Georgia Tech, the Walton Building at Walton and Cone, the Peachtree Arcade, an attic at Auburn and Pryor, 106½ Forsyth Street, scattered offices donated by Atlanta businessmen, 223 Walton Street, 162 Luckie Street, and finally the garage on Ivy Street which is the taproot of the present campus. It has been designated the Georgia Tech Evening School of Commerce, University System of Georgia Evening School, University Extension Center, University System Center, Atlanta Extension Center, Georgia Evening College, Atlanta Division of the University of Georgia and Georgia State College of Business Administration, and Georgia State, for short, which became its official name," wrote Bruce Galphin.

Finally it seemed to have found its place and its name. It occupied four buildings; another was nearing completion; three more already had been funded and let to design contract. The Board of Regents endorsed the entire master plan, and the city approved the first two pedestrian bridges across Decatur Street that would tangibly mark it as a split-level campus.

Most of the existing campus space was acquired with federal urban renewal assistance, and college officials hoped to obtain even more of the future requirements through the same method. The college already had swept aside some of the city's worst slums: rows of pawnshops, cheap hotels, rundown warehouses—areas that contributed heavily to the city's crime rate.[5]

Atlanta was soon to discover that its handsome and nearly new airport had in the space of only six years become outmoded. In 1961, after years of operation in an oversized Quonset hut, the new facility had seemed to be completely adequate. Three years later, a major new runway had to be added to relieve the enormous traffic jams already clogging the skies over Atlanta, and by the spring of 1967 every phase of operation at Atlanta airport was cramped for space. Plans for future expansion were already being discussed.

Bruce Galphin wrote in *Atlanta* magazine about how the city was becoming a convention center with a positive national reputation:

The city is beginning to have something for the tourist, too. For many decades Atlanta has been a mecca for businessmen and shopping housewives.

But beyond the Cyclorama, the bare outcropping of Stone Mountain, and drives through handsome residential sections, it has had little to show the tourist. The development of Stone Mountain and the creation of Six Flags Over Georgia, however, are modifying that image.

Given its location and transportation network, Atlanta should be a major convention center. It has been hamstrung by lack of facilities. That also is changing. The new municipal auditorium and convention center at Piedmont and Forrest Avenues will open this fall, with room for 4,500 in the cushioned seats of the auditorium and some 10,000 in the convention hall. . . .

The new auditorium will be playing its part in a cultural flowering in Atlanta. The Metropolitan Opera and other large road shows will perform there. But at the same time, an under-one-roof cultural center is being constructed at Peachtree and Fifteenth Streets—a happy memorial to the sad death of more than one hundred Atlantans at Paris' Orly Airport in 1962. The new center, made possible by private philanthropy and public subscription, will house the High Museum, the Atlanta School of Art, the Atlanta Symphony, and Municipal Theatre. Robert Shaw, the distinguished choral director-turned-conductor will assume the duties of the Atlanta Symphony's music director this fall. Also with private funds, Theatre Atlanta has built its own thrust-stage playhouse and transformed itself into the city's first fulltime repertory theatre.

Perhaps the most profound change in the city, though, is one most Atlantans barely notice any more. Atlanta is no longer a racially segregated city. As long as it existed, segregation was a source of national criticism and local unrest, a mark of provincialism, and an impediment to attracting industries and conventions. Yet, six years ago it was ingrained by decades of tradition and enforced state law.

Atlanta's were the first Deep South public schools to be desegregated. The event was extensively covered and reported by the national and international press. When the transition was accomplished peacefully, Atlanta won the immediate praise of the late President Kennedy and widespread press acclaim. Atlanta's business leadership played a major role in that 1961 event, along with the support of virtually every significant element of the Atlanta community. The business community again had a vital role in arranging the desegregation of public accommodations before the action was required by law. But what was a remarkable event in 1961 or even 1963 is now the commonplace of 1967. The issue is no longer a pebble in the shoe of Atlanta.

In short, Atlanta in six years has truly emerged as a national city. In both size and quality, it has become a new kind of city. The record is almost without precedent.[6]

The city expected to welcome 300,000 visitors at four hundred conventions in 1967. Among them would be 15,000 southeastern Shriners, 20,000 members of Rotary International, and 45,000 American Legionnaires. Convention business in 1967 would represent a 27 percent increase over that of 1965. Indications were that the city could conservatively anticipate a $100 million convention business by 1970.

Atlanta's willingness to do almost anything necessary to enhance its status as a convention city ran into problems when Gov. Lester Maddox announced that neither he nor any agency of state government would condone the fact that many Atlanta night club operators were selling whiskey after midnight on Saturday night. To Maddox, this was selling liquor on Sunday and it had to be stopped. The bar owners sought a compromise. On the advice of their lawyer, Wesley Asinov, they announced they would sell no alcohol after 2:00 A.M., and they obtained a temporary injunction against being closed down before that hour. The Atlanta Convention Bureau was on the side of the nightclub owners. To stop after-midnight sales on Saturday would be an extreme obstacle to Atlanta as it strove to become a top convention city. By the late 1970s a compromise had been worked out. Whiskey could be sold in Atlanta bars until 4:00 A.M. except on Saturday night, when closing time was 2:55 A.M. No bar could begin service on any day before nine o'clock in the morning.[7]

One reason for Atlanta's growth was active promotion, including advertisements in *Business Week,* the *Wall Street Journal,* and the *New Yorker.* "These ads," Galphin explained, "coupled with a plan of Forward Atlanta staff work providing brochures, mimeographs, technical reports and other materials, attracted the attention of executives everywhere who were interested in coming to Atlanta." This spate of material, plus the actions of a public relations staff, was more persuasive than the little annual booklet entitled "Facts and Figures about Atlanta," which before 1961 had been the only promotion carried on by the Atlanta Chamber of Commerce.

Since 1961, however, the advertising and public relations effort has been much more widespread and more effective. For several years the emphasis of the national advertising has been on the name of the city. "ATLANTA" appeared in larger type than any of the rest of the message. Copy was kept short, mentioning only the way of life and business in the city.

More than any other advertisement could have done, however, the city got its good image almost overnight, in stories appearing in newspapers all over the nation.

Peaceful desegregation of the public schools in 1961 was perhaps the turning point. The event attracted the national and international press to the city, and the resulting copy was highly favorable.

If anything, the tempo of national attention has accelerated since. Most daily newspapers and general interest magazines, and many special-interest publications, have carried features on Atlanta. In the week the Braves opened their first season in Atlanta in April, 1966, a partial count showed that at least two hundred publications carried feature stories on the city.

The coming of the Braves raises a vital point in an analysis of Atlanta's six-year record of growth. Forward Atlanta didn't bring the Braves, any more than it completed the expressways or built a new runway at the airport or constructed a dozen or so high-rise office buildings. But the thrust of Forward Atlanta has been important in these and other developments. The most important functions Forward Atlanta performs are not the direct activities of its own staff, but in focusing attention on the resources and problems of metropolitan Atlanta.

By identifying its most serious problems and bringing to bear the collective talents available in the city, Atlanta has been able to face these problems realistically and make substantial progress in solving them. It's one thing to list problems. It's quite another to execute the remedies. In some cities it would be almost impossible. But Atlanta has a relative handful of men who, having agreed on a policy, are able to carry it out. They can do this because they live here and are either heads of their respective businesses or are major influences in them. Other cities, too, have their so-called power structures, but the cooperation and the willingness to face change among Atlanta's decision-makers are the envy of most cities.

A section of downtown Atlanta took on a new identity late in November of 1967, and to the late Margaret Mitchell there came a lasting tribute. The movie version of *Gone with the Wind* first played at Loew's Grand Theatre, standing where Pryor, Forsyth, and Carnegie Way all merge into Peachtree Street. The intersection was named Margaret Mitchell Square, and on order of Mayor Ivan Allen, Jr., signs so designating were put up. Just a few steps away in Carnegie Library on Carnegie Way a typewriter and other memorabilia associated with the writing of *Gone with the Wind* were displayed, and they became one of the main attractions of the library.

While Margaret Mitchell Square was coming into being, only two blocks north on Peachtree the Henry Grady Hotel, named in honor of another famous Atlantan, was drawing slowly toward the day of its demolition. The governor's mansion once sat on the site and the title still resided in the state. Rep. Tom Murphy, a member of the State Properties Control Commission and House floor leader for Gov. Lester Maddox, suggested that the hotel be sold. The hotel, being leased from the state by its operators, was old, he noted. The lease was to expire in 1972, and, Murphy asked, if the lease was extended, who would spend millions to remodel a hotel that he did not own outright? Besides, he added, the government-owned property was not paying taxes, and if it were privately owned, it could be taxed. So why not sell it off and get the state out of the real estate business?

Opponents of the sale suggested that the hotel be leased on terms that required its improvement. They argued that the leaseholder would be likely to make a bundle that would enable payment of a hefty and escalating rent, as the Southern and the L&N Railroads proved in their competition to lease the

W&A. The rent payments to the public's treasury might beat the tax payments private owners would make. And they would be regular. The one-shot windfall resulting from a sale could be spent up by one administration.

The decision was to let the old building stand another four and one-half years, to the end of its ten-year lease in 1972. And so it stood, growing shabbier day by day until Labor Day in 1972, when it was blown down by dynamite. It was replaced by a towering edifice of glass designed by John Portman—the Peachtree Plaza Hotel.

Two other organizations devoted to the improvement of Atlanta took on a new and vigorous aspect in 1967. The old Central Atlanta Improvement Association was organized in 1941 by businessmen in the Five Points area. The Uptown Association, representing business leaders, organizations, and institutions, was formed in the 1960s to seek improvements in the Ponce de Leon Avenue/North Avenue Corridor. These two groups finally joined forces in 1967 under the new name of Central Atlanta Progress (CAP). The city's top businessmen have functioned as presidents of each organization. Serving in the Five Points area beginning in 1941, they were Robert F. Maddox, James D. Robinson, Jr., Jesse Draper, Fred B. Moore, Hugh I. Richardson, Ivan Allen, Jr., John O. Chiles, Ben J. Massell, Fred J. Turner, Jack Adair, Alfred D. Kennedy, Jr., and Alex W. Smith, Jr. The Uptown Association was headed from 1960 to 1966 by N. Baxter Maddox, Hix H. Green, and Virgil W. Milton. Central Atlanta Progress, from 1967 on into the 1980s, was led by Alex W. Smith, Robert M. Wood, John C. Portman, Jr., Harold Brockey, and L. L. Gellerstedt, Jr., and since 1973 by the highly competent professional city-builder, Dan E. Sweat, Jr.

In their book *Triumph of a People,* Bruce Galphin and Norman Shavin described CAP as a "commitment to maintain, through cooperation between the public and the private sectors, an economically vibrant, profitable business district."

By 1967 it was obvious that the business district was no longer "central." It had grown far beyond Five Points, north along Peachtree, West Peachtree, and Spring streets to a second business district bounded on the north by Brookwood Station, by the Coca-Cola Company on the west, and Sears Roebuck on the east. CAP's mentors, the Shavin-Galphin book noted, were six men, the top executives of their companies, organized into a twenty-member executive committee that met monthly, and a thirty-five member board of directors that met quarterly. A two-year term for its presidents was abandoned when Dan Sweat, Jr., came into the organization as executive director and then was named president in 1975. Over him in 1975–76 were L. L. Gellerstedt, Jr., as chairman, supported by six vice-chairmen: William L. Callaway, Thomas G. Cousins, Joel H. Cowan, Alex W. Smith, A. H. Sterne, and Robert Strickland.

Since then, the city-conscious, nonprofit CAP organization has known few quiet moments. Working in collaboration with city government and private interests, it sent task force after task force into the field. A central area planning program begun in 1969 led to the city housing study compiled in 1974. The study encouraged fifteen Atlanta banks and savings and loan associations to pledge $63 million for intown mortgages over the next five years, according to *Triumph of a People*. The regeneration of a twenty-one-block downtown area, called the Fairlie/Poplar Project, was executed the same way, with the city calling in CAP to provide the master plan. Flexible, CAP adapted different organizations to accomplish specific tasks. In the redevelopment of the Bedford-Pine area, for example, it formed a private company, Park Central Communities, to produce the intown housing. The developers were six banks and six private developers, among them Rich's, the Coca-Cola Company, and a nonprofit CAP subsidiary, Central Atlanta Civic Development, Inc. CAP could also work fast in an emergency. When Bowen Homes Day Care Center was destroyed by fire in 1980, a public drive quickly raised a fund to rebuild the center. As might be expected CAP was "high" on MARTA from the beginning, and conducted study after study of the effect MARTA would have on the future development of downtown Atlanta.

Going into the last half of 1967, CAP was aware that all the genius of its members and officers would be needed. Atlanta was on a collision course with crisis. Five mammoth construction projects going on simultaneously were adding 2.5 million square feet of office space to the downtown area, and downtown was growing rapidly more inaccessible. The northeast expressway was already carrying twice the load that it was designed to carry by 1970, and the completed MARTA system was still at least seventeen years away. There was also a rise in the number of poverty stricken families in the central city, for which housing, education, and fire and police services must be provided, and paid for. But the industries that could provide jobs were following the rush to the suburbs, outside the reach of the city tax system. Thus, CAP had many problems to solve.[8]

To get ideas from the best brains possible, *Atlanta* magazine in July of 1967 started a new feature, "Other Voices," a forum in which men and women of wisdom—and, it was hoped, of wit—would express their ideas as to what should be done about the more pressing issues facing Atlanta. Architect Cecil Alexander was the first guest columnist, and his strongest point was that there must be created around a strong and progressive central city a strong and progressive metropolitan area in which different neighborhoods would share with each other, and with central Atlanta, the common duties of government. "Forward Atlanta," said Alexander, "must mean 'Forward Metropolitan Atlanta' or we will be moving forward into chaos."

In the field of police protection Atlanta and the communities in the surrounding metropolitan area were already working hand-in-hand. Until 1965 police officers in metropolitan Atlanta wore fifty different badges and patroled fifty different jurisdictions in 1,724 square miles. After the mid-sixties they no longer acted alone. Under the new law enforcement techniques, they pooled their resources into a loose and wholly voluntary federation called Metro-pol—and its record is truly impressive. In its first year, 1966, Atlanta showed a 13 percent decrease in reported crime, and 10 percent in arrests. In every crime category except rape the metro Atlanta record was the best in the United States. Metropol was Atlanta's first experiment in true cooperation with its metropolitan neighbors, and in time it would lead to cooperation in other areas.

Much of Metropol's success can be attributed to police chief Herbert Jenkins, who lectured not only to his own department, but to the small-town police as well, urging them to "quit just talking about cooperating and truly do it." One thing that made cooperation easier was a new system of commu-nications training. In 1967 a powerful electronic weapon—a closed-circuit teletype system—connected police agencies throughout the Atlanta area. A stolen car in one county could be recovered in a few minutes as it passed into another police jurisdiction. Crimes committed and the description of fugitives could be passed immediately from one jurisdiction to another, and under Metropol, a standard procedure for handling investigations and arrests for different types of crimes was taught to each group of officers.

Another agency designed, like Metropol, to bring about a more law-abiding and peaceful city was the Human Relations Commission—a unique and level-headed assembly of men and women dedicated to cutting through the tangle of government red tape and creating, with the blessing of city gov-ernment, an agency able to contact private and public agencies and get action on complaints made by the central city's poorer, and most often black, cit-izens. These complaints, which in the past had often been ignored, might deal with matters as simple as uncollected garbage or as threatening as rats in the children's beds in a rented house. But out of such problems as these grew such riots as those that broke out in the Summerhill and Vine City areas. At the first open hearing of the new commission, held in the aldermanic chambers of City Hall in February of 1967, the commission began to show its form as an ombudsman for the needy of the community. It could make surveys of sepa-rate areas and list needs: play grounds for the children, sewage disposal, gar-bage collection, street repairs, the demolition of substandard housing—any-thing that needed doing. It could not finance these things, but it could identify them and urge upon the proper government agencies the need for them to act. The office of commission chairman I. C. Kaler, and Eliza Paschall's CRC Office at City Hall, breathed an atmosphere that most often is one of utmost frustration, touching on problems in every area of human need.[9]

Atlanta magazine described what the commission heard:

There are reports of indignities and discrimination suffered by indi-viduals at the hands of public agencies. Inequitable real estate practices, agents using "scare" tactics to induce owners to sell property, have come to light. Garbage un-collected, streets unpaved, sewers running open, rats and vermin running unchecked, have been mentioned. Over and over come the refrains: "Our children have no place to play, yet they are ordered off the streets. Our mothers have no one with whom to leave their children while they are at work. Our young people cannot get jobs because they are untrained, yet where can they go for technical instruction and vocational skills? Our houses are demolished, but we are not relocated. Or we are relocated into worse areas than the ones we left. Housing and health laws are not enforced. Luxury apartments, parking lots, a municipal stadium, go up in our midst in the time it takes us to get a street sign erected, yet we are told that facilities cannot be improved until the city has more money. Does anyone care? Does anyone *know?*" These are not vague and general complaints. Each charge has grown out of a specific instance. . . .

The Community Relations Commission has one thing going for it that many other similar organizations do not. It numbers among its members men and women who know the problems of these areas because they are of them. "Our Negro members are perhaps the most valuable people we have," [chairman] Kaler says. "They are sharp, tireless, and infinitely productive in their respective professions. They are quite capable of keeping us anchored to reality by saying, 'Don't kid yourself, friend. You've got five of us right here on this commission. We *Know.*' And they do know." The 20 members of the Commission represent a true cultural and socio-economic cross section of Atlanta, backed up by fine individual records of accomplishment, incredible capacities for bone-breaking work, and a common impatience with platitudes, euphemisms, and red tape. They are: Irving Kaler, chairman; Reverend Samuel Williams, first vice chairman: Miss Helen Bullard, second vice chairman; Mrs. Fred Patterson, secretary; Robert Dobbs, Archbishop Paul Hallinan, Rolland Maxwell, Joseph Haas, Clarence Ezzard, Rabbi Jacob Rothschild, Mrs. Sara Baker, J. A. Wyant, Miss Mary Stephens, M. O. "Buzz" Ryan, Hamilton Douglas, Jr., T. M. Alexander, Sr., R. Byron Attridge, Jack Sells, R. J. Butler, and Robert E. Lee. Mrs. Eliza Paschall was named Executive Director of the Commission early this year and serves full-time in that capacity, and Mayor Ivan Allen and Vice Mayor Sam Massell are ex-officio members under the terms of the ordinance.[10]

Though not a member of the commission, Grace Hamilton, first Negro woman ever elected to the Georgia legislature, had demonstrated such a genius for bringing about an understanding between the races that she had personally been responsible for accomplishing many things the commission would be called upon to do. The wife of Dr. Henry C. Hamilton, registrar of Morehouse College, and daughter of two Atlanta University professors, she was for eighteen years the secretary of the Atlanta Urban League, and in 1966 was elected to the Georgia legislature and in 1968 was reelected. From local and state recognition she moved up in 1966 to national status when President

Johnson named her as one of the eleven members of the Citizens Advisory Committee on Recreation and Natural Beauty. "She has been called 'one of Atlanta's Outstanding Citizens' by such notably outstanding Atlanta citizens as Mayor Ivan Allen, Jr., Atlanta *Constitution* publisher Ralph McGill, and Hughes Spalding, Sr., prominent attorney. Mr. Spalding was director of the Fulton-DeKalb Hospital Authority when the Hughes Spalding Pavilion of Grady Hospital was built for Negro patients. He called Grace Hamilton 'the instigator and moving force of the project, although many other dedicated people worked on it.' "[11]

There were other blacks, of course, who were demonstrating a deep understanding of how to bring black and white together in a mutual understanding of the racial problems and how to solve them without violence. One was a tall, slender young black lawyer, Leroy Johnson, a state senator who had been in the news for ten years. In 1957, at age twenty-nine, he became the first black man in the southeastern states to be employed on a solicitor general's staff. In 1962 he defeated three white candidates in a race for the Democratic nomination in the Thirty-eighth District legislative race. Then he beat a black Republican, T. M. Alexander, Jr., to become the first black man in the state legislature since Reconstruction. In 1963 the Atlanta Chamber of Commerce named him one of the city's five outstanding young men of the year, and he also received the Freedom Award from the NAACP. And in March of 1967 his fellow senators passed a resolution commending Johnson for his outstanding service, saying that he had "aided and assisted in bringing about a new image for the South," and praising his record as a "voice of responsibility and dignity" through six sessions of the Georgia legislature. His handling of himself in the role of lawmaker removed whatever doubts may have existed concerning the ability of Negroes to hold public office, and according to *Atlanta* magazine, "the ten other members of the General Assembly are now accepted as a matter of course."[12]

On the more violent side of race relations, civil rights leader Hosea Williams, who would later serve in the legislature and on the Atlanta City Council, accused Atlanta patrolman R. D. Marshall of "brutally beating and kicking him," on Saturday night, July 1, at Grady Hospital. Officer Marshall, a veteran of sixteen years, was suspended but denied all charges made by Williams. Williams, in turn, was charged with disorderly conduct, public drunkenness, failure to move on, and creating a disturbance.

After a hearing extended over several weeks, the aldermanic police committee voted 2 to 1 to reinstate patrolman Marshall on the force. Williams responded by calling for the resignation of Police Chief Herbert Jenkins and asked for an elected rather than an appointed chief.

One indication of the growing understanding between Atlantans in racial matters was the fact that school integration, brought about in 1961 despite threats of violence, by 1967 was moving forward. Said Dr. John Letson, superintendent, on the eve of opening of the 1967–68 school year: "We are beginning our most hopeful year. We're opening seven new buildings. The Atlanta School System has never been in better shape. We are doing a better job in education than we have ever done before." But the problems were bigger and more challenging. The increase in black pupils from 45 percent to 57 percent had greatly increased the number who were in need of special attention. The Head Start Program was expanded during the summer to include 2,500 preschool children. Other programs under Letson ranged from teacher education to free lunches for 20,000 Atlanta children who came to school hungry every day, to a new school to be created by the Atlanta Junior League in which children with learning difficulties due to poor hearing would receive special attention in a separate school.

One of the spectacular sights of 1967 occurred on Sunday, June 4, when the eighty-foot-long steel framework of a walkway between the twenty-second floors of the new Gas Light Tower and the Merchandise Mart at Peachtree and Harris streets was lifted into position. During the operation, which began about 6:30 A.M. and was completed a little after 2:00 P.M., traffic was rerouted.

The twenty-five-story Gas Light Tower was the fifth of the skyscrapers in architect John Portman's Peachtree Center, and, according to company president W. L. Lee, the tower would be the first tall Atlanta building to use natural gas for all its energy needs. Alongside the $10 million tower would be a mall, from Peachtree west to Ivy, containing sculpture, reflecting pools, fountains, and benches. In the ten years that had passed since Atlanta Gas Light celebrated its one hundredth anniversary, its service had expanded from 49 Georgia cities to 173, with 550,000 customers, and its operating revenues had exceeded $100 million for a twelve-month period.

The Peachtree Center development and other big construction projects downtown gave a picture of a booming Atlanta where there was work for all hands. And, indeed, the unemployment rate, overall, was only 2.3 percent. But, out of Atlanta's population of 499,000, 222,554 were black. And of these, some 97,451 lived in areas of the city inhabited largely by hard-core unemployed. These communities clustered near downtown Atlanta, and it was from them that protest riots surged, as in the Dixie Hills uprising. It was welcome news, therefore, when Washington, D.C., announced that Atlanta had been granted $4.5 million to set up work programs for 2,500 of the hard-core jobless. They would not be given the money outright. Through a new agency called ACEP—Atlanta Concentrated Employment Program—they would be taught new skills, and once trained, jobs would be sought for them. There would also be service to families, most of which were headed by women. These included community health services and baby sitting. Those who participated in the program lived in the target areas of Pittsburg, Price, Nash-Washington, Summerhill, Mechanicsville, and certain areas of West End. In these places, all close-in to central Atlanta, the jobless rate was 25 percent instead of the city average of 2½ percent—and out of 24,393 persons, 6,209 were looking for work. In the area were 14,463 families that had income of less than $3,000 a year, and 2,672 of the families could not afford to pay rent, the lowest available being $20 a month.

While some Atlantans were concerned with using federal funds to prepare idle young people, many of them without a high school education, for handling jobs that paid a living wage, a group at the other end of the intellectual and educational spectrum was concerned with its future at Georgia Tech. To consider what was wrong and what was right about the institution, a program called Tech Today was launched. "Its purpose," *Atlanta* magazine explained, "is to decide whether or not Tech and its curriculum is meeting the challenge of the modern times. Is it attracting the top students? Yes, but not enough of them, because it does not offer enough scholarships. Is it doing as much original research as many other institutions and universities? No, probably not, and without research, teaching rapidly grows out of date and loses vitality." But, said Dr. Charles Broden of Tech's Department of Physics, the research grants most available were military and commercial, and these tended to concentrate on gadgets and hardware instead of scientific principles. Other observations were that Tech's teaching load was too heavy, and its salaries were too low, and many professors were planning to leave for better opportunities elsewhere.

But one physics professor, Joseph Ford, summed up the feelings of many—"I'm betting my life on Tech," he said. And so were most of the faculty leaders. But there was no doubt that the majority of them were determined that in the age when computers talk to computers, when the secrets of nuclear reaction must be harnessed to produce controlled power as well as nuclear explosion, when computers commanding robots could take over manufacturing processes formerly done with human hands, Tech would be in the forefront of these problems, as it had been in all the simpler engineering problems of the past.[13]

The present author got an advance look at the new Six Flags park and wrote his impressions in the *Journal-Constitution:*

You may think that an amusement park is an amusement park and when you've ridden one roller coaster you've ridden 'em all. Well, maybe. But I've got a feeling that Six Flags Over Georgia, which will be opening officially in southwest Atlanta just off I-20 on June 16, is going to be something memorable in its field—not as full of whim and fantasy as Disneyland maybe, but just as much fun.

We went out the other day and wandered over the whole 270-odd acres, watching the carpenters and the painters put the last finishing touches on the Music Hall, where a romping show of the 1890's will be staged before an audience of 800 seated at little tables in the authentic glitter of gold and crimson of an old-time Music Hall. This is one of two shows that will be showing on the grounds all the time, and it will be so continuous that there will have to be two casts, and two orchestras, one of them taking over when the other gets tired.

The other is a truly spectacular puppet show called Sid and Marty Kroft's Circus. The puppet theater is an amphitheatre, marvelously colorful, with shadow boxes along the walls, and a stage equipped to handle a show as elaborate as *My Fair Lady.*

The puppets were hanging everywhere, dangling from their T-shaped boards by their black strings. Even though they are caricatures they are so realistic, when manipulated by a master puppeteer, that they are almost frightening.

We got to the porpoise pool too late to see Skipper and Dolly being fed, but that was all right. Having been fed, they were docile and friendly and came up to the side of the pool and made pleasant squeaking noises through the blow-holes in the top of their heads. . . .

The Petting Zoo, where [a baby] elephant will be on display, is a place where the kids can go and pet little goats, and sheep, and chickens if they can catch them, and a llama, and I don't know what all.

The Six Flags, of course, represent the flags of England, Spain, France, the Confederacy, the State of Georgia and the United States, and there is an English Village, a Spanish Fort (replica of the real one at St. Augustine) where kids can fire little cannon from the battlements at toy boats in a pond below, and a Confederate area (that's where the Music Hall is) and all of these have a special authenticity about them.

But the place is far from being an historical museum. It's built for fun and excitement. The rides are wonderfully scary, particularly the wild ride on the runaway mine train through the "burning" mine, or fantastic, like the dreamy float in boats through the marshes of the Okefenokee, with all the little creatures, automated and wired for sound, carrying on on the bank, or exciting, like the thundering, roaring dash on fibreglass logs, down the "Log Flume," or dizzying and breathtaking like the soaring lift above the whole area on the Flying Saucer.

There will be just one gate admission for the whole thing—$3.95 for adults, $2.95 for children under 12. For this, you can see every show and ride every ride as many times as you want to, with no other expense except what you eat and drink, or squander on silly looking hats that people like to wear when they go to places like this.[14]

Edmund Parks, travel editor of the *Montreal Star,* was attracted to Atlanta by the growing fame of Six Flags and by the birth of the area called Underground Atlanta. He described his reaction in the August 2, 1969, edition of the *Star.* After tracing briefly Atlanta's resurgence after Sherman's passing, he said:

Today, Atlanta is a dynamo, known by industrialists as the Wall Street of the South and by tourists as the locale in *Gone with the Wind*, and as a base for Southern fried chicken, mint juleps and hominy grits. These same tourists have also discovered that Southern hospitality is not a myth although the peaches may be. Integration here is sincere and much of the credit for it has been ascribed to the gentleness and the commonsense of Mayor Ivan Allen who, at 57 and after some years in office, has decided to call it a day, much to the regret of many people.

Six Flags Over Georgia is one of several tourist attractions close to the city. It derives its name from the six flags which have flown over the state—British, Confederate, Spanish, French, Georgian, and U.S.—and is spread across a good chunk of a 276-acre park reached via a broad highway nine miles west of the city. In sum, Six Flags is a miniature Disneyland with a difference, an inexpensive day out for a family; one ticket provides entrance to the park, and fun on all 75 of the lake, rail, tram or sky rides, stage shows and other attractions and includes mingling with a friendly bunch of animals meant for petting and fondling. Dad, therefore, does not have to keep fishing in his pocket for dwindling small change and need buy only soft drinks and sandwiches for his hungry brood unless, of course, Mother has packed victuals for a picnic at one of the many quiet spots on the spotless grounds. Garbage on the lawns and concrete paths is, in fact, a rarity. The 1,500-strong army of men and women college and high school students help keep it that way. These smiling, courteous, smart young people pilot the riverboats, drive trams and steam locos, provide good musical entertainment and operate the snack bars and small shops. Behind them are the executives, all young people. Typical of them is Bill Arnes, who left his job as a salesman in South Carolina because he liked the "feel and the spirit of this place. It's tremendous." His pretty blonde wife, Bonni, feels as he does. She is secretary to the Southern Travel Directors' Council. "Georgia is a great state and Atlanta is a great city. We couldn't be happier. . .", says Bonni.

(Six Flags, as forecast, by constantly increasing the excitement of its rides and shows, became one of the top amusement parks in the nation. By 1982, 15 million people had paid admission and still were coming at the rate of two million a year.)

"Twenty-five years ago no one could have predicted that on the eve of 1968, Peachtree Street would rival Madison Avenue as the hub of almost one hundred advertising agencies and counselors." With these words Betsy Fancher told in *Atlanta* magazine of one of Atlanta's rising businesses. "From Five Points to Buckhead, a new breed of button-down persuaders is masterminding a healthy percentage of the sixteen hundred messages that daily assault the wary consumer via radio, television, and the printed word." She wrote:

Farsighted firms are outgrowing their roles as ad agencies and becoming marketing consultants to a growing number of national accounts. And the electric, sky's-the-limit atmosphere has created an exodus from the think-factories of Chicago and New York to the burgeoning Peachtree Street firms which are adding a million dollars in billings every year.

The agency boom also has been the catalyst for a remarkable growth in such related professions as public relations, graphic arts, photography, modeling, television and radio production. And it has sparked an ever-expanding talent pool of writers, artists, and actors which the newcomers from Madison Avenue will assure you compares with the best in New York.

Among the national agencies moving into Atlanta were Batten, Barton, Durstine and Osborne. Local agencies that moved up to regional status during the upward surge in the middle sixties included Gerald Rafshoon and Charles A. Rawson and Associates. Other companies beginning to make a great impression on Atlanta were George & Glover, Tucker Wayne and Company, and Louis Hertz.[15]

While in Atlanta in 1967 was nurturing the copywriters, artists, models, typographers, and photographers brought into Atlanta by the burgeoning advertising agencies, another "industry" that was growing rapidly was most unwelcome.

The city, according to J. L. McGovern, executive director of the Metropolitan Commission on Crime and Juvenile Delinquency, had become "prime prey for organized crime." No Cosa Nostra yet, said McGovern in an interview with John Pennington of *Atlanta* magazine, but the Cosa Nostra, or Mafia, was always looking for new opportunities to make a crooked dollar. And in an expanding Atlanta a great many dollars were floating about:

Crime is a major industry in Atlanta, grossing possibly a million dollars a week. The known take from sex, moonshine whiskey, lottery, sports, gambling, and thievery runs to $38,736,172 a year. This does not include the floating crap games and some other forms of lawbreaking. The additional cost to the public for law enforcement, courts, and prisons (and $10,620,000 in lost taxes on illicit liquor alone) runs to an incredible figure.

Obviously this is crime on a major scale. But is it *organized* crime? This is a question asked frequently today as public officials before microphones, and judges before grand juries warn against the infiltration of organized crime into our society. The question deserves an answer, but the answer is not a simple YES or NO.

One hundred prostitutes work the city full time (as professional ladies of the evening). Their annual income is well over a million dollars. Others working on an occasional or part-time basis run the yearly take for prostitution to at least $1,500,000.

A dozen lottery companies in the city gross an estimated $6,000,000 a year. Authorities are aware about this much. Undoubtedly there is more. And bookies handle at least an equal amount in betting on major sports.

Moonshine whisky flows into Atlanta from the hills of North Georgia at a rate of sixty thousand gallons a month, seven hundred twenty thousand gallons a year—which is only 40% of what it was two years ago. The illicit liquor business grosses about $20,520,000 a year by the time it is "cut" and resold by the jigger and by the half-pint in slum area shot-houses.

In 1967 a car is being stolen every three and a half hours in Atlanta. Stolen cars in 1966 were valued at $3,230,000. Authorities recovered $2,714,250 worth of them. All stolen property, including cars, burglary, and larceny, amounted to $5,516,172 of which $2,905,910 was recovered.

To these crimes-for-profit add the crimes of violence. During the first six months of 1967 there were fifty-four murders, sixty rapes, four hundred thirteen assaults. The crime picture begins to emerge.

But, is this *organized* crime? To develop a realistic overview of crime and the threat of crime in Atlanta today *Atlanta* Magazine interviewed those closest to the subject on city, county, metropolitan, state, and federal levels. Pennington talked with Clinton Chafin, superintendent of Atlanta detectives, against the back-drop of blaring police radio; with Solicitor General Lewis Slaton of Fulton County, chief prosecutor for the Atlanta Judicial Circuit; with James McGovern of the Crime Commission; with Frank Hitt, agent in charge of the Atlanta FBI office. Major Barney G. Ragsdale, chief of the Georgia Bureau of Investigation, also was interviewed, along with federal alcohol tax specialists and others.

The answers given to the question: "Does Atlanta have organized crime?" will need qualification.

Hitt, of the FBI: "We know of no organized crime, as such, in the state of Georgia at this time."

Solicitor Slaton: "There's no national crime organization here at this time to my knowledge."

McGovern: "I base my statement solely on what I gather from the constituted agencies. I've been in contact with them all and they tell me there is no concrete evidence of infiltration of organized crime into Atlanta, organized in the classic sense of the Mafia. . ."

Chafin and Ragsdale echoed these answers. But all of the officials made it clear they were speaking of organized crime in the classic sense, of the murder and bribery and racketeering of the mob known as La Cosa Nostra or Mafia, which is a tightly controlled and disciplined organization whose tentacles are sunk deep into many cities of the United States.

Atlanta does not have La Cosa Nostra, the officials said. But Atlanta does have organized crime. "We have plenty of the rackets in Atlanta," Slaton said. "We have all of them. But they're locally controlled and locally organized and there's enough division between them that it's been kept fairly well under control."

Actually, though Atlanta was obviously a prime project for takeover by the mobs, most of the crime came from one of five sections of the city where poverty and lack of education were the greatest. By concentrating on prevention in this area, the city was setting some interesting records as a law-abiding place. Burglaries, larceny, and auto theft were less frequent in Atlanta, for example, than in other cities. And the rate of solved cases was higher. As Pennington reported:

Murders are solved at an 89% rate nationally, 96% in Atlanta; rapes 62% nationally, 70% in Atlanta; robbery 32% nationally, 67% Atlanta; assaults 72% nationally, 92% Atlanta; burglaries 22% nationally, 32% Atlanta, larcenies 19% nationally, 37% Atlanta; auto theft 23% nationally, 33% Atlanta. In every category Atlanta ranks well above the national average in the solving of crimes. This, of course, would have an influence on keeping nationally organized crime out of Atlanta.

"There is," said Pennington, "a silver lining around this dark crime cloud over Atlanta." And it was pointed out, not by Superintendent Chafin, who should brag about it, but by McGovern of the crime commission. While the national crime rate rose by 17% in the first half of 1967, it declined in Atlanta in some major areas and rose less than the amount in others. McGovern's computations were as follows: "Murder was up 20% nationally, and 33% in large cities. It was down 11% in Atlanta. Rape was up 7% nationally, up 4% in comparable cities. No change in Atlanta. Robbery was up 30% nationally, 40% in comparable cities. Up 21% in Atlanta. Assaults were up 11% nationally and in comparable cities. Down 12% in Atlanta."[16]

In 1967 the "Grande Dame" of southern portraitists, "Miss Kate" Edwards, turned eighty-nine. In *Atlanta* magazine's "Town Talk" it was reported, "The so-called 'Generation gap' simply does not exist between this amazing woman and myriad children, teen-agers and young adults who come to sit for her and seek her advice and wisdom, accumulated over eight decades." The magazine noted:

Getting a portrait done by Miss Kate in her apartment is the thing to do in Atlanta, but neither in her youth nor in the fullness of her years was she a mere social dabbler in the arts. She left her home in Marshallville, Ga. in the early 1900's to study at the Chicago Art Institute. After three years there she studied at the Academie Shaumire in Paris, and in the mid-Twenties she moved on to England, painting such luminaries as Walter de La Mare, Rose Macauley and Arnold Bennett. She came home to Georgia just in time for the crash of 1929. After doing advertising agency art work for awhile, she went back to painting portraits, and in 1967 after she was 89, she estimated that they totaled 544. And, she says, she remembers in detail each one, the set of the head, the look in the eyes. Among those she remembers are the portraits she did of Bobby Jones, Judge Elbert Tuttle, Poet Walter de La Mare, General Blanton Winship when he was Governor of Puerto Rico, Dr. Robert Park, former English teacher at the University of Georgia, and an old depression derelict whose despair she immortalized and whose name she never knew.

But it was the children's portraits—bearing what she calls "that special look of vulnerability of the young" that she particularly remembered.[17]

Miss Edwards continued painting long after her eighty-ninth birthday. In 1972, at ninety-four, she was named Atlanta's Woman of the Year. She died at her residence at the Darlington Apartments on May 23, 1980, in her 103rd year. Her sister, the late Eva Lovett, was as active in education as Miss Kate was in the painter's art. She founded the Lovett School in 1926 and remained active with its operations until she died at 92.

As 1967 drew to a close the Standard Club had just celebrated its one hundredth birthday at the "swinging dinner dance at the clubhouse in the Brookhaven area." On December 10 the Sunday paper told its story:

One hundred years ago, some readers in Atlanta's Jewish community who had moved here from Europe, formed a cultural group called the Concordia Club. In 1905 it was re-organized as the Standard Club and members acquired the home and property of William C. Sanders on the east side of Washington Street between Fair Street and Woodward Avenue. By the end of the twenties the clubhouse was moved to the north side of the city to 242 Ponce de Leon Avenue. The large red brick home with white columns was designed by the noted architect Walter T. Downing for Dr. Milton Nathan Armstrong. This served as home for the Standard Club until 1948 when its growing pains necessitated a new home. This time a new clubhouse was built in North Atlanta and here the 100th birthday was celebrated.

The closing days of 1967 gave Opie Shelton, executive vice-president and general manager of the Chamber of Commerce, the opportunity to pay his annual tribute to Atlanta and its people. The subject of his homage was Augustus H. (Billy) Sterne, president of the Trust Company of Georgia and retiring president of the Chamber of Commerce. Said he of Sterne: "This Chamber in its 108 years of existence may have had a better president than Mr. Sterne, but somehow, I doubt it."[18]

OBITUARIES

Neil Andrews, 72, had been appointed federal judge of the Northern District by President Truman in 1949. Tom Aldred, award-winning photographer of the Atlanta newspapers, died at 49. John Bent, 48, had been a photojournalist and news director of WAII-TV since 1958. Walter Turner Candler, 81, last surviving child of the late Asa G. Candler, founder of the Coca-Cola Company, had been a successful businessman and carried on the tradition of his father as a philanthropist and also continued the long family record of service to Emory University. In 1958 Emory bought Candler's handsome 150-acre Lullwater Farm, home of some of the world's champion trotting horses. The Elizabethan-style mansion, which Candler built in the 1920s, is now called "Lullwater House" and is the home of the president of Emory University. Candler established the Walter Turner Candler lecture series at Emory in 1952, which brings noted teachers and writers to the campus. He also established the J. Gordon Stipe lecture in memory of his long-time friend. A graduate of Emory at Oxford in 1907, Candler helped organize the alumni association, which in 1967 had 25,000 members in fifty states and fifty-seven countries. After graduating from Emory, Candler began his career with Central Bank and Trust Corporation and was cashier and vice-president when the firm was sold to C&S.

Arthur H. Coddington, 84, was a retired court reporter for the Georgia Supreme Court and the Court of Appeals. He was author of several books and was a past president of the Atlanta Writers' Club. He was a member of All Saints' Episcopal Church. Dr. Mauney Douglas Collins had been state school superintendent in Georgia for twenty-five years when he retired in 1957. During his term of office as superintendent, Dr. Collins saw adoption of the school lunch program, rural libraries, the twelfth grade, a teacher retirement system, the State Merit System, and trade and vocational education. He was an ordained Baptist minister and was lifetime pastor at Friendship Baptist Church at Fairburn, where he had served twenty-three years.

Eugene Cook, 63, state supreme court justice, was a cum laude graduate of Mercer University. He began his law practice in Wrightsville and became solicitor general of the Dublin Judicial Circuit. He served as attorney general longer than anyone before him. Judge Stonewall H. Dyer, 64, of the Fulton County Superior Court was a 1924 graduate of Mercer University. He began the practice of law in Newnan and served two terms as Coweta County representative. He managed the successful campaign in which Ellis Arnall defeated Eugene Talmadge in 1942 and then came to Atlanta to practice law. He was a veteran of World War I and a member of Wieuca Road Baptist Church.

C. O. Emmerich, Sr., 65, administrator of the Economic Opportunity Atlanta, Inc., since 1964, was a former chairman of the DeKalb County Commission. For twelve years he had served as business manager of Emory University. Active in DeKalb County civic life, he had been president of the DeKalb Chamber of Commerce, the DeKalb Kiwanis Club, and the DeKalb Cancer Society. For many years he was on the board of stewards at Glenn Memorial Church. Harvey Hester, a colorful figure in the business, civic, and sports life of Atlanta, died at 70. Widely known as a raconteur and gourmet, he operated Aunt Fanny's Cabin in Smyrna for nineteen years. A veteran of World War I, he was also a member of the Atlanta Athletic Club and the Atlanta Touchdown Club. Morris Hirsch, 60, was the third-generation president of Hirsch's, Inc., the oldest retail store in Atlanta. He was a graduate of the University of Georgia and was a member of the Commerce Club and The Temple. Col. Fonville McWhorter, Sr., 79, was senior investment broker at Courts and Company. He had been director of the Chamber of Commerce and was a member of First Presbyterian Church, the Capital City Club, the Piedmont Driving Club, and the Civitan Club.

Rt. Rev. Msgr. Joseph Emmett Moylan, 78, had been vicar general of the Roman Catholic Church for eleven years. He had served as pastor of Immaculate Conception and Sacred Heart, and as co-pastor of the Cathedral of Christ the King and first pastor of Our Lady of Assumption. He was named vicar general of the Diocese of Atlanta in 1956. A native of Savannah, he was a graduate of St. Bernard's Seminary in Rochester, New York. Angus Perkerson, 78, retired editor of the *Atlanta Journal-Constitution Magazine*, had served in that position for forty-four years. He began writing for the paper when he was 18, and the pages of his magazine carried the names of many writers who were to become well known—Margaret Mitchell, Ward Morehouse, and Medora Field, whom he married in 1922. He was the grandson of Fulton County's second sheriff, Thomas J. Perkerson, and son of a Confederate veteran. Glascock Reynolds, 63, pursued a full-time career as a portrait artist. His first exhibit was at the High Museum of Art in 1927, and he had many portraits of famous people hanging throughout the United States.

Ernest Rogers, 69, columnist for the *Atlanta Journal* for forty-two years, was called the "Mayor of Peachtree Street." For years he chronicled the activities up and down Peachtree with warmth, humor, and humanity. He was a son of Dr. Wallace Rogers, a minister for more than sixty-five years. Ernest Rogers was a cum laude graduate of Emory University, where he helped organize the Glee Club and was president of the student body. Dr. Lester Rumble, Sr., 73, served the Methodist Church for a period of forty-seven years. As a member of the North Georgia Conference he had served many charges, including North Decatur Methodist, St. Mark, and St. James in Atlanta. For over thirty years he had been a trustee of Wesleyan College and was on the boards of Emory University, Paine College, and Reinhardt College.

Henry J. Toombs, noted Atlanta architect, conceived the idea of the Atlanta Memorial Cultural Center. "Mr. Toombs' special pride was The Galleria joining the museum with the two auditoriums. He felt this area was the key to the entire project's architectural solution. He knew before he died it would be completed as he and his partners had designed it." Dr. Charles Bell Upshaw, 76, had been obstetrician and gynecologist in Atlanta for fifty years. A graduate of Emory Medical School, he was clinical professor of obstetrics and gynecology at his alma mater for forty-five years. He served in the Medical Corps in World War I and came back to his home town to serve as obstetrician to two generations. He was a member of St. Mark, the Rotary Club, and the Piedmont Driving Club.

NOTES

1. Norman Shavin, *Atlanta*, Feb., 1967.

2. James L. Townsend, *Atlanta*, May, 1967.

3. *Atlanta*, June, 1967.

4. Ibid.

5. Bruce Galphin, ibid., Mar., 1967.

6. Bruce Galphin, ibid., Jan., 1967.

7. *Atlanta*, Aug., 1967; Atlanta City Code, Permits and License Section, 142126.

8. Norman Shavin and Bruce Galphin, *Atlanta: Triumph of a People* (Atlanta: Capricorn Corporation, 1982).

9. *Atlanta*, July, 1967.

10. Ibid.

11. Genevieve Pou, *Atlanta*, June, 1967.

12. *Atlanta*, Aug., 1967.

13. Ibid., Sept., 1967.

14. Harold Martin, *Atlanta Journal-Constitution*, June 4, 1967.

15. Betsy Fancher, *Atlanta*, Oct., 1967.

16. John Pennington, ibid., Nov., 1967.

17. *Atlanta*, Dec., 1967.

18. Opie Shelton, *Atlanta*, Jan., 1968.

THE most profound event for Atlanta in 1968 was a tragic one. On April 4 Martin Luther King, Jr., was shot and killed in Memphis while he stood on a balcony at the Lorraine Motel. He was in the Mississippi River city to help in a strike by black sanitation workers. The nation was shocked, and the black community was both angered and grieved by the assassination. Nowhere was the sorrow deeper than in Dr. King's hometown of Atlanta, and Mayor Ivan Allen, Jr., shared that sorrow.

Since the Nobel Peace Prize dinner in 1965, Allen and King had become close friends. When King was in town, Allen would drop by his SCLC office on Auburn Avenue and they would talk for the better part of the day. King would brief Allen on what was happening in race relationships nationally; Allen would tell King what might be expected to happen in Atlanta. King, in 1967, gave Allen an autographed copy of his book *Where Do We Go from Here: Chaos or Community*—and from the points King made, Allen formed his own thinking as to what could and should be done in the field of civil rights.

"Unconsciously," said Allen, "I was using the book as a sort of white paper, to guide me in whatever I did as Mayor. Martin Luther King, Jr., had become to me, as he had to millions of people all over the world, the personification of the fight to gain equality for all people."

It is easy to understand, therefore, how Ivan Allen felt on that spring night when the television screen in his bedroom flashed the bulletin about the shooting. Dr. King was not yet dead. Allen's reaction was swift; he called Coretta King and asked if she had heard the news. She had, and she was preparing to leave for Memphis. If the mayor would help her get to the airport to catch the next plane out, at 8:25 P.M., she would be grateful. Allen and his wife, Louise, decided to go to the King home and escort Coretta King to the airport.

Mayor Allen, in his book, gives a dramatic picture of that evening. As he drove, he wondered: What would Atlanta, what would the whole nation be faced with in the next few weeks? First, John Kennedy and now, less than four years later, their greatest champion of all, Martin Luther King, had been gunned down. Racing through Vine City, a poorly lighted black neighborhood, he wondered: "What must they be thinking in these narrow, cluttered frame houses?"

They reached the Kings' house safely, to find Mrs. King ready and waiting to go to the airport. Police cars were already arriving. So, with Allen in one police car with radio connection and Mrs. King, a friend, Bernita Bennette, Mrs. Allen, and Mrs. Samuel Williams, the minister's wife, in the Allens' personal car, they roared off to the airport.

They had been at the airport only a moment when the news came. Dr. King was dead. There was no need now to rush to Memphis, so they went back to the King house, in silence, shocked and dazed. The phone rang. It was President Johnson at the White House. He talked to Mrs. King. In a moment Johnson was on the television, telling the nation of the tragedy.

"Riots," wrote Allen in *Mayor*, "had already broken out in several cities over the country." But his concern was Atlanta:

The obvious question was, would there be trouble in Atlanta, Martin Luther King's birthplace? By now, that was the major question in my mind. Could we hold together that huge Atlanta University complex on the west side of the city, the six predominantly Negro universities and colleges—Martin's alma mater, Morehouse College, among them—from whence had come the front-line soldiers in the civil-rights crusade? Without a doubt, the world had already shifted its attention from Memphis to Atlanta. The body would be brought back here, and it would be put into the ground here. . . .

Then, about midnight, I finally got in a call to the President. This was the only time in my eight years as mayor that I called the President of the United States. I simply wanted him to know that the leadership in Atlanta, Dr. King's home, was alerted to the dangers and aware of the magnitude of the situation. I guess I just wanted to talk to the President. At any rate, President Johnson returned the call within minutes.

"What does it look like down there?" he said.

"It's all right, right now, Mr. President," I told him. "I'm worried, but I'm hopeful. It's raining pretty hard, and that's a big help. It'll keep people off the streets."

"We've had a lot of rioting in the country," said Johnson.

"That's what we heard."

"We've had to commit a lot of troops already."

"Yes, sir."

"I'll do whatever's necessary, Mayor," he said, "but this stuff is breaking out all over. I hope we don't have to send anybody down there. I hope if it gets bad in Atlanta the National Guard can take care of it."

Then, just as I was preparing to leave City Hall to go home for some sleep, I had a long distance call. . . . from Robert Woodruff, the developer of Coca-Cola . . . .

"Ivan," he said, "the minute they bring King's body back tomorrow— between then and the time of the funeral—Atlanta, Georgia, is going to be the center of the universe." He paused. "I want you to do whatever is right and necessary, and whatever the city can't pay for will be taken care of. Just do it right." . . . He was, in one breath, relieving me of any worries such as how we were going to pay for necessary police protection. I can't imagine the mayor of any other city in the United States being given a blank check like that, under such trying circumstances.[1]

By the next day it had finally sunk into Allen and his top people that there was going to be an extremely large funeral, not in any sense a private funeral. It was going to be a huge coming together of people from all over the nation, many of them famous. Allen had been thinking of a crowd of perhaps 10,000 mourners; he began now to think in terms of 30,000, 50,000, even 100,000, and he had to do a hundred things at once—eliminate work crews on the downtown streets, arrange space for press and network television crews, housing for visitors, first aid stations, extra policemen and firemen:

This time we looked deeper into the entire situation, and the more we talked the more we were convinced that Atlanta was about to be the scene of the largest and most emotional funeral in the history of the United States. Reports kept trickling in from all over. Arrangements being made by the telephone company for phones and cables indicated there would be an unbelievable amount of coverage by the networks and the daily press. The SCLC was setting up an emergency headquarters, staffing it with scores of volunteers who were working around the clock to arrange for visitors from all over the world. The attorney general's office had sent in an advance detachment of men, apparently to lay some preliminary plans for security and to find out whether Atlanta's leaders were aware of the magnitude of the funeral. There had still been no violence in Atlanta, but we knew full well that it was all ahead of us.

That night, I was still jumpy. I finally ended up calling Herbert Jenkins. Herbert and I had lived through many a crisis over the past several years, most of them related to civil rights, and he always had a settling effect on me. . . . I suggested that I run by and pick him up, and that the two of us just ride around town and see what was happening.

We decided to visit every Negro neighborhood in Atlanta, get out of the car at each one, and let ourselves be seen. We went to Summerhill, Vine City, Mechanicsville, Pittsburg, Blue Heaven—all of them. Here we were, two white middle-aged gray-haired men—the mayor and the police chief of the city—walking up and down the streets, standing on the corners, talking to the people, trying to show them our concern. It was much the same strategy I had used during the rioting in Summerhill in 1966, and it seemed to be working. There were smiles and greetings from those who recognized us. And if you don't think word spreads like a brushfire in a black ghetto, you don't know much about that way of life. The grapevine rather than the newspapers or television or any other method of communications is the traditional means of spreading the word there. I would dare say that by midnight, after Herbert and I had spent three or four hours simply showing ourselves in all the Negro areas of the city, more than half of Atlanta's black population of two hundred thousand knew what we had done.

Very late that night, when Herbert and I had hung around the busy Negro commercial section at Hunter and Ashby Streets and were about to call it quits, he told me SCLC had set up its communications headquarters in the West Hunter Street Baptist Church and suggested we drop by to see what was happening. I wanted to see the Reverend Ralph Abernathy, anyway. Ralph had been Dr. King's trusted right-hand man for all of those years, the heir apparent to the top job at SCLC now that Martin was gone. . . .

In the back of my mind all along there had been great fears that the major factor in whether Atlanta was going to have serious trouble was not with the black people, but the white racists who had always referred to Dr. King as Martin Luther Coon and hated him and what he had done with an unswerving passion. I had received several telegrams and phone calls from a surprisingly large number of these people, and from some people I had respected in the past, suggesting that the city ignore the funeral. Lester Maddox, of course, was cowering in the Capitol and making an issue about the plan to lower flags in Atlanta to half-mast, and there were rumors that he was going to call up the National Guard for his personal protection. A mild hysteria was running through the conservative community and there was the possibility of still another assassination with all of the liberal leaders descending on Atlanta at one time. But here was a young Presbyterian minister saying his church [Central Presbyterian] was opening its doors to Negro visitors. Later in the day, hundreds of other white churches in the city made similar announcements. . . .

It appeared that more than one hundred thousand people would be coming into Atlanta for the funeral. Not only were the white and black churches of Atlanta opening their doors to the visitors, but many private homes, black and white, were also offering their rooms. Many of those planning to come wouldn't have the means to rent hotel rooms or dine at expensive restaurants; a lot of them just planned to come to Atlanta and worry about eating and sleeping when they got there. And then there would be the celebrities: the Kennedys, Harry Belafonte, Jacob Javits, John Lindsay, Wilt (the Stilt) Chamberlain, Jimmy Brown, James Brown, Nelson Rockefeller, Richard Nixon, Hubert Humphrey and on and on and on. The crush was going to be fantastic. . . .

At a meeting with SCLC officials that day before the funeral, we assured them that the city would immediately issue purchase orders for such things as public address systems and portable toilets along the line of march—and that we were prepared to foot the bill, no matter what the technicality might be over whether the funeral was public or private. We also finalized our security setup; in addition to the secret service and FBI and federal marshals, we would have fourteen hundred young Negro students serving as special marshals, plus five hundred uniformed city firemen and, for the first time in the city's history, every one of the thousand-plus employees of the Atlanta Police Department. We had done what we could. It was quiet again in Atlanta on Monday night as the population of the city began to swell and thousands of mourners inched through the darkness of the Morehouse College campus to take a last look at Martin Luther King, Jr. . . .

When we reached the [Ebenezer Baptist] church, there were perhaps one hundred thousand people in the immediate vicinity, all of them seemingly trying to get inside a church that could hold but eight hundred. It was a terrific crush. Squeals were going up on the sight of Jacqueline Kennedy or Jimmy Brown or Richard Nixon. The Secret Service was having a terrible time keeping the entrance clear so those invited to attend the service could get inside. Mrs. Allen and I were seated on the second row, directly behind the Vice President and his wife, and I was trying to see everything that went on. It was an anxious time for me. We could hear the jostling and wailing and yelling outside. I was talking to myself, pleading that nothing would go wrong. Many businesses had closed for the day, and there was a great deal of respect being shown for the memory of Martin Luther King. But, after all, this was the Old South. A good part of white Atlanta had stayed home. There was still great bitterness and opposition to the funeral. I could only hope that things would go as well outside as they were inside the church. . . . Inside was the greatest galaxy of prominent national figures there had ever been in Atlanta at one time: Robert Kennedy, George Romney, Mayor Carl Stokes of Cleveland, Nixon, Rockefeller, Harry Belafonte, and an endless array of others equally as famous. Coretta King, sitting with her family front and center in front of the casket, looked lovely and courageous and dignified in a black mourning veil.

Once the service was completed, it was time for the long procession to Morehouse College to begin. These thousands of people would march along behind the mule-drawn wagon carrying the body, would march down the streets of Atlanta in the broiling sun, [and] would march and sing "We Shall Overcome." . . . [In] this entire mass of nearly two hundred thousand mourners, every single one of them, was trying to honor Martin Luther King, Jr., just as he had lived his life. Just as he would have wanted it.

Except for the governor of Georgia, of course, who was in his office behind drawn blinds and a cordon of some hundred troopers. . . .

Although at least 46 people were killed in violence in 126 cities, there never was any trouble in Atlanta during these tense dramatic days."[2]

Police Chief Herbert Jenkins's memories of the funeral day are as vivid as those of Mayor Allen. "No unpleasant incident marred Dr. King's funeral. A city the size of Atlanta was not accustomed to the influx of people that arrived and the crowds that formed for the funeral, but we handled it as best we could."[3]

Though Allen, Chief Jenkins, Mayor Hartsfield, and others with responsibility for the city's safety remember these four tense and tragic days mainly in terms of keeping the peace, of avoiding a racial explosion, Coretta Scott King told the story of her husband's death and funeral in a personal way. In her book *My Life with Martin Luther King, Jr.* she tells of how life was for her and her children, and Mama and Daddy King, Sr., in the days after Martin died:

Ralph Abernathy, Martin's closest friend and companion, officiated at the service. The people who came were truly representative of the total society. There were diplomats, high government officials, congressmen, governors, legislators, mayors, aldermen, judges, professionals from the religious, educational, and business communities, civil rights leaders; and the people. They were black, white, brown, red, and yellow. They were rich and poor, old and young, believers and nonbelievers; conservatives, moderates, liberals, and militants. It was a beautiful example of brotherhood which he worked for in life and achieved in death.

Of all the tributes to her husband paid in the weeks and months following his death, the one which Coretta King felt best described his life, however, was written by two others of his most devoted friends, actor Harry Belafonte and attorney Stanley Levison:

Martin Luther King was not a dreamer although he had a dream. His vision of a society of justice was derived from a stirring reality. Under his leadership millions of black Americans emerged from spiritual imprisonment, from fear, from apathy, and took to the streets to proclaim their freedom. The thunder of millions of marching feet preceded the dream. Without these deeds, inspired by his awesome personal courage, the words would merely have woven fantasy. Martin Luther King, the peaceful warrior, revealed to his people their latent power; nonviolent mass protest, firmly disciplined, enabled them to move against their oppressors in effective and bloodless combat. With one stroke he organized his armies and disorganized his adversaries. In the luminescent glare of the open streets he gave a lesson to the nation revealing who was the oppressed and who was the oppressor.[4]

Soon after Dr. King's death Atlanta served as a way station on the "Poor People's March" to Washington. On May 9, 1968, 10,000 white and black citizens of at least three states filled the new Civic Center exhibit hall with the anthem "We Shall Overcome" as the southern leg of the march converged in Atlanta. On the evening before, Coretta King had addressed the group, saying, "My late husband is smiling on Atlanta tonight."

Washington was less lenient with the marchers than Atlanta had been, and there, in late June, the marchers' camp, Resurrection City, was closed down. The Reverend Abernathy, president of SCLC, was arrested and jailed, along with 280 of his followers. He would, however, continue his campaign for government jobs to feed the poor and provide them with jobs.

The trauma of the King death was the key event of the year, but, of course, the life of the city went on. In 1968 Atlanta was pushing steadily toward its oft-repeated goal of becoming known as an international city. One step was to create an Atlanta Committee for International Visitors, which sends bilingual representatives to meet the new arrivals (provided they are not tourists), escort them to the hotels, and arrange meetings for them with their local counterparts in various business, professional, and educational fields. One of the most efficient of these was Rose Cunningham, with the ACIV, who was born in Rumania and could speak most of the languages of middle Europe. Another was Madame Louise Suggs, French by birth and education. Working with the ACIV and other local organizations interested in making welcome the thousands of foreign visitors who come to Atlanta every year, Suggs discovered that even with careful guidance, there can be many problems. An Italian visitor arriving in Atlanta found that it was impossible for him to reach the ACIV by telephone. It was discovered that he was dialing, not the telephone number, but the zip code.

Atlanta families frequently welcomed visitors into their homes and tried to do something special for them to give them a good impression of the city. One local family sought to treat their Peruvian guests with anchovies, which came from Peru. The guests toyed with the food, but did not eat. In Peru, they finally explained, gently, anchovies are used as fertilizer. Rose Cunningham of ACIV took the group of Japanese to Stone Mountain, and though the visitors seemed impressed with the mountain, its carvings and its elevated railway, they bought no souvenirs. The reason? The souvenirs bore the marking "Made in Japan."

Though no foreign interests were involved, Atlantans were soon beginning to hear new voices over the local air waves. Charles Smithgall, onetime farm program maestro on WSB, moved to Gainesville where he thrived by publishing newspapers and operating radio stations. In 1968 he came back to Atlanta with a new idea—an all-talk radio station different from any then operating in Atlanta. Its name was WRNG, pronounced "Ring"—and it sought to get everybody in town on the air. WRNG was run by Sheldon Singer, who said, "This kind of programming knocks down all the barriers, all the walls. The larger the city, the lonelier the people—and the more they want to talk. It provides an opportunity for real communication between all segments of the community. It gives the average guy a chance to question public officials and experts on all kinds of topics, to complain, gripe or argue. Your phone is your microphone," said Singer, "when you ring WRNG radio." WRNG prospered for several years under a succession of personalities. It was not until Ludlow Porch came in 1972, with his warmth, wit, and wide range of knowledge, that WRNG became one of the best-known talk show stations in the country. Going into the 1980s, however, WRNG began to show a rating drop, and Charles Smithgall III, son of the WRNG founder, decided to change the format to an all-news station. Thus, old WRNG became WCNN— buying its news from cable television's Ted Turner. Ludlow Porch was named station manager.[5]

In 1968 old attitudes toward women were rapidly changing in Atlanta and the South, as for several years they had already been changing in other areas of the country. The "powdered, pampered products" of a chivalrous tradition that had survived plantation days were now bringing to the fore a woman more concerned with making a place for herself in the world than in spending her time in flower arrangements and afternoon teas.

Among Atlanta women who were meeting the challenges of new social and economic forces which now were drastically changing the role of women in society was Maggie Long, author of a best-selling book, *Louisville Saturday,* a public relations person for the Southern Regional Council, and journalist-in-residence at Clark College. "Women," Long noted, "have had their 'place' just as the Negro has had his 'place.' The implication is that both are inferior and both have got to use pressure to break the sociological chains." Several examples show the new Atlanta woman of 1968, as she was portrayed in *Atlanta* magazine:

Dr. Irene Phrydas, serene and soft-spoken wife of a Lockheed engineer is the mother of two daughters, an inspired cook, an avid gardener, and a dutiful member of the PTA. She is also a psychiatrist at the Emory Clinic, who, when she completes a Grady-Columbia University Extension program, will probably become the first woman psychoanalyst in the State of Georgia. She combines marriage, motherhood and a career, and an increasing number of Atlanta women are doing the same. . . .

They are also adding a new and exciting dimension to business and the professions. . . . Some of their techniques might horrify the business-school experts, but if they are decidedly feminine they are also remarkably effective. Take, for instance, willowy, red-headed Olga (Mrs. Arren) Duffey, a crack broker for Robinson-Humphries, the wife of a manufacturer's representative, and the mother of five children, all under the age of eleven. She compiles her grocery list while checking the Dow-Jones averages. . . .

June Wilson, who authors a column for career women which is syndicated in seventy-five newspapers and who is herself a public relations account executive, admits to handling male executives precisely as she does her three live-wire sons.

Faith Brunson, . . . Rich's bookbuyer, runs five book departments and is known as one of the top merchandisers in the country. . . .

Probably the most disarming technique is used by Helen Bullard, the sage and compassionate woman who heads public relations for Toombs, Amisano and Wells, and has been quietly and compellingly on the side of the angels in almost every political, cultural, and humanitarian effort the city has made in the past twenty-five years. When she reaches an impasse with some key figure she is trying to persuade to a just and progressive posture, she merely folds her hands and Buddha-like announces, "I am going to pray for you." Since no one who knows her has ever doubted that Miss Bullard had a straight line to the celestial power structure, her prayers have been known to prod recipients into immediate—and humane—action.

Most of these women feel that their sex is a decided advantage. "Women get closer to what the problem is, and how to resolve it," says Miss Bullard. "They have an intuitive gift. The thing is to use the intuition instead of trying to compete—disaster sets in when competition sets in."

Faith Brunson agrees. "For nine years I've tried to convince my boss that I think like a man. Actually, I don't at all. Men try to divorce themselves from emotion. If I divorced my own personal feelings from my judgments, I'd be the lousiest book buyer in the world."

Tiny, alert Dr. Evangeline Papageorge, associate dean of the Emory Medical School, has occasionally felt the sharp edge of masculine discrimination since she joined the Emory staff in 1928, but she is still firmly convinced that being a woman gives her a professional advantage. "I represent a mother figure to the students," she says. "They feel freer to talk to me about things that matter." . . .

Dr. Mary Boney, a professor of Bible at Agnes Scott College, and the first woman ever to be elected an elder in Decatur's First Presbyterian Church, admits candidly, "I've never felt being a woman was anything but good. If what we want is to be ourselves, we couldn't ask for more freedom."

But at Scott, Dr. Boney lives in a traditionally feminine world. Those who must make their way in a man's world would disagree. Sarah Frances McDonald, the tall, stunning, platinum-haired lawyer who is still the only woman on the Decatur-DeKalb Bar and was the first woman to serve as a director of the DeKalb Chamber of Commerce, notes that some men have an immediate aversion to women lawyers. The fact that she has overcome this is evident both in her professional success and in her list of clients which includes more men than women.

"Any smart woman can turn the initial disadvantage into an advantage," says Be Haas, the stately, dark-haired partner in Grizzard and Haas who masterminded the expansion of Forward Atlanta, the Westminster Schools, the Atlanta Speech School, and dozens of other progressive ventures. Twice named Atlanta's Woman of the Year (in Business and in Civic Affairs), she admits, "a woman can say and do things a man can't—she can disagree and crack the whip and no one minds." . . .

Women today, cheerfully donning a dozen hats, manage to run households, chauffeur children, cook meals, entertain their husbands' clients, run to the beauty parlor, and still blaze ahead in their professional fields. "They are wonderfully adaptable," smiles Helen Bullard, but as Dr. Papageorge points out, "they have gone about as far as they can go." Both business and the professions have got to make some major adjustments, notably in a more flexible work schedule, and greater opportunities for advanced education, if they are to fully tap the creative resources of the distaff side.

The future? "It's never been brighter," says Helen Bullard, quietly folding her hands, as if that much, at least, is settled. "It's clear now the old patterns are not going to work. Women can contribute new approaches to every problem, new techniques to every field."[6]

Year after year the downtown Atlanta skyline had thrust higher and higher. Now, finally, in 1968, the nagging question was being heard in the board rooms of the builders— "How are we ever going to fill them up? Where are the renters coming from?" Jim Rankin, writing in *Atlanta* magazine, was optimistic:

They were talking about overbuilding and asking the same question a little over a decade ago when the city's busiest post-war downtown builder and developer, Ben Massell, paused after completing his Peachtree Seventh and Peachtree Baker buildings before moving on to Pershing Point and other projects.

Entering the 60s, Fulton National Bank dominated the downtown skyline. Then came the massive Merchandise Mart, Commerce Building, Georgia Power Building. The Bank of Georgia rose thirty-one floors just a block off Five Points. Since then John Portman and his associates have put a blue bubble on the Peachtree Center complex, are doubling the Merchandise Mart, putting up a second Gas Light Tower across the street, and are talking about a seventy-story office building behind the towers on Ivy Street.

To the north, Mills Lane is "hanging" offices on a nineteen-story concrete silo, and one of the favorite guessing games at Five Points is: How long can Mr. Lane stand looking up at the new forty-two story First National Bank building across from his C&S headquarters?

To the southwest, Tom Cousins is putting up a two-deck parking garage over the railroad tracks between the Spring and Techwood viaducts, and on his drawing boards is a massive office and commercial building complex. To the southeast, developer and financier Raymond D. Nasher of Texas has plans for another "platform city" or "megastructure" extending over the railroad tracks by the State Capitol on eighteen acres bounded by Interstate 85 and Decatur, Hunter, and Washington Streets.

And the planning and building going on in the central business district downtown is more than matched by a multitude of office buildings and office parks already built and being developed in the suburbs.

Are we overplanning and overbuilding? If we are, much of the money market and some of the top economic prognosticators have gone mad.

Directors of Equitable Life Assurance Society weren't shooting craps in the board room when they decided to invest $20,000,000 of policy holders' money in the old Piedmont Hotel, as a site for thirty-four floors and 707,360 square feet of office space. Equitable plans to occupy only two of those floors. Life insurance companies and other major investors look long and hard before investing that kind of money, and the other recent bumps on the downtown skyline are labeled Hartford, Life of Georgia, Trust Company of Georgia, and First Federal.

It is probably belaboring the point, but Atlanta has been, and is now more than ever, the regional office headquarters for the Southeast. It also serves the Southeast as a wholesale center, a state capital, federal government center, transportation center, and a banking and insurance center.

But what has not been stressed is the factor that Atlanta, particularly its central business district, is starting to trade off a portion of its manufacturing and wholesaling activities and is intensifying its office-related and office-service functions.

This moving out of wholesaling, warehousing, and light manufacturing can be seen in the empty buildings and lofts in the area south of Five Points extending to the expressway. Except for the upper end of the bustling White-hall Street retail corridor, most of the area is in a general economic decline. This is an area that many real estate experts see as ripening for redevelopment. . . .

An interview of several real estate experts and developers to find out who the people are who are moving into these buildings and why was conducted. The consensus was that about 50% of them are expanding and improving the type and scope of representation they have in Atlanta. These are companies that have been operating in Atlanta for some years and are increasing and upgrading their staffs here, in some cases bringing in regional vice presidents and managers. . . .

Among the other 50% are those who are new to Atlanta—pulled into a happy climate where growth is feeding growth—and those companies that have decided to consolidate some of the functions that were scattered about either the metropolitan area or the Southeast.

Are many of the older buildings getting hurt? Some are, of course. Clarence Howard, whose firm manages many of the large "older" buildings as well as some of the new ones, says many of the older structures are being renovated, refurbished, and sport new facades. These are maintaining healthy occupancy rates, he says, which is another indication that "growth is feeding growth." Some buildings in the outlying areas are suffering some, said Mr. Howard, "and are having to go through a cycle of about a year to regain normal occupancy."

While the office building boosters are not worrying about how they're going to fill them up, many of them—including some of the most active developers and builders—are worrying about traffic congestion and lack of planning downtown.

Bob Bivens, executive director of Central Atlanta Progress, sees traffic congestion and downtown parking problems as the biggest threats to well-planned, healthy growth in the central business district. . . .

Predictably, the current traffic situation worries oldtime Atlantans more than newcomers. If they are from New York, Chicago, Cleveland, Los Angeles—then they've seen worse, and the smart money keeps betting that solutions are near.

In fact, New York Life Insurance Company has just agreed to make a

$3,500,000 loan to the Citizens Trust Company to build a twelve-story office building downtown. The only Negro-owned bank in Atlanta will make its headquarters in the new building at Houston Street and Piedmont Avenue when it is completed in September 1969. . . .

A lot of people have decided periodically that Atlanta is overbuilt. That usually was just before somebody asked them to move to another office, to make room for new tenants coming in.[7]

An old and unique local business institution underwent dramatic changes in 1968. The board of directors of the Cotton Producers Association elected C. W. Paris to the position of executive vice-president and general manager. He succeeded D. W. Brooks, founder of the little cotton cooperative in Carrollton, Georgia, in 1925, who moved it to Atlanta in 1933 and soon built it into a business earning a quarter of a billion dollars a year. Brooks became chairman of the board. Although it was now based in Atlanta and its name had become CPA Gold Kist, the company was still focused on the farmer and his problems. Its CPA part served farmers throughout the Southeast with feed, seed, fertilizer, pesticides, and all types of farm supply items. Through national and worldwide members its Gold Kist divisions marketed poultry, pecans, cotton, grain, and livestock for its farmer members.[8]

The little farm co-op by now had the look and manner of what it had become—a million-dollar operation with worldwide scope—and its office building demonstrated this status. In May of 1973 the company broke ground for a new building at 244 Perimeter Center Parkway, just off I-285 expressway near Sandy Springs. No towering multifloored structure like the banks and office buildings going up downtown, it was located on a fifteen-acre tract and contained 200,000 square feet of office space, enough to handle all of Gold Kist's operations as well as the Cotton States Insurance Company. In the building by 1974 the companies were doing more than $1 billion worth of business, and through these offices, more than 150 million broilers and 22 million dozen eggs were being sold.[9] By 1980 gross sales were up to almost $2 billion.

Gold Kist had also gone heavily into the insurance business. Under its president Robert E. Carpenter, the Cotton States Life and Health had net earnings of $1,665,000 going into the 1980s.

Atlanta rapidly had become home base for many new resident corporations. Atlanta's traditional accessibility had much to do with it. In addition to its historic role as a rail junction, Atlanta had taken on the status of a highway terminal, where trucks and buses competed with trains in hauling both goods and people. And it was growing in importance as an aerial crossroad, with several airlines now going and coming every day.

But, there was something else. Something intangible. A number of company presidents revealed that their decision to set up headquarters in Atlanta was due to the "climate"—not the weather, but the business climate, which exuded an aura of "corporate charisma." Included were three executives,

J. B. Fuqua, president of Fuqua Industries Incorporated, who moved his firm from Augusta to Atlanta; Henry Curtis, president of Curtis 1000, who moved south from St. Paul, Minnesota; and H. Tim Crow, vice-president of Rollins, Inc., who moved his diversified holding company from Wilmington, Delaware, after buying Orkin, the pest-control service, and Dwoskin, the wallpaper and decorator fabrics distributor in Atlanta.

Atlanta's banks were a big selling point for the incoming companies. They were, according to Henry Curtis, "less fussy than the bigger city banks, less fussy, more cooperative." Tim Crow of Rollins found them very competitive with each other, very friendly to the newcomers. One reason for moving to Atlanta, according to Fuqua, was that when a company moved to Atlanta, its stock immediately moved up several points on the big board on Wall Street. Atlanta's people were another. "There is an electricity here, it's obvious to anyone on the first day he's here that this is a bustling, thriving community like no other we've ever done business in before," said Tim Crow, a native of Montreal. Coca-Cola, Delta Air Lines, Cox Broadcasting, Genuine Parts, Atlantic Steel, Colonial Stores, and Retail Credit are classic examples of Atlanta companies, born here, and expanding over the years to national, and some to global, status.

"Then," Jim Rankin wrote in *Atlanta* magazine, "there are some of the smaller post–World War II corporations either born and reared in Atlanta or transferred here just before they 'took off.' " He elaborated:

Scientific Atlanta is one of the first that comes to mind. It began with a post office box and $700 in cash about fifteen years ago. First year losses were around $4,000. Guided by President Glen P. Robinson, the electronics manufacturer by 1968 was worldwide in scope, big in the space industry, and makes all kinds of sophisticated antenna testing devices.

American Cryogenics is another firm which began in Augusta—with $4,500 in cash and some war surplus oxygen cylinders. Since moving its headquarters to Atlanta this company has grown to eleven manufacturing plants strung from the Eastern Seaboard, through Alabama and into the Southwest, up to Reno, and to Sacramento and Santa Fe Springs, California. American Cryogenics produces acetylene, hydrogen, medical and anesthesia gases, helium, carbon dioxide, and other gases, and a wide range of cutting equipment and welding supplies. It is a major supplier of liquid oxygen for the country's space program.

Atlanta's charisma as a corporate capital was reflected in a survey made in the summer of 1967 by the Chamber of Commerce in Dallas, one of Atlanta's competitors for national corporate executive suites, plants and regional offices:

In this survey of more than two thousand top echelon types—officers of big corporations in the North—Atlanta got highest marks among seven cities, the others being Dallas, Houston, Kansas City, Oklahoma City, New Orleans, and St. Louis. The questions were drawn from a list of factors cited by *Business Week* in 1964 as considered most important by board chairmen and corporate executive officers in deciding where to locate. . . .

There are developments which are absolutely essential to a headquarters city. One is the professional personnel to handle corporate and insurance law. The eight major accounting firms in the U.S. all have substantial representation here, affirming the city is ready for growth.

Research and development has been the salvation of businesses as diverse as American Telephone and Telegraph, and Lockheed Aircraft. The area is amply supplied. More than eighty institutions, government agencies, and private firms are doing basic and/or applied research within a fifty-mile radius. Over 340 computer installations are on record.

There is constant disagreement about whether political outlook really has an effect on the development of headquarters cities. *Fortune* has argued that it has a significant effect and says this about Atlanta: "The quality of the city is good, and the single most striking reason is the leadership that exists there."

All this has brought both a construction boom and great new construction know-how. But building costs have remained reasonable. The F. W. Dodge survey said that a given building in Atlanta will cost only 72% as much as it would in New York, 94% as much as in Dallas, and 87% as much as in Los Angeles.

It has taken a combination of all these factors to make Atlanta an attractive headquarters city. And it has taken a little more. Newcomers call it "the electricity of the place . . . the competitive spirit."[10]

To the influx of married business executives and farmers, field hands, and blue-collar job hunters there was an inflow of what came to be known as "Swinging Singles." There are so-called singles bars not only in Atlanta but in every big city in the United States, from New York to Boston to Los Angeles. Such places attract millions of young college graduates to the big cities, where for the first time in their lives they are independent of their families and a planned pattern. "They come," said Sandra Grimes in *Atlanta* magazine, "with but a single purpose in mind—to meet singles of the opposite sex." The procedure follows a pattern—"a tap on the shoulder, the right 'line,' the right look and young men can meet more girls and pick up more phone numbers in one night than a year of random girl-hunting." Grimes continued:

These young singles are in a position of power and influence unknown ten years ago. They are better educated, better paid, freer from established moral codes than at any time in our history. And along with their freedom, financial solvency, and sexual liberation, they have become the darlings of the advertising world. With a little imagination, anything from apartments to sophisticated lounging pajamas can become a candidate for a single's dollar. The key is youth and glamour. Market analysts have said the singles have more discriminatory buying power than any other group. They haven't the financial burdens of the married man, and with their new affluence and swinging image to live up to, it's no wonder they are courted and wooed by sellers of everything from stretch pants to Florida vacations. Experts figure the singles nationally as a $60,000,000,000 market, and a local singles magazine declared in a full page ad that, in Atlanta alone, singles will spend $100,000,000 this year.

There are hundreds of apartment complexes in Atlanta jammed with singles and more going up every day; there is a popular magazine published for and about singles; there are several bars where unescorted single girls are welcome; and there are at least three singles clubs in operation. . . .

Apartment complexes with built-in social opportunities catering to singles have sprung up all over the United States. In Atlanta, General Apartment Company has 1,540 apartment units in operation with 450 more under construction. Their projects include The Red Lion, The LeMans, and The Bordeaux. One young man planning his strategy from The Red Lion told us that "On warm summer nights, all you have to do to meet a nice girl is step out on your front porch."

Peachtree Towne Apartments, sophisticated, beautifully designed two-bedroom units for singles, was conceived and developed by Don Davis, president of D. Davis & Company. Davis was among the first to study the singles idea in housing, and his Peachtree Towne is so widely known that young people come here from as far away as New York and California without a job or acquaintances, knowing only that they will live at Peachtree Towne. . . .

The National Association of Junior Executives, Incorporated, is the strongest and most active of the singles clubs in Atlanta with Larry Poling as president. JE now has 3,300 members; and with an estimated 83,000 singles in Atlanta, they predict this is just a beginning. They have promoted JE on radio, they have given parties at some of the best-known singles apartments, and have mailed out 10,000 applications to singles all over Atlanta. . . .

Atlanta's young adults regard their sex lives as very personal and very private, and quite different from the exposes of swinging singles published by national magazines. In a meeting with about thirty-five attractive singles at Peachtree Towne, Attorney Lurton Massee summed up the general consensus: "Sure, our sexual mores are a little more liberal than our parents' were. We all seek a close personal relationship with people we date—and the most of us expect that to be culminated in a sexual relationship. But this is not the focal point. We want a relationship we can enjoy in depth. Most of us spend most of our time thinking about who we are and where we're going."

Marriage? "Someday," they say, "but not now, not just yet." Most feel that they have opportunities for interesting careers, travel, and human experiences denied the married man or woman, and that possibly the one who waits until later in life to marry, who allows himself time for experiment, more time for interior growth, more time to become a whole person, has a better chance to succeed in marriage should he eventually decide to take that step.[11]

At the Lockheed plant in Marietta 26,000 employees put together the world's biggest airplane. Into the cargo hold of the C-5 Galaxy, which was longer than the first flight the Wright Brothers made at Kitty Hawk, they had crammed six trucks, three mounted howitzers, two tanks, and three ambulances, and still were well under the 265,000 pound maximum payload. Despite the great weight, however, the new transport could use a normal and even substandard airstrip, rolling on a unique landing gear with 28 wheels, which spread the weight so the plane could take off and land on runways no firmer than a baseball field. President Lyndon Johnson came to Dobbins Air Force Base in March to watch the first roll-out. Today, he said, it would take eighty-eight cargo planes to move an infantry brigade from Hawaii to Vietnam and their heaviest equipment would have to go by ship. Twenty C-5s could do the job, without sea shipments. Representatives of forty-one western nations, many of them air attaches for Washington, others press representatives from around the world, including Germany, France, England, and Japan, came to Atlanta to see the display put on at Dobbins by Lockheed, General Electric, and the Air Force. Lockheed had a contract to produce fifty-eight of the huge craft by January, 1971.[12]

From early spring until school opened in the fall, and on into the winter of the 1968–69 school year, education and educators were much in the news.

On April 24, for example, "Cecelia Ann Dunahoo, a Chamblee High School Senior, has completed her enrollment procedures and will be the first student admitted to Atlanta Baptist College, Georgia's newest four-year college." Dr. Kenneth Dawson, vice-president of academic affairs, said five hundred students were expected to enroll the first year, when only freshmen courses were to be offered. Dr. Dawson said that teaching assignments had been made for twenty-five faculty members, most of whom had completed the doctoral degree in their fields. (The school would later become Mercer University of Atlanta.)

Dr. Edwin D. Harrison, president of Georgia Tech, resigned. The Board of Regents announced that it regretted Dr. Harrison's leaving. Their statement read in part: "In no area has the demand been greater or more complex than in engineering and science, the principal concern of Georgia Tech. In this period of great pressure to keep up in these vital fields, President Harrison has provided leadership and has achieved results that have brought Georgia Tech to higher levels in programs of instruction, research and service." Dr. Harrison, a native of Evadale, Arkansas, and a graduate of the U.S. Naval Academy, had come to Tech in 1957 from the post of dean of engineering at the University of Toledo in Ohio. He did not comment on the rumors rampant that student unrest demanding black studies and Tech involvement in urban problems had hastened his resignation. He only stated that he felt ten years was enough as president of a school.

Georgia State College was pushing steadily ahead with its building program in this busy year. It acquired 2.3 acres of property in downtown Atlanta from the Atlanta Housing Authority for $156,617. The property was one-half of the block bounded by Piedmont Avenue, and Gilmer, Butler, and Decatur streets. The purchase moved the college into a block in which it had not formerly owned property. All the land was being used as commercial parking lots. College officials expected to acquire the remainder of the block, and the institution's master plan called for the construction of a science center on the property. The new School of Business building, six stories high and gleaming with white marble, was finished just in time for fall classes. The building was located at the intersection of Decatur and Ivy streets, one of the city's busiest intersections, only two blocks away from Five Points, and the traffic noise was constant. But the noise was no problem because a special feature of the new building was its thick walls and double thick windows.

On May 23, it was announced that "Atlanta school officials will dedicate the new Instructional Service Center to the memory of H. O. Smith, principal of Boys High School from 1920–1946." Located on a five-acre site on Forrest Hills Drive SW, the center was headquarters for the various instructional departments of the Atlanta school system. The center was dedicated to Dr. Smith because of his "efforts toward upgrading and improving instruction during his 37 years as a teacher and principal."

As winter came on there was trouble at Spelman College. Administrators suspended classes because of the feeling of unrest after students evicted a white speech and drama teacher from her classroom, vowing that she could not return. She had told a student that her remarks were those of a jackass. Students at Clark College and Spelman met and "took it upon themselves" to abolish certain school rules including compulsory attendance, curfews for women and restrictions on student attire on campus. School officials and student representatives were to meet in an effort to resolve these problems. A student release said the incident reflects the "oppressive character of our institutions."

Not far from Spelman College and the Atlanta University complex a small but symbolically important victory was won for civil rights. The Wren's Nest, home of author Joel Chandler Harris, is a tourist attraction known around the world for the characters created by Harris, notably "Uncle Remus," the black teller of stories that originated in ancient African tribal legends. But the Wren's Nest would not admit black sightseers. The Rev. Clyde Williams filed suit in U.S. District Court on behalf of his daughter, Joyce, and all members of the Negro race, claiming that the Wren's Nest was a "a place of public accommodation." Six months later District Judge Newell Edenfield ruled that the Wren's Nest was, indeed, a place of public accommodation under the Civil Rights Act of 1964, and that it must be integrated.

July 4 of 1968 brought the first public announcement of a plan to create in the heart of Buckhead a landscaped park, replacing aging buildings with a grassy open space. It was to surround a ruggedly beautiful monument that would commemorate the fact that in Indian days the huge head and antlers of a buck, killed, perhaps, by tavern keeper Henry Irby, hung before the tavern he built at the northwest corner that is now West Paces Ferry and Roswell roads. The tavern became known as Buckhead Tavern (I, 160).

Leading citizens of Buckhead, most of them bankers, got the park campaign under way. Julian Barfield, vice-president of the First National Bank and manager of its Buckhead branch, was named general chairman. The sculptured head of an antlered buck never appeared, nor was the park created immediately. But in the ensuing years Atlanta's famous anonymous donor, hearing of the plan, made a million dollars available, and in December of 1975 the park was dedicated by Mayor Maynard Jackson.

There were some angry rumbles on the school front. In July Atlanta school superintendent Dr. John W. Letson told protesting members of the Community Relations Commission that the school system had achieved "total desegregation" and that "the racial composition of schools will continue to reflect the racial composition of the city as a whole." However, CRC chairman Sam Williams, a longtime critic of the school system, charged that the board had been operating a segregated school system during the fourteen years since the U.S. Supreme Court ordered all systems to integrate. Dr. Letson replied that since 1960 the city school population had experienced a decrease of about 7,000 white students and an increase of some 25,000 Negro students.

Politics—local, state, and national—were much in the minds of Atlantans as the year began. Politics at the courthouse attracted the attention of many when the chairmanship of the Fulton County Commission passed from James Aldredge to Charlie Brown, with Walter Mitchell chosen to serve as vice-chairman. Having served as commissioner, state senator, and state representative, Brown was a political perennial. His first recommendation as commissioner was that county schools and libraries be put to use twelve months a year, and this was to come to pass. The commission approved a budget of $38 million for Fulton County.

As time moved on toward the general election in November, national politics came center stage. The *Journal* reported: "Richard M. Nixon came to town yesterday and turned Atlanta's streets into a political rallying ground. The Nixon party's three red-white-and-blue Boeing 727s landed at Atlanta airport and were met by Police Chief Herbert Jenkins, Mayor Ivan Allen and GOP chieftains Howard 'Bo' Callaway, Rep. Ben Blackburn, and Earl Patton. Police estimated that between 100,000 and 200,000 turned out to cheer

Nixon and shower him and his wife Pat with confetti as they rode down Peachtree."

The welcome to Nixon bore out certain drastic changes taking place in Atlanta and Georgia. The state's historic allegiance to the Democratic party was crumbling. Georgia comptroller general James L. Bentley, Jr., and public service commissioner Alpha Fowler had said that they had resigned from the Democratic party and that they intended to run in the 1970 Republican primary.

From Democrat-for-Wallace Lester Maddox to elder statesman Carl Vinson, Democrats in Georgia voiced shock and surprise at the decision of high state officials to abandon their party and hitch up to the Republican state organization. "That's bad news," said former congressman Carl Vinson. "I'm sorry they're leaving the party. I regret to see these gentlemen who hold very high state office leave the party."

Mayor Ivan Allen called the loss of the officials "a stunning blow" to the Democratic party in Georgia, pointing out that only 50,000 had voted in the Republican primary September 11.

The results of the general election on November 5 held no surprises. Richard M. Nixon was named as the thirty-seventh president. Herman Talmadge defeated Earl Patton for the Senate. Elliott Hagan, Ben Blackburn, and Fletcher Thompson won their races for the Congress. Leroy Stynchcombe was named Fulton County sheriff, and fluoridation was approved for Fulton County. Rapid transit was defeated; a $45 million city school bond issue was approved; and state legislators were denied four-year terms after Atlanta voters went to the polls. Atlanta was a "climb in your car and ride to work" town, and evidently many felt it should stay that way. The paper reported: "Rapid transit faced a decidedly pale future here as stunned officials tried to autopsy the resounding defeat handed the $377,600,000 bond referendum by voters in the City of Atlanta and Fulton and DeKalb Counties." In Atlanta 53,660 (58 percent) voted against rapid transit and 38,675 (42 percent) voted in favor. Oddly enough, the hotly argued referendum drew votes from less than one-half of those who cast ballots. An estimated 270,000 people voted, and only 120,000 bothered to vote on rapid transit, located last on the twelve-page ballot.

Officials of MARTA were visibly shaken by the defeat, and chairman Richard Rich remarked, "It's pretty obvious people don't want to be taxed for rapid transit." One who definitely did not share this view was the city's top official. As far back as April 4 Mayor Ivan Allen, at groundbreaking ceremonies for the Georgia State College Music and Art Building, had told Gov. Lester Maddox that the Atlanta metropolitan area had to have rapid transit.

"The development of this college means we must have transportation," Mayor Allen told the governor. "There must be a Georgia State College Station on the rapid transit system." The mayor, governor, and other state dignitaries appeared at the dedication of the $3 million structure that was to house the music and art departments and a concert hall.

And, of course, Allen's views on the value of rapid transit did in time prevail.

Several Atlanta city officials got raises, but Mayor Allen declined an increase from $20,000 to $30,000. As a result several employees made more than the mayor. The city official who most outranked Mayor Allen in salary was Earl Landers, administrative assistant to the mayor, who was drawing $22,633. Another mayor's aide, Dan Sweat, drew $19,162. Those besides Landers earning more than the mayor were Henry Bowden, city attorney; Charles Davis, director of finance; Paul Weir, water works director; and Ray Nixon, public works director. They were all raised to $21,710. Police chief Jenkins received $19,981; parks manager Jack Delius, $19,162; library director Carlton Rochell, $19,162; and airport manager Grady Ridgeway, $19,162.

While firms from all over the country were establishing branch offices or headquarters in Atlanta, several old established Atlanta area companies were selling control to stockholders from elsewhere: Bona Allen, Inc., a leading tannery and saddle-maker in the area, went under new ownership after an announcement by Tandy Corporation that it had purchased the plant. Lamar Whiting continued as president of the ninety-five-year-old company, which had been owned by the family of the founder since 1873. The company was the largest employer in Buford, Georgia.

Less than a month later Rhodes, Inc., an Atlanta-based furniture chain for ninety-three years, announced agreement had been reached for its sale to U.S. Finance Company of Jacksonville, Florida, for $19.3 million. Rhodes, which operated sixty-four retail furniture outlets in seven southeastern states, reported a profit of $1.6 million on sales of $28 million for the fiscal year ending January 31, 1968. Rhodes president Charles D. Collins made the announcement and did not anticipate any change in the Rhodes operation. The home office remained in Atlanta. U.S. Finance was a diversified investment-holding company with assets of more than $80 million.

One of the biggest business deals of the year involved not company stocks, but the buildings in which the company operated. The National Bank of Georgia Building and the Fulton National Bank Building were bought by a Nassau-based investment fund for $17 million in one of the largest real estate transactions in Atlanta history. The buyer was the U.S. Investment Fund (USIF), an international organization formed in 1967 to invest in income-producing property in the United States. The two prestigious bank–office buildings were previously owned by the Corrigan Interests of Dallas. The thirty-story NBG building was bought for $10 million, and the twenty-four-story Fulton National went for $7 million.

Another Atlanta real estate transaction was controversial and historic. The East Lake Country Club was located in an area of changing population pattern both racially and economically. In early April of 1968, 900 of the 1,500 members of the Atlanta Athletic Club, owners of the East Lake Country Club, voted to abandon use of the country club area in DeKalb County as a golf course and to put up the land for sale, so that the famous old course could be subdivided into tracts for apartments and individual houses. This brought strong protest, led by the 551 members who had voted against the sale. The golf club and course had been owned by the Athletic Club since 1907, and over the years it had been rebuilt and greatly improved. It also had brought "national renown and fame" to DeKalb County and the Atlanta region as the home course of Bobby Jones, Alexa Sterling, Watts Gunn, and Charlie Yates. Despite the protest and a court case, the sale went through.

Actually, half the original area continued as a golf course and social club, though no longer owned by the Atlanta Athletic Club; the East Lake club-house remained the center of social and civic events, and only one of the two eighteen hole golf courses was converted into residential use.

In 1983 the East Lake purchasers paid off the original $1.6 million loan on the area made famous by Bobby Jones. Meanwhile the Athletic Club had built a beautiful and challenging course and a handsome clubhouse on the banks of the Chattahoochee River, near Duluth.

The fifty-nine acres of the old Number Two Course were converted into a $14 million "city" for low-income families. Lying on Glenwood Avenue just east of I-20, the eight hundred housing units, in garden apartments and high-use structures, would be named East Lake Meadows. When finished in 1971 it was the nation's largest low-rent "turnkey" housing project, developed under the system by which public housing is developed by private companies and then turned over to the local Housing Authority. Four of Atlanta's major banks cooperated in the financing of East Lake Meadows—the Citizens and Southern National Bank, Fulton National, First National, and the Trust Company of Georgia. East Lake Meadows was one of five other turnkey low-rent projects in the Atlanta area. The others were Hollywood Courts, a 202-unit site in northwest Atlanta; the Bankhead Courts, a 500-unit development; the 220-unit Gilbert Gardens; and the 175-unit Leila Valley Apartments in southeast Atlanta. In DeKalb County another turnkey project, Gallway Manor, was developed on six acres of urban renewal land.

Two national retailers representing opposite ends of the market opened new units in Atlanta. Saks Fifth Avenue opened in Phipps Plaza at Peachtree and Lenox roads, across from Lenox Square. Saks' high fashion arrival was somewhat overshadowed by the news that cost-conscious Atlanta buyers now had three large, new discount department stores in the Treasure Island chain, a division of the J. C. Penney Company. Each store was on its own twenty-five-acre site and featured a free-standing garage and auto diagnostic center. The new Atlanta stores, the first to be developed outside Wisconsin, were at Jonesboro Road and I-285, Highway 41 and Terrell Mill Road, and at Buford Highway and I-285.

Meanwhile in the Kirkwood neighborhood black businessmen were opening small places in the previously all-white community. There was a small supermarket on Boulevard Drive and a Negro psychiatrist's office and an Afro-American cinema.

The brand-new Atlanta Civic Center was an immediate success. It had a theater and concert hall, a sports arena, and a place where huge business conventions could be held. In September of 1968, for example, the biggest "home show" ever held in Atlanta was displayed at the Civic Center. Called Home Horoscope, it presented new ideas on home building, furnishings, decoration, and gadgets brought in by two hundred exhibitors, and more than a quarter-million people attended. In March the Atlanta Symphony under Robert Shaw opened the Robert F. Maddox Hall before a capacity audience of nearly 4,000.

The *Journal-Constitution* described the scene on the first night:

The dazzling two-story lobby and the auditorium has a room to stir the imagination. Chandeliers look like explosions of light. Above them, gleaming brass pendant shapes, spotlighted from above, move in air-conditioning currents and give life to the dark blue ceiling. . . . The brightest thing in the room is the brilliant red carpet which casts a fiery reflection on the sculptural shape of the free standing staircases, covered with vinyl that looks like gold leaf. To the left is the entrance to Robert Maddox Hall. The hall, tuned like a giant fiddle, gave a superb performance on opening night—aided by the musicians of the Atlanta Symphony Orchestra. . . .

The middle [of the center] is a handsome open plaza. Fountains splash here into a reflecting pool and sycamore trees growing in the sunny northeast corner have already started to leaf out.

North of the plaza is the exhibit hall containing meeting rooms of various sizes, plus one tremendous column-free room covering one and one-half acres in space.

The man largely responsible for the auditorium's design is Harold Montague, an architect with Robert & Company, the firm which planned the civic center.

The nine brilliant chandeliers as well as the carpeting was a last minute gift from the City of Atlanta. The chandeliers were inspired by those in a music hall in Vienna and Mr. Montague drew up the plans and specifications, finally giving the job of executing them to Rambusch in New York—a firm that did the lighting for the Met in New York and at the Fox Theatre here. The 900 crystals involved in the three fixtures were collected from all over the world. Paul Miller who worked as an apprentice at Tiffany's put the works together.

Robert F. Maddox Hall was named on opening night for the man who was Mayor of Atlanta in 1909 when the old auditorium-armory was opened with the city's first music festival.

Opera will be grand when it comes—not this season but next. Compared to the Fox, the stage is much deeper but not nearly so wide. The Fox was designed in the days of burlesque and long chorus lines, but it is only 35 feet deep. The stage in the new auditorium is 50 feet deep, and the roof above the stage is 85 feet high, tall enough to handle any kind of set or backdrop.

. . . Atlanta's Civic Center is a $9,000,000 bargain. Of this $1,500,000 was paid for the land, $2,500,000 for the exhibition hall and $4,500,000 for the auditorium—and the rest for parking and landscaping.

This was only one-tenth as much as the cost of New York City's Metropolitan Opera House. But there was not that great a difference in the sight or sound.

By autumn of 1968 the Civic Center was joined by an even more spectacular cultural center—the new Memorial Arts Center, where all the performing arts may be seen under one roof. The new center was located on a six-acre tract between Fifteenth and Sixteenth streets on land whose social roots are rich in history. For on this site stood several handsome homes, noted for hospitality and the cultural interest of their owners.

Presenting the arts in such elegant surroundings as the High Museum Memorial Arts Center was not cheap, as Atlanta was soon to discover. President Charles Jagels explained to coworkers at a luncheon at the Capital City Club that the high cost of operating the new facility—including air conditioning, lighting, and cleaning—"is one of the penalties of our success." Campaign volunteers reported that they had raised $408,830, or 86 percent of their goal of $474,000, money needed for this first year's expenses.

The $13 million center housed the High Museum of Art, the Atlanta Symphony Orchestra, the Atlanta School of Art, and theater, ballet, and opera components of the Atlanta Municipal Theater.

It must not be assumed from the above that art and music, the dance, and the theater were available only to Atlanta's social and well-to-do. Art in Atlanta in all forms was available in 1968 to the poor slum dweller as well as to the rich and high born. A $325,000 Creative Atlanta program made seventeen weeks of workshops in drama, dance, music, puppetry, painting, and sculpture available to ghetto children, and it produced some of Atlanta's best entertainment on slum streets. The program was announced May 20 at a joint meeting of local art agencies with Economic Opportunity Atlanta, the Atlanta Council on Children and Youth Services, the Atlanta public schools, the Atlanta Department of Parks and Recreation, the Atlanta Public Library, and the Georgia Commission on the Arts. This summer program was aimed at more than 5,000 indigent youngsters in fourteen target areas.

During the ten years up to 1968, 75,000 persons had been moved out of

their homes by urban renewal, expressways, construction, housing code enforcement, and public housing evictions. Despite model cities, public housing,
and other efforts, a shortage of decent low-income housing remained. By the
end of 1969 the metro Atlanta area was expected to increase in population by
90,000, and Mayor Allen said that 17,000 housing units had to be built
by 1971 to meet the needs of persons who would be put out of their homes
by government action. Most of the displaced would be Negro, poor, and disadvantaged.

The Atlanta area had a population of 1,380,000 in 1967. By 1969 the
prediction was for 1,475,000. A housing market analysis prepared by the Federal Housing Administration showed that the median after-tax income of all
families in the area in October of 1967 was $7,950. About 28 percent of all
families and 47 percent of all renter households had after-tax income of less
than $5,000, and 17 percent of all families and 7 percent of renters had $12,500
or more. Thus, housing for Atlantans needed to come in all size and price
ranges. For the city's poor the greatest need was in the $30- to $50-per-month
rental range. The FHA analysis pointed out that there was public housing in
the metro area with a total of over 11,050 units.

B. J. Phillips, a crusading young reporter for the *Constitution,* was not
content to tell Atlanta's housing story in terms of dull statistics. She wrote:

Meet the other part of Atlanta, with pretty names like Vine City, Summerhill, Cabbage Town and Buttermilk Bottom. It doesn't live like you do—
it sleeps five to a bed, eats the same thing day in and day out; it doesn't dream
the American dream; it doesn't think like you do and it doesn't care about you
because it doesn't think you, in turn, care about it. Housing is deplorable and
rent varies from house to house and landlord to landlord. But the one con-
sistency is the disrepair of the houses and the inadequacies of decent places to
live. The average family has eight members, usually with the father missing,
and they are making do in a three room unit. The toilet may be stopped up or
ripped from the wall, generally the roof leaks and always the wind comes
through the cracks in the floor. Naturally, gas bills are high in an effort to heat
such poorly insulated housing. Lighting and water costs are minimal, but
there are the rats. Prices at the small corner store are higher than those in
super markets and selective buying is prohibited because of lack of transportation.

The view from the ghetto is narrow, and right or wrong, there is little
faith in Society as a whole, and there is continual unrest, not just in the teen-
agers, but deep down unrest of people who have seen themselves work all
their lives in Atlanta for nothing.

Phillips's crusading spirit in time led to a drastic change in the upper
editorial management at Cox newspapers. After an article attacking a local
public utility for seeking a rate increase, at the same time the papers also were
planning a rise in rates, high authority told Pulitzer Prize-winning editor Eu-

gene Patterson to tell Phillips to mend her ways. Patterson's answer was that he did not tell his good writers what to write. The result was that both Patterson and Phillips left.

Patterson went to the *Washington Post* as managing editor, then to Duke University as professor of political science, and, finally, to Florida where he became president and chief executive officer of the *St. Petersburg Times*. Phillips, her reportorial zeal undiminished, remained in the South as a regional correspondent for *Time* magazine.

A voluminous plan, proposed by local model neighborhood planners, marked the beginning of implementation of ideas being generated since the local Model Cities program was established about a year earlier. Major features of the Atlanta plan included: (1) A circumferential bus route around the entire model neighborhood, cutting across the six or seven existing routes. The new route would be operated by the Atlanta Transit Authority under government subsidy. (2) Operation of six mobile recreation centers and the establishment of store-front libraries under supervision of the Parks Department and the Atlanta Public Library. (3) Development of a nonprofit housing development to sponsor and construct 431 new housing units planned for the area. (4) Construction of a new educational complex to contain a high school and middle school. An extended day-care center was planned, as were year-round educational and recreational facilities. (5) A group medical practice building for the area, which had neither dentists nor physicians. (6) Establishment of a foster home for delinquent children to be administered by Fulton County Juvenile Court. (7) Provision of new business in the model neighborhood area with technical assistance to existing business.

The first year "supplemental" funding requested of the Department of Housing and Urban Development was $7,349,000. Another $10 million was already assigned through the program for neighborhood development.

The biggest and most tragic local disaster of 1968 occurred on May 29, when seven small children under three and two adults were killed in a fiery blast at the Hapeville Day Nursery at 724 North Central Avenue. The children had just had their lunch and had been put to bed for their afternoon nap when a bulldozer ripped open a gas line while preparing for an addition to the nursery. Two adults died in the flames as they tried to pass the children out the windows to safety. Thirty-five other children were rescued by nursery workers and passers-by before fire completely engulfed the building.

Crime in all its forms from lottery to robbery to rape and murder was much in Atlantans' minds and consciences in 1968. But murder was of main concern to police. The *Constitution* commented:

Sadly, Atlantans are killing and being killed at the fastest rate in the city's history. The number of homicides now [November] totals 135 for the year which is seven short of the all-time record set in 1967. So far this year there have been 34 more slayings than at the same time last year. . . . The majority of homicides grow out of minor arguments among husbands and wives, long-time friends, casual acquaintances and even brothers and sisters. According to Det. Supt. Clinton Chafin, the most disturbing fact of the daily violence is that people are being killed over "incidents so minor as to be pitiful." Most of these are spur-of-the-moment killings with the perpetrators giving no thought whatsoever to the consequences of their acts. Chafin believes better housing, better economic conditions and more community projects to improve living standards might help curb the slaughter. He believes the problem is more a social one than one for the police.

Records kept by homicide officers show that pistols, usually a cheap hand gun, were used in more than 70 of the 135 killings. Knives, shotguns and rifles followed in order.

Many Atlantans were engrossed in the matters that had always concerned them: with their gardens in the spring and sports in the summer and fall and their churches and church leaders—and with social events both simple and elaborate the year round. On January 27, 1968, for example:

Representatives of foreign lands dined and danced with Atlanta socialites at the brilliant and gala Diplomats Ball held at the Piedmont Driving Club.

The affair, topping the social calendar for the mid-winter season, was actually the Piedmont Ball, an annual charity event sponsored by the Women's Auxiliary of Piedmont Hospital. . . . Proceeds of the evening go to the new Pediatrics Wing at Piedmont Hospital.

Honor guests were His Excellency William P. Fay of Ireland and Mrs. Fay; Jacques LaPrette, Minister Counselor at the French Embassy in Washington; His Excellency Juan Yriart of Uruguay and His Excellency Egidio Ortona of Italy. Atlanta's French consul, Arthur Harris, was receiving congratulations on his Legion of Honor Medal from France which he had just received the day before. John Fornara, Atlanta's Italian consul, was also present.

On June 27 the *Northside Neighbor* described a venerable and distinguished Atlanta organization called the Nine O'Clocks:

For 85 years, the Nine O'Clocks has engendered a patriotic fraternalism amongst its members and curiosity and envy in the bosom of outsiders. Just what is this organization that has remained virtually unchanged throughout the years? Bobby Byrd best characterizes this venerable social institution with the least description—"It is not an organization with an axe to grind—a charitable cause to champion—or a movement to mobilize. The sole aim of the Nine O'Clocks is to gather twice annually and entertain themselves in such a unique fashion that it maintains an unprecedented pattern.

Keeping step with the Jet Age, Nine O'Clocks pepped up their parties and have given the most spectacular affairs ever recorded by Atlanta social reporters. With the swelling of the rolls to 450 members in 1968 the Nine

O'Clocks have entered their 85th year—still commanding loyalty from nonagenarians and remaining enigmatic to outsiders.

In late August, the *Northside Neighbor* again was bearing down heavily on Atlanta social history:

What was once the servants' quarters of the magnificent old Inman home has now become the choicest place in town to lunch. Through the efforts of 12 civic-minded Northside women the Swan Coach House on Slaton Drive is what it is—a beautiful and charming place to dine, shop and entertain.

When the handwriting was on the wall for the tearing down of the Old Coach House connected with the High Museum, Mrs. Ivan Allen, Jr. suggested to a group of her friends, all active in supporting the Museum, that they approach the Atlanta Historical Society, newly housed in the Swan House, to rent at a nominal fee, the estate's coach house for a non-profit restaurant-boutique establishment. The directors of the society agreed and the Forward Atlanta Arts Foundation, Inc. was born.[13]

Atlanta's interest in pro sports was whetted twice in 1968. In mid-March Commissioner Pete Rozelle announced that the annual spring meeting of the NFL and AFL would be held in Atlanta—the first time this gathering of the pro football magnates had been held outside a two-team city. And on Sunday, July 14, before 34,283 fans at the new stadium, Henry Aaron knocked his five-hundredth home run, thus joining the ranks of baseball's elite sluggers as he helped the Braves beat the San Francisco Giants.

Two distinguished religious leaders, one black and Methodist, one white and Roman Catholic, made news in Atlanta in 1968. Dr. Harry V. Richardson, president of Interdenominational Theological Center since its inception in 1958 and a national leader in theological education for Negroes, would soon retire but would continue as president emeritus of the institution that he helped found ten years before while serving as president of Gammon Theological Seminary. Holding degrees from Western Reserve University, Harvard University, and Drew University, he was also ordained an elder in the AME church in 1932. He was named president of Gammon Theological Seminary in 1948 and ordained an elder in the Methodist church the same year.

On July 15, eight hundred people attended the installation of Thomas Andrew Donnellan, formerly bishop of Ogdensburg, New York, as the new head of the Catholic Archdiocese of Atlanta. At services in the Cathedral of Christ the King on Peachtree Street at Wesley Road, the fifty-four-year old prelate praised his Atlanta predecessor, the late Archbishop Paul J. Hallinan.

OBITUARIES

An editorial in the *Constitution* during October made this tribute to a longtime city leader:

Ivan Allen, Sr. was a leader among the bright and ambitious young men who were attracted by the possibilities of the young city of Atlanta before the turn of the century.

He grew up in Dalton and came here in 1895 to found a successful business and have a part in almost every worthwhile undertaking which resulted in the development of this area.

Name any group which has been helpful in the economic advance of the place and the chances are that Mr. Allen was a founding member and at one time the head of the organization. The same goes for groups with the aim of making mankind's lot a little better, such as the Community Chest and the Boy Scouts.

Mr. Allen's energy was exceeded only by the variety of his interests and the result was a well-rounded and full life. History and old maps were hobbies, with the result that Georgians enjoy his gift to the state of Fort Mountain Park, and students have a fine collection of maps to study (at the public library). Politics was an enduring interest. He served as senator from Fulton County, and gave years of volunteer service to various boards and commissions. More than 30 years ago he was preaching the need for county consolidation and other reforms in state government, some of which have come partly as a result of his efforts.

Mr. Allen's devotion to Atlanta and the city's advancement was fervent and single-minded. He loved the place, knew it had a great future and worked to help the city fulfill its promise during all his years here. He brought up a son, Ivan Allen, Jr., the city's mayor, in the same faith and the contribution father and son together have made is incalculable.

Now Ivan Allen, Sr. is dead at the age of 92, He outlived his generation and his deeds will outlive him, for much of the Atlanta he left when he died is a living memorial to his devotion to the place and his efforts on the city's behalf.

Among his many accomplishments, Allen was instrumental in the establishment of Oglethorpe University, and he headed the city's first Forward Atlanta campaign in 1925. The founder of one of the nation's largest office supply firms, he helped create the Atlanta Retail Merchants Association, the Atlanta Convention Bureau, and the Southeastern Fair. He was a past president of the Atlanta Chamber of Commerce.

Green B. Adair, 81, was a grandson of Atlanta pioneer and millionaire E. M. Marsh. He began his career in radio by going to work for station WGST in the early 1930s and was there thirty-seven years, retiring as sales executive at 80. Dr. Wayne Starr Aiken, 75, had the distinction of being the first graduate of Emory Medical School in 1915. He became chief physician and surgeon for the Georgia Power Company and then joined Dr. Thomas Hinman and Dr. Samuel Silverman in plastic surgery at Atlanta Southern Dental College. He was a deacon at the Druid Hills Presbyterian Church and president of the Men's Bible Class. He was a Mason and a Shriner. Fred W. Ajax, 59, was director of campus affairs at Georgia Tech, where he had served for thirty-seven years. A naval veteran of World War II, he returned to Tech and was the driving force behind the development of that school's placement office.

William Alexander Cunningham, 82, enjoyed the reputation of having his Georgia football teams whip Georgia Tech the first four of his eight seasons as head coach of all major sports at the university during the interrupted 1910–1919 span. He and his entire Georgia football team joined the army in 1917 and served in France. Mrs. A. Thomas Bradbury, 59, the former Janette Lane, was the wife of a prominent Atlanta architect. She was president of the Atlanta Music Club and past president of the Atlanta Girls' Club and the Atlanta Civic Ballet Association. Mrs. Charles M. Brown, 93, the former Mamie Fickett, daughter of a pioneer Atlanta family and an authority on the city's history, was the mother of Fulton County Commissioner Charlie Brown. Loyd Sandford Burns, 82, pioneer landowner in DeKalb and Gwinnett counties, was organizer of the first Bank of Tucker.

Mrs. Charles Howard Candler, Sr., 87, was the wife of the philanthropist and financier and eldest son of Asa G. Candler. She made special contributions to the field of music and for many years underwrote the concert series at Emory. She gave money to establish Glenn Memorial Church as a memorial to her father, Wilbur Fisk Glenn. William K. Jenkins, 77, retired theater executive and civic leader, was the founder and president of the Georgia Theatre Company, a statewide chain of movie houses that included the Fox. He began his career in 1913 with the late Arthur Lukas. A graduate of Georgia Tech, he was a member of First Presbyterian Church, the Chamber of Commerce, Rotary, the Piedmont Driving Club, the Capital City Club, Variety Club, and a director of the First National Bank. W. S. Kirkpatrick, 83, former managing editor of the *Atlanta Journal*, began his newspaper career in Atlanta in 1912 with the *Georgian*. In 1940 he went with the *Atlanta Journal*. An adept gardener, he belonged to the Men's Garden Clubs of Atlanta and Decatur.

Dr. James Calhoun McDougall, 80, ear, nose, and throat specialist in Atlanta for more than fifty years, was chief of staff of St. Joseph's Infirmary. He was a graduate of the University of Georgia and Emory Medical School, where he later became a professor. During World War I he served in France with the Emory Unit. A director of the Fulton National Bank, he was also a member of the Cathedral of St. Philip and was a life member of the Piedmont Driving Club and the Capital City Club. James W. C. McKay, Sr., 62, teacher, coach, and administrator at Woodward Academy (Georgia Military Academy) for thirty-three years, was a former president of East Point Rotary Club and vice-president and director of the South Fulton Chamber of Commerce. Mrs. John McKee, longtime teacher and journalist, had taught English and journalism at Hoke Smith High School and was adviser for the school's newspaper for sixteen years. The former Catherine Brantley, she was a member of Central Presbyterian Church. Dr. William E. Pafford, 72, who for twenty-seven years served with the Georgia State Department of Education, had served as executive secretary of the Southern Association of Colleges and Schools. For many years he served as director of the State of Georgia YMCA.

E. Ralph Paris, Sr., 74, division manager of Atlanta Casket Company, was a founder of United Family Life Insurance Company. He was a graduate of Duke University and a veteran of World War I. He had been president of Atlanta Rotary and Family Service Society and was chairman of the board of stewards at First Methodist. His memberships were at the Piedmont Driving Club, the Capital City Club, Peachtree Golf Club, and the Racquet Club. Col. Charles T. Pottinger, Sr., 82, was a veteran of both world wars. He was a manufacturer's representative of air conditioning equipment and was a member of Rotary, YMCA, and St. Luke's Episcopal Church. Domenico P. Savant, Georgia Tech's first dean of engineering in 1935 and professor until his retirement in 1954, was a native of Nole, Italy. He was a master's graduate of Harvard and became head of the electrical engineering school at Tech in 1919.

Judge Sidney Trenholm Schell, 57, who had been appointed by Governor Maddox to fill the unexpired term of Judge Stonewall Dyer, was a graduate of the University of Kentucky and Atlanta Law School. He was past master of his Masonic lodge, an Elk, and a Shriner. Walter H. Scott, 90, founder of the DeKalb County Bank of Avondale Estates (now a C&S branch), was onetime sales manager for National Biscuit Company. He was a member of the First Baptist Church of Decatur, treasurer of Decatur Elks' Club, the Lions Club, and president of DeKalb Chamber of Commerce. Furman Smith, 58, senior partner in the law firm of King and Spalding, was a member of the board of directors of the Atlantic Company, E. T. Barwick Industries, Crawford & Company, and Oxford Industries. He was a summa cum laude graduate of Mercer and a member of Rotary, the Capital City Club, Shakerag Hounds, and Holy Spirit Catholic Church.

Harry Sommers, 77, a native of Philadelphia, came to Atlanta in 1922 to manage the Packard agency, and in 1924 he opened the Chrysler-Plymouth agency, which he operated until his retirement in 1966. Sommers served in World War I and was a Republican national committeeman for sixteen years. He was twice president of the Atlanta Community Chest and the Atlanta Chamber of Commerce. A member of the Nine O'Clocks, he also held membership in the Piedmont Driving Club, the Capital City Club, and Peachtree Golf Club. Robert Leonard Sommerville, 61, was a transplanted Scotsman who had lived in Atlanta for twenty years and "parlayed his British accent into a bond of confidence with the people of Atlanta." He came to America in 1948 and was a professor at Emory University until 1954, when he and six other Atlantans bought the bus system and he became president. The *Journal-Constitution* noted, "He guided the system through the turbulent years of bus desegregation and the exciting era when Atlanta grew into a big city and emerged with one of the few public mass transit systems in the country still earning a profit. Besides his involvement with the bus company he has served two Mayors in the front line of civic work for his city including chairmanship of the Citizens Advisory Committee on Urban Renewal."

Robert Spector, 77, native of Russia and founder of Spector Lumber Company in 1928, was on the board of directors of Ahavath Achim Synagogue and active in projects for the Atlanta Jewish Home and B'nai B'rith. Luther E. (Luke) Swensson, 57, general manager of all the Sears Roebuck stores in metropolitan Atlanta, was president of the board of trustees of Northside Hospital, member of the executive board of the Boy Scouts of America, the Retail Merchants Association, and the Atlanta Convention Bureau. Frank Daniel Wood, 80, was the retired southern manager of Moody's Investors Service and active in Boy Scout work for more than forty years. His awards included the Silver Beaver and Silver Antelope and the Scout Master's Key. He had been a Mason for more than sixty years and was a member of the Church of Our Saviour.

Ruben Eugene Warbington, 43, nationally known sports figure, was a member of the All American Skeet Team in 1967 and 1968 and was a past director of the River Bend Gun Club. H. P. (Bob) Whitehead, Sr., vice-president of Georgia Power Company, was a graduate of Carnegie Institute. He was also a director of Georgia Power Company and Southern Electric Generating Company. John C. Warr, 56, general manager of the Georgia Baptist Children's Home, had been employed there since 1950. He had previously been an instructor and registrar at Berry School, from which he had graduated.

NOTES

1. Ivan Allen and Paul Hemphill, *Mayor: Notes on the Sixties* (New York: Simon & Schuster, 1971).

2. Ibid.

3. Herbert T. Jenkins, *Keeping the Peace* (New York: Harper and Row, 1970).

4. Coretta Scott King, *My Life with Martin Luther King, Jr.* (New York: Avon Books, 1970).

5. Interview, Ludlow Porch, Mar. 22, 1983.

6. Maggie Long, *Atlanta*, May, 1968.

7. Jim Rankin, ibid., Feb. 1968.

8. *Northside News*, July 4, 1965.

9. Harold H. Martin, *D. W. Brooks, A Good Man, A Great Dream* (Atlanta: Gold Kist, Inc., 1982).

10. Jim Rankin, *Atlanta*, Mar., 1968.

11. Sandra Grimes, ibid., May, 1968.

12. *Atlanta*, Apr., 1968.

13. Irene Croft, *Northside Neighbor*, Aug. 28, 1968.

1969 AND INTO THE 1970S

ON THE evening of February 3, 1969, Ralph McGill was having dinner at the home of a friend, John Lawhorn, a young black man from Ohio, who was a genius as a teacher of small children by use of music. They were talking about how Lawhorn, with McGill's help, had established a series of fine music schools in slum areas of Atlanta, taking slow-learning youngsters off the streets in a city torn by racial tension, using music as an instrument for teaching them reading and the use of words and numbers.

After dinner they went into the living room. McGill, sitting in a big easy chair, was talking about how to raise money for a new dream Lawhorn had—a bus equipped as a traveling music school—when suddenly he stopped. He stood up, said shakily to his wife, Mary Lynn, "I think we should be going now," and began to fall. Lawhorn caught him and lowered him gently to the floor. The doctor arrived quickly, but it was too late. McGill was dead.[1]

A summary of McGill's impressive journalistic and civic career was published in *Atlanta* magazine in February, 1969, along with an interview done shortly before his death:

When Ralph McGill was named executive editor of the *Atlanta Constitution* in 1938 there was a parade in his honor. A mob of robed Ku Klux Klansmen marched on Forsyth Street displaying placards denouncing McGill and his newspaper. Today, thirty years later, his published views on discrimination and bigotry have not changed, but the KKK is almost out of existence.

A friend of Presidents, long-time champion of the Negro, winner of the Pulitzer, holder of many honorary degrees, including one from Harvard, the celebrated publisher of the *Constitution* has written a daily column for forty years. It is syndicated in more than a hundred newspapers and attracts millions of readers.

He has been threatened, attacked, and abused; he is loved by many for his compassion and hated by many for his unrelenting stand on civil rights.

Ralph McGill is almost certainly Atlanta's best known citizen and is certainly among its most distinguished. . . .

It is difficult not to see McGill's passing as the end of an era: most young people of today, even the informed ones, are not concerned with the Ku Klux Klan, White Citizens Councils, the county unit system, or most of the other evils which McGill fought throughout his distinguished career. That the young are not so concerned with these matters is testimony to the effectiveness of McGill's journalism: conditions *have* improved in the South, and Ralph McGill is one of the reasons.

Although the "racial question" has moved into another dimension since McGill began championing civil rights in the 1950's, it was he who broke the ground and laid the foundation for better understanding between whites and blacks in the South. It was McGill (they called him "Rastus" in the provinces, and in some parts of Atlanta) who bore the burden, almost alone and in a time when it was not fashionable, of standing for racial justice and toleration amid widespread hysteria. For this, he was vilified by whites throughout Georgia and the South, and he gained little love from the militant young blacks who consider him a reminder of the dark days when whites led Negroes in the quest for racial equality.

It is one of those tragic and dark ironies of the South that it rejects its best educated and most qualified leaders, preferring the rhetoric of demagogues to the reason of learned men. It is therefore not surprising that the large body of white Southerners should reject McGill, a man of great personal courage, who loved the South, as he put it, as one loves a crippled child. But McGill bore a very special message, as did his contemporary Martin Luther King, Jr., and that message had to do with the brotherhood of man. It will not be denied.

Atlanta extends its sympathies to the McGill family and to the entire South, which has lost a bright light in a dark passage.

McGill, indeed, did pass on at a time when the "racial question" was moving into new dimensions. While the integration of the public grade schools held the attention of white and black alike, changes were under way in white Atlanta's relations with the black colleges of the Atlanta University Center. Since the founding of these institutions, shortly after the Civil War, to provide educational opportunity for former bondsmen, white Atlanta had in great degree ignored Atlanta University, Clark College, Morehouse, Morris Brown, Spelman, and the latest addition to the Center in 1958, the Interdenominational Theological Seminary. As a result of this unawareness, the schools had been supplied over the years by donations from afar—especially from black churches, from zealous reformers throughout the nation, and from northern foundations. In 1967 Dr. Benjamin Mays, retired president of Morehouse, reported that the six Atlanta University institutions had received less than $1.5 million from Atlanta sources in 100 years. That, too, has begun to change. Beginning in 1967 the C&S Bank endowed a Mills B. Lane Chair in Finance and Accounting at Atlanta University. An unnamed southern foundation gave Morehouse $62,800 for land acquisition, and the Callaway Foundation announced its support of one professional chair each at Atlanta University, Clark, Morehouse, Morris Brown, and Spelman. Also, Clark College has worked out an internship program with a number of large Atlanta and national firms to prepare black graduates to take their place in the hitherto all-white business world. Companies cooperating were Coca-Cola, Davison's, U.S. Gypsum, Pure Oil, IBM, General Electric, Metropolitan Life, All State, C&S Bank, Gulf Oil, Lockheed-Georgia, and Rich's.

"Without question," wrote Bruce Galphin, "one of the major reasons for Atlanta's reputation for progressiveness is the maturity and the leadership of the center's facilities. Nationally, the six institutions are recognized as one of the top two or three centers of Negro higher learning. All of the institutions are accredited. They have several outstanding departments. Many of the nation's leading Negroes in government, education, business, and the arts are graduates of the Center."

As of January 1969 nearly half of all black students of higher learning in Georgia were enrolled at the Center. About a third of all seminary-trained Negro ministers in America earned their degrees at ITS. Some six hundred graduates of Morris Brown were teaching in the Atlanta public school system. Morehouse was one of only four colleges in Georgia with a Phi Beta Kappa chapter (the others: Emory, Agnes Scott, the University of Georgia). Clark was the innovator and the directing college in a thirteen-school program for accelerated, rather than remedial, studies by underprepared students. Spelman was the oldest and still the leading college in America for Negro women. Atlanta University was not only the city's oldest institution of higher learning, but one of the top three Negro schools in America. Both through formal programs and informal participation of faculty members, it played a major role in Atlanta's black community.

"In view of these achievements," Galphin concluded in *Atlanta,* "it is all the more remarkable that the Center is so little known to white Atlanta. It may well be that the six AU institutions are Atlanta's most over-looked assets."[2]

One of the hallmarks of the growing cities of the late 1960s and early 1970s was the planned office park development. Atlanta had already begun to move in this direction with Corporate Square, Executive Park, and other projects. In 1969 another major project was getting off the ground, as described in *Atlanta:*

Now, Rockefeller money has come into the act. Final plans for the $53,000,000 Interstate North office park on I-75 northwest of Atlanta were announced in early 1968 by Cousins Properties, Inc. [developer of Corporate Square]. An impressive principal partner in this project is David Rockefeller, a New Yorker of some renown, who does not invest the family money lightly. Located on a 248-acre site at the intersection of I-75 and I-285 in Cobb County, Interstate North has been in various stages of planning and development for more than two years.

In developing the park, Tom Cousins will follow the "cluster concept" of building location, in which the structures are placed relatively close together around a mall that will also include restaurants, shops, and landscaped parks. . . .

Interstate North is planned as a seven-year development project which will eventually include 1.6 million square feet of office space in a succession of multi-level office clusters, plus individually located buildings.

Cousins Properties owns 50% of the investment and is responsible for the development, planning, construction, marketing, and management once completed. . . .

As Cousins points out, the site of Interstate North is situated between two major focal points: Marietta and its Lockheed-Georgia industrial complex to the northwest, and Atlanta to the southeast, from which a major expansion thrust is to the northwest toward the intersection of I-75 and I-285.

In the previous four years Executive Park, developed by Mike Gearon, had proved the office park concept a success in Atlanta. "The Park's blue-chip tenants include such entities as Sinclair Oil, Phillips Petroleum, Republic Steel, National Cash Register, and Johns-Manville. When the last of some thirty buildings opens its doors, fifteen thousand white-collar workers will be employed. A 250-room motel, an employee cafeteria, a plush restaurant, several service shops, and other amenities will be part of the complete picture. Executive Park's office buildings are of striking architecture, one to four stories tall, and they nestle in a sylvan setting off boulevards that roam through what used to be a dairy farm."

Another project under way was Presidential Park, "a sixty-seven acre development with a projected one-million square feet of office space." Tim Sims emphasized his development's accessibility, with some reason: the project was located at the intersection of I-85 and I-285, about a fifteen-minute drive from a major portion of north and northeast Atlanta.

"Blaine Kelley, president of The Landmark Group, . . . has developed Landmark Office Center at I-85 and North Druid Hills Road and has just announced two more projects, the first at I-285 and North Fulton Freeway (a $10,000,000 development) and the second, a smaller unit, located at the entrance to the Atlanta Municipal Airport."

George Adcock, the *Atlanta* writer, asked a key question:

Do these office parks pose a threat to the economic growth of downtown Atlanta? That is an open question. Gearon sees the trend as benefiting the whole area. Anyway, he says, "The geographic center of Atlanta is no longer downtown. It's at Ansley Park golf course. And the center of disposable income is close to North Druid Hills Road."

Gearon adds that, "Our idea is not to compete with downtown Atlanta. A company coming to Atlanta has already decided where it wants to go. Our aim is to offer a building designed to function according to the company's needs."

Undoubtedly, one of the main attractions of the office park is convenience. Since most of the executives and upper echelon employees live on the north side, Gearon and his fellow developers ask, "Why not put their offices near their homes?"

"The fact is," says Gearon, "the reason most companies decide to locate in Atlanta is its predominance as an air center in the South. They're not here because of a relationship to downtown; that's totally irrelevant."

"Perhaps," thinks Gearon, "too many people think every office market should be patterned after New York. This is just not necessarily true. Atlanta is particularly suited to suburban office development because of the large, undeveloped areas in close proximity to downtown."

To say the least, not everybody agrees with this expressed point of view. Architect John Portman, whose Peachtree Center is generally credited with revitalizing downtown Atlanta, believes that by moving to the suburbs a business becomes isolated and its executives and personnel never get integrated into the mainstream of the community.

"If you don't have a strong vibrant core," he has said, "the city will lose its personality and become a series of disjointed units." Portman feels that the problems of congested traffic and parking difficulties can—indeed, must—be alleviated by rapid transit and municipal parking.

Altogether, it is estimated that more than five million square feet of office park space are presently in some phase of planning or construction, especially along the Perimeter Highway (I-285). These include a major project by Crow, Pope & Carter, Northlake, at La Vista Road and I-285; plans for a combination office park-retail center on the Perimeter and Northside Drive by Charles Barton; Mike Gearon's 440-acre Perimeter Center, which will rise at the Perimeter and Ashford-Dunwoody Road; nearby, another smaller Gearon office park, Perimeter Park; another Crow, Pope & Carter project, Cumberland, near Paces Ferry Road and I-285; the Meyerhoff Corp's plans for Executive Square at Memorial Drive and the Perimeter; plans by local developers Jon R. Gray and R. Marvin Ingram to develop one hundred acres at Clairmont Road and I-85, including 1.3 million square feet of office space.

Many of these developments will include apartment complexes and residential areas.

In addition to the pure office parks, there are several aesthetically appealing, mixed-purpose developments that include both office and warehouse space: North Park, on I-285 at I-85; Chamblee Industrial Plaza on Peachtree Industrial Boulevard near I-285, and Piedmont Interstates North on I-85 at I-285.

With plenty of his own commercial interests at stake downtown, developer Tom Cousins nevertheless believes that the recent rejection of the rapid transit proposal by the voters last November is bound to give the office park concept a shot in the arm. "After all," he said, "business is going to go where the people are."

Charles Ackerman, head of the leasing firm Ackerman & Co., believes 1969 will be a strong year for office parks, drawing on such sources as companies which are disenchanted with New York City as a headquarters location.

"New York offices are desperate to cut down overhead," says Ackerman.

"And they know that they can pay three or four dollars less per square foot of office space in Atlanta. Besides, living in New York is becoming untenable."

"The year 1968 could be called the year that the concept of office parks matured," says Ackerman. Not the least of the concept's advantages, Ackerman believes, is that it enables the developer to create a total environment himself, including those things he knows a company needs or wants.

"Besides," he reflects, "companies are in very strong competition for clerical help. Free parking is like an increase in salary. And the labor market is increasingly desirous of working near where it lives."

As for the inner city, Ackerman believes that such stabilizing factors as the Merchandise Mart, good hotels, convention sites, and public transportation facilities insure continued growth for the downtown area.

At Corporate Square and Interstate North, Ackerman notes, the buildings are clustered so that an employee need not return to his car once he has parked it in the morning. The shops, professional offices, and restaurant facilities are located around the office mall. . . .

"We're a mobile society," observes Bob Nagel of Pope & Carter. "The northwest and northeast areas used to be the bed-rooms for those who worked downtown; now Cobb, DeKalb, Gwinnett, and Clayton Counties are becoming bedrooms, too."

Although some developers think that the boundaries of the Perimeter Highway constitute the boundaries of significant office park development, there are indications that the end is not in sight. For example, Gwinnett Center, on the Buford Highway several miles to the north of the Perimeter, is rapidly building forty thousand square feet of office space. This is a drop in the bucket, to be sure, but a harbinger of things to come.[3]

In the April 1969 *Atlanta* magazine Jim Montgomery, a reporter for the *Constitution*, explained what being a major airline center meant to Atlanta:

The screaming jetliners that annually shuttle an exploding population already larger than Metropolitan New York's into and out of the Atlanta Municipal Airport, also and almost incessantly assault the auditory nerves of thousands who live and work nearby.

Every twenty-four hours upward of one thousand landings and take-offs pound the runways—one every ninety seconds on the average, nearly two a minute in peak periods.

That includes private and piston-engine craft, but three out of four are commercial, the great bulk of them jets.

Prohibit their restless comings and goings here, mused one academic economist who jets around to distant seminars and seashores, and Branch City, U.S. of A., would turn into Dry Branch.

Deprive them of near-instant access to the rest of the globe, he explained, and few, if any, of the corporate headquarters offices now nestled here could afford to remain so long as they wished to survive in the modern business jungle. An Atlanta sans jets in the jet age likely would be an Atlanta sans the chief executives and countless subordinates of Coca-Cola, Fuqua Industries, Genuine Parts, and Rollins, Inc., to mention a few—and it goes without saying, Delta Air Lines.

As for the countless regional, divisional, zone, district, and what-have-you offices that occupy and keep expanding in the downtown skyscrapers and suburban office parks, most all would shrivel into few-man local branches at best if their star salesmen and technicians and supervisors could not speed within hours to new opportunities awaiting exploitation or to old customers demanding repair parts and service. . . .

And, in the absence of jet-thrust commuting time, what of the Braves, the Falcons, the Hawks, the Chiefs? Back to the minor leagues, the ranks of the semi-pros.

But there is no aggregate measure of the Atlanta jobs and dollars that depend on the airlines, indirectly as well as directly. They influence so many lives, and among those unknowingly affected may be a peanut vendor at the stadium or an apartment owner in DeKalb County.

Atlanta's booming convention business depends . . . heavily on commercial aviation . . . A substantial majority of the 330,000 homo sapiens scheduled to mill around the 550 conventions being held in Atlanta this year would have to do their milling around some other place, were it not for the big jetliners.

According to the Atlanta Convention Bureau, the 1969 gatherings will pump some $60,000,000 into the city's economy—an average of $150 per delegate for an average three-day stay.

In 1968, the bureau said, 440 conventions generated aggregate delegate spending of some $50,000,000.

The agency also boasts that the convention business is what permitted the addition here, during the last three years, of five thousand new hotel and motel rooms. It said the city now has fifteen thousand guest rooms, exceeding all but six other cities, and that ten thousand of them are available for convention customers.

And just about all of them nourished by jetliners. . . .

When the new $20,000,000 terminal opened in 1961, it accommodated in that year approximately 3,400,000 arriving and departing passengers. By 1967, that had more than tripled to 11,700,000. Now, it's in excess of thirteen and a half million—or a bit over ten times Metro Atlanta's present population of 1,300,000—and the planners say that's only the beginning.

Would you believe forty million in 1980? That's barely a decade away. But Atlanta evidently won't be able to sustain that kind of growth. At least, say the seers, the number of passengers flying into and out of the city will have risen to only seventy-three million per annum by the year 2,000.

The only reason no one's laughing now is that all the planners have notoriously underestimated the growth to date.

Already, there are more than nineteen thousand employees earning more than $150 million a year on commercial air transportation payrolls here—the majority of them, or more than twelve thousand, working for the airlines. Included are approximately seven thousand seven hundred with Delta, three thousand four hundred with Eastern, seven hundred with Southern, four hundred with United, and three hundred-plus with Piedmont, Northwest, and TransWorld combined. . . .

But airport facilities already are taxed to capacity at peak hours, and efforts to double that capacity by 1972 at a cost of possibly more than $380 million are being implemented even though practically everyone concedes that the expansion probably will suffice only until about 1980.

If the planners are right, the annual number of landings and take-offs at this one airport—which approached a record 400,000 last year—will, in eleven years, hit 700,000.

Consequently, there is no little debate about pushing ahead with so costly a "temporary" expansion of the existing airport, where there will be no room for any significant further expansion. . . .

But the city is determined to proceed with the expansion on the grounds that the present airport will continue as the primary terminal here and that the expanded facilities are needed before a new airport could be completed.

Jim Montgomery's figures in 1969 were amazingly accurate. A new terminal was built at the existing airport. By 1983, with the completion of new runway and plane-parking capacity, it was possible to handle 75 million—the figures predicted for the year 2000. By then, the airlines were employing not 19,000 employees earning more than $150 million a year, as in 1969, but 27,000 at an average salary of $30,000 a year for a total of roughly $810 million. This direct infusion into the Atlanta economy as it moved through the market, buying food and clothing, rent and medicines and automobiles, provided some $3 billion in stimulus to local business.

Outstanding air connections, new hotels, the new stadium, and the new civic center combined to make Atlanta a major convention center. Two massive meetings in 1969 illustrate.

A conclave of 45,000 Jehovah's Witnesses came in July. It was followed by the considerably more boisterous and definitely more bibulous ingathering of some 60,000 American Legionnaires and their wives in August.

Jehovah's Witnesses living in Atlanta opened their hearts and homes to their fellow Witnesses from around the country and the world. The Witnesses carried out their entire program, except for sleeping, at the Atlanta Stadium. Delegates ate, went to school, and practically lived in the stadium for twelve hours a day. Tents housed dramas, Bible group discussions, and other religious programs, but the most noticeable tent was the "Kitchen," under 50,000 square feet.

The mammoth American Legion Convention, assembled in its 51st national session, marched through Atlanta 60,000 strong, delegates and wives. It was the largest convention ever hosted by Atlanta. Speakers included the Legion's National Commander William C. Doyle, of Vineland, New Jersey; Secretary of Defense Melvin Laird; U.S. Air Force Chief of Staff General John D. Ryan; actor Pat O'Brien; astronaut Col. Frank Borman; and George Meany, president of the AFL-CIO. President Richard Nixon received the Legion's Distinguished Service Medal.

During the convention, a granite and bronze monument honoring men who died in World War I, World War II, the Korean War, and the Vietnam War was unveiled at the State Capitol on the Hunter Street side. The memorial was presented to the state by Georgia Legionnaires but was presented on behalf of the national organization by National Commander William C. Doyle as a "memorial to our comrades who have gone before us." Atop the six-foot-high granite monument, which was presented to the Legion in memory of all veterans by the Elberton Granite Associates, Inc. of Elberton, Ga., was a flame that would burn constantly.

"This industry goes like a skyrocket," declared James Hurst, executive vice-president of the Atlanta Convention and Visitors Bureau. He and his compatriots worked hard to build Atlanta as a convention city. There were only six cities with more conventions in 1969—New York, Washington, Miami, Chicago, San Francisco, and Atlantic City. (By 1980 Atlanta would rank third, behind New York and Chicago.)

Hurst noted that Atlanta's convention bureau budget in 1969 was only $125,000, a fraction of the comparable budgets expended by the six cities with more conventions. San Francisco and Miami each spent $1 million annually, the top budget. Some convention bureaus over the country were funded by tax dollars or through local chambers of commerce. Most, like Atlanta's, got their financial backing from local civic and business interests (hotels, banks, air lines).

Those attending conventions spent an estimated $60 million in Atlanta in 1969. But Hurst worried that Atlanta did not have enough square footage of display space to match its bedroom capacity. Atlanta's new Civic Center had only 70,000 square feet, but most cities competing for the top conventions already had 100,000 to 200,000 square feet, Hurst said.

The development of Atlanta as a convention city not only increased passenger plane loadings of the big airlines in and out of Atlanta, it brought national organizations to the city and thousands of business executives flying in and out in their company planes. At Hartsfield, a company calling itself Hangar One handled more general aviation and executive traffic than all other Atlanta aviation companies combined. In a single week companies such as Frito-Lay, Humble Oil, Ford, Alcoa, IT&T, General Acceptance, Johns Manville, North American Van Lines, Container Corporation of America, Burlington Industries, Citizens & Southern National Bank, and West Point–Pepperell flew into Hangar One to drop off executives either to do business in Atlanta or meet connecting flights.

Hangar One was the trademark of Southern Airways Company, which was started in Augusta in 1929 and in 1969 was run by Jess Childress, a pilot of World War II who joined the outfit in 1946 and had what is conceded to be the finest business aircraft terminals in the country.

Childress estimated that 95 percent of Hangar One traffic came from the business sector flying in company-owned planes. They serviced an average of 1,500 aircraft a month, ranging from the small two-seater jobs to large corporate jets. The average day's gasoline volume was between 3,000 and 4,000 gallons. On the day of Martin Luther King, Jr.'s funeral 29,000 gallons were pumped. On that day Richard M. Nixon, the Kennedy families, New York's Gov. Rockefeller, Michigan's Gov. George Romney, Sammy Davis, Jr., and Harry Belafonte all flew into Hangar One.

One of the principal attractions for Atlanta's visiting conventioneers was Underground Atlanta, the historic shopping and entertainment district below the viaducts that was conceived in 1966. The years from 1969 to about 1973 were the peak of its success. In the mid-1980s city planners still dreamed of restoring the glory. A brief account of the rise and fall of Underground follows.

By mid-February 1968 Sen. Culver Kidd and Rep. Rodney Cook and Sen. Ford Spinks, chairman of the Senate Tourism Committee, had considered the Underground area and were pondering the possibility that state aid might be made available for the restoration. Out of their meeting, and others soon to follow, was created Underground Atlanta, Inc., a private company headed by Atlantans Jack Patterson, Steve Fuller, Jr., J. Grant New, and David Cowles. Their first task would be to obtain rights and leases from the owners for the storefronts still standing there and permission to close in open spaces.

The debut of the area as a historic site and a place of entertainment took place informally soon thereafter. On April 16, 1968, the Atlanta Dogwood Festival Association of the Women's Chamber of Commerce, spurred on by chairman Jo Anne Kennedy, held in the Underground area a joyful "Festival of Old Atlanta." By now Patterson, as president of Underground Atlanta, Inc., and Fuller, as vice-president, had begun to spend the $4 million it would cost to restore the heart of the original Atlanta to the look and functions of the city's earliest days. Hariette Speer, as chairman of the 1968 Dogwood Festival, had much to do with arranging the program and with preparing the announcement, which briefly traced the history of the area.

Speer, in her communique "Festival of Old Atlanta," gave a brief summary of the area's history:

Atlanta is beginning to reclaim its past.

A city of skyscrapers, Atlanta has been growing upward so fast that most people have forgotten the gloomy Underground labyrinth sprawled as a monument to the past under the railroad viaducts which progress built over the original streets of a once bustling community.

An opportunity to revisit the past and explore the streets where banks, saloons, and packing houses flourished before the turn of the century is being offered during the Atlanta Dogwood Festival the third week of April.

On Tuesday, April 16, the Atlanta Women's Chamber of Commerce is sponsoring "Festival of Old Atlanta" under the Central Avenue Viaduct, site of a proposed development by private interests to create a permanent tourist attraction.

This is the heart of the city—the dusky birthplace of a railroad terminus which grew into the metropolis of Atlanta.

Atlanta is not an old city, by comparison. It started in 1837 as the eastern Terminus of the Western and Atlantic Railroad which was pushing through to Chattanooga; and the Western Terminus of the Georgia Railroad which would bring adventurous passengers from Augusta and the Atlantic Seaboard.

On December 24, 1842, the streets of Terminus were thronged with wagons and people come to watch the locomotive *Florida* begin its inaugural trip over the new rails to Marietta.

In 1843 Terminus became known as Marthasville, named for the youngest daughter of Governor Wilson Lumpkin. In 1845 the Post Office recognized it as Atlanta—renamed from the Western & Atlantic Railroad—and a city charter was issued in 1847.

Progress changed the shape of the city and eventually lifted nearly all downtown activity from railroad level to the level of steel and concrete bridges. But as late as the mid-1920's, railroad tracks were very much a part of the downtown scene.

The Broad Street overpass was the first one built, in 1852, but more than 40 years elapsed before the second, on Forsyth Street, opened in 1893. Others followed at intervals, and when the Pryor/Central Avenue/Wall Street viaducts were built in 1929, Atlanta's original busy streets were left to the silence of a twilight world, knowing only the rumble of present-day delivery trucks which still come and go from Underground warehouses.

Early in the 1870's, old Whitehall, Alabama, and Pryor Streets down by the tracks were the boundaries of a lively open area known as Humbug Square which attracted a continuous stream of carnivals, medicine shows, and circuses.

If streets and buildings could talk, 1968's "Festival of Old Atlanta," in the same general area, would evoke nostalgic sighs from cobblestones which have long been covered with cement; and from peeling, barricaded store fronts which received the cream of Atlanta's society through ornate doorways.

At 10:00 A.M. on April 16, Underground Atlanta streets will once again glow with the soft light of gas lamps, provided for the day by the Atlanta Gas Light Company. Antique automobiles (from the Southeastern Region Antique Automobile Club of America) will be parked in front of crumbling granite arches which once adorned impressive entrances of Atlanta's bustling businesses.

Pretty girls in antebellum dresses will distribute old-fashioned handbills about Atlanta's history, and direct visitors past the Georgia Railroad Freight Depot (oldest building in Atlanta, built in 1869), beyond the old Lowry Bank (forerunner of First National and the Trust Company of Georgia) to a series of historical exhibits. There will be old telephones from Southern Bell Telephone and Telegraph Company, dolls from Lila Benton Doll Hospital and the president of the Atlanta Doll Club, firearms from the Georgia Arms Collectors Association, photographs from the Atlanta Historical Society, money and Confederate postage stamps. The city's Parks and Recreation Department will demonstrate old skills such as weaving. And a model four-car open platform train and locomotive from the Railroad Model Club of Atlanta will remind viewers of Atlanta's long-time importance as a transportation center.

Kenney's Alley, the picturesque sunlit cobblestoned passageway crossing old Pryor Street south of Alabama, will be Artists' Row. There will be paintings on exhibit, and artists from the Atlanta Artists Club will sketch and entertain visitors.

A carnival atmosphere will prevail all day. An ornamental band wagon, made before the turn of the century and loaned by Starr's Musical Museum at Stone Mountain, will ring out sentimental melodies. And there will be corn dogs, cotton candy, Coca-Cola, popcorn, ferris wheel for small children, and old movies (Charlie Chaplin vintage, courtesy of Ruby Red's Warehouse).[4]

The reaction of those who went underground to see the spruced up old storefronts, banks, shops, and saloons was such that Atlanta Underground, Inc., backers were convinced they had a gold mine here. They pushed on with its development, putting some $4 million into the project of restoration, and then hired the prestigious Atlanta architectural firm of Jova, Daniels/Busby to see to it that the mood and look of the old city were restored. By June of 1969, 22 charter tenants had signed leases, and Patterson and Fuller confidently expected that within three years there would be 150 businesses at work in Underground Atlanta.

So, there came into being a place of history combined with commerce. In mid-winter of 1969–70 William A. Evans, writing in *Southern Scene*, a magazine of Southern Airways, devoted half a dozen pages of text and pictures to the Underground as it existed then, and as it soon would be. In addition to the shops, boutiques, saloons, and playhouses, he described Grandma's Biscuit

Shop, Burning of Atlanta Bar, and Sergeant Pepper's, a modern discotheque, where young folk who knew little about General Sherman and cared less could dance and drink the night away; or the Mad Hatter, where, in a splash of color, they danced to hard rock bands. But there were many others worthy of attention, Evans pointed out. Among them there were three shops and three museums which call for special attention. "The first of the shops is the Knit Wit, whose specialty is knit clothing for both men and women. The second is The Humbug, named for its location in the 19th century Square, which stocks old-fashioned gifts, many with individual historical implications. The third shop in this group is the First Edition, a book shop in a Victorian library setting. It offers many volumes, old, new, and rare." He continued:

The three museums will attract men and women and youngsters, all who like to examine the paraphernalia of by-gone days. The Phoenix is an old print shop furnished with a unique display of antique printing devices and machines. (Run by ex-advertising man C. Worth Kendrick, it sells press proofs of old, almost forgotten, comic strips, and will set the visitor's name in ancient wooden type faces.) The Phoenix and the Musical Museum, the second of the group, can keep one mesmerized for hours. The Musical Museum is a rarity with its large collection of musical machines—player pianos, calliopes, and whole-band instruments. The third museum is Major Fellow's Battlerama, a historical display of Civil War sights and sounds.

Even if the visitor does not find a shop or store or restaurant or saloon to interest him, he surely can pass some pleasant hours wandering around the softly illuminated area, marveling at the gaslighted architecture and imaginatively making himself a part of the romantic, often tragic, history of old Atlanta. If his imagination is intensely active, he can supplement the scenes of *Gone with the Wind* or step back into the dead days when Atlanta was a busy railroad town and its people were so much like today's Atlantans, always busy and sometimes bawdy, but proud of a rich heritage.

But, of course, Underground Atlanta is not yet what it will be. When it is entirely rejuvenated, it will be a bustling community, drawing thousands of people into its viaduct-umbrellaed streets and businesses. It lies within a stone's throw of Five Points, Atlanta Stadium, the government complex, and many of the city's prominent hotels.

And soon it did become "a bustling community" drawing thousands of people from all over the nation, tourists just passing through en route to and from Florida, and conventioneers in ever-growing numbers. In *Southern Living* magazine of February 1973, Caleb Pirtle III was writing of what had happened in the six years since two young Tech graduates, Jack Patterson and Steve Fuller, joined with David Cowles to bring back to Underground Atlanta the gaslight glow of its early days.

Said Pirtle: "Beneath the viaducts of Atlanta comes the sound of music and good times, drifting upward from restaurants, boutiques and dance halls that line the original streets of the city. And Jack Patterson summed up what had happened: 'We preserved a piece of working history. It's not a cold museum. It's full of life, with money changing hands. It's become a vital part of the Atlanta economy. The business volume here approaches $100 per square foot.'"

In 1973 Underground Atlanta did flourish. Among its 80-odd shops, stores, and saloons were places that appealed to everyone. The Mad Hatter, which was "Wild, primitive and successful, . . . frenzied, frantic and popular," charged $3.00 to dance to rock bands under psychedelic lights on its 2,000 square-foot light dance floor. It opened the night the state legislature dropped the drinking age in Georgia from twenty-one to eighteen. So to be sure its prices fit the teenagers' pocketbooks, on Wednesday nights it charged only a penny for a glass of beer and a quarter for a mixed drink.

By contrast, Pirtle found The Bucket Shop to be a "meeting place, quiet and informal," with no music to distract the patron who might like to sip his drink while studying the Dow-Jones averages, which were posted every hour on a bulletin board.

The Chimeric Theater attracted still another type—the visitor who came to Underground not to dance or drink, but to spend thirty-three minutes looking at scenes of Old Atlanta flashed before him by three Cinerama projectors, thirty slide projectors, three special effects projectors, and a myriad of lighting effects. As its creator said, "it gives the audience the startlingly vivid impression it is eavesdropping on history."

Observers also were seeing in this parade of history a forecast of what soon would happen to Underground—a revival of the rowdy old Humbug Square. This change, of course, did not come all at once. In the *National Observer* of January 25, 1971, Atlanta writer Stephen Green described what Underground had become, and much, but not all, of what he saw pleased him very much.

"In less than three years," he wrote, "investors have turned a forgotten cellar of Atlanta into a swinging collection of restaurants, cabarets, boutiques, a theatre, and 'schlock' shops." These shops, he noted, "carry the usual assortment of overpriced imports, leather goods, modish clothing, and Zodiac-related trash." Green interviewed a bartender at Ruby Red's Warehouse, who had almost bought a pair of "genuine Navajo Moccasins" at one of these shops, until he discovered they were marked "Made in Japan." The bartender assured him that Atlanta residents did not patronize these shops, which offered overpriced and inferior goods. The locals came to Underground to hear the music and to eat. "It's the tourists," the bartender told Green, "that get caught in the shops."

Several of Underground's nineteen restaurants and saloons, Green discovered, did offer distinguished dining and entertainment at reasonable prices. Two of them which he particularly favored were Dante's Down the Hatch, a night club featuring fondues and possibly the biggest wine cellar in

Atlanta. Another was the Chessboard, owned by Anita and Irving Chess, whose fixed price for a formal dinner was $12.00.

Like all students of Atlanta's history, Green was aware of the reputation of that area of Underground known in the 1870s as Humbug Square. In 1973, however, he said that in this area there were no go-go girls or strip joints, B-girls or hustlers. The area also had some of the lowest crime rates in America, and parking areas were both lighted and patrolled.

This happy situation, however, did not long prevail. By 1973 the railroads still operating through the area were causing problems. It will be remembered that Underground came into being because the people working around the Zero Mile Post built viaducts above the tracks and moved the entrances to their ground-level stores to the second levels. Now, the L&N Railroad was threatening to put a fence along one entrance so that Underground revelers would not walk into the path of a moving train. Since many Atlantans came across the tracks to eat their lunch, this would put several restaurants, including Grandma's Biscuits, out of business. Also, it was learned in March of 1973 that MARTA planned to take one set of tracks for a rapid transit line connecting the main MARTA station near Underground. The squabble between the railroads and the Underground continued for more than a year, with fewer and fewer people coming to Underground, and more and more businesses there beginning to lose money. There were many other reasons that Underground was starting to lose its popularity.

The newspapers reported:

The first club in the underground, Ruby Red's Warehouse, will probably be forced to move from the area by MARTA's plans. Others such as the Mine Shaft and the Blarney Stone also must decide to relocate in the underground or move elsewhere. . . .

On a good night, thousands of milling, drinkswilling fun-seekers wind their way down cobblestone streets and narrow corridors amid a complex of 17 bars and clubs, 20 restaurants and eateries and 28 shops and boutiques.

But the crowds are not always so large as in the early heydays, especially on week nights. Underground Atlanta, Inc. (UAI), the firm that owns or controls the properties and then leases them to the tenants of 90% of the businesses considered to be underground, is in deep financial trouble.

The Underground's problems have been mounting for several years. Some believe that initial success led UAI to try to expand too fast, which drained its resources, forced it to seek rescue financing.

As time went by, the local and return trade declined.

"Maybe we became famous too fast," said one observer. "When Atlantans saw how tourists and visitors flocked there, they thought the Underground was a tourist-trap, a ripoff."

And then came MARTA with its right-of-way plans, which UAI says have led to delays and indecision.

"MARTA pushed us from a financial bind to a crucial financial bind," said UAI marketing director Peter Gordy, . . .

The fact that the Underground attraction to Atlantans has declined has many reasons: The novelty is wearing off, the idea that the area has become Honkey-tonk, a tourist trap, the fear of being mugged, the idea that many of the better known and original nightspots have failed or moved out, competition from the city's increasingly sophisticated entertainment world, and inflation's pinch on the average man's leisure expense allotment.

Fencing the area and charging a 25¢ entry fee failed to save the area, and by 1981 it was dead. Even Dante Stephenson's Down the Hatch club had moved to the Lenox Square area and closed its Underground location.

In the *Journal* Ron Hudspeth brought back the image of Underground's good years with a recital of the memories he shared with so many other Atlantans of the late sixties and the seventies:

I really hate to see Underground croak. I feel like I owned a piece of that rock. I'm certain I'm not alone.

Underground was a phenomenon. It lived, but a phenomenon just the same. In its heyday, which lasted only a couple short years in the early 70's, it outstripped New Orleans' Bourbon Street and Chicago's Rush Street for fun and class.

This week they snuff out Underground's gas street lights for good. There's no one to pay the bills. The place has been dying for years. So long, in fact, I'm glad the mercy killing has finally arrived.

Now, there will be only memories. But, oh, what memories for anyone who knew Underground Atlanta in its glorious zenith.

At its height, around 1972, Underground was all things to all people. Families loved it. Singles loved it. Maybe that accounts for the diverse popularity of a place like Muhlenbrink's located near Underground's entrance.

One night the entire cast of "The Waltons" arrived to party. Contrast John-Boy and Co., with the evening Gregg Allman showed up with Cher. Gregg drank his Chivas Scotch mixed with liquid Coke and then disappeared into the bathroom to snort the powdered variety.

The partying became so profuse in those days that the joke around Atlanta was the Legislature was about to change the divorce laws to make the grounds adultery, incompatibility and Underground.

The club's names—P. J. Kenney's, The Bucket Shop, Blarney Stone, Bank Note, Ruby Red's, The Palace, Scarlett O'Hara's, Down the Hatch— provide special memories.

Sometimes old Alabama Street was so crowded it was a Peachtree Mardi Gras. Recall the monkey and his vendor? A friend was enticed one evening to give that little monkey a $20 bill. "He'll give you change," insisted a by-stander. The monkey hasn't been seen since.

Out of Underground came musical acts ranging from Banks & Shane, now Atlanta traditions, to the late Cortez Greer, who quite possibly would have hit the big time had he not tragically died.

And why did it all fade so quickly? And why, despite thousands and thousands of dollars in studies and the total efforts of folks like Dante Stephensen, cannot Underground be revived?

Underground faded for a number of reasons and you've probably heard most. A false fear of crime, inconvenient and over-priced parking, watered-down drinks and cover charges instituted by unscrupulous proprietors attempting to ride the gravy train.

All those possibly had a bearing on Underground's demise, but more than anything else it was a victim of the times.

When Underground peaked in the early '70's, Atlanta was a much different place. DeKalb and Cobb were dry and almost void of nice restaurants. Interstate 285 was barely completed and not yet dotted with Steak & Ales, fast food chains and neighborhood pubs.

Underground was not only *the* place, it was the only place.

Many of those using the airport and occupying the new office parks and downtown skyscrapers desired and could afford expensive housing, and articles in *Atlanta* magazine indicated that Atlanta had plenty of fine houses to offer. "Within the city limits of Atlanta last year more than 530 new homes were built at an average price of less than $20,000. But in some areas of the city, and in many areas of Great Atlanta's Metropolitan Area, homes costing $45,000 and much more were being constructed in what seems to be unceasing abundance."

Not all high-priced homes were located in the traditionally posh West Paces Ferry and Habersham areas. In fact, the most expensive new subdivisions were being developed outside the city limits—far out in the northern limits of Fulton County, across the Chattahoochee River near Roswell and into Cobb County. These homes were not the homes of Atlanta's "establishment," but they were just as expensive. For example, there was speculative building in one of the new subdivisions on the banks of the Chattahoochee that brought $125,000 homes to market. In another northside development several homes sold for more than $100,000—all of them speculative homes. Houses priced in the $70,000-to-$80,000 range were regularly sold in another development north of Sandy Springs on the Chattahoochee. One writer noted:

A recent survey of such neighborhoods in the Atlanta area revealed nearly fifty areas—old and new—where houses began at $45,000 or over. Included in the list are such older areas as Ansley Park, where only a portion of the homes fit this range. But with the trend of renovating going on in Ansley Park, any of the older homes are potentially worth $45,000 or more when rebuilt and rescued from the termites. Also included are the "establishment" areas of Tuxedo Park (that plush area north of West Paces Ferry Road between Habersham and Northside Parkway) where $45,000 would not make a down payment on many of the fine homes.

Older areas notwithstanding, most of the high-priced new building is going on farther out—in such subdivisions as Winterthur, Rivermeade, Whitewater Creek, Rivershore Estates, and North Harbor. They are being developed by a number of companies—Spratlin & Associates, Goodsell Properties, Inc., Chathambilt Homes, Inc., Bob Johnson Homes, Inc., and others. These developments are all in the northern half of the Greater Atlanta Area. Scattered homes in the $50,000 range can be found all over the Atlanta area, but only in the northwest section of Atlanta and Fulton County is there a plethora of such residences.

Most of the new building is in Fulton County outside the Atlanta city limits. DeKalb County has only a few—Victoria Estates near Emory University, and Cambridge Park, the Cousins Properties, Inc., development near the Peachtree Country Club, to mention a couple.

The bulk of Atlanta's high-priced residential real estate, then, is in the posh northwest side, west of Roswell and Peachtree roads and east of Interstate 75 between Atlanta and Marietta. This area does not include Tuxedo Park or the Nancy Creek section which have long been the bastions of wealth and prestige in Atlanta. A new group of wealthy young families is springing up to meld with traditional Atlanta society. There are the corporate executives. They may not be presidents of their firms, but they are vice presidents, treasurers, and directors who pull down handsome salaries and bonuses. They are doctors and dentists whose hours are filled with patients and whose pocketbooks and bank account are filled with cash. They are the innovators—men who came to Atlanta with an idea and a little cash and "made it big." They don't mean much to the old-timers whose daddies and granddaddies fit the same categories fifty or a hundred years ago; but by the same token, the old-timers don't mean much to the new breed, either.

To real estate appraisers, addresses such as Camden Road (extension), Hawick Drive, Rivermeade Drive, Hanover West Drive, Christophers Walk, Wyngate, Arden-at-Argonne, Sentinel Post Road, Paran Valley Court, Londonberry Road, Glencastle Drive, Long Island Drive, Winterthur Drive, and Rilman Road mean as much today as West Paces Ferry, Tuxedo, Habersham, or Blackland. These streets, plus some twenty-five others, are where the homes start at $45,000 or more—usually more.

With this many expensive homes being built and sold, a logical question is "who buys them?" The answer in Atlanta is "no particular group." About the only thing the buyers have in common is a desire for an expensive home and the ability to pay for one. In Winterthur, the Spratlin development where homes range between $90,000 and $500,000, for example, the buyers so far have included a doctor, a manufacturer, an airline pilot, and the financial vice president of a large, locally based company.

A recent Spratlin analysis of the northside Atlanta housing market revealed that the "average" buyer of a home in the $40,000 and above range was between forty and fifty-five, with two teen-aged children and perhaps an in-law living with them. About 40% of these buyers were new-comers to Atlanta, while the other 60% were moving up from a smaller house in the city. Incomes ranged from $20,000 up, and these people expect to live in Atlanta for a long time, if not permanently. These families "appreciate quality and location more than just space . . ." the survey says, and they are "usually quite definite about what they want."

Appraiser Reynolds Couch of the firm of Wight, Couch and Ward, attributes the expanding market for $45,000-and-up homes to the "great affluence of the corporate executive. These men are brought in from somewhere else. They don't want to try and crack the 'establishment' in Habersham. They are not really accepted in West Wesley. They have no desire to live with the old guard, so they go out a little farther, but pay the same as they would have paid in Tuxedo Park or somewhere else close in." . . .

Adding to the cost is the special equipment found in most of today's higher-priced homes. Nearly all these homes have air conditioning and many have carpets over hardwood floors. Kitchen equipment is better and more expensive. Garages are no longer just a shelter for the one family car. They now must provide for two and even three cars, plus storage space for tools and such. Dens, family rooms, playrooms, offices, and libraries all tack extra dollars onto the selling price. While basements are not considered "living area" they are important.[5]

At the other end of the housing spectrum, many Atlantans lived in homes barely adequate or worse. Public housing tenants complained of unruly youths and of rats and pigeons. Neighborhood groups in Vine City staged a massive clean-up effort with help from the city and from C&S Bank. "This is the spirit that built this country," C&S head Mills B. Lane commented. "All the money in the world can't build a model city. It takes people. This is just wonderful."

Atlanta's ghetto housing was much in the news and on the minds of concerned citizens throughout the spring of 1969. Nineteen young Atlantans, chosen as The Outstanding Young People in Atlanta—TOYPA for short—decided that their first project would be a tour of Atlanta's slums, and the production of an original motion picture explaining the problems of the poverty areas. Their tour, sponsored by Economic Opportunity Atlanta, took them to Grady Homes, Wheat Street, Buttermilk Bottom, Cabbagetown, and Reynoldstown. They saw much that had been done to improve the lot of Atlanta's poor—and much that needed doing. In Buttermilk Bottom, just behind the Atlanta Civic Center, for example, sixty-five prefabricated houses were being prepared for people displaced by urban renewal in that area.

In DeKalb County, in a unique arrangement between private and public money, the first of 350 applicants moved into low-cost housing units in Decatur. The *Constitution* reported:

> Last week ten families hauled their belongings into Gateway Manor, a project being built on six acres of urban renewal land.
>
> Their finished brick veneer, all-electric apartments of one to three bedrooms sit in rows on a landscaped area, while across the street construction goes on.
>
> Rent on the units, which have such "luxuries" as air-conditioning and private patios, is scaled, according to ability to pay.
>
> The new residents are living in a development owned by private interests, but leased by public authorities.
>
> Decatur Savings and Loan Association, which purchased the property, will lease the full 111 housing units to the federally-financed Decatur Housing Authority as soon as construction is finished this fall. Until that time, applicants will move in as space becomes available.

New legislation and a changing public mood made 1969 an important year in the move toward racially integrated housing in Atlanta and the nation. *Journal* business writer Tom Walker explained:

> Open housing for all races is not just the black man's problem in Atlanta, it is a citizen's problem for all, says the president of an organization of black real estate brokers in Atlanta. . . .
>
> Theme of the board [Empire Real Estate Board] is "democracy in housing," a goal which has come at least within legal reach since the Fair Housing Act of 1968 and a subsequent U.S. Supreme Court ruling that had the same effect: To make racial discrimination in the sale and renting of houses and apartments illegal.
>
> While the legal barriers are down, others remain, and Thorpe has no illusions about the continued resistance which black brokers will have in their efforts to implement open housing.
>
> The housing pattern in Atlanta follows what has become a classic pattern: white families have moved (or are moving) from the core of the city, mainly as a result of inner city commercial and industrial encroachment into one-time all-residential neighborhoods.
>
> Into the houses vacated by white families—houses often in the early stages of deterioration—move Negro families. And in many instances, more than one family will move into a previously single-family dwelling, accelerating the deterioration of those houses.
>
> Thus is created a slum which spreads outward until it is stopped through a program such as urban renewal. Not every neighborhood becomes a slum, of course. Many, such as the Cascade Heights area of Southwest Atlanta, are communities of fine homes that rival the best in the city.
>
> For some, the exodus into the suburbs is to avoid living in an integrated

neighborhood, and Thorpe believes the only way to stop the exodus from the city is to open all sections of metro Atlanta to all families, regardless of race.

The alternative, said Thorpe, is the gradual creation of an all-black city of Atlanta, surrounded by all-white suburban neighborhoods occupied by people who live out and work in. The black population meanwhile would consist largely of persons who live in but work out.

"Locating (black) people will require a lot of cooperation from fair housing groups," said Thorpe. This will involve convincing the seller that if he has a dwelling to put on the market, he must make it available to anyone who is prepared to buy, white or black.

Black brokers and salesmen have traditionally been confined to helping black families find homes, but they are equally capable of serving the white community, Thorpe said.

In fact, as long as the Negro real estate broker is limited to black families as his clientele, "we'll have only a limited growth potential" as a business, Thorpe explained.

The Empire Real Estate Board which Thorpe heads is a professional organization of Negro brokers who wanted to have a vehicle to lobby for their goals and objectives. The Empire Board was organized in 1939 by seven brokers. Now 22 companies are members or allied members.

The Empire Board is affiliated with a national organization, the National Association of Real Estate Brokers, which was organized in 1948 to offset, as the association declared at that time, "a system which perpetuated segregation in housing at every level of our government."

The National Association of Real Estate Brokers is the black counterpart of the National Association of Real Estate Boards, the latter being an association of real estate boards which, in the South at least, have been all-white organizations for the most part.

The Atlanta Real Estate Board, largest in Georgia, integrated for the first time this year when Wilson Realty Co. was admitted to membership. The head of this company, J. R. Wilson, was one of the charter members of the Empire Board although his firm is not in the Empire Board now.

The Empire Board has been active in civil rights outside the strictly real estate business. For example, the board paid the bond for Negroes arrested during lunch counter sit-ins in 1960 and holds one of the oldest licenses of the National Association for the Advancement of Colored People.

The board financed the legal fight that led to the breakdown of the so-called "Atlanta wall" in the early 1960s—a wall put up in an effort to stop the movement of Negro families into Southwest Atlanta white neighborhoods. The board also was one of the first major contributors to the Southern Christian Leadership Conference, the organization founded by the late Dr. Martin Luther King, Jr.

Would members of the Empire Board be in favor of merging the board with the Atlanta Real Estate Board or some other metro Atlanta association of Realtors?

"Not any time soon," said Thorpe.

"There has been no great exodus of blacks out of the Empire Real Estate Board to the Atlanta Board, and there won't be," said Thorpe.

"If that should happen," Thorpe added, "blacks might dissolve themselves in a white group and lose their identity and effectiveness . . . You need black organizations that can afford to speak out, that challenge injustice."

Though since the advent of the open housing law, a black prospective home buyer could make a court case out of discrimination, no massive assault on white suburbia had yet occurred, according to research conducted in 1969 by the Owens-Corning Fiberglass Corporation and *House and Home* magazine. "This is mainly because black families, though inconvenienced by their present housing in many cases, feel more comfortable with other families who share their problems and heritage. But," the researchers concluded, "it won't be too much longer before Negro families form a massive surge that will put additional pressure on the demands for housing."

Walker noted other important changes in the Atlanta housing pattern. Throughout the nation in the 1960s, there had been an upswing in apartment building and a decline in the construction of single-family homes. The upsurge in apartment building, said Walker, reflected a demographic change—a shift in the age distribution of the nation's adult population.

In spite of tight money in steadily rising mortgage interest rates, Walker pointed out, the period between April 1, 1968, and April 1, 1969, was the peak in residential construction during the 1960s. In Atlanta 22,132 residential units were constructed, more than half of which were apartments.

Many black Atlantans could afford fine housing and other signs of affluence. Atlanta had been the center of black capitalism for many years, long enough to have second- and third-generation wealth in many families.

Norris B. Herndon, one of the wealthiest Negroes in America, headed the insurance company his father founded. A multimillionaire, his colonnaded home in the Atlanta University area was a showplace in northwest Atlanta. Another wealthy black was L. D. Milton, president of the Citizens Trust, a black bank. His bank was building a new twelve-story headquarters. He borrowed $3.5 million construction money from four white Atlanta banks, and a "white" insurance company took over the long-term financing. Milton, Virginia-born and the son of a slave, had the confidence of Atlanta bankers from the beginning. He grew up in Washington, D.C., graduated from an Ivy League school (Brown University at Providence, R.I.) and came to Atlanta in the fall of 1920 to teach at Morehouse College. His first business venture was the purchase—with his friend Clayton R. Yates, another ambitious young Negro—of a bankrupt drugstore on Auburn Avenue. They expanded this into five stores, and the Yates-Milton team had been a famous leader in the Atlanta black community ever since. They bought the shaky Citizens Trust with $330,000 borrowed, with the backing of Ryburn Clay, president of Fulton National Bank. By 1969, Citizens Trust's assets had reached $20 million. Milton was president; Yates, chairman of the board of Citizens Trust and of another Auburn Avenue financial institution, Mutual Federal Savings and Loan Association.

J. B. Blayton, president of Mutual Federal, was another highly successful black businessman. In 1925 he and fourteen other black investors put $100 each into founding the savings and loan association, and its assets reached $9.7 million by 1969. By contrast, a white savings and loan organization founded about the same time now pays out that much in annual dividends. White companies, Blayton noted, draw business from both white and black men. Black-owned businesses have very few white customers, which limits their growth.

This did not apply to the Paschal brothers, James and Robert. At La-Carousel, the night club they operated, 65 percent of those who came to eat, drink, and listen to big-time jazz bands were white. When they borrowed a million dollars from Citizens Trust and Atlanta Life to build a motor hotel adjacent to LaCarousel, it was the largest Negro-to-Negro financial transaction in Atlanta's history.

The Paschal brothers' humble beginning, as shoe-shine boys, paper carriers, door-to-door cosmetic salesmen, and finally, restaurant, night club, and motel operators, was far different from that of Norris B. Herndon.

Herndon, one of the richest men in Atlanta of any race, inherited wealth from his father, Alonzo F. Herndon, a former slave who came to Atlanta from Social Circle to establish one of the world's finest barbershops and then founded the Atlanta Life Insurance Company. His wealth in 1969 was estimated at $15 million; his insurance company had assets of $70 million. He contributed heavily to Negro colleges and causes, including civil rights organizations. He left the day-by-day management of the insurance company to Eugene M. Martin, a native of Atlanta who had attended Atlanta University.

Though black-owned Atlanta Life Insurance Company will happily sell policies to anyone, in 1969 it had no white policy holders to speak of, and only two non-Negro employees—one of them a Chinese.

Despite the successes cited here, white aversion to doing business with Negro owners had made it extremely difficult for the black businessman in Atlanta in the past. Sixty-year-old W. L. Calloway, one of Atlanta's leading Negro real estate men, recalled threats from antiblack clubs like the Columbians, the burning of houses he had bought for resale, and the difficulty in getting financing. This last difficulty was finally overcome when Mills Lane began providing financing for Negro developments.

One black Atlanta businessman, however, had considerable success working for or with whites in Atlanta and throughout the South. Herman

Jerome Russell, born in Atlanta's Summerhill slum section in 1930, grew up to become a plasterer, then a plastering contractor, and by 1969 he was one of the hottest success stories in the Negro business world as a builder of apartment complexes, nursing homes, and shopping centers. He did not forget his beginnings as a plasterer, however. Beside his desk in his Fair Street office were blueprints of jobs in which he was the plaster subcontractor. Among them were Phipps Plaza, the Equitable Building, the University Hospital in Augusta, a building at the University of Georgia in Athens, and the Peachtree-Fourteenth Street complex. Over 99 percent of his business was from the white market, and of his 250 employees, 25 percent were white.

Several incidents and developments marked the changing racial relationships of Atlanta in this last year of the 1960s. Martin Luther King, Sr., Atlanta pastor and father of the slain civil rights leader, was made the first Negro foreman of a Fulton County Grand Jury. Names of the new jury were drawn from a box prepared by the previous county grand jury, and of the twenty-three members, fourteen were Negroes, the largest number court officials could remember ever being named to serve on the jury here. They immediately named Dr. King their foreman.

Black business, not big banking, insurance, and real estate operations as cited earlier, but small operations, was the subject of efforts in the beginning of the year. The Southern Christian Leadership Conference had opened a state office on Auburn Avenue. There a people's cooperative would be aimed at establishing and maintaining black business, beginning with the buying and selling of wholesale groceries as a part of the project until a Negro grocery business could be started. At about the same time more than two hundred persons gathered on the Atlanta University campus to discuss how blacks could enter the business community. Sponsors included the Atlanta Community Relations Council, and the principal speaker was Chamber of Commerce President Frank Carter. Carter urged that established Atlanta businessmen should cooperate with the fledgling black capitalists' ventures, helping them through the early stages of development. Accountants and bankers should be especially helpful, Carter indicated, for starting a new business in Atlanta was an expensive proposition—ranging from $218,000 for a housing development to $1,800 for a janitorial service.

Not only in business, but in the arts, Negroes were having a growing influence in Atlanta. The naming of black leaders to the Atlanta Arts Alliance was part of a determined effort to extend the benefits of the arts into all segments of the community.

Not all Atlanta organizations in 1969 were as willing to accept black members as was the Arts Alliance, however. Attorney Maynard Jackson, candidate for vice-mayor, and state representative William H. Alexander were rejected when their names were offered for membership in the exclusive Atlanta Lawyers' Club. Ten "no" votes were sufficient to keep out a prospective member. The rejection of Jackson and Alexander seemed the greatest rift in in the civic membership since the 1950s, when a law school dean was re-buffed by a group of his former students.

DeWitt Smith, a black police officer who reported that he saw white officers beating black prisoners, also found himself in trouble and was reportedly expelled by the Fraternal Order of Police for violating his fraternal oath by calling a press conference to report the beating.

Two black dignitaries stopped over in Atlanta in this year. Carl Stokes of Cleveland, first black mayor of a major American city, came in early May to attack the Vietnam war effort and to plead that those billions be spent in the rebuilding of American cities, "to respond to the need of poor blacks, poor whites, and the elderly."

The most noted black visitor of the year, however, was Emperor Haile Selassie I, King of Kings for 24 million Ethiopians, who visited Atlanta on July 10 to lay a wreath on the grave of Dr. Martin Luther King, Jr. "Unsheltered beneath a blazing sun, the 76-year old monarch gently laid a wreath, red and yellow carnations, on King's tomb in South View Cemetery. He then moved by motorcade to Morehouse College, King's Alma Mater, where he received an honorary degree. . . . In his address before 2,200 in the school gymnasium at Morehouse, the Emperor described King as 'a man who struggled to the bitter end for the rights of his people, a man who believed in equality and justice for all men . . . we regard him as a citizen of the world.'"

Atlanta, too, in the year after King's death, began to realize the depth of his influence, in the nation and the world, and Selassie's visit was only one of many tributes to him. The *Journal-Constitution* reported another one. "Dr. Martin Luther King, Jr. received tribute in death that never was accorded him in life when the Georgia Legislature convened and some of those closest to the slain civil rights leader were introduced on the Senate floor. Among those presented by Senator Leroy Johnson, Georgia's first black senator in modern times, were Dr. King, Sr., Mrs. Rosa Parks, whose refusal to step to the rear of a bus set off the Montgomery bus boycott and Dr. Horace Ward, of Atlanta, the Senate's only other Negro member. The event would have been King's 40th birthday." Shortly thereafter the Atlanta Diocese of the Episcopal Church designated that the birthday—January 15—be observed with the Feast of a Martyr. The Council of the Diocese also recommended that King's birthday be designated as a state and national observance.

Honors continued throughout the year. On the afternoon of October 19 the newly organized Martin Luther King, Jr., library was opened at 671 Beckwith Street SW. The library, intended mainly for research, contained 1,500 books and many historic documents dealing with the civil rights movement and the whole spectrum of black history.

For Dr. Martin Luther King, Sr., the year was one of recurring tragedy. Martin Luther King, Jr., had been assassinated in Memphis on April 4, 1968. Another son, A. D. King, who served with the elder King as minister at

Ebenezer Baptist Church, was found dead in the swimming pool at his home in late July of 1969. He drowned while taking a late-night dip.

Many educational institutions celebrated anniversaries or other notable developments in 1969. One of Atlanta's most prestigious schools reached a sort of sixtieth birthday. Westminster was formed during the Korean War by Dr. William L. Pressly, president, who came to Atlanta from Chattanooga, where he had been headmaster of McCallie School. The new institution was the reincarnation of a school established in 1909 as North Avenue Presbyterian Church's Day School. Within two years, Westminster absorbed by merger the Washington Seminary, which had long been Atlanta's leading private school for girls. The new Westminster opened with an enrollment of 240, a faculty of eighteen, and a budget of $75,000. Its budget for 1969 was $1.65 million, its faculty, 168. Its library had 20,000 volumes; there were fifteen buildings valued at $7 million, a 1,400-seat chapel auditorium, and a new gymnasium. Westminster laid strong emphasis on athletics, believing that competitive sports as well as quality classroom work were essential to complete education. The school had an endowment of $1,538,341, and by acquiring the former Fritz Orr Day Camp, adjacent to the campus, it acquired valuable acreage in the Northside's most exclusive residential section, a form of endowment in itself.

An *Atlanta Journal* feature described the school and Dr. Pressly:

More than 2,000 students of the school area are scattered now around the world, concentrated mainly in the Atlanta region. When the Bobbies, Susies or Jims happen to meet their former prexy they discover he not only remembers them, but knows indeed how much momentum they have developed in life. He knows what they are doing, where they are living, who they have married, the names and ages of their children. . . .

Westminster's rules of behavior have always been strict. There was a long time when students were summarily expelled if it became known they had partaken of spirituous liquor in any shape, at any place, under any circumstances, including their own homes with their own parents. Though standards continue to be taut, this stricture as well as others has now been ameliorated. Westminster is letting parents themselves assume responsibility for their teen-agers' actions. . . .

Westminster integrated its student body in 1965 without incident and without lowering its stiff entrance examination requirements. Now black students, who number fewer than twenty, rank scholastically and athletically with their fellows and are apparently at ease in the atmosphere of the school.

The assassination of Dr. Martin Luther King was keenly felt. For weeks, groups met spontaneously and informally to discuss the meaning of the murder, and their responsibilities in social change. . . .

Westminster is billed firmly as a Christian school. Two full years of Bible study, including both Old and New Testaments, are required for graduation. Daily prayers, scripture readings, weekly chapel services and a spiritual emphasis week twice yearly are scheduled. The school's motto is biblical: "And Jesus increased in wisdom and stature and in favor of God and man." A year ago Dr. William Holmes Borders, Negro pastor of the Wheat Street Baptist Church, was leader for spiritual emphasis week. Plans have been made for a similar visit from the Reverend M. L. King. . . .

On January 6 ground was broken for a new $2 million library and academic building at Clark College. The three-story, fully air-conditioned building would house the college's science, mathematics, and foreign language departments, and construction was to take about one year.

On the negative side, the destruction of Atlanta's Clark Howell School by fire was a critical loss to blind children, not only in Atlanta, but all over the nation. Destroyed in the blaze was one of the best collections of Braille and large-print books in the country, about 14,000 volumes. The library served not only the blind children of Atlanta but was available to other Braille libraries. The 14,000 volumes represented hundreds of tedious hours of work by volunteers who were trained to copy books into Braille. They were considered irreplaceable by Atlanta school officials.

A directive from the federal Health, Education and Welfare Department called for the complete desegregation of Fulton County schools. "In an angry and fighting mood, Fulton County Superintendent Paul D. West declared he would not submit to federal officials by the May 2 deadline to end operation of racially separate high schools in College Park." West met in Washington with Fifth District Rep. Fletcher Thompson and agreed "not to accede to any threats or intimidations to abandon the neighborhood school concept in order to achieve integration." Charging that HEW officials were trying to "intimidate" the county board, West said the trouble stemmed from "the Johnson administration dying with all its fangs showing." West further believed that the Nixon administration would not abandon the neighborhood school idea.

In the middle of summer the Fulton County Board of Education acceded to the school desegregation demands of HEW by voting to close the all-black Eva Thomas High School in College Park. Early in July, Fulton County presented a plan for the desegregation of two College Park high schools. The plan called for assignment of 36 white children to the Eva Thomas School, which had 262 Negro students. According to the letter from HEW, Eva Thomas School must have at least 25 percent white students. Dr. West said that it was "the practical truth" that white parents "just aren't going to send their children down in the middle of a black community to school."

HEW stated that no plan would be acceptable unless it achieved a "racial balance" in Eva Thomas School and College Park High School. West said that the board had informed HEW that closing Eva Thomas and moving students and faculty to College Park, Lakeshore, Briarwood, and Headland would be the least disruptive of three desegregation alternatives given the school system by the federal agency. He added, "This will be a very, very expensive item for the taxpayers, to have to close a new school which is one of the most beautiful in the system."

Impatient and impulsive black leaders, not satisfied with the attempts at desegregation in Atlanta schools, called at the year's end for the replacement of Bill Wainwright as president of the Atlanta Board of Education and for the firing of board attorney A. C. (Pete) Latimer.

Clarence Coleman, convenor of the coalition, and civic leader Charles Black made the demands at the Butler Street YMCA Hungry Club Forum. The manifesto called for quality education in all schools, an end to the alleged assigning of poor white teachers to black schools and superior black teachers to white schools, and an end to waste. They wanted to give black businesses and banking and insurance institutions an opportunity at school funds and to eliminate all vestiges of a dual school system by equalizing pay increases and increasing black administrators.

In July, Georgia Tech bid farewell to retiring president Dr. Edwin D. Harrison, and the next month the school greeted its new and seventh president, Dr. Arthur G. Hansen, a forty-four-year-old educator with a background in engineering and mathematics. The new president had been dean of the Engineering School at Tech for three years. He held a Ph.D. in mathematics from Case Western Reserve University and degrees from Purdue in electrical engineering and mathematics. He had taught at four colleges before coming to Tech.

On his first day on the job President Hansen announced some personnel changes, which included abolishing two vice-presidencies, changing the responsibilities of two others, and creating three new positions. He pledged a new emphasis on providing students with the cultural aspects of living in a complex society and said Tech would become more involved in looking at the problems that technology had raised, such as pollution and transportation problems.

In August the Atlanta Board of Education passed a $72.6 million general fund budget for 1969–70. Salary appropriations accounted for the major portion of the $9 million increase over the previous year, with teacher salaries being raised from $6,000 to $6,200 in February and from $6,200 to $6,500 in September. Allocations for instructional supplies were increased from $5.30 to $6.50 for high school students and from $3.20 to $4.00 for elementary students.

Emory University could point with enormous pride to its new library for advanced studies, which was dedicated on October 31. Named for longtime friend and alumnus Robert W. Woodruff, the library incorporated all the best features of a university library. On the tenth floor were housed the special collections, including the papers of Joel Chandler Harris, Charles Palmer, Ralph McGill, D. W. Brooks, and other people of note. The library included

239,267 square feet of floor space and would house 1 million books. It had seating capacity for 1,456.

While Emory students were enjoying their new library facility, the students at Georgia Tech welcomed a new nine-story graduate addition to the Price Gilbert Memorial Library. The building cost $3.9 million.

Politics kept the town agog through much of the year. Maynard Jackson, the man who tried to retire Herman Talmadge from the U.S. Senate and was defeated 3 to 1, announced March 7 that he would attempt to be the city's first Negro vice-mayor. Jackson had made no secret of his plans to run, but speculation ranged from the offices of mayor to vice-mayor to alderman. His announcement apparently predicted that the present vice-mayor, Sam Massell, would vacate the office by running for mayor. Jackson came from a prominent Georgia family, long active in civic and religious affairs in the black community.

Earlier in the year Alderman Everett Millican had announced that he would be a candidate for mayor. At the time he expressed his stand on the issues facing the city, saying the number-one requirement for the city was financial stability. Equal education should rank almost at the top of the priorities, and there continued to be a need for low-income and middle-income single family homes, he said. Millican served on the Board of Aldermen from 1928 through 1934, from 1960 to 1962, and from 1965 to 1969.

Speaking before the Atlanta Press Club, Negro legislator Julian Bond said that he believed it was possible for Atlanta to elect a black mayor, but not without difficulty. He further added that he would be inclined to back Dr. Horace Tate, the city's only announced black mayoral candidate, but he sidestepped total endorsement pending the entrance of other possible candidates. He left no doubt he was throwing his influence behind Maynard Jackson, running against Alderman Milton Farris for vice-mayor.

The city elections were scheduled to be held October 7, and there was a total of 217,856 Atlantans eligible to vote, of which 130,569 were whites and 87,017 were Negroes. Thus, racially the ratio of whites to Negroes was almost 60-40. In Fulton County city areas, Negroes made up 40.67 percent of the total registration, and in DeKalb-Atlanta they were 32 percent of the total. These numbers were significant because for the first time in modern city history, substantial numbers of Negroes were candidates for city offices.

Three days before the city election, six candidates for mayor campaigned before two hundred persons at the Hungry Club Forum, but the two candidates for vice-mayor stole the show. Attorney Maynard Jackson received the loudest applause when he stressed the need to make the city's number-two office "the voice of the people." Those who spoke as candidates for mayor were Dr. Horace Tate, Alderman Rodney Cook, Vice-Mayor Sam Massell, Alderman Everett Millican, Socialist Linda Jenness, and Howell Smith. Cook and Massell went into a runoff. Mayor Allen endorsed Cook.

With the substantial support of the Negro community, Massell took

63,632, or 54.97 percent of the votes cast. Cook took 51,289 votes, or 45.02 percent of the total. "His substantial vote in the white community did not offset Massell's lopsided margin in the black community," wrote Raleigh Bryans in the *Journal* of October 22. "Massell's victory takes effect January 5, when he will assume office, giving Atlanta the unique one-two ethnic punch of a Jewish mayor and a Negro vice-mayor."

In late October, as Mayor Allen prepared to leave office, a longtime force in city government decided to retire. Earl Landers was administrative assistant to both mayors William B. Hartsfield and Ivan Allen, Jr. "Due to him," said Doris Lockerman in *Atlanta* magazine, "Atlanta has been remarkably free from graft, corruption and hanky-panky in the government over these many years." Her complimentary portrait of Landers continued:

Others are in the limelight, taking the bows. There in the background, where the going is often rough and demanding you can always find Earl Landers. . . .

If you had to label him, you would have to say that he is a liberal conservative. He is the fellow who negotiated the settlement of last year's garbage strike. Many like to claim the responsibility for Atlanta stadium, but, deep in our hearts we know that without his expertise it might never have been built. The Atlanta Airport is another of our assets which is in great part Earl's handiwork. . . . I asked the man declared to become his successor to describe Earl Landers. "Solid, honest, loyal, fair, stable, a man to lean on" . . . were some of the words he used.[6]

The 1968 standards required car manufacturers to reduce the auto exhaust emissions by 50 percent, and the 1970 standards would require another 50 percent reduction on the 1968 standard. Even with improvements, so many more cars would be on the road in ten years that the volume of auto exhaust would be about the same.

In a study made in 1967 Atlanta ranked fifty-first among sixty-five urban areas in the United States in terms of the severity of its air pollution problem. Fulton County experts said 80 percent of Atlanta's pollution came from carbon monoxide—mostly from automobiles. Still, a major producer of pollution in Atlanta had always been the city's own incinerator on Magnolia Street. It had $450,000 worth of pollution control equipment installed to bring it up to county standards for the first time in history.

Although the city of Atlanta had passed an ordinance against burning within the city limits, it had little effect on fires in general, for the year 1969 was plagued with burning buildings—homes, offices, and warehouses. The most spectacular fire was one of the largest in Atlanta's history and turned the huge Mead paper warehouse into a $7 million canyon of flame. In 1968 Atlanta firefighters answered 13,557 alarms and fought 6,918 fires. In 1969 the department had forty-four engines and nineteen ladder trucks.

Not fires, but firefighters made news the first two weeks of August when Negro firefighters chanted the old cry of racism. About forty Negro employees of the Atlanta Fire Department visited Mayor Ivan Allen on August 8 to complain that they were still subjected to racial abuses within the department and suffered discrimination in promotions. William Hamer was spokesman for the group and said that the men he represented were called "boy" and "nigger" at the station houses, were made to sleep in a segregated area, and had to shine the station captain's shoes. Mayor Allen listened to testimony from nineteen Negro firefighters and then asked Fire Chief P. O. Williams and Alderman William T. Knight to give him a report as soon as possible.

Ten days later Chief Williams submitted his findings of alleged discrimination against Negro firemen in a memorandum to Mayor Allen. Dealing primarily with office procedure for addressing grievances, the chief fired off a memo to all personnel in the department to address one another by their surnames and officers by their rank. One of the sore spots in the controversy with the black firefighters was the denial of their entrance into the department's social club at Lake Allatoona. In Williams's letter, it was noted that the club was a private organization controlled by a board of trustees that determined policies for membership. It was supported entirely by dues and was maintained through voluntary services of the members.

On August 26 the confrontation came. William Hamer, accompanied by five other Negro firefighters, argued with the Board of Firemasters that segregation existed within the Fire Department and had plagued Negroes since their initial hiring in 1963. Hamer argued that the blacks should have been given an opportunity to participate in the current rewriting of the department's rules and regulations handbook. Alderman Q. V. Williamson, present at the hearing, gave Hamer a copy of the suggested regulation changes and asked him to return it in three days with his suggested changes.

Williamson, the city's only Negro alderman and the first in Atlanta's modern history, summed up the issue thus: "It's common knowledge that discrimination against blacks joining the fire department existed openly prior to 1963 because they were not permitted to be foremen. Now, all these men are actually saying is that discrimination still exists, but has gone underground."

Williamson was elected vice-president of the Board of Aldermen early in the year and was third in line of command of the city government. From Friday, March 13, through the weekend, Williamson served in a way as Atlanta's first Negro mayor because both Mayor Ivan Allen and Vice-Mayor Sam Massell were out of town.

In October, Williamson was no longer the only Negro alderman in Atlanta. As a result of the fall election, four new Negro aldermen were named. They were: Ira L. Jackson, a businessman; Joel C. Stokes, a prominent banker; Marvin Arrington, an employee of Emory University, and H. D. Dodson, a commercial photographer.

The election of the new black aldermen drew attention to the interesting fact, as the *Journal* reported:

Black people are now filling 246 kinds of jobs in city government, whereas 10 years ago they worked in only 14 mostly menial and custodial jobs. Carl Sutherland, retiring head of the city's Personnel Department, said that of the city's 8,159 employees, 37% are black. He stated that more blacks than whites are being hired at City Hall, but admitted there was a dearth of black people in city department administrative positions.

"Since most of the high-level jobs in city government are filled by career employees with long service, it will take quite some time for black people to move into these high-level jobs," he added.

These comments raised an outcry from incoming Mayor Sam Massell, Vice Mayor Maynard Jackson and Negro senator LeRoy Johnson. Mr. Johnson's comment was "Our thrust is to get black people into department head jobs. What we really need in this city is a black director of personnel . . . ."

Sutherland said when he hears demands about why more blacks are not in City Hall's employ, "I show them the statistics and they are usually favorably impressed. According to recent charts, Negroes hold 3,206 out of 7,023 positions in City Hall Departments."

Changing times and changing life-styles brought an end at last to one ancient Atlanta business institution—the once-busy National Stockyards on Brady Avenue in northwest Atlanta. The last animal left there was one lone mule, owned by Ben Burnett, president of McClure-Burnett Commission Company, and it was up for sale. The complexities of urbanization had caught up with the cattle farm, where 1,500 to 2,000 head a day had been paced through the auction ring. McClure continued to maintain an office in Atlanta, but he moved his mule and cattle auctions to barns in Rome and Toccoa, Georgia.

Another Atlanta institution—no mule barn, but a landmark food purveyor—passed from the civic scene late in 1969. Old-time lovers of the Tenth Street community on Peachtree bade a sad farewell to a longtime favorite shopping place—Roxy's Delicatessen. Opened in 1923 by Jack Franco, it bowed out because of the hippie community that is surrounding it. The hippie community, in fact, was much in the news in 1969, mainly in the area of drug abuse.

Crime in every form, indeed, had been rampant in the Atlanta metro area during 1968, and predictions, which proved accurate, were that 1969 would be even worse. "Atlanta's predicted and 'disturbing' increase in crime last year was borne out in new indictment figures that show some of the most alarming gains were in murders and abuses of the narcotics laws." Fulton

District Attorney Lewis Slaton said that the newly released total of indictments—4,037—was a 25 percent rise. Of this figure, 140 were for murder; 312 were for assault with intent to murder; 139 cases involved narcotics; 319 were for robbery and 761 for burglaries.

And, Atlanta, as forecast, did keep up the unhappy pace in 1969. By the middle of October the crime situation was such that "an angry, red-faced, sometimes shouting Governor Maddox" threatened to order state troopers to Atlanta to bring "law and order" to a city he saw as besieged by "bums, criminals, anarchists and drug addicts."

Maddox charged that "sorry, no good, cowardly" Atlanta city and police officials had condoned, encouraged and sometimes joined with those who echoed the Communists' cry of "police brutality." Maddox said he did not want to order state action but felt either the police had to stop crime or vigilante groups had to do it "or the anarchists will take over."

This tirade was apparently triggered by word that Atlanta police had slowed down their arrests of hippies in Piedmont Park. "In surrendering Piedmont Park to filthy and lawless elements, Atlanta officials have created another island of immunity for those who will, to proceed with sexual immorality, drug abuse and other lawless acts," Maddox charged. Mayor Allen and Police Chief Herbert Jenkins replied that they would meet with the governor and be happy to consider his recommendations.

"Police brutality" was charged against Atlanta uniformed officers by one of their own number in September. DeWitt Smith, a five-year veteran of the department and a Negro, accused five of his white fellow-officers, including a lieutenant, of beating, stomping, and choking and kicking two Negro prisoners who had been brought into city jail. Smith, trying to choke back tears, told the story of what he had seen. Mayor Allen expressed confidence that Chief Jenkins would take whatever action was necessary, and Jenkins pledged to do so. But placating words from high civic authority did nothing to quell the rising tide of black anger.

On Monday morning, September 15, about fifty angry Negroes pushed past Mayor Ivan Allen, Jr.'s police aide at City Hall and demanded that Allen temporarily suspend Chief Jenkins and place the department under a committee of aldermen and citizens. Allen refused and told the group that Jenkins was as interested as anyone else in getting the truth of recent allegations of police brutality. Two days afterward, Jenkins strongly recommended the hiring of civilian turnkeys to handle prisoners at City Jail.

In meetings at the Greater Calvary Baptist Church and at the West Hunter Street Baptist Church, Lonnie King, head of the local office of the NAACP, the Rev. Joseph Boone, director of the Metropolitan Atlanta Summit Leadership Conference, and Jesse Hill, cochairman of the conference, presented blacks who testified that they had been brutally handled by police. As a result, the clamor to oust Chief Jenkins increased in vigor, and a suit was filed in federal court demanding that this be done. Joining in this legal action, which Atlanta City Attorney Henry Bowden described as being purely political, in addition to the above were the SCLC, the African Soul Brothers, the Bankhead Court Civic League, and the Tenants United for Fairness (TUFF). By mid-September the FBI had been called in, according to Atlanta's Special-Agent-in-Charge Frank V. Hill, and the Fulton County grand jury was asked to conduct its own special probe.

By October 1 the charges of brutality by police against the blacks had been somewhat overshadowed by similar charges in which Atlanta's hippie colony, most of them white, were the victims. The confrontation came to a climax on a Sunday afternoon in Piedmont Park. Chief Herbert Jenkins told the story in his personal history *My Forty Years on the Force*. After describing the hippie community, known as "the strip," lying along Peachtree from Fifth Street north to Fourteenth, he said:

There were many cases reported in the beginning wherein teenagers from very proper homes would drive their cars to Piedmont Park, quickly change into their hippie clothes, and then walk to the strip for several hours of excitement. Returning to their cars, they would change back to straight clothes and drive home. These kids were interested only in looking and satisfying their curiosity. But then more unsavory types were attracted to the strip and the term flower children became a misnomer. As late as the winter of 1969 drugs were virtually non-existent in Atlanta. The arrival that summer of thousands of kids from other parts of the nation who were heavy into the drug culture created a massive drug problem for Atlanta police which has yet [1973] to abate.

There were different opinions among public officials, civic leaders and the police of what approach and policies should be applied by the police to control the situation. There were those who insisted on a hard-nose policy— go in there with enough police with night sticks, tear gas, and necessary force to clean the hippies out and/or lock them up. But it had been clearly demonstrated in the civil rights movement that to arrest hundreds of demonstrators (actually, in the case of the hippies, the only demonstrating was walking the sidewalks) for minor violations did not correct anything. Usually such efforts just created more problems. I agreed with the group that insisted a more tolerant approach be used, and that every effort be made to control the situation without the use of force or arrests. Thus only flagrant violators would be arrested and force used as a last resort. The police officers assigned to the strip were carefully selected so that those officers who were in sympathy with this policy and understood it and could make it work would be assigned to the hippie community. But there was such a wide difference of opinion among public officials, the citizens, and the police that this was not always possible.

This conflict reached an explosive point in Piedmont Park on a Sunday afternoon in August of 1969. Large groups of hippies had gathered in the park and grass and other drugs were being sold openly and used openly. The relationship between the police and the hippies had been declining all summer as drug usage accelerated. A decidedly bad element had infiltrated the hippie movement. Pressure was intense from residents of the community to "do something" about the situation. What happened was a confrontation between the police and the hippies when the police tried to make a drug arrest. A near riot developed—the news media were on the scene and the cameras were grinding. Ultimately, many arrests were made and several people were injured, including some police. It had been a nervous summer and not only were the police and hippies uptight but countless Atlanta parents of children in the metropolitan area who had been unable to keep their children away from the strip and away from this particular rock concert in the park and had accompanied them to Piedmont Park for the concert. Many of these parents entered into the fray, some against the police but many taking it as an opportunity to beat up some hippie. A lot of hippies were battered that day not by the police but many by irate parents and neighborhood residents.[7]

Jenkins was called before the grand jury to report on this incident, as well as the charge of brutality filed by the black leaders. His eloquence and obvious sincerity seemed to have prevailed, for the grand jury in its presentments released on Sunday, November 2, called the recent charges of police brutality "exaggerated and lacking in substantial evidence." To Chief Jenkins, the grand jury's probe had obviously been "an excellent job of investigation."

The grand jury's findings by no means ended the confrontation between police and hippies and drug users and peddlers in general. Drug raids continued throughout the fall, with large amounts of marijuana and narcotics being confiscated by the authorities. In most cases the people arrested were very young—in their middle teens. In December, though, a twenty-seven-year old Atlantan who police said was the king pin of the LSD traffic at pop festivals was arrested while attempting to deliver fifteen pounds of marijuana and 900 LSD tablets to Cocoa, Florida. A long-haired man, he was known in hippie circles as "Atlanta Schroder." When his apartment, which he shared with several others, was searched, 5,000 LSD tablets were confiscated. Schroder, being absent, was not among the eighteen arrested in this raid.

Thus the city continued the pressure on its hippie area. Raids by local and state officers sparked a near-riot and the arrest of thirty-eight persons. The raids, conducted in the Fourteenth Street, Peachtree, and Piedmont Avenue areas, were greeted with catcalls, obscenities, and a shower of bricks and bottles when a crowd of nearly two hundred people gathered. The raids followed a two-month investigation of the area. The officers had search warrants for five places and arrest warrants for eleven individuals who had sold drugs to undercover agents. Det. Lt. J. R. Shattles charged in his report that "most of the agitators came out of the *Speckled Bird* [underground newspaper] office and instigated the hostile action toward police."

State drug inspectors also were hard at work in the Atlanta area trying to break up a narcotics ring. On August 12 it was announced in headlines that they had been successful and that three doctors and a dentist had lost their federal narcotics licenses.

Joseph Weldy, the state's chief drug inspector, put investigator Richard Andrews to work—seventy to eighty hours a week—searching through druggists' files to find names of people who seemed to be buying abnormally large amounts of narcotics. One of the ways the drug racket worked was for a person to go to a physician and fake an illness, get a legal prescription, and then steal a pad of prescription blanks, duplicate the real one many times, and then use them at different drug stores. The crackdown on prescriptions resulted in a rash of drugstore burglaries for narcotics.

Another series of burglaries involved a ring of drugstore burglars who were distributing stolen prescription drugs widely in the Fourteenth Street–Piedmont Park area. The stealing of drugs continued, and police made numerous raids throughout the year in an attempt to ferret out the ringleaders. One of the most frightening aspects of drug abuse was the increase of users in the schools.

Local juvenile court judges and police officers described DeKalb and Fulton high schools as places where drug usage was common and on the upswing. DeKalb Juvenile Court Judge Curtis Tillman believed there were 100 addicts for every case he heard and declared that no high school in the Atlanta area was without its drug sources.

Although Atlanta police kept busy with their efforts to nab drug abusers and murderers, they also had the job of keeping up with a rampant lottery operation in the Atlanta area. Accusations were brought against sixteen persons, including two Atlanta police, for allegedly conspiring to operate a multi-million-dollar lottery with headquarters in Atlanta, which was described by law enforcement officials as the largest in Georgia. Of the two police officers, one was a former detective on the lottery squad. Most of the evidence against the sixteen was obtained through wiretaps on the phones of three of the people.

Atlanta's booming lottery operation, which paid off at 500 to 1 instead of the usual 400 to 1, naturally attracted the attention of big-time racketeers elsewhere. Two of these were Gilbert Beckley of New York and Tito Arini of Miami, who came to Atlanta and soon, according to FBI Agent Donald Burgers, had completely taken over the operation of the Atlanta lottery. Beckley's triumph was shortlived. By October 10 he had been arrested.

Following close on the heels of the arrest of New Yorker Gilbert Beckley was the raid conducted by six Atlanta law enforcement agencies. They battered their way into a closely guarded gambling casino in Cobb County.

Housed in a brick home near Acworth, the casino was outfitted with gambling tables, chips, and croupier sticks. Eight men were arrested and placed under $10,000 bonds each for commercial gambling. The officers seized $17,000. The raid followed a two-month investigation by police departments of Cobb and DeKalb Counties, the GBI, the Cobb County Sheriff's Department, and the district attorney offices of Fulton and Cobb County. One officer said the operation might have had "interstate ties with organized crime."

The gambling activities named above were less fearful to Atlanta women than the brutal crime of rape, which was on the increase in the Atlanta area. The year was a busy one for police officers who were involved in those cases.

The bizarre and nationally publicized criminal act which set Atlanta agog, however, involved not rape but the kidnapping for ransom of a beautiful young Emory University co-ed—and her burial alive in a luxuriously appointed "capsule." The perpetrator of this weird act was a psychopathic Alaskan born in 1945 named Gary Krist, son of a salmon fisherman. By his own admission he was a habitual thief by the age of nine, and by 1963 he was drifting across country stealing cars, for which he served two prison sentences. In 1966 he was jailed again, in California, but he escaped in a midnight jail break in which a fellow prisoner was killed. In Miami he met Ruth Eisemann-Schier, a twenty-seven-year old student from Honduras. With her, he worked out a plan to kidnap somebody wealthy, hide him or her in a hole in the ground, and collect a fat ransom. For their victim, they chose Barbara Mackle, daughter of a Miami multimillionaire developer, Robert Mackle.

As Frazier Moore reported, the capsule was "a fiberglass-reinforced-plywood box equipped with (among other things) a ventilation arrangement, water pump, light, mattress, food, water, tranquilizers, bedpan and toilet paper. It was buried and the kidnappers were ready.

Barbara Mackle was ill and was staying with her mother in a motel near Emory. Krist knocked on the door. He forced his way into the room, with Ruth on his heels. They chloroformed Mrs. Mackle and forced her daughter into the car. Moore's account continues:

By 8:30 A.M., Barbara was imprisoned in the capsule, which was buried in the ground and covered without a trace. Then Gary phoned the Mackle home in Miami, to advise that instructions were contained in a note he'd planted in the front yard several days before.

Within hours that Tuesday morning, Gary and Ruth were on the road to Miami, where they planned to collect the ransom, then skip the country.

After collecting the half-million dollars (and losing touch with Ruth, who hopped a bus for Houston), Gary fled from Miami up the road to West Palm Beach. There, he phoned a startled FBI receptionist in the Atlanta office to tell her where his victim had lain for four days and three nights. She was rescued, unharmed in the late afternoon of December 20, 1968. In West Palm

Beach he bought a 16-foot runabout, piloted it through the cross-state canal system, and on reaching the Gulf at Fort Myers, found himself shadowed by a Coast Guard plane. Abandoning his new strategy of crossing the Gulf for Texas, he found cover in the sprawling root system of a dense mangrove island.

He had been without sleep for almost five days, when, shortly after midnight on Sunday, December 22, he was apprehended by a Charlotte County sheriff's deputy. "We didn't capture him," one of the lawmen cracked. "We rescued him."

Charged with kidnapping for ransom, Gary stood trial in DeKalb County in May, 1969. He was given life in prison. Facing the same charge a few days later, Ruth plea-bargained her way to a seven-year sentence, of which she served three years before being deported.

When Frazier Moore interviewed Krist nine years later, he was working as a laboratory technician at the Georgia State Prison at Reidsville. For Barbara Mackle, the ending was a quietly happy one. She survived the ordeal both physically and mentally, married her college sweetheart, and, seemingly, put the whole fearful incident out of her mind.

Until 1969 Atlanta had no place where needy and homeless women might check in for one night, a week, a month, or longer, as men for years had been able to do at the Union Mission on Ellis Street. In September the mission opened a woman's division able to house sixty at 910 Ponce de Leon NE. The only qualification for getting into the home was to be a female, to need help, and to be willing to cooperate. The house was open to all women in need of shelter, food, clothing, guidance, and counseling. The Mission charged $1.00 per day whether or not the woman could pay. A record was kept, and some paid, some did not. The executive director was Rev. Russell Strange.

In 1969 some Atlantans were beginning to have head-shaking doubts about the value of the new stadium to the city, as a source of income. Jim Montgomery of the *Journal-Constitution* did some checking around and came up with the unhappy news that for the moment, at least, the city and county were footing a fairly heavy bill for what was expected to have been a sure-fire money-maker:

According to a Stadium Authority financial report, the City of Atlanta and Fulton County in 1967 contributed $472,318.26 of the $968,407.50 payment due that year to meet principal and interest on the $18,000,000 of revenue bonds sold in 1964 to finance the stadium. The other $496,089.24 came from stadium revenues. By contract the city and county are obligated to pay any of the annual principal and interest that can't be met by stadium revenues.

In 1968, the joint city-county contribution jumped to $900,057.93, the increase resulting from the Stadium Authority's agreement to reimburse the Braves for the moving and legal expense associated with departing Milwaukee. Totaling $1,474,900.79, the expenses are being recovered by the Braves through omission of rental payments to the Stadium Authority. Earl Landers, administrative assistant to Mayor Ivan Allen, says the expenses will be paid in full by mid-1970. He estimates also that the City of Atlanta and Fulton County will have to contribute about one-half million dollars a year on the principal and interest on the revenue bonds which will be retired in 1993.

However, Montgomery noted, it was only fair to point out that a detailed study by Georgia Tech, done in 1967, indicated that the Braves had had a significant economic impact on the city since 1966. More than $9 million was spent the first season in connection with baseball, and as this money circulated up to $30 million in income for Atlantans was generated.

Come September, however, one-half million dollars in taxes, more or less, was of little concern to Atlanta sports lovers. On Tuesday night, September 30, Atlanta fans of the Braves knew the ecstasy of winning the National League's Western Division championship. Before a crowd of 46,357 cheering, screaming, foot-stomping supporters, the Impossible Dream arrived in Atlanta Stadium, when Atlanta beat the Cincinnati Reds 3–2 to win the division pennant.

"It's almost too much," said Mayor Ivan Allen, the man who had nerve enough to start building a major league stadium on borrowed money. "This is my last year in office and I just didn't think it would happen in my time."

But the happy hour was destined to be short-lived. The youthful New York Mets defeated the Braves three in a row to take the National League championship before a screaming wild crowd in Shea Stadium. Clete Boyer pretty well summed up the Braves' championship series performance. "We hit the ball good enough," he said, "but we played sloppy in the field and got bad pitching."

In this year of 1969 the groundwork was laid for many improvements in Atlanta institutions that took place over the next few years. The powerful Aldermanic Finance Committee earmarked $4 million of bond funds to several projects—with the largest chunk of $1 million going to the Cyclorama. The breakdown of approved funds was: Cyclorama, $1 million; urban renewal, $775,000; public library, $500,000; acquisitions and development of parks, $500,000; streets, bridges, and culverts, $475,000; storm water sewers, $440,000; and traffic signals, $350,000. The $1 million for the Cyclorama would go toward restoration of the painting and renovation of the present building or engineering for a new one. The half-million dollars for the library would be used to buy adjacent land to expand the downtown branch.

There was a steady mounting of discontent against the war in Vietnam, and it came to a head in Atlanta and the nation on October 15 when "Moratorium Day" was observed across the land. But Gov. Lester Maddox called for opposition to the antiwar moratorium and asked citizens to fly the American flag and drive to work with their automobile headlights on. Atlanta's Mayor Ivan Allen wired John Lewis, chairman of the Vietnam Moratorium Committee, that flags at City Hall would be flown at half-staff, not in protest as Lewis had required, but in honor of the soldiers who had died.

Antiwar rallies were being planned at Georgia State University, the University of Georgia, Agnes Scott, and Emory. Spelman was the only one of the black schools in the Atlanta University complex to close.

Atlanta, of course, had its softer, gentler side, its fondness for music and the arts, for drama and the dance, and as the years went by even the hippie strip on Peachtree changed its life-style. It became the haunt of painters and poets, of actors and musicians and dancers.

In 1969, however, the Metropolitan Opera was still the city's most notable social-cultural-artistic event, though, there too, certain changes were taking place, as the *Constitution* described:

Opera-loving Atlanta will be on a new diet for the 1969 Metropolitan's week-long season opening Monday, May 5.

But, will they like it? Tradition bound for years, the music lovers will face many changes. The 1969 season will be at the Atlanta Civic Center. Since 1947 fans have been swarming into the Fox Theatre where, with luck, they have enjoyed the same seats for years. And, at intermission there were the "bourbon breaks" at the Georgian Terrace Bar. And the Georgian Terrace also was noted for the "rocking chair brigade" on the front porch. Here, people could watch the outdoor and pre-performance activities, which to many was a better show than what was going on in the theatre.

So, now on the eve of the opening of the 1969 Metropolitan Season (*Der Rosenkavalier* is the opening night opera), Atlanta is facing a social and cultural change. The opera will be at the new Civic Center where the seating capacity is 4,591 as opposed to the 4,000 at the Fox. But, there is no bar across the street.

But, Alfred Kennedy, president of the Atlanta Music Festival Association, promises there will be also more room for parking space. As usual, the Piedmont Driving Club will provide bus service for its members.

Atlantans whose love of art led them to their tragic death were remembered in 1969 when litigation for the disastrous crash seven years earlier finally ended. The *Constitution* reported:

The largest settlement in history for a single airplane disaster was made here when Air France paid $5,200,000 to the survivors of 62 persons who died in the 1962 Paris airplane crash that killed more than 100 Atlantans. . . .

The hush-hush settlement was made in February when U.S. District Judge Edward T. Gignoux of Portland, Me. signed an order dismissing 42 cases involving the 62 deaths which have been in litigation for more than six years.

The settlement was discussed and the order was signed after the judge and lawyers for both sides conferred in chambers without a court reporter. The amounts of the individual settlements were not placed in court records although many Atlanta attorneys and insurance men were informed of the settlement.

The final settlement of $5,200,000 averages out to more than $84,000 for the survivors of each of the 62 persons who died. The Warsaw Convention, an international treaty ratified by more than 100 countries, sets a maximum liability of $8,300 per person in the event of a disaster if simple negligence is proven. Each of the plaintiffs in the cases settled in February received more than $8,300. The survivors of about 60 of the victims settled with the airline without litigation.

Before the case was settled, the chief lawyers for the plaintiffs, Lee Kreindler of New York and William H. Schroder of Atlanta, had alleged that there was wilfull misconduct on the part of the airline because the Boeing 707's stabilizer was not set correctly for take-off and the pilot attempted to stop the plane after it had passed the point on the runway where no attempt should be made to stop it . . . . They also maintained that the flight, a charter plane, was not covered by the Warsaw Convention.

The Fifth U.S. Circuit Court of Appeals ruled that the flight did not come under the Warsaw Convention.

E. Smythe Gambrell of Atlanta was chief lawyer for Air France.

Members of the Atlanta Jewish Community made news by good works in 1969. On May 18 Mayor Allen broke ground for a new Atlanta Jewish Home, located on a 10.5-acre site at the intersection of Howell Mill Road and Margaret Mitchell Drive in northwest Atlanta. When completed, the 120-bed facility offered complete rehabilitation, occupational, and medical services. It replaced the old home on Fourteenth Street, which had been in operation since 1951.

In October the Lions of Judea AZA Chapter of the B'nai B'rith Organization won second prize in the United States from *Parents* magazine's annual youth group achievement awards for Service to the Community. Thirty boys fifteen to seventeen years old organized a league of five baseball teams in the Perry Homes and raised money for bats and balls and uniforms and sponsored fifty Perry Homes youngsters in a twelve-game series. Also hailed by *Parents* magazine were the Daughters of Torah Chapter of B'nai B'rith girls, who presented a talent show.

In November the Protestant Radio and Television Center in Atlanta celebrated its twentieth anniversary. Located on Clifton Road near Emory, the PRTVC was the only institution of its kind in the world, according to Dr.

Edward Arnold, president. "The center, sponsored by five religious denominations and four educational institutions, produces films, recordings and tapes for radio and television and for personal or group use. The religious and educational materials are broadcast and distributed worldwide. . . . Sponsoring organizations for the center are the United Methodist, Presbyterian U.S. (Southern), Presbyterian U.S.A. (Northern), Lutheran Church in America, and the Protestant Episcopal churches, and Agnes Scott College, Emory University, Candler School of Theology and Columbia Theological Seminary."

The Center produced the "Protestant Hour" radio program, which was broadcast weekly over 561 stations in the United States and worldwide through the Armed Forces Network. Two other radio programs were "Be Still and Know," a brief daily meditation distributed to 1,330 stations and the Armed Forces Network, and "Banners of Faith," a half-hour inspirational weekly service for twenty-eight participating denominations for the armed forces.

By mid-July two strikes, one basically racial, the other based on wages and hours, disrupted the Atlanta economy. Members of three civil rights organizations, the Atlanta Branch of the NAACP, the Atlanta Urban League, and the Metropolitan Atlanta Summit Leadership Congress, joined twenty-six former maintenance employees in picketing the Peachtree Seventh Building demanding that the General Services Administration cancel its contract with a cleaning service. According to Morris Dillard, executive secretary of the Atlanta NAACP, his pickets were protesting "the simple exploitation of Atlanta people." Work hours, said Dillard, had been increased, causing a heavier load to fall on each worker; also, he said, adequate cleaning equipment was not permitted. Women were required to lift barrels weighing from 70 to 100 pounds, and two had been injured on the job as a result, though they received no pay when injured in the line of duty. Furthermore, Dillard pointed out, "Workers are referred to as 'boy' or 'girl' by the contractor. This denies them human dignity."

On July 14 a new dispute flared up at the General Motors Lakewood Plant on McDonough Boulevard in southeast Atlanta. There 4,200 workers were idled on April 28, when 3,200 members of the Atlanta local 34 of the United Auto Workers called for a shutdown. By mid-July the strike was already the longest on record dealing solely with local issues not covered by GM's contract with the national union.

Similar strikes against GM around the country based on the merging of two divisions into one assembly division had idled 40,000 workers in addition to the 4,200 in Atlanta, and had cut company production by 6,000 cars and 1,500 trucks daily.

In another strike with racial overtones printers received backing from an unexpected source. Preachers working in the SCLC's "Operation Breadbasket" announced they would support the striking printers at the famous

Negro newspaper, the *Atlanta Daily World*. The preachers said they would ask members of their congregations to refuse to buy the newspaper or advertise in it, and "large businesses will be asked to withhold their advertising" until agreeable working conditions existed. In a press release the preachers said that *World* publisher C. A. Scott had failed to keep promises to negotiate with the printers' local union despite a National Labor Relations Board ruling that he must do so.

As it was in the beginning of the city's history, and as it would continue for generations thereafter, in 1969 the location of streets, roads, and highways kept Atlantans alert and often made them sad or angry. In January of 1969 the route at issue was Georgia 120, linking Marietta and Lawrenceville. A historic preservation group had urged Jim Gillis, state highway director, to "reconsider" proposed changes that it claimed would damage several antebellum mansions in Roswell. The buildings listed were Mimosa Hall, Holly Hill, Bullock Hall, and a Presbyterian church.

Atlanta's city traffic engineer Karl Bevins shared the view of the historians that old landmarks should be preserved where possible—but his job was to keep the traffic flowing swiftly and smoothly, without congestion. In Atlanta, with a metropolitan population of 1,335,000, the average daily traffic on the combined I-75 and I-85 south of Brookwood Station was 127,400 cars in 1968–69. By 1975 it was expected to be 148,308. On the northwest freeway (I-75) it was 60,018. By 1975 it would be up to 89,078. I-20 east would jump from 82,695 to 125,680, and I-20 west from 84,397 to 138,856. Slightly less congested, but still stop-and-go at peak hours, I-85, the northeast freeway, would move up from 88,431 to 98,626 in 1975.

In August a massive downtown traffic jam caused by a combination of commuters, conventioneers and visitors, stalled cars, and a shooting inspired an editorial in the *Constitution*. It summed up the problems facing MARTA—and what was planned for the years immediately ahead:

> The final action at Tuesday's meeting of the board of the Metropolitan Atlanta Rapid Transit Authority tells us something. The board voted to hold future meetings at 3:00 P.M. instead of 3:30, so members will have a chance to get home before the afternoon traffic crush.
>
> That, thankfully, was not all MARTA did to cope with Atlanta's growing automotive snarl. The board voted unanimously for a two-year budget which would prepare a new rapid transit proposal for submission to the voters by late 1971 or early 1972.
>
> Involved is a budget of $1,693,000 for the next two years, to be derived from local, state and federal sources.
>
> Among immediate plans are new studies of routes and rolling stock and for public understanding of a future rapid transit proposal.
>
> The need for rapid transit, as part of the total transportation structure of

the metropolitan area, becomes increasingly apparent, to even the most detached observer of the expressways.

Voters only last November rejected a proposal for a rapid transit system, apparently because it was based on increased ad valorem taxes. Additional areas of financing are one of the concerns as MARTA again turns to its blueprints. Construction costs are up, along with the cost of money, so in many respects the task facing rapid transit planners is increasingly difficult.

There is hope of significant federal financing, perhaps through a trust fund similar to that which builds the Interstates and the expressways.

The important matter for today, this week, however, is that MARTA is moving purposefully toward a goal most of us know is inevitable.

A growing, vital Atlanta cannot cope, in this last third of the century, if it does not have a workable method for the mass movement of people. The automobile, with one or two persons to the car, obviously is not the answer, even if we stack freeways on top of freeways.

As MARTA turned its thoughts to a multimillion-dollar rapid transit rail system to serve the five-county Atlanta area, one famous old interstate transportation system asked permission to discontinue its service to Atlanta because of the competition of the automobile traveling on the expressways. According to the *Journal*, "The Louisville & Nashville Railroad Co. will ask the Interstate Commerce Commission for permission to discontinue the last remaining L&N passenger train into Atlanta. Claiming an out-of-pocket loss on the Atlanta–St. Louis service of $688,000 last year, L&N is requesting that it be allowed to stop the 609-mile run effective August 13." Said the *Journal*:

Loss of the service won't be earth shattering to Atlantans. Only about 15 passengers use Train No. 3 into the city and Train No. 4 out each day. Of more importance to the city, in particular the development of the downtown area, is the fact that should L&N be allowed to stop the service, the air rights now occupied by Union Station will go back to the state and will be leasable from the State Properties Control Commission.

The Union Station property, long a toilet for derelicts, divides a section of air rights now under lease to Peachtree Whitehall Co., one of the Massell Companies. The Peachtree Whitehall leaseholds lie across Spring Street from a large section of air rights now under development by Cousins Properties, Inc.

The air rights over this area have often been mentioned as a key in the redevelopment of the downtown area.

The tracks under the station will remain in use by the railroad, but the space above 23 feet over the tracks goes back to the state. . . .

Decision to remove the Atlanta–St. Louis service will sever the city's last link with rail passenger service to the Midwest and West. Southern Railway Co. still operates five passenger trains in and out of Terminal Station, all serving the Eastern Seaboard, with one connection to New Orleans and one to

Cincinnati, and Seaboard Coast Line Railroad Co. operates the Silver Comet out of Terminal Station to Richmond, Virginia. But the ICC has under advisement a request to cancel that run. Bob Etheridge, L&N's Atlanta passenger Service Manager said that the interstate highway system is responsible for destroying the railroads' business. Freight and express now move by truck, and 88% of all intercity passenger travel is now by automobile. Planes carry about 8%, while rail travel accounts for only 1½%. Buses account for the remainder.

On December 17 the ICC ruled that the L&N must continue its passenger service to Atlanta for at least six more months. It declared that the road's mishandling of the train, failing to keep it clean and comfortable in an attempt to save money, was the reason for the decrease in passenger traffic. The decision also created a problem with what could be done with the thirty-nine-year old Union Station, for the destiny of the gaunt, gray, and nearly lifeless old station and the $1 million property it occupied depended on when The Georgian would be discontinued. Typically, The Georgian arrived at 9:50 A.M. and departed at 5:15 P.M., carrying fifteen persons in two cars. "Otherwise the station is lifeless. Freight and all other passenger trains use the Terminal Station on Spring Street. At night, the Union Station's dignified Doric columns and granite arches are sought out as shelter from winter winds by itinerants and homeless alcoholics."

Not only railroads, but city-operated bus lines found the private automobiles in competition with their services. In July the Atlanta Transit System, Inc., was pressing for a five-cent fare hike, to 35¢. They had just increased from 25¢ to 30¢ in December of 1968. The rise was essential, according to Transit System President William Maynard, to take care of increases in driver salaries that would take place in June of 1971 and 1972. The reaction of Atlanta bus riders was a cry of outrage, and twenty Atlanta organizations were urging their members to boycott the buses. The groups represented the National Domestic Workers Union, various civil rights organizations such as NAACP and SCLC, groups such as Emmaus House, *The Great Speckled Bird*, Operation Breadbasket, and the Young Socialists Alliance.

(Nothing prevailed. Fares climbed steadily over the 1970s and in 1983 a single bus fare, train or bus, was 60 cents, except for senior citizens, who rode for half price.)

Atlanta is a city of railroad buffs, who would never forget that the city owed her existence to the railroads. The prospect that Atlanta in a relatively few years might be without railway passenger service, steam, diesel, or otherwise, stirred the Atlanta Chapter of the National Railway Historical Society to action. The local group owned seven steam locomotives, plus one "ancient" diesel and an electric. They welcomed a famous locomotive to town in November. The guest was the Flying Scotsman, British Locomotive No. 4472. Built in 1922 at a cost of $24,000, this locomotive ran for forty years from London to Edinburgh, sometimes racing at a speed of 100 miles an hour, the first train to reach that speed. Then it was retired, when British millionaire Alan Pegler rescued it and restored it to its original splendor at a cost of $120,000. A newspaper story told of its arrival:

The Flying Scotsman and its British delegation aboard were greeted at the Terminal Station by General Louis W. Truman, director of the State Department of Industry and Trade; and Frank Carter, representing Mayor Ivan Allen who was out of the state. Sidney Ansley, the British Consul stationed in Atlanta also was on hand.

The British presented the Atlantans with a bottle of fine Scotch whiskey. The Atlantans in turn presented the British with a giant over-sized bottle of Coca-Cola.

The soft drink was poured over the front of the Flying Scotsman as a gesture of friendship and goodwill. The Scotch was consumed in its entirety, likewise in a gesture of friendship and goodwill.

In another field of transportation, Atlanta held a unique position. Women had been driving cabs here since World War II, and some fifty of them still were in 1969. But about half of those were in what owner Arch Gary believed was the only all-woman-driven fleet in the world. And the women drivers, Atlanta police reported, were much safer drivers than men. Their driving records were examined carefully before they were issued permits, and there were few complaints from their customers.

Cabs the women drove did not have radios, according to Wilma Cosgrove, who drove for Gary, so most of the trips the women got were from cruising downtown or waiting in taxi stands at the airport or the bus terminal. "Company officials said that radios are kept out of women's cabs intentionally. This eliminates the need for women to answer calls in unfamiliar neighborhoods and gives them some discretion about whom they pick up."

Like Atlanta's lady cab drivers, Atlanta's two women bus drivers have outstanding safety records. In 1969 Edna Stephens of Decatur had driven the Clairmont–Emory–Atlanta Avenue–Georgia Avenue route for twenty-one of her twenty-five years as a driver. Her best friends, she said, were her passengers. Many of them she had transported from babyhood, through their school and college years, and on to marriage. Martha Jones of Forest Park was the other woman driver. Her father was a streetcar driver when she was born, and he urged her to take up that profession. She never did drive a streetcar, but she did serve as a conductor on a two-man car and went on from there to drive a trolley bus, and now was driving a motor bus. Both women took up driving during the shortage of manpower during World War II. Many other women also were hired as drivers during this period but went on to other jobs, or to homemaking, when the war was over. (As of March 11, 1983, there were 120 women driving MARTA buses—but only one operator of Atlanta trains. There were, however, several women supervisors who could take over and drive the train in case of an emergency.)

The Atlanta Central Library was much in the public mind in this year of 1969. Built in 1900, with a gift of $145,000 from philanthropist Andrew Carnegie, it was designed to serve a population of 70,000 and hold 50,000 books. Going into 1969, it housed just under 700,000 books, provided service for 650,000 patrons, and operated on a budget of $1,079,000. Yet it was essentially the same building as it was when first completed in 1900. Some $100,000 had been spent on it from 1963 through 1965, enlarging rooms, brightening walls, lowering ceilings, and installing elevators. It was clear that the 5,000 square feet added was not enough. A new and much larger building was needed. Nor had the outside appearance been changed. The once handsome old facade, with its stately columns, sorely needed a face-lifting.

In the *Journal-Constitution* Maxine Rock described the library's needs:

There is something sad about the old central building of the Atlanta Public Library. It squats on the corner of Forsyth and Carnegie Streets in downtown Atlanta, and its dull gray concrete columns have a forlorn, neglected look about it.

A steady stream of people enter the building through a narrow hallway, file through two creaking turnstiles, and are confronted with an awesome jumble of catalog cabinets, reference rooms, and jumbled books. It is not the type of library one would expect to have in a major metropolitan area.

"I hope they knock this place down," sighed Carlton Rochell, the library's new director. "It's about as friendly looking as a mausoleum."

Rochell, who came from Tennessee in January 1968 to succeed the late John Hall Jacobs as library director, has managed to infuse some life into the old building despite its inadequacies. The rooms are brighter now, the book collection is broader and personnel are more enthusiastic. But the main problem remains: the library is too small.

"The entire library system—physical facilities and finances—is too small for a city like Atlanta," said Rochell. "We're studying our needs now, and what we are coming up with is a gap of about one-half million books we should have acquired over the years, but didn't," he added. "Even though we get money from about four different sources, it all adds up to about half of what we need."

What's the answer? To Rochell it is new building—"a very beautiful, attractive, colorful, efficient central library building three stories high and extending the entire length of the block from Forsyth to Fairlie Street." He estimates the cost at about $5,800,000.

"You need brains, books and buildings to have an effective public library system," Rochell said solemnly, "and to get it all you need budget. We need more professional people—at least double the number we have now—and more than double the nonprofessionals.

"We need more books, especially reference volumes. We need special services, like records and tapes; bookmobiles; a children's program; discussion groups and film programs; even a nice branch area where children can do their homework.

"We need branch libraries in shopping centers—bright, open places where people feel comfortable, and can get to the books they need easily." Rochell tapped his pipe thoughtfully. "In the past, libraries have catered too much to the educated upper and middle classes," he mused.

"We must stop neglecting the other segments of our community, and start helping them to achieve an education through books and other library services."

And, in time, what Rochell dreamed of did come to pass. Despite desperate efforts by some of Atlanta's most noted citizens, who formed an ad hoc committee to save the old Carnegie Library building, the wrecking balls came at last. By April of 1977 all books had been moved to three floors of a building near Central City Park. The wreckers were at work by March 3 and on the cleared site at Forsyth Street and Carnegie Way there began to arise a more than $10 million modernistic structure, designed to be one of the most efficient library buildings in the world.

In deference to the wishes of those who treasured the memory of the old structure—among them architect Joseph Amisano; Milton Farris, the county commissioner; Franklin Garrett, the city historian; Helen Bullard; Stephens Mitchell; and Ben Fortson, secretary of state—one concession was made. The old facade with its tall columns was taken down, carefully, and placed in storage at the city prison farm on Key Road, until a proper use could be found for it.

And, finally, on Sunday afternoon, May 25, 1980, the new library building was dedicated at Carnegie Way and Forsyth streets, later known as Margaret Mitchell Square. Marcel Breur and Hamilton Smith were the architects, Stevens and Wilkinson were the associate architect and consulting engineers, and the George Hyman Construction Company and the Ozanne Company were the general contractors. The mammoth building stood ten stories tall, with eight floors above street level and two below—with two floors still unfinished. There were 245,000 square feet of space in one building, which would house one million volumes. Presiding at the dedication was Mary Lu Mitchell, chairman of the library board of trustees, and Mayor Maynard Jackson passed on the keys to Ella G. Yates, the new library director.

Nature lights no flares and rings no bells to mark the passing of time from one decade to another. In Atlanta the 1960s merged into the 1970s with the only joyful noises arising from New Year's parties in homes and private clubs to mark the occasion. But the newspapers were aware of what the decade had meant to the city—and what they hoped the next one would mean. They were also aware that Atlanta banks and business houses liked to put big ads in special editions designed to attract special attention.

The papers, therefore, on January 18, 1970, put together seven separate sections of fifteen pages each under the title:

The titles and authors were: "A Decade of Spirit" by Phil Garner; "A Decade of Beauty" by Celestine Sibley; "A Decade of Play" by Furman Bisher; "A Decade of Courage" by Jack Spalding; "A Decade of Achievement" by Margaret Shannon; "A Decade of Movement" by John Pennington; and "A Decade of Planning" by Hal Gulliver.

In the opening article, "A Decade of Spirit," Garner described Atlanta as "a mercantile trader, seductress of country youth, mirror of illustrious careers, magnet of the rural poor, and standard bearer of an elusive phenomenon called the New South."

In the section titled "A Decade of Courage" Jack Spalding named and described the actions of the topflight Atlantans, old and young, black and white, who led the city into the seventies after ten years of extraordinary growth. They had one thing in common, Spalding pointed out, courage, the courage to "look facts in the face and act justly despite old prejudices and emotional convictions." Thus, Atlanta "developed the sort of courage to face up to the race problem instead of continuing to evade it." This one single fact, said Spalding, had contributed as much as anything to the city's national reputation and to its general prosperity.

"It has not been a one-way sort of courage. It has taken courage for black leadership to counsel moderation and try to control black militants for the sake of the city. It has taken courage for white leadership to do the same with white militants. Among the leaders listed in this section devoted to men of action and courage, was, of course, Mayor Ivan Allen, Jr. who retired, a tired but satisfied man, after eight years in office, turning City Hall over to his Vice Mayor Sam Massell."

The creation of the stadium was the beginning of a sports explosion in Atlanta (which at last had reached the status of big-league city, and among the athletes who added an extra luster to its fame was Henry (Hank) Aaron, slugging outfielder of the Atlanta Braves.

On Monday night, April 8, 1974, in the fourth inning of Atlanta's game with the Los Angeles Dodgers, Aaron set 53,775 fans to leaping and screaming in Atlanta Stadium when he hit his 715th home run, thus breaking the supposedly unbreakable record of 714 set by Babe Ruth, which had stayed unbeaten for thirty-nine years.

Aaron, however, was more quietly proud of what he was able to accomplish over the years, in breaking down the barriers which in the past had relegated the black athletes to competition only with each other. Though Jackie Robinson had been the first black man to break down the doors of segregation in the big leagues, Aaron and two of his companions, Felix Montilla and Horace Garner, broke down the barriers in the South in the early fifties by playing for Jacksonville in the South Atlantic League. And in the process, they helped open doors for Negroes in many nonsports areas, including public accommodations.

Another outstanding black man in Atlanta in the 1960s and 1970s was Dr. Benjamin Mays, a nationally famed educator, civic leader, minister, and writer. Those who knew him considered him a black thorn in the white conscience. Always a champion of the civil rights movements, a crusader for enlightened justice against the ghosts of fear and prejudice, he had been president emeritus of Morehouse College in Atlanta since his retirement in May, 1962. Elected to the Atlanta Board of Education at the age of seventy-four, Dr. Mays won respect as a man possessing the moral courage to be one of the first in his lifetime openly to attack racial discrimination and for his ability to instill that courage in others.

Eleven years later in 1981, at eighty-six, Dr. Mays was still being honored when he received the 1981 Shining Light Award from WSB Radio and the Atlanta Gas Light Company for his "greatness" as an educator and humanitarian. The award is reserved for people who make everlasting contributions to the city and to mankind. The Atlanta City Council also renamed Sewell Road from Cascade Road to Fairburn Road as Benjamin E. Mays Drive. The road leads to the school that already bore Dr. Mays's name.

In 1976 an observer declared, "Benjamin Mays is indeed the living embodiment of black progress in America." One speaker at a banquet honoring Mays described the legendary man perfectly: "The man here is an original. He was 22 when he graduated from high school. He was 46 when he became president of Morehouse College. He was 52 when he was permitted to vote. And he was 76 when he became the first black president of the Atlanta Board of Education. They don't make men like that anymore."

Another outstanding Atlanta figure is an educator of national renown. Dr. Noah Langdale, the 250-pound president of Georgia State University, was called "a unique combination of brains and brawn." A native of Valdosta, Dr. Langdale was Phi Beta Kappa and was named an "outstanding student" at the University of Alabama when he graduated in 1941. He kept on going to school until he had earned three more degrees—an LLB from Harvard University Law School, an MBA from the Harvard Graduate School of Business Administration, and finally an LLD from the University of Alabama. He was the principal figure in the rise of Georgia State University. The newspaper story profiling Dr. Langdale noted:

In 1961 Georgia State was a small college with an enrollment of 3,447. Today [early 1970] it is a sprawling big city university with 12,833 students.

Last fall it became the first school in Georgia to change from a college to a full-fledged university since the University of Georgia was created in 1785. . . .

A five-minute walk from downtown Five Points, Georgia State is a rarity for the South—a university with no dormitories and no controls over the private lives of its students.

The burgeoning campus spreads over 19½ city acres with plans to expand onto a total of 44 acres. It is a concrete campus convenient for the businessman, the secretary, the commuter, the urban dweller.

When Langdale came in 1957, the total value of campus buildings was some $3 million. Going into 1970 Georgia State was worth $24 million in buildings in existence or committed—and a planned campus amounting to $75 million. When he first came there was a fine college of business administration supported by a junior college of arts and sciences—and the one degree offered was in business administration. In 1970 there were twenty-five degrees offered in 150 fields, including graduate programs in business, the arts and sciences, education, and urban life. There were more than 2,000 graduate students working in their fields. There were also ten programs offering the Doctor of Philosophy degree.

The Chamber of Commerce put together a little booklet to pass out to visitors in which the city's accomplishments through 1969 were summarized. Starting off with the civic cliché that Atlanta's confident *attitude* was the by-product of her lofty *altitude*—1,050 feet above sea level—which made her the highest big city in the country next to Denver, Colorado, the booklet continued in this vein:

Metro Atlanta's many public school systems are educating some 305,000 students in 324 elementary schools and 82 high schools.

Only two other U.S. cities' airports emplane more passengers; only three outrank Atlanta in air carrier operations. Between 11:00 A.M. and 6:00 P.M. the Atlanta Airport is often the busiest in the world.

Metro Atlanta has close to 25,000 private housing units. Construction in an average year totals about $450 million. And doesn't include residential additions or alterations.

The Roman Catholic Archdiocese of Atlanta oversees some 14 grammar schools and five high schools.

The City alone has more than 3,000 acres in parks.

Total "non-agricultural employment" (that is manufacturing plus construction, transportation, wholesale trade, retail trade, finance, insurance, real estate, services and government) provides jobs for about 579,000 Atlantans.

Atlanta has more than 100 firms concerned with banking, investments, savings and loans. The Sixth Federal Reserve District has headquarters here.

Some 40 religious creeds and denominations worship in over 1,500 Metro churches and synagogues.

. . . the five-county metro area has added an average of 23,000 plus wage and salary jobs in each year since 1960. Atlanta claims 47.5 percent of all new jobs created in Georgia.

More than 3,000 different commodities—from chemicals to textiles to airplanes—are produced here by some 1,700 manufacturers.

Some 20 degree-granting colleges, universities and institutions are located here.

There are close to 939,000 telephones in the metro area, the largest geographical toll-free dialing area in the world.

The chamber's booklet mentioned churches, but it did not point out that many of the downtown churches had followed their congregations to new places of worship in the suburbs. Some just closed their doors. But many stayed in the central city and worked with the flood of inmigrants who needed special attention. Regular worship services on Sunday and on Wednesday night were not enough to serve these people. Among those who stayed downtown were Trinity Methodist, First Methodist, Central Presbyterian, Immaculate Conception Roman Catholic, the Baptist Tabernacle, Sacred Heart Roman Catholic, and St. Luke's Episcopal Church. Among them they provided prison rehabilitation, work with homeless men and women, counseling operation of food pantries, and many other services the newcomers needed.

In some areas of culture and the arts, Atlanta clung to old patterns. As recorded earlier, Atlanta's "affair" with the Metropolitan Opera Company began in 1910, and it survived as the city's outstanding social as well as musical event, even though it did not come back from 1929, the year of the great market crash, until 1940. It then was closed by the outbreak of World War II. After the 1943 season the opera did not come back to Atlanta until the spring of 1947, when it opened its first season at the Fox Theater. There racial tensions seemed soothed by the music, and in 1962 the first integrated audiences watched Strauss' *Electra* without untoward incidents. By 1969 the Met had moved from the Fox, with its fading grandeur, to the Atlanta Civic Center, but labor problems between artists and management for a time indicated that the Met would not be able to celebrate its sixtieth anniversary in

Atlanta in the 1970 season. But it did, and going into the 1980s, it remained one of the city's main musical, cultural, and social events.

The papers that in 1970 had put out a special edition glorifying the metropolis as "Amazing Atlanta" in 1975 were publishing a doleful requiem called "City in Crisis." Beginning on March 24, and continuing through April 13, a staff of *Journal* and *Constitution* reporters took a dubious, sometimes almost a despairing, look at what had happened since 1969. Their decision, based on interviews with prominent Atlantans: "A Decade of Prosperity and Good Will has faded. This is a City in Crisis." An editor's note pointed out that throughout the 1960s Atlanta had been Camelot. Spared racial turmoil and blessed with experienced leadership, the city became a great center of commerce and a Mecca for emerging blacks. But by 1975 political power had shifted. New leadership arrived with new problems, and there were tensions among the people.

"What's happening to Atlanta? Will the dream survive?" the editors asked.

The answer, over the next seven days of first-page reporting by Bill Shipp, executive editor; Lewis Grizzard, special assignments editor; and reporters Sharon Bailey, Frederick Allen, and Sam Hopkins was a tentative "Yes."

The day after the "Crisis" series began, the city was struck a devastating blow that was not of man's own making. On March 24, 1975, a tornado danced a destructive path along eight miles of northwest Atlanta, killing three persons, injuring 117, and doing damage estimated by insurance adjusters at $85.5 million. The worst windstorm in Atlanta's history, it left 1,000 homeless, tore the porch and three columns off the governor's mansion, dropped huge power poles onto a building at Cross Creek Apartments, and lifted the roof off apartments in Perry Homes.

Nor were the doleful strains of the "Atlanta in Crisis" series too greatly exaggerated, but the "ifs" were many: If the black leaders of the inner city and the white civic leaders of the unincorporated surrounding areas could agree on a consolidation plan in which rapid transit, water and sewer and garbage collection, and police services could be expanded and improved and paid for by county and inner-city resources, all might be well. In sum, the papers' conclusions were simply these: In the words of John Portman, "Blacks are going to have to share their political powers. Whites are going to have to share their economic powers." Above all, blacks, now in the majority in both city and county government, were going to have to handle their duties in such a way that whites seeking to invest in Atlanta could do so with confidence that the crisis—the soaring crime rate, a declining economy, the need for a second airport, an increasingly black public school system as a result of the white flight to the suburbs—could not endure.

But there were thousands of Atlantans who still shared Louise (Mrs. Ivan) Allen's views, expressed to new Mayor Sam Massell as she accepted the

Woman of the Year Award in 1970: "Atlanta is a wonderful city, Sam. Take care of it."

And each of those who succeeded her husband in the mayor's office strove, in his own way, to do this. Mayor Sam Massell and his vice-mayor and president of the Board of Aldermen, Maynard Jackson, were to face the challenges of the first years of the 1970s. Then Maynard Jackson as mayor, and after him Andrew Young, faced the problems brought on by a changing lifestyle, changing traffic patterns, and an ever-widening metro area.

The so-called crisis of 1975 passed, and in the late 1970s and the first half of the 1980s metropolitan Atlanta once again was among the nation's most vibrant and vital growing cities contributing significantly to the national image of a prosperous Sunbelt. But a later historian will have to chronicle the ebb and flow of the seventies, eighties, and beyond.

OBITUARIES

Brig. Gen. Edgar Dunlap (Sandy) Beaver, 86, founder and president of Riverside Military Academy, was a former member of the State Board of Regents. He was a 1903 graduate of the University of Georgia and a charter member of the Football Hall of Fame. He was named to the Board of Regents by Gov. Eugene Talmadge in 1933. He had founded his nationally known academy in 1903. Dr. Immanuel Ben-Dor, 68, was a professor of biblical archeology at Emory University's Candler School of Theology. Dr. Ben-Dor received his early education in Russia and Poland and was graduated from the university in Austria. He did the work for his Ph.D. in oriental studies at the University of Rome. Richard B. Belser, Georgia Tech professor, was expert in the field of electronic communication devices. Mrs. Claude S. Bennett was president and chairman of the board of Bennett's Jewelers.

Mrs. Eugene R. Black, Sr., 93, was the daughter of the late Henry W. Grady, former editor of the *Constitution*, and mother of the president of the World Bank. She was one of the founders of the Sheltering Arms Day Nursery and was the widow of a former president of the Atlanta Federal Reserve Bank. Thomas W. Cliff, retired school official, had been in city educational circles since 1917, when he joined the Atlanta School System. He served as teacher, principal, assistant superintendent, and business manager until 1962, when he retired. Olive Bell Davis, local author, was a member of the Atlanta Writers' Club, the DAR, and the UDC. Isabel Dew, assistant principal and mathematics instructor at North Fulton High School, was a member of the original ten teachers on the faculty. She was a graduate of Girls High, Agnes Scott, and Emory University and was chosen STAR teacher at North Fulton in 1960. Chief Justice W. H. Duckworth, 74, had served on the Supreme Court since 1938. He was a graduate of Young Harris and a veteran of World War I. He had managed Ed Rivers's successful campaign for governor.

Edgar F. Fincher, 68, Atlanta surgeon and former professor of neurology at Emory University School of Medicine, had done brain surgery in Atlanta since 1930 and was on the staffs of eight hospitals. A graduate of Boys High and Emory University, he was a member of many neurosurgical groups, medical groups, St. Mark's Methodist Church, the Capital City Club, the Commerce Club, and Highlands Country Club. Dr. Edward L. Floyd, 82, had served as principal of old Boys High School and Commercial High School. He was a Phi Beta Kappa graduate of the 1913 class of the University of Georgia and entered the school system in 1917 as a history teacher. C. M. Frederick, 89, was former treasurer of Retail Credit Company, which he joined in 1901. He was a member of the Piedmont Driving Club, the Capital City Club, and the Ansley Park Golf Club. Robert Cecil Frost, Sr., 78, the founder and president of Buckhead Realty Company, was a veteran of World War I.

Hugh Hodgson, 76, head of the University of Georgia's music department, was a pianist, organist, composer, and choirmaster as well as a teacher. He was a major influence on Atlanta's musical life, and for over forty years he was director of music at St. Luke's Church, where his funeral was held. Dr. Malvern Dumah Huff, 90, a professor at Emory School of Dentistry for forty-six years, had been a practicing dentist for sixty-eight years. He was a member of Rotary, Druid Hills Golf Club, and Second Ponce de Leon Baptist Church. James E. (Johnny) Johnson, 49, was foreman of the pressroom for Atlanta newspapers for more than twenty years. Charles Alfred Jones, Sr., 86, had taught at Georgia Tech for forty-seven years and had been head of the textile department.

State Senator Dan I. MacIntyre III, 51, was a Republican who served District 40, encompassing most of northside Atlanta. He was a member of the insurance firm founded by his grandfather, Dan MacIntyre, in 1895 and was a graduate of Georgia Tech. He was a World War II veteran and a member of the Peachtree Presbyterian Church. John Markland, city manager of Decatur since 1958, was a member of Rotary and the East Lake Country Club. Kenneth P. Mages, vice-president for finance and treasurer of Rich's, Inc., was a graduate of Marquette University and had long been associated with merchandising. His activity in civic affairs included being president of the Leukemia Society of America. He was a member of the Capital City Club, the Commerce Club, and Sleepy Hollow Country Club in New York. Dr. Carl Mauelshagen, former head of the History Department at Georgia State, did extensive research and publication on the activities of the Salzburgers and Moravians in early Georgia after he retired from the university system.

Mrs. Ed Miles, the former Florence Early, proofreader and copy editor of the *Atlanta Journal*, was a native of England and attended Temple University and Oglethorpe College. Wiley H. Montague, Sr., 62, had been president of the AFL-CIO in Georgia since 1958. He belonged to many labor-related organizations and was a Mason and a Shriner. Robert Whitaker, 65, a member of the administration of Emory University, had been assistant to the president since 1959. Whitaker had served on many civic undertakings, including the Community Chest, the Red Cross, and the Chamber of Commerce. Wilson Wilkes, 52, was known to his friends as "Flicker." He was appointed Georgia's budget officer by Governor Sanders and retained by Governor Maddox. He had served in the House of Representatives and the Senate.

NOTES

1. Harold H. Martin, *Ralph McGill, Reporter* (Boston: Little, Brown, 1973).
2. Bruce Galphin, *Atlanta,* Jan., 1969.
3. George Adcock, ibid.
4. Hariette Speer's account is on file at the Atlanta Historical Society.
5. Opie Shelton, *Atlanta,* July, 1969.
6. Doris Lockerman, *Atlanta,* July, 1969.
7. Herbert T. Jenkins, *My Forty Years on the Force, 1932–1972* (Atlanta: Center for Research in Social Change, Emory University, 1973).

INDEX

CPSIA information can be obtained at www.ICGtesting.com
Printed in the USA

242575LV00004B/6/P